CATALOGUE OF
THE GUPTA GOLD COINS
IN THE BAYANA HOARD

CATALOGUE OF

THE GUPTA GOLD COINS

IN THE BAYANA HOARD

BY

DR. ANANT SADASHIV ALTEKAR,

M.A., LL.B., D. LITT

Professor of Ancient Indian History and Culture, Patna University, Hon. director, K. P. Jayaswal Research Institute, Patna, and Chairman, Numismatic Society of India

WITH FORTY EIGHT PLATES

GYAN

COL. H. H. SHRI BRAJENDRA SAWAI MAHARAJA BRAJENDRA SINGHJI BAHADUR BAHADURJUNG OF BHARATPUR.

FOREWORD

I have great pleasure in presenting to the world of scholars this Volume of the Catalogue of the Gupta gold coins in the Bayana Hoard.

When the discovery of this hoard was made in 1946 and the coins were brought to Bharatpur, I realised that it was a find of historical importance. I therefore decided to invite Dr. A. S. Altekar, the Chairman of the Numismatic Society of India, to come to Bharatpur with a view to assess the value of the hoard. Dr. A. S. Altekar visited Bharatpur in May 1947, subjected the coins to a preliminary examination and reported to me that the hoard was of a unique importance, as so big a hoard, and with so many types and varieties, had never been discovered and recovered. A proper classification of the coins, he added, would require a prolonged examination and a scientific catalogue of the hoard, adequately illustrated, would be a boon to the world of scholars.

It became clear to me that I should spare no troubles in getting the catalogue of the hoard published in an adequate manner, so that the world of Indology may have a worthy book for study and reference. I therefore decided to invite Dr. Altekar once more to Bharatpur for the purpose of classifying the coins and taking down notes for the preparation of the Catalogue. A large staff was placed at his disposal, so that the preliminary work may be finished as soon as possible. The Archaeological Department also extended its kind cooperation by sending its photographer to photograph the important coins of the hoard, selected for illustration. Dr. Altekar could complete his work in connection with the Catalogue only after studying the hoard during two more visits in 1948 and 1949.

The press copy of the work was ready towards the end of 1949, but circumstances had, in the meanwhile, changed both in India and at Bharatpur and the publication of this work was delayed for a short period.

I, however, felt that my original plan should not be departed from and that I should have the pleasure and privilege of placing before the students of history this book of sterling importance. I accordingly informed Dr. Altekar that he should proceed with the work, as originally planned. With a view to get the coins illustrated in the best possible manner, it was decided to get the plates prepared in England by the collotype process. One of the best presses in India was selected for printing the work.

I hope and trust that the work, that I am instrumental in publishing, will materially advance the bounds of our knowledge in the field of Indology in general and Numismatics in particular. The Gupta Age, they say, was a golden age in ancient Indian history; the publication of this Catalogue of the Gold Coins of the Bayana hoard may show that it was a golden age, both in the literal and figurative senses.

This Catalogue will undoubtedly enable the scholars to study all the coins in the hoard in full details. It is, however, likely that many of them may like to see the rare coins of the hoard in original. I, therefore, decided to present a representative set of the coins to the National Museum of India, so that it may be possible for future generations also to get a glimpse of the rich contents of the priceless hoard. I was happy to hand over this representative set to Dr. Rajendra Prasad, the President of India, in March 1951, along with the interesting copper pot in which they lay deposited, for being handed over to the National Museum. All visitors to the National Museum can see and study this representative set.

I am very thankful to Dr. A. S. Altekar for the prolonged labour he has bestowed upon this work in order to ensure that it should come up to the highest standards of critical scholarship. I am grateful to the Archaeological Department for its deep interest in this work; it sent its expert photographer to photograph the coins and supplied their photographs for publication. Mr. D. C. Chaturvedi, Head Master, Government High School, Bharatpur, was of great help.

I am also grateful to Dr. Rajendra Prasad, the President of India, for kindly allowing me to dedicate this volume to him. Our scholar-President was the first to conceive and launch forth a scheme of the National History of India, and it is but in the fitness of things that this volume should be dedicated to him.

SAWAI BRAJENDRA SINGH OF BHARATPUR

CONTENTS

3. CHANDRAGUPTA I

4. KĀCHA

5. SAMUDRAGUPTA

6. RĀMAGUPTA

7. CHANDRAGUPTA II

8. KUMĀRAGUPTA I

9. SKANDAGUPTA

10. SUCCESSORS OF KUMĀRAGUPTA I

IV COINAGE AND COIN TYPES

1. Chandragupta I

2. Samudragupta

(i) STANDARD TYPE

(ii) *Aśvamedha* TYPE

(iii) BATTLE-AXE TYPE

(iv) ARCHER TYPE

(v) LYRIST TYPE

(vi) TIGER-SLAYER TYPE

3. KĀCHA

4. CHANDRAGUPTA II

(vi) *chakravikrama* TYPE

5. KUMĀRAGUPTA I

(i) ARCHER TYPE

(ii) SWORDSMAN TYPE

(iii) HORSEMAN TYPE

(iv) KĀRTIKEYA TYPE

(v) *Chhatra* TYPE

(vi) TIGER-SLAYER TYPE

(vii) LION-SLAYER TYPE

(viii) ELEPHANT-RIDER LION-SLAYER TYPE

(ix) RHINOCEROS-SLAYER TYPE

(x) *Aśvamedha* TYPE

(xi) ELEPHANT-RIDER TYPE

(xii) LYRIST TYPE

(xiii) *Apratigha* TYPE

(xiv) KING AND QUEEN TYPE

6. SKANDAGUPTA

(xv) *Chhatra* TYPE

7. SKANDAGUPTA AND HIS SUCCESSORS

8. SILVER CURRENCY OF THE GUPTAS

9. COPPER COINAGE OF THE GUPTAS

V METROLOGY

COINS OF THE CATALOGUE

Chandragupta I

Samudragupta

KUMĀRAGUPTA I

(Skandagupta) Kramāditya

Successors of Kumāragupta I

(Not represented in the hoard)

LIST OF PLATES

PREFACE

The Numismatic Society of India has great pleasure in offering to the scholarly world this volume of the Catalogue of Coins of the Bayana Hoard, published under the gracious patronage of His Highness Lt.-Col. Sri Brajendra Singhji, the Maharaja of Bharatpur.

This book will be found to be an interesting one from several points of view. It is the Catalogue of the biggest hoard of ancient Indian gold coins that was ever discovered and recovered in the history of Indian Archaeology. It gives an accurate and full description of the 1821 coins of the hoard which were recovered, recording carefully the size and weight of each. As many as 449 coins of the hoard have been illustrated in beautiful plates prepared by the collotype process. The symbol on each coin is illustrated along with its description by special types prepared for the purpose.

In the case of the rather rare types, care has been taken to illustrate every coin in the hoard, lest important details should be lost to the students of numismatics. Thus all the coins of Chandragupta I (10 in number), Kācha (16 in number) and Skandagupta (1 in number) have been illustrated.

In the case of Samudragupta, every one of his twenty coins of the *Aśvamedha* type, nine of the Battle-axe type, six of the Lyrist type, three of the Archer type and two of the Tiger-slayer type, has been illustrated. The reader can see all the three coins of the Couch type of Chandragupta II.

In the case of Kumāragupta I, every coin of his rather rare or new types like the Swordsman type (10 coins), the Kārtikeya type (13 coins), *Chhatra* type (2 coins), Lyrist type (2 coins), Elephant-rider type (3 coins), Elephant-rider Lion-slayer type (4 coins), Rhinoceros-slayer type (4 coins), *Aśvamedha* type (4 coins), *Apratigha* type (8 coins) and King and Queen type (1 coin), has been illustrated.

In the case of the more common types also, the selection for illustration has been made on liberal lines. Thus 32 out of the

52 coins of the Lion-slayer type of Chandragupta II, 30 out of 82 coins of his Horseman type and 17 out of 57 coins of his *Chhatra* type are put on the plates. Even in the case of the Archer type of this ruler, which was produced in mass quantity, 83 out of 798 coins have been selected for the plates. Equally liberal principles have been followed in making selections from the common types of Kumāragupta I. Thus 35 out of his 183 coins of the Archer type, 60 out of his 305 coins of the Horseman type, 15 out of his 36 coins of the Tiger-slayer type and 30 out of his 53 coins of the Lion-slayer type have been illustrated. The plates thus offer for examination 459 coins of the hoard, 188 more than the gold coins illustrated in the *Catalogue of the Coins of the Gupta Dynasties in the British Museum*.

The selection of coins for illustration was guided by several considerātions. Naturally care was taken to see that it should be possible for the reader to reconstruct the entire legend with the help of a group of coins. Some coins showed peculiarities of palaeography; some time the script was very small, **(Pl. IX. 9, Pl. XII. 14-15)**; sometimes it was very bold **(Pl. II. 7, 14)**, sometimes the palaeography showed the peculiar feature of the combination of the so-called Eastern and Western varieties **(Pl. II. 12, III. 13)**. All the coins necessary for the visualisation of these peculiarities can be seen on the plates. Some coins have been selected, because they gave good portraits of the king or the queen **(Pl. II. 14,)** others because they were beautiful specimens of art, some because they showed peculiarities in dress **(Pl. III. 8, II. 14, X. 3, 9)**, coiffeur **(Pl. X. 6, XI. 14)**, ornaments, footware **(Pl. II. 11, III. 7)**, horse accoutrement **(Pl. XXII. 1, 12)** etc., and others because they showed the mistakes of mint masters, as when there was double striking **(Pl. III. 1)**.

It is hoped that the coins illustrated will offer ample data for the study of some aspects of the material civilization of the age.

As observed already, the Bayana hoard is the biggest hoard of Gupta gold coins that has ever been recovered. Unfortunately about three hundred coins of the hoard were melted down by the villagers before the police arrived on the scene and recovered the remaining 1821 coins. It is quite possible that some rare or unique coins of the hoard may have been lost owing to the natural greed for gold of the illiterate villagers. But even the coins that have been recovered display a remarkable variety, and only two types e.g. the Standard and King and Queen on the Couch types of Chandragupta II, (each known so far from a solitary specimen) are missing in it.

The special importance of the Bayana hoard lies in the fact that it discloses a number of types and varieties that were so far unknown. The most interesting coin in the hoard is the *Chakravikrama* type coin of Chandragupta II. We all know that this emperor was a great devotee of Vishṇu. But no one had ever thought that he might have issued a coin type, showing himself as a direct recipient of a *prasāda* from Vishṇu, manifesting himself before his royal devotee for that purpose. And yet this is what we visualise on the single coin of the unique *Chakravikrama* type, for the first time disclosed in this hoard. The hoard shows that Kumāragupta I was perhaps the greatest devotee of the science of Numismatics in the Gupta dynasty, for it discloses for the first time as many as five new types of his,—(i) the King and the Queen type, (ii) the *Chhatra* type, (iii) the Lyrist type, (iv) the Rhinoceros-slayer type and the Elephant-rider Lion-slayer type. The hoard contained only one coin of Kramāditya (Skandagupta); but it discloses a new type of that ruler, *viz*, the *Chhatra* type.

The hoard has disclosed a large number of new varieties of the known types as well. Among the noteworthy ones of this category the following may be mentioned, the *Garuḍadhvaja* variety of Kācha, the varieties of the Archer type of Chandragupta where the king is also having a sword or hunter by his side, the variety of the Lion-slayer type of the same ruler where the king is not stringing the bow, but defiantly looking at the lion before him, the Lion-retreating type, where the king is shooting arrow at the lion sulking back. Attention is drawn to several other new varieties in the Introduction.

It is not unlikely that the anonymous owner of this hoard had selected his coins, at least in some cases, not only for their gold value, but also for the rarity of their types and varieties and the excellence of art showed by them.

There was a remarkable revival of Sanskrit in the Gupta Age; the Gupta emperors were first to start the practice of giving the coin legends in beautiful metrical lines. Our hoard discloses several new poetic hemistiches. Notable among them are the following :—

Pṛithivītalāmbaraśaśi Kumāragupto jayatyajitaḥ
Jayati nṛiporibhirajitaḥ
Pṛithivītaleśvarendraḥ Kumāragupto jayatyajitaḥ
Bhartā khaḍgatrātā Kumāragupto jayatyaniśam

These lines would show that the poets of the Gupta age were particularly fond of using figures of speech like *upamā*, *utprekshā*, *ślesha*, etc. The coins in the hoard enable us to complete a number of legends that could not be properly deciphered so far. They also enable us to correct a number of earlier mistakes. For instance, the coins of the hoard conclusively show that the reading *Śripratāpa* on one of the rare types of Kumāragupta I has now to be abandoned in favour of *Apratigha*.

In presenting this catalogue to the readers, I have taken an opportunity to present a fresh and upto-date study of the Gupta numismatics in the Introduction, which extends over 158 pages. During the 40 years that have elapsed since Mr. Allan published his Catalogue, a lot of new numismatic material has come to light; it has been fully utilised for the present work. After giving an account of the discovery of the hoard in section I of the Introduction, I have referred to other earlier hoards of Gupta gold coins in section II, in order to bring out clearly the importance of this hoard. Section III deals with the history of the Dynasty. As there are now several books on Gupta history treating it in great details, I have contented myself only with a general account of it, sufficient enough to understand the Gupta numismatics.

Section IV of the Introduction, extending over 80 pages (xl-cxx) deals with the coinage and coin types. Here the treatment is exhaustive and comparative. Not only are the coin types in the hoard described, but attention is also drawn to the few types and varieties that are not represented in it; the number of coins of each type at the different Museums is also stated and references are given to the corresponding varieties in Mr. Allan's *Catalogue of the Coins of the Gupta Dynasties in the British Museum*. The full text and translation of the legend in each type and variety is given while discussing it; its text in the original script is given in the plates later. The principles that have governed the division of coins into classes and varieties are explained and the points of resemblance and difference between them have been clearly brought out. The attribution of some coin types like the King and Queen type of Chandragupta I and the *Chakradhvaja* type of Kācha is still a matter of great controversy. In such cases all the earlier views have been discussed before expounding my own. The evolution of the Standard type of Samudragupta from its prototype supplied by the late Kushāṇa coinage and its growing Indianisation are also fully described. The various details of the motifs on the *Aśvamedha* type of Samudragupta have been more fully brought out than was so far done in earlier works.

The Bayana hoard was most probably buried early in the reign of Skandagupta. It naturally does not contain the gold coins of his successors. In **Pl. XXXII** of this work, I have, however, given the principal coin-types of the gold coinage of all the later Gupta rulers, with a view to enable the readers of the work to have a fairly good idea of the gold coinage of the entire dynasty.

The Introduction also gives a brief account of the silver and copper coinage of the Gupta dynasty, but the coins in these metals have not been illustrated on the plates in the present work.

The hoard placed at my disposal a very large number of coins of each variety and type. It therefore became possible to study their metrology in great details and to draw several new conclusions; this is done in Section V of the Introduction. It became possible to offer a new explanation of the abnormally low and high weight standards shown by some Gupta coins. Three different weight standards of the weight of 121, 124 and 127 grains could be distinguished in the reigns of Chandragupta II and Kumāragupta I and it could be demonstrated how the latter emperor was issuing some varieties to particular weight standards only. Thus the coins of the var. A of class I of the Archer type of this king are all issued to the standard of 124 grains, the coins of the variety B to the 121 grains standard. The latter standard is usually followed by the *Apratigha* type also. Many other types of this emperor exclusively follow the standard of 127 grains. The conclusions about metrology based upon the study of the coins of this hoard were usually confirmed by the weights of the corresponding varieties as recorded in the *B.M.C., G.D.*

Section VI of the Introduction deals with the palaeography of the coin legends. It has been pointed out for the first time that the so-called Eastern variety is confined only to the coins of the early rulers and there also to the letters *ma* and *ha* only. *Sa*, *sha* and *la* show no Eastern forms.

Section VII of the Introduction gives a detailed study of the Symbols occurring on the Gupta coins, extending over 20 pages. It is shown that the symbols have no religious significance and that they can neither refer to the mint cities nor to the mint-masters, neither to the dates of the issue, nor to the number of coins issued in one mint operation. They appear to be merely decorative devices. Section VIII of the Introduction discusses the data of the coins for ascertaining the fashions of dress and ornaments and varieties of furniture and weapons in the Gupta age. This section was written at my special request by my friend Dr. Motichand, the Director, Prince of Wales Museum, Bombay.

Pls. I-XXXI of the work illustrate 459 coins from the hoard. **Pl. XXXII** illustrates the important types of coins of the later Gupta rulers not represented in the hoard. The next five plates, **XXXIII-XXXVII,** give the legends on the coins in the original script from drawings specially made at my request by my esteemed friend Mr. C. Shivaramamurti, Superintendent, Archaeological section, Indian Museum, Calcutta In these plates Mr. Shivaramamurti gives not the idealised but the actual forms of Gupta letters as they occur on the coins.

Facing each plate of legends, there is a page which gives their rendering in the Devanāgarī script. This will facilitate the task of their decipherment.

Pls. XXXVIII-XLVII contain drawings of costumes, furniture and weapons prepared under the supervision of my esteemed friend Dr. Motichand, the Director, Prince of Wales Museum, Bombay. These plates, along with their description given by Dr. Motichand, vividly show how coins can be of great help in reconstructing the history of some aspects of the contemporary material civilization.

Some of the coins of the Bayana hoard have now been distributed. Out of its 1821 coins, the Palace Cabinet, Bharatpur has 78 coins, the National Museum, New Delhi, 209, the Bharat Kala Bhavan, Banaras, 78, the Patna Museum 59, the Prince of Wales Museum 20, and the Patna University 18. It was my intention to identify all these coins with the coins described in the Catalogue, but owing to the absence of time and facilities, this was not possible. Appendix II of the book, however, gives a list of such coins in the above Museums, as could be definitely identified. These include the most rare and unique coins of the hoard. This Appendix will enable the student of numismatics to know to which Museum he is to repair in order to study these rare and unique coins in the original. Other Appendices supply the Genealogical and Chronological Table, the General Index and the Indices to Types and Symbols.

In conclusion I have to express my thanks to several individuals and institutions for the help offered to me in the preparation and publication of this work. The foremost among these is H. H. Lt.-Col. Sri Brajendra Singhji, the Maharaja of Bharatpur, who regarded it as his duty to the world of scholarship to adequately and sumptuously publish this Catalogue. He spared neither trouble nor money in achieving this desideratum. The numismatists all over the world will feel grateful to His Highness for offering them such a valuable Catalogue, which will long remain indispensable to the students of Indian numismatics. Prof. K. C. Sharma, M.A., LL.B., then also Superintendent of Archaeology, Bharatpur, enthusiastically organized the arduous work in connection with the examination and classification of the hoard, and toiled hard in the task. Mr. Kailash Narain Mehra, M.SC., Lecturer, M. S. J. College, Bharatpur, and Mr. Dinesh Chandra Chaturvedi, M.A., B.SC., Head Master, Government High School, Bharatpur, offered their valuable co-operation in the accurate weighing of the coins. Messrs. Jhamanlal, Shamsundar, Debiprasad, and Chhotelal, teachers in the Bharatpur High School, helped me in measuring the dimensions of the coins. I am thankful to all these gentlemen for their valuable assistance. I am indebted to Mr. C. Shivaramamurti, M.A., Superintendent, Archaeological Section, Indian Museum, Calcutta, for the preparation of the excellent plates of the legends in Gupta characters, and to Dr. Motichand, Director, Prince of Wales Museum, Bombay, for the plates of costumes, furniture and weapons, prepared under his supervision. He also prepared a note on this topic, included in the Introduction, and supplied a description of the plates, published at the end of the Catalogue. Mr. P. L. Gupta, M.A., offered me valuable help as my assistant, while working at Bharatpur. Mr. C. R. Singhal, the Hony. Treasurer of the Numismatic Society, was of great assistance in getting the moulds of symbols prepared in Bombay. I am indebted to the authorities of the British Museum for permitting me to reproduce some of the coins of the successors of Kumāragupta I, published by them in their *Catalogue of the Coins of the Gupta Dynasties*. The then Director General of Archaeology in India, Dr. R. M. Wheeler, and Dr. V. S. Agarwal, the then Superintendent, National Museum, New Delhi, placed the services of the departmental photographer, Mr. S. G. Tiwari, at my disposal in 1947 for photographing the coins at Bharatpur. I am indebted to the department of Archaeology for supplying very good sets of the photographs of coins for the purpose of study and plate making. My daughters Usha Altekar, M.A., Lecturer in Sanskrit, Patna Women's College and Padma Altekar, Research Assistant in the Department of Ancient Indian History and Culture, Patna University, helped me in the preparation and verification of the Indices.

Patna;
Ganesh Chaturthi,
12-9-1953

A. S. ALTEKAR

ABBREVIATIONS AND TRANSLITERATION

ABBREVIATIONS

A.B.O.R.I.	Annals of the Bhandarkar Oriental Research Institute.
A.H.D.	Ancient History of the Deccan by J. Dubreuil.
A.S.I.,A.R.	Archaeological Survey of India, Annual Reports.
B.M.C.,A.K.	Catalogue of the Coins in the British Museum, The Andhra Dynasty, the Western Kshatrapa Dynasty, etc. by Rapson.
B.M.C.,G.D.	Catalogue of the Coins in the British Museum, the Gupta Dynasties, etc. by Mr. J. Allan.
C.A.S.R.	Cunningham, Archaeological Survey Reports.
C.I.I.	Corpus Inscriptionum Indicarum.
C.G.E.	Coinage of the Gupta Empire by Dr. A. S. Altekar
E.I.	Epigraphia Indica.
I.A.	Indian Antiquary.
I.C.	Indian Culture.
I.H.Q.	Indian Historical Quarterly.
I.M.C.	Catalogue of the Coins in the Indian Museum, Calcutta, Vol. I, by V.A. Smith.
J.A.S.B.	Journal of the Asiatic Society of Bengal.
J.B.O.R.S.	Journal of the Bihar and Orissa Research Society.
J.I.S.O.A.	Journal of the Indian Society of Oriental Art.
J.N.S.I.	Journal of the Numismatic Society of India.
J.R.A.S.	Journal of the Royal Asiatic Society.
Kat. Sr. Su.	Kātyāyana Śrauta Sūtra.
Num. Chr.	Numismatic Chronicle.
Pr. A.S.B.	Proceedings of the Asiatic Society of Bengal.
P.M.C.	Catalogue of the Coins in the Punjab Museum, Lahore, Vol. I, by Dr. R. B. Whitehead.

TRANSLITERATION

आ ā, ई ī, ऊ ū, ऋ ṛi, औ au, ङ ṅ, च् ch, छ्, chh ञ्, ñ
ट् ṭ, ठ् ṭh, ड ḍ, ढ ḍh, ण् ṇ, श ś, ष sh, ळ् ḻ, ज्ञ् jñ, विसर्ग ḥ

INTRODUCTION

I. The Discovery of the Hoard

§ 1. The Bayana hoard of Gupta gold coins, of which the Catalogue is being given in the present work, was discovered on the 17th of February, 1946 in a field lying east of the village of Nagla Chhela, but within the jurisdiction of the village Hullanpura, 7 miles south-east of the Railway junction Bayana in the former Bharatpur State, 129 miles south of Delhi. The village is surrounded by hills and H. H. Shri Brajendra Sawai Maharajadhiraja Shri Brajendra Singhji, the Maharaja of Bharatpur, had been there for a shoot in January 1946. To quote the words of His Highness, "I had been there on a small shooting expedition and it certainly gave me the most pleasant surprise to learn that the shoot had brought about the discovery of these coins. For it was in the quest of empty cartridges that three children of the village Nagla Chhela suddenly lighted upon the edge of the pot showing through the earth."[1]

§ 2. The field where the hoard was discovered really lies, as stated above, within the boundary of the village Hullanpura lying to the east of Nagla Chhela; but since the coins were recovered by the villagers of Nagla Chhela, it was first reported that the find-spot was included within its boundaries. The hoard should therefore be correctly described as Hullanpura (Bayana) hoard, but for the sake of convenience, it is being designated as the Bayana hoard.

§ 3. There are no relics of any old structures near the find-spot of the hoard; nor are they to be seen anywhere else either in or near Hullanpura or Nagla Chhela. There is absolutely nothing to suggest that the antiquity of the place can go back to the Gupta period. Karoli, which is about five miles from the place, has yielded some medieval sculptures, which are at present lodged near the palace at Barentha, about 8 miles

---

[1] *J.N.S.I.*, IX, 1.

from Nagla Chhela. Bijayagadh, which is two miles south-west of Bayana and eight miles north-west of Nagla Chhela and Hullanpura, was however an important centre of administration in the Gupta period; a Yaudheya inscription of *c.* 300 A. D. and another of a king named Vishṇuvardhana, dated 372 A. D. have been found there.[1] The unknown owner of the present hoard, probably a resident of Bijayagadh, had buried it in a field of his own at Hullanpura at the time of the Hūṇa invasion. Very likely he was killed in the disturbances, and so the hoard remained undisturbed till 1946.

§ 4. The actual place where the hoard was discovered is the eastern embankment of a low-lying field to the east of Nagla Chhela, belonging to one Bhoreya Gujar. The embankment is hardly two feet in height, and the pot which contained the hoard, was just below the surface, hardly six inches under the ground. Its edge was accidently detected when a small shrub above it was removed by three children named Jitamall, Babu and Tulsi searching for empty cartridge shells. The discoverers of the hoard thought that the pot contained copper buttons and showed them as such to their parents. The latter took no time in detecting the real metal and brought home the pot. There is reason to hold that about 285 coins were distributed among the villagers or transformed into ornaments.[2] With a successful promptitude, of which we have few instances on record, the Bharatpur State authorities managed to get hold of the remaining hoard and could recover as many as 1821 pieces. These are being described in the present work.

§ 5. In order to give the reader a clear idea of the contents of the hoard, we give at the outset its broad classification.

Classification of the Coins in the Bayana Hoard.

Total Number: 1821

Chandragupta I, 10 coins.

King-and-Queen type, Nos. 1-10 10

---

[1] *C.I.I.*, Vol, III, p. 251-3.

[2] The villagers paid Rs. 12,680 to the state authorities as the price or 282 coins melted down by them at the rate of Rs. 45 a coin.

SAMUDRAGUPTA, 183 COINS.

Standard type, Nos. 11-153	143
Aśvamedha type, Nos. 154-173	20
Battle-axe type, Nos. 174-182	9
Archer type, Nos. 183-185	3
Lyrist type, Nos. 186-191	6
Tiger-slayer type, Nos. 192-193	2

KĀCHA, 16 COINS.

Chakradhvaja type, Nos. 194-209	16

CHANDRAGUPTA II, 983 COINS.

Archer type, Throne reverse, Nos. 210-250	41
Archer type, Lotus reverse, Nos. 251-1007	757
Horseman type, Nos. 1008-1089	82
Chhatra type, Nos. 1090-1146	57
Lion-slayer type, Nos. 1147-1188	42
Couch type, Nos. 1189-1191	3
Chakravikrama type, No. 1192	1

KUMĀRAGUPTA I, 628 COINS.

Archer type, Nos. 1193-1375	183
Swordsman type, Nos. 1376-1385	10
Horseman type, Nos. 1386-1690	305
Kārtikeya or Peacock type, Nos. 1691-1703	13
Chhatra type, Nos. 1704-1705	2
Tiger-slayer type, Nos. 1706-1741	36
Lion-slayer type, Nos. 1742-1794	53
Elephant-rider-Lion-slayer type, Nos. 1795-98	4
Rhinoceros-slayer type, Nos. 1799-1802	3
Aśvamedha type, Nos. 1803-6	4
Elephant-rider type, Nos. 1807-1809	3
Lyrist type, Nos. 1810-11	2
Apratigha type, Nos. 1812-1819	8
King-and-Queen type, No. 1820	1

(SKANDAGUPTA) KRAMADITYA, 1 COIN.

Chhatra type, No. 1821	1
Grand total	1821

II. Importance of the Discovery and earlier Hoards

§ 6. The discovery and recovery of a big Gupta hoard, containing as many as 1821 gold coins, is undoubtedly the most sensational numismatic discovery so far made in the history of Indian archaeology. Never before was so big a hoard of gold coins of ancient Indian period ever discovered and recovered. This will become clear, if we take a survey of the earlier hoards and aquaint ourselves of their contents and the way in which they were disposed of.

§ 7. Kalighat hoard.[1]

The earliest known hoard of Gupta gold coins was the one found in 1783 at Kalighat on the eastern bank of the Hugli near Calcutta. It is said that the hoard, which was found deposited in a brass pot, contained more than 200 coins. Nab Kishen, who discovered the hoard, presented it to Warren Hastings, who was then the Governor-General of Bengal. Hastings sent 'a greater part' of the hoard to the Directors of the East India Company, requesting that the coins might be distributed among the most eminent public and private collectons. 24 of the coins were sent to the British Museum, 'nearly an equal number' to the museum of Mr. Hunter, some to the Ashmolean Museum at Oxford, some to the Pulbic Library at Cambridge and some to distinguished individuals. Few coins still remained and eventually the Directors of the East India Company melted them down in what Mr. Allan has aptly described as a mercenary fit. Ancient Indian epigraphy and numismatics were altogether unknown even in their faintest outlines in 1783 A.D., and so there was no possibility of studying and classifying these coins before they were distributed or melted down. As a matter of fact nobody in India, England or Europe could have deciphered these coins at that time. They were believed to be Persian darics, probably because most of them being of the Archer type, appeared to show some resemblance to the coins of Darius. To judge from the coins of this hoard in the different collections to which they were presented, the hoard appears to have consisted mostly of the issues of

---

[1] Allan, *B.M.C.G.D.*, pp. cxxiv-vi.

the later Gupta emperors, most of whom issued coins only of the Archer type.

§ 8. Bharsar hoard.[1]

The next important hoard was the one found at Bharsar near Banaras in 1851 A.D. The hoard consisted of 160 coins of which only 90 could be recovered; and of these only 32 have been classified and described. It appears that most of the coins in the India Office Collection belonged to this hoard. 65 cions of the hoard were sold away as being very defective. 32 coins of this hoard, of which we have definite information, belonged to the following rulers:—

1. Samudragupta		
	Standard type	2
	Archer type	3
	Lyrist type	1
2. Chandragupta II		
	Archer type	8
	Horseman type ..	2
3. Kumāragupta I		
	Archer type	2
	Horseman type ..	4
	Tiger-slayer type ..	1
	Peacock (Kārtikeya) type	1
4. Skandagupta		
	Archer type	6
5. Prakāśāditya		
	Horseman type	2

§ 9. Jessore hoard.[2]

A small hoard of gold Gupta coins was discovered at Muhammadpur near Jessore in Bengal in 1852. This also could not be classified and described properly. The hoard contained the *rājalīlā* coin of Narendrāditya, a coin of Śaśāṅka and a specimen of the late imitations of Gupta coins. A number of silver coins of Chandragupta II, Kumāragupta I and Skandagupta are also said to have been found in the hoard, but there is no

[1] *J.A.S.B.*, 1852, pp. 399-400; *B.M.C.G.D.*, Introduction, pp. cxxvi-vii; *J.A.S.B.*, 1884, pp. 150-1.

[2] *J.A.S.B.*, 1852, pp. 401-2; *Ibid*, 1884, p. 152.

record kept of them. It is not very likely that a large number of silver coins of Chandragupta II could have been found in this hoard; they were rare in Eastern India even during the reign of that emperor. The hoard may have, however, contained some silver coins of Kumāragupta I and Skandagupta.

§ 10. Allahabad hoard.[1]

According to the information supplied by Cunningham to V.A. Smith, a hoard of about two hundred gold coins of Kumāragupta was found near Allahabad in *c.* 1864. Cunningham obtained 4 specimens from the hoard, but was not in a position to classify the remaining coins or note their types. Smith's statement[2] that the hoard consisted of 200 pieces of the Peacock type of Kumāragupta I does not seem to be correct. The Peacock type is relatively rare and the hoard is not likely to have contained as many as 200 of its specimens.

§ 11. Hugli hoard.[3]

In 1883 a hoard of Gupta gold coins was discovered near Hugli in Bengal, a careful classification of which has been handed down to us. It was a small hoard of 13 coins only, in which the following kings and types were represented;—

Samudragupta,	Standrad type	..	1
Chandragupta II,	Archer type	..	5
Kumāragupta I,	Archer type	..	3
,, ,,	Horseman type	..	3
,, ,,	Lion-slayer type	..	1
	Total	..	13

§ 12. Tanda hoard.[4]

A hoard of 15 Gupta gold coins was discovered in 1885 at Tanda, an ancient place in Rai Bareily district of U.P. We have a description of only seven coins of this collection, of which one was of Chandragupta I, five of Samudragupta of the Standard type and one of Kācha. Smith, who had

---

[1] *J.A.S.B.*, 1884, p. 152.
[2] *J.A.S.B.*, 1889, p. 49.
[3] *J.A.S.B.*, 1884, p. 152.
[4] Allan, *B.M.C.G.D.*, p. cxxviii; *Proc. A.S.B.*, 1886, p. 68.

seen the hoard, has left us a more detailed account. He says that two of the coins belonged to Chandragupta I and the remaining 23 consisted of the coins of Kāchagupta and specimens of the *Aśvamedha* and Battle-axe types of Samudragupta.[1] Unfortunately he did not note the exact number of each class.

§ 13. Kotwa hoard.[2]

This hoard was found in 1886 near Kotwa in the Gorakhpur district of U.P., scattered below some bricks in an old *ḍīh*.[3] It consisted of 17 coins belonging to Chandragupta II and Kumāragupta I. Their analysis is as follows:—

Chandragupta II		
	Archer type, Lotus reverse. ..	5
	Lion-trampler type.	1
Kumāragupta I,		
	Archer type	1
	Horseman-to-right type ..	5
	Horseman-to-left type	1
	Peacock (Kārtikeya) type ..	2
	Lion-trampler type	1
	Unidentified	1
	Total ..	17

§ 14. Basti hoard.[4]

This hoard was found in August 1887 after heavy rains on the site of an old town in Muza Sarai, close to the Basti Jail in U.P. Eleven coins were apparently found, but only ten could be recovered. They were all the issues of Chandragupta II, nine being of the Archer type, Lotus reverse, and one being of the *Chhatra* type.

§ 15. Hajipur hoard.[5]

This hoard was discovered in August 1893 among thick rubbles in a small walled enclosure close to the bazar of Hajipur

[1] *J.A.S.B.*, 1884, p. 153.
[2] *J.R.A.S.*, 1889, p. 46.
[3] *Dih* denotes a deserted town or village site.
[4] *Pr. A.S.B.*, 1887, p. 221.
[5] *Ibid.* 1894, p. 227.

in Bihar. 22 coins were found, but only fourteen could be recovered; they were as follows:—

Chandragupta I, King-and-Queen type	.. ..	1
Samudragupta, Archer type ..	.. .. ..	1
,, Battle-axe type	.. .. ..	1
,, Standard type	.. .. ..	2
Chandragupta II, Archer type, Throne reverse	.. .. ..	2
,, Archer type, Lotus reverse	.. .. ..	1
,, *Chhatra* type	.. .. ..	3
,, Lion-combatant type	.. ..	1
,, Lion-trampler type	.. ..	2
Total	..	14

§ 16. Tekri Debra hoard.[1]

A hoard of 40 gold Gupta coins was discovered at Tekri Debra in the Mirzapur district of U.P. in 1909. This is the first Gupta hoard to be scientifically analysed and adequately published. It however consisted only of 40 coins, which belonged to the following kings and types :—

Samudragupta, Standard type	.. .. ..	2
,, Battle-axe type	.. .. ..	1
Chandragupta II, Archer type	.. .. ..	15
,, Lion-slayer type ..	.. ..	9
,, Lion-retreating type	.. ..	1
,, Horseman type, left	.. ..	3
,, ,, right	.. ..	5
Kumāragupta I, Archer type	.. .. ..	1
,, Lion-slayer type	.. .. ..	1
,, Horseman type	.. .. ..	2
Total	..	40

§ 17. Kasarva hoard.

This hoard was found in the village Kasarva in the district of Ballia in U.P. and consisted of the following 17 coins.

[1] *Num. Ch.*, 1910, pp. 398-408, Pl. XIV.

Samudragupta,	Standard type	..	11
„	*Aśvamedha* type	..	3
„	Battle-axe type	..	1
Kācha		..	1
	Total	..	16

§ 18. Mithathal hoard.[1]

This hoard was found at Mithathal in the Hissar district of the Punjab in 1915-6. It consisted of 86 coins, of which 26 were melted down. Of the rest we are told that 33 were the coins of Samudragupta and the rest were of the later Kushāṇas. No details are available of the types of Samudragupta represented in the hoard, but one of them was of that rare variety of the Battle-axe type, where the king is on the left side and the attendant on the right side.

§ 19. Jaunpur hoard.[2]

This hoard was found in the building, popularly known as Jai Chandra's Mahal, in Jaunpur in U.P. It is said to have consisted of a small number of coins, but no details have been noted of their contents.

§ 20. Gopalpur hoard.[3]

This hoard was found near the village of Gopalpur in the Gorakhpur district of U.P. It consisted of 20 pieces, of which 7 are stated to have been the issues of Chandragupta II. We do not know anything about the rest.

§ 21. Jhusi hoard.[4]

This was found at Jhusi, opposite Allahabad, and is stated to have consisted of about 20 to 30 pieces. Ten coins were of Kumāragupta I, two being of the Archer type and eight of the Peacock or the Kārtikeya type.

§ 22. It will be seen from the above account of the various hoards of the Gupta gold coins found so far, how they were all small in size and how very few of them could be scien-

---

[1] *A.S.I.A.R.*, 1926-7, pp. 233-4.
[2] *J.A.S.B.*, 1884, p. 150.
[3] *J.A.S.B.*, 1884., p. 152; *J.R.A.S.*, 1893, p. 49.
[4] *J.R.A.S.*, 1893, p. 49; *J.A.S.B.*, 1884, p. 152.

tifically analysed and adequately published. The Bayana hoard probably consisted of about 2,100 coins, of which as many as 1821 pieces could be recovered, thanks to the promptness of the Maharaja and the government of Bharatpur. In the present Catalogue we are giving the size, weight and detailed description of each one of these 1821 coins and illustrating 459 of them in the plates. So big a collection of Gupta gold coins has nowhere been so far described and illustrated. The credit of recovering the hoard and getting it published goes entirely to H. H. Sawai Brajendra Singhji, the Maharaja of Bharatpur, who took the keenest interest in the matter and spared no trouble or expense to achieve his cherished desire to place before the numismatic world an adequate and scientific account of the hoard in the present Catalogue, which is being published under his gracious patronage.

III. History of the Gupta Dynasty

§ 23. We propose to give here the history of the Gupta dynasty as a back-ground to the study of the coins of the Bayana hoard. We do not, however, desire to discuss in detail the controversial or minor points connected with the dynasty; we shall content ourselves with its history in broad outlines.

I. Śrīgupta, *c.* 270-290 A.D.

§ 24. The term Gupta dynasty is given for the sake of convenience to the house founded by Śrīgupta in *c.* 270 A.D. in Magadha, primarily because the names of most of its rulers ended with the term Gupta. The sacred texts show that it was customary to add this affix to the names of the members of the Vaiśya and Śūdra communities,[1] and inscriptions disclose the existence of a number of families in the early centuries of the Christian era, which bore the surname Gupta.[2] Even in the Suṅga period, we come across individuals described as Gotiputas, obviously because their mothers belonged to Gupta families. Probably most of these Gupta families of the early period were originally members of the Vaiśya class, who

---

[1] गुप्तदासात्मकं नाम प्रशस्तं वैश्यशूद्रयोः । *Vishṇupurāṇa* quoted by Kullūka at Manu II. 32.

[2] See Lüder's List, Nos. 5,11,67,94,96,156,194,663,680-2 etc.

often changed the scales for the sword, as was common at that time. We need not suppose that they were all interconnected by blood relationship or that Śrīgupta, the founder of the Gupta dynasty, was descended from any one of them. He simply belonged to one of the numerous families that were known as Gupta from their family custom of usually having Gupta-ending personal names. The *gotra* of this family was most probably Dhāraṇa.[1]

§ 25. The founder of the dynasty, Śrīgupta, flourished from *c.* 270 to 290 A.D. He is most probably identical with the king Śrīgupta (Chi-li-ki-ta), who is described by the Chinese traveller Itsing as the builder of a temple for Chinese pilgrims at Mili-kia-si-kia-po-no (Mrigaśikhāvana), 40 *yojanas* to the east of Nālandā on the bank of the Gaṅgā. Itsing gives the time of this ruler Śrīgupta in round numbers as about 500 years before the time of his visit in *c.* 680 A.D. This would place him in *c.* 180 A.D., i.e. about 90 years before the time above assigned by us to Śrīgupta. But when we note how the Chinese pilgrim gives the time only in round numbers, as stated in the tradition handed down from ancient times by old men, the discrepancy of about ninety years in a period of 500 years need not be taken as an insuperable objection in identifying the two rulers.

§ 26. We may therefore accept as a working hypothesis that Śrīgupta of Itsing is identical with Śrīgupta, the grandfather of the first Gupta emperor Chandragupta I. This will enable us to determine the place of his patrimony. Itsing states that Śrīgupta had endowed the temple he had built at Mṛigaśikhāvana with 24 villages. It must therefore have been located in his own kingdom. Mṛigaśikhāvana was located about 40 *yojanas* or 200 miles to the east of Nālandā and was in Varendra or northern Bengal.[2] The original patrimony of the

[1] Vākāṭaka inscriptions describe Prabhāvatīguptā, the daughter of Chandragupta II, as *Dhārṇasagotrā* (*E.I.*, XV. 41). Her husband's *gotra* was Vishṇuvṛiddha, so Dhāraṇa was most probably the *gotra* of her father. We cannot, however, be quite sure on the point.

[2] Prof. Jagannath has, however, identified Mṛigaśikhāvana with Sarnath relying upon its western direction, as given in Beal's translation; *I.H.Q.*, 1946, p. 23. It is difficult to say which translation is correct. There is, however; little evidence to connect the early Guptas with the Banaras region.

Guptas was thus located in south-east Bihar and included a part of north-western Bengal as well. We cannot be more definite about its extent in the present state of our knowledge.

§ 27. Later official Gupta records never fail to differentiate between the titles of the first two Gupta rulers and their successors; the former are always given the humbler title *mahārāja*, while the latter are invariably described as *mahārājādhirājas* or emperors. It is clear that the political power and prestige of the first two rulers were much less than those of their successors. There are several instances to show that the title *mahārāja* denoted feudatory status in the Gupta period; but the same was not always the case in the earlier times, as the rulers of the independent dynasties like those of the Bhāraśivas and the Vākāṭakas were content to use the humbler title *mahārāja*, though they were not feudatories. It would appear that very probably Śrīgupta and Ghaṭotkacha were petty rulers, rather than feudatories; if they were feudatories, we do not know the names of their suzerains.

§ 28. It has been no doubt suggested that Bihar continued to be under the imperial sway of the Kushāṇas down to the 4th century A.D., and that Śrīgupta and Ghaṭotkacha must have been their feudatories.[1] There is, however, hardly any evidence to support this view. The contention that the coinage of the later Great Kushāṇas is still extremely abundant in the markets of Patna, Gaya and Banaras is inaccurate; we come across copper coins of the *early* Kushāṇa emperors in eastern U. P. and Bihar, and not those of the *later* Great Kushāṇas. The coins of the later Kushāṇa emperors are rarely found in Bihar. In the excavations at Bhita in U. P. and Patna in Bihar only the coins of the early great Kushāṇa emperors upto Vāsudeva I were found; those of their successors were conspicuous by their absence. There is ample evidence to show that the Yaudheyas of the Eastern Punjab, the Nāgas of Padmāvatī and the Maghas of Kauśāmbī had ousted the Kushāṇas and become independent in the 3rd century A.D.[2] The view that Śrīgupta and his son Ghaṭotkacha were the feudatories of the

---

[1] R.D. Banarji, *The Age of the Imperial Guptas*, pp. 2 ff.

[2] Majumdar and Altekar, *The Age of the Vākāṭakas and the Guptas*, Chap. II.

Kushāṇas and that Chandragupta I became an emperor as a consequence of his overthrowing the Kushāṇa empire, can no longer be maintained.

§ 29. Very little is known about the career of Śrīgupta. He was a man of liberal views, for we find him making arrangements for the stay of Chinese Buddhist pilgrims at Mṛigaśikhāvana. His generous endowment of the revenue of 24 villages would suggest that his kingdom could not have been an insignificant one. He, however, did not start issuing any coins; he was perhaps not important enough to take that step.

2. Ghaṭotkacha, c. 290-305 A.D.

§ 30. Ghaṭotkacha, the son and successor of Śrīgupta, is even a more shadowy figure than his father. We may, however, well presume that he must have made his own contribution to the growing glory of his house. For, a recently discovered inscription from Bundelkhand describes the Gupta royal family as descended from Ghaṭotkacha and not Śrīgupta.[1] Ghaṭotkacha may well be presumed to have extended the political influence of his family and paved the way for his son to assume the imperial title. One of the most important steps that he took in this direction was to arrange the marriage of his crown-prince Chandragupta I with the Lichchhavi princess Kumāradevī.

§ 31. The Lichchhavis had a hoary history and their name carried great prestige. In Indian royal genealogies, a king is usually found describing himself as the grand-son through the daughter of a particular personage, only when the maternal grand-father is known to have been of considerable help to his grand-son. Official Gupta genealogies never fail to describe Samudragupta as a *Lichchhavi-dauhitra* or the grand-son through a Lichchhavi princess. It is therefore clear that the Gupta-Lichchhavi union, which Ghaṭotkacha had the foresight to bring about, was regarded as of particular importance even by the great conqueror Samudragupta. There can be no doubt that the Lichchhavis wielded considerable prestige at this time.

---

[1] *Proceedings and Transactions of 12th Benares Session of the All-India Oriental Conference, p.* 588.

Vaiśālī, about 40 miles to the north of Pāṭaliputra, was their capital in the days of Bimbisāra. Where they were ruling by the beginning of the 4th century A.D. we do not know. An inscription from Nepal refers to a Lichchhavi family ruling at Pushpapura or Pāṭaliputra.[1] It is not unlikely that the Lichchhavi family to which Kumāradevī, the bride of Chandragupta, belonged may have ruled at this city. It is, however, more probable that Pāṭaliputra was in the hands of the Guptas and that the family of Kumāradevī was ruling at Vaiśālī.

§ 32. In spite of the growing power of his kingdom, Ghaṭotkacha issued no coins. The solitary coin, bearing the name *Ghaṭo* under the arm, is probably an issue of a son of Kumāragupta I and not that of the father of Chandragupta I. The reasons for this view will be explained later in § 229. Ghaṭotkacha has left us no contemporary record.[2]

3. Chandragupta I, *c.* 305-325 A.D.

§ 33. Ghaṭotkacha died in *c.* 305 A.D. and was succeeded by his son Chandragupta I. The new king bore a name of imperial association and the Lichchhavi alliance had given him a point of vantage. His power rose rapidly as a result of the union of the resources and territories of the Lichchhavis and the Guptas. The Lichchhavis were the masters of Mithilā, and the Guptas were ruling over a portion of southern Bihar and north-western Bengal. All these territories were united into a powerful kingdom by the Gupta-Lichchhavi matrimonial alliance. Chandragupta, however, was not content only with this development; he extended his sphere of influence and activity and succeeded in annexing eastern U.P. up to Allahabad and the province of Oudh as well. This conclusion is rendered almost certain by a well known verse in the Purāṇas,[3] which describes the extent of the Gupta kingdom, obviously at the end of the reign of Chandragupta I, and states how it included Magadha, Sāketa (Ayodhyā) and the Gangetic valley

---

[1] B. Indraji, *Inscriptions from Nepal*, No. 15.

[2] The seal of Ghaṭotkachagupta found at Vaiśālī cannot be attributed to the second king of the house. It bears no royal title.

[3] अनुगंगाप्रयागं च साकेतं मागधांस्तया ।
एतान्जानपदान्देशान् भोक्ष्यन्ते गुप्तवंशजाः ॥ *Vāyu P.*, 99. 383.

up to Prayāga (Allahabad). It is also confirmed by an analysis of the Allahabad pillar inscription, which shows that Samudragupta had not conquered any portion of the territory in the above area. The inclusion of Ayodhyā and Allahabad-Banaras tract in the Gupta kingdom was not due only to peaceful diplomacy. Probably some battles had to be fought and the crown-prince Samudragupta may well be presumed to have taken a prominent part in them.

§ 34. Chandragupta I eventually decided to assume the imperial title *mahārājādhirāja*, no doubt justified by the additions he had made to his ancestral kingdom. Probably this he did at a formal coronation, which took place rather late in his reign. It is usually assumed that the Gupta era marks the assumption of the imperial title by Chandragupta I at this formal coronation; this is the most probable hypothesis but lacks conclusive proof. The initial date of the Gupta era is either the 20th of December 318 or the 26th of February 320 A.D. according to different calculations; the latter date seems to be the more probable one.

§ 35. Chandragupta I is the earliest Hindu ruler, whose inscribed gold coins have been handed down to us. No ruler either of the Maurya or the Suṅga or the Sātavāhana dynasty issued any gold coins. The practice was started by the foreign Greek and Kushāṇa rulers; Chandragupta was the first national king to adopt it. Probably he started his gold coinage at the time when he assumed the imperial title. This took place rather late in his reign, when his conquests had invested him with sufficient importance. On his gold coins **(Pl. I. 1-10)**, we have the names and figures of the king and the queen on the obverse and the name of the Lichchhavis on the reverse. It is clear that in spite of the growing greatness of the Guptas, the Lichchhavis insisted in maintaining their separate identity in the dual kingdom; we have not yet got a single coin of Chandragupta I, where the name of the Lichchhavi clan and princess does not appear on the reverse and obverse respectively. The recently published Standard type coin of Chandragupta does not go against this view; for the coin in question was an issue of Chandragupta II, and not of Chandragupta I.[1]

[1] The view that this coin type belongs to Chandragupta I has been no doubt advanced, but does not seem tenable; see *J.N.S.I.*, XI, pp. 151 ff.

4. Kācha, *c.* 325-330 A. D.

§ 36. Chandragupta had several sons and selected Samudragupta amongst them as his successor at an impressive Darbar held for the purpose. The selection did cause a heart burning to those of his brothers, who had aspired for the imperial throne, and it would appear that one of them, Kācha, successfully contested the throne and ruled for some time.[1] His coins are usually found associated with those of Chandragupta I and Samudragupta in the Gupta hoards. It was at one time held by the present writer that Kācha may be identical with Rāmagupta, the eldest son of Samudragupta, according to the literary tradition.[2] But the discovery of the copper coins of Rāmagupta in Mālwā has weakened this theory. One and the same ruler could not have issued the coins with the name of Rāmagupta on copper coins and Kācha on gold ones, even if he had these two names. It is possible to argue that Rāmagupta of the copper coins was a local ruler in Mālwā, and not the Gupta emperor mentioned in literary works; but this does not seem probable. (See also §§ 142-46).

The coins of Kācha are not quite rare; he may well have ruled for about five years. For his coins, see. § 138-§ 141.

5. Samudragupta, *c.* 330-370 A.D.

§ 37. After overthrowing Kācha, Samudragupta ascended the throne in *c.* 330 A.D. The fratricidal war must have encouraged fissiparous tendencies and induced feudatory princes to rebel; the opening verses of the Allahabad pillar inscription, which are unfortunately fragmentary, vaguely refer to the enemies of the emperor, with whom he had to fight . But he soon overcame the opposition and re-established the imperial position of his house.

§ 37. The view of R.D. Banerji that the Gupta kingdom was overrun by king Chandravarman of Pushkaraṇa towards the end of the reign of Chandragupta I or soon thereafter,[3] is as

---

[1] Verse 5 of the Allahabad *Praśsasti* probably referred to the war of succession; but as it is incomplete, we cannot be definite upon the point. Kācha might have also been a king of another dynasty, who ousted Samudragupta for a while; but this eventuality appears to be extremely improbable.

[2] *J.N.S.I.* IX, 131.

[3] Banerji, *The Age of the Imperial Guptas*, p. 10.

untenable as the theory of Dr. Jayaswal that the Vākāṭakas had shattered the rising Gupta empire in *c.* 330, Samudragupta being reduced to the position of a Vākāṭaka feudatory.[1] Banerji's view presupposes that the king Chandra of Mehrauli inscription is identical with king Chandravarman of Pushkaraṇa, which is hardly probable. Dr. Jayaswal's theory is based upon his identification of king Chaṇḍasena of the *Kaumudīmahotsava* with the Gupta king Chandragupta I. This is hardly possible. There is no evidence whatsoever to show that the Vākāṭaka emperor Pravarasena I had ever conquered the Guptas[2]. It will be shown later (§ 137) how the title *rājā* on the Tiger-slayer type of Samudragupta does not at all show that he had been reduced to a feudatory status and how it was due to the numismatic convention of having only a short legend on the reverse. It appears very unlikely that the Gupta power had suffered an eclipse either at the end of the reign of Chandragupta I or at the beginning of that of Samudragupta. It is very probable that the rebellion of Kācha had created a disturbance at the beginning of the reign, but it was put down in a short time.

§ 38. Samudragupta has the rare good fortune of an authentic, official and detailed account of his achievements being handed down to the posterity in the form of his Allahabad pillar inscription, inscribing his achievements in war on a pillar originally raised to describe its sinfulness by the great Aśoka. Unfortunately Harisheṇa, who was entrusted with the draft of the inscription, was more of a poet than a historian; he, for instance, tells us how his patron had scored victories in hundreds of battles, but does not enlighten us about the times and places of most of them. Of course it must be admitted that had he done so, his panegyric could probably not have been a prose poem, as it undoubtedly is.

§ 39. Samudragupta was not only a great conqueror, but an able administrator of clear vision. He was undoubtedly inspired by the vision of an all-India empire, which could protect the country from foreign aggression and promote its progress in different departments of arts and sciences. He, however, realised that in the circumstances of the age, the whole of India

[1] *A.B.O.R.I.*, IV, 30-40.
[2] *I C*, IX, 99-106.

or even a greater part of it could not be welded into a centrally administered empire. He therefore annexed those kings' kingdoms only, which could be effectively assimilated in his empire. To this unfortunate category belonged nine kings of the Gangetic plain, Rudradeva, Matila, Nāgadatta, Chandravarman, Gaṇapatināga, Nāgasena, Achyuta, Nandi and Balavarman.[1] Of these Gaṇapatināga, Nāgasena and Nāgadatta were the Nāga rulers ruling at Padmāvatī (near Gwalior) and other neighbouring places in U.P. Achyuta was the king of Ahichchhatra in Bareily district. The dominions of other rulers cannot be precisely located at present, but they must have been contiguous to or included in modern U.P. It is not possible to accept the view that Rudradeva of this list was either a Śaka or a Vākāṭaka ruler and that Balavarman was a ruler of that name of a dynasty ruling in Assam; all these rulers were outside the limits of Āryāvarta, where they are expressly described as ruling in the Allahabad pillar inscription.

§ 40. After annexing these kingdoms, Samudragupta probably turned his attention to the petty chiefs ruling in the forests of Central India on the flanks of the Vindhya range in the Jabalpur division. Their subjugation was obviously an initial step of the grand campaign in the Deccan, which the emperor was contemplating. In the course of this campaign Samudragupta first overthrew Vyāghrarāja of the Great Forest and Mahendra of south Kośala, who were ruling in the districts of Raipur, Bilaspur and Samabalpur, and then invaded the eastern Deccan. There he defeated Svāmidatta of Koṭṭūra in Ganjam district, Damana of Eraṇḍapalla and Kubera of Devarāshṭra in Vizagapattam district, Mahendragiri of Pishṭapura and the Sālaṅkyāyana king Hastivarman of Veṅgi ruling in the Godavari district, and Maṇṭarāja, who had his small principality near the Kolair lake. He then penetrated further and attacked Ugrasena of Pālakka in Nellore district and the Pallava king Vishṇugupta of Kāñchī or Conjeeveram. Other kings mentioned in connection with this southern campaign are Nilarāja of Avamukta and Dhanañjaya of Kusthalapura. Their kingdoms are

[1] For the identification of the kings mentioned in the Allahabad inscription, see, Allan, *B.M.C.G.D.*, pp. xxi-xxx; Dubreuil, *A.H.D.*, pp. 58-61. *Bhandarkar*, *I. H.Q.* I. pp. 250-60

not yet identified, but they were probably somewhere in the northern part of the Madras State. The view that Damana of Eraṇḍapalla was ruling at Erandol in Khandesh and Kubera of Devarāshṭra was ruling in Mahārāshṭra is now shown to be incorrect. There is thus no evidence to show that the southern invasion of Samudragupta resulted in the overrunning of Mahārāshṭra as well. The Vākāṭakas, who were ruling there, are not mentioned either in the category of the feudatories or that of the tributories in the Allahabad record. Samudragupta's expedition was confined mostly to the Madras State. No districts of that State were, however, annexed to the Gupta empire; for we are expressly told that the kings of the Deccan were uprooted, but replanted in their dominions, obviously on their acknowledging the overlordship of the conqueror and agreeing to pay him a tribute.

§ 41. The Allahabad inscription enables us to ascertain the extent of the empire of Samudragupta. It included practically the whole of Bengal, Bihar, U. P., the State of Delhi and a part of the Eastern Punjab. The Yamunā was the western boundary till its confluence with the Chambal. Then the empire extended from Padmāvatī near Gwalior to Erakiṇa or Eran in Sagar district. The line from Eran to Jabalpur was the southern boundary and then it moved rather irregularly to Allahabad.

§ 42. The powerful ruler of this mighty empire naturally inspired awe among his neighbours, and we are told how the kings of Samataṭa, Ḍavāka and Kāmarūpa on the Assam frontier, of Nepāla and Kartṛipura (in Jullundur district) in the north and the ruling authorities in the republics of the Mālavas (in Mewar), the Arjunāyanas (in Bharatpur district), and the Yaudheyas (in northern Rajputana and the Eastern Punjab), and the Madras (in the Central Punjab) vied with each other in offering him their submission in a variety of suitable ways. The same course was followed by the Ābhīras (in Bhilsa-Jhansi area), the Prārjunas, the Sanakānīkas and the Kākas (near Bhopal and Sanchi) and Kharaparikas (in Damoh district of M.P.).

§ 43. Rulers of the kingdoms beyond this belt of feudatories like the Kidāra-Kushāṇa king of Peshawar and the Saka Mahākshartrapa of Western India, as also the kings of several islands like Ceylon, and possibly Java and Sumatra, showed natural anxiety to cultivate cordial and friendly relations with Samudragupta by sending him presents and proposing matrimonial alliances. There is no doubt that as a result of his conquest and successful foreign policy, Samudragupta secured for his house an undisputed position of pre-eminence in India, which it retained for about a hundred years.

§ 44. Samudragupta was a staunch Hindu and he decided to celebrate the successful termination of his campaigns by the performance of a Horse sacrifice, which the Vedic texts have prescribed for a victorious emperor. This sacrifice was no doubt not held in abeyance for a long time, as claimed by the court poet of Kumāragupta I, but there can be no doubt that Samudragupta's Horse sacrifice must have eclipsed in glory and grandeur the Horse sacrifices performed by the Bhāraśivas and the Sālaṅkyāyanas. To commemorate its performance a new type of gold coinage was issued, which ranks very high among the products of fine art in ancient India **(Pls. IV-V. 1-5)**. We shall describe this type in due course (§ 107-§ 116). The sacrifice was most probably celebrated towards the end of the reign of the emperor, for it is not mentioned in his Allahabad inscription; had it been performed earlier, the court poet would never have failed to give its glowing description.

§ 45. Though a Hindu by birth and tradition, Samudragupta could appreciate the religion and philosophy of other sects like Buddhism and Jainism as well. Literary tradition states that the famous Buddhist scholar and philosopher Vasubandhu was hospitably received in his royal court. The request of the Buddhist king Meghavarṇa of Ceylon was conceded and he was permitted to build a *vihāra* (monastery) at Bodhgayā for the reception of Ceylonese pilgrims.

§ 46. Samudragupta had a versatile personality, as remarkable for physical power as for intellectual pre-eminence, artistic predilections, political sagacity and administrative insight. His portrait on the coins **(Pl. II)** shows that he had a well-built and tall figure, which had been developed into a powerful and muscular body by active and varied exercises. He was fond of hunting and on the coins of his Tiger-slayer type we find him shooting a ferocious tiger at close quarters **(Pl. VI. 9-10)**. His intellect had been sharpened by the study of different subjects and sciences; but it had not made him dry; for he was also a poet and a musician. Of his poetic compositions, none has been handed down to us, but his interest and skill in music is attested to by a beautiful series of gold coins, where we find him seated on a couch and absorbed in playing music upon a lute **(Pl. VI. 3-8.)** His numerous victories, which are referred to in his coin legends, had not maddened him; he annexed the kingdoms only of those kings whose territories could be effectively amalgamated into a strong central state, that could be administrated from Pāṭaliputra. He allowed other kings to rule as feudatories even after their defeat. His political and cultural vision extended beyond the borders of India, for the rulers of Ceylon and other islands, like Java, Sumatra, Bali, etc. were encouraged to cultivate friendly political and cultural relations with the new and rising imperial power of India. Subsequent discoveries may show that the credit of the spread of Indian culture to Indonesia has to be largely given to the far-sighted policy of the Imperial Guptas, first enunciated by Samudragupta.

The precise date of the death of Samudragupta is not known. There is sufficient evidence to show that he had a long reign of about 40 years and we may place his death in *c.* 370 A.D.

§ 47. Samudragupta paid considerable attention to his coinage. He was not content to issue coins in a single type. He introduced a pleasing variety in his coin-types and his example was emulated by his successors, as a consequence of which we possess in Gupta gold issues the most artistic series of gold coins ever issued in ancient India. So far six coin types of Samudragupta are known.[1] Of these the Standard, the Archer and the Battle-axe types refer to his military activities and the *Aśvamedha* type commemorates their successful culmination. The other two types give us a glimpse into some of the hobbies of the great emperor. The Tiger-slayer type shows that the emperor took keen interest in wild game and the Lyrist type discloses how he used to spend his rare leisure hours in his palace in playing on the lute. The statement of Harishena that his patron excelled Tumburu in musical skill was thus not without some founda-

[1] See §§ 96-137 for the description and discussion of the coin-types of Samudragupta.

tion. Whether Samudragupta composed any poems, as claimed by Harisheṇa, we do not know. But there is no doubt that he is the first king in ancient Indian history to introduce metrical legends on coins; and it is not improbable that he may have himself composed some, if not all of them.

6. Rāmagupta, *c.* 370-375 A.D.

§ 48. The question about the successor of Samudragupta has not yet been satisfactorily solved. Till the year 1925, every body believed that Samudragupta was succeeded by Chandragupta II, as stated in the official genealogy given in all records. The discovery of the extracts from a lost drama *Devīchandraguptam* in the *Nāṭyadarpaṇa*,[1] a newly discovered work on dramaturgy, disclosed for the first time that a king named Chandragupta had saved his brother Rāmagupta's wife Dhruvadevī from an unnamed Śaka king by disguising himself in female attire in order to impersonate her, when she had been demanded by the Śaka enemy as the price for raising the siege and allowing Rāmagupta to retire. This disguise was the most striking part of the incident, as it had given the name to the drama, viz. *Devīchandraguptam*.[2] This interesting episode was well known to poet Bāṇa of the 7th century and his commentator Śaṅkarārya; for it appears from the *Harshacharita* and its commentary that a Śaka king had been killed by Chandragupta, because he was coveting his brother's wife Dhruvadevī.[3] One of the extracts from the *Nāṭyadarpaṇa* suggests that Dhruvadevī had begun to entertain a feeling of disgust for her husband on account of his cowardice[4], and her rescuer had

[1] For a full discussion of the problem of Rāmagupta, see Altekar, *J.B.O.R.S.*, XIV. 223 ff; XV. 134 ff.; Bhandarkar, *Malaviya Comm.* Vol. pp. 189 ff; Mirashi, *I.H.Q.*., X. 48 ff; S. Konow, *J. B. O. R. S.*, XVIII, 17 ff.

[2] यथा देवीचन्द्रगुप्ते द्वितीयेंडके..शकस्य ध्रुवदेवीसंप्रदानेऽभ्युपगते राज्ञा रामगुप्तेन अरिवधनार्थं पियासु: प्रतिपन्नध्रुवदेवीनेपथ्य: कुमारचन्द्रगुप्तो विज्ञपयन्नुच्यते ।
J.B.O.R.S., XIV, p. 226

[3] शकाधिपति: चन्द्रगुप्तभ्रातृजायां ध्रुवदेवीं प्रार्थयमान: चन्द्रगुप्तेन ध्रुवदेवीवेषधारिणा स्त्रीवेषजनपरिवृतेन व्यापादित: । *Ibid.*, p. 227.

[4] पत्यु: क्लीबजनोचितेन चरितेनानेन पुंस: सत: ।
लज्जाकोपविषादभीत्यरतिभि: क्षेत्रीकृता ताम्यते ॥ *Ibid.*, p. 227.

to feign madness in order to save himself, probably from his elder brother.[1] Epigraphs tell us that Dhruvadevī was also the name of Chandragupta's own wife. In Hindu families two brothers' wives do not bear the same name. The literary evidence, when correlated to the epigraphical one, thus tends to show that Dhruvadevī, wife of Chandragupta, was originally the wife of his elder brother Rāmagupta, Chandragupta being her second husband. Rāmagupta may have died a natural death, but since there is a vague reference in a Rāshṭrakūṭa copper plate to a famous donor from the Gupta dynasty having besmirched his fair name by murdering his brother and marrying his widow, it is fair to assume that Chandragupta may have connived at his brother's murder by the infuriated army, and the drama may have ended with the ultimate marriage of its hero with the lady whom he had rescued at the risk of his own life.

The surrender of Dhruvasvāminī is referred to in a single verse quoted by Rājaśekhara and the whole incident, as given in outline above, with many more suggestive details, is narrated in the *Majmalu-t-Tawārīkh*, a 12th century work, as the story of Rāwal and Barkamāris.[2] This story discloses the additional fact that Dhruvadevī had been originally betrothed to Chandragupta, but was eventually married to his elder brother against her wish.

§ 49. On the strength of the above evidence, which is mostly literary, it has been argued with fair plausibility that the eldest son of Samudragupta was Rāmagupta. He succeeded him in due course, but was signally defeated by a Śaka king, who imposed a humiliating peace upon him. His younger brother Chandragupta, however, saved the situation by killing the Śaka king in his harem by impersonating his sister-in-law Dhruvadevī. How exactly Rāmagupta's life ended, we do not know. But it is clear that he did not live long and was succeeded by his younger brother Chandragupta, who eventually married his brother's wife, whose honour he had saved at the risk of his own life.

§ 50. Epigraphical evidence, however, does not support the above reconstruction of history. It no doubt shows that

[1] इयं स्वापायशंकिनः कृतकोन्मत्तस्य कुमारचन्द्रगुप्तस्य प्रवेशप्रतिपादिकेति ।
Ibid., p. 228.

[2] *Ibid.*, XV, p. 138.

Dhruvadevī was the wife of Chandragupta II, but no official Gupta genealogy ever mentions the name of Rāmagupta as the son of Samudragupta and the predecessor of Chandragupta II. The whole incident has an air of improbability about it, and it appears difficult to believe that the fortunes of the great Gupta empire should have sunk so low within a decade of the death of Samudragupta as to compel his successor to agree to the surrender of his crowned queen. One is loath to believe that Chandragupta, the idol of the nation for a long time, should have murdered his own brother and married his widow. We have discovered the gold coins of almost every Gupta emperor, and it is inexplicable why we should have so far found no gold coins of Rāmagupta, if he was a historic personage.

§ 51. We have yet no sufficient evidence to pronounce the final opinion about the historicity of the Rāmagupta episode, but it appears fairly probable that Chandragupta II was preceded on the throne by an elder brother named Rāmagupta. Clear contemporary evidence is not yet available to show that Chandragupta had murdered his brother; it may be that he died rather abruptly by the sheer feeling of utter shame, and later scandal may have suspected foul play, especially because Chandragupta married his brother's widow. It may be that Rāmagupta may have been killed by the infuriated army and Chandragupta may have only connived at the murder, as he could not prevent it. The marriage with an elder brother's widow was, however, permitted by Dharmaśāstra writers and Chandragupta's conduct in marrying Dhruvadevī, though now appearing strange to us, would not have excited much comment in contemporary times. The omission of the elder brother's name in the official Gupta genealogies may be due to the obvious desire to omit a collateral whose name need not have been included in the genealogical list,[1] and who had brought disgrace on the dynasty by his infamous conduct.

§ 52. The recent discovery of the copper coins of Rāmagupta at Besnagar tends to support the historicity of the literary

---

[1] The dynastic list of a house has to mention all the collaterals, who had ascended the throne, but not so the genealogical list, which is intended to show the descent only.

episode.[1] It is no doubt possible to argue that Rāmagupta of the Mālwā coins may have been a local ruler. We, however, do not come across any other rulers with Gupta-ending names in contemporary times, nor was Rāmagupta a particularly popular proper name. It is well known how Samudragupta had already occupied the territory upto Eran, within 40 miles of Besnagar, where the coins of Rāmagupta have been found. The coinage in ancient India was local and it is quite likely that a need for small copper currency, similar to the Nāga coinage current earlier there, may have been soon felt by the Gupta administration. Rāmagupta on his accession may have decided to meet it by issuing coins of the type which we have now found, which closely imitate the Nāga coinge. Or, it may be that even Samudragupta might have started this currency, and its specimens may be discovered, if a careful search is made for them in Mālwā. Tiny coins of the type issued by Rāmagupta were not current in Bihar and U.P. and were therefore not issued in those provinces. It is not unlikely that gold coins of Rāmagupta may still be discovered in future. It may be pointed out that no gold coins of Budhagupta were discovered for a long time, though he was a mighty Gupta emperor and had ruled for about 25 years. They came to light as late as 1949. Rāmagupta had a much shorter reign and it is no wonder if his coins have not yet come to light.

§ 53. It appears that Rāmagupta wanted to excel his famous father by achieving fresh conquests. Impelled by this desire, he seems to have invaded the territories of Piro, the Kidāra Kushāṇa[2] king of the Western Punjab, but was signally defeated and compelled to flee. During the course of his retreat, he seems to have taken shelter in a Himalayan fort, where he was besieged by the pursuing conqueror. The beleaguered force was reduced to a desperate condition and the only way to effect an escape appeared to be to accept the ignominous peace terms dictated by the conqueror, who demanded, *inter alia*, the surrender of the

---

[1] *J.N.S.I.*, XII. 103 XIII. 128 ; see below § 237 also.

[2] The term Śaka was probably used to denote at this time all foreigners of the Scythian extraction including the Kushāṇas and the Kidāra Kushāṇas, like the term English in the last century, which was vaguely used to denote all Europeans in popular parlance. Literary tradition could easily have described a Kidāra Kushāṇa ruler like Piro as a Śaka.

Gupta queen. Chandragupta, the younger brother of the emperor, volunteered to save the situation by going to the harem of the conqueror disguised as Dhruvadevī. He was probably accompanied by a few hundred crack soldiers disguised as his maid-servants.[1] The whole enemy camp must have been in jubilation at the acceptance of the ignoble peace and therefore off its guard. Chandragupta and his 'maid-servants' must have taken the advantage of the situation and killed the conqueror and the pick of the army officers, when they were altogether off their guard. The beleaguered force may have launched an attack, when utter confusion followed the unexpected assasination of the Śaka king and the leading officers of his army, helping the escape of Chandragupta and its own safe retreat. Chandragupta must naturally have been hailed as the national hero by the whole country and Rāmagupta's end may have been hastened by the sheer sense of shame and disgrace. Or, he may have been killed by a clique in the army, Chandragupta being believed to have connived at it. How he died we do not know. On his death Chandragupta naturally ascended the throne. He later married his widowed sister-in-law, as the current custom and the rules of the Smṛitis permitted this step. It is not unlikely that she may have been originally betrothed to him, as stated in the *Majmul-ūt-tawārīkh*.

The reign of Rāmagupta may be placed between *c.* 370-375 A.D. The earliest known date for Chandragupta II is probably 376 A.D.[2]. See. § 237 for copper coins of Rāmagupta.

7. Chandragupta II, *c.* 375-414 A.D.

§ 54. Chandragupta had to face a sea of troubles at his accession. He had to remove the Śaka menace and put down the revolts in the empire that must have been encouraged by the debacle of the imperial army in the Punjab. The king Chandra of the Mehrauli pillar inscription is most probably Chandragupta II. If so, this record would show that Chandragupta first put down

[1] This is suggested by the statement of the commentator of the *Harshacharita* and expressly averred by *Majmulu-t-tawarkh.*

[2] If the reading *pañchame varshe* were certain in the Mathura record of 381 A.D., the accession of Chandragupta could be placed with certainty in the year 376 A.D. It is, however, doubtful whether the reading is *prathame* or *pañchame*. If the former is the case, the accession year of Chandragupta would be 381 A.D.

some revolts in Bengal, and then he succeeded in driving back the Kidāra Kushāṇas to the Indus Valley. We may presume that the first ten years of his reign (*c.* 375-385 A.D.) were spent in this work. The Western Punjab, however, was not annexed to the Gupta empire, but the Scythian chiefs were allowed to rule there as Gupta feudatories.

§ 55. Sometime after 390 A.D., Chandragupta launched an attack against the Śaka Kshatrapas of Western India. One of his records refers to his encampment at Bhilsa in Mālwā, while out to conquer the enemy, who could have been none other than the Śaka potentate.[1] The campaign was signally successful, for Chandragupta not only defeated the Western Kshatrapas but completely annihilated their power, and annexed to his empire their dominion, consisting of Mālwā, Gujarat, and Kathiawar. The completion of the campaign against the Śaka Kshatrapas has to be placed sometime before 409 A.D., which is the earliest year occurring on the silver coins of Chandragupta, issued to replace the currency of the fallen dynasty.

§ 56. We do not know of any other political events of the reign of Chandragupta II. The names of two of his queens are known, Dhruvadevī and Kuberanāgā. The latter was probably a princess of one of the Nāga dynasties defeated by Samudragupta. Her daughter was Prabhāvatīguptā, who was married to the Vākāṭaka king Rudrasena II. She was unfortunately widowed early in her life and her father Chandragupta had to help her in carrying on the administration as the regent for her young son. This extended the sphere of the Gupta influence to the bank of the Godāvarī, if not to that of the Kṛishṇā. It penetrated further downwards when the Kadambas succeeded in marrying a princess of theirs to a prince in the Gupta family, as stated in a record of king Kakusthavarman of that dynasty.[2] Which Kadamba princess was married to which Gupta prince is, however, not known.

---

[1] Cf. the statement in the Udayagiri (Mālwā) inscription:—
कृत्स्नपृथ्वीजयार्थेन राज्ञैवेह समागतः । *C.I.I.*, III, p. 25

[2] गुप्तादिपार्थिवकुलाम्बुरुहस्थलानि स्नेहादरप्रणयसंभ्रमकेसराणि ।
श्रीमन्त्यनेकनृपषट्पदसेवितानि योऽबोधयद्दुहितृदीधितिभिर्नृपार्कः ॥
E.I., VIII, p. 3

§ 57. Chandragupta II had a long reign of about 36 years, for 93 G.E. (412-3 A.D.) is his last known date. The empire was in a prosperous condition, as is shown by the account of the Chinese pilgrim Fa Hien. The addition of the maritime provinces of Gujarat and Kathiawar, with the new trade openings they secured, must have added immensely to the resources of the empire. Literature and art also flourished under the enlightened patronage of Chandragupta; most probably the famous poet Kālidāsa flourished in his court and the gold coins issued from his mint are remarkable for their artistic beauty and variety.

§ 58. The reign of Chandragupta II is remarkable for its numismatic activity. Minting of gold coins was done more extensively during his rule than in any prior or later reign. In the Bayana hoard his gold coins are more numerous than those of his successor Kumāragupta I, though the latter lived nearer to the time of the interment of the hoard. An account of his gold coinage and its special features will be given in § 147-§ 185. The conquest of Mālwā, Gujarat and Kathiawar necessitated the issue of silver currency, for the residents of this area were accustomed to it for more than three hundred years during the Scythian rule. Chandragupta's silver coins are few; probably he started minting in the white metal towards the end of his reign. The silver currency was, however, confined to the new provinces of the empire during the reign of Chandragupta II. This emperor also started issuing copper coins. They were however not issued extensively as was done by the Kushāṇas; for we have so far found only a few specimens of his copper coinage.

The last known date of Chandragupta is 93 G.E. or 412. A.D. His death took place within a year or two of this date, for in 96 G.E., or 415-6 A.D., we find his son Kumāragupta I ruling the empire.

8. Kumāragupta I, *c.* 414-455 A.D.

§ 59. There is an interval of three years between the latest known date of Chandragupta II and the earliest known date of Kumāragupta I. Some scholars have therefore advanced the view that Kumāragupta was preceded on the throne by his brother Govindagupta Bālāditya, whom he ousted within a year or two.[1] There is, however, no sufficient evidence to warrant this conjecture. It is no doubt true that Kumāragupta had a uterine brother named Govindagupta, but there is no evidence to show that he had ever ascended the throne. The Vaiśālī seal describes Govindagupta as a mere *mahārāja* and not as a *yuvarāja* or heir-apparent.[2] It is clear that *yuvarāja* was somebody else, and that person was obviously Kumāragupta. It has no doubt been argued that the Buddhist tradition states that Bālāditya, the successor of Vikramāditya, definitely ascended the throne and he may be identical with Govindagupta, who may have ruled for a short time before Kumāragupta. There is, however, no shred of evidence to prove that Govindagupta bore the title of Bālāditya.

§ 60. Kumāragupta had a long reign of more than forty years, from *c.* 414 A.D. to 455 A.D., but very few political events of his life are known. The emperor was named after Kumāra, the generalissimo of gods, but his name does not seem to have inspired sufficient martial enthusiasm in him to egg him on to fresh aggressive expeditions. There is no evidence to show that he attempted any fresh conquests. No doubt he performed Aśvamedha sacrifice as shown by some of his coins, but the record of his military achievements was undoubtedly very poor, as compared to that of his father, who did not care to perform that sacrifice. The discovery of a hoard of his silver coins in Satara district need not show that central and southern Mahārāshṭra were added by him to the Gupta empire. The hoard may have been the savings of a Maharashtrian merchant trading in Gujarat. There is nothing whatsoever to indicate that Kumāragupta ever contemplated any expansion of his power in the north-west. He was content to rule over the large empire he had inherited, and the performance of the Aśvamedha by him may have been due rather to the desire to re-emphasise his

[1] Saletore, *Life in the Gupta Age.*, pp. 27-30. Mandsore Inscription of Mālava Saṁvat 521 (465 A.D.) no doubt calls Govindagupta a king, but it gives him no imperial titles. This record would suggest that Govindagupta was an imperial viceroy in Mālwā. *E.I.* XXVII, p. 15.

[2] महाराजाधिराजश्रीचन्द्रगुप्तपत्नी महाराजश्रीगोविंदगुप्तमाता महादेवी श्रीध्रुवस्वामिनी। *A.S.I.A.R.*, 1903-4, p. 107 ff.

sovereign position than to the commemoration of any fresh conquests. There is no doubt that from the military point of view, Kumārăgupta's administration was not much of a success. His nephew's son, the Vākāṭaka king Narendrasena, was in a sea of troubles in *c.* 445 A.D. It does not appear that Kumāragupta offered him any help.

§ 61. Not only was Kumāragupta not able to extend the sphere of his influence, but he was also unable to defend successfully the empire he had inherited. A tribe named Pushyamitra rose in rebellion towards the end of his reign. The empire was shaken to its foundation and the Gupta armies must have suffered several reverses in the initial stage of the conflict. The crown-prince Skandagupta then took charge of the campaign and brought it to a successful close, though he had to spend a night sleeping on bare ground during its course.[1] Unfortunately the Pushyamitras cannot yet be satisfactorily identified. Very probably they are the Pushpamitras of the *Vishṇupurāṇa*[2] and they seem to have been ruling in the Narmadā valley. The Bamnala hoard of Gupta coins found in the former Indore state[3] was probably buried during the course of the turmoil caused by the Pushyamitra rebellion, which made life and property unsafe in the Narmadā valley inducing the people to bury their treasures and flee for their lives.

§ 62. During the greater part of the reign of Kumāragupta I, however, there was tranquility and prosperity in the empire, which is reflected in his coinage. His gold coinage is extensive and shows as many as fourteen types (§ 186-§ 223). Their artistic merit is high and many of their metrical legends have considerable poetical merit as well. He extended the silver currency to the Gangetic plain and issued for his home provinces a new type of silver currency showing no traces of foreign influence. He, however, practically discontinued the issue of the copper currency; we get very few specimens of it. People were generally accustomed to the use of cowries for small daily transactions; Kumāragupta probably thought that copper currency was hardly worth the trouble and expense it involved.

---

[1] विचलितकुललक्ष्मीस्तम्भनायोद्यतेन क्षितितलशयनीये येन नीता त्रियामा ।

Bhitari Pillar Inscription.

[2] Transl. by Wilson, IV, p. 213.

[3] *J.N.S.I.*, V, p. 135.

Kumāragupta died in G.E. 136 (455-6 A.D.) but before hearing the good news of the success of his crown-prince against the Pushyamitras and other enemies of his house.

9. SKANDAGUPTA, *c.* 456-468 A.D.

§ 63. The history of the Guptas after the death of Kumāragupta I teems with several problems, which we are not yet able to solve satisfactorily, partly owing to the paucity of the material and partly owing to its being vague and inconclusive.

§ 64. It has been suggested that there was a war of succession at the death of Kumāragupta I, and that Purugupta, the elder brother, was ousted by Skandagupta, the younger one.[1] There is, however, no sufficient evidence to support this veiw. It is by no means certain that Purugupta, brother of Skandagupta, was either his elder brother or that Skandagupta's mother was not the crowned queen, he therefore having no legitimate title to the throne. It is true that the mother of Purugupta, Anantadevī, is called Mahādevī in the Bhitari seal of Kumāragupta II, which altogether omits the name of Skandagupta. But Skandagupta also may well have been born of the same queen and the omission of her name in his records may be quite accidental.[2] And supposing we assume for the sake of argument that Skandagupta was not like Purugupta born of the crowned queen, it does not follow that simply because of that circumstance, he could not have been selected as the crown-prince by his father. The choice of a king in this respect was often governed more by ability than by seniority; in the Rāshṭrakūṭa dynasty, for instance, we find Dhruva deliberately selecting a younger son Govinda as his successor in preference to Stambha, who was the elder one.[3] Kumāragupta may well have done the

---

[1] *J.A.S.B.*, 1921, pp. 253 ff.

[2] It may be pointed out that in the Bhitari pillar inscription, there is a sudden change from prose to poetry after the name of Kumāragupta; prosaic statements about the father and mother of each ruler are replaced by a poetic description of the glorious achievements of the new king, and while doing so, the poet may well have forgotten to mention the name of the mother of the emperor. In the Bihar pillar inscription, there is a big lacuna at the place where the queen-mother's name was expected to occur; the conclusion, therefore, that in both these records the king has deliberately avoided the mention of his mother's name, because she was not a crowned queen, is not quite convincing.

[3] Altekar, *Rāshṭrakūṭas and their Times*, p. 59

same. We have undisputed evidence in the Bhitari pillar inscription to show that it was Skandagupta who eventually succeeded in restoring the fortunes of his dynasty, when his aged father was probably confined to his death-bed. Skandagupta, though completely successful on the battlefield, could report his glorious achievements only to his mother, his father having died in the interval.[1] It is difficult to believe that Kumāragupta would, under these circumstances, have nominated as his successor anybody other than the son, who was entrusted with the all-important mission of restoring the fortunes of his dynasty, whose very existence was in a very precarious condition. The statement in the Junagadh inscription, that the Goddess of Royal Fortune selected him as her lord in preference to all other princes,[2] need not necessarily imply that his choice was not made by his father. It is simply a poetic way of describing the great victory of Skandagupta, but for which he could not have succeeded his father as an emperor in spite of his prior selection as the crown-prince; the very continuance of the Gupta empire had become doubtful owing to the rebellion of the Pushyamitrās and others. The military position of Skandagupta must have been unchallengeable at the time of his father's death, when he had just crushed the power of the Pushyamitras, and it seems extremely unlikely that his brother Purugupta could have thought it expedient to put forth his claim at that time, even if he was, and Skandagupta was not, the son of the crowned queen. There is no doubt that Purugupta also became an emperor, but his accession has to be placed after the death of Skandagupta

[1] पितरि दिवमुपेते विप्लुतां वंशलक्ष्मीं निजभुजविजितारिर्यः प्रतिष्ठाप्य भूयः ।
जितमिति परितोषान्मातरं सास्रनेत्रां हतरिपुरिव कृष्णो देवकीमभ्युपेतः ॥

Bhitari pillar inscription, v. 6.

[2] समेत्य सर्वान्मनुजेन्द्रपुत्रान्लक्ष्मीः स्वयं यं वरयाञ्चकार ।

C.I.I. Vol. III, p. 50, v.5.

This verse occurs after the description of the defeat of several kings, which spread the fame of Skandagupta to the country of even the Mlechchhas. It further refers to Lakshmī preferring Skandagupta not from among his brothers, but from among all the sons of all kings. Had this verse occurred immediately after the description of the death of Kumāragupta I, or had it referred to Lakshmī preferring Skandagupta from among his brothers, the theory of a war of succession would have been plausible.

and not prior to his accession. He no doubt ruled for a short time as shown also by a Sarnath inscription;[1] but the shortness of his reign may be due to his succeeding an elder brother who had lived to an advanced old age, rather than to his being successfully ousted by his rival brother soon after his accession. We may therefore take it as almost certain that Kumāragupta I was succeeded in 456 A.D. by his crown-prince Skandagupta, who was also most probably his eldest son.

§ 65. Skandagupta had successfully met the challenge of the Pushyamitras before his accession, but further and even more serious troubles were in store for him. India began to be invaded by the Hūṇas at about the middle of the 5th century and their hordes soon penetrated within the boundaries of the Gupta empire. When exactly this happened we do not know, for the inscriptions referring to Skandagupta's overthrow of the Hūṇas are not dated. It, however, appears very probable that Skandagupta was called upon to face the new menace soon after his accession.[2] We know few facts about the Hūṇa war; our epigraphs only record its successful termination. We have seen already that the Western Punjab was never held or garrisoned by the Gupta armies, and so Skandagupta could have opposed the invaders only on the Satluj, if not on the Yamunā. The latter alternative is rendered fairly plausible by the contents of the Bayana hoard. The last king represented in it is [Skandagupta] Kramāditya. Obviously sometimes during his reign

---

[1] A dedicatory record at Sarnath shows that in G.E. 154 i.e. 473 A.D. Kumāragupta II was on the throne. Skandagupta was alive in 467 A.D. So Purugupta could not have ruled for more than three or four years. The view that Kumāragupta of the Sarnath record is different from Kumāragupta, the son of Narasiṁhagupta and grandson of Purugupta, does not seem to be probable.

[2] The Junagadh inscription, dated in the year 458 A.D., refers to the fame of Skandagupta being sung in the land of the Mlechchhas as well. If the Mlechchhas here are identified with the Hūṇas, as is very likely, the above conclusion woud be plausible. But the reading of the word Mlechchha in the above record is not quite certain.

The circumstance that only one coin of Kramāditya i.e. Skandagupta was found in the Bayana hoard will also suggest that he had just ascended the throne at the time of its interment due to the panic created by the Hūṇa invasion. It is, however, not quite certain that the hoard originally contained only one coin of Skandagupta; for about 285 coins in it could not be recovered; see § 4. Quite an appreciable number of the missing coins may well have been the issues of Skandagupta.

life and property became unsafe in the Bharatpur region (corresponding to ancient Matsya), inducing rich persons to bury their treasures and flee away for safety. It seems almost certain that the cause of this panic was the Hūṇa invasion, which had succeeded in penetrating upto the Yamunā. Skandagupta's armies could meet the invaders only on that river. It is likely that the emperor may have pushed back the Hūṇas to the Satluj; the Central and Western Punjab, however, continued to be in the possession of the invaders. Even this achievement was no mean one, for the Hūṇas were at this time at the height of their power and had crushed a number of kingdoms in Asia and Europe. Well may the victories of Skandagupta have been sung by the young and the old in every corner of his empire.

The empire continued undiminished down to the death of Skandagupta; for he continued to hold effectively even its outlying provinces like Gujarat and Kathiawar.

§ 66. Gupta mints were fairly active during the reign of Skandagupta. His silver coinage is as copious as that of his father; he supplanted some of its types by introducing new ones like the Bull and the Altar types.[1] But his gold coinage is much less copious and shows only three certain types **(Pl. XXXII. 1-3).** The financial strain of the Hūṇa war had also told upon the treasury, for many of his gold coins are heavily adulterated. He however introduced the national *suvarṇa* standard of 144 grains in the gold currency. But what extra quantity was given in weight in the new pieces was more than counterbalanced by the dross that was mixed in them.

10. Successors of Kumāragupta I, (*c.* 454-540 A.D.)

§ 67. The last known date of Skandagupta is 467 A.D.; thereafter he died, and being probably issueless, was succeeded by his younger brother Purugupta. The Gupta history during the next ten years is shrouded in considerable mystery and the scanty and uncertain material we possess does not enable us to unravel it. We shall therefore review it only in a cursory manner. To facilitate its quick grasp, we give below a genealogical tree; known dates of kings are given in brackets after their names.

[1] *B.M.C.G.D.*, pp. 121-2.

Kumāragupta I = Anantadevī

- Skandagupta (467 A.D.)
- Purugupta = Chandradevī
  - Budhagupta (476, 495 A.D.)
  - Narasiṁhagupta = Mitradevī
    - Kumāragupta II (473 A.D.)
      - Vishṇugupta

Purugupta, Skandagupta's successor, had a short reign and was succeeded by his son Narasiṁhagupta Bālāditya. He also ruled for a short time; his son Kumāragupta II was a king in 473 A.D.[1] Kumāragupta II had an uncle named Budhagupta, whom we find ruling as the emperor in 476, as also in 495 A.D. He had a son named Vishṇugupta, who also is known to have ruled as king from the evidence of coins and seals. We have, however, no known dates for Vishṇugupta, and therefore we do not know whether he succeeded his grand-uncle Budhagupta or preceded him. Vishṇugupta may have been too young to rule at the death of his father Kumāragupta II in *c.* 476 A.D., and may therefore have been preceded by his grown-up and experienced grand-uncle Budhagupta. Or he may have ruled for a short time and been deposed by his grand-uncle. In the former alternative his reign will have to be placed after 495 A.D., which is the last known date of Budhagupta; in the latter alternative he will have to be presumed to have ruled for a few months before 476 A.D., which is the earliest known date of Budhagupta. A third alternative is also possible. The empire may have been divided at the accession of Budhagupta sometime between 473 and 476 A.D., the new emperor taking over its larger portion and permitting Kumāragupta II to rule over a small dominion somewhere in Bengal. All the above theories have their own advocates and plausible arguments can be advanced in favour of each of them. But no theory can be regarded as conclusively proved.

[1] This date is supplied by a votive image inscription found at Sarnath; *A.S.I.*, *A.R.*, 1914-5, p. 124.

We have to await the discovery of fresh evidence to solve the mystery, in which the whole situation is shrouded.

§ 68. The decade between the death of Skandagupta in *c.* 467 and the accession of Budhagupta in *c.* 476 A.D. was undoubtedly full of troubles. Three emperors Purugupta, Narasiṁhagupta Bālāditya and Kumāragupta Kramāditya rose and fell before the accession of Budhagupta in *c.* 476 A.D. The remarkable shortness of their reigns cannot be due entirely to their meeting premature but natural deaths. There was apparently a struggle for the throne, and there were some other aspirants for it, besides the above four members of the royal family. We have a unique coin issued by a ruler named Ghaṭotkacha, who appears to have declared independence in eastern Mālwā in *c.* 460 A.D. He may also have competed for the imperial throne. The same may have been the case with Prakāśāditya, who appears to have ruled at about this time.

It seems to be very probable that Purugupta and his son Narasiṁhagupta Bālāditya were unable to check these fissiparous tendencies. Both of them may have died natural deaths. But the appearance of Budhagupta on the scene as emperor in 476 A.D. was probably due to his decision to supersede his grand-nephew in order to restore the failing fortunes of the family. He was undoubtedly a man of grit and ability and succeeded in establishing the Gupta authority from Bengal to Mālwā. Brahmadatta and Jayadatta were his governors in northern Bengal; the territory between the Narmadā and the Yamunā was in charge of another governor named Suraśmichandra, and the Parivrājaka and Uchchhakalpa kings, who were ruling in Central India, were recognising his sovereignty. Whether Mālwā, Gujarat and Kathiawar were under his sway, it is difficult to say. We get no silver coins of his issued in the types current in these provinces, which would suggest that he had lost control over them. An early Maitraka king Droṇasiṁha is said to have been crowned by his feudal lord, the ruler over the entire earth, at about 500 A.D.;[1] this may suggest the continuance of Gupta overlordship over Kathiawar down to the beginning of the 6th century A.D. But the allegiance was only a nominal formality,

[1] Fleet, *C.I.I.*, III, p. 165.

for neither the personal name of the emperor nor the name of his dynasty is mentioned in their records. It appears almost certain that the Guptas lost all effective control over Gujarat and Kathiawār, and also probably over Mālwā soon after 470 A.D.

§ 69. What was the fate of Kumāragupta II when Budhagupta ascended the throne by *c.* 476 A.D.? It is natural to presume that he must have been deposed, if he was not already killed in the struggle for the throne. But neither event seems to have occurred. Kumāragupta II has left us a numerous gold coinage; his coins in the British Museum are more numerous than those of any successor of Purugupta, including Prakāśāditya.[1] It is therefore difficult to believe that Kumāragupta had a short reign of a few months, which was terminated by his dethronement or death in *c.* 476 A.D. It is most probable that the empire was divided and Budhagupta had the magnanimity to allow his nephew Kumāragupta II to rule with full imperial title and the privilege to issue coins. He and his son Vishṇugupta seem to have ruled contemporaneously with Budhagupta, probably in southern Bengal, where their coins are usually found. Budhagupta continued to rule down to 496 A.D.

§ 70. Purugupta had a very short reign and has left us no coins. Coins once attributed to him are now proved to be of Budhagupta by better specimens found in recent times (see § 230). Neither Purugupta nor any of his successors, with the solitary exception of Budhagupta has left us any silver or copper coinage. The coins of Narasiṁhagupta, Kumāragupta II and Vishṇugupta are all in the Archer type conforming to the *suvarṇa* standard of 144 grains; they are all heavily adulterated, gold being only about 57%.

§ 71. We have no definite information about the successors of Budhagupta, whose reign terminated in *c.* 496 A.D. A Gupta king named Vainyagupta is known to be ruling in Bengal in 507 A.D.;[2] another named Bhānugupta is seen to be fighting against the Hūṇas in Mālwā in 510 A.D.[3] It is most plausible

---

[1] The British Museum possesses six coins of Prakāśāditya, twelve of Narasiṁhagupta Bālāditya, eighteen of Kumāragupta Kramāditya, three of Vainyagupta and fifteen of Vishṇugupta.

[2] Gunaighar record, *I.H.Q.*, 1930, p. 45.

[3] Fleet, *C.I.I.*, III, p. 92.

to assume that Vishṇugupta was succeeded by Vainyagupta in southern Bengal and Budhagupta by Bhānugupta at Pāṭalīputra. Of these two emperors, we have the coins of Vainyagupta,[1] which were long mistaken to be the coins of Chandragupta III. No coins of Bhānugupta have been found so far.

§ 72. The Gupta empire further shrank at the beginning of the 6th century. Mālwā was lost to the Hūṇas by *c.* 500 A.D. Mahārāja Mātṛivishṇu was ruling as a feudatory of the Guptas in 484 A.D.;[2] his younger brother had to transfer his allegiance to the Hūṇa conqueror Toramāṇa in *c.* 500 A.D. Bhānugupta tried to retrieve the situation; we find a general of his being killed in Mālwā in 510 A.D,[3] obviously while fighting for his master against the Hūṇas. We do not know the details of the various phases of the conflict between the Guptas and the Hūṇas. But there can be no doubt that the Guptas lost Mālwā and probably all the territories between the Yamunā and the Narmadā by *c.* 520 A.D.

§ 73. The Gupta history after 520 A.D. becomes still more obscure. We know neither the *āditya* epithet of Bhānugupta nor the duration of his reign. It is therefore difficult to determine the identity of the Gupta king Bālāditya, who according to Yuan Chwang, finally broke the Hūṇa power by *c.* 530 A.D. It may be that Bhānugupta's *biruda* was Bālāditya. In that case it would appear that he continued his struggle against the Hūṇas from 510 to about 530 A.D., when it was crowned with signal success by the overthrow of Mihirakula. If, however, Bhānugupta had not the title of Bālāditya, we shall have to suppose that Bālāditya was his son, who completed the work begun by his father. It appears that he received considerable assistance in this task from king Yaśodharman of Mālwā, who also claims to have defeated the Hūṇa king Mihirakula. It is clear that king Bālāditya, who defeated the Hūṇas in *c.* 530 A.D., is different from king Narasiṁhagupta Bālāditya, the son and successor of Purugupta; for the latter's son Kumāragupta II had already succeeded him before 473 A.D. It is however probable that Bālāditya,

---

[1] *I.H.Q.*, 1933, p. 784.
[2] Fleet, *C. I.I. III*, p. 159.
[3] *Ibid.* p. 92.

the conqueror of the Hūṇas, may also have borne the name of Narasiṁhagupta. In that case some of the coins bearing the legend *Nara* under the arm may have been issued by him.

§ 74. The overthrow of Mihirakula did not prolong the life of the Gupta empire. Yaśodharman of Mālwā attacked it from the west and carried his arms to the Brahmaputrā, if we are to trust his official record. His success was, however, short-lived, for we find the Gupta suzerainty recognised at Puṇḍravardhana in northern Bengal in 543 A.D. But the raid of Yaśodharman accelerated the fissiparous tendencies and encouraged the feudatories to assert their independence. The most prominent among these were the so-called later Guptas of Magadha and the Maukharis of Kanauj. These dynasties were ruling in the very heart of the Gupta empire, and when they became independent by *c.* 550 A.D., the old Gupta empire automatically came to an end. The three early Maukhari kings Harivarman, Ādityavarman and Īśvaravarman, who were ruling from *c.* 500 to 540 A.D., were mere feudatories, but the 4th king Īśānavarman not only assumes the imperial title *Mahārājādhirāja*, but claims to have defeated the Gauḍas in Bengal, the Andhras in the eastern Deccan and the Sūlikas, probably further south-east. He ruled from *c.* 540 to 560 A.D. and the victorious march of his armies to Bengal and the eastern Deccan presupposes the disappearance of the imperial Gupta power in the Gangetic plain. In the home province of Magadha, the imperial Gupta dynasty was ousted by the family of the so-called later Guptas of Magadha. Its founder Kṛishṇagupta, whose reign may be placed at the beginning of the 6th century, was probably a collateral member of the Imperial Gupta family, but the nature of his exact relationship with it is not known. Kṛishṇagupta and his son and grandson Harshagupta and Jīvitagupta were probably loyal feudatories of Budhagupta, Bhānugupta and Bālāditya II. It was king Kumāragupta of this family, who alone could come forward to oppose the advance of the Maukharis under Iśānavarman; neither Bālāditya, the victor of Mihirakula, nor any of his successors, figures in the Maukhari records as the opponent of the imperial expansion of Īśānavarman. No epigraphical record is found mentioning any scion of the Imperial Gupta family after *c.* 545 A.D., its end being caused by the declaration of independence by king Kumāragupta of the Later Gupta dynasty and by the imperial expansion of the Maukharis under Īśānavarman, leading to the incorporation of most of the home provinces of the Gupta empire in the new kingdoms.

IV. Coinage and Coin-types

1. Chandragupta I

(Pl. I. 1-10)

§ 75. We have shown already how Śrīgupta and Ghaṭotkachagupta, the grand-father and father of Chandragupta I, were rulers of no great consequence; they were ruling over a small kingdom (§ 24-§ 32). They naturally did not think of introducing any coinage of their own. We have so far found no coins of Śrīgupta. A unique coin exists in the Leningrad, formerly the Petrograd Museum, which bears the inscription *Ghaṭo* under the king's arm **(Pl. XXXII. 4)**. It is not, however, possible to attribute this coin to Ghaṭotkachagupta, the father of Chandragupta I. Its reverse type, Lakshmī seated on lotus and holding lotus in her left hand, was introduced in the Gupta coinage by Chandragupta II; it could not have occurred on the coinage of his great grand-father, even if we assume that he may have issued his own currency. The coin in question has therefore to be attributed to a later ruler in the Gupta dynasty. Probably it was issued by Ghaṭotkachagupta, a grandson of Chandragupta II, who is known to have been ruling in Mālwā as the viceroy of his father Kumāragupta I.[1] Though Bayana, near which this hoard was buried, is not far from Mālwā, where Ghatoṭkachagupta was ruling, his coins are not represented in our hoard; probably he had not become independent when the hoard was buried in *c.* 455 A.D., though he was acting as the governor of Mālwā in 435-6 A.D.

§ 76. As shown already before (§ 33-§ 35), Chandragupta I was the real founder of the greatness of the Gupta dynasty. When he had extended and consolidated his kingdom, he may have decided to commemorate his military achievements by a formal coronation at which he assumed the imperial title *mahārājādhirāja*. This formal coronation probably took place late in

[1] *E.I.*, Vol., XXVI, p. 115.

his life, as was the case with the Maratha king Shivaji in later times. It was probably on this occasion that he started the Gupta era and ordered the issue of his gold coins.

§ 77. The coins that were sent out for circulation from the imperial mint on this occasion bore on the obverse the names and figures of the emperor Chandragupta and of his crowned Queen Kumāradevī of Lichchhavi extraction. As the name of the emperor Chandragupta appeared on the obverse, early numismatists[1] naturally attributed these coins to him. While editing the Catalogue of the Gupta coins in the British Museum in 1914, Mr. Allan dissented from this view and maintained that the above coins could not be attributed to Chandragupta I, but were commemorative medals issued by Samudragupta in commemoration of his father and his own Lichchhavi descent, the obverse legend simply stating who the figures were.[2] Mr. Allan's arguments were critically analysed and examined by the present writer in 1936 and his conclusion was that the coins in question were issued by Chandragupta I and were not commemorative medals issued by his son.[3] He still holds this view and it has not yet (1952 A.D.) been controverted by any scholar.

§ 78. We shall here briefly summarise the arguments of Mr. Allan and state why they appear to us as untenable and inconclusive. Mr. Allan holds that the coins were not the issues of Chandragupta I on account of the following main reasons:—

(1) Compared to the Standard type coins of Samudragupta, Chandragupta-Kumāradevī coins show a less slavish imitation of the original Kushāṇa prototype; the latter should therefore be placed chronologically later than the former. This would obviously lead us to the conclusion that Chandragupta-Kumāradevī pieces were commemorative medals issued by Samudragupta later in his reign, and were not current during the rule of Chandragupta I.

(2) Kushāṇa coins were not current in Bihar and Oudh over which Chandragupta I ruled; his mint-masters therefore could not have selected the devices on one of the Kushāṇa types as the prototype for their only coin-type. We should there-

[1] Eg. Smith in *J.R.A.S.*, 1889, p. 63.
[2] *B.M.C.G.D.*, p. lxviii.
[3] *J.A.S.B.*, 1937, *N.S.*, pp. 105-111.

fore place the origin of the Gupta coinage at a time when the north-western boundary of the kingdom touched the dominions of the later Kushāṇas in the Punjab; this happened late in the reign of Samudragupta. Chandragupta-Kumāradevī coins should therefore be regarded as commemorative medals issued by Samudragupta towards the end of his reign, and not as coins issued by his father during his own rule.

(3) The reverse type of the coins usually attributed to Chandragupta is Goddess seated on lion. If this type was popularised in the reign of Chandragupta I, one cannot understand why it should occur on no types issued during the long reign of his successor Samudragupta. If, on the other hand, we assume that these coins were commemorative medals issued by Samudragupta, one can understand how their reverse type was copied in the next two reigns for the Lion-slayer types of Chandragupta II and Kumāragupta I.

(4) Chandragupta I ruled for a comparatively long period, and it is unlikely that as he was a *mahārājādhirāja*, he should have been content to issue a joint coinage throughout his reign. There is no parallel for a joint coinage and it is contrary to all numismatic laws for a series to open with such a remarkable development from its prototype.

(5) The right of coinage has never been the jealously exercised symbol of sovereignty among the Hindus, as it was amongst the Mahomadans. Some of the greatest Hindu sovereigns, e.g. Harshavardhana, do not appear to have struck coins at all. While it may be correct to state that Ghaṭotkacha did not strike coins, as he was a mere *mahārāja*, it certainly does not follow that Chandragupta I struck coins on his assumption of the title *mahārājādhirāja*.

§ 79. The above arguments of Mr. Allan are no doubt plausible, but they fail to carry conviction to us, if we carefully examine the contemporary political situation.

We have shown already (§ 31-§ 33) how Chandragupta I had received material assistance from the Lichchhavis in raising the structure of the Gupta empire. It is even possible that the Gupta empire during the reign of Chandragupta I was a kind of dual kingdom, where the Lichchhavis exercised considerable authority. It is quite probable that one of the terms of the matrimonial alliance between the Guptas and the Lichchhavis may have been that the Lichchhavi princess Kumāradevī should be not merely a queen consort but a queen regnant. When the coinage was started late in the reign, the proud Lichchhavis may well have insisted that the name of their clan as well as of their princess should appear on the imperial coinage.[1] We have a parallel case in English history when William III, the husband of Princess Mary, who was the heir to the British throne after the death of her father James II, was invited to come to rule over England. William was not prepared to come to England as a mere prince consort; the British Parliament was not willing that the English Princess should cease to be a regnant queen. The compromise effected was that both William and Mary should be regnant sovereigns and that the busts and names of both of them should appear on the coinage of their joint reign. William continued the joint coinage till the death of Mary in 1694; it was only after this event that he began to issue coins in his own name only. In India it appears that Kumāradevī survived her husband and so the coinage continued to be joint throughout the reign of Chandragupta I.

§ 80. When the political situation during the reign of Chandragupta I is thus fully understood, it will be readily conceded that Mr. Allan's argument (No. 4 above), that there is no parallel for a joint coinage and that it is contrary to all numismatic laws for a series to open with such a remarkable development from its prototype, loses most of its force. The pressing logic of the political situation compelled Chandragupta I to remain content with the joint type throughout his reign. There is further no evidence to show that he ruled for a long time. If we assume that his formal coronation as an emperor took place at the time when the Gupta era was started, it would appear that like the Maratha king Shivaji in later times, he did not sur-

---

[1] A suggestion has no doubt been made that the terms of the matrimonial alliance may have been dictated on the battle-field, where the Lichchhavis were overthrown (*J.N.S.I.*, V, p. 40); but this is not probable. Samudragupta would not have taken pride in calling himself a *Lichchhavi-dauhitra*, if the power of his maternal grand-father had been crushed on the battle-field before his mother's marriage (*J.N.S.I.*, V, 145).

vive that ceremony for a long time.[1] His son was on the throne in the fifth year of that era.[2] Coinage was also started probably on the occasion of the formal coronation. It could be issued only for four or five years and we can well understand how it was confined to a single type. And even if we assume that it was started much earlier, we have shown already how the logic of the political situation left no alternative to Chandragupta but to stick to the joint type throughout his reign.

§ 81. It is true that as maintained by Mr. Allan, (argument No. 2 above), the coins of Chandragupta I show a less slavish imitation of the Kushāṇa prototype than is done by the Standard type coins of Samudragupta. Their obverse is no doubt one step further removed from the prototype by the addition of the figure of the queen on that side. We have, however, shown already (§ 79) how this element of originality was really dictated by the political alliance of the Guptas with the Lichchhavis. The latter were most probably insistent that the figure and name of their princess, as also the name of her clan, should appear on the coinage that was being issued; hence the striking departure from the prototype shown by the obverse of the coins of Chandragupta I. We cannot merely on that account place this coin type late in the reign of Samudragupta.

§ 82. The relatively greater originality of the reverse of the coins of Chandragupta I, where the goddess is shown seated on a lion, and not on a high-backed throne, as on the coins of later Kushāṇas, is more difficult to explain. Most probably Durgā mounted on lion was the tutelary deity of the Lichchhavis; hence she might have been introduced on the reverse, where the name of the clan has been inscribed. Even if such was not the case, the greater originality of the reverse type would not necessitate the assumption that these pieces were issued by Samudragupta as commemoration medals. For instance, the

[1] Shivaji was coronated in 1674 when he was 44, and died in 1680. He could issue his coinage for six years only. His gold *hons* are rare.

[2] The genuineness of the Nālandā plate of Samudragupta, dated in the the 5th year of the Gupta era, is not above suspicion. It would, however, show that the general belief in 6th century, when the plates were probably forged, was that Samudragupta had ascended the throne soon after the starting of the Gupta era. There must have been some foundation for it.

reverse motifs of the Lyrist and Tiger-slayer types **(Pl. VI. 3-9)** of Samudragupta, where the goddess is shown seated on a wicker stool and standing on a crocodile respectively, undoubtedly show greater originality than the reverse of some of the Archer type coins of Chandragupta II, **(Pl. VIII. 1-15)** where the goddess appears seated on the high-backed throne. Are we then to conclude that the Archer type coins of Chandragupta II of the above variety were issued earlier than the Lyrist and the Tiger-slayer type coins of his father Samudragupta, merely because they show a more slavish imitation of the prototype? It may be also pointed out that *siṁhavāhinī* goddess appears on some coins of Huvishka and Kanishka III.[1]

The argument No. 3 of Mr. Allan about the non-occurrence of the *siṁhavāhinī* type on the reverse in the long reign of Samudragupta has also not much force. We have already observed how *siṁhavāhinī* occurs on the reverse of the coins of Chandragupta, because she was probably the tutelary deity of the Lichchhavis, whose name appears on the reverse. In the later reigns this reverse type occurs only when the obverse shows the Lion-slayer type. In other words the *siṁhavāhinī* on the reverse was connected with the lion-hunting on the obverse. There was no such connection suggested on any coin-type of Samudragupta; hence this device did not make its appearance in his reign.

Let us now consider the second of Mr. Allan's argument given above. It is not at all necessary to assume, as Mr. Allan does, that the origin of the Gupta coinage should be placed late in the reign of Samudragupta, when the memorable conquests of that emperor made the Gupta empire the immediate neighbour of the Kushāṇa kingdom. We should, however, not forget that famous centres of trade and pilgrimage like Pāṭalīputra, Gaya, Banaras, Allahabad and Ayodhya, were all included in the kingdom of Chandragupta I, and several Kushāṇa gold coins must have been brought with them to these places by traders and pilgrims, who must have come to these cities from the Punjab in considerable numbers during the 3rd and 4th centuries. Gupta mint-masters therefore could have easily procured[2]

[1] *P.M.C.*, vol. I, pl. XX. X; *J.A.S.B.*, 1933. N.p. 7; *C.G.I.*, pl. I. 6-7

[2] *J.N.S.I.*, XII. 121.

some of the Kushāṇa coins when they wanted to make a selection of their prototype even in the reign of Chandragupta I, when the Gupta empire had not annexed the western districts of U.P. It may be added that one Later Kushāṇa gold coin with Ardoxo reverse was actually recovered at Kumrahar near Pāṭalīputra during the excavations of 1912-3. It was deposited in the Patna Museum, but was stolen later. Its accession number was 2092.

It is true that some of the great Hindu emperors did not care to issue coins.[1] But among the Gupta rulers Chandragupta I was the first to assume the imperial title; most probably he also started the Gupta era. It is therefore natural to assume that the coins bearing the name of this ruler and his queen were issued by him.

§ 83. The greatest objection to the Commemoration Medal theory of Mr. Allan is the absence of the name of the commemorator on these coins. Among the Indo-Bactrian rulers Agathocles, Antimachos and Eucratides issued a number of commemorative medals, commemorating their predecessors or parents. In each such case, we find the name of the persons commemorated on the obverse, but the name of the commemorator never fails to appear on the reverse. If Samudragupta had really issued the coins under discussion as commemorative medals, it was but natural that the names and figures of his parents should have appeared in the place of honour on the obverse; but his own name or at least his *biruda* should have appeared on the reverse. In issuing these commemorative medals, Samudragupta must have been anxious to proclaim his own filial devotion; as it is, there is nothing whatsoever on these so-called commemorative medals to show that they had been issued by that emperor. In the Gupta coinage we have clear instances of commemorative medals in the *Aśvamedha* coins of Samudragupta and Kumāragupta I. But the legends on the reverse of both these types, *Aśvamedhaparākramaḥ* and *Aśvamedhamahendraḥ* contain

[1] Mr. Allan's statement that Harshavardhana did not issue any coins is not correct; for the silver coins bearing the name *Śīlāditya* were issued by that emperor. Some other Hindu emperors, however, like Chālukya Pulakeśin II, Rāshṭrakūṭa Govinda III or Paramāra Bhoja are not so far known to have issued any coins.

significant *birudas* that at once enable us to identify their issuers. If we are to assume that like the *Aśvamedha* coins, the Chandragupta-Kumāradevī coins were also commemorative medals issued by Samudragupta, it is indeed strange that he should not have put at least his *biruda* on these coins, as he did on the *Aśvamedha* type.

It will be thus seen that the coins showing Chandragupta and Kumāradevī on the obverse were not commemorative medals struck by Samudragupta. They were undoubtedly coins issued by Chandragupta I himself during his own reign.

§ 84. The hoard contains only ten coins of Chandragupta I, all of which have been illustrated on **Pl. I. 1-10.** Chandragupta's reign had ended nearly 125 years before the date of the secretion of the hoard; he is the earliest king of the hoard and therefore his coins are naturally the fewest. It may be, however, pointed out that the Lucknow Museum possesses only four coins of this ruler, the Indian Museum six and the British Museum nine.[1] The *B.M.C.G.D.* illustrates or describes seven more coins of this ruler, two from the St. Petersberg Museum, two from the Indian Museum, and one each from the Berlin Museum, Dr. Hoey's collection and the Bodleian Collection. The collection of Chandragupta I's coins in our hoard is thus by no means small.

§ 85. The Mauryas, the Suṅgas, the Kaṇvas, the Nāgas and the Maghas, who were the distant or immediate predecessors of the Guptas in Madhyadeśa, had issued no gold currency. Gupta mint-masters could therefore think of no indigenous prototype, when they had to determine the norm of their new coinage. The gold coins of the later Kushāṇas were not the popular currency of Magadha at the beginning of the 4th century, but a few of them used to reach the shroffs and temples of Pāṭalīputra, Gayā, and Banaras with the pilgrims and traders from the Punjab, who must have been visiting these famous places fairly frequently.[2] These later Kushāṇa coins showed on the

[1] The reference to the number of the coins of any particular king in any museum made in this work is based upon its published catalogue. Later additions, being not recorded in print, could not be taken into account.

[2] In the Kumrahar excavations of 1912-3, two gold Kushāṇa coins were unearthed, one showing Śiva on the reverse and the other goddess seated on high-backed throne. These coins were subsequently stolen. Their register numbers are 2091 and 2092.

obverse, king standing to left, dressed in coat and trousers and offering oblations on an altar. The king usually holds a standard in the left hand and there is a *triśūla* in his front. The reverse showed two different types; in one case there was Śiva standing by his mount bull, and in the other there was goddess Ardoxo, seated on a high-backed throne, holding a fillet in the right hand and a cornucopiae in the left. The Guptas were devout Vaishṇavas, and it is therefore natural that Chandragupta should have preferred the Ardoxo type to the Śiva one for the reverse of his coinage. The political alliance with the Lichchhavis and the necessity to include the crowned queen on the obverse along with the emperor, rendered it necessary that the obverse motif of the king offering oblations at the altar should be given up; in its stead was introduced the motif of the king offering a present to Kumāradevī on the occasion of the memorable matrimonial alliance with the Lichchhavis. The *triśula* in front of the king on the prototype was not retained on the new coin-type, partly because there was no room for it and partly because the Guptas were not Śaivas but Vaishṇavas. The dress of the king, however, betrays clear Kushāṇa influence. He no doubt wears an Indian close-fitting cap and not the peaked Kushāṇa head-dress; but his trousers and tailed coat unmistakbly betray their Kushāṇa origin. The king holds a crescent-topped standard in his left hand precisely in the manner of the Kushāṇa prototype. The king's name is written vertically under his left arm, as was done on the later Kushāṇa coins under the Chinese influence from Central Asia.

§ 86. The reverse of Chandragupta's coins shows Ardoxo as on the original prototype; the goddess holds a fillet or noose (*pāśa*) in the right hand and a cornucopiae in the left, as on the prototype. There is also a symbol in the left upper corner, and the back of the throne can be seen on the right side as on the Kushāṇa coins. The goddess, however, is seated on a lion and not on a throne. What suggested this departure is difficult to state. On some rare coins of the later Kushāṇa king Kaneshko, the goddess on the reverse appears seated on lion;[1] the same is the case with some of the coins of Huvishka.[2] It is not impos-

[1] *J.A.S.B., N.S.*, 1931-3, p. 7.
[2] *P.M.C.*, I. pl. XX, No. X.

sible that the Gupta mint-masters might have borrowed the idea of showing the goddess as seated on the lion from these rare types[1]. Since, however, the name of the Lichchhavis appears on the reverse, it is not unlikely that the goddess on that side was connected with them. Most probably *Siṁhavāhinī Durgā* was the tutelary deity of the Lichchhavis; that is probably the reason for the goddess of the reverse appearing as seated on lion rather than on the high-backed throne. Definite proof, however, is not yet available to show that Durgā was the deity of the Lichchhavis.

§ 87. Attention may be drawn to a few more points of the coin type of Chandragupta I. The process of Indianisation of the foreign prototype was started from the very beginning; we have seen already how the Kushāṇa peaked head-dress is replaced by a close-fitting cap bordered with pearls in the case of the king. The dress of the queen is entirely Indian; she wears a graceful *sari*, probably in the *vikachchha* fashion, and an upper garment hanging gracefully over her shoulders and under her arms. Her hair is tied in a knot behind the head, and earrings, necklace, armlets and bangles can be clearly seen on her person.

§ 88. The object which the king is offering to the queen is unfortunately not very clear. It is a small one, and is sometimes held between the thumb and the forefinger **(Pl. I. 7-8).** This suggests that it was most probably a ring. Sometimes, however, it is shown as clasped by all the fingers, its thick conical head peeping out above the thumb **(Pl. I. 2-4).** This object with a conical top has a fairly long handle on one coin in the Prince of Wales Museum, Bombay,[2] and on another in the Provincial Museum, Lucknow. On our coins **Pl. I. 2-4** it is clear that this long handle is concealed in the finger clasp and only the conical top appears. This object is obviously *sindūra-dāni*,[3] still in use among Hindu ladies of Northern India. In **Pl.**

---

[1] It is true that the above coin types were rare even in the Punjab, but we sometimes find rare types being selected as prototypes even in distant provinces. Thus the copper coinage of Bhūmaka, issued in distant Gujarat, has for its prototype an obscure coin-type issued jointly by Spalirises and Azes. See Rapson, *B.M.C.A.K.* p. cvii and pl. IX, 237-42, *P.M.C.* Vol. I, pl XIV, 396.

[2] *J. N. S. I.*, XI, Pl. 1. 9

[3] *Sindūradānī* with a long handle is used by Hindu ladies to put *Sindūra* between the parting of the hair on the head.

I. 6, however, the object presented looks like a circular bangle, but it is held rather curiously over the thumb. It is clear that the marriage gift given by the king on the occasion of the matrimonial alliance with the Lichchhavis is intended to be shown on the obverse. The gift, however, may have consisted of a ring, a bangle, a *sindūradānī* and several other ornaments. Different objects were selected for being shown on different dies by the different mint-masters; hence the absence of uniformity in their depiction on our coins.

§ 89. Usually there is a crescent between the king and the queen. Its significance can only be conjectured. On Kshatrapa and Gupta silver coins on the obverse, we get a number of crescents and circles; and there can be no doubt that they are unmeaning imitations of the corrupt Greek legend that used to occur there on the Greek prototype. It is not impossible that the crescent here may also have been suggested by the meaningless traces of the Greek legend occurring on later Kushāṇa coins. But if the idea was to produce an unmeaning imitation of this feature of the prototype, crescents and circles should have appeared in larger numbers, especially on the coins of Chandragupta I, which had no circular legend to accommodate. On the other hand we get only one crescent, usually between the king and the queen. The standard, which the king is holding in his left hand, is also crescent-topped. It is very likely that the crescent top of the standard and the crescent between the king and the queen may have a reference to the name of the king, Chandragupta. It may have been also intended to suggest that the rise of the new Gupta empire was as welcome to the people as the appearance of the crescent moon after the no-moon day. The precise and definite significance of the crescent is not yet possible to determine. It appears later on some coins of the Standard type of Samudragupta and other types of some later kings; see **Pl. II. 14-15; Pl. IV. 8-10; Pl. XXXI. 8-14.**

The crescent top of the banner can be seen only in the case of **Pl. I. 1,4,6.** In other cases, it is off the flan. It is interesting to note that among the coins of the present hoard, not in a single case do we see the fillet attached to the standard.

§ 90. Departing from the prototype, the Gupta mint-masters have shown the goddess on the reverse as seated on the lion, and not on a high-backed throne. Her identity is not easy to determine. The cornucopiae or the horn of plenty would suggest Lakshmī, the Goddess of Fortune, the consort of Vishṇu, the tutelary deity of the Guptas. On the other hand the mount lion would suggest *Pārvatī*, who is usually shown as *siṁhavāhinī*; she may have been the tutelary deity of the Lichchhavis, whose name appears on the reverse. The point cannot be settled at present.

§ 91. The mint-masters should have shown no back of the throne behind the lion. This they have done in some cases, e.g., **Pl. 1.1,4.** In other cases, however, the back of the throne is retained, though the throne itself is absent, probably through the sheer force of convention and habit. The back of the throne is most clear in the case of **Pl. I. 6,** where the right side hind leg of the throne is visible along with its horizontal back; in other cases, *e.g.*, **Pl. I. 2,3,8,** only the right side leg on the back is visible. In **Pl. I. 7-8** the right side leg on the back of the throne is extended almost to the end of the flan; this practice was the origin of the vertical line, separating the legend from the goddess, which appears on several later issues **(Pl. VI. 3,4).**

§ 92. The feet of the goddess are resting not on a lotus[1], but on a circular mat, which is bedecked with a pearl border. Usually the reverse has only one symbol in the upper left corner. But sometimes there is a corresponding symbol in the right corner also as in **Pl. I. 1.**[2] It is, however, not unlikely that this triangular symbol may be a portion of the back of the throne, conventionally treated.

§ 93. The cornucopiae, which the goddess holds in her left hand, is altogether unknown to Hindu tradition and iconography. Its presence, like that of the coat and trouser in the case of the king, shows how strong was the element of conservatism in the realm of numismatics. Later on the cornucopiae was replaced by the lotus and the fillet was considered to be a *pāśa* or noose.

§ 94. The legends on the coins of Chandragupta are simple. On the obverse, behind the queen we have Srī Kumāradevi,

[1] As stated in *B. M. C. G. D.*, p. 1.

[2] See also *B. M. C. G. D.*, pl. III. 11-13.

the name of the illustrious personage behind whom it is engraved. The transposition of the honorific epithet Śrī to the end, which we notice on a rare coin,[1] does not occur on any piece of this hoard. The name of Chandragupta is written vertically, partly under his left arm, and partly outside the staff of the standard held by him in the left hand. On the reverse, we have *Lichchhavayaḥ* written along the border on the right.

2. Samudragupta[2]
(Pl. I. 11—Pl. VI. 10)

§ 95. All the six known types of Samudragupta are represented in the hoard; it contains no new types of this emperor. The Standard type is the most numerous one; it is represented by 143 coins. The next most numerous type is the Aśvamedha one, of which we have twenty specimens. Then come the Battle-axe type with nine specimens and the Lyrist type with six. The number of the coins of the Archer and the Tiger-slayer type is very small, there being only three specimens of the former and two of the latter. All told there are thus 183 coins of Samudragupta in the hoard.

(i) Standard Type
(Pl. I. 11—Pl. III. 15)

§ 96. The Standard type was already known as the most popular type of Samudragupta and the above analysis of our hoard confirms this conclusion. The devices on the obverse and the reverse of the only type of the last reign were determined by the exigencies of the Lichchhavi alliance. The situation had now changed and the new emperor could claim to be a successor of both the Guptas and the Lichchhavis. The dual type coinage of the earlier reign was no longer necessary, and the mint-masters therefore naturally proceeded to copy more closely the Kushāṇa prototype, which they had to modify in the earlier

[1] *B.M.C.G.D.* Pl. III. 10.

[2] In §36 above we have assumed as a tentative hypotheses that Kācha was an elder Brother of Samudragupta, who preceded him. We should, therefore, have discussed his coins earlier than those of Samudragupta. We have, however, followed here the order of the coins in the plates, which were arranged in 1949 before the discovery of the coins of Rāmagupta. For the coins of Kācha, see § 138-146.

reign. Probably coins of this type were also very common in the new north-western districts added to the Gupta empire by Samudragupta; hence the mint-masters may have started a closer imitation of the Kushāṇa prototype.

On the Standard type, we have on the obverse the device of the king standing and offering oblations on a low altar in front of him. This motif is undoubtedly borrowed from the later Kushāṇa coins current in the Punjab, to which we have already referred (§ 85). The Gupta emperor wears the Kushāṇa coat and trousers, but the peaked turban is replaced by a close fitting pearl-bordered cap. The trident in front of the king on the Kushāṇa prototype is replaced by the Garuḍa standard. The Guptas were not Saivas but Vaishṇavas; it is therefore but natural that Samudragupta should have decided to replace the trident on the obverse by *Garuḍadhvaja*,[1] the emblem of Vishṇu, the tutelary deity of the new house. On some large coins the Garuḍa standard is clearly away from the king's right hand, but in most cases it is behind it. The object offered by the king on the altar is not incense but a *puroḍāśa*;[2] it is distinctly round in form, as can be seen on several coins; cf. **Pl. II. 14, III. 1**, etc. Usually the flames are shown as coming out of the altar. In no case in our hoard does the altar with the flames look like a *Tulasī-vṛindāvana* or *Sivaliṅga*, as it does on some specimens illustrated in the *B.M.C.G.D.* Pl. II. 4, I. 14, VIII.4.5, etc. On some coins, which are here grouped into a separate variety, we have a crescent, either above the Garuḍa standard or above the head of the king; its significance is difficult to determine, as stated in § 89.

§ 97. There is no consensus of opinion about the object held by the king in his left hand. It is described as a spear

---

[1] It appears that the Garuḍa standard was introduced first by Samudragupta and not by his father. The statement in l. 24 of the Allahabad pillar inscription, *Garutmadaṅkasvavishayabhuktiśāsana*, suggests that the royal charters issued by Samudragupta were stamped with the imperial emblem of Garuḍa; the forged Gaya grant of the emperor has this seal. The emblem introduced by Samudragupta was continued by his successors. The view of Smith that the emblem of Garuḍa was copied from imperial Rome (*J. R. A. S.*, 1889, pp. 23-4) ignores the well known association of Garuḍa, the mount of Vishṇu, with the Vaishṇava faith since early times. We have a Garuḍadhvaja raised by Heliodorus, a Greek follower of Bhāgavata sect, in honour of Vishṇu, at Besnagar in Central India as early as *c.* 125 B. C.

[2] As stated, for instance, in B. *M. C. G. D.*, p. 1. *Puroḍāśa* is a round sacrificial offering made of flour.

by Smith and a standard by Mr. Allan and a sceptre by Mr. P.L. Gupta. On the later Kushāṇa coins the object in the king's left hand has sometimes a *triśūla* top and sometimes a *chakra* one.[1] It was therefore probably a standard in the case of the Kushāṇa prototype, and the same was probably intended to be the case on the Gupta imitations. It is true that the object is a tapering one on several specimens and thus looks like a spear; cf. **Pl. III. 7,11.** In other cases, however, it has a flat and rounded top and looks like a sceptre or *rājadaṇḍa*; cf. **Pl. III. 12-14**, etc. The staff of this object is, however, usually decorated with a fillet, which we do not find associated with a spear or a sceptre. It may be therefore least objectionable to describe the object as a standard. The Indian tradition was not in favour of the king carrying his own standard; this type, therefore, though so popular in the reign of Samudragupta, was soon discontinued after his death.

§ 98. The reverse of the Standard type is a closer imitation of the prototype, because the goddess is shown as seated, not on the lion as on the coins of Chandragupta I, but on a high-backed throne, as on one of the main varieties of the later Kushāṇa coins. The back of the throne is shown only on the right side; on the left side it was displaced by the symbol. Sometimes all four, sometimes three and sometimes only two legs of the throne are visible on the coin. The goddess holds a fillet in her right hand and a cornucopiae in her left, as on the Kushāṇa prototype, and there is a circular mat under her feet. She wears a *sari*, an upper garment and several ornaments like earrings, necklace, bracelets, armlets, etc.

§ 99. There is usually one symbol in the upper left corner, but some coins have a corresponding symbol on the right side as well. It appears as quite distinct from the back of the throne in several cases; cf. **Pl. II. 1-2, III. 15**, etc.

§ 100. In the Standard type, the Gupta mint-masters undoubtedly copy the prototype supplied by the coins of the later Kushāṇas. But their coins are artistically very much superior to those they copy, and their metal very much purer. It is probably the latter circumstance which would explain the complete

[1] *I. M. C.*, Pl. XIV. 1 and 3.

absence of the later Kushāṇa coins in the present and several other hoards of Gupta coins. Hoarders naturally did not care to include in their treasures coins of doubtful intrinsic value, when better ones were available in plenty.

§ 101. To Samudragupta belongs the credit of introducing poetical legends on Indian coins for the first time. Revivial of Sanskrit was a marked feature of the Gupta age; Rājaśekhara observes how Vikramāditya, probably Chandragupta II, had ordered that Sanskrit should be spoken even in his harem. According to the Allahabad record, Samudragupta was himself a poet of high merit.[1] It is therefore but natural that he should have felt that his coin legends should be in Sanskrit poetry, announcing his achievements in adequate and appropriate language. It is not unlikely that he himself might have composed some, if not all of his metrical legends.

The obverse legend on the Standard type is a line in Upagīti metre, running as follows:—

Samaraśatavitatavijayo jitaripurajito divaṁ jayati.

"(Emperor Samudragupta), who has defeated (all) his enemies and scored victories on a hundred battle-fields, wins heaven (also by his good works)"

The legend on the reverse is simply *Parākramaḥ* 'valour' which was the *biruda* of the emperor.[2]

§ 102. The Standard type was the most popular type of Samudragupta; we may well presume that it was issued throughout his long reign and in the different provinces of his empire. Mr. Allan has conjectured that this type was probably started not at the beginning of his reign, as its legend refers to his numerous victories.[3] This however does not seem to have been the case. The legend is poetical and its expression *samaraśata* need not be literally interpreted as a hundred battles; some of these might well have been won by him as a crown-prince as well.

§ 103. Gupta gold coins are not dated, and so it is not easy to determine the relative chronology of the different coins of one type. Out of the 143 Standard type coins included in this

---

[1] Cf. *Kavimativibhavotsāraṇaṁ chāpi kāvyaṁ*, Allahabad pillar inscription, l. 16.

[2] Cf. *Tasya..parākramāṅkasya* in the Allahabad pillar inscription, l. 17.

[3] *B. M. C. G. D.*, pp. lxvii-viii.

hoard, some of course must have been issued at the beginning and some at the end of the reign. It is usual to assume that the coins like those illustrated in **Pl. II. 12-14,** which show the back of the throne very clearly, were issued earlier than the pieces like those illustrated in **Pls. II 9-10, III. 12-14** etc, where the back of the throne is not visible at all. This may be so, but we cannot ignore the geographical factor also. Coins showing the back of the throne very distinctly may have been discontinued in Bihar very soon, as the people there were not familiar with the Kushāṇa prototype. But the back of the throne may have been continued in the north-western part of the kingdom down to the end of the reign, as the Kushāṇa prototype was familiar to the people there. It is worth noting that the back of the throne appears distinctly on several coins of the Archer type of Chandragupta II,**(Pl. VIII. 5,6,8,13,** etc**)**, the son of Samudragupta. Nor can we say that the coins, which are artistically inferior, were issued early in the reign, as compared to those which are of superior artistic merit. It is quite possible that the mints in small and outlying towns could not be supplied with first class artists and therefore continued to issue inferior specimens for a fairly long time. It has to be admitted that we are not yet in a position to determine the relative chronology of the different coins of the Standard type.

§ 104. In *B.M.C.G.D.* Mr. Allan has divided the Standard type of coins in two varieties, variety *α*, consisting of those where Samudra only is written vertically under the left arm and variety β, where Gupta is added to the above inscription and engraved vertically outside the standard. Our variety A corressponds to the veriety *α* of the *B.M.C.G.D.*; it is interesting to note that the circular legend on all the 77 coins of this variety begins on the right at I; it never begins on the left at VII or VIII. **Pl. I. 11-15** and **Pl. II. 1-11** belong to this variety.

§ 105. As many as 16 coins with Samudra only in the field showed a crescent on the obverse either above the Garuḍa standard or above the king or in between them. We have therefore constituted these coins into a separate variety, here called B, and they are illustrated on **Pl. II. 12-15** and **Pl. III. 1.**

Another group of this class consisting of 18 pieces shows some distinctive features. In their case also the circular legend begins at I and we have Samudra only in the field. But all the coins of this class are of a distinct and different fabric. They are usually neat, small and carefully manufactured, their circular legend usually showing most of the medial vowels except when the flan happens to be too small to accommodate them. The king's torso is somewhat thrown back at the waist. The Garuḍa standard is usually behind the right hand of the king and not away from it. The folds of the *sari* of the goddess on the reverse are usually seen collected between her legs; the latter are not covered by one of the ends of the *sari* being taken over them both. Their weight is remarkably uniform, viz. 119 grains, and they have one common symbol . We have therefore grouped these coins in variety C. Five of these are illustrated in **Pl. III. 2-6.**

Coins of the variety D of our Catalogue have the circular legend on the obverse beginning on the left at VIII, and so differ from all the coins of the preceding varieties, where it begins at I. No coins of this class show a crescent, as those of the variety B, nor are they small and neat as those of the variety C. *B.M.C.G.D.* has only one coin of this class (No. 8), which it does not differentiate from its variety B. We have constituted these coins into a different variety, as they are as many as 25 in number. Six of these are illustrated on **Pl. III. 7-12.**

Variety E of this Catalogue corresponds with variety β of the *B.M.C.G.D.* Coins of this variety differ from those of the varieties A,B,C and D in having not merely *Samudra* but *Samudragupta* in the field of the obverse. As in earlier varieties, *Samudra* is written vertically under the left arm; *Gupta* is also similarly engraved, but outside the standard. In no case does the circular legend begin at I in this variety, as it invariably does in the varieties A,B and C. The crescent is also conspicuous by its absence on all the specimens. This variety resembles the var. D in having the circular legend beginning at VIII, but differs from it in having the king's full name Samudragupta in the field. Three coins of this variety are illustrated on **Pl. III. 13-15.**

§ 106. Although the hoard contains as many as 143 coins of the Standard type, we do not find a single coin among them with the *biruda Vikrama*. One of the Standard type coins of

Samudragupta found at Bamnala in Central India[1] showed the *biruda Vikrama* on the reverse instead of the usual one *Parākrama.* This hoard tends to show that the occurrence of the *biruda* of *Vikrama* on the solitary coin in the Bamnala hoard is probably due to the mistake of the mint-master in using the obverse die of the Standard type of the earlier reign along with the reverse die of the Archer type of the later one. If Samudragupta had really started using the *biruda* of *Vikrama* on his Standard type, we would naturally have found at least some coins with that *biruda* in our present hoard, which contains such a large number of them. That *biruda* may also well be expected to occur either singly or in a compound on some coins of the other types as well issued by the emperor. It does not however so occur at all.

(ii) Aśvamedha Type
(Pl. IV. 1—Pl. V. 5)

§ 107. Samudragupta had revived the Aśvamedha sacrifice, which had been in abeyance for some time. It is therefore but natural that he should have issued a special coin type to commemorate the occasion. The sacred texts tell us that each of the four priests (*ritviks*) was to be given a thousand golden *śatamānas* as his honorarium (*dakshiṇā*).[2] Each of the two lute players, who were to sing daily about the victories and pious works of the sacrificer throughout the year, was also to be given a fee of a hundred coins, probably in gold.[3] The Aśvamedha coins were probably first intended to be given as *dakshiṇā* on the occasion of the horse sacrifice. Later on they were issued to the public as well, probably to announce the successful termination of the great event.

§ 108. Aśvamedha sacrifice was performed towards the end of the reign of Samudragupta, when he had returned victorious from his various campaigns in Madhyadeśa, Central India and the Eastern Deccan, after establishing his claim to undisputed supremacy in the country. The coins commemorating the event are fairly numerous; they seem to have been issued in large quan-

[1] *J. N. S. I.*, V. p. 135.

[2] तेभ्यश्चत्वारि सहस्राणि ददाति शतमानांश्च तावतः । शतमानं दक्षिणा सौवर्णम् । *Kāt. Sr. Sūtra.*, XX. 6. 22.

[3] वीणागाथिभ्यां पृथक् शते ददाति । *Ibid*, XX. 7.

tity. In our present hoard they number 20 and are thus more numerous than any other type of this ruler, excepting of course the Standard type. The British, the Indian and the Lucknow Museums respectively possess seven, two, and five pieces of this type; and the *B.M.C.G.D.* refers to six more.

§ 109. The Aśvamedha coins are among the best specimens of the numismatic art of ancient India, and they show no foreign influence whatsoever. The horse on the obverse looks noble and graceful and seems to be resigned to its impending doom. The *yūpa* (sacrificial pillar) in its front is artistically engraved. The figure of the queen on the reverse is slim and graceful; her attitude is one of alertness, as befits her role. Obviously the best artists were selected for cutting the dies and they were fully conscious of the importance of the event and were determined to see that the artistic merit of the coins they were striking was commensurate with the importance of the occasion.

§ 110. The obverse of the Aśvamedha type shows the horse standing before the *yūpa*. On a few specimens only there is a strap round its neck; see **Pl. IV. 7, V. 4;** it was probably not intended to show the animal as tied to the *yūpa*. The horse is uncaparisoned, but on several specimens beads seem to have been plaited into its mane; see **Pl. IV. 2,7,8,10,13.** This was in accordance with the direction of the sacred texts. The *Kātyāyana-Śrauta-Sūtra*, for instance, tells us that a hundred beads of gold were plaited in the hair of the horse; those on the head were strung by the *mahishī* or the crowned queen, those on the mane by the *vāvātā* or the favourite queen and those in the tail by the *parivriktā* or the discarded queen.[1] Our specimens show the beads over the head and the mane **(Pl. IV. 6-7)**, but not on the tail. In addition to the beads plaited in the horse's hair, several coins show a string of beads over the back of the horse, but at a considerable height above its body; cf. **Pl. IV. 11-13.** This string of beads is probably merely an ornamental decoration in the motif of the coin type, but was probably suggested by the plaiting of the horse's hair by beads, as required by the sacred texts.

[1] अभ्रश्यमाणान्मणीन्सौवर्णानेकशतमेकशतं केशपुच्छेषु आवयन्ति भूर्भुवः स्वरिति प्रतिव्याहृति । 123. 8. The commentary adds, भूरिति महिषी अश्वस्य शिरोरोमसु भुव इति वावाता ग्रीवारोमसु स्वरिति परिवृक्ता पुच्छरोमसु ।

§ 111. Under the horse each coin shows the letter *si*; it is obviously an abbreviation of *siddham* and refers to the auspicious nature of the occasion. The horse is standing on a platform, below which we have either slanting lines **(Pl. IV. 8-10)**, or several dots **(Pl. IV. 1,3)**. On a few coins there is a smaller platform above this larger one, whose significance is not yet clear **(Pl. IV. 2,7)**. It has been suggested that this may be the slab of gold on which the priest (*hotṛi*) sat;[1] but it is not clear why this slab should be shown under the horse.

The larger platform under the horse is probably the *vedī* or the altar. In rare cases it is connected with the *yūpa* by a perpendicular line **(Pl. IV. 11,13)**; in most cases, however, the base of the *yūpa* is seen half over this *vedī*. The sacred texts state that if the *yūpa* was set up entirely within the altar, the scrificer would win the world of gods; if outside the altar, the world of men, if set just at the edge of the altar, then both the worlds.[2] The mint-masters seem to be attempting to satisfy the last mentioned condition, when they show the *yūpa* as half within and half outside the altar.

§ 112. In their representation of the *yūpa*, the Gupta engravers were moved partly by artistic considerations and partly by the regard for the sacred texts. In every case the *yūpa* is shown as having a base or platform, usually in two tapering steps. This is not required by the sacred texts; they on the other hand lay down that the ground round the *yūpa* was to be made even by being beaten down.[3] Artistic considerations, however, dictated that the *yūpa* should have a proper platform and the mint-masters were bent upon supplying it, whether the sacred texts permitted it or not.

Pennons or clothes that are shown as flying from the top of the *yūpa* over the horse on every specimen of this type seem also to be dictated by artistic considerations. The *Śatapatha-Brāhmaṇa* no doubt states in one place that the *yūpa* should be wrapped in 17 clothes; but they were apparently wound round the staff of the *yūpa* and not flying like pennons from its top. There was a standard fastened ceremoniously on the chariot of the conqueror

---

[1] *B. M. C. G. D.*, p. lxxvii.

[2] *Taittiriya-saṁhitā*, VI. 6. 4.

[3] ब्रह्म वनित्वा इति पांसुभिः पर्यूहति । *Kātyāyana-Śrauta-Sūtra*, VI. 3, 9. Commentator says, कुट्टनेन च पांसूनवटेऽवः प्रवेशयेत् ।

at the beginning of his victorious campaign.[1] It may be that it is shown here as attached to the *yūpa* with a view to add to its gracefulness. It is, however, more probable that a pennon or a piece of cloth was tied near the top of the *yūpa* and allowed to fly as a standard; for the *Rāmāyaṇa* describes how each of the 21 *yūpas*, that were erected at the time of the Aśvamedha sacrifice of king Daśaratha, was decorated with one piece of cloth.[2]

In the other details of the *yūpa* the Gupta engravers closely follow the requirements of the sacred texts. There were no hard and fast rules about the exact height of the *yūpa*. To judge from the height of the horse, the height of the *yūpa* was probably intended to be about 10 feet. The shaft of the *yūpa* was to be eight cornered, but that detail could probably not be shown distinctly as the coins were very small. The sacred texts require[3] that the *yūpa* shaft should not be straight, but that it should have a bend in the centre as well as at the top, both the bends being in the same direction. The *yūpas* on all our coins show this characteristic without exception.

All the *yūpas* show a girdle near their middle, which is usually shown as wound round twice.[4] Its two ends are shown as hanging down, sometimes on the same and sometimes on the opposite sides of the *yūpa*. The girdle or *raśanā* was made of *kuśa* grass and its length was to be 18 feet.[5] It is no wonder that it is shown as hanging down the *yūpa* over a considerable distance. The direction of the sacred texts that the two ends of the *raśanā* should be tied together enclosing the *yūpaśakala*[6]

---

[1] केतुं कृण्वन्नकेतवे इति ध्वजं प्रतिमुञ्चति । *Taittirīya-Brāhmaṇa*, III. 9.4.

[2] प्राप्ते यूपोच्छ्रये तस्मिन् षड्बैल्वाः खादिरास्तथा ।
तावन्तो बिल्वसहिताः पर्णिनश्च तथापरे ।
.. .. ..
शोभार्थं तस्य यज्ञस्य काञ्चनालंकृता भवन् ॥
एकविंशतिरूपास्ते एकविंशत्यरत्नयः ।
वासोभिरेकविंशद्भिरेकैकं समलंकृताः । *Rāmāyaṇa*, I, 14. 22-27.

[3] अथ य एष आनत उपरिष्टादुपनतो मध्ये सोऽन्नाद्यस्य रूपं तस्मात्तादृशमन्नाद्यकामः कुर्वीत । *Śatapatha Br.*, XI, 7, 2.

[4] *Śatapatha Br.*, XI, 7, 3, 2.

[5] त्रिगुणा त्रिव्यामा कौशी रशना तया नाभिमात्रे त्रिवृतं परिव्ययति संसृज्य अन्यतरस्यान्तं प्रवेशयति यूपशकलमस्यामवगूहति । *Kātyāyana Śrauta Sūtra*, VI, 3, 13-14.

[6] This was a small piece of the branch of the tree from which the *yūpa* was cut out.

in the knot is not followed by the mint-masters; for the two ends of the *raśanā* are usually shown as hanging down separately.

A wooden 'ring', ten fingers long and narrow in the centre, which was technically known as a *chashāla*, was put on the *yūpa* just near its end.[1] It can be seen on the *yūpas* of most of our coins, and is denoted by two dot-like objects that can be seen very clearly on **Pl. IV. 2,6-11, 12-15** etc. The two dots, however, do not denote two objects; *chashāla* looks like two contiguous dots because its narrow centre is exaggerated on the coins by the engravers. Near the *chashāla*, a piece of cloth is fastened to the *yūpa* and flows from it like a penon; we have already discussed its significance.

§ 113. On the reverse of the Aśvamedha type, we have a graceful female figure standing on a circular mat, treated as a lotus, and facing left. She holds a *chauri* in her right hand resting on the right shoulder and a small piece of cloth in the left hand, which often looks like a mere rope hanging by her side. This figure has obviously to be identified with Dattadevī, the crowned queen of Samudragupta, who had to wait upon the horse during the sacrifice. The queen wears a *sari* and a bodice and several ornaments, as befitted her exalted position. The sacred texts lay down that the queen was to fan and wash the horse;[2] the *chauri* which she holds in her right hand was obviously intended for the former purpose. The queen is nowhere shown as holding any water gourd in her hand on any coin. In Pl. V. 14 of the *B.M.C.G.D.*, Mr. Allan thinks that there is probably a gourd near the feet of the queen. The object is by no means clear in the plate; but if it is really a gourd, it would be probably for washing the horse. No object like a gourd, however, appears on any coins in the Bayana hoard.

---

[1] अग्राच्चषालं पृथामात्रं (दशांगुलं) अष्टाश्रि मध्यमसंगृहीतम् । (Com. says:—मध्ये उलूखलवत्संकुचितम्) । द्वयंगुलं त्र्यंगुलं वा अतिक्रांतं यूपस्य निसृतं भवेत् ।

Kātyāyana Śr. Sūtra, VI. 1. 27. 8.

[2] त्रि: पुनः परियंति ।......एभिरेव एनं तल्लोकैर्धुवंते । *Ibid*, XIII. 2. 8. 4.
Com. says:—धावित्रैरुपवीजयंति एनमश्वं राजानमिव ।

पात्नेजनहस्तां वाचयीत यन्नमस्त आतान इति । *Ibid*, VI. 6. 1.
Com. says:—पात्नेजनो मुखाद्यवयवशोधनार्थं जलकलशः सा हस्ते यस्याः सा ।

The object looking like a small piece of cloth, which the queen holds in her left hand, is probably a small towel which she is keeping with her in order to cleanse the horse after its bath.

§ 114. Lastly we have to consider the spear-like perpendicular object which is shown before the queen. Smith thought that it was a standard or a staff;[1] Mr. Allan suggests that it may be a ceremonial or sacrificial spear.[2] The object undoubtedly looks pointed like a spear, but the latter weapon was not required at any stage of the Aśvamedha sacrifice. The object also differs considerably from the spear, as it has two circular ornamental appendages to it, one at its centre and the other near its top.

After the horse was killed, the sacred texts lay down that the three queens were to extensively puncture its body by *sūchis* or needles in order to facilitate the passage of the sword into its body. The crowned queen was to use a golden needle, the favourite one a silver one and the discarded one a copper one.[3] It appears that the spear-like object before the queen is this 'needle'; its circular appendages may have been intended to enable the queen to grasp it firmly when piercing the hard skin of the horse. To us this appears to be the most plausible explanation of the object in front of the queen.

§ 115. The name of Samudragupta does not occur in the legend of the Aśvamedha coins either on the obverse or on the reverse. They can, however, be confidently attributed to that emperor on account of the reverse legend *Aśvamedhaparākramaḥ*. The Allahabad Pillar Inscription states that *Parākrama* was the *aṅka* or characteristic title of Samudragupta, and the inclusion of this word in the reverse legend clearly indicates that the issuer was none other than Samudragupta. On the earlier specimens the obverse legend was indistinct towards its end, and taking his clue from the metre and such traces of letters as could be seen, Mr. Allan had read it as *Rājādhirājaḥ prithivīmavitvā divaṁ jayatyaprativāryavīryaḥ*. Later on, on a coin found in Balia

---

[1] *I. M. C.*, I, p. 101.
[2] *B. M. C. G. D.*, lxxviii
[3] तिस्र: पत्न्य: असिपंथानं कल्पयंति अश्वस्य सूचिभिर्लोहराजतसौवर्णाभि: ।
Kātyāyana Ś.S. XX. 7. Com. says:—अश्वस्य शरीरे असे: सुखेन प्रवेशार्थं सूचिभिर्वितुद्य त्वचं जर्जरां कुर्यु: ।

district, traces of letters *hṛi*, *va*, *ja* and *ma* were found towards the end ; therefore the concluding part of the legend was read by Dr. Venis as *divaṁ jayatyāhṛitavājimedhaḥ*.[1] On two coins of the present hoard **(Pl. IV. 6, 13)**, the concluding word *vājimedha* is certain, though its medial vowel marks have not come out well. There can therefore now be no doubt about the concluding portion of the legend. It is a hemistich in Upagīti metre meaning, 'The king of kings, who had performed the Horse sacrifice, after having protected the earth, (now) wins the heaven.' It is interesting to note that only one of the coins of the present hoard, **Pl. V. 1** seems to contain that variant of the present reading, where its first part is *Rājādhirājaḥ pṛithivīṁ vijitya*, 'The king of kings, after having conquered the earth.' This variation occurs on one coin in the Hoey collection. On our coin the wòrd *vijitya* does not come out entire; the first letter is missing, the second is a clear *ja* and the third is a *ta*. *Pṛithivīṁ vijitya*, 'after having conquered the earth,' is no doubt a better reading for a legend on the Aśvamedha coin than the reading *Pṛithivīmavitvā*, 'after having protected the earth.' Why the former is common and the latter so rare, it is difficult to understand.

§ 116. There are no new variations in the main features of the Aśvamedha type as seen in our collection of 20 coins. So far, however, the legend on the obverse was known to be beginning either near the top of the *yūpa* at XII or near its base at VIII. On one coin of our hoard, however, it begins near the hind legs of the horse at VI, which is a new feature disclosed by our hoard; see **Pl. V. 4**.

(iii) Battle-axe Type
(Pl. V. 6-15)

§ 117. Our hoard contains only 9 coins of the Battle-axe type, as against the same number in the British Museum, 1 in the Indian Museum and 3 in the Lucknow Museum. Curiously enough, most of them are considerably worn out. Why the coins of this type alone should be so much more worn out than

---

[1] *J. A. S. B.*, 1914, p. 255; *ibid*, 1915, p. 478.

The expression in the coin legend, *āhṛitavājimedhaḥ* reminds us of the expression *chirotsannāśvamedhāhartuḥ* used of Samudragupta in the inscription of Kumāragupta I.

those of the coins of even Chandragupta I, issued earlier than them, or than the coins of the Standard type of this emperor, which were issued right from the beginning of his reign, is still a mystery.

§ 118. The Allahabad Pillar Inscription does not contain the description of Samudragupta as *Kṛitāntaparaśuḥ*, Battle-axe of the God of Death, though the epithet is invariably applied to him in later official documents. There can, however, be no doubt that the epithet was popular with the emperor in his own reign as well, as the abbreviation of the epithet, *kṛi*, is used on some coins of the present type as a substitute for his proper name Samudragupta occurring under the left arm, even when the full epithet *Kṛitāntaparaśuḥ* figures on the reverse. This type obviously refers to the military activities of the ruler. The obverse shows the king standing in the same posture as that on the Standard type. He, however, holds a battle-axe in place of the standard in the left hand and his right hand is resting on the waist. In some cases a sword is seen hanging from his belt; see **Pl. V. 6,8.** In place of the altar of the Standard type, we have here a dwarf standing before the king and looking up to him. The *Garuḍa* standard of the Standard type is replaced by a crescent-topped banner; what is its precise significance, we do not know. The crescent-topped banner was used on the coins of Chandragupta I, as we have seen already; it also finds place on the Tiger-slayer type of the present emperor.

§ 119. The significance of the obverse scene can only be conjectured. Kings in ancient India used to have several dwarfs as attendants, and our present type shows one of them. He may have come to the royal presence to deliver a report or to take orders. On most of the coins of this type the king seems to be surveying a distant scene, apparently from a point of vantage, probably the events of a battle progressing in the neighbourhood. The dwarf is perhaps awaiting the instructions of the imperial commander-in-chief to be carried to the general in the battle-field. The circular legend on the obverse is *Kṛitāntaparaśurjayatyajitarājajetājitaḥ*; it describes the irresistible prowess of the emperor and states that 'Victorious is the conqueror of unconquered kings, himself invincible and a veritable battle-axe of the God of Death'. The legend is a line in Pṛithvī metre.

§ 120. The reverse of this type shows the goddess seated on the throne, but Indianisation of the motif is carried further apace. The throne can be distinctly seen only in three cases **(Pl. V. 6, 8, 14).** On the remaining coins it is to be rather inferred from the posture of the feet of the goddess; for a lotus rather than a throne appears under her. It seems as if the mint-master could not make up his mind as to whether the goddess should be seated on the throne or appear as seated on lotus (*padmāsanā*), or on a throne entirely covered with a big lotus. She continues to hold a noose in the right hand and a cornucopiae in the left, but the latter has been replaced by a lotus bud in one case **(Pl. V. 6.)**, showing thereby that the process of identifying Ardoxo with Lakshmī was nearing completion. There is a symbol in the left upper corner on all the coins of the type. The symbol in the right corner appears only on some coins, e.g. *B. M. C. G. D.*, Pl. IV. 8, 9; none of them is represented in our hoard. The legend on the right is *Kṛtāntaparaśuḥ*, 'the battle-axe of the God of Death.'

§ 121. Only two varieties of the Battle-axe type are represented in the hoard, variety A having *Samudra* under the left arm and variety B having the letter *Kṛi*; the former corresponds to the variety α and the latter to the variety β of the *B.M.C.G.D.* The sub-variety of the former, where the goddess holds a lotus in place of cornucopiae in her left hand is represented by a single coin in the hoard, **Pl. V. 6.** On one of the coins of this variety in the *B. M. C. G. D.*, Pl. IV 16, the dwarf is shown as carrying a spear or a staff in his left hand. Such is not the case on the solitary coin of this variety in our hoard. The rare variety having *Samudra* between the dwarf and the king and *Gupta* under the latter's left arm[1] is not represented in the Bayana hoard, as also another scarce variety where the ralative position of the king and the dwarf is reversed.[2]

(iv) Archer Type
(Pl. V. 15—Pl. VI. 2)

§ 122. The Archer type is one of the rarest types of Samudra-

[1] *B. M. C. G. D.*, Pl. IV. 15; *J. A. S. B.*, 1904, Pl. 1. 1., *C. G. I.*, Pl. III. 4.
[2] *A. A.*, Pl. XVIII. 10; *A. S. I., A. R.*, 1926-7, p. 234, Pl. XXIII; *C. G. I.* Pl. II. 15, 17.

gupta. We have only three coins of this type in the Bayana hoard **(Pl. V. 15. VI. 1-2)**; the British and the Indian Museum have four coins each and the Lucknow Museum possesses only one. The Archer type was destined to become the most popular one in the succeeding reigns; it continued in use down to the end of the dynasty. We do not know why it was so scarce in the long reign of Samudragupta; probably it was started late in the reign.

§ 123. The Archer type represents another direction of the effort of the Gupta mint-masters to Indianise the foreign prototype. The standard in the left hand of the king in the Standard type was superfluous in view of the Garuḍa standard appearing in his front as well. King as his own standard-bearer is also repugnant to Hindu tradition. The standard in the king's left hand was therefore replaced by the battle-axe in the Battle-axe type; here we find it supplanted by the bow. The offering of oblations on altar by an individul wearing coat, trousers and boots was inconsistent with the Hindu ideas of purity and religious etiquette. In the Archer type, therefore, we find the king shown as holding an arrow in the right hand and not as offering any oblation with it. The reverse of this type, however, shows no effort at Indianisation, as does the reverse of the Battle-axe type; the goddess continues to be seated on high-backed throne, holding a fillet or noose (*pāśa*) in the right hand and a cornucopiae in the left. The latter is not yet replaced by the lotus.

§ 124. The name Samudra is written only under the king's left arm in this type; it does not occur between the bow and the bowstring or outside the bow, as on many coins of Chandragupta II. Two varieties may be distinguished according to the legend on the obverse. The legend in variety A is *Apratiratho vijitya kshitiṁ sucharitairdivaṁ jayati*; 'The matchless warrior, having conquered the world, wins the heaven (as well) by his meritorious deeds.' It is a line in the Upagīti metre.

The legend in the variety B is slightly different; it reads *Apratiratho vijitya kshitimavanīśo divaṁ jayati*, 'The matchless warrior, the protector of the earth, having conquered the world, wins the heaven.' The reverse legend on both the varieties is the same, viz. *Apratirathaḥ*, 'a matchless warrior.' It may be pointed out that Samudragupta is described as *prithi-*

vyāmapratirathaḥ, 'a matchless warrior on the earth' in the 24th line of the Allahabad Pillar Inscription; obviously *apratirathaḥ* was his favourite epithet.

125. The Bharsar hoard of Gupta coins is said to have contained three coins of the Archer type, where the king on the obverse was seen offering oblations on altar by the right hand in stead of holding an arrow in it. The legend on the reverse of these coins was *Parākramaḥ* and not *Apratirathaḥ*.[1] These coins have not been illustrated, and therefore we connot be sure of their constituting a new variety in this type. Our hoard contains no coins of this variety, supposing it actually existed.

(v) Lyrist Type
(Pl. VI. 3-8)

§ 126. There are six coins of the Lyrist type in the Bayana hoard, two of the larger size and four of the smaller one. The British Museum possesses five coins of the former and only one of the latter type. The Indian Museum has two coins of the larger variety and only one of the smaller one. In the Bamnala hoard found in Central India, the solitary coin of this type belonged to the smaller variety.[2]

§ 127. The coins of this type are divided in two varieties. Variety A consists of the coins of large size and high artistic merit, having foot-stool superimposed with the letter *si* on the obverse and no symbol on the reverse. The coins of the variety B are smaller in size and poorer in workmanship; they have a symbol on the reverse, but no foot-stool or the letter *si* on the obverse. The letter *ha* in the legend on the coins of the variety A is of the eastern variety; it appears in the western form in the legend on the coins of the variety B. It is, therefore, very probable that the coins of the variety A were issued from the mint at the capital Pāṭaliputra, where very good artists were available, and where the eastern variety of the Gupta characters was more popular. The coins of the variety B seem to have been issued from provincial mints in Central India and Northern U.P., where mints could get the services of artists of mediocre

[1] *J. R. A. S.*, 1889, p. 71. The legend *Parākramaḥ* occurs on the Standard type; it is not unlikely that these three coins may have belonged to it.

[2] *J. N. S. I.*, V., p. 140.

ability and in which territory the western variety of the Gupta alphabet was more familiar. This theory would explain why the variety B should be represented by four and variety A by only two coins in the Bayana hoard, and why the variety A should be altogether absent in the Bamnala hoard. In the outlying districts where the coins of the Bamnala and the Bayana hoards were probably collected, the coins of the variety A do not appear to have been common. Most of the coins of the variety A were found in Oudh and Banaras.

Though the coins of the variety B are smaller in size, their average weight is higher than that of the average coin of the variety A.

128. Coins of the variety A of the Lyrist type are among the finest specimens of the Gupta art. They are thin, broad and well struck and in singularly low relief. The king's body is graceful and the gestures of his hands natural. The coins show no trace of foreign influence on the obverse; on the reverse also the case is nearly the same, save for the presence of the cornucopiae in the hand of the goddess. The king wears Indian dress consisting of a *dhoti* and a close-fitting cap; his torso is bare. He is shown as seated on a cushioned high-backed couch; the depressions produced in the cushions by the pressure of the body of the king or of his lute are very vividly shown; see **Pl. VI. 3-4**. One of the king's feet is resting on a foot-stool and His Majesty is shown playing on a stringed lute lying on his lap by the fingers of his right hand. One expects the left hand to be placed under the lute in order to support it. It is, however, just above the instrument; probably the idea is to show its fingers gesticulating appreciation, as is very common with most musicians. The king's torso is bare, as observed already above; the idea may be to represent His Majesty seated on the terrace of his palace on a summer evening, and engaged in spending his rare leisure hours in music, which was obviously his favourite hobby, and in which his courtiers thought that he excelled even the divine musicians Nārada and Tumburu. Coins thus supply numismatic evidence to confirm the claim made in Allahabad inscription in this connection.

§ 129. The lute of Samudragupta's coins has a long hollow belly covered with a board of seven strings. It thus resembles this musical instrument as depicted in the early sculptures of Bharhut, Besnagar and Amaravati and is markedly different from its modern counterpart which has a straight, long and narrow sounding board with a gourd at one or both ends. The lute of this latter type goes back only to the Pāla period (c. 800 A. D.), and is not to be seen in Gupta sculptures.[1]

§ 130. The letter *si* occurs on the pedestal of the variety A of this type, as it does under the horse of the Aśvamedha type of this ruler. It is not unlikely that this type was suggested by the Rājanya lute-player daily singing *gāthās* (verses) composed by himself during the year preceding the actual performance of the Aśvamedha sacrifice, as required by the sacred texts.

The daily scene of the court musician playing on the lute throughout the year preceding the celebration of the Aśvamedha sacrifice, may well have suggested to Samudragupta the idea of issuing the Lyrist type, revealing his favourite hobby to his subjects. The letter *si* occurring on the obverse of variety A may be suggestive of the above connection of this type with the Aśvamedha sacrifice.

§ 131. The reverse of the type shows the goddess seated on the wicker stool facing left. This is quite a new variation and shows how the mint masters were becoming more and more successful in freeing themselves from the Kushāṇa prototype. Smith no doubt points out that this type is an exact copy of Demeter as represented on a rare coin of Paros island;[2] but unless it is shown that this rare foreign coin type had reached India, we cannot accept the theory of foreign influence in the case of this motif.

The reverse motif of goddess seated on a wicker stool became subsequently popular; it is to be seen on the Horseman types of Chandragupta II and Kumāragupta I.

(vi) Tiger-slayer Type
(Pl. VI. 9-10)

§ 132. The Tiger-slayer type is so far the rarest type of Samudragupta. Before the discovery of the Bayana hoard only two of its specimens existed in each of the British and the Lucknow

[1] *J. A. O. S.*, 1930, p. 244.
[2] *J. R. A. S.*, 1889, p. 24.

Museums and our hoard also contains the same number. They are illustrated on **Pl. VI. 9-10.**

§ 133. The coins of the Tiger-slayer type are valuable not only on account of their extreme rarity, but also on account of their high artistic beauty. They show no vestige of any foreign influence either on the obverse or on the reverse. The king discards the Kushāṇa coat and trousers and wears a *dhoti*, a turban and the usual Indian ornaments. He is shown facing left and stringing a bow, held in the left hand, to the ear by his right hand in order to shoot at a tiger leaping at him. The king's attitude is energetic; he is dauntlessly trampling the tiger by his right foot and the beast is shown as about to collapse. As on the Battle-axe type, there is a crescent-topped banner in front of the king; its significance is difficult to determine.

§ 134. The reverse also shows no trace of the Kushāṇa influence, for the usual seated goddess gives place to a slim female figure, gracefully attired and standing on a crocodile. Her identity is difficult to determine. The view that she is Varuṇānī, the wife of Varuṇa or Rati, the wife of Kāma, does not appear to be probable. Varuṇa may be suggested by the name of Samudragupta, but it is doubtful whether that can warrant the conjecture of the reverse goddess being the consort of Varuṇa. For, in that case she would have appeared on several types of the emperor and not only on his rarest type. The mount of the goddess is *makara* or crocodile and not fish; this would go against her identification with Rati. Makara or crocodile is the mount of the Gaṅgā and both the Gaṅgā and the Yamunā figure prominently in the Gupta sculptures. It is therefore possible that the deity on the reverse is the river goddess Gaṅgā. The goddess, however, holds lotus in her left hand, which may suggest her identification with Lakshmī. No definite identification of the goddess can be suggested with confidence at present.

There is a crescent-topped standard on the reverse side of this type in front of the goddess. Why this standard should appear both on the obverse and reverse sides of this type, is a mystery at present.

§ 135. The device on the reverse of the Tiger-slayer type

---

[1] *J. A. S. B.*, 1884, i, p. 177.

closely resembles that of the reverse of the Aśvamedha type. The female figures on both are slim and graceful and their posture is the same. The crescent-topped banner bears a close resemblance to the *sūchi* of the reverse of the Aśvamedha type. The lotus reaching over the shoulder of the goddess in the Tiger-slayer type is occupying the place of the *chauri* over the queen's shoulder in the Aśvamedha type. Both the types may therefore well have been contemporary.

§ 136. The Tiger-slayer type has no metrical legend either on the obverse or on the reverse. In variety A, the legend *Vyāghraparākramaḥ* occurs on the obverse and *Rājā Samudraguptaḥ* on the reverse. In variety B, the same legend *Vyāghraparākramaḥ* occurs both on the obverse and the reverse. *Parākrama* was the special epithet of Samudragupta, and so we can confidently ascribe the coins of the variety B also to him, though his personal name does not occur on them.

§ 137. The simple title *rājā* prefixed to the king's name in the reverse legend of the variety A has given rise to several conjectures. Smith thought that the legend showed that the coins were issued when Samudragupta was a mere crown-prince;[1] Jayaswal felt that the legend would warrant the conclusion that the type was issued when Samudragupta was reduced to a feudatory status by the Vākāṭakas.[2] Both conjectures are unjustified. The reverse legend gives the simple title *rājā* to Samudragupta, simply because the numismatic convention prescribed a short legend on that side; a legend like *Mahārājādhirāja-Samudraguptaḥ* was out of question on the reverse. It may be pointed out that the reverse legend on the Lyrist type of Samudragupta is shorter still; for it is simply *Samudraguptaḥ* without any title whatsoever. On this type, however, the obverse legend contains the title *Mahārājādhirāja*. But on the Swordsman type of Kumāragupta I the reverse legend is simply *Śrī-Kumāraguptaḥ*, and the metrical legend on the obverse, *Vijitāvaniravanipatiḥ Kumāragupto divaṁ jayati*, contains no royal title. Are we to conclude that they were issued when Kumāragupta had ceased to be even a feudatory? It will be quite unsafe to determine the status of a Gupta king from the short legend on the reverse of one of his coin types.

---

[1] *J. R. A. S.*, 1889, p. 65.

[2] *History of India*, p. 118.

3. KĀCHA[1]

(Pl. VI. 11—Pl. VII. 11)

§ 138. The Bayana hoard contains 16 coins of Kācha, as against his seven coins represented in the British Museum, three in the Indian Museum and four in the Provincial Museum, Lucknow. Fifteen of these coins belong to variety A, which is already well-known to us from several specimens. The 16th coin **(Pl. VII. 11)** constitutes a new variety, here called variety B.

§ 139. The obverse of the coins of the variety A **(Pl. VI. 11-Pl. VII. 10)** shows the king standing to left in a posture remarkably similar to that of Samudragupta on his standard type. Like Samudragupta, Kācha also is shown offering oblations on altar; but in variety A the Garuḍa standard is missing in his front and he is seen holding a *chakradhvaja* (wheel standard) in his left hand. Under the left arm is engraved the issuer's name Kācha, the medial *ā* being quite clear in several cases, e.g. **Pl. VI. 12-13**, etc. The circular legend, beginning at 1, reads as follows:—

Kācho gāmavajitya Karmabhiruttamairdivaṁ jayati

"Having conquered the earth, Kācha (now) wins the heaven by his excellent works." It is a hemistich in Upagīti metre.

§ 140. The reverse of the coins of Kācha closely resembles that of the Aśvamedha and the Tiger-slayer types of Samudragupta. As on the above two types, the female figure is standing to left; there is a mat under her feet, as is the case with the queen on the Aśvamedha type and not a crocodile, as we see under the feet of the goddess on the Tiger-slayer type. The cornucopiae, which the goddess holds in her left hand, reminds us of the Kushāṇa prototype, but the graceful manner in which the flower is held in the right hand shows how the Gupta mint-masters were trying to show both originality and artistic sense. The monograms on the coins of Kācha are remarkably graceful, complex and original. The reverse legend is *Sarvarājochchhettā*, 'the exterminator of all kings.'

§ 141. Variety B **(Pl. VII. 11)**, which is disclosed by the present hoard for the first time, bears a general resemblance to

[1] See *ante*, p. 52, note 1.

variety A, but it shows slightly greater Indianisation. The king on the obverse wears a *dhoti* instead of the Kushāṇa trousers. The object in his left hand is not completely on the flan; but it is most probably a *chakradhvaja* rather than an ordinary standard, as in variety A. The goddess on the reverse holds a noose instead of a flower. The most striking feature of this variety is the presence of *Garuḍadhvaja* on the obverse, which is absent in variety A.

§ 142. The question of the identity of Kācha cannot yet be finally settled. Some think that Kācha is identical with Samudragupta, others hold that he is different from him. Among the latter, some opine that he was an elder or half-brother of Samudragupta, others think that he is identical with Rāmagupta of the literary tradition. How evenly balanced the arguments are in this controversy can be easily realised when we note how Smith advocated the identity of Kācha and Samudragupta in 1889,[1] how he abandoned this view and accepted the opinion of Rapson that the two were different rulers in 1893[2] and how he veered round to his first opinion in 1902.[3] Fleet accepts the identity of the two rulers and Mr. Allan thinks that the attribution of the coins of Kācha to Samudragupta can no longer be doubted.[4]

§ 143. *Sarvarājochchhettā*, the legend on the reverse of the coins of Kācha, no doubt appears as the exclusive epithet of Samudragupta in the later Gupta official records; however, we need not merely on that account ascribe Kācha coins to Samudragupta, becuse Samudragupta's own records do not show the use of that epithet for that emperor. The obverse legend on the coins of Kācha is no doubt a close paraphrase of the obverse legend on the coins of Samudragupta. This circumstance, however, cannot necessarily show that the two rulers were identical;[5] it may perhaps show that the two kings were not far re-

---

[1] *J. R. A. S.*, 1889, pp.75-76.

[2] *Ibid*, 1893. p. 95

[3] *I. A.*, 1902, pp. 259-260.

[4] *B. M. C. G. D.*

[5] The legend on the Kācha coins paraphrased by Kumāragupta I on his Swordsman type, where we have *Gāmavajitya sucharitaiḥ Kumāragupto divaṁ jayati*; so the paraphrasing of a legend need not necessarily show that the paraphraser lived close to the time of the king, whose legend is paraphrased by him.

moved in time. Gupta emperors like Chandragupta II, who had also secondary or alternative names like Devagupta, usually confine themselves to one name only, written on their coins under their arm. If Kācha was an alternative name of Samudragupta, it is not likely that he would have departed from this practice. And supposing that Kācha was another name of Samudragupta, why should it have been restricted only to the *Chakradhvaja* type? Why should not the name Samudra have occurred on some specimens of the *Chakradhvaja* type and the name Kācha on some specimens of the Standard, the Archer and the Battle-axe types? Why should not *Chakra* standard of Kācha have occurred on some of the coins of the Standard, the Archer and other types of Samudragupta, if the two were identical? Gupta kings no doubt often use different *birudas* on the reverse like *apratirathaḥ*, *Kritāntaparaśuḥ* etc., but they use only one personal name on the obverse under the arm. This circumstance tends to show that Kācha was different from Samudragupta.

§ 144. Our difficulties are, however, not solved by this assumption. The identity of Kācha continues to baffle us. At one time scholars were inclined to take Kācha as an abbreviation of Ghaṭotkacha and identify the king with the father of Chandragupta I. This, however, is an untenable view. Firstly, the name of the king is Kācha and not Kacha, and Kācha can hardly be regarded as an abbreviation of Ghaṭotkacha. Secondly, Ghaṭotkacha was a mere feudatory and could hardly have issued any coins.

§ 145. After the discovery of the copper coins of Rāmagupta in 1951 in Mālwā, the most plausible view to suggest is that Kācha was probably an elder brother of Samudragupta, who successfully contested his succession for some time. Allahabad pillar inscription seems to refer to this contest in its fragmentary verses; in the Gupta coin hoards, the coins of Kācha are usually found associated with those of Chandragupta I and Samudragupta. His name was probably omitted deliberately in Gupta genealogies as that of an impious son, who had dared to challenge the succession as formally authorised by his father.

§ 146. We may, however, add that the available evidence does not exclude the possibility of Kācha being a king not belonging to the Gupta dynasty, and challenging its supremacy sometimes after the death of Chandragupta I and before the accession of Chandragupta II. The identity of Kācha can be finally settled only by the discovery off resh and conclusive evidence. [See § 36 also.]

4. Chandragupta II

(Pl. VII. 12—Pl. XVIII. 14)

§ 147. Out of 1821 coins of the Bayana hoard 983 belong to Chandragupta II; Kumāragupta I, his son whose reign had terminated just before the immurement of the hoard, has only 628 coins. This would suggest that the output of the gold coins of the Gupta mints was at its maximum during the reign of Chandragupta II, which was probably the most prosperous period in the Gupta age.

§ 148. 983 coins of Chandragupta II of this hoard contain all known types of the emperor excepting two. The Standard type of this ruler, which is so far known from a single coin in the Bhārata-kalā-bhavana,[1] Banaras Hindu University, is unrepresented in the hoard. The idea of representing the emperor as his own standard-bearer was distasteful to Indian sentiment, and Chandragupta seems to have soon decided to discontinue the type, which was not revived by any of his successors. The other type of this emperor not represented in the hoard is the King-and-Queen-on-the-Couch type. This type is so far known from a single published specimen, whose subsequent whereabouts are unknown;[2] it is therefore not surprising that it should not be in our hoard. The *Chakravikrama* coin of this hoard is a unique coin of its type, so far not known from any second specimen. We shall refer to it later in § 182-§ 185.

§ 149. The Archer, the Couch, the Lion-slayer, the Horseman, the Chhatra, and the Chakravikrama are the types of Chandragupta represented in the hoard. Of these the Archer type was already known to be the most popular one, the British Museum having its 34 specimens and the Provincial Museum, Lucknow, and the Indian Museum, Calcutta, having 18 each.

[1] *J. N. S. I.*, Vol. IX, p. 146. Dr. Chhabra has suggested that this coin-type should be attributed to Chandragupta I (*Ibid.* XI, p. 15), but his arguments do not appear conclusive.

[2] I saw a specimen of this type with a dealer in Lucknow in 1948; I am not sure whether it was not the same coin which was published in 1888.

The Bayana hoard contains 798 coins of this type; they are thus more numerous than those of any coin-type of any emperor represented in the hoard. This type continued to be popular in the subsequent reigns and remained the only coin-type for gold coins with most of the later Gupta kings. The Lion-slayer type seems to have been suggested by the Tiger-slayer type of Samudragupta. The Couch type is an adaptation of the Lyrist type of the same ruler, and the King-and-the-Queen-on-the-Couch type, not represented in our hoard, is a further modification of it.

§ 150. Chatra, Horseman and Chakravikrama types are the innovations of Chandragupta II. The Chhatra type was probably intended to emphasise the supreme overlordship (*ekachchhatratva*) of the emperor. He was perhaps famous as a cavalry leader; it was probably because of this circumstance that the Horseman type was ordered to be issued. Both Chhatra and the Horseman types were fairly common and popular in the reign. The Chakravikrama type shows the emperor as receiving a gift from God Vishṇu, manifesting himself before his devotee for that purpose. Chandragupta was a devout Vaishṇava and hence it is natural that he should have thought of this type. But why it should have been so scarce, we do not know.

§ 151. It is worth noting that the Aśvamedha and the Battle-axe types of Samudragupta were not continued in the new reign. In spite of his extensive conquests, Chandragupta performed no Aśvamedha sacrifice, probably due to his Vaisṇava leanings; hence he naturally issued no coins of that type. The Battle-axe type was not continued by Chandragupta, probably becuse *Kritāntaparaśu* had become a special and personal epithet of Samudragupta; his son was perhaps reluctant to issue that type and use that epithet for himself. We have shown already how the Lyrist and the Tiger-slayer types of Samudragupta reincarnate themselves as the Couch and Lion-slayer types in the reign of his son. Of these the latter was very popular. Chandragupta naturally did not care to continue the *Chakradhvaja* type of king Kācha. He was no doubt himself a Vaishṇava like Kācha, but his open rebellion against Samudragupta naturally made Chandragupta reluctant to follow his coin type.

(i) Archer Type

(Pl. VII. 12—Pl. XIII. 5)

§ 152. The Archer type, which is represented by 798 coins in the Bayana hoard, was undoubtedly issued as a mass production, but it should not be supposed that the coins of this type present a dead uniformity. The creative vein was the most characteristic feature of the Gupta art, and it urged the mint-masters to attempt ever new variations within the frame work of the main type. The name of the king Chandra is written sometimes under his left arm, sometimes between the bow and the bow-string and sometimes outside the string. Sometimes the string of the bow is inside and sometimes it is outside; sometimes the bow is held at the top and sometimes by the middle at its back. Usually the bow is in the left hand and the arrow is in the right; but sometimes the position is reversed. Generally the Garuḍa standard is on the left, but sometimes it is on the right also. On several coins the king's head is adorned with different varieties of beautiful crowns, but very often he is bare-headed with curly hair falling down like a wig on the neck.

Class I: Throne Reverse

(Pl. VII. 12—Pl. IX. 5)

§ 153. Coins of the Archer type are usually divided into two classes, class I with the Throne reverse and class II with the Lotus reverse. Our hoard contains 41 coins of class I, the British Museum, the Indian Museum and the Lucknow Museum having 7,4, and 2 coins respectively of this class. All the coins of this class known so far are issued to the weight standard of 121 grams. The coins of this class bear closer resemblance to the Kushāṇa prototype than those of the class II; the goddess on their reverse appears on high-backed throne, which is replaced by a lotus in class II. It was therefore thought that the coins of class I were issued either early in the reign when the Kushāṇa influence was still dominant or in the north-western part of the empire, where the foreign prototype might have continued to be copied down to the end of the reign.[1] The Bayana hoard may well be presumed to have been collected in the north-western

[1] *B. M. C. G. D.*, p. lxxviii.

part of the Gupta empire and yet it contains only 41 coins with the Throne reverse as against 757 with the Lotus reverse. We may therefore well assume that the Throne reverse was discontinued even in the north-western part of the empire early in the reign of Chandragupta II.

§ 154. In class I of the Archer type, the obverse shows the king dressed usually in Kushāṇa coat and trousers and holding the bow in the left hand and the arrow in the right, as was the case with the Archer type of Samudragupta. There is also a Garuḍa standard in his front. The coins of this class are divided into four varieties. In variety A, **(Pl. VII. 12—VIII. 12)** the name Chandra is written vertically under the left arm; it corresponds with variety *a* of the *B.M.C.G.D.* In variety B, the bow is held with the string inwards and the name of the king Chandra is written vertically between the bow and the bow-string **(Pl. VIII. 13—Pl. IX. I)**. It corresponds with the variety β of the *B.M.C.G.D.* The variety C differs from the above variety in having the bow-string outside **(Pl. IX. 2)**; it is a new variety disclosed by the Bayana hoard. In variety D, the bow is held at the middle with its string outside, Chandra being written vertically outside the string **(Pl. IX. 3-5)**. This variety corresponds with the variety γ of the *B.M.C.G.D.* The obverse legend on all these varieties is '*Devaśrīmahārājādhirāja-Śrī-Chandraguptaḥ.*,' 'His Majesty glorious Chandragupta, king of kings.' The same legend occurs on class II also.

§ 155. The reverse of all these varieties shows the goddess seated on the throne, whose back is visible in some cases and invisible in others. The right hand of the goddess is sometimes empty **(Pl. VIII. 1-3)**, but sometimes it is scattering round coins **(Pl. VIII. 4-5)**. In the left hand, the goddess holds sometimes a cornucopiae **(Pl. VIII. 4-10)**, and sometimes a lotus **(Pl. VIII. 1-3)**. Coins of this class, which show the goddess on the reverse seated on a backless throne but with her feet resting on a lotus, and holding a noose in the right hand and a lotus instead of the cornucopiae in the left hand **(Pl. VIII. 3. 11-2)**, may be regarded as forming the transition to class II. *B. M. C. G. D.* has only one coin of this transition type illustrated on Pl. VI. 7.

§ 156. The rare coins of the Archer type of this class which show no name of the king written vertically on the obverse, but show the sword hanging under the left arm,[1] are not represented in the Bayana hoard.

Class II: Lotus Reverse
(Pl. IX. 6—Pl. XIII. 5)

§ 157. The obverse of the coins of class II bears a general resemblance with that of the obverse of class I; the circular legend is also the same. King is generally bare-headed, but he usually wears a *dhoti* instead of trousers; he, however, continues to wear the Kushāṇa coat. The goddess on the reverse is now definitely identified with Lakshmī; she is seated on a lotus and holds another lotus flower in her left hand, the right hand usually holding a *pāśa*.

§ 158. The different varieties of this type have been determined usually by the variations on the obverse. The most numerous variety is the variety A, where *Chandra* is written vertically under the left arm of the standing king **(Pl. IX 6—Pl. XI. 11)**. Out of 757 coins of this class, as many as 700 belong to the variety A. It corresponds with the variety *β* of the *B. M. C. G. D.* The variety B **(Pl. XI. 12—Pl. XII. 2)**, where a hunter is shown as hanging by the side of the king, is a new discovery disclosed by our hoard. The same observation holds good of the variety C **(Pl. XII. 3-6)**, where a sword is hanging by the side of the king instead of the hunter.[2] Varieties D, E and F are also new. Variety D resembles variety A in the obverse, but differs from it in the reverse, inasmuch as the right foot of the goddess is shown as hanging down the lotus, the left one being tucked up **(Pl. XII. 7-8)**. Variety E **(Pl. XII. 9)** differs from all other varieties in having no vertical legend Chandra on the obverse. Variety F is quite peculiar; its reverse legend is Chandragupta instead of the usual one Śrivikramaḥ **(Pl. XII. 10)**. In variety G, the position of the bow and arrow is reversed; the bow is held in the right and the arrow in the left hand **(Pl. XII. 11-12)**. The *B. M. C. G. D.*, has one coin of this variety (Pl. VII. 19), but there the king is looking to right and not to left, and his left hand rests upon the hip and is not holding any

---

[1] *J. A. S. B.*, 1894, p. 168.

[2] The name of the king is written under his left arm; this differentiates this variety from the coin published in *J. A. S. B.*, 1894, p. 168.

arrow. Variety H partially resembles variety A; it differs from it, inasmuch as the king looks to right though his body is turned to left **(Pl. XII. 13—Pl. XIII. 2)**. This variety corresponds with variety γ of class II of the *B. M. C. G .D.*, Pl. VI. 18. Variety I **(Pl. XIII. 3-5)** of this class shows the king holding the bow in the left hand by its middle with its string outside, *Chandra* being written vertically outside the string. This variety was so far known from a solitary specimen published by Mr. Prayag Dayal.[1]

§ 159. On four coins of this class in the British Museum, there is a wheel (*chakra*) above the Garuḍa standard (B.M.C.G.D., Pl. VII. 15-17); this peculiarity is to be seen on none of the coins of this hoard, though it contains as many as 757 specimens of it. Coins with this peculiarity were found in the Kalighat hoard and were probably the issues of an eastern mint; that may explain their non-occurrence in the Bayana hoard collected in the north-western part of the Gupta empire. The Indian Museum has five coins of the Archer type weighing about 141 grains, which have been attributed to Chandragupta II.[2] The arguments advanced in support of this view are by no means convincing, and the circumstance that not a single coin out of 757 pieces of this type in the present hoard should belong to the heavy weight standard of 140 grains further weakens the theory that the specimens in the Indian Museum were issued by Chandragupta II.

(ii) Horseman Type
(Pl. XIII. 6—Pl. XV. 3)

§ 160. The Horseman type of Chandragupta II represents an innovation of the emperor in the Gupta coinage. Chandragupta was probably himself a renowned horseman and he may therefore have conceived the idea of representing himself on some of his coins as riding on his horse and marching to the battlefield to win martial glory.[3] Coins of this type were not quite numerous so far; the British, the Indian and the Lucknow Museums had

---

[1] *J. A. S. B.*, 1920, p. 89.

[2] *I. M. C.*, I., p. 106-7.

[3] The Horseman type was quite a common one with the Indo-Scythian and Indo-Parthian rulers, but had been discarded by the Kushāṇas. Whether Chandragupta got his inspiration from the coins of the above rulers, we do not know. There is no marked resemblance between the two types.

12, 5 and 11 coins respectively of this type. In the Bayana hoard we have, however, 82 coins.

§ 161. On the Horseman type, the obverse shows the king riding his horse, which is caparisoned. The mane is usually plaited and the rein, the leather strap on the neck and the strap passing under the tail can be clearly seen on several specimens. The last mentioned object is sometimes seen decorated with a beautiful circular ornament **(Pl. XIII. 8)**. The king often looks bare-bodied and one can see several ornaments on his person like the necklace, earrings and armlets. His head is usually bare; the hair is arranged in tresses falling like a wig upon the neck. In one case **(Pl. XIV. 14)**, however, it is represented as dishevelled and flying behind, obviously as a consequence of his riding very fast. The obverse legend on all the coins is *Parama-bhāgavata-mahārājādhirāja-rī-Chandraguptaḥ*, 'Chandragupta, the overlord of kings and a devout worshipper of Vishṇu.'

On the reverse of all the coins of this type there is goddess Lakshmī seated on wicker stool facing left. Usually she holds a noose in the right hand, her left hand resting on waist and holding a lotus with a long stalk. Some of the coins have a symbol and others are without it. The legend on the reverse is *Ajitavikramaḥ*, the invincible Vikrama.

§ 162. It is not easy to classify the coins of this type. The direction of the horse, whether to right or to left, obviously suggests itself as a suitable criterion. Smith had followed this principle, but Mr. Allan rejected it on the ground that the distinction is quite an artificial one, because it separates coins of very similar fabric.[1] Mr. Allan has divided the coins in two classes, class I consisting of those which have a symbol on the obverse and class II of those which are without it. This division also does not appear to be particularly significant. We propose to follow Smith and first divide the coins into two classes according to the direction of the horse, and then to distinguish varieties in these classes according to the weapons carried by the king. In class I, variety A, the king is facing left and carrying no weapons **(Pl. XIII. 6-12)**. In variety B, the king is carrying a sword hanging by his left side **(Pl. XIII. 13-Pl. XIV. 2)**. In variety

[1] *B. M. C. G. D.*, p. lxxxv.

c, the the king is carrying the bow in his right hand; sometimes its upper end can be seen near the king's head **(Pl. XIV. 3-4)**, and sometimes its lower end can be noticed above the horse's haunch **(Pl. XIV. 5-6)**.

§ 163. In class II **(Pl. XIV. 8—XV. 3)** the coins of our hoard show only one variety, where the king carries no weapons. As the king faces right in this class, his left side is invisible, and so the sword dangling by the left leg could not be naturally shown. In spite of his facing right, however, the king could have been shown as wielding a bow, as is done in the British Museum Catalogue (Pl. X. 8-9). The coins of this variety, however, are not represented in our hoard.

(iii) Chhatra Type
(Pl. XV. 4—Pl. XVI. 7)

§ 164. The Chhatra type is another innovation of Chandragupta II. The type was introduced probably with the idea of emphasising his imperial status (*ekachhatratva*) in the country. There are 54 coins of this type in the Bayana hoard; the British Museum and the Indian Museum have each six coins of this type and the Lucknow Museum only one.

§ 165. On the obverse side of this type, we find the king standing to the left and offering oblations on a small altar in his front. The motif is borrowed from the Standard type of Samudragupta, which was most popular with that emperor. The king, however, is in Indian dress; the Kushāṇa costume worn by his father is discarded. In some cases he wears a graceful crown **(Pl. XV. 6-7)**, and in others a close fitting cap bedecked with pearls **(Pl. XV. 9-10)**. Very often, however, his head is bare showing frizzled hair; cf. **Pl. XVI. 2-3**. There is a dwarf behind, holding an umbrella over the head of the emperor. Very often, however, the umbrella is not above but away from the head **(Pl. XVI. 3-4)**. Sanskrit literature no doubt refers to female umbrella-bearers, but there is no coin on which the umbrella-bearer can be distinctly seen to be a woman.

Class I: With prose legend
(Pl. XV. 4-6)

§ 166. Following Mr. Allan, we have divided the Chhatra type into two classes according to the obverse legend.

In class I the legend is *Mahārājādhirāja-śrī-Chandraguptaḥ*. There were only two coins of this class known so far, one in the Indian Museum and the other in Dr. Hoey's collection. Our hoard has five coins of this classs, of which three have been illustrated **(Pl. XV. 4-6).**

Class II: With metrical legend

(Pl. XV. 7—Pl. XVI. 7)

§ 167. In class II the obverse remains essentially as above, but the prose legend is replaced by the metrical hemistich, *Kshitimavajitya sucharitairdivaṁ jayati Vikramādityaḥ*, 'Having conquered the earth, Vikramāditya wins the heaven (also) by his meritorious actions.' The metre is Upagīti.

§ 168. A number of varieties have been distinguished in this class based on the peculiarities on the reverse. In variety A, **(Pl. XV. 7-11)** Lakshmī stands facing on a conventional lotus, holding a noose in the right hand and a lotus with a long stalk in the left. In variety B, the goddess is standing on a low pedestal and is turned three-fourths to the left **(Pl. XV. 12-13).** Variety C resembles variety B, but the goddess is standing not on a pedestal but on a mat **(Pl. XV. 14—Pl. XVI. 3).** In variety D, **(Pl. XVI. 4-6),** the goddess is walking to left. Her standing posture in variety C is not much different from her walking posture in variety D. Legs are crossing each other in a similar fashion. There is, however, a circular mat under her feet in variety C, which suggests that she is standing and not walking. The absence of the mat in variety D lends support to the view that she is intended to be shown as walking there. It is, however, possible to argue that the mat is off the flan on these coins and that the variety D, therefore, does not exist. This view, however, does not seem to be a correct one; for the mat could not have been off the flan on all the coins. In variety E **(Pl. XVI. 7)** the posture of the hands and feet of the goddess clearly suggest that she is running to left . Why the goddess should have been thus shown as double-marching, it is difficult to understand. *B. M. C. G. D.* publishes one coin of this type, Pl. VIII. 9.

§ 169. Thomas had thought that the Chhatra type coins of Chandragupta should be ascribed to Chandragupta I.[1] He had

[1] *J.R.A.S.*, 1869 p. 92.

mainly relied upon the close resemblance of the reverse motifs of standing goddess on these coins with that on the Aśvamedha and Tiger-slayer types of Samudragupta. But this is not a conclusive argument; for this motif occurs as late as the reign of Kumāragupta I, as it is seen on the latter's Swordsman type. The reverse legend Vikramāditya was exclusively associated with Chandragupta II, and is not known to have been used by Chandragupta I. We cannot, therefore, ascribe these coins to that ruler. It is no doubt true that the reverse motif of the Chhatra type, Goddess standing facing left, closely resembles the reverse motif of the Aśvamedha and the Tiger-slayer types of Samudragupta, but that is no sufficient reason for ascribing these coins to his father.

(iv) Lion-slayer Type
(Pl. XVI. 8—Pl. XVIII. 10)

§ 170. The Lion-slayer type of Chandragupta II was obviously suggested by the Tiger-slayer type of his father. The coins of the latter type are rare, while those of the Lion-slayer type of Chandragupta II are much more common. The Bayana hoard contains 42 coins of this type; the British Museum possesses 13, the Indian Museum 10 and the Lucknow Museum 12. As on the Tiger-slayer type, we find the king standing and shooting arrow at the lion in his front. There is, however, no crescent-topped standard between the lion and the king. The reverse shows wide difference; instead of the goddess standing on a crocodile, as on the prototype of Samudragupta, we find her seated on the lion, which is sometimes facing left and sometimes facing right. The reverse motif is copied from the coinage of Chandragupta I, but it seems to have been suggested by the presence of the lion on the obverse. In the next reign also we find the Lion-slayer motif on the obverse associated with the *siṁhavāhinī* goddess on the reverse.

Many of the coins of this type are artistically of a very high merit. The tall and the muscular body of the king, his energetic and determined attitude when engaged in the deadly fight, and the agony of the lion as it is being pierced by the arrow are all portrayed with remarkable skill; see **Pl. XVII. 1-9.** The king usually wears a *janghia*, a turban and a waist band, but in some varieties the last mentioned object is omitted.

§ 171. Normally a bowman holds the bow in the left hand, and strings it by the right. On all the specimens of this class, where the king is facing right, we find the bow being wielded in this natural manner **(Pl. XVII. 1-9)**. But the specimens where the king is facing left show the king holding the bow in the right hand and stringing it by the left **(Pl. XVII. 11-14)**, which is undoubtedly an unnatural procedure. This may be due to the engraver having overlooked this point; but it is equally probable that he may have deliberately intended to show the king as an ambidextrous archer.

§ 172. We have divided the coins of this type in three classes; class I consisting of Lion-combatant type, where the king and the lion are pitted against each other, class II where the king is shown as actually trampling upon the lion and class III, where the lion is shown as retreating. This classification was first suggested by Smith, but Mr. Allan did not accept it, because the legend on both was identical and the attitude of the king on them hardly showed any difference (*B. M. C. G. D.*, p. lxxxii). It is, however, obvious that the mint-masters must have decided to show the king as trampling upon the lion on some specimens to emphasise his reckless courage; it would therefore be but natural that we should recognise Lion-trampler as a distinct class. For the same reason, those rare coins where the lion is shown as retreating from the king should be regarded as constituting a different class.

§ 173. Mr. Allan has classified the coins of the Lion-slayer type by their legends, class I consisting of those which have the legend *Narendrachandraḥ prathita..divaṁ jayatyajeyo bhuvi siṅhavikramaḥ*, class II, where the legend has been conjecturally restored as *Narendrasiṅha-Chandraguptaḥ pṛithivīṁ jitvā divaṁ jayati*, and class III, where the legend is *Mahārājādhirāja-śrī-Chandraguptaḥ*, sometimes preceded by *Deva*. His class IV, however, has the same legend as class I and has been distinguished from it simply because the king is attacking the lion by the sword. Class II of Mr. Allan consists of a single coin, where the legend is quite uncertain. It would therefore be more convenient to accept the classification first suggested by Smith, and divide the coins into three types, Lion-combatant, Lion-trampler and Lion-retreating. It is obvious that the mint-masters must have deliberately decided to show the king as trampling upon the lion on some coins in order to emphasise his reckless courage. Where they have shown the lion as retreating, the idea must be to emphasise how even the king of the beasts was compelled to beat retreat before the king of men. We have therefore divided the Lion-slayer type into three classes, Lion-combatant, Lion-trampler and Lion-retreating.

§ 174. The varieties in the attitude of the king on the obverse, and of the posture of both the goddess and the lion on the reverse and of the objects in the hands of the former are so numerous that it is impossible to suggest a scheme of classification of varieties within these three classes which may not lead to some overlapping. For the sake of convenience, we have first divided the coins according as the lion on the obverse faces left or right and then noticed further varieties according to the posture of the goddess and the objects in her hands.

Class I : Lion-combatant Type
(Pl. XVI. 8—Pl. XVII. 10)

§ 175. The var. A of this class **(Pl. XVI, 8-13)** consists of the coins where the king faces left, and the goddess on the reverse is shown as seated facing on lion couchant to left; the goddess holds a noose in the right hand and a lotus in the left. **Pl. XVI. 12-13** are included in this class because the king's right foot, though in touch with the lion's body, is clearly shown as away from it, and not as trampling upon it. The legend on all the coins of this variety is *Narendrachandraḥ prathitaraṇo raṇe iayatyajeyo bhuvi siṁhavikramaḥ*, 'The moon among the kings, who is famous for his warfare, who is valorous like a lion and who is invincible, is victorious on the battle-field'. The metre is Vaṁśasthavila. The letters *raṇo raṇe*, which were for a long time impossible to read, are quite clear on **Pl. XVI. 12-13.** In varieties B, C, and D, the king faces right, the legend being the same. In the variety B, the king faces right **(Pl. XVI. 14.—XVII. 1-5)**, the goddess holds a noose in the right hand and a lotus in the left. The variety C **(Pl. XVII. 6-9)** differs from the variety B in showing the right hand of the goddess empty. The single coin of the variety D **(Pl. XVII. 10)** differs from the variety C in showing the king on the obverse as not stringing the bow at all, but merely holding it in his left hand. This variety was unknown before the discovery of the Bayana hoard. The mount of the goddess on all these varieties is seated couchant to left, but in varieties C and D, it is seen slightly raising its head. The coins of the varieties B, C, D are undoubtedly among the most beautiful specimens of the Gupta numismatic art. The bare muscular body of the king is shown in the most graceful manner. Our variety A corresponds with variety ζ of the *B. M. C. G. D.*; our varieties B and C are both included in variety η of the latter.

Class II : Lion-trampler Type
(Pl. XVII. 11—XVIII. 9)

§ 176. Class II consists of the Lion-trampler coins; they show a greater variety on the reverse than the coins of class I. In varieties A to D, the king is seen facing left. In variety A **(Pl. XVII, 11)** the goddess on the reverse is seated to left astride the lion; in variety B **(Pl. XVII, 12)** her mount is walking to right; in variety C, **(Pl. XVII. 13)** it is couchant to left. In variety D **(Pl. XVII. 14)** the lion is walking to right as in variety B, but it is distinguished from it because it has a different legend, viz., *Deva-śrī-mahārājādhirāja-śrī-Chandraguptaḥ*. In varieties B, C, and D, the goddess holds a noose in the right hand and a lotus in the left. The variety A differs from them in having the left hand hanging down empty by her side. The weight of the coin of the variety B is 138.5 grains, which is rather unusual. In varieties E, F, G and H, the king on the obverse is facing right. In variety E **(Pl. XVIII. 1-2)**, the goddess is shown seated on a lion couchant to left, both her legs hanging down, and she having a noose in the right hand and a cornucopiae in the left. The cornucopiae may suggest that this variety may have been intended for the northern part of the empire. In variety F **(Pl. XVIII, 3-4)**, the feet of the goddess are folded on the back of the lion and her right hand is opened out and empty, the left hand holding the lotus as in variety B. In variety G **(Pl. XVIII, 5-6)**, the goddess is seated astride the lion facing left, her right hand holding a lotus and the left hand hanging empty by her side. In variety H **(Pl. XVIII, 7-9)**, the mount of the goddess is walking to left and she holds a noose in the right hand and a lotus in the left. It is possible to further subdivide this variety; in **Pl. XVIII, 7,** we find the goddess folding her legs on the back of her mount, but facing left. In **Pl. XVIII, 8,** she sits facing, but the lion is walking to left. In **Pl. XVIII, 9,** she faces left, while her left leg is dangling over the head of the lion walking to left. The legend on the coins of class II is the same as that on the coins of class I, except in variety D, where we have the prose legend, *Devaśrī-mahārājādhirāja-śrī-Chandraguptaḥ.* The legend on the reverse is *Siṁhavikramaḥ.*

CLASS III : LION-RETREATING TYPE (Pl. XVIII. 10)

§ 177. Class III of the Lion-retreating type is represented by a single specimen in our hoard **(Pl. XVIII, 10).** The king on the obverse is facing to right and the lion is shown as beating a hasty retreat before him. The legend is the usual metrical one. The goddess on the reverse is shown as seated facing on lion couchant to left, having a noose in the right hand and a lotus in the left, which has not come out on the flan. There is no coin of this variety in the British Museum. The Provincial Museum, Lucknow, has got one coin similar to it, but there the king is attacking the lion by the sword and not shooting it by the arrow.

§ 178. The following is a tabular statement showing which varieties of our hoard correspond with which varieties of the *B. M. C. G. D.*

Bayana Hoard	B. M. C. G. D.
	Class I.
Var. A, **Pl. XVI. 8-13**	Var. ζ, Pl. IX. 4
Var. B, **Pl. XVI. 14-XVII. 5**	Not in the *B. M. C. G. D.*
Var. C, **Pl. XVII. 6-9**	Var. η, Pl. IX. 7-8
Var. D, **Pl. XVII. 10**	Not in the B. M. C. G. D.
	Class II.
Var. A, **Pl. XVII. 11**	Var. ε, **Pl. IX. 1,** with this difference that the king is facing right and not left.
Var. B, **Pl. XVII. 12**	Var. δ, **Pl. VIII 16-17,** with this difference that the king is facing left and not right.

Var. c, **Pl. XVII. 13**	Var. ζ, Pl. IX. 5
Var. d, **Pl. XVII. 14**	Not in the *B. M. C. G. D.* The rev. is similar to *B. M. C. G. D.* Pl. IX. 5
Var. e, **Pl. XVIII. 1-2**	Var. α, Pl. VIII. 11-12 ; the feet of the goddess, however, do not hang down.
Var. f, **Pl. XVIII. 3-4**	Var. γ, Pl. VIII. 14.
Var. g, **Pl. XVIII. 5-6**	Var. ϵ, Pl. IX. 1
Var. h, **Pl. XVIII. 7-9**	Not in the *B. M. C. G. D.*
	Class III.
Pl. XVIII. 10	Not in *B. M. C. G. D.*; its Pl. IX. 13 from Lucknow Museum partly resembles this coin, with this difference that the king is attacking with a sword.

Coins not represented in our hoard are the following:—

B. M. C. G. D., class II, where the legend seems to be *Narendra-siṁha-Chandraguptaḥ pṛithivīṁ vijitya divaṁ jayati*; Pl. IX. 10.

B. M. C. G. D., Class III, var. *α*, Pl. IX. 11 ; Lion-retreating type, king facing left and not stringing the bow, and goddess seated upon couchant lion.

B. M. C. G. D. Class III, var. *β*, where the obverse is as above, but the goddess on the reverse is seated upon a lion walking left ; Pl. IX. 12.

Lion-combatant type ; king facing left and the legend *Chandra* written in the field on right; goddess facing seated on lion couchant to left having a noose in r. hand and a lotus in the l. *J. A. S. B.*, 1923, N. *S.* Pl. III. 7.

(v) Couch Type

(Pl. XVIII. 11-13)

§ 179. The Couch type is one of the rarest types of Chandragupta II. There are only two specimens of this type in the British Museum and one each in the Indian Museum, the Lucknow Museum and the Prince of Wales Museum, Bombay. Our hoard contains three specimens only.

The Couch type was obviously suggested by the Lyrist type of Samudragupta. On the obverse of both, we find the king seated on a high-backed couch; but Chandragupta II was probably not a musician like his father, and therefore did not care to be shown as playing on a lute. The reverse of one of the varieties of this type shows the goddess seated to left, not on a wicker stool as on the Lyrist type of Samudragupta, but on a backless throne; the resemblance between the two is still striking.

§ 180. The variety A **(Pl. XVIII. 11)** of this type shows the king looking at a lotus bud hanging down from a long stalk held in the hand as a *līlākamala*. The legend is *Paramabhāgavata-mahārājādhirājaśrī-Chandraguptaḥ*. The reverse shows the goddess seated to left on a backless throne, which is covered by a lotus; her right hand is holding a lotus with a long stalk , while the left hand is hanging by her side. The legend *Vikramādityaḥ* is on the left and there is no symbol.[1] In both varieties B and C the king is holding a lotus flower in the right hand; the legend is *Devaśrīmahārājādhirājaśrī-Chandraguptasya*. Their reverses, however, differ. In variety B, the legend *Śrī-Vikramaḥ* is written on the left and the right hand of the goddess is empty **(Pl. XVIII. 12)**. In variety C, the legend is written on the right as usual, and the right hand of the goddess is holding a noose **(Pl. XVIII. 13)**.

§ 181. Our hoard does not contain any specimen of the unique variety of this type in the Indian Museum which has the mysterious legend *rūpākṛiti* on the obverse.

(vi) Chakravikrama Type
(Pl. XVIII. 14)

§ 182. The *Chakravikrama* type is the most unique type of the Bayana hoard. Only one coin of this type was found in it, and no specimen of it exists in any museum or private collection. The obverse shows god Vishṇu standing on an elevated platform to right, with a double halo not only round his head, but almost round his entire body. He holds a mace in his left hand and is offering by the right one three round objects to the nimbate personage standing before him, who is obviously none other

[1] The Provincial Museum, Lucknow, and the Prince of Wales Museum, Bombay, each possess one coin of this variety. The latter has been recently illustrated in *J. N. S. I.*, XI, Pl. I. 12.

than Chandragupta himself. The king is resting the left hand on the hilt of his sword and extending the right one to receive the divine gift. The three circular objects of the divine *prasāda* (favour) are obviously symbolical. They may refer to the three worlds being gifted to the devotee king, or may more probably refer to the *prabhuśakti*, *mantraśakti* and *utsāhaśakti*, which together contribute to the might of a ruler. The obverse has no legend; this is rather unusual. The reverse shows a goddess, most probably Lakshmī, standing three fourths to left; she holds a lotus in the left hand and is pointing to some object by her forefinger, which, however, is not on the flan. The object upon which the goddess is standing is indistinct. The reverse side has the legend *Chakravikrama*. This legend reminds us of similar legends like *Ajitavikrama* and *Siṅhavikrama*, which occur on some other coin-types of Chandragupta II. We may therefore be reasonably certain that this type also was issued by the same emperor.

§ 183. Chandragupta II was the first Gupta emperor to assume the Vaishṇava title of *Paramabhāgavata*. It is, therefore, but natural that his mint-masters should have conceived the idea of representing the emperor as the recipient of a *prasāda* (favour) direct from Vishṇu himself. The divine personage in front of Chandragupta has a *gadā* or mace in his hand, and it is therefore natural to identify him with Vishṇu himself. It has been recently[1] suggested that this personage is not Vishṇu, but a personification of his weapon *chakra*, known in Indian sculpture as a Chakrapurusha. *Chakra* is no doubt often denoted in the human form as a Chakrapurusha in several Gupta sculptures. But we do not find Chakrapurusha represented all by himself; he is generally associated with and by the side of Vishṇu, nor is he seen holding a *gadā* in his hand. If a miracle was intended to be represented on the coinage, the mint-masters would obviously have preferred to show the emperor as receiving the *prasāda* not from a Chakrapurusha but from *Chakradhārin*, the wielder of the *chakra*, i.e. Vishṇu himself.

§ 184. It is not easy to translate the reverse legend *Chakravikrama*. We do not know to which of the personage on the obverse it is referring. If it refers to Vishṇu, it would mean, 'One who is valorous on account of *chakra* or divine disc.' If

[1] *J. N. S. I.*, XIII, p. 181.

it refers to the king, it may mean, 'one who possesses the valour of the invincible *chakra* (of Vishṇu).

§ 185. All the known types of the gold coinage of Chandragupta II are represented in the Bayana hoard with the exception of two rare types. The first of these is the one which shows on the reverse the king and the queen seated on a couch, the former offering a cup to the latter. The obverse of this type is closely similar to that of the obverse of the Standard type of Samudragupta, the king dressed in Kushāṇa coat and trousers offering oblations on altar by right hand and holding a standard in the left.[1] The second is the Standard type, which is known from a unique specimen in the Bharat Kalabhavan of Banaras Hindu University. The obverse of this type is exactly similar to the obverse of the Standard type of Samudragupta, the king offering oblations by the right hand on an altar before him and holding a standard in the left hand, Garuḍa standard being in his front. The reverse shows the goddess seated on a backless throne, having a noose in the right hand and a cornucopiae in the left.[2]

5. Kumārgupta I
(Pl. XIX. 1—Pl. XXXI. 14)

§ 186. Numismatic activity continued unabated in the reign of Kumāragupta I. His coins in the hoard are, however, only 628 in number, as compared to 983 of his father. They, however, show very much greater variety; for we have got 14 types of this ruler represented in the hoard, as against 6 of his father. We find the mint-masters continuing the Archer, the Horseman and the Lion-slayer types, all of which had been very popular in the preceding reign. Why the Chhatra type, fairly common in the preceding reign, should be represented only by two specimens in this huge hoard is a mystery; so far it was not known at all.

§ 187. Kumāragupta revived a number of types of the earlier reigns. Prominent among these known so far were the Tiger-slayer and the Aśvamedha types of Samudragupta; our hoard, however, now shows that he had also reintroduced the Lyrist type of that mighty emperor. The King-and-Queen type of Chandragupta I

[1] *Pr. A. S. B.*, 1888, pp. 129-30, Pl. VI.

[2] *J. N. S. I.*, 1947, p. 146, Pl. VII, 3.

was also revived with suitable modifications; it is represented by a single specimen. This type was so far altogether unknown.

§ 188. The so-called '*Pratāpa*', (here described as '*Apraṭigha*'), the Swordsman, the Kārtikeya, the Elephant-rider and the Elephant-rider-Lion-slayer types are the innovations of Kumāragupta, but they were already known to us before the discovery of this hoard. The Rhinoceros-slayer type, represented by four specimens in our hoard, is quite a new and beautiful type, so far quite unknown. Subsequent to the discovery of this hoard, a fifth coin of this type came to light, and it has been published in *J. N. S. I.*, Vol. XI., p. 9.

We now proceed to describe and comment upon the above types.

(*i*) Archer Type
(Pl. XIX. 1—Pl. XXI. 5)

§ 189. The Archer type, which was the most popular type of his father, is seen continued by Kumāragupta. It seems to have been issued fairly copiously, for nearly 27% coins of this emperor—183 in all—represented in the hoard belong to this type. The British, the Indian and the Lucknow Museums possess 11, 6, and 4 coins respectively of this type. We do not, however, see that striking variety on the obverse of this type, which can be seen on the coins of the Archer type of Chandragupta II. We had classified the coins of this type of Chandragupta mainly by the position of the vertical legend *Chandra* on the obverse. We shall follow the same principle here. Mr. Allan has classified the coins in the *B. M. C. G. D.* by their legends on the obverse; we shall follow this principle in determining the varieties in each class.

Class I
(Pl. XIX. 1—Pl. XX. 4)

§ 190. Class I of the Archer type consists of coins where the king's name Kumāra is written vertically on the obverse. There are 82 coins of this class in the Bayana hoard. It is noteworthy that Kumāra is written sometimes under the arm and sometimes outside the bow, but never between the bow and the bow-string. The weight standard of 121 grains is generally followed in this class.

§ 191. In variety A of class I the bow is held at the top with string inside, Kumāra is written under the left arm and the circular legend is *Mahārājādhirāja-śrī-Kumāraguptaḥ* **(Pl. XIX. 1-5)**. In variety B, we have the same circular legend, but the bow is held by the middle with string outside, *Kumāra* being written vertically outside the bow-string **(Pl. XIX. 6—Pl. XX. 1)**. Varieties A and B correspond with varieties ε and η of the *B. M. C. G. D.* Variety C is similar to variety B, but its legend is different **(Pl. XX. 2-4)**. It seems to have contained the words *Guṇeśo mahītalaṁ*. The specimens in our hoard are in a poor condition and do not enable us to complete the legend. The reverse legend in all the varieties is *Śrī-Mahendraḥ*.

Classes II—III

(Pl. XX. 5-13; Pl. XX. 14—Pl. XXI. 5)

§ 192. Class II consists of coins where only the initial of the king's name, *Ku*, is engraved on the obverse. There is a crescent above *Ku*; this letter is always written under the king's left arm, and never between the bow and the bow-string or outside the bow-string. There are 73 coins of this class in the Bayana hoard. We have divided the coins of this class in three varieties according to the obverse legends. In variety A **(Pl. XX. 5-7)**, the legend is *Vijitāvaniravanipatiḥ Kumāragupto divaṁ jayati*, 'King Kumāragupta who has conquered the earth, wins heaven.' Metre is Upagīti. This variety corresponds with the variety α of the *B. M. C. G. D.* It is interesting to note that the metrical legend introduced by Kumāragupta on this variety was destined to be used by a number of his successors of Gupta and later dynasties down to the time of Harshavardhana in the 7th century. The variety B, **Pl. XX. 8-12**, differs from the variety A only in the circular legend, which reads as *jayati mahītalamekaḥ Śrī-Kumāraguptaḥ sudhanvī*, 'The excellent archer Kumāragupta conquers the earth.' This variety probably corresponds with the variety γ of the *B. M. C. G. D.* In variety C, the legend seems to be the same, but it apparently stops with *Śrī-Kumāraguptaḥ* **(Pl. XX. 13)**. This variety is not represented in the *B.M.C.G.D.* Class III **(Pl. XX. 14—Pl. XXI. 5)** consists of the coins which have neither *Kumāra* nor *Ku* in the field on the obverse. Their legend is *Paramarājādhirājaśrī-Kumāraguptaḥ*. They correspond with variety δ of the *B.M.C.G.D.*

Coins of classes II and III are all minted in the heavier standard of 128 grains. There are none among them, which weigh 120 grains or so. In class I coins of the 128 grains standard are exceptional.

§ 193. The reverse of the Archer type shows Lakshmī seated on the lotus. Usually she holds a lotus in the left hand and a noose in the right. In some cases, however, her right hand is scattering wealth in the form of round coins **(Pl. XX. 9-13)**; in some cases she is holding a rosary **(Pl. XIX. 12)**. She is usually seated with folded legs on the lotus **(Pl. XIX. 2-3)**, but in some cases the legs are considerably raised up, and elbows of the two arms are resting on them **(Pl. XIX. 8-11)**. On a few coins one of her legs is folded up and the other is hanging down **(Pl. XIX. 14-15)**. The legend is *Śrī-Mahendraḥ*.

(*ii*) Swordsman Type
(Pl. XXI. 6-15)

§ 194. The Swordsman type is one of the rare types of Kumāragupta. It was so far known by two specimens in the British Museum and one specimen each in the Indian Museum and Lucknow Museum. The Bayana hoard contains 10 specimens of this type.

The present type recalls the Standard type of Samudragupta; the king stands facing left offering oblations by his right hand on an altar, there being the Garuḍa standard before him. The type is, however, Indianised. The king does not wear the Kushāṇa trousers and overcoat; he wears a *dhoti* and a crested head-dress, but is otherwise bare-bodied. In his left hand he is holding not a standard as on Samudragupta's coins, but a sword hanging by his side. His initial *Ku* is written not under his left arm but outside the sword. The reverse also shows no trace of foreign influence; the goddess is seated on a lotus and is holding a noose in the right hand and a lotus in the left, as on the Archer coins, class II, of this ruler. The legend on the obverse '*Gāmavajitya sucharitaiḥ Kumāragupto divaṁ jayati*', is adapted from the Chhatra type of Chandragupta II, only the word *kshitim* of the original is substituted by its synonym *gām*. The metre is Upagīti and the translation is, 'Having conquered the earth, Kumāragupta wins heaven by meritorious deeds.' It is interesting to note that on the Chhatra type of Chandragupta II also, the king is offering oblations on an altar as on the present type.

§ 195. The reverse legend of this type is simply *Śrī-Kumāraguptaḥ*; it has no regal title whatsoever. This will show how we cannot draw any conclusion from the king's titles on the reverse of Gupta gold coins; they were traditionally very brief and were not at all intended to give an accurate idea of the status of the emperor among the contemporary kings. In the present case it is pertinent to note that the mint authorities did not care to insert any imperial title in the reverse legend, even when the obverse metrical legend contained no word denoting the royal or imperial position of Kumāragupta.

(*iii*) HORSEMAN TYPE

(Pl. XXII. 1—XXV. 15)

§ 196. The usual impression that the Horseman type was the most popular type of Kumāragupta I is confirmed by the Bayana hoard; for out of 628 coins of this ruler represented in the hoard, as many as 305 belong to this type. The British Museum has 15 coins of this type, the Indian Museum 13 and the Provincial Museum, Lucknow, 8.

We had classified the coins of the Horseman type of Chandragupta II mainly with reference to the weapons borne by the king. They play only a minor part on the coins of Kumāragupta I. We have therefore classified his Horseman type coins with reference to their reverse. Class I consists of those coins, where the goddess is all alone, and class II of the coins where she is feeding a peacock. Beautiful metrical legends on the obverse are the most characteristic feature of the Horseman type; we have therefore distinguished the varieties in each class with reference to them. The reverse legend on this type is *Ajita-Mahendraḥ* throughout.

CLASS I

(Pl. XXII. 1-15)

§ 197. In variety A of class I (**Pl. XXII. 1-6**), the legend is *Pṛithvītalāmbaraśaśī Kumāragupto jayatyajitaḥ*, 'Kumāragupta, who is a veritable moon in the firmament in the form of earth's surface, and who is invincible, conquers (the enemies).' The metre is Upagīti. This variety corresponds to variety *a* of class I of the *B. M. C. G. D.*; Mr. Allan, however, was unable to read the legend completely. The specimens in our hoard, however, enable us to decipher the complete legend. The accoutrement of the horse in this variety is very artistic; particularly noteworthy is the circular ornament under the rein and the starry ornament on the haunch of the horse. The king bears no weapons, and his sash is flowing behind him. The reverse of this type is markedly similar to that of the reverse of the Horseman type of Chandragupta II; we have the goddess seated on a wicker stool, but she carries not a noose, but a lotus with long stalk in her right hand and her left hand, resting on waist, is empty. Mr. Allan's observation that this hand is possibly holding a lotus with long stalk is not supported either by the coins he has published,[1] or by those in the present hoard **(Pl. XXII. 1-6)**. Variety B **(Pl. XXII. 7)**, which is represented by a single coin in this hoard, discloses a new legend *Jayati nṛiporibhirajitaḥ*, 'Victorious is the king, never conquered by the enemies.' The king is riding to left and is holding a bow in his right hand. The goddess on the reverse is seated to left, as in variety A, but she holds a noose in her right hand, and a lotus in the left, as on the Horseman type coins of Chandragupta II. There is no symbol. Variety C **(Pl. XXII. 8-15)** has the legend *Kshitipatirajito vijayī Kumāragupto divaṁ jayati*, 'The unconquered and victorious king Kumāragupta wins the heaven.' The metre is Upagīti. This variety corresponds with class I, variety β, of *B. M. C. G. D.* The king carries no weapons in this variety, nor is the sash flowing behind him except in one case **(Pl. XXII. 9)**. The reverse is exactly like that of variety B, except in one case, where the goddess holds a flower in the right hand instead of the noose **(Pl. XXII. 9)**.

§ 198. The assignment of the coin on **Pl. XXII. 9** to this variety is only tentative. The goddess on the reverse is carrying no noose in her hand, as she does on the other coins of this type. The posture of her right hand is exactly similar to that of the goddess in variety C of class II, where she is feeding a peacock in her front. If we minutely examine the coin, we can perhaps detect the faint outlines of a peacock in front of the goddess. There is also a symbol on this coin, as occurs on those of class II, variety C. The king on this coin has a sash flying behind

[1] *B. M. C. G. D.*, p. xc.

him, as on the coins of class II, variety C; but there he is facing left and not right, as on the present coin. The legend on our coin is too fragmentary and indistinct to permit us to decide as to whether it ended with *divaṁ jayati* as in the present variety, or with *iayatyajitaḥ*, as in variety C of class II.

Class II
(Pl. XXIII—Pl. XXV)

§ 199. Coins of class II, where the goddess on the reverse is seen feeding a peacock, are divided into five varieties. In var. A **(Pl. XXIII. 1-15)**, the legend is *Guptakulavyomaśaśī jayatyajeyojitamahendraḥ*, 'The invincible Mahendra who is unbeaten, a veritable moon in the firmament of the sky in the form of the Gupta family, is successful.' The metre is Upagīti. The king rides to right and the bow is in his left hand. The bunch of grapes, which the goddess in this variety is offering to the peacock, is distinct and graceful. This variety corresponds with class II, variety α, of the *B. M. C. G. D.* In variety B **(Pl. XXIV. 2-15)**, the legend is *Guptakulāmalachandro Mahendrakarmājito jayati*, 'The spotless moon in the firmament of the Gupta family, the invincible (hero) who is as valorous as Mahendra, conquers (the enemy).' The metre is Upagīti. On the coins of this variety king faces left and carries a bow in his right hand; a sword also hangs by his side. The sword is, however, rather long and is more or less parallel to the leg. On the reverse of this type, in the bunch of grapes offered to the peacock, twigs are more prominent than the grapes attached to them. The idea is probably to suggest that the feeding is coming to an end, the peacock having eaten most of the fruits in the bunch. There is a symbol in the upper left corner, which is rather unusual in this type. We find it only in one other variety, namely variety E below. This variety corresponds with variety β of class II of the *B. M. C. G. D.* Variety C **(Pl. XXV. 1-9)** closely resembles the variety C of class I. In both cases the king faces right and is without any weapons. The goddess is, however, sitting all alone in class I, variety C; but she is feeding the peacock in class II, variety C. She is holding the twig of the fruits usually between the thumb and the forefinger. The legend on this variety was so far considered to be identical with the legend on variety γ of class I of the *B. M. C. G. D.*;[1] but on two coins of this hoard **(Pl. XXV. 2, 9)** the concluding letters can be distinctly read as *jayatyaja*. We must therefore read the legend as *Kshitipatirajito vijayī Kumāragupto jayatyajitaḥ* and not as *Kumāragupto divaṁ jayati* as in class I, variety C. This variety corresponds with class II, variety γ, of the *B. M. C. G. D.* The variety D, which is represented by a single coin **(Pl. XXV. 10)**, introduces a slight variation in the above legend, *Kshitipatirajito vijayī Kumāragupto divaṁ jayati*. This variety is apparently not represented in the *B. M. C. G. D.* In variety E **(Pl. XXV. 11-15)**, our hoard discloses another new legend, *Pṛithivītaleśvarendraḥ Kumāragupto jayatyajitaḥ*, 'Kumāragupta, a veritable Indra on the surface of the earth, himself invincible, conquers (the enemy).' The metre is Upagīti. This legend begins on the left at VIII. The king is riding to right in this variety, and is armed with a bow held in the left hand with string inwards. On the reverse the fruits in the hand of the goddess can be distinctly seen, and there is a symbol in her front as in variety B above. This variety was unknown before the discovery of the Bayana hoard; it, however, appears probable that the solitary coin of class I variety δ of the *B. M.C. G. D.*,[2] which is only described but not illustrated, belongs to this variety. Mr. Allan does not state where the legend begins on this coin; if it commences at VIII and if the reverse has a symbol, our conjecture above would be quite correct.

§ 200. The Horseman type coins of Kumāragupta throw a lot of light on the contemporary accoutrement of the horses in the Gupta period; what they enable us to visualise is confirmed by literary evidence. The horse of Chandrāpīḍa, as described by the *Kādambarī*,[3] had a number of jingling jewel necklaces interspersed with pearls; pearl necklaces can be distinctly seen on **Pl. XXV. 12-15**. The *Harshacharit* refers to the stud in the necklace woven in several threads.[4] This stud can be distinctly seen woven in a multi-thread necklace on **Pl. XXV. 1-10**. The *Harshacharit* further states that the accoutrement of royal horses was

---

[1] *B. M. C. G. D.*, p. 71.

[2] *B. M. C. G. D.*, p. 155.

[3] पदे पदे रणितरत्नमालेन स्थूलमुक्ताफलप्रायेण अरुणेनाश्वालंकारेण उपशोभितमिन्द्रायुधमद्राक्षीत् । *Kādambarī*, p. 130.

[4] बहुगुणसूत्रग्रथितग्रीवागंडकैस्तुरंगै . . . । *Harshacharit*, p. 63 (Cowel's edition).

golden and used to make a jingling sound, as they moved or gallopped.[1] It is quite possible that the graceful, circular and starry ornaments that we see on the neck and haunch of the horse in some varieties **(Pl. XXII. 1-5)**, may have been golden in the case of royal horses and silvery in the case of the feudatories and generals. The horse is usually seen having a crest in most cases; cf. **Pl. XXII. 8-15**

(*iv*) Kārtikeya Type
(Pl. XXVI. 1-13)

§ 201. Kumāragupta was named after Skanda *alias* Kumāra, whose mount was peacock. His Kārtikeya type,[2] which is an innovation of the reign, was obviously intended to be a numismatic homage to the deity after whom he was named. One would naturally have expected that the coins of this type should have been issued in large numbers; but somehow such is not the case. It is no doubt stated by Smith that the Allahabad hoard consisted of 200 coins, mostly of the Peacock type[3], but his information was based on hearsay report. The Bayana hoard contains only 13 coins of this type, as against 183 of the Archer type and 305 of the Horseman type. The British Museum has 9 coins of this type, the Indian Museum 5 and the Lucknow Museum 2. It would appear that the idea of issuing the Kārtikeya type was conceived late in the reign.

§ 202. The reverse of the Kārtikeya type shows the deity riding his mount, peacock, armed with his characteristic weapon *śakti* or spear[4] in the left hand, and apparently scattering something by his right hand upon an object which looks like an altar. The obverse shows the king standing to left and offering a twig of

---

[1] शिन्जानशातकौम्भजयनशोभिनि वाजिनि. . . । *Ibid*, p. 23.

[2] Gupta coin-types are usually described from their obverse, and previous writers have therefore described this type as Peacock type, because the obverse shows the king as feeding a peacock. The reverse of this type, which shows god Kārtikeya himself, is, however, more important than the obverse, whose motif occurs on the reverse also of some other types. We have therefore described this type as the Kārtikeya and not as the Peacock type.

[3] *J. A. S. B.*, 1884, p. 152.

[4] The breasts of the deity are rather prominent like those of a female, but the hair is dressed like that of a male. This circumstance along with the fact that the deity holds a *śakti* in the left hand would show that it is intended to be a male and Kārtikeya and not a female, as Smith was inclined to think. *I. M. C.*, I, p. 113.

grapes to a peacock in his front. The obverse legend begins with *Jayati svaguṇairguṇa*(*ā*) and ends with *Mahendrakumāraḥ*. The intervening letters, which are indistinct, are probably *-ravindaḥ*.[1] The legend meant, 'A lotus of good qualities (as it were), Mahendra-Kumāra is victorious by his own merits.' The reverse legend is *Śrī-Mahendrakumāraḥ*.

§ 203. The type shows two varieties. In variety A, Kārtikeya on the reverse is facing three-fourths to left and the king on the obverse is offering fruits to the peacock which is actually reaching them **(Pl. XXVI. 1-10)**. In variety B, the deity on the reverse is seated facing on the peacock, and the king on the obverse wears a coat and is apparently pointing at something by his forefinger to the peacock, whose head is under the king's elbow **(Pl. XXVI. 11-13)**. In variety A, the king is standing erect, in variety B, he is slightly stooping forward.

(*v*) Chhatra Type
(Pl. XXVI. 14-15)

§ 204. The Chhatra type, which was so popular in the previous reign, was but very sparsely issued by Kumāragupta. No coins of this type were known before the discovery of the Bayana hoard, and it also contains only two specimens of it. The obverse is similar to that of the Chhatra type of the preceding reign. The king is standing to left, with his left hand on the sword, and offering oblations on an altar, which is off the flan. The dwarf is standing behind him, holding a parasol over his head. The legend is incomplete; it begins with *Jayati mahītalaṁ*, but its concluding part is off the flan. The reverse is also similar to the prototype; it shows the goddess standing to left and holding a noose in the right hand and a lotus in the left. The legend is *Śrī-Mahendr-ādityaḥ* **(Pl. XXVI. 14-15)**.

(*vi*) Tiger-slayer Type
(Pl. XXVII. 1-15)

§ 205. The Bayana hoard contains 36 coins of the Tiger-slayer type. There are fifteen coins of this type in the British

[1] In *Num. Chr.*, 1935, p. 235, Mr. Allan has abandoned his earlier reading *Jayati svabhūmau* in favour of *Jayati svaguṇai*. Mr. C. Sivaramamurti has suggested *guṇaratnābdhiḥ* instead of *guṇāravindaḥ*. The word is very indistinct.

Museum, nine in the Indian Museum and one in the Lucknow Museum.

In his Tiger-slayer type, Kumāragupta is obviously trying to revive one of the rarest types of his grand-father, which somehow had not found favour with his father. As on the Tiger-slayer type of Samudragupta, the king is facing left and holding the bow in the right hand and stringing it by the left. The crescent-topped banner between the king and the tiger is also taken from the prototype. Samudragupta's obverse legend, *Vyāghraparākramaḥ*, is however slightly improved and enlarged into *Śrīmāṁ vyāghrabalaparākramaḥ*, 'His Majesty having the strength and valour of a tiger.' The same is the case with the reverse legend; the simple title *rājā* used on Samudragupta's coins is replaced by *adhirājaḥ*; we have *Kumārguptodhirājaḥ* in the place of *Rājā Samudraguptaḥ*. This change seems to be deliberately introduced to emphasise the imperial status of the issuer; for *adhirājaḥ* means a king over kings. As on Samudragupta's type, the goddess on the reverse is standing on a crocodile,[1] three-fourths to left, and holding a lotus in her left hand. On the coins of Kumāragupta, however, she is represented as feeding a peacock by her right hand. The reverse motif therefore shows only a partial resemblance to the reverse of the Tiger-slayer type of Samudragupta. It also reminds us of the reverse of class II of the Horseman type of this emperor where the goddess is feeding a peacock.

§ 206. We have divided the coins of this type in two varieties, variety A **(Pl. XXVII. 1-12)** consisting of coins having the letter *Ku* in the field on the obverse, and variety B, which has not this letter. Our hoard contains 32 coins of variety A and only 4 of variety B **(Pl. XXVII. 13-15)**.

(*vii*) Lion-slayer Type
(Pl. XXVIII. 1—Pl. XXIX 15)

§ 207. The Bayana hoard contains fifty-three coins of the Lion-slayer type as against twelve in the British Museum, two in the Indian Museum and one in the Lucknow Museum. These

[1] In his Introduction, Mr. Allan states that the goddess is standing on a lotus flower (p. xcii); in the Catalogue, however, we find him rather hesitating on the point (p. 81); but the crocodile is quite clear on several specimens of our hoard; cf. I. **Pl. XXVII 3, 5.**

coins may be divided into two classes, the Lion-combatant class and the Lion-trampler class; in each class we can distinguish varieties by the differences in legends. The reverse motif on the coins of all the varieties is goddess seated on lion, usually couchant to right. She is nowhere seen sitting astride the lion, nor is the latter anywhere shown as walking, as on some coins of this type of Chandragupta II. The reverse legend is either *Srī-Mahendrasiṁhaḥ* or *Siṁha-Mahendraḥ*.

CLASS I

LION-COMBATANT TYPE

(Pl. XXVIII. 1-13)

§ 208. On the coins of this class, the king is standing at close quarters to the lion and shooting an arrow at it by the bow. Sometimes his foot is in contact with the beast, but he is not shown as trampling upon it as in class II.

§ 209. The variety A of this class, **(Pl. XXVIII. 1-7)**, which corresponds with the variety δ of the *B. M. C. G.D.*, has the obverse legend beginning at VIII; it runs *Kumāragupto yudhi siṁhavikramaḥ*, 'In war, Kumāragupta is as valorous as a lion.' The metre is Vaṁśasthavila. The reverse shows the goddess seated on a couchant lion, facing; she holds a lotus in the left hand and is scattering wealth (round coins) by the right. The reverse legend is *Siṁha-Mahendraḥ*, and we have the symbol in its usual place.

In variety B **(Pl. XXVIII. 11-12)** the obverse legend also begins with *Kumāra*, but it is incomplete and probably different from that in the variety A. The symbol on the reverse is the same as that in var. A, but the right hand of the goddess is opened out and empty. The legend is *Siṁha-Mahendraḥ*.

On the coins of var. C **(Pl. XXVIII. 8-10)** the obverse legend is not yet completely deciphered; it begins with *Kshitipati* and probably was followed by *rajitamahendraḥ Kumāragupto divaṁ jayati*, 'King Kumāragupta, who is invincible Mahendra, wins the heaven.' On the reverse of this class, goddess is to be seen gracefully reclining on her left arm resting on the thigh. She is holding a lotus in her right hand; her left hand, which is akimbo, is empty. The legend is *Srī-Mahendrasiṁhaḥ*. This variety corresponds with variety β of the *B. M. C. G. D.*

Variety D **(Pl. XXVIII. 13)** is a new discovery of the Bayana hoard. It is the only coin of the Lion-slayer type of Kumāragupta, where the king is facing left. It is a coin of the Lion-combatant class, because the king is not trampling upon the beast. The king has frizzled hair and wears a short-sleeved coat with buttons artistically arranged in a line at the centre. He is holding the bow by the right hand and stringing it by the left, as we find it on the coins of this type of Chandragupta II, where the king is facing left. The obverse legend on this type is too indistinct to decipher. On the reverse the lion is couchant to left, and the symbol is in the centre and not at the top. The goddess is holding an indistinct object in her right hand and a lotus with a long stalk in the left. The legend is intended to be *Śrī-Mahendrasiṁhaḥ*.

CLASS II

LION-TRAMPLER TYPE

(Pl. XXVIII. 14—Pl. XXIX. 15)

§ 210. In variety A, which corresponds with the variety α of the *B. M. C. G. D.*, the king is facing right and trampling upon the lion **(Pl. XXVIII. 14—Pl. XXIX. 7)**. He wears a *pagaḍi* and wields the bow in the left hand and strings it by the right. The circular legend is *Sākshādiva nārasiṁhaḥ siṁhamahendro jayatyaniśam*, 'Narasiṁha as it were incarnate, (the king) Mahendra (as it were) among the lions, is ever victorious.' The metre is Upagīti. The second word of this legend can be read fairly clearly on one coin of the hoard **(Pl. XXVIII. 14)**. The goddess on the reverse is holding a noose in the right hand and a lotus in the left, but the latter looks more like a cornucopiae than a lotus. It is likely that this variety was issued in the northern part of the empire, where the memory of the cornucopiae might still have been lingering. The legend is *Śrī-Mahendrasiṁhaḥ*.

Variety B **(Pl. XXIX. 8-15)** is represented by eleven coins, but they do not enable us to read the entire obverse legend. The opening word *Kumāra* is clear on many coins. The legend seems to have ended with *vikrama*, for on some coins *kra* or *krama* can be seen at X or XI; see **Pl. XXIX. 8-11**. It is therefore likely that the legend was a short one and read *Kumāragupto yudhi siṁha-*

vikramaḥ,[1] 'Kumāragupta, who is as valorous in war as the lion.' This legend would be the same as that occurring on class I, var. B. The goddess on the reverse of this variety holds a rosary in her right hand, whose palm is opened out; her left hand resting on the knee holds a lotus with a long stalk. She is usually slightly reclined to right. The legend is *Srī-Mahendrasiṁhaḥ*. The coins of this variety were quite rare before the discovery of this hoard. They were unrepresented in the British or the Indian Museum and were known from a solitary specimen published in *N. S.*, XXXIX, p. 225.

(*viii*) Elephant-rider-Lion-slayer Type

(Pl. XXX.1-4)

§ 211. This type was so far known from the cast of a single specimen, which was once offered for sale to the Lucknow Museum,[2] but which now remains untraced. The Bayana hoard contains four beautiful specimens of this type. The type tries to combine the Lion-slayer type, which has been already described and the Elephant-rider type, which will be soon dealt with in § 217.

The emperor is seen seated on an elephant with an attendant behind him holding a parasol over his head. The elephant is furiously marching to right, and trying to trample the lion in its front by its front left leg. The emperor is also attacking the common enemy by a dagger in his right hand. The lion is to be seen cleverly anticipating the move of the elephant by trying to bite its right fore leg by its mouth before the left one crushes him down. His jaw is widely opened for the purpose. Great indeed is the skill shown in portraying the fury of the ponderous elephant, the cleverness of the supple lion and the determination of the agile emperor. The obverse legend begins with *Kshataripu* and ends with *ti ripūn;* it may have been identical with that on type xi below; see § 218. The reverse shows goddess standing three fourths to right, but looking back to left,

---

[1] Mr. Allan conjecturally restores the legend as *Kumāragupto vijayisiṁha-mahendro divaṁ jayati; B. M. C. G. D.* p. 79. This, however, seems improbable because of the clear presence of the letter *kra* at IX on some coins.

[2] *J. A. S. B.*, 1917 p. 155.

holding a lotus in the left hand and an uncertain object in the right in front of a peacock standing behind her. The legend is seen partly on the left and partly on the right, which is quite an unusual feature on the reverse of gold Gupta coins. It begins at X and reads *Siṅhanihantā Mahendragajaḥ*, 'The elephant of the king Mahendra, the destroyer of lions.'

(*ix*) Rhinoceros-slayer Type

(Pl. XXX. 5-8)

§ 212. The Rhinoceros-slayer type represents another effort at originality made by the mint-masters of Kumāragupta; it was unknown before the discovery of the Bayana hoard.[1] We have only four coins of this type **(Pl. XXX. 5-8)**; they are artistically very beautiful. So far we had Lion-slayer and Tiger-slayer types; Kumāragupta is seen adding the Rhinoceros-slayer type to them. On the present type, however, the king is not shown hunting the animal on foot; here we find him riding a horse. The type is thus a combination type like the Elephant-rider-Lion-slayer type.

§ 213. The obverse shows the king riding a caparisoned horse to right and leaning forward to attack the rhinoceros by the sword. Suddenly confronted by the wild beast, the horse raises its head slightly frightened. The rhinoceros bravely stands at bay, turning back its head to attack the king. The animal is skilfully engraved, its single horn on the head, left eye, two ears and the circular spots on the body being all clearly shown. The legend on this beautiful type is naturally in poetry. The king is attacking the rhinoceros by sword or *khaḍga*, which Sanskrit word also means a rhinoceros. The unknown author of the metrical legend makes a pun on the word *khaḍga* and describes the emperor as '*Bhartā khaḍgatrātā Kumāragupto jayatyaniśam*', 'Ever victorious is the lord Kumāragupta, who is *khaḍgatrātā*, protector by the sword (*khaḍgena trātā*), as well as protector from rhinoceroses ((*khaḍgebhyastrātā*).' The metre is Upagīti. The reverse of this type is quite unique; it shows the goddess Gaṅgā standing three-fourths to left on a crocodile, and holding a lotus with the

[1] One coin has since been acquired by the Provincial Museum, Lucknow, and published in *J. N. S. I.*, XI, p. 9.

long stalk in her right hand. The left hand of the goddess is hanging by her side, and she is pointing at something by the forefinger of the right hand. Behind the goddess is a female attendant holding a parasol over her head, which is also quite a novel feature on the reverse. The reverse legend is on the left and probably reads *Śri-Mahendrakhaḍgaḥ*, 'Rhinoceros (killed by) Mahendra.'

(*x*) Aśvamedha Type

(Pl. XXX. 9-12)

§ 214. Only two coins of the Aśvamedha type, lying in the cabinet of the British Museum, were known before the discovery of the Bayana hoard. The type is undoubtedly a scarce one; the Bayana hoard contains only four of its specimens. One more was recently acquired by the Provincial Museum, Lucknow. Samudragupta had issued a large number of coins of the Aśvamedha type; one wonders why Kumāragupta should apparently have issued only a few of them.

§ 215. The two coins in the British Museum showed marked departure from the Aśvamedha type of Samudragupta; their obverse showed not a bare but a caparisoned horse, and standing to right and not to left. Our hoard has two coins of this type **(Pl. XXX. 9-10)**. But it shows a new variety showing a closer imitation of the prototype. It is represented by two specimens **(Pl. XXX. 11-12)**, where we have a bare horse standing to left as on the coins of Samudragupta. The reverse is the same as that of the Aśvamedha type of Samudragupta. It shows the queen standing to left, holding a towel in her left hand and a *chouri* in her right, resting over her right shoulder; there is the *sūchi* or sacrificial needle in her front.

§ 216. The Aśvamedha coins of Kumāragupta, known so far, showed a very fragmentary legend on the obverse; they were attributed to Kumāragupta because of the reverse legend *Aśvamedha-Mahendraḥ*. The obverse legend on the coins of the Bayana hoard is much better preserved and we can distinctly read *Kumāragupta* on one specimen under the horse **(Pl. XXX. 11)**. The reading of some of the words is still uncertain; but most probably the legend read as *Devo jitaśatruḥ Kumāraguptodhirājaḥ*, 'King

Kumāragupta, who has conquered the enemies, is king of kings'. The reverse legend is *Srī-aśvamedha-Mahendraḥ*.

The Aśvamedha coins of Kumāragupta are artistically much inferior to those of his grandfather. The horse and the pedestal of the *yūpa* are much less graceful. The *yūpa* is usually off the flan and one can see neither its *raśanā* (girdle) nor its *chashāla* on any specimen. The letter *si* also figures nowhere on the coins. The queen on the reverse is plumpy, bent, and short-statured and her figure can bear no comparison to the slim, tall, and graceful figure of Dattadevī occurring on Samudragupta's coins.

(*xi*) Elephant-rider Type

(Pl. XXXI. 1-3)

§ 217. The Elephant-rider type of Kumāragupta was so far known from a solitary specimen in the Indian Museum.[1] The name of the king is illegible on this coin, but it was conjecturally attributed to Kumāragupta I on account of its weight and style. The Bayana hoard contains three coins of this type; they enable us not only to attribute this type definitely to Kumāragupta I, but also to read most of its legend.

§ 218. The obverse of this type shows the emperor riding an elephant furiously marching to left. There is an attendant behind him holding an umbrella over his master, as on the Elephant-rider-Lion-slayer type. The obverse legend is most probably *Kshataripurājatrātā Kumāragupto jayati ripūn*, 'Kumāragupta, whose enemies have been destroyed, and who protects feudatory kings, conquers the enemies.' The metre is Upagīti.

The reverse shows Lakshmī standing, facing on a conventional lotus, holding a lotus creeper with leaves, buds and flowers in her right hand and a cornucopiae in the left. The cornucopiae is treated almost like a lotus, as in variety A of class II of the Lion-slayer type of the present ruler; see **Pl. XXIX. 1-7**. There is a conch in the right lower field, which is quite a novel feature. The reverse legend is *Srī-Mahendragajaḥ*; it describes the elephant on the obverse and compares it by *double entendre* with Indra's elephant.

(*xii*) Lyrist Type

(Pl. XXXI. 4-5)

§ 219. The Lyrist type of Kumāragupta was altogether unknown before the discovery of the Bayana hoard; it also contains only two of its specimens. The type obviously represents an effort to revive the Lyrist type of Samudragupta. The obverse shows the king seated on a high-backed couch and playing on a lute placed on his lap, as on the prototype; the legend is also the same, with the only change of the name, viz., *Mahārajādhirājaśrī-Kumāraguptaḥ*. The reverse, however, shows considerable departure from the prototype. It no doubt shows the goddess facing to left. She is, however, seated on a couch like the king on the obverse, and not on a wicker stool, as on the coins of Samudragupta. Her left hand rests on the couch and is not holding a cornucopiae, as on the prototype. The right hand does not hold a noose but a flower, which the goddess is shown as smelling. The legend *Śrī-Kumāraguptaḥ* is on the left and not on the right.

It is not impossible that the reverse may be showing the figure of Kumāragupta's queen, rather than a goddess.

(*xiii*) Apratigha Type

(Pl. XXXI. 6-13)

§ 220. The mystery surrounding the solitary specimen of the type conveniently described as the Pratāpa type by Mr. Allan is but partially removed by the discovery of eight of its specimens in the Bayana hoard. These coins show that the legend on the reverse is *Apratigha* and not *Śrī-pratāpa*, as suggested by Mr. Allan. The reverse shows Lakshmī seated facing on a large beautiful full-blown double petalled lotus, both her hands being empty. The symbol is on the left at the centre and there are four dot-like objects above it.

§ 221. The obverse shows three persons standing. The central one is a male figure standing facing, with hands folded on chest. He wears a simple *dhoti* with its pleats hanging between the legs. There is either a protuberance on the head, as on the Buddha figures, or alternatively the hair is tied in a knot on the top of the head. The figure wears no ornaments or royal insignia and looks more like a Buddhist layman or monk, but is expressly described as Kumāragupta in a legend written vertically but to be read horizontally, partly on the right and partly on the left of the central standing figure. To the proper right of Kumāragupta is a male figure standing profile to right and apparently holding a shield in the left hand; in the right hand he is holding a Garuḍa-standard which can be seen between the two figures. To the proper left of Kumāragupta, there is a female figure standing to left with the right hand bent up in the attitude of *vitarka* or argumentation.

On either side of the central figure there is a vertical legend in two short lines to be read horizontally. The bottom of the letters is towards the central figure; in the line on the right they are to be read from top to bottom and in the line on the left from bottom to top. The letters on the right are rather blurred, but *Kumāra* is fairly clear on **Pl. XXXI. 12.** The letters on the left are quite distinct on almost all the coins and there can be no doubt that they read *guptaḥ*. The name of Kumāragupta is thus written vertically on the obverse at the usual place [1].

Several letters of the long circular legend are well preserved on **Pl. XXXI. 6, 9-11,** but no scholar has yet succeeded in combining them into an intelligent legend, though their photographs have been placed for study before the world of scholars since February 1949. Assuming that the legend begins at XII, the first seven letters appear to be *Papurapaparapa* **(Pl. XXXI. 6).** The following three letters are less like letters and more like the numerical figures for 50, 50, and 2. One can, however, hardly expect numerals in the midst of a legend. Prof. Mirashi has read this part of the legnd as *Pratāpa paramādhāraḥ.*[2] It gives a good sense as describing Kumāragupta; the reading of the letters *ta, ma and dha* in the above legend is, however, doubtful. The next nine letters are read by Prof. Mirashi as *Śrīprathamakramākramavapuḥ,* which he takes to be a cadence in the Śārdūlavikrīḍita metre. These can be the opening letters in this metre, but with two first letters missing. Whether such a truncated line

[1] Prof. R. C. Majumdar thinks that this vertical legend in two lines may be Mihirakula rather than Kumāragupta. There are serious difficulties in accepting this view. See *J. N. S. I.,* XII. 72-3.

[2] *J. N. S. I.,* XII. 68-71

in Sārdūlavikrīḍita could have been combined with a line in the Anushṭubh is very doubtful. The letters Srīprathama are fairly clear on **Pl. XXXI. 10.** The next three letters *Kramakra* can also be read as *Kumara,* but the second letter *ma* is rather doubtful. It looks also like *kha* or the numerical figure for 50. After *pu* of *vapu,* there is a distinct *pu* or *pra.* A large portion of the legend on the left has been preserved on **Pl. XXXI. 11-12,** but the letters are all indistinct. At IX one can perhaps see traces of *Kumāra* again : see **Pl. XXXI. 8-10** With the help of the present specimens it is not possible to offer any intelligent reading of the long circular legend.

§ 222. The significance of the obverse showing Kumāragupta in non-regal dress with a military attendant on one side and a lady arguing with him on the other is very difficult to understand. The mystery could have been perhaps solved, had we been able to read the obverse legend. This, however, is not yet possible, though we have now got eight specimens of the type.

We may, however, hazard a conjecture about the meaning of the obverse motif. The legend on the reverse usually bears a close connection with the motif of the obverse and refers to the principal figure occurring there. Here it is *apratigha* and means invincible. This may refer to the principal figure on the obverse side, namely Kumāragupta. He, however, appears in non-regal dress and is seen folding his hands, and the lady on the right is violently arguing with him. Can it be that the motif refers to the abdication of the king on religious grounds and the effort made by his queen and general or crown-prince to dissuade him? Kumāragupta was firm in his resolve and is therefore described on the reverse as invincible.

It may be passingly observed that the obverse motif of three standing figures reminds us of a coin-type of Huvishka, which shows on the obverse the three deities, Skanda-Kumāra, Viśākha and Mahāsena. The resemblance is, however, only a superficial one and does hardly enable us to solve the mystery connected with the interpretation of the present type.

(*xiv*) King-and-Queen Type.

(Pl. XXXI. 14)

§ 223. In his King-and-Queen type, which was altogether unknown before the discovery of the Bayana hoard, Kumāragupta is reviving the only known coin-type of Chandragupta I. The hoard contains only one coin of this type. On the obverse, we have the king and the queen standing and facing each other, as on the prototype. The posture of the queen, who is facing right, is exactly similar to that of Kumāradevī; the hands of both the queens are exactly in the same positions. The king is facing left. But he is no longer holding a standard in his left hand, which fashion was given up long ago; his left hand rests on the hip, grasping the hilt of a sword. Like Chandragupta I, he is offering by his right hand a gift to the queen, which in the present specimen can be distinctly made out to be a bunch of flowers. Between the king and the queen there is a crescent, as on some coins of Chandragupta I. There are traces of an inscription behind the standing king, but the legend is fragmentary and illegible. Probably there was a similar inscription behind the queen which is off the flan. To judge from the prototype, both these inscriptions should have given the names of the king and the queen. The name of the Crowned Queen of Kumāragupta is not known so far. Had it been preserved on the coins of the present type, some of the problems connected with the successors of Kumāragupta would have been solved. On the reverse we have the goddess seated on a lion couchant, as on the prototype. Her left hand resting on waist is empty, the foreign cornucopiae in the prototype being given up; the right hand holds a lotus with a long stalk instead of a noose. The reverse is markedly similar to that of the variety c of class I of the Lion-slayer type of the present emperor; see **Pl. XXVIII. 8-10.** In both cases the goddess is seated facing on a lion couchant to right. In both cases her left hand is empty and resting on the waist and right hand is holding a flower. The most characteristic common feature is, however, the graceful *tribhaṅga* posture of the goddess; she is seen reclining to left, leaning on her left arm resting on her slightly raised knee. It is quite possible that both the reverses were engraved by the same artist. The reverse legend is *Śrī Kumāraguptaḥ.*

6. Skandagupta
Chhatra Type
(Pl. XXXI. 15)

§ 224. Kramāditya is the last ruler represented in the hoard; we have, however, recovered only a single coin issued by him. This coin is of the Chhatra type and bears a close resemblance to the coin of that type issued by Kumāragupta. The obverse shows the king standing three-fourths to left and offering oblations on an altar, which however is off the flan. There is a dwarf behind, holding a parasol over the emperor. The reverse shows the goddess standing to left, holding a noose in the right hand and a lotus with long stalk in the left.

§ 225. The identification of the king, who issued this coin, is not free from difficulties. The legend on the obverse is incomplete; it begins with *Vijitāvanira*, but its concluding portion, which must have contained the issuer's name, is off the flan. The reverse legend gives the issuer's *biruda* as *Kramāditya*. Kramāditya was the *biruda* of Skandagupta, and his silver coins bear the legend, *Vijitāvaniravanipatirjayati divaṁ Skandaguptoyam*, which could well have been the legend on this coin also, since it begins with *Vijitāvanira*. It is therefore most probable[1] that the solitary Chhatra type coin of Kramāditya, found in the Bayana hoard, is an issue of Skandagupta, the son and the successor of Kumāragupta I.

§ 226. About three hundred coins of this hoard were melted down before it could be recovered. It is not unlikely that most of the coins of Skandagupta, who was the last ruler, were at the top of the pot containing the hoard, and therefore were first to be sent to the melting pot by the villagers. It is therefore quite likely that the hoard may have contained a few dozen coins of

[1] We cannot, however, exclude another possibility. Ghaṭotkachagupta, who was most probably a son of Kumāragupta I, was ruling as governor of Mālwā in *c.* 435 A. D. If we identify this Ghaṭotkachagupta with the king known from the solitary coin in the St. Petersberg Museum, which has *Ghaṭo* on the obverse and the legend Kramāditya on the reverse (*B. M. C. G. D.*, Pl. XXIV, 3), it will follow that Ghaṭotkachagupta had the *biruda* of Kramāditya as well. Since this coin has also the same *biruda* on the reverse, it is not impossible that it might have been issued by Ghaṭotkachagupta, the governor of Mālwā in *c.* 435 A. D., who may have disputed the accession of Skandagupta and issued a few coins, bearing his *biruda Kramāditya.* This theory is possible, but not probable.

Skandagupta. If, however, it really contained a single coin of that ruler, it will follow that the Hūṇa invasion, which led to the immurement of the hoard, took place very early in the reign of Skandagupta, as is also suggested by the Bhitari pillar inscription.

7. Gold Coinage of Skandagupta and his Successors

§ 227. In the present Catalogue of the coins of the Bayana Hoard of Gupta Gold Coins, which publishes the largest number of the gold coins of the dynasty, it would be convenient for the reader, if we give a brief account of the gold coins of the kings not represented in it, as also of the silver and copper coinages of the dynasty. This will enable the readers of the volume to have a fairly complete idea of the coinage of the Gupta empire.

§ 228. Skandagupta, the successor of Kumāragupta I, is represented in the Bayana hoard, as shown above, by a solitary coin of the Chhatra type, which was not known so far. His other certain coin-types are two, the Archer-type **(Pl. XXXII. 1-2)** and the King-and-Lakshmī type **(Pl. XXXII. 3)**. The Archer type is of the usual nature, and has nimbate Lakshmī on the reverse. It shows no variety in the device of the obverse, nor is its circular legend read completely so far. It was issued in two denominations, one **(Pl. XXXII. 1)** followed 132 grains standard of the earlier reign and the other **(Pl. XXXII. 2)** that of 144 grains. This latter standard was an innovation of Skandagupta, probably prompted by the desire to issue gold currency of the *suvarṇa* standard of 80 *rattis* or 144 grains, mentioned in the Smṛiti literature.[1] The coins of the *suvarṇa* standard, though heavier in weight, are considerably adulterated; what Gupta government gave by one hand was thus taken away by the other. The King-and-Lakshmī type of Skandagupta **(Pl. XXXII. 3)** reminds us of the King-and-Queen types of Chandragupta I and Kumāragupta I; some numismatists maintain that it is not King-and-Lakshmī type but the King-and-Queen type.[2] The former view, however, seems to be more probable, and the type seems to illustrate on the coins the situation described by the poet in the Bhitari pillar inscription, where we are told how Lakshmī voluntarily accepted Skandagupta as her lord. In this type king is standing with

---

[1] *Manu*, VIII. 134.
[2] *J. N. S. I.*, VIII, 18.

Lakshmī in front of him, who is holding an uncertain object in her hand, which she is offering to the king. This reminds us of the Chakravikrama type of Chandragupta II, where Vishṇu is seen offering *prasāda* or a present to the emperor.

There is a solitary gold coin of the Horseman type, with the legend *Kramājitaḥ* on the reverse in the Bodleian collection[1]. If the legend is a mistake for Kramāditya, it would be an issue of Skandagupta, who had adopted that *biruda*.

§ 229. Skandagupta had two brothers Ghaṭotkachagupta and Purugupta. The solitary Archer type coin in the St. Petersberg Museum, with *Ghaṭo* under the arm, was probably issued by the former **(Pl. XXXII. 4)**. Purugupta had a short reign and no coins of his have been discovered so far. A coin of Archer type having a blurred legend under the left arm published in *B. M. C. G. D., XXI.* 23 was for a long time attributed to Purugupta. This coin had the legend Vikrama on the reverse and weighed about 144 grains. Other coins, therefore, which belonged to this heavy weight standard and had the biruda *Vikrama* on the reverse, (*B. M. C. G. D.*, XXI. 24-25), were also attributed to the same king.[2] New and clear specimens have, however, now conclusively shown that *B. M. C. G. D.*, Pl. XXI. 23 has the legend Budha under the arm and not Pura, as was once supposed.

§ 230. Purugupta was succeeded by his son Narasiṁhagupta, and the latter by his son Kumāragupta II. Both these kings issued coins only in the Archer type, showing no variations **(Pl. XXXII. 5-6)**. They conform to the *suvarṇa* standard, but are heavily adulterated. Kumāragupta's successor Budhagupta had a long reign and succeeded in reasserting the Gupta power and prestige. We have now discovered two coins bearing his name Budha under the left arm and giving the legend *Vikrama* on the reverse; both these coins are now in the cabinet of the Banaras Hindu University. The coin in the *B. M. C. G. D.*, Pl. XXI. 23 also belongs to the same class. There is now, therefore, no doubt that Budhagupta issued gold coins of the Archer type of the heavy weight standard of 144 grains. One of these coins is illustrated in **Pl. XXXII. 7**.

§ 231. Budhagupta was probably succeeded by his grand-

---

[1] *B. M. C. G. D.*, p. c.

[2] *Ibid*, p. 134.

nephew Vishṇugupta and the latter by Vainyagupta, whose relationship to the former is not known so far. Both these kings issued gold coins only in the Archer type and in the *suvarṇa* denomination, but heavily adulterated; see **Pl. XXXII. 8-9.** The reverse of these coins has Lakshmī seated on the lotus, as is the case with the coins of all the successors of Skandagupta. Prakāśāditya, who issued gold coins where the obverse shows the king riding a horse and slaying a lion **(Pl. XXXII. 10)**, most probably belongs to the Gupta dynasty, but it is not yet possible to identify him. Jayagupta, who issued Archer type coins with Lakshmī on the reverse **(Pl. XXXII. 11)**, undoubtedly copies a Gupta type, but it is very doubtful whether he belonged to the Gupta dynasty. The same is the case with king Samāchāradeva, who seems to have ruled in Bengal sometimes in the 6th century A. D. The coins of Samāchāradeva are of the Archer type and give his *biruda* on the reverse as Narendrāditya; see **Pl. XXXII. 13.** Saśāṅka, the opponent of Harsha, also issued gold coins, which closely imitate the reverse motif of the gold coinage of the Guptas, *viz.* goddess seated on lotus; his obverse, however, shows Siva standing by the side of the bull; see **Pl. XXXII. 12.** Rude imitations of Gupta coins, but weighing only about 85 grains, were issued by some unknown rulers of Eastern Bengal in the 7th century; their obverse is an imitation of the Archer type, but the reverse shows the eight-armed goddess standing to left; see **Pl. XXXII. 15.** Some of these coins have a horse on the reverse, perhaps suggesting that the issuer had performed a Horse sacrifice; see **Pl. XXXII. 14.**

8. Silver Currency of The Guptas

§ 232. Chandragupta II was the first Gupta emperor to issue silver currency. He had to take this step as a natural consequence of his conquest of Gujarat and Kathiawar, the residents of which provinces were long accustomed to the silver currency under the rule of the Kshatrapas. Gupta silver coins conform closely to their prototype. The obverse shows the typical Kshatrapa bust with long hair and moustaches, as also clear traces of degraded Greek letters, which were mechanically copied by the Kshatrapa mint masters from the Indo-Greek prototype. The reverse, however, shows some innovation. The three-arched hill was replaced by *Garuḍa*, which was the insignia of the Gupta dynasty; but the crescent and star were permitted to continue. The year of issue, when given on the obverse, was naturally in the Gupta era. The weight standard is the same as that of the Western Kshatrapas; for all the Gupta silver issues weigh about 30 grains. The reverse legend does not give the names and titles of the king and his father, as on the prototype; it is either *Paramabhāgavata-mahārājādhirāja-śrī-Chandragupta-Vikramādityaḥ* or *Śrī-Guptakulasya Mahārājādhirāja-śrī-Chandragupta-Vikramāṅkasya*. Chandragupta's silver coins are scarce, showing that they began to be issued late in his reign. For the illustrations of these coins, see *B. M. C. G. D.*, Pl. X, 14-20; *C. G. D.*, Pl. XVI. 1-7.

§ 233. Kumāragupta I has left us ample silver currency. In the western provinces of his empire, he continued the type issued by his father, changing only the legend which is either *Paramabhāga-vata-rājādhirāja-śrī-Kumāragupta-Mahendrādityaḥ* or its abbreviation in some form or other. He, however, issued a new silver type for the Gangetic plain, showing hardly any Kshatrapa influence, except in size and weight. The bust of the king on the obverse is strikingly different from the stereotyped Kshatrapa bust, and may be an attempt at portraiture; there are also no traces of degraded Greek letters. The date is given not behind the king's head, as on the Kshatrapa coins, but in front of it. The reverse shows a fan-tailed peacock; this bird was the mount of god Kumāra or Kārtikeya after whom the emperor had been named. The circular legend is *Vijitāvaniravanipatiḥ Kumāragupto divaṁ jayati.* When the Gupta empire was in great financial stress as a result of the wars with the Pushyamitras, we find Kumāragupta issuing in his western provinces silver-plated currency, very crude in execution and incomplete in the legend; it follows the usual Kshatrapa prototype. For the illustrations of silver types of Kumāragupta I, see *B. M. C. G. D.*, Plates XVI-XVIII; *C. G. D.* Pl. XVII.

§ 234. Skandagupta continued to issue both the main silver types issued by his father for the different provinces of his empire. In Western India, however, he issued two new types, the Bull type and the Altar type. Their obverses, however, continue to copy the Kshatrapa original. The obverse legend on the Western type is *Paramabhāgavata-mahārājādhirāja-śrī-Skandagupta-Kramādityaḥ* or its abbreviation; that on the type intended for the Gangetic plain is the same as that on the coins of his father, with slight alterations, *Vijitāvaniravanipatirjayati divaṁ Skandagupto'yaṁ*. The year of issue is also given, and it enables us to prolong the emperor's reign to 148 G. E. or 467 A. D. For the illustrations of the silver coins of Skandagupta, see *B. M. C. G. D.*, Plates XX-XXI; *C. G. D.*, Pl. XVIII. 6-23.

§ 235. Among the successors of Skandagupta, only Budhagupta issued silver coins, and very few of them have been found. None of them imitate the western type, showing that Gujarat and Kathiawar were lost to the empire for all practical purposes. The silver coins of Budhagupta have the bust of the king on the obverse and the fan-tail peacock on the reverse, the legend being *Vijitāvaniravanipatiḥ-śrī-Budhagupto divaṁ jayati*. One of them is dated in 175 G.E. and enables us to prolong the emperor's reign to 494 A. D. Toramāṇa, the Hūṇa rival of Budhagupta, has copied this type, as also the Maukhari and the Pushyabhūti rulers, who succeeded the Guptas in the Gangetic plain.

For the illustrations of the silver coins of Budhagupta, see *B. M. C. G. D.*, Pl. XXIV. 13-15; *G. G. D.*, Pl. XVIII. 26-29.

9. Copper Coinage of the Guptas.

§ 236. Chandragupta II is the only Gupta emperor, who can be said to have issued a copper currency. No copper coins of any of his predecessors are known and only half a dozen pieces of his successor Kumāragupta have so far been found. Copper coins of Chandragupta II can be seen in *B. M. C. G. D.*, Plates X-XI and *C. G. D.*, Pl. XVI, and those of Kumāragupta I in *B. M. C. G. D.*, Pl. XVIII and *C. G. D.*, Pl. XVIII.

Copper coins naturally cannot compare with the gold issues in artistic beauty; they are also usually worn out considerably. They, however, show considerable variety of type. In some cases the obverse shows the bust of the king; in others, we find His Majesty offering oblations at the altar. A third type is the reproduction of the Chhatra type of the gold currency, The reverse is usually divided into two halves, the upper one having Garuḍa and the lower one the legend *Mahārāja-śrī-Chandraguptaḥ*. A few coins, however, have the short legend *Chandra* on the obverse and vase on reverse. The metrology of the copper coinage is difficult to understand, as the weights of the pieces are irregularly graded. The highest weight is 101 grains; then we have pieces weighing 87, 64, 57, 49, 35, 28, 18, 12 and 5 grains.

The copper coins of Kumāragupta are very scarce; only six have so far come to light. Their obverse shows either Standing King or Altar and the reverse either Garuḍa or Lakshmī; see *B. M. C. G. D.*, Pl. XVIII; *C. G. D.* Pl. XVIII.

§ 237. In 1951 tiny copper coins were discovered in Mālwā bearing the name of Rāmagupta.[1] They have the name of the king on the obverse and Couchant Lion on the reverse. The legend on the coins, when pieced together, distinctly reads as Rāmagupta. The script is the Gupta one and we know of no contemporary ruler having the name of Rāmagupta other than the elder brother of Chandragupta II. It is therefore likely that these coins are the issues of Rāmagupta, who figures in the literary tradition as the elder brother of Chandragupta II. This theory, if proved by further conclusive evidence, will go against the view that Rāmagupta is identical with Kācha. His gold coins may be found later; we had no trace of any gold coins of Budhagupta, who had ruled for 25 years and had re-established the prestige of his house, till the year 1948.

V. Metrology

§ 238. The weights of modern coins are very accurately adjusted by governments. Such, however, was not the case in ancient time. The Greeks were fairly careful about their coinage, but the weights of their coins issued in ancient India do not come up to the modern standard in their accuracy. Thus the weights of the silver drachms of Demetrius vary from 61 to 55 grains, those of Eucratides from 67 to 52 grains, when the standard weight of the coin concerned was 67.2 grains. Coins issued by the Indo-Bactrian rulers during the decadence of their rule show even greater variations. The Roman coins also show a similar variation in weight. The gold *aurei* of Julius Caesar vary in weight from 120 to 125 grains. After his death, the weight of the Roman

---

[1] *J. N. S. I.*, XII, p. 103 ; XIII, p. 128.

aureus gradually declined and was ranging between 114 to 121 grains.

§ 239. The gold coins of the Imperial Guptas also show similar variations. Very often well-preserved coins of the same type show a variation of 4 or 5 grains. We can explain this circumstance only on the assumption that the mint authorities in ancient India, as those in ancient Greece or Rome, were not as careful as those in modern states in weighing the flans of their coins. Gold was much cheaper in terms of silver or copper than what it is now. A difference of three or four grains or two *rattis* amounts to about Rs. 3 or 4 now, but it was equal to twelve annas or one rupee only in the pre-war days. It was, however, a difference of only about two or three annas in a twenty rupee piece of the gold coin in the Gupta period. Such minor variations in weight were, therefore, probably overlooked. Or it may be that each coin may have been weighed at the time of its exchange. Now also gold ornaments are re-weighed even when their weights are written or stamped on them by firms of repute. We should not forget that gold coins were used on rare occasions, when big sums had to be paid for the purchase of land or on the occasion of making perpetual deposits in banks.

§ 240. The traditional standard weight of a gold coin according to Manu was 80 *rattis* or about 140 grains.[1] We have, however, so far found no coins issued to this weight standard by any pre-Gupta government or guild. The Indo-Greeks issued a few gold coins to the weight standard of a stater, weighing 133.2 grains. The Kushāṇas followed the standard of the Roman *aureus,* weighing about 121 grains. We have seen already how the Gupta gold coinage was considerably influenced by the Kushāṇa prototype in several respects; and metrology was no exception. Early Gupta emperors generally issued coins to the standard of 120 grains. Since this weight standard is not known to Indian tradition, and is identical with that of the Roman and Kushāṇa gold coins, the conclusion is inevitable that the Gupta emperors adopted this standard, because it was well established in the Roman and Kushāṇa empires and had acquired an international recognition.

---

[1] *Manu*, VIII. 134.

§ 241. There are ten coins of Chandragupta I in our hoard; the lightest of them No. 1 weighs 117.6 grains and the heaviest, No. 2, weighs 121.3 grains. The weights of well-preserved coins like Nos, 3, 4, 7 and 8 vary between 120 and 121 grains. It is thus clear that the coins of this emperor were intended to conform to the standard of 121 grains, which was the average weight of the Roman *aurei* and the Kushāṇa gold coins.

§ 242. Samudragupta continued this weight standard throughout his long reign, and with reference to most of his types. The average weight of well-preserved coins of the Standard type varies between 119 and 121 grains. Among the 143 specimens of this type, there are however 19 coins (Nos. 11, 19, 21, 26, 28, 33, 47, 51, 59, 64, 79, 89, 93, 97, 99, 127, 128, 129), which though not worn out in any appreciable degree, weigh between 110 and 114 grains. The *B. M. C.* collection of 17 coins of this type also has 2 specimens weighing between 110 and 114 grains. Whether the lower weight of these coins was due to a different standard of metrology being followed, or whether it was due to mere carelessness of the mint-masters, we do not know. Mr. Allan has suggested that different districts may have had different weight standards,[1] but this does not seem to be likely. Mints for the gold coins could not have been spread district-wise. The weights of coins Nos. 48, 55 and 89 of the Standard type are 108.4, 100.4 and 100.7 grains respectively. One coin in the *B.M.C.G.D.*, No. 5, also weighs only 108.4 grains. It is worth noting that some of these coins like No. 48 are large in size and well-preserved in condition, and still their weight is abnormally low. These coins could certainly not have been accepted as of the same value as those weighing about 120 grains. But it is doubtful whether this abnormally low weight denotes any different denomination. If such were the case, we would have got many more specimens of that denomination. The denomination would be that of a 4/5 *dīnāra*, which is rather unnatural. It would appear that as the weight of each coin was not very accurately adjusted, the flan of the last piece to be issued in one particular minting operation, for which a specific quantity of gold had been previously given by the authorities, would often be much under the normal

[1] *B. M. C. G. D.*, Introduction, p. cxxxii.

weight; if about two dozen coins had happened to be issued, each about only half a grain excess in weight, the last coin would be 108 grains in weight instead of 120. The last piece was, however, allowed to be stamped and issued, even if only about 100 or 108 grains in weight, because the public was expected to accept it at its actual weight. Coins weighing about 100 to 108 grains are to be found in later reigns also in several types. We have probably to explain these on this theory of their being 'remainder' pieces.

Three coins of the Standard type, Nos. 27, 64 and 71, weigh 123, 122.4, and 123.8 grains respectively. A Battle-axe type coin in the B. M. C. also weighs 123.4 grains. Here the excess of weight is due probably to carelessness. If half a dozen coins in one minting operation are issued half a grain less in weight, the flan of the last 'remainder' coin will be about three grains above the normal weight, as is the case with the above coins.

§ 243. Among the twenty coins of the Aśvamedha type as many as 14 weigh only approximately 115 grains. Three weigh only about 112 grains, while the remaining three weigh in the vicinity of 120 grains and conform to the normal standard. In the B. M. collection of nine coins of this type, five approximate to the standard of 118 grains, two weigh 115 grains and two 112 or 113 grains. It is difficult to state whether in the Aśvamedha type there were really three or four different weight standards of 112 115, 118 and 121 grains or whether these variations in weight are due to sheer carelessness.

§ 244. In the other types of Samudragupta also, we see similar variations in weight. In the Lyrist type, smaller variety, all coins follow the standard of 120 grains. But the larger variety of this type, curiously enough, has some coins following the lighter weight standard. In our hoard coin No. 186 weighs only 108.9 grains and in the B. M. collection of five coins, one piece weighs 111 and another 112 grains.

§ 245. Out of the two coins of the Tiger-slayer type one weighs 117.6 grains and the other 119 grains. Both seem to follow the 120 grains standard. In the B. M. collection, one coin of this type weighs 116.6 grains and the other 112 grains. The latter, however, is much worn out. The coins of the Tiger-slayer type may therefore be presumed to have been issued to the standard of 120 grains. In the Archer type of this ruler we have two coins; one, which is slightly worn out, weighs 115.6 grains and the other, which is well-preserved, weighs only 108.2 grains. Obviously the latter is a 'remainder' coin, the last piece to be issued in a particular minting operation. The five coins described in the *B. M. C. G. D.* were all issued to the standard of 120 grains; their actual weights vary between 116.4 and 120 grains.

§ 246. The nine coins of the Battle-axe type in our hoard are rather worn out. Most of them weigh in the vicinity of 115 grains, only one (No. 176) weighing 118.2 grains. In the *B. M. C. G. D.* most of the coins weigh in the vicinity of 118 grains, only one, which was probably a 'remainder' coin, weighing 111.8 grains. These coins were probably intended to conform to the standard of 120 grains.

§ 247. Out of 16 coins of Kācha eight weigh between 116 and 120 grains, seven between 112 and 116 and one (No. 196) weighs only 107.4 grains. In the B. M. collection of seven coins, three weigh between 116 and 118 grains and four between 111 and 115 grains. Kācha seems to have issued coins to two standards, one of 115 grains and the other of 118 grains.

§ 248. During the reign of Chandragupta II, the lighter weight standard of about 115 grains seems to have been abandoned. Among the 798 coins of the Archer type of this ruler, only seven weigh between 110 and 115 grains. They are probably 'remainder' pieces. In this coin type we can perhaps distinguish three weight standards of 121, 124 and 127 grains respectively. About 525 coins weigh in the vicinity of 121 grains, about 170 in the vicinity of 124 grains, and about 110 in the vicinity of 127 grains. In the B. M. collection of 34 coins, 7 belong to the standard of 127 grains, 6 to that of 124 grains, and 18 to that of 121 grains. Three pieces weighing between 129.5 and 132 grains, apparently follow a higher standard. All the B. M. pieces of this heavy weight standard have a wheel on the obverse.

§ 249. It appears that some of the varieties of the Archer type were issued to a particular weight standard. Thus among the 41 coins of class I (the Throne reverse), there is none issued to the standard of 124 or 127 grains; all coins weigh about 119 or 120 grains. The same is the case with the seven coins of this class in the British Museum. In class II, Lotus reverse, all the coins of variety C, where the king holds a sword by his side, are found issued to the standard of 127 grains. All the four coins of variety D, which shows the goddess on the reverse with her left foot tucked up, are issued to the standard of 121 grains. The same is the case with the two coins of the variety G in our hoard, where the king holds the bow in the right hand, and with the single coin of this variety in the *B. M. C. G. D.* (No. 101). The 17 coins of the variety H of this class, where the king is looking to right, are all issued to the standard of 120 grains; the same is the case with the single coin of this variety in the *B. M. C. G. D.*, No. 100. The 18 coins of the variety B of class II, where the king holds a hunter, appear, however, to have been issued to all the three standards; for three of them weigh about 121 grains, three weigh about 124 grains and the remaining 12 about 127 grains.

§ 250. In Chhatra type of Chandragupta II, out of 57 coins of our hoard 51 belong to the 121 grains standard and six to the 124 grains standard. Out of the nine coins of this type in the *B. M.* two belong to the 124 grains standard and 7 to 121 grains standard. No coins were issued to the 127 grains standard in this type. In the Horseman type, a great majority, i. e. 63 out of 82, belong to the 121 grains standard; 15 weigh in the vicinity of 124 grains and six in that of 127 grains. In B. M. collection of 15 coins, nine follow the low standard of 121 grains, two the intermediate standard of 124 grains and 4 the higher standard of 127 grains. In the case of this type also we thus have all the three weight standards. Out of the 42 coins of the Lion-slayer type, 34 belong to the 121 grains standard and 7 to the 124 grains standard; the remaining piece, No. 1171, is abnormally heavy, weighing as much as 136.5 grains. In the B. M. collection of 20 coins of this type 14 are of 121 grains standard, two of 124 grains standard and two of 127 grains standard. Two coins weigh less than 115 grains, one weighing 111 grains and the other 115.4 grains. Both these are probably 'remainder' pieces. All the three coins of the Couch type of Chandragupta II belong to the 120 grains standard. The same is the case with one of the two coins of this type in the B. M. The other, however, weighs 114.7 grains only.

§ 251. In the reign of Kumāragupta I, the standard of 121 grains became very rare; it is also confined to certain well-defined types and varieties. To this category belong most of the coins of the Archer type, class I, variety B, where the king holds the bow by the middle. Out of 58 coins of this variety, 52 are of the 121 grains standard and only 6 belong to the heavier standard of 127 grains. The B. M. has six coins of this type; out of them 5 belong to the 121 grains standard and one to the 124 grains standard. All the 10 coins of the variety C of class I, which differ from variety A only in its legend, *Guṇeśo mahītalam*.., also belong to the 121 grains standard. The same is the case with the two coins of this variety in the B. M. Out of the eight coins of the 'Apratigha' type, seven belong to this weight standard, the eighth belonging to 124 grains standard. It is interesting to note that the solitary coin of this type in the B. M. weighs very low, *viz*. 115 grains.

§ 252. All the coins of the variety A of class I of the Archer class, where the bow is held at the top and the legend is *Mahārājādhirājaśrī-Kumāraguptaḥ*, belong to the 124 grains standard without any exception. The same is the case with the solitary coin of this type in the British Museum and with the two coins in the Indian Museum (*I. M. C.*, I. p. 112, Nos. 9-10).

§ 253. All other coin types of Kumāragupta I were issued to the 127 grains standard. All the coins of the Archer type of classes II and III are above 126 grains in weight, two weighing as high as 130.2 and 130.1 grains.

In the Horseman type, class I, varieties A, B, and C, all the 47 coins belong to the above standard. In the B. M. only variety C is represented, and two of its coins belong to 124 grains standard and 7 to 127 grains standard. Out of the 97 coins of class II, variety A of the Horseman type, 94 belong to the 127 grains standard. Nos. 1440, 1509 and 1527, which weigh 108.5, 106.7 and 118 grains respectively, must be regarded as abnormal in their weight; they are most probably 'remainder' pieces, as explained earlier. The B. M. coins of this variety also belong to this standard except one, which belongs to 124 grains standard.

§ 254. In the Horseman type class II, variety B, it appears that coins were issued to both the 127 and 124 grains standards.

Out of the 83 coins of this variety, 69 weigh in the vicinity of 127 grains, 13 in that of 124 and one in that of 121. The latter coin may be regarded as exceptional, but not so the group of 13 coins weighing 124 grains. In the B.M. collection of six coins of this variety the 124 grains standard preponderates; for four out of six coins follow that weight standard, as against one which follows the 127 grains standard. The remaining sixth coin, which is worn out, weighs 110 grains; it is most probably a 'remainder' piece. All the coins of class II, varieties C, D, and E of the Horseman type are of the 127 grains standard, except No. 1662 of class II, variety C, which weighs only 107.8 grains and is obviously a 'remainder' coin. The same is generally the case with the coins in the B. M.

§ 255. The Tiger-slayer type is mostly issued to the 127 grains standard. Out of 36 pieces of this type, 34 follow this weight standard, only one being of the 124 grains standard and the remaining coin, No. 1718, weighing 108 grains, is obviously a 'remainder' piece. Out of the eight coins of this type in the B. M. six belong to the 127 grains standard, one belongs to 121 grains standard and one to 124 grains standard.

All the 13 coins of the Kārtikeya type in our hoard belong to the 127 grains standard; the same is the case with all the coins of this type in the B. M. In the Swordsman type we have 3 coins of the 124 grains standard and 7 of the 127 grains standard; the four coins of this type in the B. M. are evenly divided between these two weight standards. It may be, however, observed that the coins of this type appear to follow the standard rather of 125 grains than that of 124 or 127 grains.

§ 256. In the Lion-slayer type of this ruler, 127 grains standard preponderated. Out of 53 coins, 49 are issued to this standard. One, however, weighs as high as 131 grains. All the remaining three coins follow the 124 grains standard. Out of the 14 coins of this type in B. M. 9 follow the 127 grains standard and 3 that of 124 grains. The remaining two coins weigh 115 and 113 grains, and they are obviously 'remainder' pieces.

The coins of all the remaining types of Kumāragupta I, the Rhinoceros-slayer type, the King-and-the-Queen type, the Chhatra type, the Lyrist type, the Aśvamedha type, the Elephant-rider type and the Lion-slayer type belong to the 127 grains standard. One coin of the last mentioned type weighs 115 grains; it is very much worn out, and is probably a 'remainder' piece. The weights of the two Aśvamedha coins in the B. M. C. are 124.5 and 128.4 grains and that of the single coin of the Elephant-rider type is 124.1 grains.

§ 257. The single coin of Kramāditya of our hoard, which is in a good state of preservation, weighs 130.2 grains. It obviously belongs to the standard of 132 grains, which became common in the reign of Skandagupta Kramāditya.

§ 258. A few words may be said about the metrology of the gold coins of the successors of Kumāragupta I. Skandagupta issued coins to two different standards; the coins of his Chhatra and King-and-Lakshmī types are issued to the standard of 132 grains, which was but rarely adopted in the earlier reigns. His Archer type with the legend *Śrī-Skandaguptaḥ* on the reverse also conforms to this standard. But this emperor started issuing coins conforming to a much higher standard, the standard of 144 grains, which was obviously intended to conform to the traditional *suvarṇa* standard of 80 *rattis* or about 144 grains mentioned in the Smṛiti literature. The *suvarṇa* standard coins of the Archer type of this ruler have all of them the legend *Kramāditya* on the reverse in lieu of *Śrī-Skandogupta,* which occurs on the coins of the 132 grains standard. All the successors of Skandagupta gave up lighter standards of the earlier reigns and issued coins to the *suvarṇa* standard, weighing between 142 and 148 grains. But what extra was given in weight was taken away in purity. For the coins of these rulers contain only about 50% of gold.

VI. Palaeography

§ 259. The palaeography of the Gupta gold coins calls for a few remarks only. The characters are usually well engraved, but they are often compressed and their forms distorted for want of sufficient space. The characters on the coins resemble those in the contemporary lithic and copper records, as will be seen from their drawings in **Pl. XXXIII-XXXVII.** They however do not show anywhere the so-called eastern form of the letters *la*, *sa* and *sha*. Eastern forms of the letters *ma* and *ba* appear sometimes on the coins of the earlier emperors. They are relatively most common on the coins of Samudragupta and tend to become rarer and rarer in later reigns, till they disappear in the reign of Kumāragupta I and his successors.

§ 260. On the coins of Chandragupta I, preserved in the Bayana hoard, we do not get the so-called eastern form of *ma*; but we get it on one coin in B.M.C. No. 28, where the name of the queen is given as *Kumāradevī-śrī* and not as *Śrī-Kumāradevī*. The Standard type has usually the western *ma* with the triangular base. In some cases there is no triangle in the lower limb of the letter, and we have only two slanting lines meeting on the base line. It is interesting to note that the eastern *ma* is more common than the western *ma* in variety E of Standard type, where the full name of the emperor is given; see **Pl. III. 13-15.** It is however doubtful whether these different forms were really characteristic of different regions and can justify us in placing coins with the so-called eastern *ma* in eastern mints and those with the so-called western *ma* in western mints. For though we find the so-called eastern *ma* on both the sides of some coins, as on **Pl. II. 2, 4,** there are others like **Pl. II. 12, Pl. III. 13** where the eastern *ma* appears on one side and the western *ma* on the other. These coins make it clear that the same die-cutters very often used both the forms, and that they were current or not unintelligible in all the parts of the Gupta dominions. In the Archer type, the eastern *ma* is more common than the western; it occurs on two out of three coins in our hoard and on four out of seven coins in the B. M. In the Lyrist type, the larger coins use western *ma* with eastern *ha*; in the smaller type we have both the letters in the western form. In the Battle-axe type of Samudragupta, the eastern *ma* is common in that variety which has *Samudragupta* in the field; coins of the other varieties have usually the western *ma*. Out of 16 coins of Kācha in our hoard eight use the western and eight the eastern *ma*. In the B. M. collection of eight coins of this ruler, 5 use the western and three the eastern form of this letter. In the reign of Chandragupta II the eastern form of *ma* practically disappears. It is to be seen only in class I of the Chhatra type of this emperor, where it occurs on three out of five coins. On none of the remaining 980 coins of this emperor, does the eastern *ma* make its appearance.

§ 261. The other letters in the coin legends show a general

resemblance to their forms on the contemporary lithic records. Thus *a*, *ka* and *ra* have a long vertical; in rare cases do we see a tail developing only in the case of *ra*. The right hand limb of *ga* and *śa* is longer than the left hand one. *Ṇa* is bipartite and *na* has a loop in the lower limb. The lower limb of *ta* is usually a semicircle, which is sometimes not joined to the upper horizontal line. *Tha* is denoted by a circle opening on the right; *da* is also open to right. Both the limbs of *pa* are of equal height and *ba* is denoted by a square. The forms of *ma* have been already commented upon. *Ya* is generally tripartite, both its limbs being usually denoted by curves. From the reign of Kumāragupta I, however, we begin to get a *ya*, where the left limb becomes a straight line in continuation of the base line; see **Pl. XX. 8.** The subscript *ya* is bipartite. *Va* has usually a triangular base; the round base is rare both in its case as well as in the case of *ma*. On coins No. 43 and 58, **Pl. I. 15, Pl. II. 4,** belonging to the Standard type of Samudragupta, we see a round *va* along with the eastern form of *ma*. In the conjunct *vya* in the legend on the Tiger-slayer types of both Samudragupta and Kumāragupta I **(Pl. VI. 9-10; Pl. XXVII. 1-15)**, *va* is round in form. The same is the case with the conjunct *vyo* in the legend *Guptakulavyomaśaśī* occurring on one of the varieties of the Horseman type of Kumāragupta I; see **Pl. XXVIII. 11-15.** As already pointed out, the letters *sa* and *sha* do not show the eastern forms.

§ 262. Medial vowels display no peculiarities. *Ā* is usually denoted by a line slanting to right and attached to the letter at the top; in some rare cases, as in the name Kācha under the arm and *rūpākṛiti* on the Couch type of Chandragupta II, it is denoted by a short parallel line above the letter. Medial *i* is denoted by a short curve to left and *ī* by a similar curve to right. The latter, however, is frequently denoted by a curve open at the top, both its ends being curved. The form of medial *u* differs with the forms of the letters to which they are attached; in the case of *su*, it is a mere elongation of the vertical; in the case *gu* and *śu*, it is denoted by a high curve attached to the right of the right limb and opening upwards; in the case of *ku*, it is a curve open to the right and attached to the bottom of the vertical. Medial *e* is denoted by a slanting line to left at the head of the letter; an additional similar line slanting to right denotes medial *o*. Medial *ṛi* is denoted by a short slanting stroke to the left of the letter. Subscript *ra* is denoted by a tail or curve attached to the bottom of the letters like *ka* or *da*.

VII. Symbols

§ 263. The problem of the significance of the symbols occurring usually in the upper left quadrant of gold Gupta coins is difficult to solve. These symbols do not occur on copper or silver coins of this dynasty, nor do they occur in the above manner on any earlier series of indigenous coinage. We have to look to the foreign currencies of the north-west in order to understand the origin of these symbols. They first make their appearance on the coins of the Indo-Bactrians, where, however, they are clear monograms standing for the combination of easily distinguishable Greek letters like P, K, E, H etc. On the coins of the Indo-Parthian and Indo-Scythian rulers, Greek monograms continue, but are associated with the monograms of Kharoshṭhī letters as well. Kharoshṭhī monograms are usually single letters like *ka*, *śi*, *ti*, *mi*, *kha*, etc; they are rarely combinations of letters.

The correct and certain interpretation of these monograms on the Indo-Bactrian, Indo-Scythian and Indo-Parthian coins is not yet known to us; but it is generally agreed that the letters that can be clearly distinguished on them must be either the initial letters of the names of the cities, where the coins were issued, or of the mint-masters who issued them, or of the governors or generals, who were associated with the king in the administration.

§ 264. With the advent of the Kushāṇas, the monograms change their character. They cease to be combinations of Greek or Kharoshṭhī letters and appear to resemble decorative motifs or symbols. Thus on the coins of Soter Megas we have 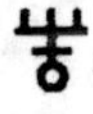, on the coins Wima Kadphises we have  and . These can hardly be regarded as combinations of Greek or Kharoshṭhī or Brāhmī letters. Wima Kadphises was a great devotee of Siva and Soter Megas was most probably his general; and so we can possibly interpret the three-pronged symbol as having a Shaivite significance. No such significance can, however, be suggested for his four-pronged symbol , which is continued by Kanishka.

Huvishka accepted this four-pronged symbol for his copper currency; but on his gold coins we see a new four-pronged symbol , though the old one also occasionally makes its appearance on a few pieces. The coins of Vāsudeva show a further modification of the above four-pronged symbol; its open triangle is now converted into a parallelogram. On the coins of the later Kushāṇas we see a further modification of the four-pronged symbol, which now assumes the form of . This symbol is one of the most common symbols that occurs on the coins of Chandragupta I and Samudragupta.

§ 265. We cannot suggest any definite significance to the symbols appearing on the Kushāṇa coins. But since usually, though not invariably, only one or two symbols appear on most of the coins of each ruler, we can say that each of them was to some extent associated with one particular king. It is very doubtful whether it had any religious bearing. A suitable religious significance obviously suggests itself with reference to the three-pronged symbol of Wima Kadphises. But none such can be offered about the four-pronged symbols appearing on the coins of Kanishka and Huvishka. For, we find the same symbol associated with the deities drawn from the Greek, Zorastrian, Vedic, Buddhist and Pauranic pantheons.

§ 266. Artistic variety was in the very life blood of the votaries of Fine Arts of the Gupta period, and it would have been a wonder if the Gupta mint-masters had confined themselves to the few symbols that had occurred on the Kushāṇa coins. They are soon seen discarding the symbols occurring on the coins of Kanishka, Huvishka and Vāsudeva. The four-pronged symbol 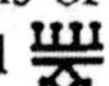 occurring on the coins of later Kushāṇa rulers like Kanishka III and Sita is continued by Chandragupta I, but he introduced several artistic variations in it like , 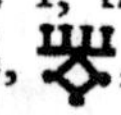, 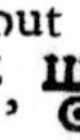, etc. A number of new and original symbols are also seen making their appearance, e. g. , , . The number of symbols on the coinage of Samudragupta is very much more numerous than that on the coins of his father, and the same is the case with the coinage of Chandragupta II.

§ 267. Can we assign any significance to these symbols ? It was to some extent possible to associate one symbol with one particular ruler in the case of the Kushāṇas; that is impossible in connection with the Guptas. Each one of the early great Gupta emperors had several symbols on his coins. Chandragupta I and Kācha had short reigns and small kingdoms, and yet they had not less than half a dozen symbols, some of which are continued by their successors. Symbols ,  and their variations occur on the coins of Chandragupta I, Kācha, Samudragupta, Chandragupta II and Kumāragupta I. The symbol  and its variations occur in all reigns except that of King Kācha. The three-pronged symbol , introduced by Samudragupta, continues in all subsequent reigns. We can hardly point to any symbol or group of symbols as characteristic of any particular reign.

§ 268. Smith has suggested that most probably the symbols had some religious significance.[1] This also does not appear to be the case. The goddess on lion on the coins of Chandragupta I and II is most probably Durgā, but the three-pronged symbol is but rarely to be seen on any of these coins. The Kārtikeya (Peacock) type coins of Kumāragupta I should have shown some Shaivite symbols; they, however, show no symbols at all. Chandragupta II was certainly a Vaishaṇva, but *chakra* (wheel) or *padma* (lotus) appears but rarely on his coins. The goddess standing on the fish or crocodile on the Tiger-slayer type of Samudragupta is most probably the river Gaṅgā. But no symbol whatsoever appears on the specimens of this type. There can be no doubt that the goddess, seated on lotus and carrying a lotus in her hand, who figures on the Archer type coins of Chandragupta II, is Lakshmī, but no symbol that can be connected with Vaishnavism appears on this type even in a single case. It is quite clear that the symbols are not connected either with the religious leanings of the emperors or with the deities that appear on their coins.

§ 269. Can we connect the symbols with mint-cities or mint-masters ? This also does not seem to be the case. The kingdom of Chandragupta I was a small one and his coinage was probably confined to a short period towards the end of his reign. And yet we find eight different symbols on his scanty

---

[1] *J. R. A. S.*, 1889, p. 33.

coinage. It is rather difficult to assume that Chandragupta I should have found it necessary to appoint eight mint-masters during the short period of his reign when his mints were active, or that he should have had eight mint-cities. It should further be noted that symbols like , , and persist through several successive reigns. The same mint masters could not be regarded as functioning over three or four generations. The theory of the symbols being connected with particular mint-cities is difficult to be proved, for there are no data to enable us to associate any particular symbol with any particular city. Nor are the findspots of the Gupta gold coins carefully noted; they are not usually disclosed by the dealers. Even if they were known, they would not be of much use; for gold coins travel over long distances unlike the copper ones. It is possible to argue that the symbol which occurs on twenty-two out of seventy-seven coins of the var. A of the Standard type coins of Samudragupta, may be the mint-mark of a city in the north-western part of the Gupta empire, where the present hoard was obviously collected. But we are not in a position to identify this mark with that of any city in particular in that region, supposing the coins had not travelled much further away from it; for there is nothing to help us in the matter.

§ 270. It appears most probable that the Gupta mint-masters regarded the four-pronged symbol they had inherited from the Kushāṇa prototype as merely a decorative element, which they were at liberty to diversify in any artistic or graceful way they liked. We cannot otherwise explain the great divergence in the symbols like , , , , , etc. During the reign of Samudragupta, six different types were introduced, each usually having several variations. The number of symbols also increased to more than double of what it was in the earlier reign. We do not, however, usually find any particular symbol associated with any particular variety. Thus the 77 coins of the variety A of the Standard type have about a dozen symbols. Several artists were engaged perhaps in different places to cut the dies and they had probably full freedom to introduce such artistic symbols as they liked. It is, however, quite likely that some of the rather peculiar symbols that occur only on the coinage of

Samudragupta may be associated with particular artists or cities. For instance, the symbol , which occurs on 12 coins of the Standard type and is nowhere to be seen on later coinage, may be the choice of a particular artist in a particular mint. Same is even more certainly the case with rare symbols like , , and , which appear on very few or solitary coins. The symbol , which appears on some coins of Chandragupta I and on five out of the 10 known specimens of the Tiger-slayer type of Samudragupta, may be the mint-mark of a paticular engraver. The complex symbol and its minor variations may quite possibly represent the artistic fancy of the engravers associated with a particular mint city of the empire. But we cannot be quite sure about the correctness of these conjectures; they are nothing but mere speculations.

§ 271. In the early Gupta period, symbols were certainly not connected with particular types or varieties. The coins of the Couch type of Chandragupta II are few. They show three distinctive varieties, and yet two of them, which alone have symbols, show the same common symbol, *viz.*, . So symbols did not vary with varieties in early times. Nor was any symbol characteristic of any particular type. We have only seven specimens of the rather rare Archer type of Samudragupta represented in the Bayana hoard and the British Museum, and yet they show two dissimilar symbols and . The few specimens of the Battle-axe type, however,show us only two varieties of the well-known four-pronged symbol, and , with their minor variations. But we cannot associate the symbols with this this type, for they are to be seen quite frequently on the Standard type as well. The forty one coins of the Archer type, throne reverse, of Chandragupta II show five different symbols. Variety B of the Archer type, Lotus reverse, of Chandragupta II has only 18 coins; but they have as many as five different symbols, *viz.*, , , , and . In variety D of this type there are only four coins and they show two different symbols and . Class I of the Chhatra type has only five coins and they show two symbols and . Forty-two coins of the Lion-slayertype of Chandragupta II have thirteen different symbols. This diversity in symbols on the coins of the same type and sometimes of the same variety can only be explained on the assumption that the die-cutters had more or less a free choice to accept an old symbol or to introduce a variation in it or to invent a new one according to their individual artistic fancy.

§ 272. The only exception to this conclusion with reference to the early Gupta coins would be the coins of Samudragupta of the small fabric of the Standard type, which are for the first time found in the Bayana hoard. All the 18 coins of this variety have the symbol ; it is quite possible to argue that they were minted at one centre only or by one and the same mint-master. But since we cannot make any such plausible suggestion about any other early type or variety, it is difficult to be certain about its correctness even in the case of this variety of the Standard type.

§ 273. It appears that sometimes in the reign of Chandragupta II, probably towards its close, it began to be felt that the number of symbols should be reduced and that they should, if possible, be associated with particular types or varieties. Only four out of the 82 coins of the Horseman type of this ruler have the four-pronged or four-dotted symbols, the rest have all three-pronged or three-dotted symbols. They, however, show seven different varieties.

§ 274. The Archer type was issued by Kumāragupta I in mass quantity; yet the symbols on it are not many. In class I most of the symbols used are three-pronged or three-dotted ones; only two coins (Nos. 1201 and 1203) have four dots or prongs at the top. In class II variety A of this type, all symbols are either three-pronged or three-dotted, and they show only two or three varieties. Variety B has a peculiar symbol of five or seven dots differently arranged, or or ; no other symbol occurs in it. Class three of this type has only two symbols, and .

§ 275. With the issue of the Horseman type of Kumāragupta I, the symbols begin to become scarce, and particular ones among them become confined to particular varieties of the different types. The symbol makes its appearance only on variety B of class II of the Horseman type. Here though we have 83 coins, they all show one and the same symbol . The varieties of the Lion-slayer type of this ruler have, as a rule, one peculiar symbol for each variety. Thus 19 coins of variety A, class II, with the legend *Sākshādiva narasiṁhaḥ* have one and the same symbol in our hoard; the coins of the varieties A and B of class I have either or .

§ 276. In the Tiger-slayer type of Kumāragupta I, we have two symbols and with their minor variations. The variety B has only the last symbol. In variety A both the symbols occur almost in equal numbers. The coins of the rather rare types of Kumāragupta I have one peculiar symbol each. Thus the Swordsman type of ten specimens has the symbol , the Rhinoceros-slayer type has , the Chhatra type has , as also the 'Apratigha' type. It is true that none of these symbols is peculiarly associated with one type only; thus is quite a common symbol. But it is worth noting that within each of the above types, its own symbol appears and none other.

§ 277. It may be passingly observed that diversity of symbols disappears with the diversity of types in the case of the coinage of the successors of Kumāragupta I. The coins of Skandagupta have only two symbols and , the latter occurring only once. The three-pronged symbol is the only symbol occurring on the coins of Ghaṭotkachagupta, Budhagupta and Kumāragupta II. The coins of Narasiṁhagupta have usually this same symbol, which is replaced by its cognate form in a few cases. The coins of Prakāśāditya show a unique and original symbol ; none other has been used on his coinage.

§ 278. On the later Kushāṇa coins there was only one symbol on the reverse. The early Gupta types, however, show in some cases two symbols, one in the upper left and the other in the upper right corner. Some coins of Chandragupta I, nearly 25 percent coins of the Standard type of Samudragupta and a few coins of his rare Archer type have two symbols. The practice, however, grows quite rare in later reigns; it can be seen only on a few coins of the variety E, class II, of the Horseman type of Kumāragupta I (**Pl. XXV. 14-15**).

It is not possible to suggest any intelligent reason for this practice of introducing an additional symbol on the right. The left side of the back of the throne was displaced by the symbol in every case; the idea of introducing a counter-balancing symbol on the right might have occurred, when the back of the throne began to be eliminated on the right side as well. In some cases this can be clearly proved, *e. g.*, **Pl. I. 1, II. 10**, etc. In several other cases, however, the additional symbol on the right is in addition to the back of the throne, *e. g.*, **Pl. I.11; II. 2, 5; III. 15**, etc.

§ 279. The symbols on the Kushāṇa coins occur usually on the reverse; on a few coins of Wima Kadphises, we get an additional symbol on the obverse as well. I have not so far seen any Gupta coin having a symbol on the obverse. Smith, however, has stated that coin No. 688 of the Bodleian collection is a Standard type coin of Samudragupta having 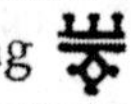 on the reverse and  on the obverse.[1] He further observes that the obverse symbol appears to be twice struck. It is probable that this obverse symbol, if it really exists, must be due to a mistake of the engraver.

§ 280. The usual place of the symbol is the upper left quadrant; sometimes it is shifted lower down to the middle, as on the coins of Kācha, on the single specimen of variety B of class III of the Archer type and on all the coins of the 'Apratigha' type of Kumāragupta I. The reason for this displacement of the symbol in all the above cases is the same. The object in the right hand of the goddess trespasses upon the usual place of the symbol, and so it had to be shifted to the centre, if it was not to be omitted altogether. It is only in rare cases that the symbol is shifted to the upper right quadrant. This occurs on the coins of Rhinoceros-slayer type of Kumāragupta I, where the parasol over the goddess' head displaced the symbol; it could not be shifted to the middle on the left owing to the engraving of the legend at that place, so it had been engraved in the upper right quadrant.

---

[1] *J. R. A. S.*, 1889, p. 30.

§ 281. Several engravers, however, preferred to drop the symbol altogether, when it became impossible to accommodate it at the usual place. Thus on the Tiger-slayer type of Samudragupta, **Pl. VI. 9-10**, we have no symbol, because the top of the crescent-banner usurps its place. On the Aśvamedha type coins both of Samudragupta and Kumāragupta I **(Pl. IV-Pl. V. 1-5, Pl. XXX. 9-12)**, there is no symbol, because its place is taken by the top of the *sūchi* in front of the standing queen. The pointed object in the right hand of the goddess on the single coin of the variety F, class II, of the Archer type of Chandragupta II **(Pl. XII. 10)**, rendered the inclusion of the symbol very difficult, and so it was dropped. Lotus in the right hand of the goddess effectively ousts the symbol in the case of (i) the variety A of the couch type of Chandragupta II, **(Pl. XVIII. 11)**, (ii) some of the coins of the Lion-slayer type of Chandragupta II **(Pl. XVIII. 5-6)**, (iii) the variety C of class I of the Lion-slayer type of Kumāragupta I **(Pl. XXVIII. 8-10)**, (iv) King-and-Queen type of Kumāragupta I **(Pl. XXXI. 14)** and (v) the Elephant-rider type of Kumāragupta I **(Pl. XXX. 1-3)**. In the case of the Elephant-rider-Lion-slayer type **(Pl. XXX. 1-4)** part of the legend on the reverse was accommodated in the left quadrant and so the symbol had to be dropped. The symbols had begun to lose their popularity in the reign of Kumāragupta I, and they occur on only one out of the seven varieties of his Horseman type. In the remaining six varieties of the type the lotus or the bunch of grapes in the hand of the goddess usually renders the inclusion of the symbol impossible. This difficulty, however, did not arise in the case of some individual coins of the different varieties of this type, e. g., **Pl. XXII. 11, 14, Pl. XXV. 7-8,10**, etc. Nevertheless symbols have been excluded from them, probably bacause not much importance was attached to them at this time. The omission of the symbol in the Lyrist type, variety A, of Samudragupta **(Pl. VI. 3-4)** is more difficult to understand. The place of the symbol is empty there; and it is accommodated in the variety B of this type. We can perhaps explain the absence of the symbol in variety A of this type as due to the personal dislike of the gifted artist, who was responsible for conceiving the device of this extremely graceful coin-type. Eight out of 30 coins of the class II of the Horseman type of Chandragupta II have no symbol. This omission is hard to explain, for the room of the symbol is empty and it is actually occupied by the symbol in the remaining specimens of this variety. Perhaps here also the personal dislike of the artist for the symbol was responsible for its exclusion in the case of the above coins.

§ 282. To conclude, the symbol was accepted by mint authorities on the Gupta gold coins as a decorative element from the Kushāṇa prototype. Even on the Kushāṇa coins, it was not a monogram, as it was on the earlier coinage of the Indo-Bactrians and Indo-Scythians. On the Kushāṇa coins, however, the symbols were very few, each king usually having only one or two. The Gupta mint-masters were swayed by the creative vein and decided to introduce as many artistic variations as possible. Each die-cutter was apparently given full freedom to exercise his own ingenuity, and as a consequence we have more than 90 different symbols on the Gupta coinage, as against six or seven figuring on the Kushāṇa coinage. In the beginning particular symbols were not, as a rule, confined to any particular type or variety. Even in so scarce a type as Archer type of Samudragupta we have several symbols. Later on in the days of Kumāragupta I, particular symbols very often began to be associated with particular types or its particular varieties.

§ 283. The Gupta artist felt that the proper place for the symbol was the upper left quadrant. If that place happened to be occupied by some indispensable and significant object like the flower in the hand of the goddess, the symbol was usually dispensed with. It is in rare cases like the coins of Kācha that we find the displaced symbol accommodated lower down on the left side. Only in rare cases, it was transferred to the upper right quadrant, as in the case of the coins of the Rhinoceros-slayer type **(Pl. XXX. 5-8)**.

With these preliminary observations, we shall proceed to describe and analyse the main symbols occurring on the coins of the different Gupta kings.

Chandragupta I

§ 284. Symbols occur on all the coins of Chandragupta I in our hoard. On their reverse there is usually only one symbol in the upper left quadrant, but there is an additional symbol 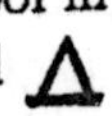

on the right side of coin No. 1. The symbols on the coins of this ruler are simple. The most common symbol is 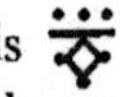; it is on coins Nos. 4, 6, 7 and 8. On coin No. 2, the parallelogram in the above symbol is replaced by a circle and the dots above the horizontal line are joined to it by short vertical lines. This symbol occurs on coin No. 3, but it is incomplete. The type for this symbol was not prepared through oversight; it will be  with three prongs above as on symbol  in stead of the four dots. The symbol on coin No. 1 is the most complicated one on the coins of this ruler; on it is .

The following are among the symbols on the coins of this ruler, not represented in our hoard:—

, , ,  and .

Samudragupta

Standard Type

§ 285. The Standard type is the most numerous type of Samudragupta, and naturally it shows a great variety of symbols. It shows all the symbols of Chandragupta I, except . Usually the coins have only one symbol on the left in the upper quadrant, but 30 out of 143 coins have an additional symbol on the right, which is usually smaller in size and simpler in composition.

Among the symbols in this type, the symbol  and its variations ,  and 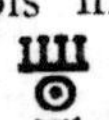 are most common. They occur on about 36 coins. The symbol  and its variations ,  and 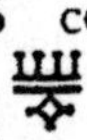 occur about 20 times. The symbol  is slightly less frequent. On some of the coins of this type in the British Museum, the pendant parallelogram of this symbol assumes a very flat shape on account of want of sufficient space; see Pl. II. 3 of *B. M. C. G. D.* Symbol , which becomes very common in later reigns, is seen occurring on all the eighteen coins of variety C of this type. This may suggest that all the coins of this variety were issued from the same mint. In variety E, symbol 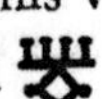 and its variation  are to be seen; on the coins in the *B. M. C. G. D.* of this variety symbol  is more common.

Among the rarer symbols occurring in this type are , , , , , , and . The symbol on coin No. 56 approaches the form of the symbols on the coins on Kācha.

The symbol does not occur in the Standard type. It is no doubt shown on one coin of this type in the *B. M. C. G. D.*, p. 2; but the illustration of this coin in Pl. I. 4 in the above *Catalogue* shows that its correct form is , but with three dots above in the place of three prongs.

Some coins of the Standard type show an additional symbol on the right. It is usually one of the following, *viz.*, , , or . The symbol , which occurs on one of the coins of this type in the *B. M. C. G. D.*, does not occur in our hoard.

OTHER TYPES OF SAMUDRAGUPTA

§ 286. In the Lyrist type, variety A, we do not find any symbols engraved. The coins of the variety B have two symbols and , the former being more common than the latter. The three coins of the Archer type have three different symbols, , and . The last symbol is incomplete. The first symbol occurs on all the four coins of this type in the *B. M. C. G. D.*; the coin in the White King Collection has the second of the above symbols. On the Battle-axe type only two symbols occur, and ; the former of these, which is more common than the latter, occurs in its varying forms like and . The specimens of this type in the *B. M. C. G. D.* have also these two symbols only. But some of them have a symbol on the right as well; no coin of this type in our hoard, however, has two symbols. Symbols do not occur on the Tiger-slayer type, the Aśvamedha type and the Lyrist type, variety A. The probable causes for their discontinuance on this type have been discussed above already (§ 281.)

Kācha

§ 287. Kācha has used five different symbols on his coins. Of these and its minor variations occur six times and occurs once only on the solitary coin of the variety B; both these symbols had occurred on the coins of Chandragupta I and Samudragupta. The remaining two symbols are new and they are remarkable for their complexity and gracefulness. The symbol occurs on eight coins. The second symbol is , and it occurs on one coin only. The symbol , which occurs on a solitary coin in the *B. M. C. G. D.*, Pl. II. 6, is not represented on the coins of our hoard.

The symbol on Kācha coins is engraved not in the upper left quadrant but in the centre of the left side. The reason is not difficult to understand. The flower in the hand of the goddess, facing left, usurps the usual place of the symbol, and so its place is shifted to the centre. It was probably felt that the disappearance of the symbol on the Aśvamedha and Tiger-slayer types, which was caused by the usurpation of the place of the symbol by the point of the *sūchi* or the standard, should be remedied by changing its place to the centre.

Chandragupta II

Archer Type

Class I

§ 288. In class I of the Archer type of Chandragupta II, the symbol with its different variations occurs 15 times, the symbol occurs seven times, the three-pronged symbols and are a little less frequent. The most artistic symbol in this type is , which occurs about eight times. This symbol seems to be a modification of , which was so common on the coins of Kācha.

Class II

§ 289. Class II of the Archer type with Lotus reverse has 757 coins and shows a large variety of symbols. In variety A of this class there are 700 coins, of which 616 have clear symbols. Out of these nearly 50% or 298 have the symbol . Its variety occurs 32 times. In fact symbols with three prongs or dots at the top are more common on this type than the symbols with four prongs or four dots. Among other more common symbols of the former type may be mentioned symbols , and , which occur 139, 36 and 24 times respectively.

Symbols and , though common elsewhere, are rather rare in this variety and occur 11 and 16 times only. Symbol occurs 14 times. We have a number of artistic varieties of the symbol with three dots at the top. Among these may be mentioned , and , which occur 24, 16 and 11 times respectively with minor variations. Among rarer artistic varieties of the three-dotted symbol may be mentioned , which occurs three times and , which occurs once only. Among other rare symbols may be mentioned , which occurs thrice, , and , which occur once. The last mentioned symbol may be due to the engraver's mistake as well; the slipping of the instrument may have given rise to the central line.

Symbols with four prongs or dots at the top are relatively less common, as pointed out already. Among these , which is rather rare in other classes and varieties, is the most common here and occurs 16 times. Symbol , which is quite common elsewhere, occurs only 13 times in this variety. Its variation occurs twice. Symbol and its variations are rather rare and are seen only on about eight coins. Among its artistic sub-varieties may be noticed , which occurs four times, which occurs eight times, and which occurs once. Among the rare symbols may be mentioned , and , each of which occurs once only.

§ 290. The variety B of the Archer type, class II, has only 18 coins, but shows seven different symbols. Of these is the most common; it occurs eight times. Others are mostly three-pronged or four-pronged symbols; of these occurs once and twice. In the variety C of this class, which has ten coins, symbol is very common. The four coins of variety D have the two symbols and , the former occurring thrice and the latter once. The single coin of the variety E, which has no *Chandra* under the arms, has the symbol . The variety F, which has *Chandragupta* on the reverse, shows no symbol at all, probably because the peaked object in the hand of the goddess is trespassing on its place. In the variety G, the symbol occurs on both the specimens; and in the variety H, it occurs on 13 out of 17 coins, the other symbols being and . The *B. M. C. G. D.* specimen of this variety has . On one coin of this variety we have two symbols, on the left and a group of four dots on the right. The four coins of the variety I, where the king holds the bow by the middle, show the symbols and ; the first occurs once and the last three times.

CHHATRA TYPE

§ 291. All the five coins of class I of this type have symbols with four constituents at the top; the same is the case with the coins of this class in *B. M. C. G. D.* Of these the symbol occurs on three coins, and and on one coin each. The variety A of class II having 16 coins has a number of artistic and complex symbols. Of these occurs four times, and occur two times and and occur once only. The two coins of variety B of this class show two symbols and .

In variety C of 17 coins, the most common symbol is . It occurs twelve times. The symbol occurs twice, and the symbol once.

In variety D of 16 coins, the most common symbol is ; it occurs about eight times. Its variation occurs thrice. The symbols and occur once each only.

On the solitary coin of the variety E, we have the symbol . The *B. M. C. G. D.* does not show any additional symbols in this type.

HORSEMAN TYPE

Class I

§ 292. In variety A, where the king has no weapons, all symbols have three elements at the top. The symbols and occur nine times each, and symbol occurs seven times. The artistic symbol occurs once only. In variety B of 13 coins, where the king is with sword, there are only two symbols; of these  occurs ten times and  three times. In variety c, there are only ten coins, but they show considerable variations in symbols. The symbol  occurs on three coins; symbols ,  and  occur once each.

Class II

§ 293. In variety A, eight coins out of 30 have no symbols. The reason is difficult to understand, as already explained before in § 281. The common symbol in this variety is , which occurs five times. Other symbols occurring here are , , , , ,  and 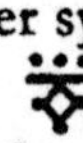. They occur once or twice only.

The symbols with four dots or prongs at the top are very rare in the Horseman type represented in the Bayana hoard. 50% of the coins in the *B. M. C. G. D.*, however, have symbols with four dots or prongs. Were they characteristic of any eastern mint which was perhaps poorly represented in the Bayana hoard?

Couch Type

§ 294. The Couch type, variety A, has no symbol, probably because the lotus in the hand of the goddess trespasses on its place. In varieties B and C we have the same symbol 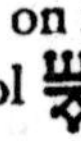, which also occurs on both the coins of this variety in the *B. M. C. G. D.* In variety B, the right hand of the goddess is empty and opened out, and in variety C, it is holding a noose hanging down. So the usual place of the symbol was available for its being engraved, which was not the case in variety A.

Lion-slayer Type

§ 295. The coins of this type have rather an unusual variety of symbols. We come across one unusual symbol on **Pl. XVII** 13, which appears to be . It is however likely that the symbol is incomplete. The three-dotted symbol 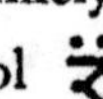 is most common; it occurs on 11 out of 42 coins. Symbols with 4 prongs or dots occur on 5 coins. Among interesting symbols of this class may be mentioned ,  and . Six coins of this type have no symbols. In most of these cases the goddess is facing left and holding a lotus in right hand, which occupies the place of the symbol. In a few cases, however, the place is empty, the goddess holding a noose. Some of the symbols occurring on the coins of this type included in the *B. M. C. G. D.* are not represented on the specimens in our hoard. They are , and .

In the Lion-slayer type coins of the Bayana hoard, coins with 4 dots or prongs at the top are very few; they are only 5 out of 42. In the British Museum collection, they are more numerous, being seven as against nine, which have three dots or prongs at the top.

Chakravikrama Type

§ 296. The symbol on the unique Chakravikrama type appears to be incomplete. It looks like , but may have been perhaps intended to be .

Kumāragupta I

Archer Type

Class I

§ 297. The symbols occurring in this class are not many. The three-pronged symbol shows two varieties; the most common among them is , which occurs 10 times. Its variation is rather rare and occurs once only. The symbol is very common; it occurs 34 times. Its variation occurs in four cases. The rather rare symbol occurs in two cases. The variation is very rare and occurs twice only. The symbol is the only four-headed symbol occurring in this variety and it occurs once only.

Class II

§ 298. In variety A, we have a few symbols only. The symbol is most common; it occurs 23 times. Symbols and occur three and five times respectively.

In varieties B and C, the most common symbol is with its variations and . No other symbol occurs in these two varieties. Whether , and are deliberate variations or whether they are due to the carelessness of the engraver, it is difficult to say.

Class III

§ 299. Class III has only two symbols and . Of these the former along with its variation occurs 19 times and the latter 3 times.

Lion-slayer Type

Class I

§ 300. There are few symbols in this class. In variety A of class I common symbols are and ; occurs once only. Variety B shows only. In variety C, we have no symbol and the solitary coin of variety D has the symbol .

Class II

§ 301. All the coins of variety A have the symbol except in one case, No. 1783, where the symbol is indistinct and may be . The coins of this variety in the *B. M. C. G. D.* also have usually the three-pronged symbol , the four-pronged one occurring in one case only. The variety B has the peculiar symbol on all its coins.

Horseman Type

§ 302. The coins of the Class I, varieties A, B, C, and D, have no symbols. The place of the symbol is usurped by the lotus in the right hand of the goddess facing left.

In class II, variety A, there is no symbol, its place being occupied by the twig from which the bunch of grapes is hanging down.

In variety B, a symbol has been introduced in its usual place. It consists of four dots separated by a vertical line having a dot at its top, two dots being on each side, . Sometimes the symbol is carelessly drawn and only four dots or the vertical line and some of the dots are visible.

In varieties C and D there is no symbol. A noose is hanging down from the right hand of the goddess. The usual place of the symbol is empty, but it is not engraved there. The reason for this is difficult to understand.

In variety E **(Pl. XXV. 11-15),** we have a rather unusual symbol consisting of a simple parallelogram without any horizontal line at its top. At first sight, it would appear as if the horizontal line has been crowded out for want of space, but a careful examination of the specimens shows that such is not the case. On three specimens of this variety, we have an additional symbol on the right; it is .

Swordsman Type

§ 303. A symbol regularly figures on the Swordsman type in the usual place. It is the common symbol . In one case the symbol has two instead of one horizontal line; this may be a mistake in engraving. The three specimens in the *B. M. C. G. D.* also have this very symbol, it being wrongly shown as 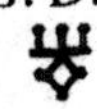 in the case of coin No. 202 in that *Catalogue*

Rhinoceros-slayer Type

§ 304. The Rhinoceros-slayer type shows one and the same symbol  on all its specimens.

Chhatra and 'Apratigha' Types

§ 305. The two coins of the Chhatra type, as also the eight specimens of the 'Apratigha' type, have the common symbol . In the case of the 'Apratigha' type, however, the symbol appears not in the upper left quadrant, but lower down at the centre.

Tiger-slayer Type

§ 306. Only two symbols occur on this type, the three-pronged and four-pronged ones 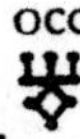 and 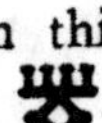. In variety A, the former occurs 14 times and the latter ten times. In variety B of three coins, however, only the symbol 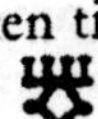 is seen to occur. As usual in some cases 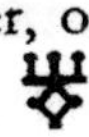 becomes indistinguishable from 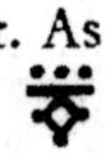 and 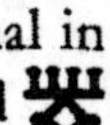 from .

The specimens of this type in the *B. M. C. G. D.* also have these two symbols, almost in equal proportion.

Types Without Symbols

§ 307. Several types of Kumāragupta have no symbols. They are the following ones.

King-and-Queen and Elephant-rider Types

These types show no symbol, because the flower in the hand of the queen or the goddess usurps its place.

Elephant-rider-Lion-slayer Type

In this type the legend on the reverse has been engraved on the left; and so there was no place for any symbol.

Aśvamedha Type

As in the case of the Aśvamedha type coins of Samudragupta, there is no symbol on the coins of this type of Kumāragupta I also. The reason is the same; the *sūchi* in front of the queen leaves no place for any symbol either at the top or at the centre.

Kārtikeya Type

The coins of the Kārtikeya type of our hoard, as also in the *B. M. C. G. D.*, show no symbol. This circumstance is rather inexplicable, for the place of that symbol is quite empty; no object in the hand of the goddess is occupying its place.

Symbols on the Coins of Later Gupta Kings

§ 308. For the sake of convenience and completeness we may review here the symbols occurring on the coins of the successors of Kumāragupta I. It is worth noting that like the coin-types, symbols also become few and monotonous with the later Gupta emperors. Only one symbol 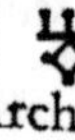 is seen to occur on the King-and-Lakshmī type and the Archer type of Skandagupta. This three-pronged symbol is the only symbol occurring on the coins of Ghaṭotkachagupta and Budhagupta. The coins of Narasiṁhagupta Bālāditya show this symbol along with the cognate one 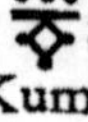; the latter, however, figures rather rarely. The coins of Kumāragupta II, the son of Narasiṁhagupta, usually show the three-pronged symbol . The coins of Prakāśāditya, whose identity is yet not known, introduce quite a new symbol like its type; it is  and it occurs uniformly on all his coins. The coins of Vishṇugupta Chandrāditya show a rather unexpected variety of unusual symbols. Besides the usual symbol , they show the unusual symbols  and . The last symbol occurs on one of the coins of the Lion-slayer type of Chandragupta II in the *B. M. C. G. D.* The only symbol occurring on the coins of Vainyagupta seems to be the usual one .

There are no symbols on the coins of Saśāṅka, Narendrāditya, Jayagupta, Vīrasena and Harigupta, who issued coins imitating the Gupta types, nor on the ancient imitations of the Gupta coins current in Bengal in the 7th and the 8th centuries.

VIII. Costume, Furniture and Weapons

§ 309. Gupta gold coins supply a rich material for the study of contemporary costumes, weapons, furniture and horse-accoutrement, which has not yet been properly studied. I therefore suggested to my friend, Dr. Motichandra, Director, Prince of Wales Museum, Bombay, who is a well known authority on Fine Arts in India, to kindly prepare a note on the subject for being included in this *Catalogue.* Dr. Motichandra not only kindly agreed to this suggestion, but also got the necessary drawings and sketches prepared under his personal supervision. I am very grateful to him for all this trouble. As this note will be of great use to the students of Numismatics and Fine Arts, I am including it in this section. I may add that though I generally agree with the views and conclusions set forth by Dr. Motichandra in this note, there are also some minor points of difference between us, as may be apparent in a few cases, if the reader carefully compares the description of some figures given in this note with their description in the body of the *Catalogue*.

§ 310. The Gupta period is not only distinguished for its political achievements, but also for its art, architecture and other spheres of material culture. To take an instance, the fashions in hair-dressing, costumes[1] and ornaments in this period

[1] For the study of costume in Gupta period, see Motichandra, *J.I.S.O.A.*, 1944, pp. 1-97; *Prāchīna Bhāratīya Veshabhūshā*, Chapter X.

show an artistic trend of mind which delighted in elegant innovations. The artistic arrangement of pleats and folds of *dhotī* and *sārī*, the graceful way of wearing *dupaṭṭā* and the carefully arranged knot's of *kamarband* testify that the people were not unaware of the aesthetics of dressing. Such was the importance of dressing properly that the art is indicated by five words in the *Amarakośa*, namely, *ākalpa*, *veśa*, *nepathya*, *pratikarma* and *prasādhana*.

§ 311. For the study of Indian costume in the Gupta period, besides the sculptures at Mathurā and Sāranāth and the paintings of Ajaṇṭā and Bāgh, there are a very large number of Gupta coins bearing the portraits of kings, queens and goddesses. A very significant fact in the costume of the kings is that they wear tunics and trousers like the Kushāṇa kings, though they also appear in purely national costume. The convenience and also the elegant cut of sewn garments must have appealed to the highly artistic but practical commonsense of the Guptas. This commonsense in the sphere of dress is also reflected in changing from heavy woollen material of the Kushāṇa costumes to thin and at times diaphanous material, which suited well with the climatic conditions of the Gangetic plain. The coarseness and heavy barbaric cut of the Kushāṇa garments gave place to elegance and finish. In this age the top-boots of the Kushāṇas also lost their heaviness and were reduced to the shape of modern riding boots.

§ 312. The introduction of sewn garments in India during the Kushāṇa period on an extensive scale influenced the costume of those who came in close contact with the court. The servants, both male and female, wore well-cut tunics and at times shorts. A minority of this class was probably of foreign origin, but the majority wearing sewn garments were Indians. It is interesting to note that the *Antagaḍadasāo*[1] mentions female foreign slaves wearing their own national costumes. These slaves serving in the palaces must have exercised certain influence on the costume of the servant class as a whole. The adoption of sewn garments by the horse-riders and a section of soldiers of the Gupta period also reveals Śaka influence.

§ 313. The common articles of wear in Gupta costume are *dhotī*, *dupaṭṭā*, *sārī* and *kamarband* worn in such a manner as to

[1] Translated by L. D. Barnett, pp. 28-29.

impart a peculiar grace to the wearer. The *Amarakośa*[1] mentions four synonyms for *dhotī* and five for *chādar*. In what way they differed from one another, it is difficult to say. The sewn garment of a woman is called *chola* and *kūrpāsaka*.[2] No further details are given, but *chola* seems to have been a tunic, and *kūrpāsaka*, also mentioned by Kālidāsa,[3] seems to have been a close-fitting bodice. Both of them appear on Gupta coins. *Chaṇḍātaka* seems to have been a sort of petti-coat. Women often wore *vaikakshya* passing across their chest. *Kañchuka*,[4] as an article of wear, is mentioned by Bāṇa, and it seems to have been the same as *chola*.

§ 314. The costume of a Gupta king is described in the *Mudrārākshasa* as a *vārabāṇa* decorated with the circles of pearls and jewels, tiara and the flower garland worn across the chest.[5] There is little doubt that *vārabāṇa* here is the same as the tunic with pointed ends appearing on Gupta coins. The circles on them indicate the decoration of pearls and jewels. According to Bāṇa the *dhotī*, which kings and men of status wore, had its one corner set in front a little below the navel; the pleated end was tucked behind and it was so girt up as to show a part of the thighs.[6] This method of wearing *dhotī* is common on the coin portraits.

§ 315. Soldiers, according to Bāṇa, wore tunic (*kañchuka*) and *vārabāṇa*. Their shanks were covered with trousers (*svasthaṅgaṇā*, Hindi *suthnā*), and they wore *chīnacholaka* over their tunics. We are further informed that these were made of *stāvaraka* decorated with pearls and sequins.[7] It is interesting to note that *stavaraka* here is derived from the Pahalavi *staur*. The *istabrak* of the Qurān is also the same. It was a thick cloth, apparently decorated with pearls and jewels.[8] It is possible that *vārabāṇa* appearing on Gupta coins was made of this material. Besides these the soldiers wore *chādar* (*āchchhādana-paṭa*).

---

[1] *Amarakośa*, II, 6, 117-18.
[2] *Ibid.*, II, 6, 118.
[3] *Ṛitusaṁhāra*, IV, 6; V, 8.
[4] *J.I.S.O.A.*, 1944, p. 16-17.
[5] *Mudrārākshasa*, ed. by K. T. Telang, pp. 129-30, Bombay, 1928.
[6] *J.I.S.O.A.*, 1944, p. 18.
[7] *Ibid.*, 18-20.
[8] Richard Jeffry, *Vocabulary of Foreign Words in Quran*, Baroda, 1938.

§ 316. Usually the kings on Gupta coins are shown wearing full boots decorated with buttons. On the authority of the *Bṛihat-Kalpasūtra-Bhāshya*[1] these boots could be identified with *khallakā*, *ardha-khallakā*, *khapusā* and *jaṅghā* types. The *ardha-khallakā* type covered half the leg, the *samasta-khallakā* covered the full leg; the *khapusā* covered the knees and the *jaṅghā* and *ardha-jaṅghā* covered either full or half thighs. Apparently these shoes had fasteners.[2] They were sewn or fastened with two, three or even more lines of sewing and fastenings.[3]

§ 317. An analysis of the costumes of the kings and queens and the goddesses reveals the following interesting details. Chandragupta I wears a helmet or close-fitting cap, which is usually beaded, and tunic with pointed ends with embroidered front or neck. At one place **(Pl. XXXVIII. 2)**, traces of oblique lines perhaps indicate fasteners. He either wears trousers or *dhotī*, with a pleated corner dangling between the legs, and boots reaching a little below the knees **(Pl. XXXVIII. 2)**. His tunic was often secured with a *kamarband* **(Pl. XXXVIII. 3)**.

§ 318. The dress of Samudragupta is more varied. In Archer type he either wears a beaded skull cap **(Pl. XXXVIII. 5)**, often decorated with streamers **(Pl. XXXIX. 14)**, which was hemispherical **(Pl. XXXVIII. 8)**, conical **(Pl. XXXVIII. 9)** or peacked **(Pl. XXXIX. 13)**. He usually wears the tunic with pointed ends secured by a *kamarband* or a belt. He wears trousers of *chuṛīdār* type **(Pl. XXXVIII. 5)**, trousers with pleats **(Pl. XXXVIII. 8)** and *shalwār* **(Pl. XXXIX. 13)**. He also wears *dhotī* in combination with the tunic and *dupaṭṭā*. The buttoned top boots are worn. In Lyrist type he merely wears a skull cap and a short *dhotī* **(Pl. XXXIX. 16)**.

In the Archer type he wears a turban, with a plaque, tight fitting tunic, *kamarband* and *dhotī* **(Pl. XXXIX. 17)**.

§ 319. Chandragupta II in his Archer type wears a skull cap with streamers **(Pl. XXXIX. 18)**, beaded conical cap **(Pl. XL. 19)**, tasselled cap **(Pl. XL. 21)** and beaded helmet **(Pl. XL. 23)**, tunic secured by a *kamarband*, *chūṛīdār* trousers, *shalwār* **(Pl. XL. 24)**, *dhotī* worn in various ways, sometimes

[1] Vol. IV, 3847.
[2] *Ib.*, 3851.
[3] *Ib.*, 3869.

pleated and its one end tucked behind and shorts (Pl. XL. 26).

In Horseman type Chandragupta II is shown wearing a tunic, *kamarband*, beaded cap with streamers, shorts, *dhotī* and trousers (Pl. XLI. 33-4).

In Chhatra type he wears a turban, the usual tunic with *kamarband*, shorts, *dhotī*, and *paryastaka* or decorative sash attached to *dhotī* (Pl. XLII. 35-36).

In Lion-slayer type, the dress appropriate to the occasion is simple. The king wears a flowered cap, light turban with a plaque, head-scarf, half-sleeved tunic without pointed ends, shorts, *dhotī*, *laṅgot* and *kamarband* (Pl. XLII. 37-42).

In Couch type the dress consists of hemispherical cap, *dupaṭṭā* and *dhotī* (Pl. LII. 43).

§ 320. Kumāragupta I in Archer type wears a beaded hemiphercical cap, light tiara, half-sleeved tunic, beaded at the neck, sleeves and front, its sweeping ends reaching the feet, *dhotī*, knickers, *kamarband*, a belt and shoes (Pl. XLIII. 43-49).

In Swordsman type he wears a half-sleeved tunic, belt and short *dhotī* (Pl. XLIII. 50.) In Chhatra type he wears a *dhotī* and *kamarband* (Pl. XLIII. 50).

Costume of Women.

§ 321. On the coins of Chandragupta I two types of women's costumes are shown. In one type the goddess Ardoxo wears what may be described as Śaka or Pānjābī tunic, *sārī*, *dupaṭṭā* and belt (Pl. XLIV. 52). Kumāradevī wears a veil[1], *dupaṭṭā*, bodice and long *sārī* (Pl. XLIV. 53-4).

In Standard and Aśvamedha types the goddess wears beaded veil,[1] bodice, tunic, *chādar*, *dupaṭṭā*, *paryastaka* and *sārī* (Pl. XLIV. 56-59). Dattadevī, queen of Samudragupta, wears a veil[1], *sārī* and *kamarband* (Pl. XLIV. 60). In Battle-axe type the goddess wears a *chadar*, bodice and *sārī* (Pl. XLIV. 61). In Lyrist type her dress consists of a bodice, *chādar* and *sārī* (Pl. XLV. 62). On the coins of Kācha she wears a bodice, *dupaṭṭā* and *chādar* (Pl. XLV. 63). In the Archer type of Chandragupta II, she wears a half-sleeved bodice, *sārī* and the zone (Pl. XLV. 64-5). In Horseman type as well, her costume consists of a bodice and *sārī*. In the Chhatra type she wears a bodice, spiralled headdress, *kamarband*, *dupaṭṭā*,

[1] I do not think that any veil in the sense of a thin piece of cloth covering the face is worn by any queen or goddess. A.S.A.

sārī with shorts underneath and the zone **(Pl. XLV. 67-9)**. In the Lion-slayer type she wears a bodice, *dupaṭṭa*, *kamarband*, and *sārī* **(Pl. XLV. 70)**.

§ 322. Certain interesting points emerge from the description of the costume of the Gupta kings described above. They wear usually a tunic with or without pointed ends. The former may be *vārabāṇa* of Sanskrit literature and the later *chola* or *kañchuka*. Such sewn garments also appear in Ajaṇṭā and Bāgh paintings,[1] though it is remarkable that kings in Ajaṇṭā paintings usually wear the national costume. It may be that as they represent the Bodhisattvas, the convention disallowed them wearing foreign costume. Similarly, soldiers wear trousers, but not the kings.

As shown above, the kings on Gupta coins are often shown wearing caps and helmets. Caps begin appearing in Indian art, though rarely, in the 2nd century B.C.[2], but in the first century B.C., with the appearance of the Śakas, they came in vogue.[3] In Gandhāra sculptures of the early centuries of the Christian era caps are fairly common.[4] In the art of Mathurā also caps are common.[5] By the second century A.D. caps reached as far south as Amarāvatī.[6] In Ajaṇṭā paintings kings frequently wear caps.[7] It is thus clear that the Guptas were introducing no novel feature in their costume while using caps. It is, however, strange that early Sanskrit literature has no word for caps. *Ṭopī* for caps first appears in the *Jasaharachariu* in the 10th century.[8] In the 11th century Kshemendra refers to an article of wear called *ṭippikam*,[9] which is possibly a cap. The *Ardha-ṭuppikā* of the *Samayamātṛikā*[10] is possibly the skull cap.

The Gupta kings are also shown wearing, though rarely, shorts or *jāṅghiā*. They appear in Ajaṇṭā paintings.[11] Perhaps they were designated as *ardhōrukas* worn by both men and women.

---

[1] *J.I.S.O.A.*, 1944, Figs. 30, 51, 52, 53, 55, etc.
[2] Motichandra, *Prāchīna Bhāratīya Veshabhūshā*, Fig. 48.
[3] *Ib.*, Figs. 83-89.
[4] *Ib.*, Figs. 155-159.
[5] *Ib.*, Figs. 194-200.
[6] *Ib.*, Figs. 248-249.
[7] *Ib.*, Figs. 296, 298, 299.
[8] I, 6, 4. Ed. by P. L. Vaidya, Poona, 1931.
[9] *Narmamālā*, I, 47.
[10] VIII, 55.
[11] *Prāchīna Bhāratīya Veshabhūshā*, Figs. 355, 374-380.

§ 323. There are some interesting points in the costume of the queens, who wear regularly full tunic or bodice. *Kañchuka* is a very ancient garment mentioned in Pālī literature.[1] It appears frequently in the terra-cotta figurines of the first century B.C. and in Gandhāra[2] and Mathurā[3] sculptures. It also appears at Ajaṇṭā.[4] The bodice known as *kūrpāsaka* seems to have been frequently worn at Ajaṇṭā.[5] On one coin **(Pl. XLV. 69)** the goddess is shown wearing what appears to be shorts or *ardhōruka*, also appearing at Ajaṇṭā.[6]

§ 324. Furniture and weapons do not call for any detailed remarks in this Introduction.

Detailed description of costumes, furniture and weapons, illustrated in **Pls. XXXVIII-XLVII.**, is given at the end of the *Catalogue*.

ADDENDUM

§325. In §§ 2-3 of the Introduction we have given information about the antiquity of Hullanpura and Nagla Chhela, in the vicinity of which the hoard was found, and of Bijayagadha, to which its owner probably belonged. We should as well say a few words about the antiquity of Bayaṇa, after which the hoard has been named for the sake of convenience. Bayana is only two miles from Bijayagadha, but its antiquity does not seem to be going back to the Gupta period, as is the case with that of the latter place. In the town of Bayana itself there is a mosque, which was originally a Jain temple. On one of the plasters of this building, there is a Sanskrit inscription, dated in *Saṁvat* 1100, in praise of a Jain teacher named Maheśvarasūri, who died in that year. This inscription shows that Śrīpatha was the ancient name of the city of Bayana. At another place in the town called Ukha-mandara, there is a second Sanskrit inscription, about a century earlier, which also refers to the place as Śrīpatha.[7] There is, however, no evidence to show that the antiquity of Śrīpatha is about five centuries earlier than this record. It is more likely that the owner

---

1 *Bhikkhunī Patimokkha*, IV, 40, 96.
2 *Prāchīna Bhāratīya Veshabhūshā*, Figs. 172, 173, 175, 176.
3 *Ib.*, Figs. 213-217.
4 *Ib.*, Figs. 385, 393, 397, 400, etc.
5 *Ib.*, Figs. 385, 408-09.
6 *Ib.*, Fig. 392.
7 *I.A.* XIV. pp. 8-10.

of our hoard was a citizen of Bijayagadha than that of Sripatha, whose antiquity cannot so far be proved to be of the Gupta age.

How the name Sripatha was changed into its modern form Bayana is not easy to guess. The town continued to bear its ancient name down to *Samvat* 1503, as is shown by a third Sanskrit inscription, found at the place and dated in that year.

Carlleyle's effort to connect the name of Bayana with Bāṇāsura is hardly convincing.[1] The same is the case with the following derivation suggested by Cunningham; 'Pathāyām-purī, I believe, to have been the original name of the place Bayana. For by the simple elision of '*th*', Payampuri or Bayanpur might easily be shortened into Bayana.'[2] No such name as Pathāyām-purī ever existed; it is simply a mistake due to misunderstanding the wrong locative expression *Srī-śrī-pathāyām puri*, occurring in the local metrical record.[3]

---

[1] *I.A.*, XV 23.9; *C. A. S. R.*, XX, p. 65.
[2] *C. A. S. R.*, VI. p. 41.
[3] *I. A.*, XIV, 10.

CHANDRAGUPTA I—10 COINS

King and Queen type : 10 coins

No.	Wt.[1]	Size[2]	Obverse	Reverse
			King standing l., usually nimbate, wearing close-fitting tailed coat, trousers, pearl-bordered head-dress, earrings, armlets and shoes, holding in l. hand a crescent-topped standard,[3] and offering with r. hand, bent and raised up, an object, which is a ring in some cases, and a bangle or a *sindūradānī* in others, to Kumāradevī, who stands before him facing r., usually nimbate, wearing a *sari*, and an upper garment, earrings, necklace, armlets and bangles. Usually a crescent between the heads of the king and queen. On the right, on either of the standard,	Goddess Ambikā (?), nimbate, wearing a *sari*, an upper garment across her shoulders, bangles, necklace and a circular pearl ornament round the head, seated facing on lion couchant to r. or to l. holding a *pāśa* (noose) in outstretched r. hand and a cornucopiae in l. resting on l. shoulder; the feet of the goddess usually rest on a circular mat with beaded or pearl border; behind her, traces of the back of the throne visible in some cases; border of dots all round. Symbol in the upper l. corner; but sometimes a second one also in the upper r. corner.

[1] Weight is always given in grains.
[2] Size is always given in inches.
[3] On some coins of this ruler, the standard is adorned with a fillet; see *B.M.C.G.D.*, Pl. III. 15. In our hoard there is no coin of this variety.

No.	Wt.	Size	Obverse	Reverse
			Cham चं *gu* गु *dra* द्र *pta* प्त or *Cha* च *gu* गु *ndra* न्द्र *pta* प्त[1] **Pl. XXXVII. 71** On the left behind the queen[3], *Srī-Kumāradevī* श्रीकुमारदेवी । **Pl. XXXIII. 2**	Legend on r., *Lichchhavayaḥ*[2]. लिच्छवयः । **Pl. XXXVI. 43**
1	117.6	.85	King and queen both not nimbate; no crescent between them. Trousers have decorative buttons in front right up to the waist; buttons of the coat are very clearly visible. Head-dress of the queen is clear. Standard has no fillet. The object offered is very small and is held between the thumb and the forefinger; it may possibly be a ring. *Cha* *ga* *ndra* *p*	Lion couchant to r. Back of the throne not visible. End of the *sari* passes over both the legs. Circular mat under the feet. Symbol on l, ,two rows of 4 dots touching each other; alternatively it may be Symbol on r, △ *Lichchhavayaḥ*. **Pl. I. 1.**

[1] Reference to plate after the legend in Devanāgarī gives a reference to Pl. XXXIII and following, where the legends are given in original Gupta characters.

[2] The variant spelling *Lichchhivayaḥ*, which occurs in some inscriptions and apparently on one coin (*J.R.A.S.*,) 1893, p. 94), is not to be seen on any coin in our hoard.

[3] There are three or four dots between the feet of the king and the queen on one coin published in *J.R.A.S.*, 1893, p. 95. We have no such coin in our hoard.

No.	Wt.	Size	Obverse	Reverse
			Sra-Kumāradeva. Normal condition.[1]	
2	121.3	.8	King and queen nimbate and no crescent between them. Object presented is not clear; it is clasped by all the fingers and its thick end is peeping above the thumb. It is most probably a *sindūradānī,* the handle of which is clasped in the closed fist and the top of which is peeping out side. Pearl ornament on the queen's head is partly visible. King wears leather boots reaching the knees. Crescent top of the banner is off. *Cha gu* *ndra pta* *Srī-Kumāradeva.* Normal condition.	Lion couchant to l. Folds of the *sari* between the legs of the goddess. No mat under her feet. Back of the throne slightly visible on r. Symbol on the l. a variation of  but with three vertical lines only; none on r. *Lichchhavayaḥ.* **Pl. I. 2.**
3	120.1	.75	King and queen nimbate and traces of crescent between them. Pearl ornament on the king's head is clear; he wears boots, as on No. 2.	Lion couchant to l. Back of the throne partly visible on r. *Sari* folds between two legs. No mat under feet.

[1] In the case of the coins of early rulers, the condition of the coin is often given to enable the reader to know whether it is the cause of any abnormality in weight.

No.	Wt.	Size	Obverse	Reverse
			Object offered by king is *sindūradānī* as on No. 2. Crescent top of the standard off. *Sra-Kumāradeva.* *Cha gu* *ndra pta* Normal condition; gold looks impure.	Symbol on l. or but incomplete; none on r. *. chchhavayaḥ.* **Pl. I. 3.**
4	120.4	.78	King and queen nimbate and crescent with a dot in the centre between them. King wears high shoes as on No. 2. Object offered to the queen is *sindūradānī* as on No. 2. Queen's hair tied in a knot behind the head; the upper garment is quite distinct. She wears no head-dress. Crescent top of the banner is clear. *Cha gu* *ndra pta* *Srī-Kumāradeva.* Normal condition.	Lion to l. *Sari* folds between two legs. Circular mat below the feet of the goddess. Symbol on l. roughly drawn; none on r. *. chchhavaya,* truncated. **Pl. I. 4.**
5	119.8	.7	King and queen nimbate; crescent between them. Object offered not clear. *Cha gu* *ndra pta*	Lion to r. Folds of the *sari* between legs. Symbol on l. , none on r. *Lachchhavayaḥ.* **Pl. I. 5.**

No.	Wt.	Size	Obverse	Reverse
			partly visible. *Śrī-Kumāradeva.*	
6	118.4	.85	Both king and queen nimbate and a crescent between them. The figure of Kumāradevī is blurred. The object offered to her clearly looks like a circular bangle held over the thumb. *Cha gu* *ndra pta* *Gupta* is only partly visible. *Śrī-Kumāradeva*, blurred and truncated. Normal condition; very yellow gold.	Lion to r. *Sari* end over both knees. Back of the throne clearly visible. Symbol on l., , roughly drawn; none on r. *Lachchhavayaḥ*. **Pl. I. 6.**
7	121	.8	King and queen both nimbate and a crescent between them. The object offered is not clear at all. King wears high shoes as on No. 2. *Cha gu* *ndra pta* Legend behind the queen blurred and truncated.	Lion to l. *Sari* folds between two legs. Mat below feet partly visible. A line to r. separating the legend from the goddess.[1] Symbol on l. , none on r. *Lachchhavaya*. **Pl. I. 7.**
8	120.8	.75	King and queen both nimbate and a crescent	Lion to l. Line separating the legend stops

[1] A comparison of this line with the back of the throne as visible on Pl. I.6 enables us to understand the genesis of the line, which is seen separating the goddess from the legend on several coins of later Gupta kings. It arose owing to a careless joining of the back of the throne to its leg; later on this joining was made straight and the line was retained even when there was no throne on the reverse as on the Lyrist type of Samudragupta.

No.	Wt.	Size	Obverse	Reverse
			between them; queen's hair tied in a knot on the head. Object offered to the queen is not clear. *Cha gu* *ndra pta* *Pta* is partly visible. *Sra-Kumāradava*, truncated.	half way and is surmounted by a loop. *Sari* folds between two legs. Symbol on l. , none on r. *Lachchhavaya*, truncated. **Pl. I. 8.**
9	120.7	.8	King and queen both nimbate and a crescent between them. Object offered is apparently held in the palm; its nature is not clear. *Cha gu* *ndra pta* *Gupta* is partly visible. *Sra-Kumāradeva* Normal condition.	Lion to l. *Sari* folds between two legs. No carpet under the feet of goddess. Symbol[1] on l. , none on r. *Lachchhavaya.* **Pl. I. 9.**
10	120	.75	Name of the queen almost off the flan. Object offered is not distinct. Crescent between the king and the queen. *Cha gu* *ndra pta* *. Ku. . . va.*[2]	Lion couchant to l. Throne not visible, but there is a line on the r., separating the legend from the goddess. Symbol on l.  or , none on r. *Lichchhavaya.* **Pl. I. 10.**

[1] The figure below the horizontal line of this symbol looks more like a circle than a parallelogram.

[2] The number of the dots given at the beginning or in the middle of a legend stands for the number of letters missing in it on the particular coin. The missing letters in a legend at its end are not indicated by dots; they can be ascertained by referring to the complete legend, as given at the beginning of each type or variety.

SAMUDRAGUPTA : 183 COINS

Standard type : 143 coins

Variety A : 77 coins

(Legend beginning at I and *Samudra* under left arm)

No.	Wt.	Size	Obverse	Reverse
			King standing l. nimbate, wearing coat, trousers, close-fitting cap, earrings and necklace, holding in l. hand standard adorned with fillet and offering oblations on altar by r. hand. In some cases the altar looks like a *Tulasīvṛindāvana* with a plant and oblations appear like round *puroḍāśas*.[1] Behind the altar is a *Garuḍa* standard adorned with fillets; it is sometimes away and afar from the r. hand, sometimes it is behind it. Beneath king's l. arm, written vertically, *Sa* स *mu* मु *dra.* द्र	Goddess Lakshmī, nimbate, seated facing on throne, wearing *sari*; upper garment (*dupaṭṭā*) covering both arms, circular pearl ornament round the head, earrings, necklace and armlets, holding a noose in r. hand out-stretched and a cornucopiae in the l. resting on l. shoulder; her feet rest on a circular mat; traces of the back of the throne on r. in most cases. The number of the legs of the throne visible varies from two to four. Border of dots. Symbol on left; sometimes on r. also. The legend *Parākramaḥ*

[1] *Puroḍāśa* was an oblation made of floor offered in Vedic sacrifices.

No.	Wt.	Size	Obverse	Reverse
			Circular legend beginning at I, *Samaraśatavitatavijayo jitaripurajito divaṁ jayati* समरशतविततविजयो जित-रिपुरजितो दिवं जयति । **Pl. XXXIII. 3** Metre, Upagīti.	पराक्रम: on the right, the 3rd letter being sometimes spelt as *kra* and sometimes as *kkra*. **Pl. XXXVI. 44.**
11	114.1	.8	Garuḍa standard away from the r. hand and without fillet. *Sa mu dra.* *Samaraśatavitata . jaya ..raparaja* Normal condition	Two legs of the throne are visible. Symbol  *Parākramaḥ.*
12	121.8	.83	Garuḍa standard behind the r. hand and without fillet. *Sa mu dra.* *Samaraśatava....ya jatara*	Four legs of the throne are visible. A line between the goddess and the legend. Symbol on l.  Symbol on r.  *Parākramaḥ.*
13	117	.77	*Sa mu dra.* *Samara*, in bold characters. Slightly worn.	Throne is crude and all its legs are visible. Symbol  Legend truncated.
14	116.8	.87	*Sa mu dra.* Legend blurred. Normal condition.	Two legs of the throne visible. Symbol  *Parākramaḥ.*

No.	Wt.	Size	Obverse	Reverse
15	120.7	.75	*Sa* *mu* *dra.* *Samaraśatavatata* Good condition.	All legs of the throne visible. *Sari* end is across both the legs. Symbol  *Parākramaḥ.*
16	120.8	.75	*Sa* *mu* *dra.* *Samaraśatavatatava* Good condition.	All legs of the throne visible. Symbol on l. incomplete, only the parallelogram and one horizontal line being visible; on r.  *Parākramaḥ.*
17	117.8	.83	Pearl border of the cap very clear. King wears waistband over the coat. One round *purodāśa* visible in hand. *Sa* *mu* *dra.* *Samaraśatavatatavajaya* *jata* truncated; last two letters on l. Good condition.	Two legs of the throne visible. Carpet below the feet. Symbol on l. ; it is carelessly executed, upper left side protruding above the lower left one. Symbol on r, 
18	116.1	.8	*Sa* *mu* *dra.* . . . . *jaya jatara* Good condition.	Two legs of the throne visible. Symbol on l. ; Symbol on r.  *Parākramaḥ* truncated.
19	113	.82	*Sa* *mu* *dra.* Circular legend blurred. Condition worn out.	Four legs of the throne visible. Symbol  *Parākramaḥ.*
20	117.1	.8	One round *purodāśa* visible.	Four legs of the throne visible.

No.	Wt.	Size	Obverse	Reverse
			Sa *mu* *dra.* *Samaraśatava*	Symbol Legend off the flan, traces of *kra* only being visible.
21	114.2	.92	*Sa* *mu* *dra.* *Samaraśa* A large and well preserved coin, but low in weight.	Four legs of the throne visible. Symbol *Parākramaḥ.*
22	120.1	.75	*Sa* *mu* *dra.* . . . . *raśatavatata.* Small coin but well preserved.	Two legs of the throne visible. Symbol The second line of the symbol is shortened owing to the noose coming too near it. *Parākra*
23	114.9	.8	Flan not well prepared; there are undulations on its surface. One round *puroḍāśa* visible in hand. *Sa* *mu* *dra.* Legend on l. blurred; *tara* on r. A well preserved coin.	Four legs of the throne visible. Symbol *Parākramaḥ.*
24	118	.78	*Sa* *mu* *dra.* *Samaraśatavatata.* *Ma* of *mu* is eastern.	Symbol *Parākramaḥ.* *Ma* is eastern.
25	120.8	.75	*Sa* *mu*	Three legs of the throne are visible.

No.	Wt.	Size	Obverse	Reverse
			dra. *Samaraśatava,* partly truncated.	Symbol off. *Parākramaḥ.*
26	111.6	.8	*Sa* *mu* *dra.* *Samaraśatavatatava,* in clear and bold letters. Very slightly worn out; low weight.	Two legs of the throne visible. Symbol, but incomplete. *Parākramaḥ.*
27	123	.75	*Sa* *mu* *dra.* (I) *Samaraśatavatata.* (VIII) *jaya ja*	Two legs of the throne visible. Symbol on l. Symbol on r., *Parākramaḥ.* **Pl. I. 11.**
28	114.9	.8	*Sa* *mu* *dra.* . . . . *jatarapa* A well preserved coin.	Four legs of the throne visible. Symbol but incomplete. *Parākramaḥ.* Letter *ma* is crammed for want of space.
29	121.8	.8	*Sa* *mu* *dra.* *Samaraśatavatata.jaya jata*	Symbol *Parākramaḥ.*
30	120.8	.88	*Sa* *mu* *dra.* *Samaraśatavatata.jaya jata*	Two legs of the throne visible. Symbol *Parākramaḥ.*
31	115.7	.89	*Sa*	Two legs of the

[1] Roman numerals I, VII, etc. preceding a part of the legend, refer to the places of these numbers on the dial of a clock, and are given to indicate the place where the particular part of the legend can be found on the coin.

No.	Wt.	Size	Obverse	Reverse
			mu *dra.* *Samaraśatavatata* Three cracks in the edge. A well preserved coin, large in size but low in weight.	throne visible. Symbol  *Parākramaḥ.*
32	115.8	.8	*Sa* *mu* *dra.* *Samaraśatava* Very slightly worn out.	Three legs of the throne visible. Symbol , but incomplete. *Parākramaḥ.*
33	114	.85	*Sa* *mu* *dra.* ......*tatavajaya jatara* Condition normal.	Two legs of the throne visible. Symbol , incomplete. *Parākramaḥ.*
34	115.2	.79	*Sa* *mu* *dra.* ....*jataripa* Legend blurred. Slightly worn.	Two legs of the throne visible. Symbol  Legend off the flan; the lower part of *kra* alone is visible.
35	118.3	.78	Flan had slipped while striking, giving rise to two *śa*s. Standard away from r. hand. One *puroḍāśa* is clear. *Sa* (half only) *Sa* *mu* *dra.* (II) *Samaraśata*...... (VIII) *jatarapu*; blurred and truncated. Normal condition.	All legs of the throne visible. Two pillows on either side of the goddess. Symbol on l. incomplete, but probably 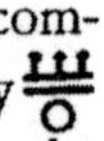 with a dot in the centre of the circle; the first vertical line is probably off the flan. *Parākramaḥ.* **Pl. I. 12.**

No.	Wt.	Size	Obverse	Reverse
36	115.2	.8	Standard behind r. hand and without fillet. *Sa* *mu* *dra.* *Samaraśatavata....* *jatara* A well preserved coin.	All legs of the throne visible. Symbol incomplete, but probably  *Parākramaḥ.*
37	115.8	.82	Standard away from r. hand. *Sa* *mu* *dra.* (I) *Samaraśatavatata* (VII)...*jataraparaja.* Letters on the left are truncated. Normal condition.	Two legs of the throne visible. Left hand of the goddess clearly visible under the cornucopiae. Symbol  *Parākramaḥ.* Pl. I. 13.
38	116.7	.8	*Sa* *mu* *dra.* *Samaraśatavatata..ya* *jatara.*	Two legs of the throne visible. Symbol 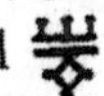 *Parākramaḥ.*
39	116.2	.78	*Sa* *mu* *dra.* *Samaraśata* Very slightly worn out.	Four legs of the throne visible. Symbol  *Parākramaḥ.*
40	121.6	.79	*Sa* *mu* (*dra.*) (II) *Samaraśa*...(VII) *tavijayo jita*; medial vowels are very clear.	Two legs of the throne visible. Symbol  on l. but carelessly drawn. Symbol on r.  *Parākramaḥ.* Pl. I. 14.

No.	Wt.	Size	Obverse	Reverse
41	118.4	.8	*Sa* *mu* *dra.* Circular legend off.	Two legs of the throne visible. Left hand resting on the waist. Symbol on l. Symbol on r. *Parākramaḥ.*
42	118.6	.8	*Sa* *mu* *dra.* *Samaraśatava* Very slightly worn.	Two legs of the throne visible, as also its back. Symbol *Parākramaḥ.*
43	119.7	.79	*Sa* *mu* *dra.* (I) *Samaraśatavatatava* Eastern variety *ma* and round *va.*	Four legs of the throne visible. Symbol but carelessly engraved. *Parākramaḥ.* *Pa* is round in form. **Pl. I. 15.**
44	114.7	.78	*Sa* *mu* . *.maraśata* Very slightly worn.	Three legs of the throne visible. Symbol or Legend off.
45	119.4	.75	*Sa* *mu* *dra.* Circular legend off.	Two legs of the throne visible. Symbol incomplete. *Parākramaḥ.*
46	116.8	.88	*Sa* *mu* *dra.* *Samaraśatava..... .tarapa* A large and well preserved coin.	Two legs of the throne visible. Symbol *Parākramaḥ.*
47	114.1	.8	*Sa* *mu* *dra.*	Two legs of the throne visible. Symbol

No.	Wt.	Size	Obverse	Reverse
			Circular legend fragmentary and blurred. Two cracks in the edge.	*Parākramaḥ* blurred.
48	108.4	.8	*Sa* *mu* *dra.* Circular legend off. A large and well preserved coin, remarkably low in weight.	R. hand of the goddess rests on the throne; only two of its legs visible. Symbol on the r., a variation of , the upper part being like that of ; symbol on l. . *Parākramaḥ.*
49	117	.84	Standard behind r. hand. *Sa* *mu* *dra.* *Samaraśatavata* Normal condition.	Two legs of the throne visible. Symbol 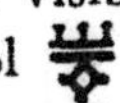 *Parākramaḥ.*
50	114.9	.85	*Sa* *mu* *dra.* *Samaraśatavitatavi* Somewhat worn.	Symbol on l.  Symbol on r.  *Parākramaḥ.*
51	116	.85	One *puroḍāśa* held between two fingers. *Sa* *mu* *dra.* (I) *Samaraśatavatata*	Two legs of the throne visible. Symbol on l. ; symbol on r.  *Parākramaḥ.* **Pl. II.** 1.
52	111.4	.85	*Garuḍa* on the standard is crude and turning its head towards the king.	Four legs of the throne visible. Symbol on l. a variation of 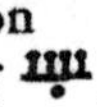, with

No.	Wt.	Size	Obverse	Reverse
			Sa *mu* *dra.* (I) . . . *śatavatatavaja.* (VIII) *jataripuraja* Very slightly worn.	two horizontal lines instead of one. Symbol on r.  *Parākramaḥ.* **Pl. II. 2.**
53	121	.84	*Sa* *mu* *dra.* *Samaraśatavatata* . . . *jatari* Slightly worn.	Four legs of the throne visible. Symbol on l. ; symbol on r.,  *Parākramaḥ*
54	116.4	.78	Standard behind r. hand. *Sa* *mu* . Normal condition.	Two legs of the throne visible. Symbol on r. 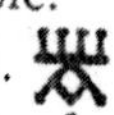; symbol on l.  *Parākramaḥ.*
55	100.4	.9	Two flames over the altar look like an upturned goad. Buttons of trousers clear. *Sa* *mu* *dra.* Circular legend blurred. Weight of the coin is remarkably low. Its condition is normal.	Two legs of the throne visible. Symbol  *Parākramaḥ.* **Pl. II. 3.**
56	115.6	.85	*Sa* *mu* *dra.* *Samaraśatavitata* . . . *.taripurajito*	Four legs of the throne visible. Symbol  *Parākramaḥ.*
57	114.3	.8	Round *puroḍāśa* in king's hand.	Four legs of the throne visible.

No.	Wt.	Size	Obverse	Reverse
			Sa *mu* *dra.* *Samaraśatavi* Normal condition.	Symbol on l. incomplete. Symbol on r. ⋏ *Parākramaḥ.*
58	116.6	.85	*Sa* *mu* *dra.* (I) *Samaraśatava.....* (VIII) *.taripurajito di* *Ma* is of eastern variety on both sides and *va* is round. There is a small loop above the right limb of *ta*, which makes it appear like a *śa* to some extent. Normal condition.	Four legs of the throne visible. Symbol  *Parākramaḥ.* Flan had slightly moved during striking giving rise to a double border at the top; symbol is also partly double-struck. **Pl. II.** 4.
59	116.3	.86	*Sa* *mu* *dra.* *Samaraśatavitata...* . *....jato* *divaṁ* Somewhat worn.	Two legs of the throne visible. Symbol on l. , on r. Δ *Parākramaḥ.*
60	112.9	.78	*Sa* *mu* *dra.* Circular legend blurred. Somewhat worn out.	Four legs of the throne visible. Symbol  *Parākramaḥ.*
61	119.7	.8	*Sa* *mu* *dra.* *.maraśata...vijaya* *jita* Slightly worn on the obverse.	Two legs of the throne visible. Symbol incomplete. *Parākramaḥ.*

No.	Wt.	Size	Obverse	Reverse
62	118.3	.86	*Sa* *mu* *dra.* *Samaraśatava* Normal condition.	Two legs of the throne visible. Symbol 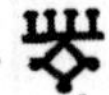 *Parākramaḥ.*
63	116.9	.85	*Sa* *mu* *dra.* Circular legend off the flan. Slightly worn out.	Two legs of the throne visible. Symbol  *Parākramaḥ.*
64	122.4	.75	*Sa* *mu* *dra.* . . . . *jito divaṁ ja* Normal condition.	Two legs of the throne visible. Symbol 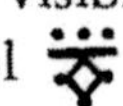 *Parākramaḥ.*
65	113.6	.85	*Sa* *mu* *dra.* Circular legend blurred. Two cracks in the edge. Coin worn out.	Two legs of the throne visible. Symbol on l.  Symbol on r.  *Parākramaḥ.*
66	116.2	.75	*Sa* *mu* *dra.* Circular legend blurred. Very slightly worn out on obverse only.	Two legs of the throne visible. Symbol on r. . Symbol on l.  *Parākramaḥ.*
67	118.4	.85	*Sa* *mu* *dra.* (I) *.maraśatavitatavaja* Slightly worn out	Four legs of the throne visible. Symbol on l. , but dots differently arranged. Symbol on r.  *Parākramaḥ.* **Pl. II. 5.**

No.	Wt.	Size	Obverse	Reverse
68	117.4	.8	*Sa* *mu* *dra.* *Samaraśatavata* Normal condition.	Four legs of the throne visible. Symbol *Parākramaḥ.*
69	116.3	.8	*Sa* *mu* *dra.* Circular legend blurred. One crack in the edge. Very slightly worn out.	Two legs of the throne visible. Symbol *Parākramaḥ.*
70	119.9	.8	The legend under the l. arm looks like *Chandra*, but it is really *Samudra*, *sa* being blurred, looks like *cha*, *mu* being joined to *dra* below looks like *ndra*. It is true that the posture of the king is somewhat different from his posture on other Standard type coins, but the coin is of Samudragupta, as shown by the reverse legend. (I) *Samaraśatavatatava-jaya*, blurred.	Two legs of the throne visible. Folds of the *sari* of the goddess are between her legs. Symbol *Paparakramaḥ*, the second *pa* being engraved by mistake. **Pl. II. 6.**
71	123.8	.82	*Sa* *mu* *dra.* Circular legend blurred. One crack in the edge.	Four legs of the throne visible. Symbol on l. Symbol on r. *Parākramaḥ.*

No.	Wt.	Size	Obverse	Reverse
			A large and well preserved coin.	
72	120.4	.74	As above but no crack. Flan surface not well dressed. Normal condition.	Four legs of the throne visible. Symbol  *Parākramaḥ.*
73	117.5	.8	*Sa* *mu* *dra.* (I) *Samaraśatavata*, very clearly engraved.	Two legs of the throne visible. Symbol  *Parākramaḥ.* **Pl. II. 7.**
74	119.6	.79	*Sa* *mu* *dra.* (I) *Samaraśatavatata* . . . . (VIII) *jata dava jayati* . . *Ti* is between the head of the king and Garuḍa. A well preserved coin.	Reverse side apparently double struck; hence the symbol, the throne and the legend are all blurred. Symbol blurred, probably  **Pl. II. 8.**
75	117.3	.79	One *puroḍāśa* visible in king's hand. *Sa* *mu* *dra.* . . *raśata* Normal condition.	Four legs of the throne visible. A line between the goddess and the legend. Symbol  *Parākramaḥ.*
76	121	.75	*Sa* *mu* *dra.* . . . . (VIII) *taraparajata dava jayata.* Letters are small but distinct. Normal condition.	Two legs of the throne visible. Symbol a variation of 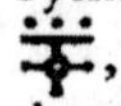, with two rows of three dots instead of one. *Parākramaḥ*, in small characters. **Pl. II. 9.**

No.	Wt.	Size	Obverse	Reverse
77	115.2	.78	*Sa* *mu* . *Samaraśatava.....* *jatarapurajata* Slightly worn out.	Four legs of the throne visible. Symbol The symbol is unusual, but its shape is distinct. *Parākramaḥ.*
78	118.1	.82	*Sa* *mu* *dra.* *Samaraśatavata...ya* *jatara* Normal condition.	Two legs of the throne visible. Symbol on l. Symbol on r. △ *Parākramaḥ.*
79	116	.85	Trousers lined with decorative buttons. *Sa* *mu* *dra.* (II) *Samaraśa* (VII) *tavatatavajaya* This is a clear case of the die itself not having the entire legend. Normal condition.	Two legs of the throne visible. Symbol on l. Symbol on r. △ *Parākramaḥ.* **Pl. II. 10.**
80	114.1	.8	*Sa* *mu* *dra.* *.maraśatavatata* Very slightly worn.	Four legs of the throne visible. Symbol *Parākramaḥ.*
81	117	.79	One *puroḍāśa* visible in king's hand. *Sa* *mu* *dra.* *Samaraśatavatata* Slightly worn.	Three legs of the throne visible. Symbol *Parākramaḥ.*

No.	Wt.	Size	Obverse	Reverse
82	118	.75	*Sa* *mu* *dra*. . *Samaraśata*. . *tavajaya* *jatara* Normal condition.	Two legs of the throne visible. Symbol 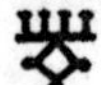 *Parākramaḥ*.
83	116.4	.85	Cap of the king is clearly discernible. The standard in the king's hand has a peculiar ornamentation in the middle, somewhat resembling that of the *sūchi* on the Aśvamedha coins of this ruler; see **Pl. V. 5.** *Sa* *mu* *dra*. (I). . *raśatavatata*; traces of letters on l. A large and well preserved coin.	Two legs of the throne visible. Symbol a variation of , but with two horizontal lines. Legend is blurred, but *Para* is clear. **Pl.II. 11.**
84	117.2	.78	*Sa* *mu* *dra*. . . *raśatavatata* Normal condition.	Four legs of the throne visible. Symbol on l. 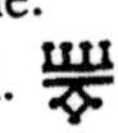 Symbol on r. Δ *Parākramaḥ*.
85	120.2	.83	*Sa* *mu* *dra*. *Samaraśatava*. . . . . *raja* Normal condition.	Two legs of the throne visible. R. elbow of the goddess rests on throne. Symbol 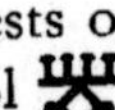 *Parākramaḥ*.
86	117.8	.83	*Sa* *mu*	Four legs of the throne visible.

No.	Wt.	Size	Obverse	Reverse
			dra. *Samaraśa* A well preserved coin.	Symbol incomplete. *Parākramaḥ.*
87	116.8	.9	Only the figure of the king is visible along with the standard in l. hand. Apparently with a view to convert this coin into bullion, it was first hammered and then cut into three pieces of which two only have been preserved, which when joined together, make the coin nearly but not entirely complete. The hammering has rendered both the sides very much blurred.	Reverse side completely blurred. Symbol indistinct. Faint traces of the legend.

Variety B : 16 coins

(As in variety A, but with a crescent on the obverse)

No.	Wt.	Size	Obverse	Reverse
88	115.3	.9	Standard behind r. hand and a crescent above it. *Sa* *mu* *dra.* *Samaraśata...... jatara* Slightly worn.	Two legs of the throne visible. Symbol *Parākramaḥ.*
89	100.7	.78	Crescent above standard partly visible. *Sa* *mu* *dra.* (1) *Samaraśatavata*	Two legs of the throne visible. Symbol *Parākramaḥ.*

No.	Wt.	Size	Obverse	Reverse
			(VII) *tavayaya jatarapura* Condition good; weight remarkably low.	
90	113.7	.84	Standard without fillet. King wears high boots, and the crescent is above his head. *Sa* *mu* *dra.* (I) *Samaraśama*(*ta*)-*vata* (VII) *tavajaya jatarapura* *Ma* is misengraved for *ta*. *Va* has round lower limb, and *ma* under arm is of the eastern variety on the obverse and of the western variety on the reverse.	Four legs and back of the throne visible. Symbol *Parākramaḥ.* **Pl. II. 12.**
91	117.8	.75	Crescent above the standard. *Sa* *mu* *dra.* *Samaraśatavatata. jayo.*	Two legs of the throne visible. Symbol *Parākramaḥ.*
92	116.5	.87	Faint traces of crescent above the standard. *Sa* *mu* *dra.* *Samaraśata.... jaya jatara*	Four legs of the throne visible. Symbol *Parākramaḥ.* Three cracks on the edge.
93	116.5	.83	Standard behind r. hand and a crescent above it.	Three legs of the throne visible, as also its back.

No.	Wt.	Size	Obverse	Reverse
			Sa *mu* *dra.* *Samaraśatavata* Somewhat worn.	Symbol *Parākramaḥ.*
94	114.3	.83	*Garuḍa* on the standard blurred owing to a defect in the die; crescent above it. No fillet attached to the standard in king's hand. *Sa* *mu* *dra.* (I) ..*raśata*...... ... (VIII) *pura jatara*; Letters are blurred and truncated. Coin fairly well preserved.	Four legs of the throne visible, as also its back. Symbol *Parākramaḥ.* Pl. II. 13.
95	118.5	.82	Standard without fillet behind r. hand and crescent above it. *Sa* *mu* *dra.* *Samaraśatavata*.... *jata* A well preserved coin.	Four legs of the throne visible. Symbol on l. Symbol on r. *Parākramaḥ.*
96	118.1	.8	Crescent above the standard. *Sa* *mu* *dra.* ....*rapu-* *rajata*	Three legs of the throne visible. Symbol *Parākramaḥ.*

No.	Wt.	Size	Obverse	Reverse
97	116.1	.88	Standard behind r. hand and crescent above it. *Sa* *mu* *dra.* *Samaraśatavitata .jaya* *jata* A large and slightly worn out coin.	Four legs and back of the throne visible. Symbol *Parākramaḥ.*
98	116.5	.9	Crescent above the standard. *Sa* *mu* *dra.* (I) *Samaraśatavatata . .* *ya* (IX) *jatarapu* *Pu* looks like *pta.* Very slightly worn.	Four legs and back of the throne visible. Five dots above the cornucopiae. Symbol *Parākramaḥ.* **Pl. II. 14.**
99	116.9	.8	Standard behind r. hand and crescent above it. *Sa* *mu* *dra.* *Samaraśatavatata .jaya ja* Normal condition.	Three legs of the throne visible. Symbol, but incomplete. *Parākramaḥ.*
100	113.5	.82	Crescent above the standard. *Sa* *mu* *dra.* *Samaraśa*	Two legs of the throne visible. Right hand of the goddess rests on the throne. Symbol *Parākramaḥ.*
101	116.1	.79	Crescent above the standard. *Sa* *mu*	Two legs of the throne visible. Symbol *(Pa)rākramaḥ.*

No.	Wt.	Size	Obverse	Reverse
			dra. *Samaraśata..... ..tara*	
102	117.3	.88	Crescent over king's head. *Sa* *mu* *dra.* (I) *Samaraśatavata...* (VII) *ya jatarapurajata dava* *Ma* in *mu* is of the western variety.	Four legs and back of the throne visible. Symbol , but central dot blurred. *Parākramaḥ.* *Ma* is of the eastern variety. **Pl. II. 15.**
103	116.4	.82	Crescent over king's head. *Sa* *mu* *dra.* Circular legend off the flan. Obverse side is double-struck ; we have two heads, two haloes, two *Garuḍadhvajas*, two altars and two groups of *puroḍāśas*. *Ma* is of the eastern variety both on the obverse and the reverse.	Four legs and back of the throne visible. Symbol  *Parākramaḥ.* **Pl. III. 1.**

Variety C : 18 coins

(Small and neat fabric)

No.	Wt.	Size	Obverse	Reverse
104	121.6	.72	King wears half-pant or short *sakachchha dhoti* along with leather boots. *Sa* *mu*	Two legs of the throne visible. Symbol  *Parākramaḥ*, truncated. **Pl. III. 2.**

No.	Wt.	Size	Obverse	Reverse
			dra, truncated. (I) . . *raśata* . . . . . . (VII) *jatara purajato divaṁ jaya* Letters on r. hand blurred and truncated; those on l. have clear medial vowel marks. Normal condition.	
105	120.2	.7	*Sa* *mu* *dra.* *Samaraśata* . . . . . . *jitaripu*	Two legs of the throne visible. Symbol , but incomplete. *Parākramaḥ.*
106	121.9	.75	King wears half-pant or short *sakachchha dhoti* along with leather boots. *Sa* *mu* *dra.* *Samaraśatavatatava* . . . . . . *rajata.* Normal condition.	Two legs of the throne visible. Folds of the *sari* between the legs. Symbol *Parākramaḥ.*
107	119.5	.75	*Sa* *mu* *dra.* *Samaraśatavitata* . . . . *taripurajito divaṁ ja* Normal condition.	This side is double-struck. Two legs of the throne visible. Symbol Folds of the *sari* between the legs. Legend blurred.
108	120.8	.75	*Sa* *mu* *dra.* . . . . *rajito diva* Normal condition.	Four legs of the throne visible. Symbol *Parākramaḥ.*

No.	Wt.	Size	Obverse	Reverse
109	121	.78	King wears long *sakachchha dhoti.* *Sa* *mu* *dra.* . . . .*to* *divaṁ ja* Normal condition.	Two legs of the throne visible. Folds of the *sari* between the legs. Symbol *Parākramaḥ.*
110	119.5	.72	King wears short *sakachchha dhoti* with leather boots. *Sa* *mu* *dra,* truncated. (I) *Samaraśatavatata...* (VIII) . .*raparajato* *divaṁ jayati.* Letters *jayati* are above Garuḍa and rather compressed for want of space.	Two legs of the throne visible. Part of Goddess' head truncated. Symbol *Parākramaḥ.* **Pl. III. 3.**
111	119.3	.75	*Sa* *mu* *dra.* . . . *śatavitatavaja.* . .*rapara* Normal condition	Two legs of the throne visible. Symbol *Parākramaḥ.*
112	120	.73	*Sa* *mu* *dra.* *Samaraśatavatata*... ... *parajata.*	Two legs of the throne visible. Symbol *Parākramaḥ.*
113	119.6	.72	King's leather boots are prominent and he is wearing *sakachchha dhoti.* *Sa* *mu*	Two legs of the throne visible. Symbol , though it look like *Parākramaḥ.*

No.	Wt.	Size	Obverse	Reverse
			dra. . . . . (VII) *jato divaṁ . . ti.* Letter *ti* is clear; it is between Garuḍa and the king's head, *jaya* is crowded out by the bird's head.	Note the doubling of *k* in *kkra* **Pl. III. 4.**
114	119.8	.78	King wears *sakachchha dhoti.* *Sa* *mu* *dra.* *Sa. . . . .* *rajito di. jayata.* Normal condition.	Two legs of the throne visible. Symbol *Parākramaḥ.*
115	121.3	.7	*Sa* *mu* *dra.* *Sa. . . . .* *jatarapurajito divaṁ ja* Normal condition.	Two legs of the throne visible. Folds of the *sari* between the legs. Symbol *Parākramaḥ.*
116	119.1	.7	King wears *saka-chchha dhoti.* *Sa* *mu* *dra.* . . . . *.tara.* *rajata dava* Normal condition.	Two legs of the throne visible. Symbol *Parākramaḥ.*
117	119.8	.78	King's hair tied in a knot at the top of the head. *Sa* *mu* *dra.* (I) *Samaraśatavitata*	Two legs of the throne visible. Symbol *Parākramaḥ.* **Pl. III. 5.**

No.	Wt.	Size	Obverse	Reverse
			(VIII) *purajata dava ja* Letters on the left are truncated.	
118	118	·79	*Sa* *mu* *dra.* *Samaraśatavatatavaja.* . . . . . .*ta divaṁ* Coin slightly truncated at the top, apparently to adjust weight.	Two legs of the throne visible. Symbol *Parākramaḥ.*
119	121.6	·79	King wears *sakachchha dhoti*. His hair is tied in a knot on the head. *Sa* *mu* *dra.* (I) *Samaraśatavatata*. . . . . (VIII) *rapurajito divaṁ jayati.* Normal condition.	Two legs of the throne visible. Symbol *Parākramaḥ.* Subscript of *kra* is covered by the cornucopiae. **Pl. III. 6.**
120	118.2	·71	*Sa* *mu* *dra.* . . . .*ta dava jayati.* Somewhat worn.	Two legs of the throne visible. Symbol *Parākramaḥ.*
121	121.6	·75	Coin is poor in execution; king's figure is rather tall and crude; he is wearing *sakachchha dhoti* with leather boots. Garuḍa standard behind r. hand, and the fillet is tied to it in a peculiar manner.	Throne is rather narrow and high-backed. Symbol *Parākra* **Pl. III. 7.**

No.	Wt.	Size	Obverse	Reverse
			Sa *mu* *dra.* Circular legend quite blurred; traces of a few letters only.	

Variety D : 25 coins

(Legend beginning on l. at VIII)

No.	Wt.	Size	Obverse	Reverse
122	116.4	.84	*Sa* *mu* *dra.* *Samaraśatavata* Slightly worn.	Two legs of the throne visible. Symbol *Parākramaḥ.*
123	117.6	.8	King's trousers have ornamental buttons right up to the waist. Garuḍa standard is adorned with a fillet. *Sa* *mu* *dra.* (VIII) *.marasatavitata* (I) *vajaya* Last four letters are truncated. *Ma* is of the eastern variety both on the obverse and reverse. Normal condition.	Two legs of the throne visible. Symbol on l. Symbol on r. Δ *Parākramaḥ.* **Pl. III. 8.**
124	114.6	.8	*Sa* *mu* *dra.* *.mara....tavajaya ja* Normal condition.	Four legs of the throne visible. Symbol on l. Symbol on r. Δ *Parākramaḥ.*
125	116.3	.79	*Sa* *mu*	Two legs of the throne visible.

No.	Wt.	Size	Obverse	Reverse
			dra. . . . .*rajata* Normal condition.	Symbol  *Parākramaḥ.*
126	117.4	.8	*Sa* *mu* *dra.* . .*raśatavatatavaja* Coin slightly cut at the top to adjust weight.	Two legs of the throne visible. Symbol  *Parākramaḥ.*
127	118.3	.85	*Sa* *mu* *dra.* . . . . .*vatatavaja* Slightly worn.	Two legs of the throne visible. Symbol  *Parākramaḥ.*
128	113.2	.8	*Sa* *mu* *dra.* *.maraśatavatatavajaya* Somewhat worn out.	Two legs of the throne visible. Symbol  *Parākramaḥ.*
129	111.5	.8	*Sa* *mu* . *Samaraśatava* Normal condition.	Two legs of the throne visible. Symbol  *Parākramaḥ.*
130	119.4	.8	*Sa* *mu* *dra.* *.maraśata.tatavajaya* Normal condition.	Two legs of the throne visible. Symbol a variation of 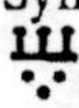 having two horizontal lines. *Parākramaḥ.*
131	117.2	.83	Buttons or bosses of the trousers right up to the waist. *Sa* *mu* *dra.*	Two legs of the throne visible. Left arm akimbo. Symbol a variation of 

No.	Wt.	Size	Obverse	Reverse
			(VIII) *.maraśatavata-* (I) *tavajaya ja*	*Parākramaḥ.* *Ma* of the eastern variety. **Pl. III. 9.**
132	121.4	.85	*Sa* *mu* *dra.* *.maraśatavi..jaya* Normal condition	Four legs of the throne visible Symbol on l. , symbol on r. Δ *Parākramaḥ.*
133	117.6	.85	Trouser buttons right up to the waist. *Sa* *mu* *dra.* (VIII) *.maraśatavata* (I) *ta vajaya* The legend was not completed on the die. Normal condition.	Two legs of the throne visible. Symbol on l. , symbol on r. Δ *Parākramaḥ.* **Pl. III. 10.**
134	115.3	.84	*Sa* *mu* *dra.* *.maraśatavatatavajaya* *jatara* Very slightly worn.	Two legs of the throne visible. Symbol 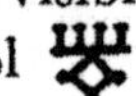 *Parākramaḥ.*
135	116	.88	Altar is crudely engraved. *Sa* *mu* *dra.* *.maraśatavatata* Good condition.	Four legs of the throne visible. Symbol 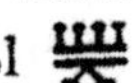 *Parākramaḥ.*
136	116.2	.78	*Sa* *mu* *dra.* ....*vijaya jatara* Normal condition.	Four legs of the throne visible. Symbol blurred. *Parākramaḥ.*

No.	Wt.	Size	Obverse	Reverse
137	122.6	.75	*Sa* *mu* *dra.* . . . . . .*tatavajaya .ta* Normal condition.	Four legs of the throne visible. Symbol incomplete; it may be either or *Parākramaḥ.*
138	110.9	.83	Standard away from r. hand. *Sa* *mu* *dra.* (VII) *Samaraśatavatata* . . (II) *ya jata* Last three letters are truncated. Good condition; abnormally low weight.	Four legs of the throne visible. Symbol but incomplete and blurred. *Parākramaḥ.* **Pl. III. 11.**
139	117.8	.9	*Sa* *mu* *dra.* *Samaraśatavatatavaja-ya jata.* Good condition.	Two legs of the throne visible. Goddess sitting cross-legged. Symbol on l. , symbol on r. *Parākramaḥ.*
140	114.6	.79	*Sa* *mu* *dra.* . . . .*tavajayo jata* Normal condition.	Four legs of the throne visible. Symbol *Parākramaḥ.*
141	114.5	.79	*Sa* *mu* *dra.* . . . .*vajaya jata* Very slightly worn.	Two legs of the throne visible. Symbol on l. , symbol on r. *Parākramaḥ.*
142	119.4	.9	*Sa* *mu* *dra.*	Two legs of the throne visible. Symbol

No.	Wt.	Size	Obverse	Reverse
			(VII) *Samaraśatavata-* (II) *tavajaya ja* Western variety of *ma* on the obverse. One crack in the edge at III. Normal condition.	*Parākramaḥ.* Eastern variety of *ma* on the reverse. **Pl. III. 12.**
143	113.5	.75	*Sa* *mu* *dra.* *...śatavatata* Legend begins at VI and not at VIII as on the other coins of this class. Normal condition.	Two legs of the throne visible. Symbol on l. , symbol on r.  *Parākramaḥ.*
144	116.3	.8	*Sa* *mu* *dra.* *..raśatavatatavajaya jata* Normal condition	Four legs of the throne visible. Symbol on l. , symbol on r.  *Parākramaḥ.*
145	119.5	.88	*Sa* *mu* *dra.* *Samaraśatavatavajayo jata*	Two legs of the throne visible. Symbol 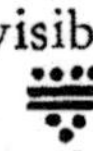 *Parākramaḥ.*
146	119	.82	*Sa* *mu* *dra.* *.maraśatavatata...* *...pura*	Four legs of the throne visible, as also its back. Symbol  *Parākramaḥ.*

Variety E : 7 coins

(*Samudragupta* in the field; legend begins at VIII)

No.	Wt.	Size	Obverse	Reverse
147	116.9	.81	*Sa* *gu* *mu* *pta.* *dra* *Samaraśatavatatava.ya*	Two legs of the throne visible. Symbol on l. , symbol on r. 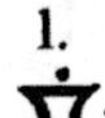.

No.	Wt.	Size	Obverse	Reverse
			jatarapara Normal condition.	*Parākramaḥ.*
148	115.9	.79	*Sa gu* *mu ptaḥ.* *dra* *Samaraśatavi* Eastern variety of *ma.*	Two legs of the throne visible. Symbol  *Parākramaḥ.*
149	115.9	.77	*Sa gu* *mu ptaḥ.* *dra* *Samaraśatavi* Eastern variety of *ma.*	Western variety of *ma.* Two legs of the throne visible, as also its back. Symbol  *Parākramaḥ.*
150	107.6	.79	Standard in the king's hand has a thick flat top like a sceptre. What king wears may be either a half-pant or a short *sakachchha dhoti.* *Sa gu* *mu pta.* *dra* Only faint traces of circular legend.	Two legs of the throne visible. Symbol 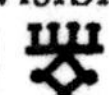 *Parākramaḥ* *Ma* is of the western variety on the reverse and of the eastern variety on the obverse. **Pl. III. 13.**
151	118	.84	King wears trousers. *Sa gu* *mu pta.* *dra* (VII). *maraśata.* (I) *tatavijaya* *Mu* is of the eastern variety. Slightly worn on the obverse.	Two high legs of the throne visible. The r. hand of the goddess rests on the throne. Symbol 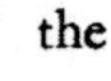 *Parākramaḥ.* *Ma* of the western variety. **Pl. III. 14.**
152	121.2	.75	*Sa gu* *mu pta.* *dra*	Two legs of the throne visible.

No.	Wt.	Size	Obverse	Reverse
			.... *jitaripurajito divaṁ* Normal condition.	Symbol  *Parākramaḥ.* *Ma* is of the eastern variety, both on the obverse and reverse.
153	114.8	.79	*Sa gu mu pta.* . ...*tatavajayo jatara* Legend on the left is almost off the flan. Die was misadjusted on the flan, leaving a considerable part blank at the top. As a consequence, lower part is off the flan. Slightly worn.	Two legs of the throne visible. Symbol on l. , symbol on r.  *Parākramaḥ.* **Pl. III. 15.**

The Aśvamedha type : 20 coins

No.	Wt.	Size	Obverse	Reverse
			Uncaparisoned horse, sometimes with a neck-strap-standing to l. on a *vedī* or low platform before a *yūpa* (sacrificial post), slightly bent in the centre and at the top with one *chashāla* at its end, which being narrow in the centre looks like two contiguous rings in several cases. *Yūpa* has an ornamental pedestal in two or three steps; a *raśanā* (string) is	Crowned queen, usually nimbate, standing l., wearing ear-rings, necklace, bangles, *kañchukī*, *sari*, headdress and an upper garment in some cases, holding in r. hand a *chauri* over r. shoulder and in l. hand a towel hanging by her side. A bead-bordered mat or lotus under the feet of the queen. Sacrificial *sūchī* (a spear-like-pointed ob-

No.	Wt.	Size	Obverse	Reverse
			tied at its centre, its two ends being sometimes on the same and sometimes on opposite sides. A pennon flies from the *yūpa* top over the horse. The mane of the horse is plaited with a string of golden beads, but in some cases another string of beads is shown over the back of the horse and separated from it. There is a crescent above the haunch of the horse in some cases. Letter *si* is under the horse, probably standing for *siddham*. In rare cases, there is a small *vedikā* (platform) under the letter *si* and above the larger platform. Under the platform of the horse there is an ornamental border made of transverse lines, extending upto the edge of the coin; sometimes, however, this border consists of dots. Circular legend begins sometimes near the head of the horse, sometimes near the	ject) before the queen usually adorned with a fillet. Dotted border all round. No symbol. Legend on r., *Aśvamedhaparākramaḥ*. अश्वमेधपराक्रमः । **Pl. XXXVI. 45.**

No.	Wt.	Size	Obverse	Reverse
			base of the *yūpa* and sometimes near the hind legs of the horse. It reads:— *Rājādhirājaḥ prithivī-mavitvā divaṁ jayatyāh-ṛitavājimedhaḥ.* राजाधिराजः पृथिवीमवित्वा दिवं जयत्याहृतवाजिमेधः । **Pl. XXXIII. 4.** Metre, Upagīti. On one coin, No. 169, the legend seems to be राजाधिराजः पृथिवीं विजित्य दिवं जयत्याहृतवाजिमेधः । **Pl. XXXIII. 5.**	
154	115.1	.9	Base of *yūpa* is two-stepped. No string of beads above the horse. One end of the *raśanā* falls behind the *yūpa* on l. and the other under the horse's neck. *Chashāla* is not visible. Neck strap is absent. Crescent above the haunch of the horse. Legend beginning at I, *Rajadharajapṛi*...... ..(IX) *tyāhṛita* Slightly worn.	Towel in the l. hand clear. The *sūchi* is divided into three parts by two circular ornamentations. *Aśvamedhaparākramaḥ.* **Pl. IV. 1.**
155	114.5	.87	The upper bent end of the *yūpa* distinctly visible, as also its *chashāla*, very narrow in the centre. The ends of the *raśanā* tied at	*Sūchi* before the queen divided into two parts by the circular ornamentation rather low on it. Circular mat is

No.	Wt.	Size	Obverse	Reverse
			the centre of the *yūpa* are falling behind it on left. No string of beads above the horse; but beads are apparently plaited in its mane. Under the horse between its legs there is a low *vedikā* or pedestal; under it the platform below which are small slanting lines. Legend, beginning at I, *Rājādhirājaḥ pritha-vamava* Slightly worn.	treated like a lotus. *.śvamedhaparākramaḥ.* **Pl. IV. 2.**
156	118	.83	*Chashāla* of the *yūpa* just visible above the head of the horse. Crescent over the haunch of the horse. Below the platform of the horse are remnants of a dotted border. Legend is blurred; it begins at I; *Raja* Letters only worn out; coin in normal condition.	Queen is not nimbate and she wears a crest ornament on the forehead. No towel visible in the queen's l. hand. One fillet on either side of the *sūchi*, which has three small circular rings near the top. *Aśvamedhaparākramaḥ.* **Pl. IV. 3.**
157	114.8	.8	Pedestal of the *yūpa* is simple; there is the dotted line above the horse. The ends of the *raśanā* fall on either side of the *yūpa*.	Queen stands on a carpet and holds the towel in the l. hand. *Sūchi* has three circular attachments in its upper half;

No.	Wt.	Size	Obverse	Reverse
			Chashāla not visible. Traces of dotted border below the platform of the horse. Legend beginning at I, *Rājādharāja prithavamavatva dava jaya.* Most of the letters are truncated and blurred. Coin slightly worn out.	there is a fillet on its either side. Carpet under the queen's feet. *Aśvamadhaparakra* **Pl. IV. 4.**
158	115.1	.8	Crescent on the haunch of the horse. String of beads is blurred. *Yūpa* is partially visible; its pedestal is simple but in two steps; *chashāla* is just visible at the end of the *yūpa*. Slanting lines prominent under the platform of the horse. Legend beginning at (XI)........(II) *vatva da. ..tya*; letters blurred and truncated. Coin is considerably worn.	The carpet under the queen's feet looks like a lotus. *Sūchi* divided into two parts by the ornamentation at its centre; both the ends of its fillet are falling on r. *Aśvamedhaparākramaḥ.* **Pl. IV. 5.**
159	115.7	.92	String of beads above the head and neck of the horse and crescent over its back. Two ends of the *raśanā* fall on opposite sides of the *yūpa*. The *yūpa* and its pedestal are fully visible; as also its *chashāla* and penons.	Queen stands on a circular mat and the towel is faintly visible in the l. hand. The edge of the queen's *sari* looks like a rope hanging in her front. Central ornamentation of the *sūchi* is distinct and graceful.

No.	Wt.	Size	Obverse	Reverse
			Letter *si* is blurred. Circular legend beginning at XI, nearly complete, but without the medial vowels; *Rajodharaja prithava-mavatva dava ja...ta* (IX) *vajamedha*. Three cracks in the edge. Normal condition.	*Aśvamedhaparākramaḥ*. **Pl. IV. 6.**
160	115.3	.83	Crescent above the haunch of the horse. *Chashāla* of the *yūpa*, which is very much bent, looks like two contiguous rings, and is quite distinct. Beads are plaited in the mane of the horse. Two rounds of the *raśanā* visible. *Si* is blurred and below it is a pedestal above the platform of the horse. Legend beginning at (XII) *Rajadharaja pri-thava* Good condition.	Queen's legs are too short; towel in her hand is distinct. Ornamentation at the centre of the *sūchi* is very broad. Mat is treated like lotus. *Aśvamedhaparākramaḥ*; medial vowel marks over *ma* and *ra* are quite distinct. **Pl. IV. 7.**
161	115.2	.94	Crescent above the haunch of the horse; beads, plaited in its mane, are distinct. Both the ends of the *raśanā* of the *yūpa* hang behind it, and the	Small towel in queen's l. hand. *Aśvamedhaparākrama*. The reverse has been thrice struck; three dotted borders can be seen on r. and

No.	Wt.	Size	Obverse	Reverse
			chashāla near its end is distinct. Slanting lines below the platform of the horse. Legend, beginning at (XI), *Rajadharaja pri . . . . tva* One crack in the edge at (I). Worn out only at the edge.	two on the l. As a result the *sūchi* is blurred, as also the legend. **Pl. IV. 8.**
162	118.4	.8	*Yūpa* is nearly complete and its pedestal is ornamental; its *chashāla* is clear. Two leather straps are visible on the neck of the horse. Small *vedikā* under *si*. Legend, beginning at (I), *Rajadharajap ritha*	Legs of the queen are too short. Ends (*gherā*) of her *sari* round her two legs look like a rope.[1] Towel clear in her l. hand. The ornamental circular object of the *sūchi* is at one third its height from the bottom. *Aśvamedhaparākramaḥ*. The tail of *kra* almost touches its horizontal line. **Pl. IV. 9.**
163	118.4	.8	Two straps round the neck of the horse; *yūpa* and *raśanā* of the usual type. No crescent or dotted line over the horse. Legend, beginning at (VIII) . . . . (I). *va jayatyāhṛi*	Queen's legs rather short and ends of her *sari* look like a rope round her feet. *Sūchi* of the normal type. *Aśvamedhaparākra* **Pl. IV. 10.**

[1] Cf, Allan, *B. M. C. G. D.*, Pl. V. 11, 13.

No.	Wt.	Size	Obverse	Reverse
164	114.2	.82	The string of beads above the head and back of the horse; crescent above its haunch. Platform of the horse is connected with *yūpa* by a vertical line above it. Legend beginning at (VII), near the pedestal of the *yūpa*, rather blurred; *Rajadharaja pritha-vamavatvā dava jayatya* Normal condition.	Queen standing on bead-bordered mat, towel in her l. hand. *Aśvamedhaparākramaḥ*. Tail of *kra* is joined to its central horizontal line and the letter thus looks like a Chālukyan *ka*. **Pl. IV. 11.**
165	113.3	.87	String of beads above the head and back of the horse, but no crescent. *Chashāla* is distinct. Slanting lines under the platform below the horse. Pedestal of the *yūpa* artistic and two-stepped. Legend, beginning at (VII), *Rajadhiraja prithavamavatva dava jaya* One crack in the edge at (III). Normal condition.	Queen standing on a Carpet. The die has moved at the top giving rise to two heads and two haloes. The earring visible is of the half visible head. Towel in l. hand clear. Both the ends of the fillet hang down on the same side of the *sūchi*. *Aśvamedhaparākramaḥ*, rather blurred. **Pl. IV. 12.**
166	111	.87	String of beads above the horse and a crescent above its haunch. Pedestal of the *yūpa* is connected with the small platform under the horse by a vertical line. *Chashāla* of the *yūpa* is faintly visible.	Reverse is considerably blurred. Queen standing on carpet; towel in the l. hand. Both the ends of the fillet of the *sūchi* fall on the same side. *Aśvamedhaparakramaḥ*,

No.	Wt.	Size	Obverse	Reverse
			Legend, beginning at (VIII) ....(V) *hritavajamadha.* Concluding letters are under the platform, but rather blurred. One crack in the edge at VI. Somewhat worn out.	blurred. **Pl. IV. 13.**
167	112.8	.81	String of beads above the back of the horse. Banner over the horse voluminous. *Chashāla* of the *yūpa* quite distinct. Slanting lines below the platform of the horse. The ends of the *raśanā* of the *yūpa* are faintly visible behind it above its pedestal. Legend, beginning at (VII), *Rajadhiraja pṛithavamatva;* The letter *tva* is crudely engraved. Normal condition.	Queen standing on carpet ; her feet very short. The *gherā* of the *sari* looks like a rope round the queen's feet. The *sūchi* here looks somewhat like a flame in a lampstand. *Aśvamedhaparākrama.* **Pl. IV. 14.**
168	115.8	.9	String of beads is indistinct; beads appear to be plaited in the mane also. Crescent above the haunch of the horse. *Chashāla* is visible. Legend, beginning at (VIII), *Rajadharaja pṛithava.vatva dava jayatyaḥrita*	Queen standing on a mat. Towel in her l. hand slightly blurred. *Aśvamedhaparākramaḥ.* **Pl. IV. 15.**

No.	Wt.	Size	Obverse	Reverse
			Letters *mava* being similar, the engraver has faild to engrave one of them. Normal condition, but part of the legend worn out; a fine coin.	
169	115.2	.8	Short string of the beads above the head and back of the horse; crescent above its haunch. Banner of the *yūpa* is voluminous, its pedestal thick and the *chashāla* at its end is distinct. The ends of the *raśanā* are blurred and fall behind the *yūpa*. Below the platform of the horse, slanting lines. Legend, beginning at (VIII)..... ...(I).*juta dava ja*. This is a clear loop below *ja*, but it seems to be due to a mistake in engraving. The legend here probably read *vijitya*, instead of *mavitvā*. **Pl. XXXIII. 5.** Normal condition.	Queen is short statured and the *gherā* of her *sari* looks like a string round her legs. Ornamental addition to the *sūchī* at its centre very prominent. *Aśvamedhaparākramaḥ*; the tails of *ra* and *kra* are joined together. **Pl. V. 1.**
170	115.1	.84	Crescent above the haunch of the horse. *Chashāla* is clear. Legend, beginning at (VII) .... (X) *mavata dava jayatyahṛita* Crack across the	Reverse is double struck and blurred. Queen is standing on the mat and the object in her l. hand is blurred. Legend almost com-

No.	Wt.	Size	Obverse	Reverse
			yūpa and the face of the horse.	pletely blurred, but *Aśvamedha* is faintly visible. **Pl. V. 2.**
171	116.4	.85	String of beads above the head and back of the horse; crescent above its haunch. Pedestal of the *yūpa* is artistic. One end of the *raśanā* falls between the *yūpa* and the head of the horse, and the other end is behind the post. Legend, beginning at (VIII) *Rajadharaja*, blurred and truncated; faint traces of letters between (I) and (V). The coin is slightly worn at the border.	Mat under the queen's feet is indistinct. Two dotted borders at the top. *Aśvamedhaparākrama*, blurred. **Pl. V. 3.**
172	114.8	.8	No crescent or string of beads above the horse; strap round its neck. Slanting lines below the platform of the horse and above the legend at the bottom. Legend, beginning near the hind feet of the horse, *Rajadharaja prithava* The coin is slightly worn on the reverse.	Queen is short statured. Ornamentation of the *sūchi* is almost at its bottom. Towel in queen's l. hand almost reaches the ground. *Aśvamedhaparākrama*, partly blurred. **Pl. V. 4.**
173	115.3	.88	Crescent behind the haunch of the horse,	The flan moved while the die was being

No.	Wt.	Size	Obverse	Reverse
			and string of beads above the head and the back. Border of slanting lines faintly visible under the platform of the horse; no letters below it. Legend beginning at IX, ...*vata dava jayatya* One crack in the edge, but not visible on the surface. Condition normal.	struck, hence this side is blurred; two dotted borders can be seen on r. side. *Aśvamedhaparākrama.* **Pl. V. 5.**

The Battle-Axe type : 9 coins

No.	Wt.	Size	Obverse	Reverse
			King, nimbate, standing l., wearing a close-fitting cap, tailed coat and trousers, half-pant or *janghia*, necklace, earrings, armlets and wristlets; one end of the *paryastaka* (decorative string round the waist) hangs between his legs; the ends of the diadem are sometimes visible behind the head. The king holds battle-axe (*paraśu*) in l. hand, r. hand resting on the waist. A sword is seen hanging from the belt in some cases. On l. in front of the king dwarf attendant (*vāmana*) looking up to	Goddess (Lakshmi ?), nimbate, seated facing on throne with lotus under her feet, holding *pāśa* (noose) in her r. hand, bent and outstretched, and cornucopiae, or lotus bud in the l. resting on the thigh. Symbol on l. legend on r. *Kritantaparaśuḥ.* कृतान्तपरशुः। **Pl. XXXVI. 47.**

No.	Wt.	Size	Obverse	Reverse
			the king, his hand resting on waist. Between the king and the dwarf is a crescent-topped standard. Under the king's l. arm, *Sa* स or *Kṛi* कृ *mu* मु *dra* द्र **Pl. XXXVII. 72, 74.** Circular legend, beginning at VIII or I, *Kṛitāntaparaśurjayatyajitarājajetājitaḥ.* कृतान्तपरशुर्जयत्यजितराजजेताऽजितः । **Pl. XXXVIII. 7.** Metre, Pṛithvī	

Variety A : 7 coins

(With Samudra under l. arm.)

No.	Wt.	Size	Obverse	Reverse
174	114.4	.9	King wears trousers and there is a sword hanging on his left side. Sleeves of the coat are rolled up. Dwarf is holding a short sword erect in the r. hand. *Sa* *mu* *dra.* Circular legend, beginning at VIII, *Kṛitantaparaśurjjayatyaji*..(II) *jajeta* Last four letters are faint. Normal condition.	The throne of the goddess is high-backed and cushioned, the depression caused by her body being clearly visible on the seat. She holds a lotus bud with long stalk in l. hand (and not a cornucopiae); noose in the r. hand is slightly away from it. Symbol *Kṛitāntaparasuḥ.* **Pl. V. 6.**

No.	Wt.	Size	Obverse	Reverse
175	115.2	.77	Coin is blurred. Dwarf is partly off the flan. Sleeves of the coat are rolled up, and the king wears a half-pant. Ends of the diadem are visible behind the head. *Sa* *mu* *dra.* Circular legend, beginning at I, *Kṛitantaparaśuja* Worn out in the lower right quadrant.	Die has slipped giving a considerable sloping border in the upper half. Throne has no back and lotus is off the flan. Cornucopiae in the l. hand. Symbol *Kṛitāntaparaśuḥ.* **Pl. V. 7.**
176	118.2	.82	King wears *shalwar* and there are three dots between him and the dwarf. Sword is hanging on the l. side of the king; it appears as hanging from the arm pit and not from the waist. R. hand of the dwarf is on the waist and the l. one is invisible. *Sa* *mu* *dra.* Circular legend is blurred; only faint traces of *Kṛitānta* are visible at I. Slightly worn on obverse.	Throne has no back. Feet of the goddess are resting on lotus. R. hand is empty, but traces of a detached noose are visible away from it; l. hand holds a cornucopiae. Symbol *Kṛitāntaparaśu.* **Pl. V. 8.**

No.	Wt.	Size	Obverse	Reverse
177	114.6	.78	Sleeves of the coat are rolled up and the king wears trousers. No sword by his side. Ends of the diadem visible behind the head. *Sa* *mu* *dra*. Circular legend, beginning at I, very much blurred, *Kritantapara* Worn out on obverse only.	The feet of the goddess rest on lotus; noose in her r. hand, bent and outstretched, and cornucopiae in the l. hand. Symbol  *Kṛitāntaparaśuḥ*. **Pl. V. 9.**
178	115.2	.75	King wears trousers and the sleeves of the coat are rolled up; he has no sword. Ends of the diadem visible behind the head. *Sa* *mu* *dra*. Circular legend, beginning at I, very much blurred. Traces of *Kṛitāntapara* are visible between I and III. Somewhat worn.	Feet of the goddess rest on lotus; there is a noose in her r. and a cornucopiae in her l. hand. Symbol  *Kritāntaparasuḥ*. **Pl. V. 10.**
179	114.4	.79	King wears half-pant and ends of the diadem are visible behind the head. Sleeves of the coat are rolled up; the king has no sword. There is a faint cres-	Throne is invisible and is to be inferred from the posture of the feet of the goddess. Lotus below feet is graceful and large. Cornucopiae in the

No.	Wt.	Size	Obverse	Reverse
			cent over the crescent-topped banner. *Sa* *mu* *dra.* Circular legend, beginning at I, blurred; there are faint traces of *Kṛitāntapa*	l. hand. Symbol *Kṛitāntaparaśuḥ*, slightly truncated. **Pl. V. 11.**
180	115.5	.8	King wears trousers and the sleeves of the coat are rolled up; there is no sword by his side. Ends of the diadem visible behind the head. Dwarf partly off the flan. *Sa* *mu* *dra.* Circular legend, (I) *Kṛitāntaparaśu* One crack at IV and one at X. Somewhat worn.	Goddess seated on a throne, which is invisible and can be inferred only from the posture of her feet. Lotus under her feet is very large. Symbol, but incomplete. *Kṛitāntaparaśuḥ.* **Pl. V. 12.**

Variety B : 2 coins

(*Kṛi* under the l. arm)

No.	Wt.	Size	Obverse	Reverse
181	113.2	.84	King wears pant and leather boots; sleeves of the coat are rolled up. Ends of the diadem are visible; no sword by his side. Under l. arm, *Kṛi.* Circular legend, beginning at I,	Goddess seated on backless throne, whose legs are not visible. Lotus below her feet is large and elegant. She holds cornucopiae in l. hand and a noose in r. Symbol

No.	Wt.	Size	Obverse	Reverse
			.........(VIII) *jata-rājajetāja* Normal condition.	*Kṛitantaparaśuḥ.* **Pl. V. 13.**
182	116	.8	King as above. Features sharply drawn. Crescent-topped banner clear. *Kṛi* under the l. arm. Legend, beginning at (VII)......*śaja-* (I) *yatyajataraja*	Goddess as above. Two legs of the throne are visible. Lotus below the feet. Symbol *Kṛitantaparaśa.* **Pl. V. 14.**

Archer type : 3 coins

No.	Wt.	Size	Obverse	Reverse
			King standing left, nimbate, wearing coat (with sleeves tucked up), trousers, pearl-bordered head-dress, necklace and armlets, holding bow with string inwards in l. hand, while r. holds arrow, in a slanting position, its pointed head resting on the ground. Two ends of the fillet on the head fall behind it. Garuḍa standard on l. Under the l. arm, written vertically, *Sa* स *mu* मु *dra.* द्र Circular legend, beginning at I, *Apratiratho vijitya kshitiṁ sucharitairdivaṁ jayati.*	Goddess (Lakshmī), nimbate, seated facing on throne with back, covered with *gaddi*, holding noose in r. hand, slightly bent and extended, and cornucopiae in the l., resting on the shoulder. The goddess wears *sari* and an upper garment thrown across the shoulders. Symbol on the l. Legend on right, *Apratirathaḥ.* अप्रतिरथः । **PL. XXXVI. 49.**

No.	Wt.	Size	Obverse	Reverse
			अप्रतिरथो विजित्य क्षितिं सुच-रितैर्दिवं जयति । **PL. XXXIII. 9.** Metre : Upagīti.	

Variety A : 2 coins

(Legend ending with *sucharitairdivam jayati*)

No.	Wt.	Size	Obverse	Reverse
183	115.6	.88	As above. *Sa* *mu* *dra.* (I) *Apra.ratha vajatya* ..(IX) *sucharitairdi* Four cracks on the coin between VIII and XI. Normal condition.	The coin is double struck on the reverse, as shown by the double dotted border at the top and the bottom. Symbol , but lower part indistinct. It may be  also. .*pratirathaḥ*, blurred. **Pl. V. 15.**
184	108.2	.9	Generally as above. Standard away from r. hand. Arrow is partly visible. Crescent at the top above the halo. *Sa* *mu* *dra.* *Ma* is of eastern variety. Circular legend, beginning at I, *Aprataratho vijitya kshtata* Medial vowels are clearly shown in some cases. A well preserved coin, but with a remarkably low weight.	Same as above. Back of the throne and its four legs are visible; it is covered with a thick *gaddi.* Mat under the feet of the goddess. Symbol , but its upper line is shorter owing to want of space. *Apratirathaḥ.* **Pl. VI. 1.**

Variety B : 1 coin

(Legend ending with *avanīśo divaṁ jayati*)

No.	Wt.	Size	Obverse	Reverse
185	120.5	.83	The king wears half-pant and high boots. Arrow is held straight and not slanting; dress and jewelry not quite distinct, but the ends of fillet are clear. *Sa* *mu* *dra.* (II) [*Apratiratho vi*]*ja* (*i*)*tya ksha*(*i*)*ta*(*i*) *mava-nī* (*śo di*) *va*[*ṁ*] *jaya*[*ti*].[1] अप्रतिरथो विजित्य क्षिति-मवनीशो दिवं जयति **Pl. XXXIII. 9.** Metre : Upagīti. Good condition.	Generally as on the preceding variety. Right hand of the goddess is at a high level. Two legs of the throne are visible and the *gaddi* on it can be clearly seen. Carpet under the feet of the goddess. Symbol incomplete; it is probably  with a dot in the centre of the parallelogram. *Apratirathaḥ.* **Pl. VI. 2.**

Lyrist type : 6 coins

Variety A : 2 coins

(With foot-stool and without symbol, large size)

			King, nimbate, to l., wearing short *dhoti*, close-fitting pearl-bordered cap, necklace, earrings and armlets, seated cross-legged on cushioned couch with a cushioned back	Goddess (Lakshmī?) nimbate, seated to l. on a wicker stool, wearing *sari*, *kañchukī*, earrings, necklace and bangles; l. hand resting on the waist; she holds a

[1] Letters in square brackets are not visible on the die. Letters in round brackets represent the emendations of the preceding letters.

No.	Wt.	Size	Obverse	Reverse
			slightly sloping, its r. side being bead- or pearl-bordered, playing on a stringed lute lying on his lap, by the fingers of his r. hand, left hand just above the lute gesticulating appreciation. Beneath the couch is a foot-stool inscribed with *si*, on which king's r. foot is resting. Legend beginning at I, *Mahārajādhirāja-śrī-Samudraguptaḥ*. महाराजाधिराजश्रीसमुद्रगुप्तः। **Pl. XXXIII. 6.**	*pāśa* (noose) in the r. hand stretched out but bent and a cornucopiae in the l. resting on the waist; border of dots all round. No symbol. Legend on the r., separated from the goddess by a line, *Samudraguptaḥ*. समुद्रगुप्तः। **Pl. XXXVI. 46.**
186	108.9	.9	The back of the couch is sloping considerably and all its four legs are visible. Legend, beginning at I, *Mahara....śra..(VIII) draguptaḥ*. The letter *ptaḥ* appears between the lute and the king's head. The letter *ha* is of the eastern variety. Note that the same coin has eastern *ha* on the obverse and a western *ma* on the reverse. Good condition and yet low weight.	No symbol. *Samudraguptaḥ*. Letter *mu* looks more like a *rva* than a *mu*. Cf. *B. M. C. G. D.*, Pl. V. 1. *Ma* is of western variety. **Pl. VI. 3.**

No.	Wt.	Size	Obverse	Reverse
187	116	.85	Slope of the back of the couch is slight. Noteworthy is the depression made by the lute end in the cushioned back of the couch. *Si* on the foot-stool truncated. Legend, beginning at I, *Maharajadhiraja-śra*-(IX) *Samudraguptaḥ*. *Ma* is of the eastern variety on the obverse and of the western variety on the reverse.	Same as No. 186. Flan had a chisel cut extending from one end to the other, which can be seen even after the striking of the die; it bisects the letter *ptah* and passes under the cornucopiae. No symbol. *Samudraguptaḥ*. *Ma* is of the western variety. **Pl. VI. 4.**

Variety B : 4 coins

(Small size and inartistic fabric; with symbol but without foot-stool)

No.	Wt.	Size	Obverse	Reverse
188	119.4	.75	Same as variety A, but the king and the couch are both crudely engraved. There is no foot-stool under the couch. The king is apparently bare-headed, torso also being bare. Legend as in variety A, but mostly off the flan. (I) *Ma*......(VII) *śra-Samudragupta*. The last six letters are truncated; the last three letters are between the end of the lute and the head of the king. *Ma* is western. Normal condition.	Same as on variety A, but the execution is less artistic. Line between the goddess and legend cut short by the cornucopiae coming over it. Symbol  *Samudraguptaḥ*. *Ma* is western. **Pl. VI. 5.**

No.	Wt.	Size	Obverse	Reverse
189	119.3	.72	Couch is very crude. King is apparently wearing a peaked cap under which hair is seen falling in two tresses, one above the other. Legend, beginning at I, *Ma* .... (VIII) *mudragupta*. Truncated traces of the letters on the right are visible. End of the lyre cuts across the subscript of *dra*. *Ma* is western. Normal condition.	As above. Left hand of the goddess rests on the edge of the seat. Her hair is tied in a knot at the top of the head. Line between goddess and the legend, its lower portion being screened by the cornucopiae. The extant portion of the line really looks like the usual back of the throne on the Standard type of this king. Symbol *Samudraguptaḥ*. *Ma* is western. **Pl. VI. 6.**
190	119.2	.75	Couch is cushioned, its back is upright; and the l. side has beaded border from top to bottom. Legend blurred. (I) *Maharajadha* .... (VIII) *mudragupta*. Both *ma* and *ha* are western.	As above. Stool is broad, its reeds being vertical. Line between the goddess and the legend touches the letters. Symbol blurred, but probably ..*draguptaḥ*. **Pl. VI. 7.**
191	119.1	.77	King's hair on the head flowing down in three stepped tresses. Legened, beginning at (I), *Maha* .... (VIII) *mudraguptaḥ*. Edge of the lute cuts across the end of the letter *dra*.	L. hand of the goddess just touches the seat. Line between the goddess and the legend, going under the cornucopiae. Symbol *Samudraguptaḥ*.

No.	Wt.	Size	Obverse	Reverse
			Ma is western in both cases. Normal condition.	*Ma* is western. **Pl. VI. 8.**

Tiger-slayer type : 2 coins

Variety A : 1 coin

(Different legends on the obv. and rev.)

No.	Wt.	Size	Obverse	Reverse
192	117.6	.85	King, nimbate, standing left, wearing high crested turban, *sakachha dhoti*, necklace, earrings and armlets, trampling upon a tiger which falls back gaping its mouth in agony and terror as the king shoots it with bow in r. hand, l. hand drawing the string back upto the ear; near the bow crescent-topped standard adorned with fillet. Ornaments on the king's body are not so clear as on *B.M.C. G. D.*, II, 4, but his figure is more graceful and energetic on the present specimen. The tiger is also more fully visible here than on the piece in the B. M. Legend on the r., fairly clear; *Vya*(*ā*)*ghrapara* (*ā*)-*kkramaḥ*. व्याघ्रपराक्रमः; **Pl. XXXIII. 8.**	Goddess Gaṅgā standing to l. on crocodile (*makara*), wearing a *sari*, a close-fitting *kañchukī*, a scarf over head, necklace, earrings. bangles, armlets and anklets and holding lotus with long stalk in l. hand, r. hand bent and out-stretched being open and empty. On the l. behind r. hand cresent-topped banner adorned with fillet. No symbol. Legend on the right, *Rājā Samudraguptaḥ*. राजा समुद्रगुप्तः **Pl. XXXVI. 48.** *Ma* is of the western variety. **Pl. VI. 9.**

No.	Wt.	Size	Obverse	Reverse
			Penultimate letter is *kkra* and not *kra*. *Ma* is of the western variety. Normal condition.	

Variety B : 1 coin

(*Vyāghraparākramaḥ* on both sides)

No.	Wt.	Size	Obverse	Reverse
193	119	.81	As above. Crescent-topped banner is clearer on this coin. The protruding tongue from the gaping mouth of the tiger is clear. Legend is less complete than that on No. 192; *Vya* (*ā*) *ghra* [*pa*] *ra* (*ā*) [*kramaḥ*[1].] Normal condition.	As above. The figure of the goddess is slim and graceful; she stands cross-legged on the crocodile, which is only partly visible on this coin. Her hands are as in var. A. Crescent-topped banner behind the r. hand is not so clear as on the preceding coin. No symbol. Legend to r., *Vyāghraparākramaḥ*, completely clear. *Ma* is of the western variety. The *B. M. C. G. D.* Pl. II. 15 has only the concluding letters *kramaḥ*. The reverse of the present coin is much better preserverd than that of the above coin in the *B. M. C. G. D.* **Pl. VI. 10.**

[1] Letters in square brackets are not on the flan; those in round brackets represent the emendations of the preceding ones.

KĂCHA : 16 COINS

Chakradhvaja type : 16 coins

Variety A : 15 coins

(Without Garuḍadhvaja on the obverse)

No.	Wt.	Size	Obverse	Reverse
			King nimbate, standing to l., wearing coat, trousers or *shalwār*, close-fitting cap, ear-rings necklace and wristlets, holding standard surmounted by wheel and adorned with fillet in l. hand, and offering by r. hand on altar an oblation, usually a round *puroḍāśa*. The wheel of the *chakradhvaja* usually causes the suppression of the r. side of the halo. Under the l. arm *Kā* का *Ka* क or *cha* च *cha* च **Pl. XXXVII. 75.** Circular legend, beginning at I, *Kācho gāmavijitya divaṁ karmabhiruttamairjayati.* काचो गामवजित्य दिवं कर्मभिरुत्तमैर्जयति । **Pl. XXXIII. 11.** Metre : Upagīti.	Goddess (Lakshmī), nimbate, standing to l., usually on a carpet, wearing *sari*, close-fitting *kañchukī* (bodice), necklace, ear-rings and bangles, holding flowers in r. hand bent up and cornucopiae resting on l. shoulder in the l. hand, placed on the waist. Border of dots all round. Symbol on the l. side at the centre below the r. hand of the goddess, and not at the top, as usual on most Gupta coins. Legend on r. *Sarvarājochchhettā.* सर्वराजोच्छेत्ता । **Pl. XXXVI. 50.**

No.	Wt.	Size	Obverse	Reverse
194	114.2	.77	King is probably wearing leather boots reaching the knees. *Kā* *cha*. (I) *Kacha gamavajatya da*. ..(IX) *bharuttamaja*. *Ma* of eastern variety. Very slightly worn.	No carpet under feet. Symbol *Sarvarājochchhetta*. **Pl. VI. 11.**
195	119.1	.79	*Kā* *cha*. (I) *Kacha ga*.... .. (VII) *kamabharuttamairjaya* [*ti*] *Ma* of eastern variety. More worn out than the above, but the weight is heavier.	Traces of carpet under goddess' feet. Symbol *Sarvarajachchhatta*. **Pl. VI. 12.**
196	107.4	.76	*Kā* *cha*. (I) *Kacha gamavajatya* .. .. (VIII) *bharuttamajja* *Ma* of the western variety with a triangular base. Slightly less worn than the above but the weight is disproportionately low.	Carpet under the feet of the goddess. Symbol *Sarvarāiochchhatta*. **Pl. VI. 13.**
197	112.5	.8	Standard without fillet. *Kā* *cha*. (I) *Kacha gamavaja*. .. (VII) *kamabharuttamaja* *Ma* of the eastern variety. Condition normal.	Traces of carpet under goddess' feet. Symbol *Sarvarājochchhetta*. **Pl. VI. 14.**

No.	Wt.	Size	Obverse	Reverse
198	116.3	.8	*Kā* *cha.* (I) *Kacha gamavajatya* . . *ka* (VII) *mabharutta-majja* *Ma* is of western variety. Very slightly worn.	Carpet under goddess' feet. Symbol , but perhaps with three dots below. *Sarvarājochchhetta.* Medial vowels, rather blurred. **Pl. VI. 15.**
199	111.4	.88	King probably wears leather boots. *Ka* *cha.* (II) *Kacho gamavajatya* . . . . . (X) *rutta* Triangle-based *ma* of western variety.	No carpet under goddess' feet. Symbol with a dot in the centre of the parallelogram. *Sarvarājochchhettā.* **Pl. VII. 1.**
200	117.2	.78	Fillet of the standard tied very low. *Ka* *cha.* (II) *Kacha gamavajatya* . . . (VII) *mabharut-tamarja* *Ma* is of the western variety and the legend on the r. is partly truncated.	Symbol but incomplete, and having additional dot in the centre of the parallelogram. *Sarvarājochchhettā.* **Pl. VII. 2.**
201	117.2	.79	Normal condition. *Ka* *cha.* . . ga. . . . . . (VIII) *kamabhiruttamairjja* *Ma* of western variety. Slightly worn.	Goddess standing on carpet but her head partly off the flan. Symbol , but three dots below instead of two. *Sarvarājochchhetta.* **Pl. VII. 3.**

No.	Wt.	Size	Obverse	Reverse
202	114	.75	*Ka* *cha*. (I) *Kacha gamavajatya* .. .. (IX) *bharutta* *Ma* of the western variety. Somewhat worn.	No carpet under goddess' feet. Symbol  *Sarvarājochchhetta.* **Pl. VII. 4.**
203	116	.75	*Kā* *cha*. (I) *Kacha gamavajatya* *da*. .. (VIII) *bharutta.* *Ma* of the western variety. Slightly worn.	Goddess stands on carpet. Symbol a variation of  with a dot in the centre. *Sarvarājochchhetta*, rather blurred. **Pl. VII. 5.**
204	118.2	.83	*Ka* *cha*. (I) *Kacha gamava*.. .. ...(IX) *ruttamja.* Worn on obverse.	Goddess on carpet. Symbol  with an additional dot bellow. *Sarvarājochchhetta.* **Pl. VII. 6.**
205	114.7	.79	Fillet is attached almost at the bottom of the standard. *Kā* *cha*. (I) *Kacha ga.vaja-tya* .. .. (VII) *bharu-ttamarjja* *Ma* is of western variety. Slightly worn.	Goddess standing on carpet. Symbol  with an additional dot in the centre. *Sarvarājochchhetta.* **Pl. VII. 7.**
206	116	.84	*Ka* *cha*. (I) *Kacha gamava*..(VII) .. *karmabhiruttamajja* Letters on the right	Carpet under the goddess' feet. Symbol 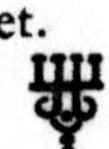, but blurred and incomplete.

No.	Wt.	Size	Obverse	Reverse
			side are truncated in some cases, while those on the left are unusually bold and large. *Ma* is of the western variety. Slightly worn.	*Sarvarājochchhetta.* **Pl. VII. 8.**
207	115	.82	*Ka* *cha* (I) *Kācha gamavajatya . .* (VIII) *karmabbaruttamarja.* A small portion of the halo on the right is also visible on this coin. *Ma* is of the eastern variety. Coin well preserved.	Carpet under goddess' feet. Symbol *Sarvarājochchhettā.* **Pl. VII. 9.**
208	114	.77	*Ka* *cha.* .. .. (VIII) *mabharuttamarjayati.* A portion of the halo on the right is also visible.	No carpet under goddess' feet. Symbol with an additional dot in the centre of parallelogram. *Sarvarājochchhetta.* **Pl. VII. 10.**

Variety B : 1 coin

(With both *Garuḍadhvaja* and *chakradhvaja* on the obv.)

No.	Wt.	Size	Obverse	Reverse
209	119.4	.75	As on variety A. *Chakradhvaja* is partly visible and is adorned with fillet. Halo is complete. On the right, there is *Garuḍadhvaja* also be-	Goddess, nimbate, standing to l. as in variety A, wearing a head dress also, holding a noose instead of flower in l. hand extended, and

No.	Wt.	Size	Obverse	Reverse
			hind the r. hand of the king. King is wearing a *dhoti* instead of trousers. Altar is broad and several flames can be seen on it. *Ka* *ch.* .. .. (VIII) *bharuttamajjayata* *Ma* is of the eastern variety. Normal condition.	a cornucopiae in r. hand, hanging down. Symbol is at the top and not in the centre as in variety A; it is 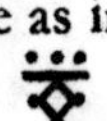 .. *rajachchhata*, truncated. **Pl. VII. 11.**

CHANDRAGUPTA II : 983 COINS

Archer Type : 798 coins

CLASS I : THRONE REVERSE: 41 COINS

Variety A : 25 coins

(*Chandra* under the left arm)

No.	Wt.	Size	Obverse	Reverse
			King, nimbate, standing to l. wearing close-fitting cap, coat, trousers or *dhoti*, sash, earrings, necklace and wristlets, holding bow in l. hand at the top, string inwards, and arrow in r. hand; Garuḍa standard on the l. behind r. hand. Under l. arm, *Chandra*, written vertically.[1] Circular legend beginning at I, *Devaśrīmahārājādhirājaśrī-Chandraguptaḥ*. देवश्रीमहाराजाधिराज-श्रीचन्द्रगुप्तः **Pl.** XXXIII. 12.	Lakshmī, nimbate, seated facing on cushioned throne with high back, wearing *sari*, upper garment, earrings, necklace; r. hand bent and extended, sometimes empty, sometimes holding a *pāśa* (noose), sometimes a garland or rosary; l. hand on waist or thigh holding sometimes a cornucopiae resting on shoulder and sometimes a lotus. The feet of the goddess rest on a circular mat; border of dots. Symbol on l. Legend on r., *Śrīvikramaḥ*. श्रीविक्रमः । **Pl.** XXXVI. 51.

[1] *Chandra* under the left arm occurs on all the coins of this type and is never off the flan; its presence, therefore, is not specifically referred to in the catalogue of the coins of this type.

No.	Wt.	Size	Obverse	Reverse
210	118.8	.78	King wears trousers. [1]*Davaśramaharajadharaja* *..ndragupta.*	R. hand bent up and empty; l. hand holds lotus. Symbol  *Srīvikrama.*
211	118.5	.8	King wears a half-pant. *Devaśramaharajadharaja śra-Chandraguptaḥ,* partly blurred and truncated.	Reverse is double-struck. There are two symbols and two circular borders. Goddess as above but very hazy owing to double-striking. Symbols  and 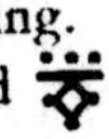 *Srīvikramaḥ.* **Pl. VII. 12.**
212	117.6	.8	*Devaśrīmaharajadha..* *śra-Chandragupa.*	Goddess as in No. 210. Symbol , but with two horizontal lines. *Srīvikrama.* **Pl. VII. 13.**
213	118.6	.72	*Davaśrīmahārāja...* *śra-Chandraga*	Goddess as on No. 210. Symbol  but with two horizontal lines. *Sravakra* **Pl. VIII. 1.**
214	117.7	.87	King wears *sakachchha dhoti.* *Devaśrimahārājādhiraja-śrī-Chandragu*	Goddess as on No. 210. Symbol  *Srīvikrama.* **Pl. VIII. 2.**

[1] In this type the circular legend begins at I, the letter after the break in the legend can be usually traced at VIII or IX. The precise clockwise places of these letters are not therefore indicated by the insertion of the Roman numerals I or VIII in the legend.

No.	Wt.	Size	Obverse	Reverse
215	117.3	.9	Die has moved during striking and so the letters on the l. appear twice but blurred. *Davaśramahā .....* *śra-Chandrandra.*	The r. hand of the goddess is bent up and empty; left hand is bent up and holds a lotus. Symbol *Śrīvikramaḥ.* **Pl. VIII. 3.**
216	118	.82	King's l. arm is passing through the bow and the bow-string. *Devaśramaharajadhara*	Goddess has a noose in r. hand and a lotus in the l. bent up. Symbol *Śrīvikkramaḥ.*
217	118.4	.72	Circular legend off. A crack in the edge at VIII.	R. hand bent up and empty; cornucopiae in l. hand. Symbol *Śrīvikrama.*
218	121.5	.75	King probably wears short *sakachchha dhoti* and leather boots; his coat has side buttons. Arrow off the flan. *Devaśri .... Chandragupta,* truncated.	Lakshmī is scattering wealth (round coins) by r. hand and holding cornucopiae in l. Folds of the *sari* between the two legs. Symbol, but crudely drawn. *.vikrama.* **Pl. VIII. 4.**
219	119.6	.76	King wears short *dhoti* and high boots. Circular legend blurred.	Goddess as in No. 218 Symbol *Śrīvikrama.*

No.	Wt.	Size	Obverse	Reverse
220	122.1	.83	King wears trousers; his coat has side buttons. *Devaśrīmaharajadharaja* blurred and truncated.	Goddess scattering coins by r. hand. Symbol *Srīvikrama.* **Pl. VIII. 5.**
221	122.4	.79	King wears a crest-jewel; his coat has side buttons, its sleeves are rolled up. He wears short *sakachchha dhoti.* *Devaśramaharajadha*	Goddess holds a noose in r. hand and cornucopiae in l. Symbol *Sravakrama,* truncated. **Pl. VIII. 6.**
222	119.9	.72	*Davaśra*	R. hand of the goddess is empty and the l. hand holds a cornucopiae. Symbol *Sravikrama.* **Pl. VIII. 7.**
223	119.4	.78	King wears a cap with crest and his coat has side buttons or bosses. *Davaśramaha.....* *śra-Chandra,* partly truncated.	Goddess as above. Symbol, but incomplete. *Srīvikrama.* **Pl. VIII. 8.**
224	119.9	.72	...........*Chandragupta*	Goddess as on No. 221. Symbol *Srīvikrama.*
225	121.3	.75	King wears a beautiful crest-jewel, *sakachchha dhoti* and high boots. Sleeves of his coat are rolled up. *Davaśramaharaja*	Goddess has noose in r. hand and cornucopiae in l. Symbol, but incomplete. *Sravakramaḥ.* **Pl. VIII. 9.**

No.	Wt.	Size	Obverse	Reverse
226	119.8	.72	*Devaśrī*	R. hand empty, l. hand holds a cornucopiae. Symbol  *Śrīvikrama.*
227	121.1	.71	*Davaśrama*	Goddess holds a noose in r. hand and a cornucopiae in l. Symbol  *Śrīvikrama.*
228	119.2	.72	*Devaśrīmaharajadhara*	Goddess as above. Symbol , incomplete. *Śrīvikrama.*
229	118.7	.75	King wears half-pant or short *sakachchha dhoti* with high boots. Under r. arm, crescent above *Chandra.* *Deva..........ndra-gapa.*	Goddess holds a noose in r. hand and a cornucopiae in the l. Back of the throne visible. Symbol  *Śrīvikramaḥ.* **Pl. VIII. 10.**
230	121.6	.76	Crescent above *Chandra* under l. arm. Circular legend off.	Goddess as on No. 227. Symbol 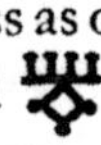 *Śrīvikrama.*
231	119.8	.72	*Devaśrī*	Throne without back. Goddess holds a noose in r. hand and a lotus in l. Symbol 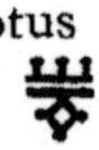 *Śrīvikrama.*
232	120.1	.8	*Devaśrīmaharajadhara... ndraguptaḥ.*	Throne without back. Noose in r. hand and lotus in l. Symbol  *Śrīvikramaḥ.* **Pl. VIII. 11.**

No.	Wt.	Size	Obverse	Reverse
233	117.5	.72	*Devaśrimaharājādhara-* *..Chandra* *Ha* is of the eastern variety. A crack in the edge at VIII.	Goddess holds noose in r. hand and lotus in l. Her feet rest on lotus and not on carpet. Symbol incomplete, but probably  *Srīvikramaḥ.* **Pl. VIII. 12.**
234	120.1	.85	........*ja śrī-Chandragupta,* in bold characters.	Throne without back. Noose in r. hand and lotus in l. Symbol incomplete. Legend off.

Variety B : 7 coins

(*Chandra* written between the bow and the bow string)

No.	Wt.	Size	Obverse	Reverse
			King standing to l. as in variety A, but *Chandra* written vertically, not under l. arm, but between the bow and the bow-string which is inwards.	Goddess as in variety A; usually holding a noose in r. hand and a cornucopiae in l.
235	121.9	.83	King wears short *dhoti* and high-heeled shoes; sleeves of his coat are rolled up. Sash is tied round the waist and one of its ends is falling down. Standard on the l. is away from the r. hand and not behind it. *Davaśramaharajadhara-ja-śra* A fine coin.	Goddess holds a noose in r. hand and a cornucopiae in l.; all four legs of the throne visible. Symbol on l. is a variation of , dot below being hollow. Symbol on r. Δ *Srīvikrama.* **Pl. VIII. 13.**

No.	Wt.	Size	Obverse	Reverse
236	120.4	.8	Standard away from r. hand. Circular legend off.	Symbol a variation of , as above. *Srīvikrama.*
237	121.4	.78	End of the sash falling along the leg. Standard away from the r. hand. *..śrīmaharaja*, truncated.	Cornucopiae in l. hand and in r. noose partially on the flan. Symbol  *Srīvikrama.* **Pl. VIII. 14.**
238	119.9	.8	King wears a peculiar circular beautiful ornament on r. arm and a big wristlet. End of the broad sash falling along the l. leg. Hair falls behind the head in thick curls. *Devaśramaha*, truncated	Noose in r. hand and cornucopiae in l. Symbol 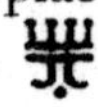 blurred. *Srīvikrama*, truncated. **Pl. VIII. 15.**
239	120.2	.77	Standard away from r. hand, circular legend off.	Back of the throne clearly visible; goddess with noose and lotus. Symbol 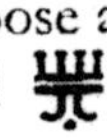, incomplete.
240	116.6	.78	As above.	Goddess with noose and lotus. Symbol  *Srīvikrama.*
241	119.8	.78	King wears an artistic crest-jewel. Coat has side buttons. *Davaśra.........* *gupta*, truncated.	Goddess with noose and cornucopiae. Symbol , incomplete. *Srīvikrama.* **Pl. IX. 1.**

Variety C : 1 coin

(Bow-string outside)

No.	Wt.	Size	Obverse	Reverse
242	119.4	.8	King standing to l., as in variety B, holding arrow in r. hand and bow at the top in l. with string outside. King wears half-pant and boots. *Chandra* written vertically between the bow and the bow-string. Circular legend, beginning at VII, [*Devaśrīmahārājādhirāja*] (II) *śrī-Chandraguptaḥ.*	Goddess seated on throne, holding noose in r. hand and lotus in l., both hands being bent up. Symbol. *Śrīvikkrama.* **Pl. IX. 2.**

Variety D : 8 coins

(Bow held at the middle)

No.	Wt.	Size	Obverse	Reverse
			King nimbate, standing to l., wearing coat, trousers, head-dress, earrings and necklace, holding arrow in r. hand and bow in the l. at the middle with string outside; Garuḍa standard on the l. usually behind the r. hand. *Chandra* written vertically outside the bow-string. Circular legend, *Devaśrīmahārājādhirāja-śrī-Chandraguptaḥ.*	Goddess Lakshmī, nimbate, seated facing on high-backed throne wearing *sari,* upper garment, earrings and necklace, and usually holding a noose in r. hand, slightly bent and stretched, and a cornucopiae in l. resting on the waist or thigh. Symbol on l. Legend, *Śrīvikramaḥ* on r.
243	113.6	.75	*..śramaharajadhara..* *Chandra*	Symbol *Śrīvikra*

No.	Wt.	Size	Obverse	Reverse
244	119.4	.74	There is a peculiar semi-circular bow-like object with two beads or pearls in its centre hanging by the r. leg of the king. *..śramaharajadhara*, truncated. Traces of letters on the r.	Four legs of the throne visible but not the back. Symbol blurred and incomplete, but probably 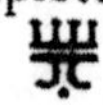 *Śrīvikrama.* **Pl. IX. 3.**
245	121.5	.75	King wears half-pant; arrow in r. hand off the flan. *Devaśrīmaharaja*	Symbol  *Śrīvikrama.*
246	120.1	.8	*..śramaharajadhiraja*	Symbol  *Śrīvikrama.*
247	121	.78	There is a peculiar semi-circular object with two beads or pearls attached to it hanging by the r. leg of the king as on No. 244. *Davaśaramaharajadharaja .. ndraga*	Four legs and back of the throne visible. Symbol probably a variation of  with an open traingle enclosing a dot below. *Śrīvikrama.* **Pl. IX. 4.**
248	119.5	.72	King wears half-pant and high leather boots. *Davaśra.......śra-Chandragupta.* Most of the letters are truncated. *Chandra* outside the bow-string displaces the letters in the circular legend.	Four legs and back of the throne visible. Goddess is scattering wealth in the form of coins by r. hand. Symbol  *Śrīvikramaḥ.* **Pl. IX. 5.**
249	120.5	.8	*..........śra-Chandragupta*	A line between the goddess and the legend. Symbol 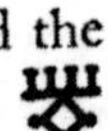 *Śravakramaḥ.*

No.	Wt.	Size	Obverse	Reverse
250	121.9	.85	King wears a close-fitting cap and half-pant. *Devaśramaharajadharaja-śrī-Chandragupta.*	Four legs of the throne are visible, but not its back. Upper garment of the goddess is clear. Symbol *Śravakrama.*

CLASS II : LOTUS REVERSE : 757 COINS

Variety A ; 700 coins

(*Chandra* under l. arm; bow held at top with string inside)

No.	Wt.	Size	Obverse	Reverse
			King to l., nimbate, standing, holding bow at the top in the l. hand, string inwards, and arrow in the r. hand. Garuḍa standard to l. behind king's r. hand. Usually the king is bare-headed and wears a coat and a *dhoti*. Sometimes the *dhoti* reaches the ankles and sometimes the knees only. In some cases the king wears trousers or *shalwār* or half-pant. Half-pant cannot be easily distinguished from short *dhoti*. Under the arm, written vertically, *Chandra*. Circular legend, beginning at I, *Devaśrīmahārājādhirāja-srī-Chandraguptaḥ.* देवश्रीमहाराजाधिराजश्रीचन्द्रगुप्तः। **Pl. XXXIII. 12.**	Lakshmī, nimbate, wearing necklace, ear-rings and bangles, seated on lotus, facing, holding, a noose in the r. hand and a lotus with long stalk in the l. The r. hand is usually extended and slightly bent. In majority of cases the l. hand rests on the knee. Sometimes however it is bent up and sometimes bent down and placed on the waist. In some cases it is stretched out. Symbol in the l. upper corner. Legend on the r. *Śrīvikramaḥ* श्रीविक्रमः, usually with the medial vowels. Border of dots.
251	121.7	.78	King in trousers. *Devaśramahārā . . . . śrī-Chandraguptaḥ.*	Symbol *Śrīvikramaḥ.*

No.	Wt.	Size	Obverse	Reverse
252	121	.83	King in *dhoti*. Poor die. *.vaśramaharaja*	L. hand bent up. Symbol *Śrīvikra*
253	121	.8	King in *shalwár*. *Devaśramaharajadha . . . Chandragupta*	L. hand bent up. Symbol *Śrīvikkramaḥ*. **Pl. VII. 14**[1].
254	129.3	.78	King in trousers. *Devaśramaha* Weight very high.	L. hand resting on knee. Symbol *Śrīvikramaḥ*.
255	121.7	.77	King in *dhoti*. Halo carelessly engraved; its l. part is detached and looks like a crescent. Legend off.	L. hand bent up. Symbol , but incomplete. *Śrīvikra*
256	120.5	.82	King wears short *sakachchha dhoti* and boots. Halo on his l. side is detached, and looks like a crescent on the Garuḍa standard. Lower part of the bow shows two dots, looking like rivets. Faint traces of *Devaśrī*.	L. hand bent up and resting on knee slightly raised. Symbol , but incomplete. *Śrīvikkrama*. **Pl. IX. 6.**
257	122.5	.77	King in *dhoti*. Crescent on Garuḍa. *Devaśramaha*	L. hand bent up. Symbol *Śrivikkra*
258	120.1	.85	King in *dhoti* and his figure is graceful. Necklace and armlets are very clear. Circular legend off.	L. hand bent up. R. hand bent up and holds a flower. Symbol *Śrīvikramaḥ*.

[1] This coin was misplaced when the plates were prepared; hence it is to be seen on Pl. VII in the midst of the coins of Class I with throne reverse.

No.	Wt.	Size	Obverse	Reverse
259	122	.78	King in *dhoti*. Halo on the l. looks like a crescent. Circular legend off.	L. hand bent up. Symbol *Śrīvikramaḥ*.
260	120.6	.77	King in *payajama*. L. side halo looks like a crescent. Profuse hair on king's head curling down. *Deva*	L. hand on knee. Symbol *Śrīvikramaḥ*.
261	120.3	.82	King in *dhoti*. Crescent above Garuḍa. *Deva*	L. hand on knee. Lotus crudely engraved. Symbol Legend blurred and illegible.
262	120.5	.76	King in *dhoti*. Buttons of coat very clearly visible. Crescent above Garuḍa. *Devaśra*	L. hand bent up. Symbol indistinct. *Śravakramaḥ*.
263	120.7	.7	King in *dhoti*. Legend under arm blurred; circular legend off. Three cracks in edges.	L. hand bent up. Symbol incomplete, but probably *Śrīvikramaḥ*.
264	119	.8	King in *dhoti*. Earring rather big. *.va........srī-Chandraguptaḥ*.	Lotus of small stalk in l. hand, which is stretched above the knee. Symbol, but incomplete. *Srivīkkramaḥ*.
265	120.6	.75	King in *dhoti*; ornamental side-buttons on coat. *Devaśrama*	L. hand on knee. Symbol *Śrīvikramaḥ*.

No.	Wt.	Size	Obverse	Reverse
266	123.1	.79	King in *dhoti*. Tresses of curly hair on the head. Circular legend off.	L. arm akimbo. Symbol *Śrīvikkramaḥ*.
267	120.7	.78	King in *dhoti*; his hair looks like a wig. *Devaśrī*	Coin is crude in appearance. L. hand on knee. Symbol, but incomplete. Legend illegible.
268	121.7	.73	King in *dhoti*. *Dava*	L. arm akimbo. Symbol Legend blurred.
269	119.1	.84	King in *dhoti*. *Devaśrīmahārāja*	L. arm akimbo. Symbol *Śrīvikkramaḥ*.
270	121.7	.83	King in *dhoti*. Circular legend off.	L. hand on knee. Symbol, but incomplete. *Śrīvikramaḥ*.
271	120.4	.75	King in *dhoti*. *Devaśrī*	L. hand bent up. Symbol blurred. Legend blurred.
272	120.2	.75	King in *dhoti*. *Devaśrīma*	L. hand bent up. Symbol, but incomplete. *Śrīvikramaḥ*, blurred.
273	126.8	.79	King in *dhoti*. *Devaśramahara*	L. hand on the knee. Symbol *Śrīvikramaḥ*.
274	125.5	.84	King in *dhoti*. *Devaśrīmaharajadha*	L. hand on knee. Symbol *Śrīvikkramah*.
275	127.2	.8	King in *dhoti* and wearing sash, whose ends hang down parallel to	L. hand on knee; noose in r. hand. Symbol a variation of

No.	Wt.	Size	Obverse	Reverse
			the ends of the coat. Circular legend off.	, but lower part being like that of 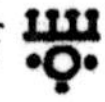 *Srīvikkramaḥ.*
276	121.9	.76	King in *dhoti.* Circular legend off.	L. hand bent up. Symbol  *Srīvikramaḥ.*
277	121.6	.8	King in *dhoti.* He wears high leather boots or something like *paṭṭis* of soldiers, right up to thigh. ....*śra-Chandraguptaḥ.*	L. hand bent up. Symbol , but carelessly engraved. *Sriviakramaḥ.* Pl. IX. 7.
278	127.5	.79	King in trousers. ....*śra-Cha*	L. hand resting on knee. Symbol , but incomplete. *Srīvikramaḥ.*
279	122.6	.79	King in *dhoti.* ...*śramahārājādharā*	L. hand on knee. Symbol  *Srīvikkramaḥ.*
280	125.9	.82	King in *dhoti.* *Devaśrīmaha*	L. hand on knee. Goddess is rather crudely engraved. Symbol a variation of , lower part being like that of 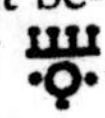. *Srīvikkramaḥ.*
281	127.7	.78	King in *dhoti.* Faint traces of truncated legend.	L. hand on knee. Symbol a variation of 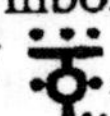, lower part being like that of 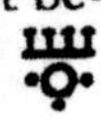. *Srīvikramaḥ.*
282	125.8	.83	King in *dhoti.* *.vaśrama*	L. hand on knee and the lotus held in it looks like a cluster

No.	Wt.	Size	Obverse	Reverse
				of four dots. R. hand slightly raised up. Symbol *Śrīvikramaḥ.*
283	121.1	·73	King in half-pant. Circular legend off.	L. hand on knee. Symbol , but incomplete. *Śrīvikramaḥ.*
284	121.7	·76	King in *dhoti.* Circular legend off.	L. hand on waist akimbo. Symbol *Śrīvikramaḥ.*
285	112.3	·79	King in *dhoti.* Circular legend off. Normal condition; low weight.	L. hand on knee. R. hand slightly raised up. Symbol *Śrivikramaḥ.*
286	124.5	.85	King in *dhoti.* *Devaśrīmahārā*	L. hand on knee. Symbol *Śrīvikramaḥ.*
287	125.4	.8	King in *dhoti.* *Chandra* under arm blurred. *Devaśramahārājā*	L. arm akimbo. Symbol blurred. *Śrīvikramaḥ.* Die crude.
288	119.9	·74	King in *dhoti.* *Devaśramaharajadha-......ptaḥ.*	L. hand on knee. Symbol *Śrīvikramaḥ.*
289	124.6	.84	King in *dhoti.* *Dava...rājādharā,* truncated. Two cracks in the edge.	L. hand on knee. Symbol blurred. *Śrīvikramaḥ.*
290	121.1	.77	King in *dhoti.* ....*draga*	L. hand on knee. Symbol *Śrīvikkramaḥ.*
291	121.2	.77	King in *dhoti.* *Devaśramahārājā*	L. hand stretched out.

No.	Wt.	Size	Obverse	Reverse
				Symbol , but incomplete. *Srīvikramaḥ.*
292	127	.78	King in *dhoti.* *Devaśramahārājā* One crack in edge.	L. hand on knee. Symbol blurred. *Srīvikra*
293	120.9	.8	King in *dhoti.* *Devaśrīmahā*	L. hand bent up and the lotus in it is crude. Symbol *Srīvikramaḥ.*
294	123.3	.75	King in *dhoti.* Circular legend off.	L. hand bent up. Symbol incomplete, but probably , lower part only being on the flan.
295	127.6	.72	King in *dhoti* and with sash. Circular legend off.	L. hand on knee. Symbol Legend off.
296	128.5	.79	King in trousers and with sash. Circular legend off.	L. hand on knee. Symbol , but it is carelessly drawn. Legend off.
297	124.3	.84	King in *shalwār* and high boots and wearing wristlets and armlets; hair on head denoted by numerous curls. ....*Chandra-guptaḥ.*	L. hand on thigh. Symbol , but it is incomplete. *Srīvikkramaḥ.* **Pl. IX. 8.**
298	121.2	.76	King in trousers. *Dava..........ndra-guptaḥ.*	L. hand bent up. Symbol *Srīvikkramaḥ.*
299	120	.74	King in *dhoti.* *Devaśrī*	L. arm akimbo. Symbol *Srīvikkramaḥ.*

No.	Wt.	Size	Obverse	Reverse
300	121.4	.75	King in *dhoti* and wearing sash. Circular legend off.	L. hand bent up. Symbol  Legend off.
301	121.4	.73	King in *dhoti*. Circular legend off.	L. hand on knee. R. arm akimbo. Symbol 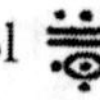, but without the dot in the circle. *Srīvikkramaḥ.*
302	121.3	.8	King in trousers. *Davaśramahārājā-......guptaḥ.*	L. hand stretched out. Symbol 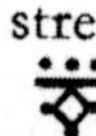 *Srīvikramaḥ.*
303	123.2	.8	King in *dhoti*. Circular legend off.	L. hand on knee. Symbol 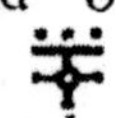 *Srīvikramaḥ.*
304	123.7	.88	King in trousers. *Devaśrīmahārājā* A thin and broad piece.	L. hand on knee. Symbol 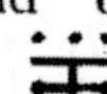 *Srīvikramaḥ.*
305	120.1	.74	King in *dhoti*. *Devaśrīma*	L. hand on thigh. Symbol 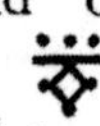, but it is incomplete. *Srava*
306	125	.83	King in *dhoti*. *Chandra* under l. arm blurred. *Devaśrīmahārājādharā*	L. hand on knee. Symbol 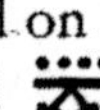 *Srīvikramaḥ.*
307	120.5	.74	King in trousers. Circular legend off. Three cracks in the edge.	L. arm akimbo. Symbol 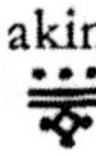 *.vikra*
308	121.1	.78	King in trousers. *.............ndra-guptaḥ.*	L. hand bent up. Symbol 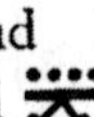 *Srīvikkramaḥ.*
309	120.3	.71	King in *dhoti*. Halo on the l. awkward in appearance and detached. Circular legend off.	L. hand bent up. Symbol 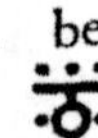, but ill engraved. *Srīvikramah.*

No.	Wt.	Size	Obverse	Reverse
310	120.8	.8	King in trousers. *Devaśrī* Two cracks in the edge.	L. hand extended. Stalk of the lotus looks like a sword. Symbol Legend blurred.
311	120.6	.7	King in *dhoti*; his coat buttons visible in the centre, as also earrings and necklace. .....*rajadharajaśrī-Chandraguptaḥ*, mostly on l; *ptaḥ* is between the head of Garuḍa and the king.	L. hand on thigh. Symbol *Śrīvikkramaḥ*. **Pl. IX. 9.**
312	121.2	.75	King in *dhoti* and with sash. Circular legend off.	L. hand bent up. Symbol *Śrīvikkramaḥ*.
313	124.3	.83	King in *dhoti*. Curly hair on head arranged in two rows. *Deva.........guptaḥ*.	L. hand on thigh. Symbol blurred. *Śrīvikramaḥ*.
314	119.9	.8	King in *dhoti*, reaching to the knees only. To the left of Garuḍa an incomplete symbol (?) *Devaśrī*	L. hand bent up. Symbol off. *Śrīvikkramaḥ*.
315	122	.75	King in *dhoti*. Circular legend off.	L. hand bent up. Symbol *Śrīvikkramaḥ*.
316	123.5	.78	King in *dhoti*. Necklace and armlets very clear. *Devaśrī........ ndraguptaḥ*.	L. hand on knee. Symbol incomplete, but probably *Śrīvikkramaḥ*.

No.	Wt.	Size	Obverse	Reverse
317	120.6	.71	King in *dhoti* and with sash. Circular legend off.	L. hand bent up. Symbol incomplete, but probably  *Srīvikkramaḥ.*
318	120.2	.75	King in *dhoti.* Button line of the coat very clear. *Deva.........Chandraguptaḥ.*	L. hand bent up. Symbol  *Śrīvikkramaḥ*
319	121.6	.73	King in *dhoti*; halo detached. Circular legend off.	L. arm akimbo. Symbol 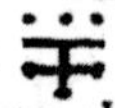 *Śrīvikkramaḥ.*
320	126.5	.84	King in *dhoti* and with sash. Buttons of the coat clearly visible. Circular legend off.	L. arm akimbo. Symbol  *Śrīvikkramaḥ.*
321	119.9	.75	King in *dhoti*, wearing high boots; sleeves of the coat tucked up and armlet on the l. arm. *Davaśriamaharajadharaśra-Chan* Arrow cuts across the letters *śri* and *dra.*	L. hand on knee, engraved crudely. Symbol a variation of 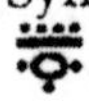, having three dots above instead of four. *Srīvikkramaḥ.* **Pl. IX. 10.**
322	120.9	.73	King in *dhoti.* *Chandra* under l. arm blurred. *Deva*	L. arm akimbo. Goddess not nimbate. Symbol  *Srīvikkramaḥ.*
323	122	.7	King in *dhoti.* Circular legend off.	L. arm akimbo. Symbol  *Srīvikkramaḥ.*
324	126.9	.74	King in *dhoti*, whose folds appear prominently. Circular legend off.	L. hand on knee. Symbol 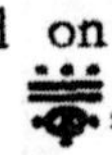, but incomplete. *Sra.kra*

No.	Wt.	Size	Obverse	Reverse
325	121.6	.75	King in *dhoti.* *Devaśrīmaharajadharaja*	L. hand on the knee. Symbol  Legend blurred.
326	122.8	.79	King in *dhoti.* *Devaśrīmaharajadha*	L. hand on knee. Symbol probably , but incomplete. *Srīvikkramaḥ.*
327	123.5	.77	King in *dhoti.* *Deva*	L. hand bent up. Symbol incomplete. *Srīvikkramaḥ.*
328	118	.72	King in *dhoti.* Circular legend off.	L. hand bent up. Symbol incomplete. *Srīvikkramaḥ.*
329	121.3	.72	King in *dhoti.* Circular legend off.	L. hand bent up. Symbol  *Srīvikkramaḥ.*
330	122.3	.82	King in trousers. *Devaśramaharajadha . . .* *Chandraguptaḥ.*	L. hand on knee. Symbol 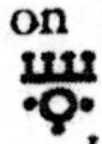 *Srīvikkramaḥ.*
331	120.3	.78	King in *dhoti.* *Davaśrīmaharajadha . .* *śra-Chandraguptaḥ.*	L. hand bent up. Symbol , blurred. *Srīvikkramaḥ.*
332	119.4	.8	King in *dhoti.* *.vaśramaharaja*	L. hand stretched. Symbol incomplete, but probably , lower part only being visible.
333	122.8	.85	King in trousers. *Devaśrīmaharajadharaja,* in small characters.	L. hand on knee. Symbol 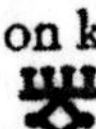 *Srīvikkramaḥ.*
334	121.6	.78	King in trousers. *Devaśrīmaha . . . .* *gu*	L. hand stretched out. Symbol , but in- complete. *Srīvikkramaḥ.*

No.	Wt.	Size	Obverse	Reverse
335	123.7	.88	King in *dhoti*. *Devaśrīmahārajadha*	L. arm akimbo. Symbol *Śrīvikkramaḥ*.
336	124.2	.82	King in trousers. *...maharajadha* Four cracks in the edge.	L. hand on the knee. Symbol , but incomplete. *Śrīvikkramaḥ*.
337	122.4	.77	King in trousers. *Dava..........* *guptaḥ*.	L. hand stretched out. Symbol *Śrīvikkramaḥ*.
338	121.3	.73	King in *dhoti*. *Devaśramaharaja......* *guptaḥ*.	L. hand bent up. Symbol *Śrīvikkramaḥ*.
339	120.1	.73	King in *dhoti*; curly hair falls on the neck. *Devaśrīma*	L. hand bent up. Symbol *Śrīvikkramaḥ*.
340	123.4	.79	King in trousers. *Devaśramahara........* *ndraguptaḥ*.	L. hand on knee and the lotus in it has a long stalk. Goddess without halo. Symbol *Śrīvikkramaḥ*.
341	124.7	.9	King in *dhoti*. *Devaśrīmaharajadha...* *śra*	L. hand on knee. Symbol *Śrīvikkramaḥ*.
342	120	.79	King in *dhoti*. *Devaśra........* *Chandraguptaḥ*.	L. hand bent up. Symbol , but blurred. *Śrīvikkramaḥ*.
343	122.5	.8	King in *dhoti*. *..śra..........* *gaptaḥ*.	L. arm akimbo. Symbol *Śrīvikkramaḥ*.
344	123.9	.8	King in *dhoti*. *Devaśrīmaha*, blurred.	L. hand resting on knee. Symbol off. *Śrīvikkramaḥ*.

No.	Wt.	Size	Obverse	Reverse
345	123.2	.88	King in *dhoti*. *Devaśramaharaja . . . śra-Cha*	L. arm akimbo. Symbol *Srīvikkramaḥ*.
346	119.9	.88	King in trousers. Ornamental rows of buttons on either side of the coat. *. . śrīmaharajadharaja . . ndraguptaḥ*.	L. hand stretched out. Symbol *Srīvikramaḥ*.
347	127.5	.77	King in *dhoti*. *Deva* One crack in the edge.	L. hand bent up. Symbol Legend truncated.
348	120.2	.85	King in *dhoti*. *Devaśrīmahāraja . . . . Chandraguptaḥ*.	L. hand bent up. Symbol *Srīvikramaḥ*.
349	123.1	.81	King probably in trousers. *Devaśrīmaha*	L. hand on knee. Symbol *Srīvikramaḥ*.
350	124.7	.82	King in *dhoti*. *Devaśramaharajadha*	L. hand on knee. Symbol off. *Srīvikkramaḥ*.
351	122.4	.8	King in *dhoti*. Curly hair on head. *Davaśra . . . . ndraguptaḥ*	L. hand on knee. Symbol *.vikramaḥ*.
352	122.6	.82	King in *dhoti*. *Dava* Three cracks in the edge.	L. hand on knee. Symbol *Srīvikkramaḥ*.
353	120.1	.77	King in trousers. *Dava . . . . śrī-Chandraguptaḥ*.	L. hand on knee. Symbol *Srīvikkramaḥ*.
354	121	.78	King in *dhoti*. *Davaśra* One crack in the edge.	L. hand on knee. Symbol *Srīvikkramaḥ*.

No.	Wt.	Size	Obverse	Reverse
355	127.8	.79	King in *dhoti*. Circular legend off.	L. hand bent up. Symbol 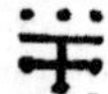 *Srīvikkramaḥ*.
356	122.6	.83	King in *dhoti*. *Deva*, blurred; rest off the flan.	L. arm akimbo. Symbol  *Srīvikkramaḥ*.
357	118.5	.72	King in *dhoti*. *.vaśra* Crack in the edge at XI	L. hand bent up. Symbol , but incomplete. *Srīvikramaḥ*.
358	119.6	.83	King in trousers. *Devaśrī* Cracks in the edge at VII and XI	L. hand on knee. Symbol  *Srīvikramaḥ*.
359	122.6	.87	King in *pāyajamā*. *Devaśrīmaharajadhiraja-śrī*	L. hand on knee. Symbol 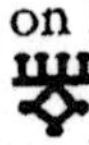 *Srīvikkramaḥ*.
360	124.7	.8	King in *dhoti*. Crescent over Garuḍa. A pellet between the waist and r. arm of the king. Circular legend off.	L. hand on knee; r. hand slightly raised. Symbol  *Srīvikramaḥ*.
361	122.4	.84	King in *dhoti*. *Dava*	L. hand on knee. Symbol 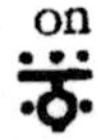, but incomplete. *Srīvikkramaḥ*.
362	126.8	.74	King in *dhoti* and with a sash across the body. Coat with ornamental buttons. Circular legend off the flan. A thick coin with several cracks in the edge.	L. arm on knee. Symbol a variation of 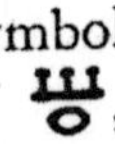, with three dots on the three sides of the circle. *Srīvikra*

No.	Wt.	Size	Obverse	Reverse
363	126.3	.8	King in *dhoti*. Coat buttons clear. Circular legend off.	L. arm on knee. Symbol 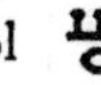, but incomplete. *Srīvakramaḥ*.
364	122.4	.87	King in trousers. *Davaśramaharajadhiraja-śra-Chandraguptaḥ*.	L. arm akimbo. Symbol  *Srīvikkramaḥ*.
365	119.5	.79	King in *dhoti*. Circular legend off. A dotted line below the king's feet.	L. hand bent up. Symbol , but incomplete. *Srīvikramaḥ*.
366	120.8	.87	King in *dhoti*. Buttons of the coat clear. *Devasramaharaja ...... guptaḥ*.	L. hand bent up. Symbol  *Srīvikramaḥ*.
367	126.1	.79	King in *dhoti*. Circular legend blurred.	L. hand on knee. Symbol  *Srīvikkramaḥ*.
368	124.2	.8	King in *dhoti*. *Davaśramaharajadha* Two cracks in the edge.	L. hand on knee. Symbol  *Srīvikkramaḥ*.
369	118.1	.83	King in *dhoti* and wearing *paṭṭis*; fillet round the forehead. *Davaśramaharajadhara-...ndraguptaḥ*; rather blurred. Three cracks in the edge at III, V and X.	L. hand stretched out. Symbol almost off the flan. *Srīvikrama* Right side is double-struck as shown by the double halo and border of dots. **Pl. IX. 11.**
370	113	.79	King in *dhoti*. Circular legend is blurred. Remarkably low weight. The coin is not worn out.	L. hand on knee. Symbol 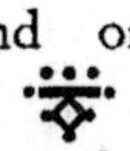 *Srīvikkramaḥ*.

No.	Wt.	Size	Obverse	Reverse
371	125.8	.83	King in *dhoti*, wearing a sash. *Davaśramaḥa*	L. hand on knee. Symbol blurred. Flan moved while striking. Legend blurred.
372	121.8	.79	King in *dhoti*. *Davaśra*	L. hand on knee. Symbol  *Śrīvikkramaḥ*.
373	127.1	.73	King in *dhoti* and sash. Legend off.	Left hand on knee. Symbol  *Śrīvikra*
374	125.4	.84	King in *shalwār* and wearing a sash, wristlets and armlets, curly hair falling on the neck. Row of buttons in the centre of the coat. *Deva*	L. hand on thigh. Symbol  *Śrīvikkramaḥ*. Pl. IX. 12.
375	125	.82	King wearing *dhoti* and sash. Sword-like object hanging from the waist. Circular legend off.	L. hand on knee. Symbol  Legend blurred.
376	124.6	.82	King in trousers. Pearl-bordered headdress. *Davaśramaharaja*	L. hand on knee. Symbol 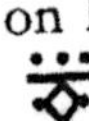 *Śrīvikramaḥ*.
377	118.7	.8	King in trousers. Circular legend off. Even bow also partly visible on the r. Three cracks in the edge.	L. hand bent up. Symbol  *Śrīvikramaḥ*.
378	121.3	.7	King in *dhoti*. *Dava* Several cracks in the edge.	L. hand on knee. Symbol 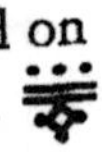 *Śrīvikkra*

No.	Wt.	Size	Obverse	Reverse
379	128.1	.85	King in short *dhoti*, reaching only to the knees, and wearing beautiful head-dress. Only faint traces of circular legend. One crack at III.	L. hand on knee. Symbol *..kkra*
380	120	.77	King in *dhoti*. *Davaśra*	L. hand bent up. Symbol *Śravakkramaḥ.*
381	121.6	.76	King in *dhoti*. Circular legend off.	L. hand bent up. Symbol *Śrīvikramaḥ.*
382	120.6	.75	King in *dhoti*. Traces of truncated circular legend.	L. hand bent up. Symbol *..kkra*
383	123.6	.82	King in *dhoti*. *Devaśrama* Two cracks in the edge, at IX and I.	L. hand on knee. Symbol *Śrīvikkramaḥ.*
384	121.7	.75	King in trousers. *.....rajadharaja-śra-Chandragu*	L. hand on knee. Symbol *Śrīvikkramaḥ.*
385	121.1	.74	King in trousers. Row of buttons on the coat very clear. *..śramaharajadharaja*	L. hand bent up. Symbol *Śrīvikkramaḥ.*
386	119.3	.75	King in *dhoti*. *Davaśrama*	L. hand bent up. Symbol , but incomplete. *Śrīvikkramaḥ.*
387	120.5	.75	King in trousers. Circular legend off.	L. hand bent up. Symbol *Śrīvikkramaḥ.*
388	121.3	.78	King in *dhoti*. *Dava*	L. hand on knee. Symbol Legend off.

No.	Wt.	Size	Obverse	Reverse
389	123.9	.85	King in *dhoti*. *Devaśrama*	L. hand on knee. Symbol blurred. *Śrīvikkramaḥ*.
390	123.6	.82	King in *shalwār*. Profuse curly hair falling on the neck in three tresses. Necklace and double armlet distinct. *Devaśramahārājādhirāja-śra-Cha*.	L. hand akimbo. Symbol  *Śrīvikkramaḥ*. **Pl. IX. 13.**
391	123.2	.85	King in *shalwār* and wearing a pearl bedecked cap. *Davaśramaharajadharaja-śra-Cha*, blurred and truncated.	L. hand akimbo. Symbol  crudely engraved. *Śrīvikramaḥ*. **Pl. IX. 14.**
392	119.8	.7	King in *dhoti*. *Davaśra*	L. hand bent up. Symbol , but incomplete. *Śrīvikramaḥ*.
393	127	.8	King in *dhoti*. Curly hair descends on the neck in tresses. Circular legend blurred.	L. hand on knee. Symbol 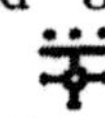, but incomplete. *Śrīvikramaḥ*. Flan moved while striking.
94	115.3	.8	King in *dhoti*. Circular legend blurred. Considerably worn.	L. hand bent up. Symbol  *Śrīvikkramaḥ*.
395	120.7	.77	King in *dhoti*. Halo on the l. detached from the head. *Devaśra*	L. hand bent up. Symbol  *Śrīvikramaḥ*.

No.	Wt.	Size	Obverse	Reverse
396	120.8	.83	King in *dhoti*. *Dava* A crude coin.	L. arm akimbo. R. hand touches the knee. Symbol  *Śrīvikkramaḥ*.
397	121	.79	King wearing a short *dhoti*. *Davaśramaha*	L. hand bent up. Symbol  *Śrīvikramaḥ*.
398	128.1	.73	King in trousers. Circular legend off. A neat coin but eight cracks in the edge.	L. hand on knee. Symbol 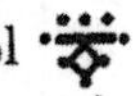 *Śrīvikramaḥ*.
399	121.8	.7	King in *dhoti*, sash tied at the waist and hanging down from a knot; unlike the hunter on **Pl. XI. 12-14,** it shows a bulge in the upper portion. Coat buttons clear in the centre. *Davaśra*	L. hand bent up. Symbol 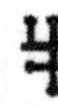, but incomplete. *Śrīvikrama*, truncated. **Pl. IX. 15.**
400	121	.8	King in trousers. ....*śrī-Chandraguptaḥ*.	L. hand on knee. Symbol  *Śrīvikkramaḥ*.
401	124	.83	King in *dhoti*. *Davaśramaharajadharaja*	L. hand on knee. Symbol a variation of , but having two horizontal lines. *Śrīvikramaḥ*.
402	124.1	.8	King in *dhoti*. ....*guptaḥ*.	L. hand on knee. Symbol 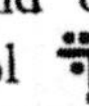 *.vikkramaḥ*.
403	123.6	.85	King in trousers. *Devaśramaharajadhara*	L. hand on knee Symbol 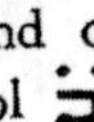 *Śrīvikkramaḥ*.

No.	Wt.	Size	Obverse	Reverse
404	120	.76	King in trousers. . . . . *Śrī.ndraguptaḥ.*	L. hand bent up. Symbol *Śrīvikkramaḥ.*
405	118.3	.71	King wearing short *dhoti*, reaching to the knees only. Circular legend off.	L. hand on knee. Symbol *Śrīvikkramaḥ.*
406	121.2	.74	King in *dhoti*. *Deva. . . . . .guptaḥ.* One crack in the edge.	L. hand bent up. Symbol *Śrīvikkramaḥ.*
407	128	.79	King in trousers. Circular legend off.	Goddess not nimbate. L. hand on knee. Symbol *Śrīvikramaḥ.*
408	123.8	.87	King in trousers. *Deva. . . . .* *ndraguptaḥ.*	L. hand on knee. Symbol *Śrīvikkramaḥ.*
409	122.3	.84	King in *dhoti*. *Dava*	L. hand on knee. Symbol *Śrīvikramaḥ.*
410	127.2	.77	King in trousers, wearing a sash. Circular legend off.	L. hand on knee. Symbol *Śrī*
411	120.9	.72	King in *dhoti* and wearing a sash. Circular legend off.	L. hand bent up. Symbol indistinct. *Śrīvikkramaḥ.*
412	121.7	.74	King in *dhoti*. Circular legend off.	L. arm akimbo. Symbol *Śrīvikkramaḥ.*
413	126.9	.8	King in *dhoti*. *Dava*	L. hand on knee. Symbol , incomplete. *Śrīvikkramaḥ.*
414	121.2	.77	King in *dhoti*. Circular legend off.	L. arm akimbo. Symbol *Śrīvikkramaḥ.*

No.	Wt.	Size	Obverse	Reverse
415	121	.73	King in *dhoti*. Circular legend off.	L. hand bent up. Symbol  Legend truncated.
416	124.7	.82	King in *dhoti*. Circular legend off.	L. hand on knee. Symbol  *Srīvikkramaḥ*.
417	121.3	.82	King in *dhoti*. Circular legend off.	L. hand on knee. Symbol  *Srīvikkramaḥ*.
418	119.8	.77	King in *dhoti*. *Dava*	L. hand bent up and touching the left knee. Symbol  *Srīvikkra*
419	121.4	.79	King in *dhoti*. *De*	L. hand bent up. Symbol 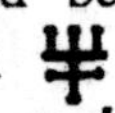 *Srīvikkramaḥ*.
420	120.2	.75	King in *dhoti*. *Deva*	L. hand bent up and resting on l. knee. Symbol  ..*kkra*
421	128.3	.77	King in trousers. Circular legend off.	L. hand on knee. Symbol 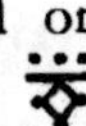 Legend blurred.
422	120.6	.78	King in *dhoti*. Circular legend off.	L. hand on knee. Symbol  *Srīvikramaḥ*.
423	123.4	.79	King in *dhoti*. Circular legend off.	L. hand on knee. Symbol off. *Srīvikkramaḥ*.
424	126.8	.77	King in trousers. Circular legend off.	L. hand on knee. Symbol 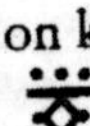 Legend blurred.

No.	Wt.	Size	Obverse	Reverse
425	121.6	.73	King wearing a short *dhoti*. Circular legend off.	L. hand bent up. Symbol  *Śrīvikkramaḥ*.
426	121.6	.74	King in *dhoti*. Circular legend off.	L. hand bent up. Symbol  *Śrīvikkramaḥ*.
427	121.5	.74	King in *dhoti*, wearing a sash. Circular legend off.	L. hand bent up. Symbol off. *Śrīvikramaḥ*.
428	120.5	.78	King in *dhoti*. Circular legend off.	L. hand on knee. Symbol blurred. *Śrīvikkramaḥ*.
429	121.1	.73	King in *dhoti*. Legend blurred and partially preserved.	L. arm akimbo. Symbol off. *Śrīvikkramaḥ*.
430	122.1	.77	King in *dhoti*. Circular legend off.	L. hand on knee. Symbol  *Śravakkra*
431	124.6	.78	King in *dhoti*. *.vaśra*	L. hand on knee. Symbol  *Śrīvikramaḥ*.
432	121	.71	King in *dhoti*. Circular legend off.	L. arm akimbo. Two legs of the goddess folded in such a way as to look like a pillow.[1] Symbol , but without a dot in the circle. *Śrīvikra*
433	119.5	.78	As above.	L. hand on knee. Symbol  *Śrīvikkramaḥ*.

[1] This fashion later became common with Prakāśāditya and Narasiṁhagupta; see Pl. XXXII. 10, and *B. M. C. G. D.*, Pl. XXII, 1-8.

No.	Wt.	Size	Obverse	Reverse
434	121.1	.75	King in *dhoti.* *.vaśra*	L. hand bent up, and resting on l. knee, slightly raised up. Symbol , but incomplete. Legend blurred.
435	120.5	.78	King in *dhoti.* Circular legend off.	L. hand bent up. Symbol blurred. *Śrīvikkramaḥ.*
436	120.3	.78	King in *dhoti.* Crescent over Garuḍa. Circular legend off.	L. hand bent up. Symbol Legend off.
437	120.7	.71	King in *dhoti.* Circular legend off.	L. hand on knee. Symbol *Śrīvikramaḥ.*
438	120.1	.7	As above.	L. arm akimbo. Symbol Legend off.
439	119	.78	As above	L. hand on knee. Symbol *Śrīvikramaḥ.*
440	124	.8	King in trousers. *Davaśrīmaha*	L. hand on knee. Symbol *Śrīvikkramaḥ.*
441	120.6	.75	King in *dhoti.* Circular legend off. The coin appears to be heavily alloyed.	L. hand bent up. Symbol *Śrīvikkramaḥ.*
442	120.9	.75	King in *dhoti.* Circular legend off. One crack in the edge.	L. hand bent up and resting on l. knee raised up. Symbol *Śrīvikramaḥ.*

No.	Wt.	Size	Obverse	Reverse
443	121.2	.78	King in *dhoti*. *Dava*	L. arm akimbo. Symbol a variation of  but without a dot in the circle. *Srīvikkramaḥ.*
444	127	.8	King in trousers. Circular legend off. One crack in the edge.	L. hand on knee. Symbol , incomplete. *Srīvikkramaḥ.*
445	123.7	.79	King in trousers. Circular legend off.	L. hand on knee. Symbol  *.vikkramaḥ.*
446	120.2	.77	King in *dhoti*. ....*guptaḥ.*	L. hand bent up. Symbol  *Srīvikra*
447	121.1	.73	King in *dhoti*. ....*chandra*	L. hand bent up and resting on l. knee raised up. Symbol  Legend truncated.
448	120.7	.78	King in *dhoti*. *Deva*........... *guptaḥ.*	L. hand bent up. Symbol 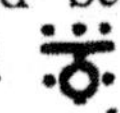 *Srīvikkramaḥ.*
449	121	.75	King in *dhoti*. Circular legend off.	L. arm akimbo. Symbol  *Srīvikkramaḥ.*
450	121.4	.79	King in *dhoti*. ....*guptaḥ.*	L. hand bent up. Symbol  *Srīvikkramaḥ.*
451	118.6	.8	King in *dhoti*. ....*śrī-Chandra-guptaḥ.*	L. hand bent up. Symbol  *Srīvikkramaḥ.*
452	120.3	.79	King in *dhoti*. *Devaśrīmahārājādharāja-* ...*guptaḥ.*	L. hand bent up. Symbol  Legend truncated.

No.	Wt.	Size	Obverse	Reverse
453	120.2	.89	King in *dhoti*. ....*ndraguptaḥ*. Four cracks in the edge.	L. hand stretched out. Symbol incomplete. *Śrīvikramaḥ*.
454	122.5	.83	King in *dhoti*, wearing a cap having a string of pearls behind. Coat is of short sleeves. *Davaśrama*........*ndraguptaḥ*; partly truncated.	L. hand stretched out, and the lotus stalk held in it touches the ground. Symbol blurred. *Śravakramaḥ*. **Pl. X. 1.**
455	128.2	.8	King in *dhoti*. *Davaśra*	L. hand on knee. Symbol *Śrīvikramaḥ*.
456	127.6	.8	King in *dhoti* and wearing sash. *Davaśra*	L. hand on knee. Symbol incomplete. *Śrīvikramaḥ*.
457	120.4	.73	King as above. Circular legend off.	L.' hand bent up. Symbol *Śrīvikramaḥ*.
458	120.7	.8	King in *dhoti*. Circular legend off.	L. hand bent up. Symbol Legend blurred.
459	120.9	.75	King in *dhoti*. *Davaśra*	L. hand on knee. Symbol *Śrīvikramaḥ*.
460	120.5	.78	King in *dhoti*, and a crescent above him. *Devaśrīmaharaja*	L. hand on knee. Symbol *Śrīvikramaḥ*.
461	125.3	.8	King in *dhoti*. *.vasrama*	L. hand bent up. Symbol *Śrīvikramaḥ*.
462	119.4	.8	King in *dhoti*. *Davaśra*.......... *guptaḥ*.	L. hand bent up. Symbol *Śrīvikkramaḥ*.

No.	Wt.	Size	Obverse	Reverse
463	124.5	.83	King in *dhoti*. ....*gaptaḥ*.	L. hand on knee. Symbol *Śrīvikkramaḥ*.
464	120.1	.76	King in *dhoti*. ....*śra-Chandra*	L. hand bent up. Symbol *Śrīvikramaḥ*.
465	123.6	.85	King in *dhoti*. *Devaśrīmahārājādha-rājāśra*	L. hand on knee. Symbol *Śrīvikkramaḥ*.
466	120.8	.78	King in *dhoti*. *Davaśramaharajadharaja* in small characters.	L. hand on knee. Symbol *Śrīvikramaḥ*.
467	128.7	.71	King in *dhoti*. Circular legend off.	L. hand on knee. Symbol Legend off.
468	121	.83	King in *dhoti*. Coat buttons clearly visible in the centre. *Davaśramaha*, in small characters.	L. hand bent up. Symbol *Śrīvikramaḥ*.
469	120.4	.76	King in *dhoti*. Circular legend off.	L. hand bent up. Symbol , incomplete. *Śrīvikkramaḥ*.
470	120.9	.73	King in *dhoti*. Circular legend off.	L. hand bent up. Symbol , incomplete. Legend truncated.
471	120.9	.74	King in *dhoti*. Circular legend off.	L. hand bent up. Symbol , incomplete. Legend truncated.
472	120.6	.8	King in trousers. *Devaśrīma*	L. hand stretched out. Symbol *Śrīvikramaḥ*.

No.	Wt.	Size	Obverse	Reverse
473	121.7	.78	King in trousers. *Davaśramaharaja*	L. hand stretched out. Symbol  *Śrīvikramaḥ.*
474	121.1	.72	King in *dhoti.* . *vaśra*	L. hand on knee. Symbol  *Śrīvikramaḥ.*
475	124.3	.88	King in trousers. *Davaśramaharajadhara-jaśra-Chandraguptaḥ.*	L. hand on knee. Symbol  *Śrīvikkramaḥ.*
476	123.2	.85	King in *dhoti.* Hair on the head looks like a wig. *Davaśramaharajadha* One crack in the edge.	L. hand on knee. Symbol  *Śrīvikkramaḥ.*
477	123	.89	King in *dhoti.* *Devaśrīmaharajadhara...* *Chandraguptaḥ.*	L. hand on knee. Symbol  Legend blurred.
478	119.1	.90	King has curly hair. *Devaśramaharajadhiraja-śra-Chandraguptaḥ.* Part of the legend blurred and truncated.	L. hand on knee. Symbol  *Śrīvikramaḥ.* **Pl. X. 2.**
479	118.8	.79	King in *dhoti.* *Davaśra*, truncated.	L. hand bent up. Symbol  *Śrīvikkramaḥ*, truncated.
480	127.3	.75	King in *dhoti.* *Devaśrīmaharajadhara*, in small characters.	L. hand on knee. Symbol  *Śrīvikramaḥ.*
481	120.9	.72	King in *dhoti.* Circular legend off.	L. hand bent up. Symbol 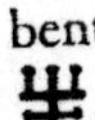, incomplete. *Śrīvikkramaḥ.*
482	120.6	.79	King in *dhoti.* Circular legend off.	L. hand bent up. Symbol 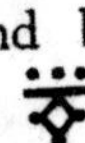 *Śrīvikramaḥ.*

No.	Wt.	Size	Obverse	Reverse
483	118.6	.75	King in *dhoti*. Circular legend blurred.	L. hand bent up. Symbol *Śrīvikramaḥ*.
484	121.6	.78	King in *dhoti*. *Davaśramaharajadhara . . Chandraguptaḥ*.	L. hand bent up. Symbol *Śrīvikkramaḥ*.
485	121	.85	King in *dhoti*. *Devaśra*	L. hand on knee. Symbol Legend truncated.
486	120.7	.73	King in *dhoti*. . . . . *ndra*	L. hand on knee. Symbol Legend truncated.
487	123.4	.78	King in trousers. *Davaśrama*	L. hand stretched out, and the lotus in it has a long stalk. Symbol *Śrīvikramaḥ*.
488	126.2	.74	King in *dhoti*. *Davaśra*	L. hand on knee. Symbol *Śrīvikkramaḥ*.
489	127.6	.8	King in trousers. Circular legend off. One crack in the edge.	L. hand on knee. Symbol Legend truncated.
490	119	.85	King in trousers. . . . . *śrī-Chandraguptaḥ*. Arrow head between *śrī* and *cha*.	L. hand bent up. Symbol *Śrīvikramaḥ*.
491	121.8	.74	King in *dhoti*. *Davaśrama*	L. arm akimbo. Symbol incomplete. *.vikramaḥ*.
492	119.9	.79	King in *dhoti*. . . . . *Chandragupta*.	L. arm bent up. Symbol *Śrīvikkramaḥ*.
493	117	.88	King in *dhoti*. Circular legend off.	L. hand on knee. Symbol off. *Śrīvikramaḥ*.

No.	Wt.	Size	Obverse	Reverse
494	119.5	.78	King in *dhoti*. *Deva* One crack in the edge.	L. hand on knee. Symbol *Śrīvikramaḥ*.
495	120.4	.73	As above, but no crack.	L. hand bent up. Symbol *Śrīvikkra*
496	124	.73	King in *dhoti*. Hair on his head thick and curly. *Devaśramaha . jadhara*	L. hand on knee. Symbol *Śrīvikkramaḥ*.
497	122.8	.81	King in *dhoti*. Circular legend off.	L. hand on knee. Symbol *Śrīvikkramaḥ*.
498	119.2	.79	King in *dhoti*. *Davaśra*	L. hand bent up. Symbol Legend truncated.
499	120.3	.7	King in *dhoti*. . . *śra*	L. arm bent up. Symbol Legend blurred.
500	121.2	.74	King in *dhoti*. *Davaśra*	L. hand on knee. Symbol incomplete. *Śrīvikkramaḥ*.
501	121.7	.8	King in *dhoti*. *Davaśramahara* Four cracks in the .dge.	L. hand bent up. Symbol *Śrīvikkra*
502	118.8	.79	King in *dhoti*. *Davaśramaharajadhara-śra-Chandraguptaḥ*.	L. hand bent up, the elbow resting on l. knee raised up. Symbol *Śrīvikkramaḥ*.
503	123.7	.78	King in *dhoti*. . . . . *Chandra* Four cracks in the edge.	L. hand on knee. Symbol *Śrīvikramaḥ*.

No.	Wt.	Size	Obverse	Reverse
504	122.4	.72	King in *dhoti*. *Dava.........Chandra-guptaḥ*.	L. hand on knee. Symbol incomplete. *Śrīvikkramaḥ*.
505	121.3	.79	King in trousers. *Davaśra*	L. hand stretched out and holding a lotus whose stalk touches the ground. Symbol  *Śrīvikramaḥ*.
506	127.2	.8	King in *dhoti*. Circular legend off. Three cracks in the edge.	L. hand on knee. Symbol , incomplete. Legend truncated.
507	119.2	.77	King in *dhoti*. *..........śrī-Cha*	L. hand bent up, elbow resting on l, knee raised up. Symbol  *Śrīvikkramaḥ*.
508	125.2	.76	King in *dhoti*. Circular legend off.	L. hand on knee. Symbol 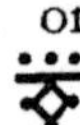 *Śrīvikramaḥ*.
509	120.5	.77	King in *dhoti*. *Devaśrī........... ptaḥ*.	L. arm on knee. Symbol 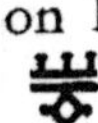 *Śrīvikramaḥ*.
510	118.6	.78	King in *dhoti* and wears leather boots. Coat has side buttons and short sleeves. *Davaśrīmaha......cha ndraguptaḥ*. One crack in the edge.	L. hand stretched out and holding the long lotus stalk at its centre. Symbol , but ill-executed. *Śrīvikramaḥ*. **Pl. X. 3.**
511	121.1	.78	King in *dhoti*. Crescent over *Garuḍa*. *Dava*	L. hand bent up. object in r. hand off the flan. Symbol  *..kramaḥ*.

No.	Wt.	Size	Obverse	Reverse
512	122.5	.79	King in *dhoti*. L. foot at right angle to the leg. *Deva*	L. hand bent up. Symbol *Śrīvikkramaḥ*.
513	119.7	.75	King in *dhoti*. ..*śrī*.........*ndra-guptaḥ*.	L. hand bent up. Symbol *Śrīvikkramaḥ*.
514	120.9	.74	King in *dhoti*. *Davaśramahara*	L. hand on knee. Symbol *Śrīvikkramaḥ*.
515	127.4	.8	King in *dhoti*. *Davaśra*	L. hand on knee. Symbol Legend truncated.
516	125.6	.86	King in *dhoti*. *Davaśra*	L. hand on knee. Symbol blurred. *Śrīvikkramaḥ*.
517	119.4	.75	King in *dhoti*. Circular legend off.	L. arm akimbo. Symbol *Śrīvikkramaḥ*.
518	127.7	.85	King in *dhoti*. Circular legend off.	L. hand on knee. Symbol *Śrīvikkramaḥ*.
519	117.7	.75	King in *dhoti*. *Davaśra*	L. hand bent up. Symbol , incomplete. *Śrīvikkramaḥ*.
520	120	.75	King in *dhoti*. *Davaśra* Two cracks in the edge.	L. hand bent up. Symbol *Śrīvikramaḥ*.
521	128	.75	King in *dhoti* and wearing sash. A crescent over the vertical legend *Chandra* under the arm. Circular legend off.	L. hand on knee. Symbol Legend blurred.

No.	Wt.	Size	Obverse	Reverse
522	127.2	.77	King in *dhoti*. Circular legend off.	L. hand on knee. Symbol Legend truncated.
523	121.8	.83	King in *dhoti* and wearing a pearl bordered cap. Coat has buttons and short sleeves. Earring is very prominent. *Davaśra.........ndraguptaḥ.*	L. hand stretched out, and holds lotus with a long stalk. Symbol *Sravikramaḥ.* **Pl. X. 4.**
524	120.9	.86	King in trousers. *Davaśramaharajadhara*	L. hand stretched out and holding the long lotus stalk at its centre. Symbol *Srīvikramaḥ.*
525	120.6	.8	King in *dhoti*. Circular legend off.	L. hand bent up. Symbol *Srīvikkramaḥ.*
526	120.7	.84	King in *dhoti*. Hair on the head indicated by rows of dots. Circular legend off.	L. hand on knee. Symbol *Srīvikkramaḥ.*
527	127.6	.79	King in *dhoti* and wearing a long sash. Circular legend off.	L. hand on knee. Symbol incomplete. *Srīvikramaḥ.*
528	125.7	.78	King in *dhoti* and wearing a sash. *Davaśra*	L. hand on knee. Symbol *Srīvikkramaḥ.*
529	122.5	.85	King in *dhoti*. Hair on the head shown by dots artistically arranged. *Davaśra.*	L. hand on knee. Symbol *Srīvikramaḥ.*
530	120.4	.74	King in *dhoti*. *Davaśra..........guptaḥ.*	L. hand bent up. Symbol *Srīvikkramaḥ.*

No.	Wt.	Size	Obverse	Reverse
531	120.3	.79	King in *dhoti*. Buttons of the coat clearly visible. *Davaśramaharaja . . . . . ndraguptaḥ*.	L. hand bent up. Symbol *Śrīvikkramaḥ*.
532	123.8	.89	King in *dhoti*. *. . śramaharajadha-rajaśra . ndraguptaḥ*.	L. hand on knee. Symbol *Śrīvikramaḥ*.
533	118.7	.7	King in *dhoti*. Circular legend off. Gold is whitish.	L. hand on knee. Symbol *Sravakkra*
534	121.3	.76	King in *dhoti*. Circular legend off.	L. hand bent up. Symbol Legend blurred.
535	121	.74	King in half-pant. *. . śra . . . . ptaḥ*.	L. hand bent up. Symbol *Śrīvikkramaḥ*.
536	121.7	.78	King in trousers. *Davaśramaharajadha-raja . . . guptaḥ*.	L. hand bent up. Symbol *Śrīvikkramaḥ*.
537	120.8	.79	King in *dhoti*. *Davaśramaharaja*	L. hand bent up. Symbol *Śrīvikramaḥ*.
538	123.5	.86	King in *dhoti*. *Davaśramaharaja*	L. hand on knee. Symbol *Śrīvakramaḥ*.
539	121.6	.75	King in *dhoti*. *Davaśra*, in small characters.	L. hand bent up, elbow resting on the l. knee, slightly bent up. Symbol *Śrīvikramaḥ*.
540	119.8	.72	King in *dhoti*. *Devaśra*	L. hand as above. Symbol off. *Śrīvikkramaḥ*.

No.	Wt.	Size	Obverse	Reverse
541	120	.77	King in *dhoti*, wearing a sash. Circular legend off.	L. hand bent up. Symbol *Śrīvikramaḥ.*
542	120.7	.77	King in *dhoti.* *Devaśrīmahārājadhara*	L. hand bent up, elbow resting on l. knee, raised up. Symbol *Śrīvikramaḥ.*
543	128	.79	King in *dhoti* wearing a long sash. Circular legend off.	L. hand on knee. Symbol Legend off.
544	118.1	.78	King in *dhoti.* Circular legend off. Three cracks in the edge.	L. hand bent up, elbow resting on the knee slightly bent up. Symbol *Śrīvikramaḥ.*
545	119.3	.71	King in *dhoti.* Circular legend off.	L. hand bent up, elbow resting on the knee, slightly bent up. Symbol Legend off.
546	119.6	.74	King in *dhoti.* Circular legend off.	L. hand bent up. Symbol *Śrīvikkramaḥ.*
547	124.7	.8	King in *dhoti.* Circular legend off. Gold is pale.	L. hand on knee. Symbol *Śrīvikramaḥ.*
548	126.3	.75	King in trousers. Circular legend off.	L. hand on knee. Symbol *Śrīvikramaḥ.*
549	119.8	.75	King in *dhoti.* *Dava*	L. hand on knee. Symbol *Śrīvikra*
550	120.7	.85	King in *dhoti.* *Davaśramaharajadhara-jaśra*	L. hand on knee. Symbol *Śrīvikramaḥ.*

No.	Wt.	Size	Obverse	Reverse
551	124.9	.79	King in *dhoti*. Circular legend off. One crack in the edge.	L. hand on knee. Symbol  *Śravakkramaḥ*.
552	120.6	.7	King in *dhoti*. Circular legend off.	L. arm akimbo. Symbol  *Śravikkarmaḥ*.
553	120.9	.73	As above.	L. hand bent up. Symbol  *Śravakkramaḥ*.
554	120.3	.73	King in *dhoti* and with sash. Circular legend off.	L. hand bent up. Symbol , but incomplete. *Śravakramaḥ*.
555	119.6	.71	King in short *dhoti*, reaching down to the knees only. Circular legend off.	L. hand on knee. Symbol  *Śrīvikkramaḥ*.
556	122.5	.8	King in *dhoti*. Circular legend off.	L. hand on knee. Symbol , lower part alone being visible. *Śravakkramaḥ*.
557	120.6	.74	As above.	L. hand bent up. Symbol 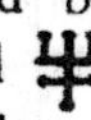, but incomplete. *Śravakkramaḥ*.
558	120.6	.72	King in short *dhoti*, reaching down the knee only. Circular legend off.	L. hand bent up and touching the knee slightly bent up. Symbol  *Śrīvikkramaḥ*.
559	127.3	.84	King in *dhoti*. Circular legend off.	L. arm akimbo. Symbol 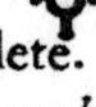, but incomplete. *Śravakramaḥ*.

No.	Wt.	Size	Obverse	Reverse
560	119	.72	King in trousers. Circular legend off.	L. hand on knee. Symbol *Śrīvikkramaḥ.*
561	114.7	.72	King in *dhoti.* Circular legend off.	L. hand bent up, and touching the knee slightly raised. Symbol *Śravakkramaḥ.*
562	119.9	.7	King in trousers. Circular legend off.	L. hand on knee. Symbol Double struck at the legend which has become indistinct.
563	121.4	.79	King in *dhoti* and wearing sash. Circular legend off.	L. hand bent up. Symbol , but incomplete. Legend blurred.
564	123.4	.73	King in *dhoti.* ....*Chandraguptaḥ.*	L. arm akimbo. Symbol *Śravakkramaḥ.*
565	120	.7	King in *dhoti.* Circular legend off.	L. hand bent up. Symbol off. *Śravakkramaḥ.*
566	123.5	.81	King in *dhoti.* Circular legend off.	L. hand on knee. Symbol *Śrīvikkramaḥ.*
567	125.6	.8	King in trousers. Circular legend off.	As above.
568	121.3	.73	King in *dhoti.* Circular legend off.	L. hand bent up and resting on the knee slightly raised. Symbol ..*kra*
569	123.3	.75	King in *dhoti.* *Davaśra*	L. hand on knee. Symbol *Śrīvikkramaḥ.*

No.	Wt.	Size	Obverse	Reverse
570	118.3	.73	King in *dhoti*. Circular legend off.	L. hand on knee. Symbol, but incomplete. *Srīvikkramaḥ.*
571	123.2	.85	King in trousers. *Dava*	L. hand on knee. Symbol *Srīvikramaḥ.*
572	121.3	.7	King in *dhoti*. Circular legend off.	L. hand bent up. Symbol *Sravakkramaḥ.*
573	127.8	.73	As above.	L. hand on knee. Symbol *..kra*
574	121.7	.75	King in *dhoti*. *Dava*	L. arm akimbo. Symbol, but incomplete. Legend off.
575	121.2	.7	King in *dhoti*. Circular legend off.	L. hand on knee. Symbol *Srīvakkramaḥ.*
576	122.6	.8	King in *dhoti*. *Davaśra*	L. hand on knee. Symbol *Srīvikkramaḥ.*
577	127.9	.76	King in *dhoti*. Circular legend off.	L. arm on knee. Symbol *Sravakramaḥ.*
578	122.3	.76	King in *dhoti*. Circular legend off.	L. arm akimbo. Symbol, but incomplete. *Srīvikramaḥ.*
579	110.9	.78	King in short *dhoti*, reaching the knees only. *Devaśramaharajadharaja* Coin in normal condition, but its weight is very low.	L. hand on knee. Symbol *Sravakkramaḥ.*

No.	Wt.	Size	Obverse	Reverse
580	121.2	.75	King in *dhoti*. Circular legend off.	L. arm akimbo. Symbol Legend truncated, only *kkra* being visible.
581	125.9	.84	As above	L. hand on knee. Symbol *Śrīvikkramaḥ*.
582	119.2	.77	King in short *dhoti*, reaching to the knees only. Circular legend off.	L. arm bent up, elbow resting on the knee slightly raised. Symbol *Śravakramaḥ*.
583	127.2	.78	King in *dhoti*. Circular legend off.	L. arm akimbo. Symbol *Śrīvikkramaḥ*.
584	127.6	.7	King in trousers. Coat buttons very clear. Circular legend off.	L. hand on knee. Symbol *Śrīvikkramaḥ*.
585	120.2	.82	King in *dhoti*. Circular legend off.	L. arm akimbo. Symbol, but incomplete. *Śrīvikramaḥ*.
586	120	.77	As above.	L. hand on knee. Symbol *Śrīvikkramaḥ*.
587	120.1	.77	King in *dhoti*. Circular legend off.	L. hand bent up. Symbol *Śravakramaḥ*.
588	120.3	.73	As above.	L. hand bent up. Symbol *Śravakramaḥ*.
589	127.6	.76	King in trousers. Beautiful frizzled hair on the head. Circular legend off.	L. hand on knee. Symbol *Śrīvikramaḥ*.

No.	Wt.	Size	Obverse	Reverse
590	118.3	.78	King in *dhoti.* Circular legend off.	L. hand bent up. Symbol blurred. *Śrīvikkramaḥ.*
591	125.6	.83	King in *dhoti.* *Dava*	L. hand on knee. Symbol *Śrīvikramaḥ.*
592	119.5	.75	King in *dhoti.* Circular legend off. The coin is worn out.	L. hand on knee. Symbol *Śravakramaḥ.*
593	127.6	.79	King in trousers. Ornamental head-dress. Circular legend off.	L. hand on knee. Symbol *Śravakramaḥ.*
594	123.1	.79	King in *dhoti.* Circular legend off.	L. hand on knee. Symbol blurred. *Śrīvikramaḥ.*
595	123.5	.75	As above.	L. hand bent up. Symbol *Śrīvikramaḥ.*
596	120.6	.79	As above.	L. hand on knee. Symbol *Śrīvikkramaḥ.*
597	123.5	.8	King in *dhoti.* *Deva*	L. hand on knee. Symbol incomplete. *Śrīvikramaḥ.*
598	120.6	.73	King in *dhoti.* Circular legend off.	L. hand bent up, elbow resting on knee slightly raised up. Symbol , but incomplete. *Śrīvikramaḥ.*
599	126.3	.79	King in *dhoti.* Circular legend off.	L. hand on knee. Symbol a variation of with four prongs above. *Śrava* **Pl. X. 5.**

No.	Wt.	Size	Obverse	Reverse
600	127.3	.82	King in *dhoti.* Circular legend off.	L. arm akimbo. Symbol *Srīvikkramaḥ.*
601	121.1	.8	As above.	L. hand on knee. Symbol *Srīvikkramaḥ.*
602	120.5	.74	King in *dhoti.* *Davaśramahara*	L. hand on knee. Symbol blurred. *Srīvikkramaḥ.*
603	120.1	.79	King in *dhoti.* Circular legend off.	L. hand on knee. Symbol *Srīvikramaḥ.*
604	127.4	.78	King in trousers; hair on head curly looks like a wig. Circular legend off.	As above, but the symbol and the legend are blurred.
605	123.8	.78	King in *dhoti.* Circular legend off.	L. hand on knee. Symbol blurred. *Srīvikramaḥ.*
606	123.2	.82	King in *dhoti* and wearing a sash. Coat has short sleeves. Hair denoted by several curls falling down to the neck. *Davaśra.....ra..* *Chandraguptaḥ.*	L. hand on knee. Symbol *Sravakramaḥ.* **Pl. X. 6.**
607	120	.76	King in *dhoti.* *Davaśra.hara*	L. hand on knee. Symbol *Srīvikra*
608	119.4	.8	King in trousers. Coat with beautiful buttons. ....*śrī-Chandraguptaḥ.*	L. hand bent up. Symbol *Srīvikramaḥ,* truncated.
609	119.1	.82	King in *dhoti.* *Davaśra*	L. hand on knee; lotus has long stalk.

No.	Wt.	Size	Obverse	Reverse
				Symbol  *Śrīvikramaḥ*.
610	121.6	.74	King in *dhoti*. *Davaśramaharaja*, in small characters.	L. hand on knee. Symbol a variation of , but with a dot in the circle. *Śrīvikkramaḥ*.
611	129.1	.75	King in trousers. Circular legend off. One crack in the edge.	L. hand on knee. Symbol  Legend blurred.
612	119.8	.72	King in *dhoti*. Circular legend off.	L. hand bent up, the elbow resting on the knee, slightly raised up. Symbol 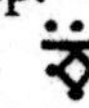 Legend truncated.
613	121.6	.78	King in trousers. Buttons on coat, as also on the sides of the trousers. ....*ndraguptaḥ*.	L. hand bent up. Sўmbol  *Śrīvikkramaḥ*.
614	125.6	.81	King in trousers and wearing a sash. Circular legend off.	L. hand on knee. Symbol 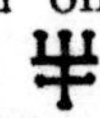, but incomplete. *Śrīvikramaḥ*.
615	123.1	.9	King in trousers. *Devaśrīmahārājādhirāja*; medial vowels very clear.	L. hand on knee. Symbol 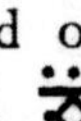 *Śrīvikkramaḥ*.
616	117	.73	King in *dhoti*. Circular legend off. Condition slightly worn; impure gold.	L. hand bent up. Symbol 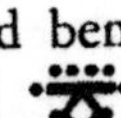 Legend blurred.
617	122.9	.8	King in *dhoti*. *Da.śrama*	L. hand on knee. Symbol blurred. *Śrīvikramaḥ*.

No.	Wt.	Size	Obverse	Reverse
618	120.4	.78	King in trousers, wearing a beautiful cap bordered with pearls. ....*Chandraguptaḥ*.	L. hand bent up. Symbol *Śravakkramaḥ*.
619	120	.73	King in trousers. Circular legend off.	L. hand on knee. Symbol *Śra.kkra*
620	125.6	.8	King in *dhoti* and wearing a long sash. Circular legend off.	L. hand on knee. Symbol, but incomplete. *Śrīvikkramaḥ*.
621	121	.89	King in *dhoti*. Circular legend off. One crack in the edge.	L. hand bent up. Symbol *Śravakkramaḥ*.
622	120.6	.7	King in *dhoti*. Circular legend off.	L. hand on knee. Symbol *Śrīvakkr*
623	120.7	.74	King in *dhoti*. Buttons of the coat clearly visible. Circular legend fragmentary and truncated.	L. hand bent up. Symbol *Śrīvikkramaḥ*.
624	123.4	.84	King in *dhoti*. Hair on the head denoted by curls in two rows. *Davaśramaharajadharajaśra-Cha*, partly truncated.	L. hand on knee. Symbol *Śrīvikkramaḥ*. Pl. X. 7.
625	123.1	.79	King in *dhoti*. *Davaśramaharajadharaja*, partly blurred.	L. hand on knee. Symbol *Śrīvikramaḥ*.
626	125.7	.89	King in *dhoti*. *Davaśramaharaja .... Chandraguptaḥ*.	L. hand on knee. Symbol *Śrīvikkramaḥ*.

No.	Wt.	Size	Obverse	Reverse
627	121.8	.76	King in *dhoti.* *Davaśramaha*	L. hand bent up. Symbol *Sravakkramaḥ.*
628	121.3	.78	King wearing a short *dhoti* reaching the knee. *..śrama*	L. hand bent up, the elbow resting on the knee slightly bent up. Symbol blurred. Legend truncated.
629	121.5	.79	King in trousers, having ornamental side-buttons. *Devaśrīmaharajadharaja-śrī-Chandraguptaḥ.*	L. hand on knee. Symbol, a variation of , with three dots on the three sides of the circle. *Srīvikkramaḥ.*
630	127.7	.79	King in trousers. *Devaśramaha..dhara*	L. hand on knee. Symbol *Sravakra*
631	119	.75	King in trousers. *..śrama*	L. hand bent up. Symbol *Srīvikramaḥ.*
632	126.5	.82	King in *dhoti* and wearing a sash. *Davaśramaharajadharaja*, in small characters.	L. hand bent up. Symbol *Sravakramaḥ.*
633	119.7	.77	King in *dhoti.* *Davaśra*	L. hand bent up. Symbol *Sravakkramaḥ.*
634	119.3	.74	King wearing *dhoti* and high leather boots. Coat has short sleeves and an armlet is above the r. sleeve. *Davaśramaharaja ....* *Chandragap.*	L. hand on knee. Symbol *Srīvikkramaḥ.* **Pl. X. 8.**
635	123.4	.78	King in *dhoti.* *Davaśramaha*	L. hand bent up. Symbol *Srīvikkramaḥ.*

No.	Wt.	Size	Obverse	Reverse
636	121.6	.78	King in *dhoti*. Circular legend fragmentary and blurred.	L. hand on knee. Symbol , but incomplete. Legend blurred.
637	123.9	.84	King in trousers. *Devaśramaharaja....* *Chandraguptaḥ*.	L. hand on knee; lotus has long stalk. Symbol *Śrīvikkramaḥ*.
638	120.5	.78	King in *dhoti*. *Davaśra........* *Chandraguptaḥ*.	L. hand on knee. Symbol *Śrīvikramaḥ*.
639	123.6	.76	King in trousers. Circular legend blurred.	L. hand on knee. Symbol *Śrīvikkramaḥ*.
640	122.7	.88	King in trousers. Hair on the head shown by two rows of curls. *Devaśrīmaharaja*	L. hand on knee. Symbol *Śrīvikkramaḥ*.
641	120.5	.75	King in *dhoti*. *Davaśra*	L. arm akimbo. Symbol *Śravakkramaḥ*.
642	120.1	.76	King in *dhoti*. *Dava.........* *Chandraguptaḥ*.	L. hand bent up. Symbol *Śravakkramaḥ*.
643	120.3	.75	King wearing short *dhoti* reaching down the knees. *.vaśra*	L. hand bent up. Symbol , but incomplete. *.vakramaḥ*, blurred.
644	121.5	.75	King in *dhoti*. *Dava*	L. hand bent up. Symbol Legend off.
645	124.2	.83	King in trousers. *Devaśramaharajadha*	L. hand on knee. Symbol , but incomplete. *Śrīvikkramaḥ*.

No.	Wt.	Size	Obverse	Reverse
646	123.3	.75	King wearing short *dhoti*, reaching down the knees. *.vaśrī*	L. hand on knee. Symbol  *Sravakkramaḥ.*
647	120.4	.77	King in *dhoti*. Circular legend off.	L. hand on knee. Symbol  *Sravakkramaḥ.*
648	121.9	.82	King in *dhoti*. Circular legend fragmentary, blurred and truncated.	L. hand on knee. Symbol  *Srīvikkramaḥ.*
649	120.3	.82	King in *dhoti*, wearing high boots; buttons of the coat very clear. *Devaśrīmaharaja . . . śra-Chandraguptaḥ.* Arrow cuts across the subjunct of *śra*	L. hand bent up. Symbol  *Srīvikkramaḥ.* **Pl. X. 9.**
650	121	.78	King in *dhoti*. A close-fitting cap or headdress on the head. *Devaśramaharajadha . . . .ndraguptaḥ.*	L. hand bent up, but not touching the knee. Symbol  *Sravikkramaḥ.* **Pl. X. 10.**
651	120.5	.75	King in *dhoti*. Circular legend off.	L. hand bent up. Symbol  *. . kra*
652	120	.77	As above.	L. arm akimbo. Symbol 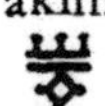 *Srīvikramaḥ.*
653	118.2	.79	King in *dhoti*. *. . . . . Chandraguptaḥ.* Crack in the edge at II.	L. hand bent up. Symbol  *Srīvikkramaḥ.*
654	119.7	.81	King in *dhoti*. *Devaśrī*	L. hand bent up. Symbol, a variation of 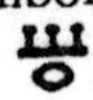, but with a

No.	Wt.	Size	Obverse	Reverse
				dot in the circle. ..*kra*
655	120.7	.8	King in *dhoti*. *Devaśrama*	L. arm akimbo. Symbol  *Śrīvikkramaḥ*.
656	123.1	.8	King in *dhoti* ....*Chandra-guptaḥ*.	L. arm akimbo. Symbol , but incomplete. *Śrīvikramaḥ*.
657	120.6	.7	King in *dhoti*. Circular legend fragmentary and blurred.	L. arm akimbo. Symbol  *Śrīvikramaḥ*.
658	129.3	.78	King in *dhoti*. Crescent over *Garuḍa*. Circular legend off.	L. arm akimbo; lotus has long stalk. Symbol  Legend blurred.
659	120.3	.78	King in *dhoti*. Legend fragmentary and blurred.	L. hand bent up. Symbol  *Śravakramaḥ*.
660	123.3	.79	King in *dhoti*. *Davaśramaharajadhara-* ....*guptaḥ*.	L. arm akimbo; lotus has long stalk. Symbol 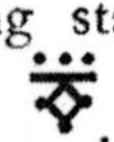 *Śrīvikkramaḥ*.
661	119.2	.75	King in *dhoti*. *Deavaśrīmaharajadharaja*	L. hand bent up. Symbol  *Śrīvikramaḥ*.
662	121	.74	King in *dhoti*. Circular legend off.	L. arm akimbo. Symbol  *Śrīvikkramaḥ*.
663	120	.77	King in *dhoti*. Circular legend blurred and fragmentary.	L. hand bent up. Symbol  *Śravakkramaḥ*.
664	119.2	.8	King in *dhoti*. Circular legend off.	L. arm akimbo. Symbol , but incomplete. *Śrīvikkramaḥ*.

No.	Wt.	Size	Obverse	Reverse
665	119.7	.75	King in *dhoti*. Circular legend off.	L. hand bent up. Symbol *Śravakkra*
666	121	.83	King in *dhoti*. *Davaśrīmaharajadhara*	L. arm akimbo. Symbol , but incomplete. *Śrīvikkramaḥ*.
667	128.5	.78	King in *dhoti*. Crescent above him. Circular legend off.	L. arm akimbo. Symbol Legend off.
668	119.9	.78	King in *dhoti*. Circular legend off.	L. arm akimbo. Symbol blurred. *Śrīvikkramaḥ*.
669	121.4	.75	King in *dhoti*. *..śramaharajadharajaśra-Chandra*	L. hand bent up. Symbol *..kkrama*
670	121.7	.75	King in *dhoti*. Circular legend off.	L. arm akimbo. Symbol Legend fragmentary and blurred.
671	120.4	.79	King in short *dhoti* and high boots. Coat is short sleeved; armlets above the sleeves. Earring, necklace and coat buttons neatly shown. *Devaśrīmaharajadha..śra.ndraguptaḥ*. Arrow across the letters *śrī* and *ndra*.	L. hand on knee. Symbol *Śrīvikkramaḥ*. **Pl. X. 11.**
672	124.5	.8	King in *dhoti*. *Davaśra*	L. arm akimbo. Symbol *Śrīvikkramaḥ*.
673	120.1	.75	King in *dhoti*. Circular legend off.	L. arm akimbo. Symbol *Śrīvikramaḥ*.

No.	Wt.	Size	Obverse	Reverse
674	121.4	.74	King in *dhoti*. *Davaśramaharajadha*, in small characters.	L. hand bent up. Symbol *Srīvikkramaḥ*.
675	119.9	.75	King in *dhoti*. Hair on the head thick and curly. Circular legend off.	L. hand bent up. Symbol incomplete. *Sravakramaḥ*.
676	118	.71	King in *dhoti*. *Devaśra*	L. hand on thigh. Symbol *Sravakkrama*
677	123.6	.82	King in *dhoti*. Hair on the head denoted by curls in two rows. *Davaśramaharajadha*, in small characters.	L. hand on thigh. Symbol *Śrīvikrama*
678	124	.87	King in *dhoti*, wearing a close-fitting pearl-bedecked cap. Coat has short sleeves and armlets are worn above them. *Devaśrīmahārājādharaja ..ndragupta*. Arrow cuts across the letter *ndra*	L. hand on thigh. Symbol carelessly drawn. *Śrīvikramaḥ*. **Pl. X. 12.**
679	121	.78	King in *dhoti*. Circular legend off.	L. hand on thigh. Symbol *Śrīvikrama*
680	124.5	.7	King in *dhoti*. Circular legend off.	L. hand bent up. Symbol *Śrīvikrama*
681	128.4	.82	King in *dhoti*. *..śra*	L. hand on thigh. Symbol *Sravakrama*.

No.	Wt.	Size	Obverse	Reverse
682	121.2	.74	King in *dhoti.* Circular legend off.	L. hand on thigh. Symbol *Śravakrama*
683	123.8	.71	King in *dhoti.* Circular legend off. Two cracks in the edge.	L. arm akimbo. Symbol Legend blurred.
684	119.2	.74	King in *dhoti.* *Davaśra*	L. hand bent up. Symbol , but incomplete. *Śravikkra*
685	119.8	.73	King in *dhoti.* *Deva*	L. arm akimbo. Symbol *Śravakkrama*
686	123.7	.8	King in *dhoti.* *Davaśramaharaja....* *Chandragupta,* in small characters.	L. arm on thigh. Symbol *Śrīvikramaḥ.*
687	123.8	.79	King in *dhoti.* *Davaśramaharajadha-raja*	L. hand on thigh. Symbol off. *Śrīvikramaḥ.*
688	120.7	.7	King in *dhoti.* Circular legend off.	L. hand bent up. Symbol *Śravakra*
689	121.1	.7	King in *dhoti,* and wears a sash also. *Davaśra*	L. hand bent up. Symbol , but incomplete. Legend off.
690	121.1	.7	King in *dhoti.* Circular legend off.	L. arm akimbo. Symbol off. *Śrīvikramaḥ.*
691	120.8	.7	King in *dhoti.* *Davaśramahara*	L. hand stretched out and holding a lotus with a long stalk. Symbol *.vakrama.*

No.	Wt.	Size	Obverse	Reverse
692	121.3	.79	King in *dhoti*. *Da............ndra-gupta*	L. hand on thigh. Symbol *Śravakrama.*
693	121.1	.75	King in *dhoti*. *Davaśramaha*	L. hand on thigh. Symbol *Śrīvikrama.*
694	121.2	.75	King in *dhoti*. *Davaśra*	L. hand bent up. Symbol *Śravakrama.*
695	121.4	.75	King in *dhoti*. Circular legend blurred.	L. hand stretched out and holding a lotus with a long stalk. Symbol *Śravakrama.*
696	117	.75	King in *dhoti*. Circular legend blurred.	L. hand on thigh. Symbol incomplete. *Śrīvikramaḥ.*
697	122.5	.75	King in *dhoti*. *Davaśrama*	L. hand on thigh. Symbol *Śrīvikramaḥ.*
698	120.1	.75	King in *dhoti*. Circular legend off.	L. hand on thigh. Symbol *Śravakrama.*
699	118.9	.72	King in *dhoti*. *Deva*	L. hand on thigh. Symbol blurred. *Śravakrama.*
700	120.6	.75	King in trousers. *Dava.maharaja...... Chandragupta.*	L. hand on thigh. Symbol *Śrīvikkrama.*
701	122.8	.75	King in *dhoti*, part of the halo is detached and looks like a crescent. Circular legend off.	L. hand bent up, elbow resting on knee. Symbol Legend blurred.

No.	Wt.	Size	Obverse	Reverse
702	121.6	.69	King in *dhoti*. Circular legend off.	L. hand bent up. Symbol *Sravakkrama*.
703	117.8	.74	King in *dhoti*. Circular legend off.	L. hand on knee. Symbol incomplete. *Sravakkrama*.
704	123.3	.78	King in *dhoti*. *Dava*.......... *gupta*.	L. hand on knee. Symbol, but incomplete. *Srīvikrama*.
705	128.8	.76	King in *dhoti*. Circular legend off.	L. hand on knee. Symbol *Sravikra*
706	126.2	.79	King in *dhoti*. Circular legend off.	L. hand on knee. Symbol *Srivakkrama*.
707	123.3	.85	King in *dhoti*. ....*Chandra-gupta*.	L. hand on knee. Symbol *Srīvikkrama*.
708	124.4	.82	King in *dhoti*. Circular legend off. One crack in the edge.	L. hand on knee. Symbol *Srīvikkrama*.
709	128.2	.74	As above, but no crack.	L. hand bent up. Symbol, but incomplete. *Sravakkrama*.
710	121.1	.78	King in *dhoti*. Circular legend off.	L. hand bent up. Symbol off. *Sravakkramaḥ*.
711	123.4	.78	As above.	L. hand bent up. Symbol *Srīvikramaḥ*.
712	128.4	.79	King in trousers. Circular legend off.	L. arm akimbo. Symbol, but incomplete. *Srīvikrama*.

No.	Wt.	Size	Obverse	Reverse
713	120	.76	King in *dhoti.* Circular legend off.	L. hand on knee. Symbol  *Srīvikrama.*
714	125.9	.8	King in trousers. Circular legend off.	L. hand on knee. Symbol  *Sravakkramaḥ.*
715	121.1	.69	King in *dhoti.* Circular legend off. Two cracks in the edge.	L. arm akimbo. Symbol  *.vakkra*
716	122.1	.8	King in *dhoti.* Circular legend off.	L. hand on knee. Symbol  *.vakkra.*
717	122.8	.75	As above.	Symbol  *Srīvikramaḥ.*
718	120.1	.7	King in *dhoti.* *Dava*	L. hand bent up. Symbol  *Sravakkrama.*
719	120.7	.73	King in *dhoti.* Circular legend off.	L. arm akimbo. Symbol , but incomplete. *Srīvikkrama.*
720	120.7	.73	King in trousers. Circular legend off.	L. hand stretched out and holding lotus with a long stalk. Symbol , but incomplete. *Sravikrama*
721	121.3	.75	King in *dhoti* and with a sash. Circular legend off.	L. hand bent up. Symbol 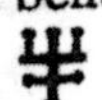 Legend off.
722	122.2	.7	King in *dhoti.* Circular legend off.	L. arm akimbo. Symbol 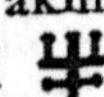, but incomplete. *.vakkrama*

No.	Wt.	Size	Obverse	Reverse
723	121.8	.74	King in *dhoti.* Circular legend off. One crack in the edge.	L. hand bent up. Symbol *Śrivikramaḥ.*
724	121.1	.74	As above, but no crack.	L. hand on knee. Symbol *Śrīvikramaḥ.*
725	120.2	.73	As above.	L. hand bent up, elbow resting on knee. Symbol *Śravakrama.*
726	120.4	.74	King wears trousers and a graceful cap. *Devaśramaharaja. . . .* *Chandragupta.*	L. hand bent up. Symbol *Śrīvikkramaḥ.*
727	120.4	.72	King in trousers. Artistic head-dress. *Devaśrīmaharajadhara .* *. . ndragupta.*	L. hand bent up. Symbol *Śrīvikkramaḥ.*
728	121.1	.82	King in *dhoti.* Hair falling on the neck down the head. Circular legend off.	L. hand bent up. Symbol *Śrīvikkrama.*
729	120.2	.76	King in *dhoti.* Circular legend off.	L. hand bent up. Symbol *Śrīvikkramaḥ.*
730	120.3	.75	King in half-pant or short *dhoti.* Circular legend off.	L. hand on knee. Symbol *Śravakkramaḥ.*
731	128.8	.73	King in *dhoti.* Circular legend off.	L. arm akimbo. Symbol, incomplete. *Śravakkramaḥ.*
732	121.2	.71	King in *dhoti.* *Devaśrīmahara,* in small characters.	L. hand bent up. Symbol Legend off.

No.	Wt.	Size	Obverse	Reverse
733	126.7	.85	King in *dhoti*. Hair on the head falling down the neck. *..śra*	L. hand akimbo. Symbol *Śrīvikramaḥ*.
734	123.5	.83	King in trousers. *Davaśrama*	L. hand on knee. Symbol *Śrīvikkramaḥ*.
735	118.2	.75	King in *dhoti*. *Davaśra* One crack in the edge.	L. hand bent up. Symbol off. *Śravakkramaḥ*.
736	120.4	.75	King in half-pant. Circular legend blurred.	L. hand on knee. Symbol off. *Śravakramaḥ*.
737	119.7	.74	King in trousers. ....*Chandraguptaḥ*.	L. hand on knee. Symbol *Śrīvikkrama*
738	118.7	.73	King in *dhoti*. Circular legend off.	L. hand on knee. Symbol *Śravakkrama*.
739	119.8	.79	King in *dhoti*. *Dava*	L. hand bent up. Symbol Legend off.
740	127	.89	King in trousers. *Devaśrīmaharajadharaja*	L. hand bent up. Symbol *Śrīvikramaḥ*.
741	121.9	.75	King in trousers. *Deva*............*gu*	L. hand akimbo. Symbol blurred. *Śravakkrama*.
742	119.9	.76	King in *dhoti*. ....*Chandragupta*.	L. hand bent up. Symbol *Śrīvakrama*.
743	116.1	.82	King in trousers. *Davaśramaharajadharajaśra-Chandragupta*.	L. hand on knee. Symbol *Śrīvikramaḥ*.

No.	Wt.	Size	Obverse	Reverse
744	120.2	.76	King in short *dhoti* and wearing high leather boots. *Davaśramaharajadharajaśra-Chandragupta*, partly truncated.	Goddess not nimbate. L. hand bent up. Symbol *Sravakkramaḥ*. Pl. X. 13.
745	121	.78	King in *dhoti*. Circular legend off.	L. hand bent up, elbow resting on knee. Symbol blurred. *Sravakkrama*.
746	123.4	.77	King in trousers. *Davaśramaha* One crack in the edge.	L. hand on knee. Symbol *Srīvikkrama*.
747	125.3	.82	King in trousers. *Da*	L. hand on knee. Symbol *Srīvikkrama*.
748	123.2	.75	King in *shalwar*. Hair arranged in three rows of curls. *Devaśrīmaharajadharajaśra-Chandragupta*, last four letters being blurred and truncated.	L. hand on knee. Symbol, perhaps with an additional dot below. *Srīvikramaḥ*. Pl. X. 14.
749	118.8	.7	King in trousers and wearing sash. Circular legend off.	L. hand bent up. Symbol *Sravakkra*
750	121.4	.74	King in trousers. Circular legend off.	L. arm akimbo. Symbol *Sravakkrama*.
751	121.6	.76	King in *dhoti*. Circular legend off.	L. hand on knee. Symbol *Sravakra*.
752	127.5	.77	As above.	L. hand on knee. Symbol *Sravakrama*.

No.	Wt.	Size	Obverse	Reverse
753	120.6	.76	As above.	As above. Symbol
754	119.5	.78	As above.	L. hand bent up; elbow resting on knee. Symbol *Śravikrama.*
755	120.1	.78	King in trousers. Circular legend off.	L. hand on knee. Symbol Legend blurred.
756	127.6	.8	King in trousers. Circular legend off.	L. hand bent up. Symbol *Śravakrama.*
757	121	.75	King in half-pant. *Deva*	L. hand bent up. Symbol incomplete. *Śravakramaḥ.*
758	121.4	.8	King in *dhoti.* *Davaśra*	L. hand bent up. Symbol *.vakkrama.*
759	121.2	.74	King in *dhoti.* Circular legend off.	L. hand bent up. Symbol Legend off.
760	124	.78	As above.	L. hand on knee. Symbol *Śravikra*
761	121.8	.76	King in *dhoti.* . . . . *ndra-gupta.*	L. hand bent up, elbow resting on knee. Symbol *Śrīvikkramaḥ.*
762	128	.81	King in half-pant. *Davaśramaharajadharaja,* in small characters.	L. hand on knee. Symbol *Śravikramaḥ.*
763	121.1	.79	King in *dhoti.* . . . . *harajadharajaśra-Chandragup,* mostly on the l. side.	L. hand on knee. Symbol *Śrīvikkrama.*

No.	Wt.	Size	Obverse	Reverse
764	126.7	.84	King in *dhoti*. Circular legend off.	L. hand on knee. Symbol *Srīvakka*
765	125.9	.82	King in *dhoti* and with sash. *Devaśrīmahārājadharaja*	L. hand on knee. Symbol *Sravakrama.*
766	119.7	.83	King in *dhoti* and wearing sash. *..śramaha.....Chandragup*	L. hand bent up and the flower does not look like a lotus. Symbol *Srīvikkrama.*
767	126	.78	King in *dhoti* and wearing sash. Circular legend off.	L. hand on knee. Symbol *Sravakka*
768	121	.79	King in *dhoti*. *Devaśrîmaharaja*	L. hand on knee. Symbol *Srīvikkramaḥ.*
769	121.4	.74	King in *dhoti*. Circular legend off.	L. hand bent up, elbow resting on knee slightly bent up. Symbol *Srīvikramaḥ.*
770	121.2	.76	King in *dhoti*. *............ndraguptaḥ.*	L. hand bent up. Symbol *Sravakkama.*
771	120.7	.75	King in *dhoti*. *Dava*	L. hand on knee. Symbol *Sravakra*
772	121.3	.78	King in *dhoti*. Circular legend off.	L. hand bent up. Symbol *Sravakkama*
773	122.1	.69	As above.	L. hand on knee. Symbol *Sravakkama.*

No.	Wt.	Size	Obverse	Reverse
774	117.4	.76	King in half-pant or short *dhoti*. Circular legend off.	L. arm akimbo. Symbol  *Śrīvikkramaḥ*.
775	126	.8	King in *dhoti*. Circular legend off.	L. hand on knee. Symbol , but incomplete. *Śrīvikkramaḥ*.
776	119.4	.78	King in trousers, wearing a coat with side buttons. *Davaśramaharaja.....ndragupta*.	L. hand stretched out and holding a lotus of long stalk. Symbol 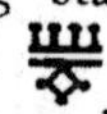 *Śrīvikkramaḥ*. Pl. X. 15.
777	119.4	.71	King in *dhoti*. ....*Chandra*	L. hand bent up. Symbol 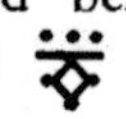 *Śravakrama*.
778	127.3	.73	King in *dhoti*. Circular legend off.	L. hand on knee. Symbol 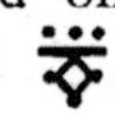, but incomplete. *.vakkramaḥ*.
779	119.5	.77	King in coat and trousers. Circular legend off.	L. hand bent up. Symbol 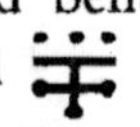 *Śravakrama*.
780	121	.75	King in coat and trousers. *Devaśrīmaharaja*	L. hand stretched out. Symbol  *Śravikkrama*.
781	125	.8	King in *dhoti*. ......*Chandraga*	L. arm akimbo. Symbol 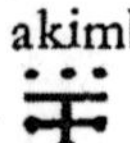 *Śrīvikkramaḥ*.
782	124.6	.82	King in *dhoti*. Circular legend blurred.	L. arm on knee. Symbol 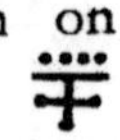 but with four prongs above instead of four dots. *Śrīvikkramaḥ*.

No.	Wt.	Size	Obverse	Reverse
783	121.4	.7	King in *dhoti*. Circular legend off.	L. hand bent up. Symbol *Śravakra*.
784	118.3	.73	King in *dhoti*. *Davaśra*	L. hand on knee. Symbol *Śrīvikkramaḥ*.
785	125.4	.8	King in *dhoti*. *Davaśra*	L. arm akimbo. Symbol *Śrīvikkramaḥ*.
786	124.8	.83	King in *dhoti* and boots and his hair on head is arranged in rows of curls. *Davaśramaharaja....* *Cha*, blurred and truncated.	L. hand on thigh. Symbol *Śrīvikkramaḥ*. **Pl. XI. 1.**
787	120.3	.8	King in trousers. *Davaśramaharajadharaja. Chandraguptaḥ*	L. hand bent up. Symbol *Śrīvakkrama*.
788	119.3	.73	King in *dhoti*. *Davaśramaharajadha*	L. hand on knee. Symbol *Śrīvikkramaḥ*.
789	126.1	.8	King in *dhoti*. *Davaśrama*	L. hand on knee. Symbol blurred. *Śrīvikkramaḥ*.
790	120.8	.74	King in *dhoti*. *Davaśramahara*, truncated.	L. hand on hip. Symbol *Śravakkrama*.
791	120.1	.84	King in *dhoti*. Circular legend off.	L. hand bent up. Symbol blurred. Legend off.
792	120	.72	King in *dhoti*. *Devaśrma*	L. hand on knee. Symbol *Śrīvikkramaḥ*.

No.	Wt.	Size	Obverse	Reverse
793	120	.77	King in *dhoti.* *Davaśra*	L. arm akimbo. Symbol *Śravakkramaḥ.*
794	120.9	.78	King in *dhoti,* hair falling on neck. Circular legend off.	L. hand bent up. Symbol Legend blurred. **Pl. XI. 2.**
795	123.4	.8	King in *dhoti.* *Davaśrama........* *draguptaḥ.*	L. hand on knee. Symbol *Śravikramaḥ.*
796	118.9	.7	King in *dhoti.* Crescent with a dot in centre to the right of *Garuḍa*, facing the bird. *Davaśra.........dra*	L. hand bent up. elbow resting on knee. Symbol incomplete. *Śrīvikkramaḥ.* **Pl. XI. 3.**
797	120.8	.74	King in *dhoti.* *..........śri-chandra-guptaḥ.*	L. hand bent up. Symbol *Śrīvikkramaḥ.*
798	123.1	.81	King in *dhoti.* *Davaśra*	L. hand on knee. Symbol *Śrivikkramaḥ.*
799	123	.82	*Devaśramaharājadharaja. .Chandraguptaḥ.*	L. hand on knee. Symbol *Śrīvikramaḥ.*
800	118	.72	King in *dhoti.* *Davaśra*	L. hand bent up. Symbol *.vakramaḥ.*
801	121	.75	King in *dhoti.* *Davaśrīmaha*	L. arm akimbo. Symbol *Śrīvikkramaḥ.*
802	120.9	.71	King in *dhoti.* Circular legend off.	L. hand bent up. elbow resting on knee slightly bent up. Symbol *Śravaka*

No.	Wt.	Size	Obverse	Reverse
803	126.6	.75	King in *dhoti*. ....*Chandra-gupta*.	L. arm akimbo. Symbol off. *Śravakkrama*.
804	123.5	.78	King in *dhoti*. *Davaśri*	L. arm akimbo. Symbol *Śrīvikkramaḥ*.
805	120.4	.75	King in *dohti*. ....*Chandra-guptaḥ*	L. hand extended, holding lotus with a long stalk. Symbol *Śrīvikkramaḥ*
806	122.7	.85	King in *dhoti* and wearing a peculiar graceful headdress, wristlets, armlets and necklace. *Davaśramahara*...... *Chandarguptaḥ*, blurred and truncated.	L. hand on knee. Symbol *Śravikkramaḥ*. **Pl. XI. 4.**
807	122.4	.9	King in trousers. *Devaśramaharaja*... *śra-Chandra*	L. hand on knee. Symbol *Śrīvikramaḥ*.
808	119.8	.8	King in *dhoti*. *Devaśrīma*	L. hand on knee. Symbol incomplete, but probably *Śravakkramaḥ*.
809	121.4	.75	King in *dhoti*. *Davaśrī*	L. arm akimbo. Symbol Legend truncated.
810	119	.78	King in short *dhoti*. *Chandra* under arm blurred. *Devaśra*	L. hand bent up, elbow resting on knee raised up. Symbol *Śrīvikramaḥ*.
811	125.9	.82	King in *dhoti*. *Davaśra*	L. hand on knee. Symbol incomplete, but probably *Śrīvikkramaḥ*.

No.	Wt.	Size	Obverse	Reverse
812	121.1	.79	King in short *dhoti.* Circular legend off.	L. hand on knee. Symbol *Srīvikkramaḥ.*
813	124	.9	King in *dhoti.* *Devaśrīmaharajadharaja-śra*	L. hand on knee. Symbol *Srīvikkramaḥ.*
814	120.9	.73	King in trousers. *......dhara*	L. hand on knee. Symbol *Srīvikkramaḥ.*
815	123.9	.8	King in trousers. *Davaśrīmahara*	L. hand on knee. Symbol *Srīvikkramaḥ.*
816	126.1	.8	King in *dhoti* and wearing sash. *............ndra-guptaḥ.*	L. hand on knee. Symbol off. *Srīvikkramaḥ.*
817	121	.75	King in *dhoti.* *....hara*	L. hand bent up. Symbol *Sravakrama.*
818	120.1	.76	King in *dhoti.* *Devaśramaharajadhara*	L. hand bent up, elbow resting on knee slightly raised up. Symbol Legend blurred.
819	120.5	.73	King in *dhoti.* *Davaśramaharajadhara-ja,* in small characters.	L. hand bent up. Symbol incomplete, but probably *Srīvikramaḥ.*
820	123.8	.76	King in coat and trousers. *Davaśramaharajadharaja*	L. hand outstretched and holding lotus with long stalk. Symbol, but in-complete. *Sravakrama.*
821	120	.8	King in short *dhoti* and coat. *Devaśrama*	L. hand bent up. Symbol incomplete. *Srīvikkramaḥ.*

No.	Wt.	Size	Obverse	Reverse
822	121.4	.72	King in trousers. *Davaśrī*	L. hand bent up. Symbol incomplete. *Śravakrama.*
823	120.4	.75	King in *dhoti.* *Devaśrī maharajadharaja-..ndragupta.*	L. hand bent up. Symbol  *Śrīvikkramaḥ.*
824	120.6	.75	King in *dhoti.* Circular legend blurred and truncated.	L. hand bent up. Symbol  *Śrīvikra*
825	119.9	.76	As above.	L. arm akimbo. Symbol  *Śrīvikkramaḥ.*
826	121	.8	King in short *dhoti.* Circular legend off.	L. hand bent up, elbow resting on knee slightly raised. Symbol , but incomplete. *Śravikkramaḥ.*
827	119.9	.75	King in trousers. Circular legend off.	L. hand on knee. Symbol 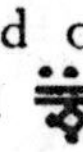 *Śravakra*
828	125.5	.83	As above.	L. hand on knee. Symbol 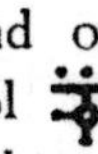 *Śravakkrama.*
829	118.8	.69	King in *dhoti.* Circular legend off.	L. hand on knee. Symbol off. Legend blurred.
830	121.8	.7	As above.	L. hand on knee. Symbol 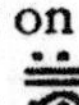 Legend blurred.
831	119.7	.74	King in *dhoti.* *Dava*	L. hand on knee. Symbol 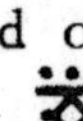 *Śravakkrama.*
832	119.8	.78	King in *dhoti.* Circular legend off.	L. hand bent up. Symbol incomplete. *Śrīvikramaḥ.*

No.	Wt.	Size	Obverse	Reverse
833	120	.78	King in short *dhoti*. *.vaśra*	L. hand bent up, elbow resting on knee slightly raised up. Symbol  *Śravakkrama.*
834	124.6	.88	King in *dhoti*. *Devaśramahara*	L. hand on knee. Symbol  *Śrīvikkramaḥ.*
835	120.2	.72	King in trousers. ....*Chandra-guptaḥ.*	L. hand on knee. Symbol  *Śrīvikramaḥ.*
836	118.8	.78	King in short *dhoti*. *Devaśra.*	L. hand bent up, elbow resting on knee slightly raised. Symbol  *Śravakrama.*
837	119.3	.79	King in *dhoti*. *Devaśra*.......... *guptaḥ.*	L. hand bent up. Symbol  Legend blurred.
838	119.3	.78	King in short *dhoti*. *Dava*	L. hand on knee. Symbol  *Śrīvikramaḥ.*
839	121.2	.79	King in short *dhoti*. *Dava*	L. arm akimbo. Symbol  *Śravakkramaḥ.*
840	120.1	.76	Coat buttons fixed on a strip. ....*śra-Chand-raguptaḥ.* Arrow cuts across the letter *śrī*.	L. hand bent up. Symbol 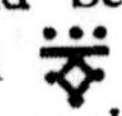 *Śrivikkramaḥ.* **Pl. XI. 5.**
841	123.7	.8	King in trousers. Circular legend off.	L. arm akimbo. Symbol  *Śrīvikkramaḥ.*

No.	Wt.	Size	Obverse	Reverse
842	121.4	.78	King in trousers. *Devaśramaha*	L. hand bent up. Symbol *Sravakkramaḥ.*
843	125	.78	King in *dhoti.* *Davaśrama*	L. hand on knee. Symbol *Sravakkrama.*
844	120.9	.75	King in *dhoti.* . . . .*ptaḥ.* Three cracks in the edge.	L. hand bent up. Symbol *Srīvikkrama.*
845	119.7	.76	King in trousers. *Davaśrama*	L. hand stretched out and holding a lotus with long stalk. Symbol *Srīvikramaḥ.*
846	122.7	.74	King in trousers with buttons on sides (?) and wearing a pearl-bedecked cap. . *va* .. *hara* . . . . . . *Chandraguptaḥ.*	L. hand bent up, elbow not resting on knee. Symbol *Srīvikkramaḥ.*
847	127.3	.82	King in *dhoti.* Circular legend off.	L. hand on knee. Symbol *Srīvikkramaḥ.*
848	125.2	.79	As above.	L. hand on knee. Symbol *Sravakkramaḥ.*
849	119.6	.78	King in *dhoti.* *Devaśramha*	L. hand bent up. Symbol *Srīvikrama.*
850	123.7	.86	King in *dhoti.* *Davaśramaharajadharaja*	L. hand on knee. Symbol *Srīvikkramaḥ.*
851	121.4	.8	King in trousers. *Devaśra . . . . śrī-Chandraguptaḥ.*	L. hand bent up. Symbol *Srīvikramaḥ.*

No.	Wt.	Size	Obverse	Reverse
852	124.4	.83	King in trousers. *Devaśrīmaharajadharaja-śra-Cha* Impure gold.	L. hand on knee. Symbol incomplete. *Srīvikramaḥ*, partly double struck.
853	121.1	.7	King in short *dhoti*. Circular legend off.	L. hand bent up. Symbol a variation of  with a dot below on either side of the circle. *Srīvikkramaḥ*.
854	119.7	.82	King in trousers. *Davaśramahara....* *śra-Chandraguptaḥ*.	L. hand on knee. Symbol  *Srīvikkramaḥ*.
855	123.6	.82	King in *dhoti*, and wearing high boots; curly hair falls on the neck in two rows; armlets on both arms. *Deva.........* *Chandraguptaḥ*.	L. hand on knee. Symbol 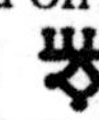 *Srīvikkramaḥ*. **Pl. XI. 6.**
856	123.2	.82	King in *dhoti*. Circular legend off. Pale gold.	L. hand on knee. Symbol 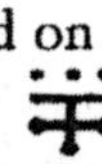 *Srīvikkramaḥ*.
857	120.8	.75	King in trousers. *Devaśramaharajadharaja-śra-Chandraguptaḥ*.	L. hand bent up. Symbol 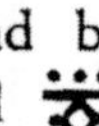 *Srīvikkramaḥ*.
858	121.1	.75	King in *dhoti*. *......jadharaja*	L. hand on knee. Symbol incomplete. *Srīvikkramaḥ*.
859	120.5	.73	King in trousers. Circular legend off.	L. hand on knee. Symbol  *Srīvikkramaḥ*.
860	120.2	.8	King in *dhoti*. *...........Chandra-guptaḥ*.	L. arm akimbo. Symbol  *Srīvikramaḥ*.

No.	Wt.	Size	Obverse	Reverse
861	119.8	.74	King in *dhoti*. *Davaśra*	L. hand raised up, elbow resting on knee. Symbol *Śrīvikramaḥ*.
862	120.3	.73	King in *dhoti*. *Davaśramaha*	L. hand on knee. Symbol incomplete. *Śrīvikkramaḥ*.
863	122.2	.8	King in *dhoti*. *Davaśramaharajadha*	L. hand on knee. Symbol *Śravikkramaḥ*.
864	121.6	.7	King in *dhoti*. Circular legend off.	L. hand bent up. Symbol *Śrīvikkramaḥ*.
865	119.6	.74	King wears high boots. Coat buttons on a strip. *Davaśramaharajadharaja-...guptaḥ*, partly truncated.	L. hand bent up. Symbol *Śrīvikramaḥ* Pl. XI. 7.
866	123	.8	King in *dhoti*. *Dava............pta*.	L. hand on knee. Symbol , but with four prongs above instead of four dots. *Śrīvikkramaḥ*.
867	123.3	.82	King in *dhoti*, curly hair on head. *Devaśrīmaharajadharaja*	L. hand on knee and holding a lotus with a long stalk. Symbol *Śrīvikkramaḥ*.
868	124.2	.79	King in *dhoti*. *Davaśra*, in small characters.	L. hand on knee. Symbol *Śrīvikramaḥ*.
869	120.6	.71	King in *dhoti*. *Deva*	L. hand on knee. Symbol , but incomplete. *Śravakramaḥ*.

No.	Wt.	Size	Obverse	Reverse
870	120.7	.7	King wearing short *dhoti*. *Davaśra*	L. hand bent up. Symbol  *Śravikramaḥ*.
871	120.6	.7	King in *dhoti*. ....*dhara*	L. hand bent up. Symbol  *Śravakramaḥ*.
872	119.9	.75	King in *dhoti*. *Davaśra.........ndra-gupta*.	L. hand on knee. Symbol , but incomplete. *Śravikramaḥ*.
873	121.4	.74	King in *dhoti*. *Devaśra*	L. arm akimbo. Symbol  *Śravikramaḥ*.
874	120.8	.75	King in *dhoti*. .....*rajadhara.Cha-ndragupta*.	L. arm akimbo. Symbol 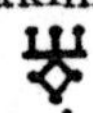 *Śrīvikramaḥ*.
875	127.9	.73	King in *dhoti*. *.vaśrama* Two cracks in the edge.	L. hand on knee. Symbol 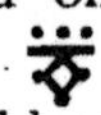 Legend blurred.
876	113.9	.75	King in *dhoti*. Circular legend off.	L. hand on knee. Symbol  *Śrīvikkramaḥ*.
877	123	.81	King in trousers. *Dava....jadha....n-dragupta*.	L. hand on knee. Symbol 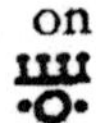 *Śrīvikkramaḥ*.
878	120.2	.72	King in *dhoti*. Circular legend off.	L. hand on knee. Symbol 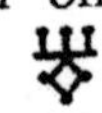 *.vakra*
879	115.3	.75	King in *dhoti*. *Davaśra*	L. hand bent up. Symbol 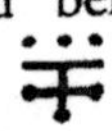 *Śravakkra*
880	120.4	.7	King in *dhoti*. *Devaśramaha*	L. hand on knee. Symbol  *Śravakkramaḥ*.

No.	Wt.	Size	Obverse	Reverse
881	123.8	.79	King in *dhoti*. *Davaśra*	L. hand on knee. Symbol *Śrīvikkramaḥ*.
882	119.5	.8	King in coat and trousers, button line of the former being clear. .... *Chandraguptaḥ*.	L. hand on knee. Symbol *Śrīvikramaḥ*.
883	127.6	.7	King in *dhoti*, his feet being off the flan. *Devaśramaha*, truncated.	L. hand on knee. Symbol , but incomplete. Legend blurred.
884	120.9	.7	King in short *dhoti*. *Davaśramahara*	L. hand bent up, elbow resting on knee slightly raised. Symbol *Śrīvikramaḥ*.
885	121.4	.75	King in short *dhoti*. ...*maharajadharaja*, truncated.	L. hand bent up. Symbol *Śravakra*
886	120	.78	King in coat and trousers. ..*śramaharaja*	L. hand on knee. Symbol indistinct. Legend blurred.
887	119	.75	King in *dhoti*. *Davaśramahara*	L. hand bent up. Symbol , but incomplete. *Śrīvikkramaḥ*.
888	120.8	.8	King in *dhoti*. *Dava*	L. hand on knee. Symbol *Śrīvikkramaḥ*.
889	124.1	.86	King in *dhoti*. *Davaśramaharajadharajaśra-Chandra*	L. hand on knee. Symbol *Śrīvikkramaḥ*.

No.	Wt.	Size	Obverse	Reverse
890	120.3	.7	King in short *dhoti* and with sash. Circular legend off.	L. hand bent up. Symbol off. *Śravakra.*
891	120.3	.7	King in *dhoti* and wearing sash. Circular legend off.	L. hand bent up, elbow resting on knee slightly raised. Symbol  *Śravakkrama.*
892	120.6	.8	As above.	L. hand bent up. Symbol  *Śrīvikkramaḥ.*
893	125.2	.78	King in *dhoti* and with sash. *Dava*	L. hand on knee. Symbol  *Śrīvikkramaḥ.*
894	119.9	.75	King in *dhoti* and with sash. Circular legend off.	L. hand bent up. Symbol  Legend off.
895	125.7	.76	King in *dhoti* and with sash. *Devaśrī*	L. hand on knee. Symbol 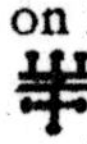 *Śrīvikkramaḥ.*
896	127.4	.8	King in *dhoti* and with sash. Circular legend off.	L. hand on knee. Symbol  *Śravakkrama.*
897	121.4	.7	As above.	L. hand bent up. Symbol incomplete. Legend blurred.
898	126	.8	King in *dhoti* and with sash. *Davaśramaharaja*	L. hand on knee. Symbol blurred. Legend blurred.
899	120.4	.72	King in *dhoti.* Circular legend off.	L. hand bent up. Symbol 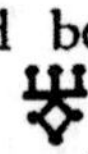 *Śrīvikkramaḥ.*
900	121.8	.75	King in *dhoti* and wearing coat with prominent buttons. Circular legend off.	L. hand bent up. Symbol  *Śrīvikkramaḥ.*

No.	Wt.	Size	Obverse	Reverse
901	126	·79	King in *dhoti*. *Dava*	L. hand on knee. Symbol *Śrīvikkramaḥ*.
902	124.2	.8	King in *dhoti*; sash round the waist. *Devaśrīmahārājadhiraja-śrī* Flan has slightly moved in striking and letters have become curiously blurred.	L. hand on knee. Symbol *Śrīvikkramaḥ*. **Pl. XI. 8.**
903	121.1	.78	King in *dhoti*. *Davaśramaharaja*	L. hand on knee. Symbol *Śrīvikkramaḥ*.
904	126.8	.71	King in *dhoti* and wearing a fine waist-band and a buttoned coat. *Devaśramaharaja*	L. hand on knee and holding a lotus with a long stalk. Symbol *Śrīvikramaḥ*.
905	123.3	.8	King in *shalwar* and high boots. Armlets on either arm over the coat. *Davaśramaharajadhara-ja . Chandraguptaḥ*. The arrow is cutting across the letter *ndra*.	Goddess not nimbate and wearing a waist-band of five straps. L. hand at waist and holding a lotus with long stalk. Symbol *Śrīvikrama*. **Pl. XI. 9.**
906	120.3	·73	King in *dhoti*. Circular legend off.	L. hand bent up. Symbol *Śravakkrama*.
907	123.2	.8	King in trousers. *Davaśramaha*	L. arm akimbo. Symbol *Śravikramaḥ*.

No.	Wt.	Size	Obverse	Reverse
908	120.9	.72	King in *dhoti*. *Chandra* under arm blurred. Circular legend off.	L. hand bent up. Symbol off. *Śrīvikkramaḥ*.
909	123.7	.85	King in *dhoti*. *Devaśrīmaharajadharaja-śra*	L. arm akimbo. Symbol *Śrīvikkramaḥ*.
910	123.2	.8	King in trousers. *Devaśramahara......* *ndragupta*.	L. hand on knee. Symbol *Śrīvikkramaḥ*.
911	122.3	.73	King wearing short *dhoti* or shorts. Circular legend off.	L. hand on knee. Symbol *Śrīvakkrama*.
912	121.3	.75	King in trousers. *Da ....ndra-gupta*.	L. hand bent up. Symbol *Śrīvikkramaḥ*.
913	121.1	.75	King in trousers. *Devaśramaharaja......* *gupta*.	L. hand bent up. Symbol *Śrīvikkramaḥ*.
914	121.8	.75	King in trousers. Circular legend off.	L. arm akimbo. Symbol *Śravikkramaḥ*.
915	120.9	.72	King in *dhoti*. *Davaśra*	L. hand bent up. Symbol Legend blurred.
916	121.1	.7	King in trousers and wearing coat with prominent buttons. *.............gupta*.	L. hand bent up. Symbol *Śrīvikkramaḥ*.
917	123.9	.8	King in *shalwar*. He is either wearing armlets over coat or its sleeves are rolled up. Three rows of pearls on the head-dress or hair dressed	Goddess not nimbate. L. hand on knee. Symbol *Śrakkramaḥ*. **Pl. XI. 10**

No.	Wt.	Size	Obverse	Reverse
			in three-stepped artistic tresses. *Davaśra........* *Chandraguptaḥ.* Right side legend is truncated.	
918	120.9	.73	King in *dhoti.* Circular legend off.	L. hand bent up. Symbol  *.vakkra*
919	122	.75	King in *dhoti.* *..śrama*	L. hand on knee. Symbol  Legend blurred.
920	119.9	.78	King in trousers. *Deva..........* *ndragupta.*	L. hand bent up. Symbol  *Śravikkramaḥ.*
921	120.8	.73	King wearing short *dhoti* and buttoned coat. Circular legend off.	L. hand bent up. Symbol  *Śrīvikkramaḥ.*
922	119.1	.75	King in short *dhoti.* *...........ndraguptaḥ.*	L. hand bent up. Symbol  *Śrīvikkramaḥ.*
923	123.8	.82	King in *dhoti;* his personality and posture are fine. *...........Chandragupta.*	L. hand on knee. Symbol 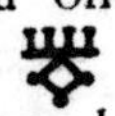 *Śrīvikkramaḥ.*
924	118.4	.7	King in *dhoti.* Circular legend off.	L. hand bent up. Symbol  *Śrīvikrama.*
925	128.1	.74	King in *dhoti* and with sash. Circular legend off.	L. hand on knee. Symbol  Legend blurred.
926	119.6	.73	King in *dhoti.* *Davaśramaharajadharaja*	L. hand on knee. Symbol  *Śrīvikkramaḥ.*

No.	Wt.	Size	Obverse	Reverse
927	120.8	.7	King in *dhoti* and with sash. Circular legend off.	L. hand bent up. Symbol 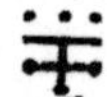 Legend off.
928	120.3	.7	As above.	L. hand bent up. Symbol off. *.vakkra*
929	120.8	.75	King in *dhoti* and with sash. Circular legend off.	L. hand on knee. Symbol  Legend off.
930	120.6	.8	King in *dhoti* and with sash. *Deva*	L. hand bent up. Symbol  *Śravakkrama.*
931	120.5	.75	King in *dhoti* and with sash. ....*śrī-Chandra*	L. hand bent up, elbow resting on knee slightly raised. Symbol blurred. Legend blurred.
932	120.3	.75	King in *dhoti* and with sash. Circular legend off.	L. hand bent up. Symbol incomplete. *.vakkama.*
933	119.4	.73	As above.	L. hand bent up. Symbol 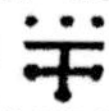 *Śravakkrama.*
934	120.8	.7	As above.	L. hand bent up. Symbol off. *.vakkama.*
935	121.6	.74	King in *dhoti*. *Davaśramaharaja*	L. hand bent up. Symbol 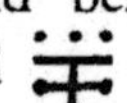 Legend off.
936	126.2	.8	King in *dhoti*. Circular legend off.	L. hand on knee. Symbol blurred. *Śrīvikkrama.*
937	127.1	.7	King in *dhoti* and wearing coat with five buttons. Circular legend off.	L. hand on knee. Symbol blurred. *Śrīvikrama.*

No.	Wt.	Size	Obverse	Reverse
938	120.6	.75	King in trousers and wearing a coat with buttons at sides and in the centre. There is a crescent over his head and the cap has a pearl decoration at the back. *Davaśramaḥa........ guptaḥ.*	L. hand on waist. Symbol  *Śravakrama.* **Pl. XI. 11.**
939	120.5	.8	King in trousers and with coat as above. *..........śrī-Chandragupta.*	L. hand stretched out and holding a lotus with long stalk reaching down to the ground. Symbol  *Śrīvikkrama.*
940	119.9	.75	King in *dhoti* and wearing coat with side buttons. Circular legend off. There is a cut on the coin.	L. hand on knee. Symbol  *Śravakkrama.*
941	118.6	.75	King in trousers wearing a coat with prominent buttons. *Davaśramaha*	L. hand bent up. Symbol  *Śravakkrama.*
942	120.7	.8	King in trousers, wearing a coat with side buttons. *..........śra-Chandragupta.*	L. hand stretched out and holding lotus with a long stalk. Symbol  *Śrīvikkrama.*
943	118.5	.7	King in short *dhoti.* Circular legend off. Gold pale.	L. hand bent up, elbow resting on knee, raised up. Symbol  *..kkra*

No.	Wt.	Size	Obverse	Reverse
944	124.8	.8	Impression blurred as the coin was hammered subsequently with a view to convert it into bullion. *Davaśramaha*	A cut across the coin at I. Symbol blurred. *Śravakkrama.*
945	118.9	.75	King in short *dhoti*. Buttons of the coat clear. Circular legend off.	Goddess not nimbate. L. hand on knee. Symbol Legend off.
946	127.5	.73	King in *dhoti*. *Davaśra*	L. hand on knee. Head of the goddess off the flan. Symbol but incomplete. *Śrīvikrama.*
947	127.9	.78	King in *dhoti*. Parallel to the bow-string there is a vertical line cutting across the word *Chandra*, which if taken as part of the legend, seems to give the reading *Samudra*. Circular legend off.	Goddess facing l. L. hand on knee. Symbol blurred. *Śravakkrama*, blurred and truncated.
948	123.9	.85	King in *dhoti* and his hair is curly. *Davaśramaharajadha . . . Chandraguta.*	L. hand on knee. Symbol *Śrīvikkramaḥ.*
949	123.4	.85	King in *dhoti* and his hair is curly. *Devaśrīmaharajadhara-jaśra.*	L. hand on knee. Symbol *Śrīvikkramaḥ.*
950	120	.73	Halo detached from the king's head. King wears a *dhoti*. *Devaśrīmaharajadhiraja-śra . . gapta*	Left hand bent up. Symbol *Śrīvikkramaḥ.*

Variety B : 18 coins.

(King as in Variety A, but with a hunter)

No.	Wt.	Size	Obverse	Reverse
			King nimbate, standing to l., holding an arrow in r. hand and bow in the l. at its top, with its string inside, wearing coat, waist-band and *dhoti*, a hunter hanging by his l. side from the waist. *Garuḍadhvaja* behind the r. hand. *Chandra* written vertically under the l. arm. Circular legend beginning at I, *Devaśrī-mahārājādhirājaśrī-Chandraguptaḥ*. देवश्रीमहाराजाधिराजश्रीचन्द्रगुप्तः । Pl. XXXIII. 12.	Goddess Lakshmi, nimbate, seated facing on lotus holding noose in r. hand usually bent and extended, and lotus in the l., sometimes bent up and sometimes resting on the knee or waist. Symbol on the l. Legend on the r. *Śrīvikramaḥ*. श्रीविक्रमः । Pl. XXXVI. 51.
951	125.6	.8	Stick and thong of the hunter are both short. *Deva*	L. hand of the goddess rests on thigh. Symbol 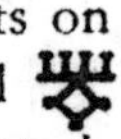 *Śrīvikramaḥ*.
952	121	.75	Sleeves of the coat are rolled up. Thong of the hunter is rather long. Circular legend off.	L. hand bent up. Symbol off. *Śrīvikrama*. **Pl. XI. 12.**
953	126.3	.78	Circular legend off.	L. hand on waist. Symbol 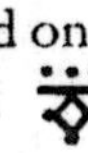 *Śrīvikra*.

No.	Wt.	Size	Obverse	Reverse
954	120.7	.7	The buttons of the king's coat are clearly visible. The handle of the hunter is small. Circular legend off.	L. hand bent up. Symbol 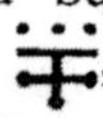, but incomplete. *.vakrama.*
955	124.7	.87	Hunter has a long stick and a relatively short thong. ....*Chandragupta.* Clipped at the top to adjust the weight.	L. hand on waist. Symbol , blurred. *Śravikkrama.* **Pl. XI. 13.**
956	125.3	.79	*Davaśramahara*	L. hand on waist. Symbol incomplete. *Śrīvikramaḥ.*
957	114.7	.8	...........*Chandragupta.*	L. hand on waist. Symbol , incomplete. *Śrīvikramaḥ.*
958	125.5	.8	Circular legend off.	L. hand on waist. Symbol  *Śrīvikrama*
959	126	.8	............*ndragu*	L. hand on waist. Symbol  Legend off.
960	125.8	.8	Circular legend off.	L. hand on waist. Symbol 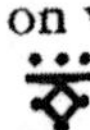 *Śrīvikramaḥ.*
961	125.7	.77	As above.	As above. *Śravakramaḥ.*
962	119.6	.67	As above.	L. hand bent up. Symbol 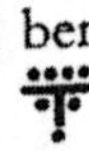 *Śrīvikkrama.*
963	125.1	.8	The king's posture and personality is stately and his coat but-	L. hand on waist. Symbol 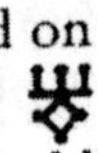 with an additional dot

No.	Wt.	Size	Obverse	Reverse
			tons are artistic. *Devaśrī*, truncated.	below. *Sravakkrama*. **Pl. XI. 14.**
964	94.4	.8	Stick of the hunter is long and its thong very short. It can be seen tied to the waist-band. *Dava* A well preserved coin, but very low in weight.	L. hand on waist. Symbol *Srīvikkrama*. **Pl. XI. 15.**
965	123.1	.8	............*gupta*.	L. hand bent up. Symbol *Srīvikkrama*.
966	124.2	.78	...........*Chandra-gupta*.	L. hand on waist. Symbol *Sravakrama*.
967	124.8	.8	Stick of the hunter is long compared to its thong. *Davaśramaharaja*, truncated and blurred.	L. hand on waist. Symbol off. *Srīvikkramaḥ*. **Pl. XII. 1.**
968	126.2	.8	Artistic row of buttons in the centre of the coat. King wears high leather shoes. ....*Chandra-guptaḥ*, in small characters.	L. hand on waist. Symbol *Sravakkramaḥ*. **Pl. XII. 2.**

Variety C : 10 coins

(King as in variety A, but with sword)

			King standing to l., nimbate, wearing ear-rings, necklace, armlets coat, *dhoti*, waistband, holding arrow in r.	Goddess Lakshmī, nimbate, seated facing on lotus, holding noose in r. hand extended and a lotus with long

No.	Wt.	Size	Obverse	Reverse
			hand and bow at the top with string inside by the l. hand; sword in scabbard, hanging by king's l. side. On the l. is *Garuḍadhvaja* behind the r. hand. Under king's l. arm, written in a vertical line, *Chandra*. Circular legend, *Devaśrīmahārājādhirāja-śrī-Chandraguptaḥ*. देवश्रीमहाराजाधिराजश्रीचन्द्रगुप्तः । Pl. XXXIII. 12.	stalk in the l. hand resting on knee. Symbol on l. Legend on r., *Śrīvikramaḥ*. श्रीविक्रमः । Pl. XXXVI. 51.
969	128.3	.7	Circular legend blurred and truncated.	Symbol  *Śrīvikrama*.
970	127.6	.73	King's curly hair is falling down his head. Hilt of the sword can be clearly seen above the scabbard. Legend blurred and truncated; traces of *Davaśrama*	Symbol 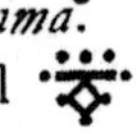 *Śravakrama*. **Pl. XII. 3.**
971	127.6	.75	Buttons of the coat clear. Circular legend off.	Symbol  *Śra.kkrama*.
972	127.3	.8	Hilt of the sword visible. *Devaśrīmaha*	Symbol  *Śrīvikramaḥ*.
973	128	.75	*Devaśramaharajadha*, partly blurred and truncated.	Symbol  *Śravakkrama*. **Pl. XII. 5.**
974	127.9	.7	Hilt of the sword clearly visible outside the scabbard. Circular legend off.	Symbol as above. *Śravakra*

No.	Wt.	Size	Obverse	Reverse
975	128.6	.71	Sword is long and its hilt is clear. Circular legend off.	Symbol Legend blurred; traces of *Sa.kra* **Pl. XII. 4.**
976	127.6	.8	King's figure is stately. ....*śrī-Chandra-gupta*, truncated and blurred.	Symbol a variation of with three prongs above. *Śrīvikkrama.* **Pl. XII. 6.**
977	127	.8	Circular legend off.	Symbol , but incomplete. *Śrivakrama.*
978	126.8	.71	Circular legend off.	Symbol blurred. *..kkrama.*

Variety D : 4 coins

(King as in variety A, but goddess on rev. with l. foot tucked up)

No.	Wt.	Size	Obverse	Reverse
			King nimbate, standing to l., wearing a cap, coat, trousers or *dhoti*, necklace, earrings, armlets, and boots, holding arrow in r. hand and bow, string inwards, at the top with the l; Garuḍa standard on l. behind the r. hand. No sword or hunter by the king's side. *Chandra* written under the l. arm. Circular legend, *Devaśrīmahārājādhirājaśrī-Chandraguptaḥ.* देवश्रीमहाराजाधिराजश्रीचन्द्रगुप्तः। Pl. XXXIII. 12.	Goddess Lakshmī nimbate, seated on lotus, facing, holding noose in outstretched r. hand and lotus in the l., resting on waist. Left foot is tucked up and the r. one is hanging down. Symbol on l. Legend on r., *Śrīvikramaḥ.* श्रीविक्रमः। Pl. XXXVI. 51.

No.	Wt.	Size	Obverse	Reverse
979	122.4	.71	King wears *dhoti* with high leather boots. *Davaśramaharajadha* Coin was deliberately clipped in the lower l. side, apparently to adjust weight.	Symbol *Śravakra* **Pl. XII. 7.**
980	120.8	.76	King wears *dhoti* and boots. *.....rajadha* Cracks in the edge at III and VII.	Symbol *Śrīvikramaḥ.*
981	118.3	.74	King wears *dhoti.* *Davaśramaharajadhi*	Symbol *Śravikramaḥ.* **Pl. XII. 8.**
982	119.8	.73	King wears trousers and boots. *Davaśramaharaja* Two cracks in the edge. Normal condition.	Symbol *Śrīvikramaḥ.*

Variety E : 1 coin

(King as in variety A, but no *Chandra* under l. arm.)

No.	Wt.	Size	Obverse	Reverse
983	117.7	.79	King nimbate, standing l. wearing cap, coat, trousers, high leather shoes, earrings, necklace and armlets, holding arrow in r. hand and bow with string outside in the l. hand, resting on waist, bow passing over shoulder and being held at its middle. End of the	Goddess, nimbate, facing, seated on lotus, wearing a *sari*, upper garment, earrings, necklace, and bangles, both hands outstretched, holding noose in the r. and lotus with long stalk touching the ground in the l.

No.	Wt.	Size	Obverse	Reverse
			sash flies across the bow. Garuḍa standard on l. behind the r. hand. No legend under the l. arm. Circular legend incomplete, but the same as in earlier varieties; *Devaśramahara....śra-Chandragu* Last three letters are separated from the rest and are at IX. Normal condition.	Symbol  *Śravikrama.* **Pl. XII. 9.**

Variety F : 1 coin

(King as in variety A, but with *Chandragupta* on rev.)

No.	Wt.	Size	Obverse	Reverse
984	129.6	.8	King standing to l., nimbate, curly hair on head, bare and muscular body, wearing a *dhoti* and sash, holding arrow in r. hand and bow in the l. at the top; *Chandra* written vertically under the arm. Staff of the Garuḍa banner is worked on lathe. Legend, apparently beginning at VII, is the same as in var. A. ....*śrī-Chandragu*, the concluding letters being on the r. side.	Goddess Lakshmī, nimbate, seated facing on lotus, r. hand extended, holding an uncertain peacked object; l. hand bent up and holding a lotus. No symbol. Legend on r., *Chandragupta*, rather blurred, but clear on the original. Letters *gupta* are sufficiently clear in the plate. **Pl. XII. 10.**

No.	Wt.	Size	Obverse	Reverse
			A crack in the coin at III. Normal condition.	

Variety G : 2 coins

(Bow in r. hand and arrow in the l. and king looking left)

No.	Wt.	Size	Obverse	Reverse
			King not nimbate, standing facing right, wearing earrings, necklace, armlets, *sakachha dhoti* and sash, upper body bare and muscular, currly hair on head, holding arrow in l. hand and bow at the top in the r., string inwards; Garuḍa standard on l. behind the r. hand; *Chandra*, written vertically under r. arm. Circular legend, beginning at (l), *Devaśrīmahārājādhirāja-śrī-Chandraguptaḥ.*	Goddess Lakshmī, nimbate, seated facing both hands extended, holding noose in the r. hand and lotus with long stalk in the l., resting on the knee, slightly raised. Symbol on l. Legend, *Śrīvikkramaḥ.*
985	120.7	.76	*Devaśramaharajadha . . śra-Chandraguptaḥ.* Letters on the left are rather blurred and *pta* is between the bow-end and the king's head.	Symbol slightly incomplete. *Śrīvikkramaḥ.* **Pl. XII. 11.**
986	120.7	.74	*Devaśrama . . . . . . śra-Chandraguptaḥ,* blurred. Normal condition.	Symbol *Śrīvikkramaḥ.* **Pl. XII. 12.**

Variety H : 17 coins

(Bow in l. hand, but king looking r.)

No.	Wt.	Size	Obverse	Reverse
			King not nimbate, standing facing right, but body turned three quarters to l., wearing short *dhoti* or *janghia*; head and upper body, which is muscular, being bare; curly hair on the head, falling behind it. Ends of the diadem behind the head. Arrow in r. hand and bow held at the top in l., string inwards. Garuḍa standard on l. behind r. hand. *Chandra* under l. arm. Circular legend beginning at (1), *Devaśrīmahārājādhirārajaśrī-Chandraguptaḥ.* देवश्रीमहाराजाधिराजश्रीचन्द्रगुप्तः । Pl. XXXIII. 12.	Goddess Lakshmī, nimbate, seated facing, legs folded and the l. one slightly raised, wearing earrings, necklace, bangles, *sari* and *kañchukī*, holding noose in r. hand stretched out, but not touching the knee and lotus with long stalk in l., also stretched out but resting on l. knee. Symbol on l. Legend, *Srīvikramaḥ.* श्रीविक्रमः । Pl. XXXVI. 51.
987	120.7	.72	*Devaśramaharajadhara-ja-śrī-Chandraga,* all on r. side and considerably blurred.	Symbol *Srīvikkrama.* Flan has moved while striking, giving rise to double border on the l. **Pl. XII. 13.**
988	120.2	.78	*Devaśramaharajadhira-jaśra,* blurred and truncated.	Symbol *Srīvikkramaḥ*, blurred. **Pl. XII. 14.**

No.	Wt.	Size	Obverse	Reverse
989	120.6	.76	*Devaśrīmaharajadhi* .	Symbol *Śrīvikkramaḥ.*
990	122.8	.72	*Davaśramaharajadhara,* truncated.	Symbol, but incomplete. *Śrīvikramaḥ.*
991	120.4	.83	*Davaśramaharaja,* blurred.	Symbol *Śrīvikkramaḥ.*
992	120.1	.78	*Dava.maharajadhara*	Symbol *Śrīvikramaḥ.*
993	120.6	.75	*Devaśrīmahārājādhara-ja*	Symbol *Śrīvikramaḥ.*
994	121.4	.74	Fillet behind the head is very clear. *Davaśramahārājādhira-jaśra*	Symbol *Śrīvikramaḥ.* Pl. XII. 15.
995	119.1	.8	Fillet behind head is very clear. *Devaśramaharajadharaja-śra-Cha.gupta,* blurred.	Symbol *Śrīvikramaḥ,* rather blurred. Pl. XIII. 1.
996	120.2	.71	Circular legend fragmentary and blurred.	Symbol *Śrīvikra*
997	120.2	.8	*Devaśramahārājādhira-jaśrī-Chandragupta.* Only traces of the last two letters are visible at IX, the remaining legend is all on the r.	Symbol *Śrvikkramaḥ.* Pl. XIII. 2.
998	120.9	.75	*..śrīmahārājādhiraja*	Symbol *Śrīvikramaḥ.*
999	121.3	.75	*Davaśrī*	Symbol on l.; on r. a group of four dots. *Śrīvikramaḥ.*

No.	Wt.	Size	Obverse	Reverse
1000	121.6	.74	Ends of the diadem visible behind the head. *..śramaharaja*	Symbol *Srīvikrama.*
1001	121.6	.74	*Davaśramaharaja*	Symbol *Srīvikrama.*
1002	120.3	.7	*..śrīmaharajadhirājaśra*	Symbol incomplete. *Srivikrama.*
1003	120	.73	*Davaśramaharajadhara-*	Symbol *Srīvikramaḥ.*

Variety I : 4 coins

(King standing r., bow in l. hand, held by the middle)

No.	Wt.	Size	Obverse	Reverse
			King nimbate, standing to r.; but body turned one fourth to l., wearing *janghia* and sash, but the upper body and the head bare, holding arrow in r. hand and bow with string outside held at its middle in the left. *Garuḍadhvaja* behind r. hand. *Chandra* outside the bow-string. Circular legend beginning at (I), *Devaśrīmahārājādhirajaśrī-Chandraguptaḥ.* देवश्रीमहाराजाधिराजश्रीचन्द्र-गुप्तः । Pl. XXXIII. 12.	Goddess, Lakshmī, nimbate, seated with legs slightly raised, facing on lotus, wearing *sari*, *kañchukī*, ear-rings, necklace and bangles, holding noose in out-stretched r. hand and lotus with long stalk in the l. Symbol on l. Legend, *Srīvikramaḥ.* श्रीविक्रमः । Pl. XXXVI. 51.
1004	111.5	.8	*Devaśramahārājādha.... dra* Normal condition, weight abnormally low.	Symbol *Srīvikkramaḥ.* **Pl. XIII. 3.**

No.	Wt.	Size	Obverse	Reverse
1005	121.6	.71	*Davaśramaharajadha....* *ndragupta.* Normal condition.	Symbol *Śrīvikramaḥ.*
1006	121.7	.75	*Devaśrīmahārājādhara-* *jaśrī-Chandra*	Symbol *Śravakkramaḥ.* **Pl. XIII. 4.**
1007	122	.78	*Devaśramaharajadhara-* *ia,* blurred and truncated.	Symbol *Śrīvikkramaḥ.* **Pl. XIII. 5.**

HORSEMAN TYPE : 82 COINS

Class I : King to left : 52 coins

Variety A : 29 coins

(King without any weapons)

No.	Wt.	Size	Obverse	Reverse
			King riding on fully caparisoned horse to l., usually wearing *dhoti*, coat and waist-band flying behind him, necklace, ear-rings, armlets, etc. Circular legend, beginning at (I), *Paramabhāgavato mahārājādhirājaśrī-Chandraguptaḥ*. परमभागवतो महाराजाधिराज-श्रीचन्द्रगुप्तः। Pl. XXXIII. 15. The letters *gupta* are usually at X, separated from the rest of the legend by the head of the horse.	Goddess, usually nimbate, seated facing l. on wicker stool, holding noose in r. hand and lotus of long stalk with leaves and roots in the l. hand usually resting on waist. Symbol usually present except in one case, No. 1035. Legend on r. *Ajitavikramah*. अजितविक्रमः। Pl. XXXVI. 53.
1008	120.6	.7	King to l. *Para..... maharaja-......gupta.*	Symbol *Ajatavakrama.*
1009	120.3	.66	King to l. .... *gupta.*	Symbol blurred. *Ajitavikramaḥ.*
1010	120.6	.7	As above. One crack in the edge.	Symbol incomplete. *Ajatavakra*

No.	Wt.	Size	Obverse	Reverse
1011	121.7	.72	King to l. *Para..... ....* *śra-Chandragupta,* in small characters.	Symbol incomplete, but probably Legend off.
1012	120.8	.75	King to l. .... *śra-Chandragupta,* in small characters. Crack in the edge at X	Symbol *.jatavakramaḥ.*
1013	127.9	.78	King to l. Legend blurred.	Stool is artistic. Symbol *.....maḥ.*
1014	134.3	.74	King to l. (I) *Paramabhagavata mahara.* (V) *dharajaśra-Chandragupta.* Letters *dharajaśra* are below the horse and blurred. Unusually high weight.	Symbol *Ajitavikkramaḥ.* **Pl. XIII. 6.**
1015	120.6	.71	King to l. *Parama.... ....* *śra-Chandragupta.*	Symbol *Ajitavikkramaḥ.*
1016	120.3	.78	King to l. *Paramabhāgavata ......* *.....ptaḥ.*	Symbol *Ajitavikkramaḥ.*
1017	121.9	.77	King to l. (I) *Paramabhāgava. ...* ....XI *gaptaḥ.* Letters were engraved under the horse, but have become blurred and illegible.	Symbol *Ajitavakkramaḥ,* blurred and truncated. **Pl. XIII. 7.**
1018	120.4	.7	King to l. *.....va. maha.....* *śrī-Chandraguptaḥ.*	Symbol *Ajatavakkramaḥ.*

No.	Wt.	Size	Obverse	Reverse
1019	121.1	.7	King to l. *Para..... .... dharajaśra-Chandra-guptaḥ.*	Symbol but incomplete. *Ajitavikkramaḥ.*
1020	120.6	.75	King to l. *Paramabhā... ....guptaḥ.*	Symbol, but incomplete. *..tavakkramaḥ.*
1021	122.3	.7	King to l. *Paramabhāga... ....gapta.*	Symbol *Ajatavakama.*
1022	121.8	.72	King to l. *Parama.... .... śrī-Cha.gapta.*	Symbol *Ajitavikkramaḥ.*
1023	127	.72	King to l. Legend off.	Symbol *Ajitavikrama.* Stool is artistic.
1024	123.4	.7	King to l. .... *śra-Chandragupta;* letters are truncated.	Symbol, but incomplete. *Ajitavikkramaḥ.*
1025	121	.85	King to l. *Paramabhāgavata ....gupta,* in small characters.	Symbol Legend blurred.
1026	119.8	.74	King to l. *Paramabhāga.. ....gupta.*	Symbol incomplete. Legend blurred.
1027	127	.8	King to l., bare-bodied; his torso is slim and muscular. The mane of the horse is beautifully plated. The saddle ornamentation on the haunch of the horse is noticeable. .... (XI) *guptaḥ.*	Goddess has slightly stretched out the r. leg. Symbol *Ajatavakrama.* **Pl. XIII. 8.**

No.	Wt.	Size	Obverse	Reverse
1028	120.1	.8	King to l. *Parama.... ....* *dharajaśra-Chandragupta.* Several cracks in the edge.	Symbol  *.jatavakkramaḥ.*
1029	121.3	.7	King to l. *Paramabhāga.. ..* *......Chandragupta.*	Symbol  *Ajitavikkramaḥ.*
1030	127.8	.74	King to l. .... *jaśra-Chandragupta.* One crack in the edge.	Symbol  *Ajitavikramaḥ.*
1031	128.1	.77	King to l. ....*rajaśra-Chandraguptaḥ.*	Symbol  *Ajatava*
1032	121	.76	King to l. *Parama.... ....* *..guptaḥ.* truncated.	Symbol incomplete, but probably 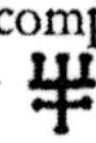 *..tavakrama.* **Pl. XIII. 9.**
1033	120.6	.68	King to l. (I) *Paramabhagavata mahara....*(IX) *Chandraguptaḥ.* Characters are small.	Stool is small. Symbol 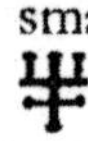 *Ajitavikramaḥ.* **Pl. XIII. 10.**
1034	120	.75	King to l. (I)*Paramabhagavata* ....(XI) *ptaḥ.* Legend is neatly inscribed.	Symbol  or  *Ajitavikramaḥ.* **Pl. XIII. 11.**
1035	124	.75	King to l. (I) *Para..... ....* (VII) *dharajaśra-Chandragupta.*	Goddess slightly reclining forward. No symbol. *Ajitavikramaḥ.* **Pl. XIII. 12.**
1036	122.1	.75	King on horse to l. *Para.... ....* *śra-Chandragupta.*	Symbol 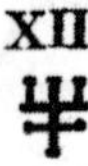 *Ajatvikramaḥ.*

Variety B : 13 coins

(King with sword)

No.	Wt.	Size	Obverse	Reverse
			King to l. as above, but sword hanging down from the belt on the l. side.	Goddess seated on wicker stool as in Var. A.
1037	119.8	.8	King to l., wearing a scull cap bedecked with pearls and a buttoned coat, sword hanging by the l. side. (I) *Paramabhāga.. ....* (VI) *dharajaśra-Chandraguptaḥ.*	Symbol *Ajitavikkramaḥ.* **Pl. XIII. 13.**
1038	120.5	.7	King to l. as above. *Paramabhāga.. .... Chandraguptaḥ.*	Symbol *.jatavikkramaḥ.*
1039	120.5	.72	King to l. as above. *Paramabhāgavata .. rajadhirajaśra-Chandraguptaḥ.*	Symbol Legend off.
1040	121.1	.75	King to l. as above. *Paramabhāgava....... .śra-Chandraguptaḥ.*	Symbol *Ajitavikramaḥ.*
1041	120.2	.75	King to l. as above. *Paramabhāgava. maharajadharajaśra-Chandraguptaḥ.*	Symbol *Ajitavikkramaḥ.*
1042	121.6	.78	King to l. as above, wearing a buttoned coat. (I) *Paramabhāgavato* (VI) *mahārājadharajaśra-Chandra.ptaḥ.* Letters are blurred but fairly clear. *O mātrā*	Symbol *Ajitavikkramaḥ,* rather blurred but legible. **Pl. XIII. 14.**

No.	Wt.	Size	Obverse	Reverse
			over *to* is quite distinct. Hoofs of the horse separate *ma* from *ha* and *ha* from *raja*.	
1043	121.2	.74	King to l. as above. .... *śra-Chandragupta*, blurred.	Symbol Legend blurred.
1044	121.6	.8	King to l., wearing a diadem, a coat and chest-band or *kamar-band*. (I) *Paramabhaga*.. ..... (VIII) *rajaśra-Chandra-guptaḥ*.	Symbol *Ajitavikkramaḥ*. **Pl. XIII. 15.**
1045	120.3	.78	King to l., bare-headed, wearing coat. (I) *Parama*.... .... (VII) *dharaja śra-Chandra.ptah*	Symbol *Ajatavikkramaḥ*. **Pl. XIV. 1.**
1046	119.9	.71	King to l. *Para*..... ....*gupta*.	Symbol Legend off.
1047	119.9	.73	King to l. *Parama*.... .... *dharajaśraChandra-gupta*.	Symbol *Ajitavikkramaḥ*.
1048	119.8	.72	King to l. (I). *Paramabhāgavata* ....(VI) *dharajaśra-Chandraguptaḥ*. Letters on the left are truncated.	Symbol *Ajitavikkramaḥ*. **Pl. XIV. 2.**
1049	118.3	.7	King to l. .... *dharajaśra-Chandra-guptaḥ*.	Symbol *Ajitavikkramaḥ*.

Variety C : 10 coins

(King with bow)

No.	Wt.	Size	Obverse	Reverse
1050	121.5	.73	King to l., holding bow in r. hand, its upper part being visible between the horse's head and the king's head. (I) *Paramabhagava*. ... .(XI) *gupta*, blurred.	Symbol, but incomplete. Legend blurred and mostly off. **Pl. XIV. 3.**
1051	121	.75	King to l. Bow is very clearly visible in front of the king's face. ....(IX) *jaśra-Chandragu*, rather blurred.	Symbol *Ajitavikkramaḥ*. **Pl. XIV. 4.**
1052	121.1	.72	King to l., bow being clearly visible before the face. Legend off.	Symbol *Ajatavikkramaḥ*.
1053	120.6	.74	King to l., with bow in the r. hand whose lower part is visible just above the horse's haunch and the upper part being behind the king's body. Legend off.	Symbol *Ajatavikramaḥ*.
1054	120.7	.75	King to the l., as above, holding the bow by the l. hand, its lower part being visible above the haunch of the horse, the upper part being in-	Reverse side is blurred considerably and the symbol is indistinct. A line between the goddess and the blurred legend.

No.	Wt.	Size	Obverse	Reverse
			visible behind the king's body. (I) *Parama.... ....* (VII) *dharajaśra-Chandragupta.* First three letters are truncated.	*Ajatavakrama.* **Pl. XIV. 5.**
1055	122.8	.72	King to l., holding bow in r. hand, as above. *Paramabhāga*	Symbol 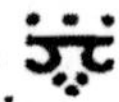 *Ajatavikra*
1056	120	.78	King to l., holding bow in r. hand, as above. *Paramabhāgavata ....* *....Chandragu*	Symbol 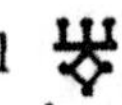 A line between the goddess and the legend on the r. *Ajitavikramaḥ.*
1057	118.8	.79	King to l. holding bow in r. hand. (I) *Paramabhāgavata ....* ....(VIII)*Chandra.pta.* Only lower part of *dra* is visible.	A dotted line between the goddess and the legend behind. Symbol blurred. *.jatavikrama.* **Pl. XIV. 6.**
1058	120.6	.72	As above. Legend mostly off, traces of *śra* and *ndra* being visible at IX.	Symbol 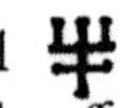 Legend off.
1059	123.1	.83	King as above, but not nimbate, bare-bodied with frizzled hair, wearing *dhoti*, necklace and armlets. Probably traces of bow above the haunch. The stirrup is quite clear. (I) *Paramabhāgavata ..* *......Chandragupta*; the letters on the left	No symbol or symbol blurred. *Ajitavikramaḥ.* **Pl. XIV. 7.**

No.	Wt.	Size	Obverse	Reverse
			side are blurred and truncated.	

Class II : King to right : 30 coins

(King without any weapons.)

No.	Wt.	Size	Obverse	Reverse
			King to r., riding caparisoned horse, wearing necklace, earrings, coat, waist-band, etc., holding neither whip nor bow in the hand and with no sword hanging by the side. Circular legend, (I) *Paramabhāgavato mahārājādhirājaśrī-Chandraguptaḥ.* परमभागवतो महाराजाधिराज-श्रीचन्द्रगुप्तः। Pl. XXXIV. 15.	Goddess seated on wicker stool to l., usually holding a noose in r. hand, but sometimes scattering round coins by it, and having lotus in l. hand, resting on waist. Symbol on some coins. Legend, *Ajitavikramaḥ.* अजित वेक्रमः Pl. XXXVI. 53.
1060	119.6	.7	King to r. Crescent behind his head. (XII) *Para* (II) *mabhāgavata* ....(XI) *ga*	Goddess to l.; her r. leg is slightly higher than the l. She is scattering seven round coins from the palm of her hand. Symbol very fragmentary. ..*tavakrama.* **Pl. XIV. 8.**
1061	120.4	.87	King to r; the sash flying behind looks like part of a bow. (I) *Parama.gavata ma* ......(VIII) *śra-Chandraga*	Wicker stool is broad and the upper garment of the goddess is falling behind. No symbol or symbol off. *Ajitavikramaḥ.* **Pl. XIV. 9.**

No.	Wt.	Size	Obverse	Reverse
1062	120.8	.78	King on horse to r. The saddle is clear. Legend, beginning at (II) *Paramabhaga*.. .... (VIII)*śra-Chandragupta*; *gu* is behind and *pta* in front of the king's face.	Symbol a variation of , without the short vertical line. *Ajitavikkramaḥ*. **Pl. XIV. 10.**
1063	119.5	.77	King not nimbate. (XII) *Para*..... ....(X) *ndragupta*. The first two letters are between the head of the king and the head of the horse.	Symbol blurred, but probably  *Ajitavikkramaḥ*. **Pl. XIV. 11.**
1064	121.2	.8	King's features are quite distinct and torso well proportioned; necklace and armlets graceful. ....(VIII)*dhara-jaśra-Chandragu* Letters *dhara* are between hoofs.	Wicker stool is very broad on this coin and is apparently covered with thick cushion. Its weaving is artistic and worth noting. A line between the goddess and the legend reminiscent of the back of the throne of earlier issues. No symbol. *Ajitavikrama*. **Pl. XIV. 12.**
1065	121.6	.73	King to r. as above. *Para*..... ....*ptaḥ*.	A line between the goddess and the legend. Symbol  *Ajitavikramaḥ*.
1066	118.4	.75	King to r. as above. ....*rajadharajaśra*	Symbol  *Ajitavikramaḥ*.

No.	Wt.	Size	Obverse	Reverse
1067	120.5	.75	King as above. Legend off.	Symbol A line between the goddess and the legend. *Ajatava*
1068	121.4	.78	King to r. as above. Legend is rather blurred but fairly distinct and complete. (XII) *Parama* (II) *bhagavatamaharajadharaja-* (VIII) *śra-Chandragupta*; Only the lower parts of the letters of the king's name are visible.	Goddess is apparently wearing a cap with a knot at the top and her upper garment is clear. The cushion over the stool is thick. Symbol *Ajitavikrama.* **Pl. XIV. 13.**
1069	120.9	.78	King to r. ......*ta maharajadha*	Symbol *.jatavakrama.*
1070	121.9	.8	King to r. ... *bhagavata* ... *jadharaja*	Upper garment of the goddess is clear. Symbol *Ajatavakra*
1071	120.5	.83	King to r., his dishevelled hair is flying behind. (XII) *Para* ....*Chandragupta.*	Wicker stool is plain. Dotted line between the goddess and the legend. Symbol *Ajitavikramaḥ.* **Pl. XIV. 14.**
1072	123.8	.81	King to r. ... *bhagavata* .... *dharajaśra-Chandra*	Upper garment of the goddess is clear. Symbol *Ajatavakra*
1073	119.9	.82	King to r. ... *bhagavata maharaja*	Line between the goddess and the legend. Symbol *Ajitavikramaḥ.*

No.	Wt.	Size	Obverse	Reverse
1074	120.1	.75	King to r. *Parama.... ....* *.... ptaḥ.*	Symbol  *Ajatavakrama.*
1075	121.4	.78	King to r., and a crescent behind his head. (XII) *Parama..vata mahāraja...* (VIII) *śra-Chandraguptaḥ.* Only the lower part of *śra* is visible and *ndra* is crowded out by the end of the sash.	Stool has apparently a heavy cushion above it. Symbol  *.jatavakrama.* **Pl. XIV. 15.**
1076	120.4	.8	King to r. Crescent over king's head. *Paramabhagavata ....* *..... ndraguptaḥ.*	Upper garment is clear Symbol 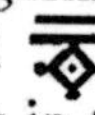 but without dot in the centre. *Ajatavakrama*
1077	120.8	.78	King to r. Crescent behind the king's head. *Parama ....* *.....ndragupta.*	One leg of the goddess is slightly lifted up. Symbol 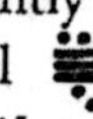 *Ajatavikrama.*
1078	118.3	.76	King to r. *Paramabhāgava*	Symbol blurred. *Ajatavakra*
1079	120.2	.73	King to r. *Parama*	A line between the goddess and the legend Symbol 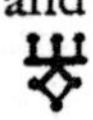 *Ajatavikrama.*
1080	120.3	.78	King to r. *... bhagavata ......* *...ndraguptaḥ.*	Artistic wicker stool. Symbol a variation of , with only one dot below instead of three. *Ajitavikrama*
1081	120.6	.75	King to r. *...... ....* *gupta.*	A line between the goddess and the legend Symbol  *.jatavakrama.*

No.	Wt.	Size	Obverse	Reverse
1082	121.9	.82	King to r. .... *maharajadhara-jaśra-Chandragupta.*	A line between the goddess and the legend. Symbol blurred. *Ajatavikrama.*
1083	118.4	.74	King to r. Legend off.	No symbol. *Ajatavakra*
1084	120.3	.75	King to r. Legend off.	No symbol. *Ajitavikramaḥ.*
1085	119.4	.75	King to r. Crescent behind his head. (XII) *Paramabha*... . ... (IX) *ndra.pta.* The letter *pta* is enormously big in size and peculiar in shape.	Wicker stool has indented angled ornamentation in the central row. No symbol. *Ajatavikkrama.* **Pl. XV. 1.**
1086	118.3	.75	King to r. Crescent behind his head. *Paramabhāgava*	No symbol. *Ajatavakrama.*
1087	122.1	.75	King to r. ......(III) *ta maharaja-dharaja..ndra.pta.* Subscript of *pta* is very big. Letters on the right are blurred.	Artistic and small stool. No symbol. *Ajitavikramaḥ.* **Pl. XV. 2.**
1088	121.6	.75	King to r. .... *gavata* .... *ndra*	Broad and artistic wicker stool. No symbol. *Ajitavikramaḥ.*
1089	121.2	.82	King to r. Legend blurred on the r. side, but *Chandragupta* is visible on the l. side truncated. *Pta* is similar to that on Pl. XV. 2	No symbol. *Ajitavikrama.* **Pl. XV. 3.**

CHHATRA TYPE : 57 COINS

Class I : 5 coins

(With the legend *Mahārājādhirājaśrī-Chandraguptaḥ*)

No.	Wt.	Size	Obverse	Reverse
			King, nimbate, standing l, offering oblations on altar before him with r. hand bent and stretched, while the l. hand rests on the hilt of the sword hanging by his side; behind him, dwarf attendant holding *chhatra* (parasol) over him. King is sometimes bare-headed and sometimes he wears an ornamental head-dress decorated with a crest. Circular legend, beginning at I, *Mahārājādhirājaśrī-Chandraguptaḥ*. महाराजाधिराजश्रीचन्द्रगुप्तः । Pl. XXXIV. 13.	Goddess Lakshmī nimbate, standing three fourth to l., on a carpet or lotus, holding noose in r. hand and lotus with long stalk and leaves in the l. Symbol on l. Legend on r., *Vikramādityaḥ*. विक्रमादित्यः । Pl. XXXVI. 52.
1090	120.8	.83	King's head-dress has a crest and his figure is tall. R. hand is opened out. L. hand of the dwarf rest on his waist. *Chhatra* is clear, but off the king's head. *Mahārājādhirāja* ... *gupta*.	Goddess is standing on a lotus. Symbol *Vakramāditya*.

No.	Wt.	Size	Obverse	Reverse
			Last two letters are blurred and *ha* is of the eastern variety.	
1091	119.4	.83	King wears *dhoti* and his *pagri* has a beautiful crest. Object offered is not clear, though the palm is opened out. (I) *Mahārājādharāja* *Ha* is of the eastern variety.	Goddess standing on lotus. Symbol *Vakramāditya.* **Pl. XV. 4.**
1092	118.7	.83	Headdress of the king is studded with pearls. He wears a *dhoti*, coat, wristlets, armlets and earrings. Altar has three flames; the king's palm is opened out, but the object offered is not clear; possibly it is incense. Dwarf's l. hand is hanging down and holds the staff of the parasol with fillets. Legend, (I) *Mahārāja....* (IX) *Chandraguptaḥ.* *Ha* is of the eastern variety. The flan seems to have slipped once and the die appears to have been impressed a second time. There are faint traces of letters above the present legend.	Goddess standing three-fourths to left, but the object she is standing upon is apparently treated both as a mat and lotus. Symbol *Vakramaditya.* **Pl. XV. 5.**

No.	Wt.	Size	Obverse	Reverse
1093	112.7	.75	King wearing *dhoti* and head-dress. His palm is opened out, but the object offered is not clear. (I) *Maharaja* A well preserved coin but low in weight.	Goddess as above. Symbol *Varkramāda* **Pl. XV. 6.**
1094	118.4	.77	As above. *Mahara*, truncated.	Goddess standing on mat. Symbol *Vikramāditya.*

Class II : 52 coins

(With the legend, ***Kshitimavajitya sucharitairdivaṁ jayati Vikramādityaḥ***)

No.	Wt.	Size	Obverse	Reverse
			King dressed and standing as in class I, but the objects offered by him are usually distinct; they are round ***puroḍāśas*** (sacrificial oblations). Circular legend beginning at I, *Kshitimavajitya sucharitairdivam jayati Vikramādityaḥ.* क्षितिमजित्य सुचरितैर्दिवं जयति विक्रमादित्यः। Pl. XXXIV. 14. Metre, Upagīti.	In this class, the goddess is sometimes facing and standing on carpet, or lotus or pedestal, sometimes she is standing l., sometimes she is walking and in one case she is apparently running to l. When facing l., one of her legs is crossed and it is not easy to state in every case whether she is standing to l. or walking. Symbol on left. Legend on right. *Vakramādityaḥ.* विक्रमादित्यः। Pl. XXXVI. 52.

No.	Wt.	Size	Obverse	Reverse
1095	119.5	.73	King wears head-dress, coat and trousers. Altar and *purodāśas* are blurred. *Kshatama*	Goddess is standing facing on mat. Her l. hand is holding lotus and is resting on her waist. A line between the goddess and the legend. Symbol  *Vakramaditya*
1096	120.7	.75	Altar and *puroḍāśas* are blurred. Dwarf's r. leg is bent and his l. hand is on waist. Legend off the flan.	Goddess standing facing. A line between her and the legend. Symbol  *Vakramāditya.*
1097	120.3	.82	Coin is blurred. *Kshitima*	Goddess standing facing and a line between her and the legend. Symbol  *Vakramāditya.*
1098	120.9	.74	*Chhatra* is off the flan, only its fillets are visible. Three *puroḍāśas* can be seen distinctly. *Kshatamavajatya suchrata*, truncated.	Goddess stnding facing on mat. Symbol  *Vakramâditya.*
1099	120.4	.84	King's head-dress has a prominent crest and he is wearing a *dhoti.* Dwarf holds the staff of the parasol in both hands, the r. one being bent up. King has opend out the palm and 11 round *puroḍāśas* can be seen falling	Goddess is standing facing, apparently on a lotus; her upper garment falls on her either side. Both her hands are slightly bent and stretched out, r. one holding noose and the l. one a lotus with a long stalk.

No.	Wt.	Size	Obverse	Reverse
			down from it on the altar below, showing three flames on it. (I) *Kshitimavajitya sucharitai*; medial vowels are distinct.	Her hair is tied in a knot on the top of the head and she wears a pearl ornament on the forehead. Symbol a variation of , having two horizontal lines instead of one. *Vikrāmāditya.* **Pl. XV. 7.**
1100	121.7	.8	King wears a *dhoti* and his head-dress has a small crest. Eight *puroḍāśas* are trickling down on the altar. (I) *Kshitamavajatya sucha*; *ma* is of the western variety on both the sides.	Goddess standing facing, l. hand resting on waist. Symbol slightly blurred. *Vakramāditya* **Pl. XV. 8**
1101	123.5	.78	Six *puroḍāśas* visible. Dwarf lifts up his r. leg, his l. hand being on waist. *Kśhatamava*.. .... *kramadatya.*	Goddess standing facing. This side is blurred. A line between the goddess and the legend. Symbol a variation of , with three prongs instead of three points. *Vakramādatya.*
1102	122.1	.78	King wears trousers. 14 *puroḍāśas* are visible. *kaśhatamava* *Ma* is of the western variety.	Goddess standing facing and her l. hand is on waist. Symbol *Vikramādatya.*

No.	Wt.	Size	Obverse	Reverse
1103	118.3	.79	King wears coat and trousers. Ten *puroḍāśas* are visible. *Kshitimajatya suchara*; *ma* is of western variety.	Goddess as on the preceding coin. Symbol *Vikramāditya.*
1104	118.3	.8	Three *puroḍāśas* are visible. (I) *Kshatamavaja* . . . . . (VIII) *dava jayata Vakrama*; blurred and truncated.	Goddess standing facing., l. hand being on waist. Symbol *Vikramāditya.* **Pl. XV. 9**
1105	121.2	.81	Seven or eight *puroḍāśas* are visible. Both legs of the dwarf are bent. (I) *Kshatamavajatya sucharata*	Goddess standing facing, her l. hand being on waist. A line between her and the legend. Symbol a variation of , having four prongs instead of four points. *Vikramāditya* **Pl. XV. 10**
1106	114.3	.78	*Chhatra* not visible, as also the *puroḍāśas*. Both legs of the dwarf are straight. *Kshatamavajatya su*	Goddess standing facing, l. hand being on waist. Symbol *Vakramāditya.*
1107	123.3	.8	This side is blurred, but the buttons of the coat are distinct. Dwarf's r. leg is bent. Legend is blurred.	Goddess standing facing and l. arm is on waist. Lotus stalk shows leaves. Symbol *Vikramāditya.*
1108	117.6	.79	Six *puroḍāśas* are visible. Dwarf is holding the *chhatra* in l. hand,	Goddess standing facing, l. hand holding the lotus being

No.	Wt.	Size	Obverse	Reverse
			both his legs being straight. (I) *Ksha ....* (III) *tya sucharita*	bent up. Lotus on which she is standing is crude. Symbol blurred. *Vikramadityaḥ.* **Pl. XV. 11**
1109	121.2	.8	King wears a close-fitting cap, coat and trousers, having side buttons or bosses below the knee. Nine *puroḍāśas* in three rows of three are visible. R. leg of the dwarf is raised up and his l. hand is on waist. .... *Vakramadatya.*	Goddess standing facing. Symbol *Vakramaditya*
1110	121.6	.82	King wears a *dhoti* and close-fitting cap. Both legs of the dwarf are straight. *Kshitimavajatya sucharata*	Goddess standing facing on mat. Symbol *Vakramaditya.*

Variety B : 2 coins

(Goddess standing on a pedestal)

No.	Wt.	Size	Obverse	Reverse
1111	119.7	.75	The king wears a cap with a knob at the top and a pearl string behind it. Three *puroḍāśas* are visible. Dwarf holds the *chhatra* by the r. hand, l. one hanging down. (I) *Kshatamava*	Goddess standing facing, three-forths to l. on a pedestal with a narrow central support, and holding a noose in r. hand, slightly bent and lotus with long stalk in the l. resting on waist.

No.	Wt.	Size	Obverse	Reverse
				Symbol *Vakramāditya.* **Pl. XV. 12.**
1112	122	.79	King as on the preceding coin. His head-dress is similar, as also the posture of the dwarf. His figure is blurred and so the dress is not clear. The knob of the cap is quite distinct. *Kyhitimava*	Pedestal of the goddess is high and broad and has two projections on either side. Symbol *Vakramāditya.* **Pl. XV. 13.**

Variety C : 17 coins

(Goddess standing on mat three-fourths to l.)

No.	Wt.	Size	Obverse	Reverse
1113	120.8	.75	King standing to l. as on varieties A & B. He is bare-headed and bare-bodied and apparently wears a *dhoti.* Object offerred not clear. Dwarf is short and has prominent breasts; but a *janghia* is worn and so he is obviously a male and not a female. He holds the *chhatra* in the r. hand and rests the l. on the waist. (I) *Kshitimavajatya sucha* .. .. (IX) *maditya.*	Goddess standing on a mat. Symbol *Vakkramādityaḥ.* **Pl. XV. 14.**
1114	119.7	.81	*Chhatra* is just visible above the head of the king; dwarf holds its	Goddess standing on mat; her l. hand is a little away from her

No.	Wt.	Size	Obverse	Reverse
			staff in both the hands. (I) *Kshata* . . . . (VIII) *va jayata Vikkramāditya.*	person, grasping at the stalk of a lotus with leaves. Symbol  *Vakkramāditya.* **Pl. XV. 15.**
1115	120.7	.81	King wears *dhoti*; his torso is bare. *Puroḍāśas* not visible. Dwarf's both legs are straight and he holds the staff of the *chhatra* in both his hands. (I) *Kshitimavaja* . . . . (VIII) *ta Vakkramadityaḥ.*	Goddess stands on a mat; the noose has several ends. Symbol  *Vikkramāditya.* **Pl. XVI. 1.**
1116	121.3	.76	King is bare-headed and wears a *sakachchha dhoti*. Object offered is not clear. Dwarf's body is turned away from the king, but he is looking back at him, supporting his l. arm on l. leg raised up, and holding the staff in the r. hand. (I) *Kshatamavaja* . . . . (IX) *Vakramadatyaḥ.* Characters are small. Five cracks in the edge, but only two extending to the surface.	Goddess standing on lotus. Symbol  Legend blurred **Pl. XVI 2.**
1117	121	.79	King wears a cap and *dhoti*. No *puroḍāśa* is visible.	Goddess stands on mat.

No.	Wt.	Size	Obverse	Reverse
			Kshatama ... . *Vikramadityaḥ.*	Symbol *Vikkramādityaḥ.*
1118	121.1	.73	King with cap and *dhoti.* Legs of the dwarf are straight and his l. hand is on waist. *Kshtamavajatya* .... *kramaditya.*	Goddess stands on mat. Lotus stalk has leaves. Symbol *Vikkramādityaḥ.*
1119	119.9	.73	King as above. The r. leg of the dwarf is bent up. *Kshatamavaja*	Goddess stands on mat. Symbol *Vikkramāditya.*
1120	120.9	.73	King as above. Altar off the flan. Both legs of the dwarf straight. *Kshatamavajitya* ....*tya*	Goddess stands on mat. Symbol *Vakkramādatya.*
1121	120.3	.75	King as above. Dwarf mostly off the flan. *Kshatama* ... . *ditya.*	Goddess stands on mat. Symbol blurred. *Vakkramāditya*
1122	120.7	.74	The r. leg of the dwarf is bent. Legend mostly off, only the last four letters *kramadatya* are partly visible.	Goddess stands on mat. Symbol *Vikkramādityaḥ.*
1123	121.6	.75	King stands on mat. *Chhatra* off the flan. Dwarf stands erect. *Kshatamavajatya su-charitairdivaṁ* ... .. *madatya.*	Goddess stands on mat. Symbol indistinct. *Vikkramādityaḥ.*
1124	124.4	.8	King has curly hair, is bare-bodied and wears a *dhoti. Chhatra* and altar both off. Staff	Object under the feet of the goddess not visible. Her r. palm is opened out

No.	Wt.	Size	Obverse	Reverse
			of the *chhatra* is visible across the body of the dwarf holding it; dwarf also has curly hair like his master. Legend is in small characters and is blurred, truncated and illegible.[1]	and is scattering round small coins, l. hand, holding the lotus rests on the waist. Symbol a variation of , with three prongs in place of three dots. *Vikkramādityaḥ.* **Pl. XVI. 3.**
1125	120.6	.76	King as before. *Chhatra* and legend off. Dwarf is rather tall and reaches king's shoulder. Legend off the flan.	Goddess stands on mat. Symbol *Vikkramāditya.*
1126	119.5	.72	King as above, his hair falling in tresses. *Kshitimavajitya* .... *Vakramadatya*; the last five letters are truncated.	Goddess stands on mat. Symbol *Vikramāditya.* **Pl. XVI. 4.**
1127	121.1	.74	Dwarf, *chhatra* and legend all almost off. *Puroḍāśas* falling off the altar on the ground. Legend off the flan.	Goddess as above. Symbol *Vakramādatya.*
1128	120.1	.78	Dwarf's l. hand on waist. *Kśhatama*	Goddess as above. Symbol *Vikkramādityaḥ.*
1129	119.6	.74	Dwarf as above. *Kshatama* ... . *madatya.*	Goddess as above. Symbol *Vakkramādatya.*

[1] Owing to an oversight, the obverse of this coin is placed in the lower row and the reverse in the upper one in the plate.

Variety D : 16 coins

(Goddess walking to l.)

No.	Wt.	Size	Obverse	Reverse
1130	122.1	.72	King wears *dhoti*, but is otherwise bare-bodied and bare-headed; his hair falls behind on the neck. Armlets and waist-band are clear. Altar is off the flan. Dwarf's body is turned away from the king, but he looks back to him, supporting his l. hand on l. leg raised up. It is not clear how he holds the staff of the *chhatra*. *Kshatamavaja*, truncated; characters are small.	Goddess is walking to l.; she has her hair tied in a knot behind the head. Lotus stalk has leaves. Symbol  blurred. Legend blurred. *. kramādatya.* **Pl. XVI. 5.**
1131	120.4	.79	*Chhatra* almost off the flan. *Kshatimavajatya . . . . madatyaḥ.*	Goddess walking to l. Symbol 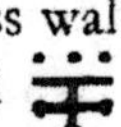 *. kkramādatya.*
1132	121	.72	King's hair is curly. Dwarf as on No. 1130. *Kshitama . . . . madatya.*	Goddess walking to l. Symbol  *Vikkramāditya.*
1133	121.6	.67	*Chhatra* off the flan. Dwarf as on No. 1130. *Kshatamavajatya . . . . kramadatya.*	Goddess walking to l. Symbol blurred. *Vakramādityaḥ.*
1134	121.1	.73	Dwarf as on No. 1130 *Chhatra* almost off. *Kshatamavaja*	Goddess walking to l., her legs crossing each other. Symbol incomplete, but probably  *Vakramāditya.*

No.	Wt.	Size	Obverse	Reverse
1135	120	.71	Dwarf as on No. 1130 *Kshitamavajatya*	Goddess walking to l.; her hair is tied in a knot at the back of the head. Symbol *Vakkramādatya.*
1136	121	.73	King is bare-headed and bare-bodied and wears *sakachchha dhoti.* Object offered not clear. (I) *Kshata*.... ....(VIII) *Vakramadityaḥ.* Small characters.	The reverse side is blurred. Goddess is walking to l., her hair is tied in a knot behind the head. Symbol , but blurred. ..*madatya*, blurred. **Pl. XVI. 6.**
1137	120.7	.72	Parasol off. Dwarf as on No. 1130. Legend off.	Goddess walking to l. Symbol blurred. *Vakra*
1138	119.5	.74	Dwarf as on No. 1130. .... *Vakramadatya.*	Goddess walking to l. Symbol incomplete, but probably *Vakramāditya.*
1139	121	.7	Dwarf as on No. 1130. Parasol off. Legend off.	Goddess walking to l. Leaves of the lotus stalk are distinct. Symbol *Vakkramādatya.*
1140	120.3	.75	Dwarf as on No. 1130. *Kshata*.... ....*madatya.*	Goddess walking to l. Symbol *Vikkramāditya*
1141	121.1	.72	Dwarf as on No. 1130. .... *Vakramadatya.*	Goddess walking to l. Symbol *Vakrama*
1142	121.8	.75	Dwarf as on No. 1130. *Kshitamavajitya*	Goddess walking to l. There is a pillar like object behind the

No.	Wt.	Size	Obverse	Reverse
				goddess. Symbol a variation of , but with four prongs above. *Vakkramāditya.*
1143	120.2	.71	Dwarf as on No. 1130. Parasol off. Legend indistinct.	Goddess walking to l. Pillar like object behind the goddess. Symbol *. . . datya.*
1144	121	.75	Dwarf as on No. 1130. Parasol off. Legend off.	Goddess walking to l. Symbol *Vakramādatya.*
1145	123	.75	Altar off the flan. R. leg of the dwarf is raised up and he holds the staff in the l. hand. *Kshitmavaja . . . . tyah.*	Goddess walking to l. Lotus stalk has leaves. Symbol *Vikramadityaḥ.*

Variety E: 1 coin

(Goddess double-marching)

No.	Wt.	Size	Obverse	Reverse
1146	118.8	.78	King wears a close-fitting cap with a pearl string attached at its back. He is bare-bodied and wears a *dhoti*. His earring is large. Dwarf is three-fourths to r., but looking back to the king and supporting himself by his l. hand on his leg raised up. Legend is in small characters. (I) *Kshatamavajatya*	Goddess is facing l., and the posture of her l. leg and hand suggests that she is double-marching. She holds a noose in r. hand and a lotus in the l. Symbol *Vakramādatya.* **Pl. XVI. 7.**

LION-SLAYER TYPE : 42 COINS

Class I : Lion-Combatant : 21 coins

No.	Wt.	Size	Obverse	Reverse
			King stands r. or l., usually wearing waist-cloth or *janghia*, sash or waist-band, which floats behind, a head-dress (in some cases), earrings, necklace, armlets and wrist-lets; usually he holds bow in l. hand and strings it to the ear by the r. hand to shoot at a lion standing in his front, but just away from him. Circular legend beginning at I, *Narandrachandraḥ prathitarano rane jayatyajayyo bhuvi siṁhavikramaḥ.* नरेन्द्रचन्द्रः प्रथितरणो रणे जयत्यजय्यो भुवि सिङ्हविक्रमः ॥ Pl. XXXIV. 17. Metre, Vaṁśathavila.	Goddess Ambikā-Lakshmī, nimbate, seated on lion couchant to r. or l. holding lotus or cornucopiae in l. hand, r. hand sometimes holding a noose, sometimes an indistinct object and sometimes being empty. Lion's head is usually bent down, but in some cases it is raised up. The goddess wears a circular pearl ornament round her forehead, earrings, necklace, armlets, bangles and anklets. She is sometimes seated facing, with both legs folded upon the lion's back and sometimes astride the lion. Legend on r. *Siṁhavikramaḥ.* सिङ्हविक्रम : । Pl. XXXVI. 54.

Variety A : 6 coins

(King facing l. and goddess holding lotus and noose)

No.	Wt.	Size	Obverse	Reverse
1147	115.3	.74	King wears a cap with a pearl string behind, coat with short sleeves, *dhoti*, and boots. Lion partly visible. (I) *Narendrachandrapra*, blurred and truncated.	Lion couchant to l. and both legs of the goddess above the back of the lion; she has a noose in the r. hand and a lotus in the l. with its stalk twisted in the middle. Symbol  or  *Saṅhavakrama*. **Pl. XVI. 8.**
1148	122	.7	A crest on king's forehead; he wears a short-sleeved coat and a *dhoti*, which is shown as clinging to the inner side of the legs. Lion partly visible. (I) *Nara..ndra pra-* .... (X) *vakrama*,	Goddess seated as on No. 1147; lotus stalk twisted. Symbol , but carelessly engraved. *Saṅhavakkrama*. **Pl. XVI. 9.**
1149	122	.82	King wears a peculiar jewelled head-dress, short-sleeved coat, *dhoti* and boots. Lion is gasping and the arrow point is piercing its jaw. (I) *Nara*... (III) *pra-* .... (IX) *ṅhavakama*.	Goddess as on No. 1147. Lion couchant to l. Symbol a variety of , but having two horizontal lines instead of one. *Saṅhavakkramaḥ*. **Pl. XVI. 10.**
1150	118.6	.77	King wears boots, *dhoti*, short-sleeved coat	Goddess seated with r. leg raised up

No.	Wt.	Size	Obverse	Reverse
			and a pearl-bordered cap with a pearl string behind; knot of the waist band is clear at the waist. (I) *Narendrachandra pra-* . . . . (X) *ṅhavakrama.*	and l. leg on the lion's back; lotus stalk twisted at its middle. Lion couchant to l. Symbol a variety of  but having two horizontal lines instead of one. *Saṅhavakrama.* **Pl. XVI. 11.**
1151	118.7	.78	King as above, but more energetic. His r. foot is beside the lion, but not trampling it. He wears buttoned coat. (I) *Narandrachandra prathatarano rane* Last four letters are clearly visible between IV and VI	Goddess as above, but l. leg hanging down; the lotus stalk is not twisted. Lion to l. Symbol incomplete, but probably 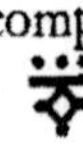 *.ṅhavikramaḥ.* **Pl. XVI. 12.**
1152	121.5	.8	King and lion as above but rather blurred. (I) *Narandrachandra prathatarano rane;* some letters are blurred.	Goddess seated as above. Symbol a variation of 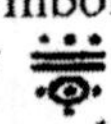 having only one horizontal line and no dot in the centre of the circle. *Siṅhavikkranaḥ.* **Pl. XVI. 13.**

Variety B : 10 coins

(King facing r. and goddess holding noose and lotus)

No.	Wt.	Size	Obverse	Reverse
1153	119.2	.77	King wears a *janghia,* otherwise he is bare-bodied and bare-headed, A crest-jewel on	Goddess nimbate, seated facing, r. leg on the back of the couchant lion to l. and

No.	Wt.	Size	Obverse	Reverse
			the forehead. Curly hair falls on the neck. (I) *Nara* . . . . (VIII) *yya bhuri saṅhavikrama.*	l. leg slightly raised; upper garment visible. Lotus stalk in the l. hand not twisted in the middle; and a noose in the r. hand. Symbol, a variation of ; having only three dots above the horizontal line instead of four. *Siṅhavikkramaḥ.* **Pl. XVI. 14.**
1154	121.1	.77	King wears a cap and *janghia*, his body being bare. (I) *Nara* . . . . (XI)*maḥ*.	Goddess as above. Symbol  *Siṅhavakkrama*
1155	119.4	.75	King's body bare and muscular; head also bare, hair falling on the neck. King wears *janghia*. . . . . (VIII) *tyajayo bhava*	Both legs of the goddess on lion's back, but r. one raised up. Lion couchant to l. Symbol a variation of , as on No. 1153 above. *Saṅhavikkramaḥ.* **Pl. XVI. 15.**
1156	119.1	.73	King as above. . . . . (VII) *jayatyaja* . . . . *nha*	Goddess as above. Lion couchant to l. Symbol  *Siṅhavikkramaḥ.* **Pl. XVII. 1.**
1157	121	.72	Coin very much blurred. . . . . *jaya*	Goddess as above. Symbol  *Saṅhavikrama.*

No.	Wt.	Size	Obverse	Reverse
1158	121.8	.75	King is bare-bodied, wears a *janghia* and there is a crest jewel on his forehead. Bow-ends almost touch his body at the forehead and thigh. (XII) *Narendrachandra* .... (VIII) *tyaja* Bow cuts across the letter *ndra* of *Narendra*.	Goddess and lion as on Pl. XVII 1. Symbol  *Saṅhavikkrama.* **Pl. XVII. 2.**
1159	119.3	.74	King is bare-bodied. and wears a *janghia*. .... (VII) *tyajayyo bhuvi*	Goddess nimbate, facing, r. leg up and l. leg hanging down, holding noose in r. hand and lotus in l. Lion couchant to l. Symbol 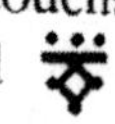 carelessly drawn. *Saṅhavikkrama.* **Pl. XVII. 3.**
1160	118.7	.75	King wears a peculiar head-dress with crest, and a *janghia*. Bow cuts across the upper paws of the lion. .... (VII) *jayya bhava sa*	Goddess and lion as above. Upper garment is clear. Symbol incomplete; a variation of  with no dot in the centre. *Saṅhavikkramaḥ.* **Pl. XVII. 4.**
1161	120.7	.8	King is bare-bodied and wears a *janghia*. Legend is mostly truncated, *ṅhavakkrama* is visible on the l.	Goddess seated as above. Symbol  *Sanhavikkramaḥ.*

No.	Wt.	Size	Obverse	Reverse
1162	120.1	.75	King's muscular body is graceful and well proportioned; the necklace is distinctly visible. .... (VII) *tyajaya bhava sa*, truncated.	Goddess and lion as above. Symbol, a variation of  with no dot in the centre. *Sanhavakra* **Pl. XVII. 5.**

Variety C : 4 coins

(King facing r., goddess holding lotus in l. hand and r. hand being empty.)

No.	Wt.	Size	Obverse	Reverse
1163	119.8	.77	King bare-bodied, wearing a *janghia*; his body is muscular and graceful, hair on the head falling on the neck. Legend off, only *tya* is visible at IX.	Goddess seated facing, r. hand bent up, open and empty, l. hand on thigh holding a lotus. Lion couchant to l., its head raised. Symbol  roughly drawn. *Sanhavakkrama* **Pl. XVII. 6.**
1164	119.3	.77	King is bare-bodied and wears a *janghia*; hair falling behind on the neck. Only the upper part of the lion's body is visible and the bow is touching it. (XII) *Narandrachandra* in small characters.	Goddess and lion as above. Symbol incomplete, possibly  *Sanhavakrama* **Pl. XVII. 7.**
1165	121	.7	King bare-headed, hair falling on the neck in curls; body muscular and graceful. *Narandrachandra pra*	R. hand of the goddess open and empty. Symbol  but incomplete. *Sanhavakkramaḥ.* **Pl. XVII 8.**

No.	Wt.	Size	Obverse	Reverse
1166	119.9	.71	King to r.; body bare and muscular, wearing *janghia*. (I) *Narandra*; traces of letters on the left.	Goddess seated facing with l. leg tucked up and r. leg hanging down, holding lotus in l. hand resting on knee and r. hand bent up and empty. Lion couchant to l. with head raised up. Symbol *. ṅhavakkrama.* **Pl. XVII. 9.**

Variety D : 1 coin

(King as above but not stringing the bow)

No.	Wt.	Size	Obverse	Reverse
1167	123	.8	King standing to r., bare-bodied and wearing a *janghia*; hair tied in a knot behind the head; holding in l. hand bow resting on the ground and arrow in the r. hand, resting on the hip. The remarkable thing is that he is not stringing the bow. *Narendrachand* . . . . . . *. . ty . yya bhu. sa*	Goddess seated as in variety C, r. hand empty, l. hand holding a lotus. Symbol *Saṅhavakra* **Pl. XVII. 10.**

CLASS II : LION-TRAMPLER : 20 COINS

Variety A : 1 coin

(King to l., goddess seated astride the lion)

No.	Wt.	Size	Obverse	Reverse
1168	120.7	.75	King to l., wearing cap, *janghia*, wristlets, armlets and necklace,	Goddess nimbate, sitting astride the lion to l., with gaping

No.	Wt.	Size	Obverse	Reverse
			trampling on lion falling on ground, l. leg on the chest of lion (faultily shown), and r. leg bent behind and treading on lion's tail; bow and arrow as on the Lion-combatant type. (I) .... (III) *ndra* .... (IX) *saṁhavakrama.*	mouth, protruding tongue, and raised head; r. hand bent up and holding a flower and l. hand empty hanging down by the side and resting on the haunch of the lion. No symbol. *Siṁhavikrama.* **Pl. XVII. 11.**

Variety B : 1 coin

(King to l. and lion on rev. walking to r.)

No.	Wt.	Size	Obverse	Reverse
1169	121	.8	King to l. as above, but r. leg bent up and planted on the chest of the lion and l. leg straight and on its tail. Loop of the waist-band tied at the waist is clear. Arrow-point almost in the gaping mouth of the lion, which is almost entirely on the flan. (I) *Narandra..* (VI) *prath.........* (IX) *ya bhuva sa*	Goddess, not nimbate, seated facing on lion with both legs folded up, but the lion is walking to r. Goddess wears *sari*, upper garment, necklace etc., and holds noose in r. hand and lotus in the l. resting on the waist. Symbol  slightly incomplete. *Saṁhvikramaḥ.* **Pl. XVII. 12.**

Variety C : 4 coins

(King to l. and lion on rev. couchant)

No.	Wt.	Size	Obverse	Reverse
1170	117	.75	King to l.; feet partly off the flan, stringing the bow as above. Cap has pearl string	Goddess, nimbate, seated facing on lion cauchant to l., with noose in r. hand and

No.	Wt.	Size	Obverse	Reverse
			attached at the back. Lion mostly off the flan. (I) *Narandrachandra pra* . . . . (IX) *sañhavakrama*.	cornucopiae in the l. resting on the thigh. Symbol [symbol] *.ñhavakramaḥ*. **Pl. XVII. 13.**
1171	136.5	.8	King to l. wearng *janghia* and cap. Legend off. Crack at X The weight is unusually high for this king.	Goddess, nimbate, seated facing on lion couchant to l., both legs folded up, holding noose in r. hand and lotus in l. A line between the goddess and the legend which is off the flan. Symbol [symbol] *Sañhavikramaḥ*.
1172	120.4	.75	King to l., wearing cap, buttoned coat and *dhoti*, trampling the lion by the l. foot, r. one being bent behind. Lion almost off the flan. *Narandrachandra prathatarāṇo raṇe*.	Goddess, nimbate, seated facing on lion couchant to l. with gaping mouth, holding noose in r. hand and lotus in the l. resting on thigh. L. leg of the goddess hangs down and the r. one is tucked up. Symbol incomplete. *.ñhavakkramaḥ*.

Variety D : 1 coin

(King to l., with a different obv. legend, goddess sitting on lion walking to r.)

No.	Wt.	Size	Obverse	Reverse
1173	122.3	.85	King facing l., with crested head-dress, wearing *janghia*, armlets and wrist-lets,	Goddess, nimbate, seated facing with both legs folded up on lion walking to r.,

No.	Wt.	Size	Obverse	Reverse
			trampling lion on the chest by r. foot; l. foot on the tail. Arrow head in lion's mouth. (I) *Devaśrīmaharaja...* (IX) *śra-Chandragapta,* standing for *Devaśrīmahārājādhira-jaśrī-Chandraguptaḥ.* Three cracks in the edge.	holding noose in r. hand and lotus in l. Symbol a variation of , with two horizontal lines instead of one. *Siṁhavikramaḥ.* **Pl. XVII. 14.**

Variety E : 2 coins

(King to r., and goddess seated facing on lion couchant, holding noose in r. hand and cornucopiae in l.)

No.	Wt.	Size	Obverse	Reverse
1174	118.6	.75	King to r. wearing cap and armlets, r. leg bent and l. leg straight and planted on lion's stomach; the king is stretching the bow held in the l. hand by his r. hand. Lion is collapsing on the ground and almost his whole body is visible. (XII) *Narandrachandra pratha* ... .. . (VII) *ya .. yya* Characters are bold.	Goddess seated facing on lion couchant to l., her legs hanging down, holding noose in r. hand and cornucopiae in the l. Symbol 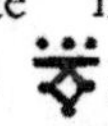, but incomplete and ill engraved. *.ṁhavakrama.* **Pl. XVIII 1.**
1175	121	.75	King as above, but lion less complete on the coin. (XII) *Narandrachandra pratha* ... .. . (VII) *ya .. ya*	Goddess as above but the r. leg resting on the lion, and the l. one hanging down. Symbol 

No.	Wt.	Size	Obverse	Reverse
				Sańhavakrama, truncated. **Pl. XVIII. 2.**

Variety F : 4 coins

(King to r., goddess holds lotus in l. hand, r. hand being empty)

No.	Wt.	Size	Obverse	Reverse
1176	121.8	.75	King as above, but his body is better proportioned. The bow is cutting across the lower portions of the letter *ndra*, whose upper part is off the flan. Faint traces of the legend on the r.	Goddess and lion as above, but the r. palm of the goddess is off the flan; it was probably opened out and empty. L. hand holds a lotus with long slalk. Symbol incomplete. *Sańhavikkrama.* **Pl. XVIII. 3.**
1177	122.1	.74	King as above. (I) *Narandrachandra prathita*; bow cuts across the subjuncts; characters are small.	Empty palm of the r. hand is clearly visible. Symbol 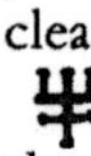 or 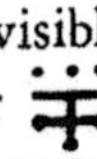 but partly truncated. *Sańhavikramaḥ.* **Pl. XVIII. 4.**
1178	122	.78	As above. (I) *Narandracha*	Palm of the r. hand is off the flan, but was most probably empty. Symbol  *Sińhavikkramaḥ.*
1179	121.5	.8	King is above. (I) *Narandra*	Goddess as above; palm of the right hand is blurred, but it was undoubtedly empty; lotus in the l. hand resting on knee. Symbol  *Sańhavakrama.*

Variety G : 5 coins

(King to r., goddess seated astride the lion to l.)

No.	Wt.	Size	Obverse	Reverse
1180	121.1	.75	King to r. as above, wearing *janghia*, waist-band, head-dress, and three armlets and trampling the lion on its belly with l. leg raised and bent ; r. leg straight. Arrow pierces right into the jaw of the lion. (XII) *Nara*	Goddess, nimbate, seated to l. astride the lion couchant to l., its head raised; goddess holds lotus in r. hand, l. hand being empty and resting on the animal's haunch. The pearl ornament on the head of the goddess is remarkable. No symbol. *Saṁhavikramaḥ.* **Pl. XVIII. 5.**
1181	118.7	.78	As above. Lion is almost complete on the coin. (XII) *Narandra*	As above. No symbol. *Saṁhavikrama.* **Pl. XVIII. 6.**
1182	121.2	.75	King to r., wearing *janghia* and trampling the lion on the belly by l. leg. (XII) *Nara*	Goddess to l., sitting astride on lion couchant to l., head raised and mouth gaping, holding lotus in r. hand, l. hand hanging empty by her side. No symbol. Legend truncated.
1183	120.2	.78	King to r., curly hair falling behind the neck, wearing *janghia* and armlets. Lion collapsing. (XII) *Narandracha*	Goddess, nimbate, seated astride on lion couchant to l., its head being raised up. Goddess holds lotus in r. hand and l. hand

No.	Wt.	Size	Obverse	Reverse
				hanging down by the side. Symbol  *Sanhavikramaḥ.*
1184	113.1	.79	King to r., wearing cap and *sakachchha dhoti*, trampling the lion by l. leg. *Nara*	Goddess seated astride on lion walking to l., r. hand half extended and empty, l. hand on waist holding a cornucopiae. Symbol, a variation of 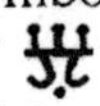 but with two horizontal lines instead of one. *Sañhavikramaḥ*

Variety H : 3 coins

(King to r. but goddess holding noose in r. hand and lotus in the l. and seated on lion walking to l.)

No.	Wt.	Size	Obverse	Reverse
1185	118.6	.77	King to r., hair tied in a knot on the head, and wearing a half-pant. Lion is massive and standing almost erect; king is trampling it with l. foot. In the original four teeth of the lion are visible. (XII) *Narandracha. . . .* .. .. *. . . .yya bhuva . . vakrama*; concluding letters are truncated.	Goddess, nimbate, facing left, seated on lion walking to l., legs of the goddess not astride but folded up. She holds noose in r. hand and lotus in the l., resting on waist. Faint traces of symbol blurred, probably 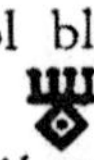 or 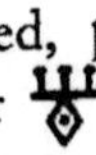. *Siñhavikramaḥ.* **Pl. XVIII. 7.**
1186	119.3	.85	King to r., hair tied in a knot on the head, and trampling	Goddess, nimbate, seated facing, but face turned to l. seated

No.	Wt.	Size	Obverse	Reverse
			the lion by l. leg. (XII) *Nara*; faint traces of the lower portions of letters on l. One crack in the edge at II.	with both legs folded upon lion walking to l., holding noose in the r. hand and lotus in the l. No Symbol. *Saṅhavakrama* The die-cutter has blundered in engraving *ṅha*; he has separated *ṅ*, which looks like *pa*, and the letter following it is intended to 'stand for an eastern *ha*. **Pl. XVIII. 8.**
1187	119.6	.78	King to r., hair on the head tied in a knot at the top, trampling by l. leg the lion, which is falling down. (XII) *Narendrachandra parathatara*	Goddess, nimbate, seated facing l. with her l. leg dangling over the head of lion walking to l., holding noose in the r. hand and a lotus in the l. resting on waist. No symbol. *Saṅhavikrama.* **Pl. XVIII. 9.**

CLASS III : LION-RETREATING : 1 COIN

No.	Wt.	Size	Obverse	Reverse
1188	119.6	.75	King to r., wearing *dhoti* (shown clinging ornamentally to the legs) and sash, l. leg straight and r. one bent up, having a peculiar dotted semicircular line (ornamental	Goddess, nimbate, seated facing, with both legs folded up on lion couchant to r., holding noose in r. hand and an indistinct lotus in the l. Symbol blurred and

No.	Wt.	Size	Obverse	Reverse
			shoe?) below that foot. Lion is retreating away and its back is visible. .... (VIII) *jayatyajayya*, truncated.	incomplete, probably  or  *.ṅhavakrama.* **Pl. XVIII. 10.**

COUCH TYPE : 3 COINS

Variety A

(King to l. and offering a lotus bud)

No.	Wt.	Size	Obverse	Reverse
1189	118.5	.8	King not nimbate, bare-headed with curly hair, wearing *dhoti*, but otherwise bare-bodied, seated three fourth to left with feet folded up, on a couch, decorated with beads or pearls and all of whose legs are visible. Spittoon under the couch. King's l. elbow rests on the back of the couch and he is offering by the r. hand a lotus bud apparently to an object of worship, which is but half visible and cannot identified. Circular legend, (XII) *Paramabha(ā)-gavatamaha (ā) [rājādhirājaśrī-Chandraguptaḥ]* परमभागवतमहाराजाधिराज-श्रीचन्द्रगुप्तः। Pl. XXXIV. 15.	Lakshmī, nimbate, seated facing l. on a lotus-covered backless throne, whose legs are visible, holding lotus with long stalk in r. hand, the l. hand hanging by the side and resting on the couch. R. leg of the goddess is raised up on the couch and the l. leg is hanging down. Foot-stool under the couch. Subscripts of *kra* and *tya* form almost a continuous line behind the goddess. No symbol. Legend, *Vikramādatya[ḥ].* विक्रमादित्यः। Pl. XXXVI. 52. **Pl. XVIII. 11.**

Variety B : 1 coin

(King holding flower in r. hand; r. hand of goddess empty)

No.	Wt.	Size	Obverse	Reverse
1190	120.6	.8	King nimbate, bare-headed, wearing a short *dhoti*, but otherwise bare-bodied, seated three-fourths to l. on a couch, whose three legs are visible. R. hand bent up and holds a lotus; the l. hand, which hangs down, rests on the couch. Circular legend beginning at VIII, [*Devaśrīmahārājā*] (X) *dhirājaśrī-Chandraguptasya.* देवश्रीमहाराजाधिराजश्रीचन्द्रगुप्तस्य। Pl. XXXIV. 16. Good condition.	Goddess Lakshmī, seated facing on throne without back, her feet resting on a lotus, holding a lotus in l. hand bent up, r. hand, which also is bent up, is empty with its palm opened out. Goddess wears *sari*, upper garment, pearl ornament round forehead, earrings, necklace and bangles. Symbol Legend on the l. and not on the r. *Śravakramaḥ.* (*Śrivikramaḥ.*) श्रीविक्रमः। Pl. XXXVI. 51. **Pl. XVIII. 12.**

Variety C : 1 cion

(King holding flower in r. hand and goddess holding noose in r. hand)

No.	Wt.	Size	Obverse	Reverse
1191	119.4	.8	King seated and dressed as in variety B. Circular legend beginning at VIII, *Davaśramaha . .* (I) *dharajaśra-Cha* (*Devasrīmahārājādhirājaśrī-Chandraguptasya*) देवश्रीमहाराजाधिराजश्रीचन्द्रगुप्तस्य। Pl. XXXIV. 16.	Goddess seated as in variety B, but holds *pāśa* in r. hand. Symbol Legend is on the r. and not l. *Srivikkrama*[*ḥ*]. श्रीविक्रमः। Pl. XXXVI. 51. **Pl. XVIII. 13.**

CHAKRAVIKRAMA TYPE : 1 COIN

No.	Wt.	Size	Obverse	Reverse
1192	116.7	.76	God Vishṇu is standing to r. with double halo round his person reaching down the knees. The two haloes are joined by rayed lines between them and the outer one is surrounded by a beaded border. The deity is bare-headed and bare-bodied, wearing *dhoti*, waist-band with ends flying behind, necklace and wristlets, holding mace (*gadā*), in the l. hand hanging by his side and offering by r. hand, bent and raised up, three round objects, held in his palm, to king standing facing him, nimbate, bare-headed, and wearing earrings, necklace, armlets, tunic and trousers with prominent folds round the legs. He is extending his r. hand, bent up, to receive the divine gift; his l. hand is placed on the hilt of a sword hanging by the l. leg. The sword is fastened by a	Within dotted border, Lakshmī, not nimbate, standing three-fourths to l., on a crude lotus, wearing *sari*, upper garment and earrings, r. hand bent up, its forefinger apparently pointing at something, l. hand hanging down, slightly bent, and holding a lotus with a long stalk having a bud as well. A conch below the r. hand. Symbol, worn, but probably either  or  Legend on r. *Chakravikramaḥ*. चक्रविक्रम: । Pl. XXXVII. 53. **Pl. XVIII. 14.**

No.	Wt.	Size	Obverse	Reverse
			strap to the king's waist, which passes through a hole in the hilt. No legend on the obverse, circular or vertical. Coin slightly worn.	

KUMĀRAGUPTA I : 628 COINS

Archer Type : 183 coins

CLASS I : 82 COINS

(With *Kumāra* in the field)

Variety A : 14 coins

(Bow held at the top and *Kumāra* under l. arm)

No.	Wt.	Size	Obverse	Reverse
			King, nimbate, standing to l., wearing *sakachha dhoti*, diadem over frizzled hair, wristlets, armlets and necklace, torso being bare; he holds arrow in the r. hand, point downwards, and bow in the l. hand at the top with string inwards. Garuḍa-standard on the l. behind the r. hand. Under the arm, written vertically, *Ku* कु *mā* मा *ra.* र Circular legend beginning at I, *Mahārājādhirājaśrī-Kumāraguptaḥ.* महाराजाधिराजश्रीकुमारगुप्तः । Pl. XXXIV. 19.	Within dotted border goddess Lakshmī, nimbate, seated, facing on lotus with folded legs, holding noose in r. hand and lotus in the l., which is sometimes bent up and sometimes stretched out, resting on knee slightly raised. Symbol on the l. Legend on the r. *Śrīmahendraḥ.* श्रीमहेन्द्रः । Pl. XXXVII. 56.

No.	Wt.	Size	Obverse	Reverse
1193	123.8	.72	*Ku* *mā* *rā*. *Mahārāja*	L. arm extended and resting on the knee. Symbol *Śrīmahendra*.
1194	123.5	.8	*Ku* *mā* *ra* *Māhārāja*	Symbol *Śrīmahendra*.
1195	123.2	.8	Diadem is very distinct. L. arm passes through the bow and the bow-string. *Ku* *mā* *ra*. *Mahā*	Both arms of the goddess are stretched out and rest on knees. Symbol incomplete and blurred, but probably *Śrīmahendraḥ*. **Pl. XIX. 1.**
1196	122.6	.88	*Ku* *mā* *ra*. . . . . *gupta*.	Symbol a variation of with four prongs. *Śrimahendra*.
1197	123.5	.82	*Ku* *ma* *ra*. *Mahārājādharājaśra-Ka*, truncated.	Symbol *Śrīmahendra*.
1198	123	.82	*Ku* *mā* *ra*. *Mahārājādharājaśra* One crack in the edge.	Symbol *Śrīmahendra*.
1199	124.2	.84	*Ku* *mā* *ra*. Circular legend off.	Symbol blurred *Śramahendra*.

No.	Wt.	Size	Obverse	Reverse
1200	123.2	.83	*Ku* *mā* *ra.* *Maharajadhiraja* Cracks in the edge at VIII and V	Symbol blurred. *Śramahendra.*
1201	123.7	.82	*Ku* *mā* *ra.* *Mahārājādharājaśra-Kamā,* partly truncated.	Symbol, a variation of , with four prongs instead of three. Legend blurred.
1202	123.3	.83	*Ku* *ma* *ra.* . . . . *gupta.*	Symbol  *Śrīmahendra*
1203	122.9	.72	Diadem not visible. *Ku* *mā* *ra.* *Maharajadharajaśra;* blurred traces of *maragupta* on the l.	L. hand bent up. Symbol  *Śrīmahendra.* **Pl. XIX. 2.**
1204	123.5	.85	Diadem is distinct. *Ku* *mā* *ra.* *Maharajadharajaśra-Kama* Crack in the edge at IX.	Both hands stretched out and folded legs look like a pillow. Goddess is neatly engraved. Symbol 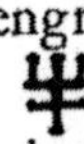 *Śrīmahendraḥ.* **Pl. XIX. 3.**
1205	123.8	.83	*Ku* *ma* *ra.* . . . . *dhirajaśrī-Kumaraguptaḥ.* Letters are broad and	Both arms stretched out and rest on knees slightly raised. Symbol 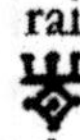 *Śrīmahenndra.* **Pl. XIX. 4.**

No.	Wt.	Size	Obverse	Reverse
			blurred and only the traces of *gupta* can be seen at VIII.	
1206	123.9	.84	Diadem distinct; profuse hair falling behind the head in several tresses. *Ku* *mā* *ra.* *Mahārājādhirājaśrī-Kumā*	Both hands stretched out and resting on knees. Symbol *Śrīmahendraḥ.* Medial vowels very clear. **Pl. XIX. 5.**

Variety B : 58 coins

(Bow held at the middle and *Kumāra* outside the bow-string)

No.	Wt.	Size	Obverse	Reverse
			King, nimbate, standing l., bare-headed, wearing coat, *dhoti* and necklace, holding an arrow in the r. hand and bow with string outside at its middle in the left. *Ku* *mā* } out side the bow-string. *ra.* Circular legend from (I), *Mahārājādhirājaśrī-Kumāraguptaḥ.* महाराजाधिराजश्रीकुमारगुप्तः । Pl. XXXIV. 19.	Goddess, usually nimbate, seated facing on lotus, holding noose in r. hand, bent and stretched out, and lotus in the l., sometimes bent up and sometimes resting on the knee. Symbol on the l. Legend on the r., *Śrīmahendraḥ.* श्रीमहेन्द्रः । Pl. XXXVII. 56.
1207	120.2	.7	*Ku* *mā* *ra* *Mahārājādhirājaśrī-Kumāragupta,* in small characters.	Symbol *Śramahendra.*

No.	Wt.	Size	Obverse	Reverse
1208	120.5	.78	*Ku* *mā* *ra*. *Mahārājādha*, truncated.	L. hand bent up and resting on knee. Symbol *Śrīmahendra*.
1209	120.6	.78	*Ku* *mā* *ra*. Circular legend off.	L. hand bent up and resting on knee. Symbol *Śrīmahendra*.
1210	120.7	.77	*Dhoti*, coat, necklace and armlets are clear. *Ku* *mā* *ra*. *Maharajadhara* One crack in the edge at IV.	Both hands resting on knees raised up. Symbol *Śrīmahendra*. **Pl. XIX. 6.**
1211	121.3	.78	*Ku* *mā* *ra*. *Mahara*	Symbol but incomplete. Legend off.
1212	120.4	.69	*Ku* *mā* *ra*. *Maharajadharaja*	L. hand bent up and resting on knee. Symbol, but incomplete. *Śramahendra*.
1213	120.7	.69	*Ku* *mā* *ra*. *Mahārā*	Symbol, but incomplete. *Mahandra*.
1214	120.7	.69	*Ku* *mā* *ra*. *Mahārājādharāja*	L. hand bent up. Symbol *Śramaha*
1215	120.9	.72	*Ku* *mā* *ra*. *Mahārājā*	L. hand blurred owing to defect in the die. Symbol Legend off.

No.	Wt.	Size	Obverse	Reverse
1216	121.7	.8	*Ku* *mā* *ra.* *Mahārājā*	Symbol, but incomplete. *.mahandra.*
1217	120.3	.78	*Ku* *mā* *ra.* *Mahārājādharājaśra*, truncated.	L. hand bent up. Symbol *.mahandra.*
1218	121	.76	*Ku* *mā* *ra.* *Mahārājādharāja*, truncated.	L. hand bent up. Symbol *Śrīmahendra.*
1219	121.7	.78	*Ku* *mā* *ra.* *Mahārājā*	L. hand bent up. Symbol *Śramahandra.*
1220	121.2	.72	*Ku* *mā* *ra.* Circular legend off.	L. hand bent up. Folded legs appear like a pillow. Symbol incomplete. *Śramahandra.*
1221	121.2	.71	*Ku* *mā* *ra.* Circular legend off.	L. hand bent up. Legs appear like a pillow. Symbol *Śramahandra.*
1222	120.6	.7	*Ku* *mā* *ra.* Circular legend off.	L. hand bent up. Symbol *Śramahandra.*
1223	121.5	.69	*Ku* *mā* *ra.* Circular legend off.	L. hand bent up. Symbol Legend truncated.
1224	120.5	.75	*Ku* *mā*	L. hand bent up. Symbol but

No.	Wt.	Size	Obverse	Reverse
			ra. Circular legend off.	incomplete. *.mahandra.*
1225	121.1	.72	Necklace clear. *Ku* *mā* *ra.* Circular legend off.	L. hand bent up. Symbol 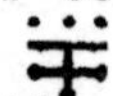 Legend blurred.
1226	122.3	.7	Circular legend off. Legend under r. arm blurred.	L. hand bent up. Symbol  Legend blurred.
1227	120.6	.7	*Ku* *mā* *ra.* *Maharaja*	L. hand bent up. Symbol 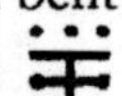, but incomplete. Legend blurred.
1228	120.7	.77	*Ku* *ma* *ra.* Circular legend off.	L. hand bent up. Symbol 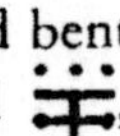, but incomplete. *Śramahandra.*
1229	116.8	.7	*Ku* *mā* *ra.* *Mahara*	L. hand bent up, but partly off the flan. Coin has errosion. Symbol 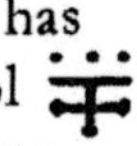, but incomplete. Legend blurred.
1230	121.5	.69	*Ku* *mā* *ra.* Circular legend off.	L. hand bent up. R. hand truncated; its object is off. Symbol off. Legend blurred.
1231	120.7	.75	*Ku* } *mā* } truncated. *ra.* } Circular legend off.	L. hand bent up. Symbol 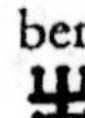, but carelessly engraved. Legend blurred. **Pl. XIX. 7.**
1232	119.3	.74	*Ku* *mā*	Noose in the r. hand is treated like a gar-

No.	Wt.	Size	Obverse	Reverse
			ra. *Mahara*	land to some extent. L. hand bent up and resting on knee slightly raised up. Symbol blurred, but probably  *Sramahandra.* **Pl. XIX. 8.**
1233	120.8	.8	King's head-dress and coat are both peculiar. Head-dress looks like a flat cap. *Ku* *mā* *ra.* *Maharajadha,* blurred.	Only half of the head of the goddess has come. Both hands on knees bent up. Object in r. hand indistinct. Symbol , but incomplete. Legend blurred. This side is double struck as shown by two disconnected dotted border lines. **Pl. XIX. 9.**
1234	117.9	.81	*Ku* *mā* . Circular legend off.	Both hands rest on knees slightly raised and bent up. Symbol 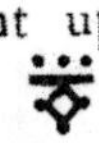, but incomplete Legend off. Either the reverse die was defective or it was not properly struck. **Pl. XIX. 10.**
1235	119.2	.78	*Ku* *mā* *ra.* *Mahārājā*	Both hands bent up and resting on knees slightly raised up. Symbol  but,

No.	Wt.	Size	Obverse	Reverse
			.	incomplete. *Sramahandra.*
1236	129	.78	Garuḍa standard almost off. *Ku* *mā* *ra.* *Maharajadharajaśra-Ku,* blurred and truncated. Crack in the edge at VI.	R. hand bent up and resting on knee too much raised up. L. hand apparently rests on waist. Symbol blurred. Legend blurred. Die was defective and it has been carelessly struck. **Pl. XIX. 11.**
1237	121	.75	*Ku* *mā* *ra.* *Maha*	L. hand as above. Symbol  *Śrīmahendra.*
1238	120.6	.78	*Ku* *mā* *ra.* Circular legend off.	Both hands bent up and resting on knees slightly raised. Symbol  *Śrīmahendra.*
1239	120.1	.79	*Ku* *mā* . Circular legend off.	Both hands resting on knees, r. hand extended, l. hand bent up. Symbol  *Śrīmahendra.*
1240	119.3	.77	*Ku* *mā* *ra.* Circular legend off.	L. hand bent up and resting on knee slightly raised. Symbol 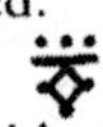 Legend blurred.
1241	118.7	.81	*Ku* *mā* . Cirular legend off.	Both hands bent up and resting on knees slightly raised up. Noose is long.

No.	Wt.	Size	Obverse	Reverse
				Symbol , but incomplete. *Śrīmahendra.*
1242	120.4	.77	*Ku* *mā* *ra.* Circular legend off.	Hands as above, but object in r. hand off. Symbol , but incomplete. *Śrīmahendra.*
1243	119.8	.77	*Ku* *mā* *ra.* *Mahārājādha*	Hands as above. Symbol *Śrīmahendra.*
1244	119.4	.75	*Ku* *mā* *ra.* Circular legend off.	Both hands bent up and resting on knees slightly raised up. Symbol off. *Śrīmahendra.*
1245	120	.74	*Ku* *mā* *ra.* Circular legend off.	Hands as above. Symbol Legend blurred.
1246	117.8	.75	As above.	As above. Symbol Legend blurred.
1247	119	.78	As above.	Both hands bent up and resting on knees. Symbol , but incomplete. *Śrīmahendra*
1248	120.3	.78	*Ku* . . Circular legend off.	Hands as above. Symbol *Śrīmahendra.*
1249	120.2	.75	*Ku* *mā* *ra.* Circular legend off.	Hands as above. Symbol , without dots. Legend blurred.

No.	Wt.	Size	Obverse	Reverse
1250	120.7	.7	*Ku* *mā* *ra.* *Mahārājādha*	Both hands bent up and resting on knees slightly raised. Symbol blurred. *Śrīmahendra.*
1251	127.8	.81	*Ku* *mā* *ra.* Circular legend blurred.	R. hand stretched out and scattering round coins or holding a garland. L. hand on knee. Symbol *Śrī..ndra.*
1252	126.8	.77	King is wearing trousers. *Ku* *mā* *ra.* Circular legend off.	As on the above, but the object in r. hand off. Symbol , but incomplete. *Śrīmahendra.*
1253	127	.78	*Ku* *mā* *ra.* Circular legend off.	L. hand bent up and resting on knee slightly raised. Symbol Legend off.
1254	127.6	.74	Head of Garuḍa and king partly off. Ample hair falling on the neck. *Ku* *mā* *ra.* Circular legend off.	L. hand rests on knee and the r. one is either scattering round coins or holding a garland. Symbol Legend off. **Pl. XIX. 12.**
1255	127	.78	*Ku* *mā* *ra.* Circular legend off.	Goddess as on No. 1250 Symbol *Śrīmahendra.*
1256	121.1	.77	Halo only on r. side. *Ku*	This side is partly blurred. R. hand rest-

No.	Wt.	Size	Obverse	Reverse
			mā *ra*. *Mahara*, blurred and truncated. Medial *ā* sign of *mā* is very prominent.	ing on thigh and dropping circular coins, nine in number. L. hand bent up and resting on knee. Symbol  *.mahandra*, blurred. **Pl. XIX. 13.**
1257	118.2	.75	*Ku* *mā* *ra*. Circular legend blurred.	Goddess as above. Symbol , but incomplete. Legend indistinct.
1258	118.4	.74	King's figure is very crude and arrow is off the flan. Halo only on r. side. *Ku* *mā* *ra*. *Mahārājādharāja*, blurred.	R. leg of the goddess is tucked up and the l. one is hanging down. L. hand on knee. Symbol incomplete, but probably . Legend blurred. **Pl. XIX. 14.**
1259	117.8	.8	*Kku* *mā* *ra*. *Maha* *KKu* misengraved for *Ku*	L. hand rests on thigh and l. leg is hanging down, the r. one being tucked up. Symbol  *Sramahandra*. **Pl. XIX. 15.**
1260	120.9	.78	*Ku* *mā* *ra*. Circular legend off.	Both knees raised, r. hand extended and l. one resting on the knee. Symbol  Legend blurred.
1261	117.8	.78	*Ku* *mā*	Goddess as above, but her l. leg is hang-

No.	Wt.	Size	Obverse	Reverse
			ra. *Mahara*	ing down. Symbol *Śramaha*
1262	119.4	.71	*Ku* *mā* *ra.* *Maharajadha*	Goddess as above. Symbol Legend off.
1263	120.2	.77	*Ku* *mā* *ra.* *Maha* Two cracks in the edge at IV and IX.	Goddess seated facing, r. leg folded up and the l. one hanging down. L. hand bent up. Symbol *Śramahandra*, blurred. **Pl. XX. 1.**
1264	117.9	.75	*Ku* *mā* *ra.* *Mahārājādha*, truncated.	Symbol, but incomplete. *Śramaha*

Variety C : 10 coins

(Same as the Variety B, but with a different legend)

No.	Wt.	Size	Obverse	Reverse
			King and bow as in variety B, but the legend is different and incomplete. It is *Guṇeśo mahītalaṁ* . . . . गुणेशो महीतलं . . . Pl. XXXVI. 37. The coins of this variety are poor in workmanship.	Goddess, nimbate, seated facing on lotus, both knees slightly bent up and supporting the two hands above, r. one extended, holding a noose and the l. one bent up holding a lotus. Symbol on l. *Srīmahendraḥ.* श्रीमहेन्द्रः Pl. XXXVII. 56.

No.	Wt.	Size	Obverse	Reverse
1265	119.5	.78	*Ku* *mā* *ra.* *Guṇaśa*	Symbo *Śramaba*
1266	119.7	.72	*Ku* *mā* *ra.* *Ga..śa ma*	Knees not bent up. L. hand on thigh. Symbol *Śramabandra.*
1267	119.1	.77	*Ku* *mā* *ra.* *Ga .. ma* Two cracks in the edge. Gold seems to be adulterated.	Goddess as above. Symbol , but incomplete. *Śramabandra.* Pl. XX. 2.
1268	120.2	.73	*Ku* *mā* *ra.* *Guṇaśa mahata*	Symbol off. *Śramabandra.*
1269	118.2	.73	*Ku* *mā* *ra.* *Gaṇaśa* Two cracks in the edge.	Symbol , but incomplete. Legend off.
1270	118.9	.73	*Ku* *mā* *ra.* Legend blurred.	Symbol *Śramaḥandra.*
1271	119.3	.78	*Ku* *mā* *ra.* Circular legend blurred.	L. hand on thigh. Symbol *Śramabandra.* Pl. XX. 3.
1272	119.9	.73	*Ku* *mā* *ṛa.* *.. śa*	Symbol , but incomplete. *..bandra.*

No.	Wt.	Size	Obverse	Reverse
1273	119.1	.72	*Ku* *mā* *ra.* Circular legend off.	Some thing like a garland in the r. hand resting on r. knee and stretched out. L. hand bent up and resting on knee, both knees slightly raised. Symbol, but incomplete. Legend off.
1274	119.2	.77	*Ku* *mā* *ra.* Circular legend off.	L. hand rests on thigh. R. hand off. Symbol *Śrīmahendra.* **Pl. XX. 4.**

CLASS II : 73 COINS

(With *Ku* under l. arm)

Variety A : 33 Coins

(With the legend, *Vijitāvaniravanipatiḥ Kumāragupto divaṁ jayati*)

No.	Wt.	Size	Obverse	Reverse
			King, nimbate, standing l., usually wearing *sakachchha dhoti* and coat, holding arrow in the r. hand and bow in the l. at the top with string inside. Garuḍa standard, sometimes having a dotted staff, behind the king's r. hand. Under the l. arm *Ku* with crescent above. Circular legend, beginning at I,	Within dotted border, Goddess Lakshmī, nimbate, seated, facing, holding noose in outstretched r. hand and lotus in the l. resting on knee. Symbol on the l. Legend on the r. *Śrīmahendraḥ.* श्रीमहेन्द्रः । Pl. XXXVII. 56.

No.	Wt.	Size	Obverse	Reverse
			Vijitāvaniravanipatiḥ Kumāragupto divaṁ jayati. विजितावनिरवनिपतिः कुमारगुप्तो दिवं जयति । Pl. XXXIV. 20. Metre, Upagīti.	
1275	126.2	.79	Staff of the standard is worked on lathe and Garuḍa is partly off. *Ku* *... vanaravanapata* *Kamaragapa dava;* *Kamara* is between the feet.	L. hand on knee. Symbol fragmentary. *Śramahandra.* **Pl. XX. 5.**
1276	126.8	.8	*Ku* *Vajatavanara ... ta*	L. hand on knee. Symbol *Śrīmahendraḥ.*
1277	127.5	.8	*Ku* *Vajatavana ..... .* *maragapta dava jayati*	L. hand on knee. Legs folded like a pillow as seen on Pl. XIX. 3. Symbol *Śramaha*
1278	126.6	.75	*Ku* *Vajatavanara*	L. hand on knee. Symbol *Śrīmahendra*
1279	126.6	.73	*Ku* *Vajatavanarava ......* *.. dava jayata*	As above.
1280	126.7	.81	Staff of the standard is worked on lathe. *Ku* Circular legend blurred.	L. hand on knee. Symbol *Śrīmahendra.* **Pl. XX. 6.**
1281	126.5	.78	*Ku* *Vajatavanara ....* *..... .. ..ta*	L. hand on knee. Symbol *Śramahandra.*

15

No.	Wt.	Size	Obverse	Reverse
1282	127.1	.72	*Ku* *Vajata*.......................... .. ..*ta*	As above, but legend *Śrama* only.
1283	127.1	.8	*Ku* Circular legend blurred.	L. hand on knee. Symbol *Śramahandra.*
1284	128	.72	King's hair falls on the neck in thick curls. *Ku* *Vajatavanara*	As above. Symbol *Śramahandra.*
1285	125.7	.76	*Ku* *Va*........ .... *jaya*	L. hand on knee. Symbol, incomplete. *Śramaha*
1286	125.6	.77	*Ku* *Vajatavanara*	L. hand on knee. Symbol *Śrama*
1287	128.4	.78	*Ku* .... *va* *jayata*	L. hand on knee. Symbol off. *Śramahandra.*
1288	126.7	.78	*Ku* *Va*	L. hand on knee. Symbol *Śrīmahendra.*
1289	126.5	.72	*Ku* *Vajatavanarava*	L. hand on knee. Symbol *Śramahendra*
1290	126.8	.77	*Ku* *Vajatavana*	As above, but legend *Śramaha* only.
1291	128.8	.76	*Ku* Circular legend blurred.	As above, Symbol, incomplete. *Śrama*
1292	126.5	.78	*Ku* *Vajatava*.......... .. ..*ta*	L. hand on knee. Symbol *Śramaha*

No.	Wt.	Size	Obverse	Reverse
1293	126.7	.74	*Ku* *Va*......... .... *dava jayata*	L. hand on knee. Symbol , in-complete *Śrīmahendra.*
1294	126.7	.76	*Ku* *Va*......... .... *dava jayati*	L. hand on knee. Symbol , in-complete. *Śrīmahendra.*
1295	128.3	.7	*Ku* Circular legend blurred.	L. hand on knee. Symbol *Śramaha*
1296	125.8	.77	*Ku* .... *dava jayata*	As above.
1297	126.1	.77	*Ku* *Vajatavanara*	L. hand on knee. Symbol *Śrīmahendra.*
1298	126.5	.77	*Ku* .... *dava ja*	L. hand on knee. Symbol *Śramaha*
1299	125.8	.79	*Ku* *.jatavanaravanapata* ..... *dava jayata*	L. hand on knee. Symbol *Śrīmahendra.*
1300	125.9	.75	*Ku* *Vajatavanarava...* .... *ta.* *Va* is just above bow-top and *ti* above Garuḍa, both separated from the rest of the legend.	L. hand on knee. Symbol or *Śrīmahandra.* **Pl. XX. 7.**
1301	126.8	.73	*Ku* *Vajata*	L. hand on knee. Symbol off. *Śrīmahendra.*
1302	126.6	.75	*Ku* Circular legend off.	L. hand on knee. Symbol *Śrīmahendra.*

No.	Wt.	Size	Obverse	Reverse
1303	125.9	.76	*Ku* Circular legend off.	L. hand on knee. Symbol *Śramaha*
1304	129	.78	*Ku* *Vija* One crack in the edge.	L. arm akimbo. Symbol *Śrīmahendra.*
1305	130.2	.72	*Ku* Circular legend off. The weights of this and of the next coin are rather high.	L. arm akimbo. Legs folded like a pillow as on Pl. XIX. 3. Symbol *Śrīmahendra.*
1306	131.1	.74	As above. One crack in the edge.	Every thing as above.
1307	124.2	.74	*Ku* Circular legend off.	L. arm akimbo. Legs folded like a pillow as on Pl. XIX. 3. Symbol *Śrīmahendra.*

Variety B : 34 coins

(Legend, *Jayati mahītalaṁekaḥ śrī-Kumāraguptaḥ sudhanvī*)

No.	Wt.	Size	Obverse	Reverse
			King with bow and arrow as in variety A, usually wearing a *dhoti*, but otherwise bare-bodied. Garuḍa standard behind r. hand. *Ku* under l. arm with crescent above. Legend is rather indistinct but seems to be, *Jayati mahītalamekaḥ śrī-Kumāraguptaḥ sudhanvī.* जयति महीतलमेकः श्रीकुमार-गुप्तः सुधन्वी । Pl. XXXIV. 21.	Goddess Lakshmī, nimbate, seated facing on lotus, l. hand on thigh, usually holding lotus, and r. hand usually opened out and empty, scattering some small round coins. Symbol on the l. Legend on the r. *Śrīmahendraḥ.* श्रीमहेन्द्र : Pl. XXXVII. 56.

No.	Wt.	Size	Obverse	Reverse
1308	126.6	.75	Profuse hair on head. Many folds of the *sakachha dhoti* on the thighs. *Ku* (I) *Jayata mahatala . .* . . . . *mvi* .	Goddess holds lotus in r. hand slightly bent up and nothing in l. hand resting on the thigh. No symbol. *Śrīmahendraḥ.* **Pl. XX. 8.**
1309	126	.83	*Ku* Legend beginning at I, *Jayata mahatala*, between king's legs, *Kuma*, between Garuḍa and the king, *mva*. The last letter looks like a *nma*, but it is intended to be *mva*.	R. hand opend and empty and two circular coins dropping down from it. L. hand rests on knee, holding lotus. Symbol ⁙ or ∴, but blurred. *Śrīmahendra.* **Pl. XX. 9.**
1310	126.8	.77	*Ku* *Jayata ma* . . . . *.dhanya* (*mva*).	R. hand is opened out and is dropping some circular coins. Symbol ⁙ *Śrīmahendra.*
1311	126.4	.79	Ample hair on head. Gold armlet on r. hand is apparently studded with pearls. *Ku* (I) *jayata* . . . . (XI). *dhanva*	R. palm opened out and three circular coins trickling down from it. Symbol blurred; it may be ⁙ or ∴. *Śrīmahendra.* **Pl. XX. 10.**
1312	126	.8	Garuḍa only partly visible. *Ku* (I) *Jayata mahatala . .* . . . . (XI)*mvi.*	Three circular coins trickling down from the r. hand. Symbol blurred; it may have been ⁙ , or ⁙ or ∴.

No.	Wt.	Size	Obverse	Reverse
				Srīmahendraḥ. **Pl. XX. 11.**
1313	126.6	.76	*Ku* (XII) *jaya* . . . *tala* . . . . *va* .	R. hand palm is opened out and some eight round coins trickle down from it. Lotus in the l. hand but partly on the flan. Symbol ⁙ *Sramahandra.* **Pl. XX. 12.**
1314	127.2	.76	*Ku* *Jayata mahata* . . . . *nvi*	R. hand slightly raised up and empty. L. hand also empty and resting on knee. Symbol ⁙ *Srīmahendraḥ.*
1315	127.3	.77	*Ku* *Jayata*	R. hand opened out and empty. Symbol ⁙ *Srīmahendra.*
1316	126.5	.84	*Ku* *Jayata*	Hands as above. Symbol ⁙ *Srīmahendraḥ.*
1317	126.4	.81	*Ku* *Jayati ma*	Hands as above. Symbol ⁙ *Srīmahendraḥ.*
1318	126.4	.79	*Ku* *Jayati mahatala* . . . . *nva.*	Hands as above. Symbol ⁙ *Srīmahendra.*
1319	127.5	.79	*Ku* *Jayata mahata*	Hands as above. Symbol ⁙ *Srīmaha*
1320	127	.83	*Ku* *Jayata mahitala* . . . . . *dha*	Every thing as above.

No.	Wt.	Size	Obverse	Reverse
1321	127.9	.81	*Ku* *Jayata mahata . . .* *. . . .* *. . . . nva.*	Noose in r. hand. Symbol ⁙ *Śrīmahendra.*
1322	127	.78	*Ku* Circular legend off.	Hands as above. Symbol ⁙ *Śrīmahendra.*
1323	126.6	.77	*Ku* . . . . *. dhanvi.*	Hands as above. Symbol ⁙ *Śrīmahendra.*
1324	128	.8	*Ku* *Jayata mahatala*	Hands as above. Symbol blurred. *Śrīmahendra.* Die had stipped during striking and it was restruck.
1325	127.4	.8	*Ku* *Jayata mahata. . . . .* *. . nma (nvi)*	Hands as above. Symbol as ⁙ *Śrīmahendraḥ.*
1326	126.8	.83	*Ku* *Jayata mahata . . . .* *. dhanvi.*	Hands as above, Symbol ⁙ or ⁙ *Śrīmahendraḥ.*
1327	127.5	.75	*Ku* *Jayata* Three cracks in the edge.	Hands as above. Symbol as above. *Śrīmahendraḥ.*
1328	126.3	.8	*Ku* *Jayata ma . . . .* *. . nva*	Hands as above. Symbol ⁙ *Śrīmahendraḥ.*
1329	125.8	.79	*Ku* *Jayata maha*	Every thing as above.
1330	128.5	.8	*Ku* Circular legend off.	Hands as above. Symbol blurred. *Śrīmahendraḥ.*
1331	126.7	.82	*Ku* *Jaya. . . . .* *. . nva.*	Hands as above. Symbol ∴ *Śrīmahendraḥ.*

No.	Wt.	Size	Obverse	Reverse
1332	126.1	.8	*Ku* *..ta mahatala .. ..* *..nva,*	Every thing as above, but symbol ⁘
1333	126.4	.78	*Ku* *Jaya*	Hands as above. Symbol ⁘ *Śrimahendraḥ.*
1334	127.3	.78	*Ku* *Jayati mahita .. ..* *.. nva.*	Hands as above. Symbol ⁘ *Śramahandra.*
1335	126.1	.79	*Ku* *Jayata mahatala*	Every thing as above.
1336	127	.8	*Ku* *Jayati mahatala*	Every thing as above.
1337	127	.8	*Ku* *Jayati maha*	Every thing as above.
1338	127.3	.8	*Ku* *Jayata maha..........* *.... nva.*	Hands as above. Symbol ⁘ *Śrīmahendra.*
1339	126	.82	*Ku* *Jayata maha....* *...... ..nva.*	Every thing as above.
1340	128.2	.75	*Ku* *Jaya*	R. hand raised up and empty. Symbol blurred. Legend blurred.
1341	127.1	.82	*Ku* *Jayata m..... ......* *.. nva.*	Hands as above. Symbol ⁘ *Śrīmahendra.*

Variety C : 6 coins

(Legend, *Jayati mahitalaṁ śrī-Kumāraguptaḥ*)

			King, nimbate, standing l., holding bow in l. hand and arrow in the r.; Garuḍa standard behind. The legend is uncertain; it	Goddess, nimbate, seated facing on lotus, with r. hand empty or dropping some small circular coins and l. hand holding

No.	Wt.	Size	Obverse	Reverse
			begins with *Jayati mahītalaṁ*, but does not end with *sudhanvī* but with *Kumāragup-taḥ*, probably it is *Jayati mahītalaṁ Śrī-Kumāraguptaḥ.* जयति महीतलं श्रीकुमारगुप्तः।	lotus and resting on the knee. Symbol on the l. Legend on the r. *Śrīmahendraḥ.* श्रीमहेन्द्रः
1342	125.3	.8	Arrow in r. hand off the flan. *Ku* *Jayata ma . . . . ptaḥ.*	R. hand empty. Symbol *Śrīmahendra.*
1343	127.7	.73	*Ku* (I) *Jaya. . . . . Śra-Kama . . pa.* Letters *Śraka* are fairly distinct at VIII and *pa* above Garuḍa. The rest are blurred and truncated. Four cracks in the edge, but not visible on the surface.	R. hand dropping four circular coins. Symbol *Śramahandra.* **Pl. XX. 13.**
1344	126.9	.82	*Ku* *Jaya . . . . pta.*	R. hand empty. Symbol *Śrīmahendra.*
1345	127.2	.83	King wears half-pant *Ku* *Jaya . . . . p.*	R. hand empty. Symbol *Śrīmahendra.*
1346	127.2	.79	*Ku* *Jayata mahata.* *. . . . . p.*	R. hand empty. Symbol *Śrīmahendra.*
1347	127.5	.8	*Ku* *Jaya . . . . p.*	R. hand empty. Symbol , blurred. *Śrīmahendra*

CLASS III : 28 COINS

(With neither *Ku* nor *Kumāra* in the field)

Variety A : 27 coins

(Legend, *Paramarājādhirājaśrī-Kumāraguptaḥ*)

No.	Wt.	Size	Obverse	Reverse
			King, nimbate, standing to l., usually bareheaded and wearing coat and *dhoti*, holding arrow in r. hand and bow in the l. at the top with string inside as in class I, but with no *Ku* or *Kumāra* written either under the arm or outside the bow. Garuḍa standard behind the r. hand. Circular legend, beginning at I, *Paramarājādhirāja-Śrī-Kumāraguptaḥ*. परमराजाधिराजश्रीकुमारगुप्तः Pl. XXXIV. 22.	Goddess, nimbate, seated facing on lotus, both legs folded, usually in a straight line, holding noose in r. hand outstretched and lotus in the l. resting akimbo on the waist. Symbol on the l. Legend on the r, *Śrīmahendraḥ*. श्रीमहेन्द्रः । Pl. XXXVII. 56.
1348	127.4	.81	*Paramarajadhara*, blurred.	Symbol incomplete, probably  Legend blurred.
1349	126.6	.78	*Paramaraja* .... *maragupta*.	Symbol  *Śrīmahendra*.
1350	126.7	.72	King is probably wearing trousers. *Para* .... *maragupta*.	Symbol  *Śrīma*
1351	126.9	.8	Top of the Garuḍa standard and feet of the king partly off. Curly hair falls be-	Goddess is neatly engraved. Symbol 

No.	Wt.	Size	Obverse	Reverse
			hind the neck in tresses. *Paramarajadharaja*, truncated.	*Śramahendra*. **Pl. XX. 14.**
1352	126.6	.72	.... *pta*.	Symbol incomplete, but probably Legend truncated.
1353	125.3	.75	*Paramarajadhara-* ......*pta*.	Symbol *Śrīmahendra*.
1354	126.3	.75	*Parama* ....*pta*.	Symbol *Śrīmahendra*.
1355	126.6	.78	*Para* .... *gupta*.	As above.
1356	125.8	.78	Coat buttons are very distinct. *Paramarajadhara* ... *maragupta*. Letters on the r. side are blurred and those on the l. are truncated; *pta* before king's face is distinct.	Symbol Lotus is rather big and goddess relatively small. *Śrīmahendraḥ*. **Pl. XX. 15.**
1357	127.2	.79	........*śra-Kamara-* .*pta*.	Symbol *Śrīmahendra*.
1358	128	.72	.............*pta*	Symbol *Śramaha*
1359	127	.75	.... *ragupta*. Buttons of the coat distinct.	Symbol *Śrīmahendra*.
1360	126.4	.8	*Paramarajadharajaśra-Kamaragupta* . Letters *rajadharaja* are truncated; *śra-Kumaragupta* are fairly distinct on the l. One crack at X.	Symbol *Śrīmahendra*. **Pl. XXI. 1.**

No.	Wt.	Size	Obverse	Reverse
1361	126.1	.72	Legend off.	Symbol incomplete. *.mahandra.*
1362	125.3	.75	The coin is small and somewhat oval. *Para*	Goddess is blurred. Symbol *Sramahandra,* blurred. **Pl. XXI. 2.**
1363	126.5	.76	*Parama.........* *pta*	Symbol *Śrīmahendra.*
1364	127.7	.8	*Para..........* *pta.*	Symbol *Śrīmahendra.*
1365	129	.8	*Paramarajadharaja..* *maragupta.*	Symbol *Śrīmahendra.*
1366	129.4	.79	*Paramarajadharaja.* *Kamara.pta.*	Symbol *Śrīmahendra.*
1367	125.8	.8	Buttons of the coat are clear. *Paramarajadharaja..* *maragupta.* Legend is somewhat blurred but fairly legible.	Symbol *Śrīmahendra.* **Pl. XXI. 3.**
1368	125.8	.77	*...........pta.*	Symbol *Śrīmahendra.*
1369	127.9	.78	*Paramarajadhara.....* *.pta.*	As above.
1370	125.8	.79	*Para.rajadhara.śra-* *Kumaragupta.*	As above.
1371	126.5	.78	*Paramarajadhara..* *Kamaragupta.*	Symbol *Śrīmahendra.*
1372	127.3	.79	*.........Kumaragu-* *ta.*	As above. Symbol
1373	125.1	.78	*...rajadharaja*	As above. Symbol

No.	Wt.	Size	Obverse	Reverse
1374	124.9	.8	*Paramarajadhara*	As above. Symbol Pl. XXI. 4.

Variety B : 1 coin

(Legend, *Jayati mahītalaṁ Śrī-Kumāraguptaḥ*)

No.	Wt.	Size	Obverse	Reverse
1375	127.3	.8	King, nimbate, standing to l., bare-headed, wearing coat and *dhoti*, holding in the r. hand an arrow and in the l. a bow at the top with string inward. No *Ku* or *Kumāra* in the field. Circular legend, beginning at VIII, *Jayata (i) maha(ī)tala(ṁ) Śra(ī) Kuma (ā) ragapa (guptaḥ)* Name of the king begins at I. जयति महीतलं श्रीकुमारगुप्तः । Pl. XXXVI. 37.	Goddess, nimbate, seated facing on lotus with legs folded, holding a flower in r. hand bent up, and a cornucopiae in the l. resting on the waist. Symbol on the l. at the middle. Legend, *Śrīmahendraḥ*. श्रीमहेन्द्रः । Pl. XXI. 5.

SWORDSMAN TYPE : 10 COINS

No.	Wt.	Size	Obverse	Reverse
			King nimbate, standing l., bare-headed, wearing diadem, apparently bare-bodied, wearing *dhoti* with waist-band, earrings necklace and armlets, l. hand grasping the hilt of the sword hanging by his side, r. hand in the posture of offering oblations on an altar, which is usually off the flan. Dagger hang-	Goddess Lakshmī, not nimbate, seated on lotus facing, holding noose in r. hand slightly bent and extended, and lotus in the l. resting on the thigh or at the waist. Symbol on the left in every case. Legend on r. *Śrī-Kumāraguptaḥ*. श्रीकुमारगुप्तः । Pl. XXXVII. 61.

No.	Wt.	Size	Obverse	Reverse
			ing from the left on the l. thigh. *Garuḍadhvaja* behind the r. hand. *Ku* with a crescent above, under the l. elbow. Circular legend begins at I; the last letter *ti* is usually at XI, between the head of the king and that of Garuḍa. *Gāmavajitya sucharitaiḥ Kumāragupto divaṁ jayati.* गामवजित्य सुचरितैः कुमारगुप्तो दिवं जयति । Pl. XXXV. 34. Metre, Upagīti.	
1376	125.9	.85	Altar is faintly visible under king's r. hand. (I)*Gamavajatya sucharitai Kumara.. .. ..ta.* Letters are bold and distinct. Crescent on *Ku* in the field is displaced.	R. hand is bent up. Symbol blurred, but probably  L. arm is akimbo. *Srī-Kumāraguptaḥ.* **Pl. XXI. 6.**
1377	122	.8	King is wearing a *shalwar*. Altar just visible. Crescent on *Ku* in the field is large. (I)*Gāmavajatya sucharata Ku* Letters are blurred.	As above. Symbol  *Sra-Kumāragupta.* **Pl. XXI. 7.**

No.	Wt.	Size	Obverse	Reverse
1378	125.3	.75	There is a crest jewel on king's head. Pedestal of the *Garuḍa-dhvaja* is clear, as also two *puroḍāśas* falling from king's hand. (I) *Gamavajatya* ....(VIII) *dava jayati*. Letters on r. blurred.	R. hand is not so much bent up as on the above two coins. L. hand rests on thigh. Symbol *Śra-Kumāra* **Pl. XXI. 8.**
1379	126	.78	There is a crest jewel on king's head. (I) *Gāmavajatya sucha-* .. .. (VIII) *dava jayati*. Letters on r. blurred.	Noose almost off the flan. R. hand on thigh. Symbol , incomplete. *Śrī-Kumāragupta*. **Pl. XXI. 9.**
1380	123.2	.77	Crest jewel of the king is clear. Pedestal of the *Garuḍadhvaja* partly visible, as also the altar. (I) *Gāmavajatya* ....*ti*.	L. hand of the goddess on thigh. Symbol , or , but incomplete. *Śra-Kumāragu* **Pl. XXI. 10.**
1381	124.5	.78	Pedestal of the *Garuḍadhvaja* partly visible. (I) .*mavajatya* ..*ra*. ....*pta dava* ..*ti*. Many letters are truncated.	Hands of the goddess as above. Symbol , but incomplete. *Śra-Kumāragu* **Pl. XXI. 11.**
1382	125.1	.73	Coin is small in size and its letters are also small. Pedestal of the *Garuḍadhvaja* and the altar partly visible. *Gamavajatya sucha*.. ....*ta*; partly truncated.	Hands of the goddess as above. Symbol *Śra-Kumāraga*, truncated. **Pl. XXI. 12.**

No.	Wt.	Size	Obverse	Reverse
1383	124.6	.79	Pedestal of the *Garuḍadhvaja* and part of the altar faintly visible. Crest jewel is distinct. (I) *Gamavajatya* .... *.va jayati.*	L. hand is akimbo. Symbol 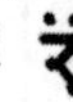 *Śra-Kumāraga* Pl. XXI. 13.
1384	123.6	.77	Pedestal of the *Garuḍadhvaja* nearly full; altar partly on the flan. *Gāmavajatya su*... ..... *dava jayata.* Letters on the left are blurred.	The hand of the goddess as above. Symbol , incomplete. *Śra-Kumāragupta.* Pl. XXI. 14.
1385	124.8	.75	Pedestal of the *Garuḍadhvaja* partly visible, but not the altar. *Gāmajatya su*... ..... *dava jayati.*	The hands of the goddess as above. Symbol 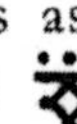, but incomplete. *Śra-Kumāragupta.* Pl. XXI. 15

HORSEMAN TYPE : 305 COINS

CLASS I : 47 COINS

(Goddess alone on rev.)

Variety A : 9 coins

(Legend, *Pṛithivītalāmbaraśaśī Kumāragupto jayatyajitaḥ*)

No.	Wt.	Size	Obverse	Reverse
			King on horseback, facing r., not nimbate, bare-headed wearing necklace, armlets, coat with buttons, half-pant and waist-band, sometimes flying behind, carrying no weapons, foot hanging in stirrup. Horse is well caparisoned; its mane is plaited. There is a circular leather ornament below the neck strap of the horse and a starry one, represented by seven dots, on its haunch. Circular legend, beginning at I, *Pṛithivītalāmbaraśaśī Kumāragupto jayatyajitaḥ.* Letter *pṛi* has both medial *i* and *ṛi mātrās*, which is quite incorrect. The first two letters of the legend are between the heads of	Goddess, nimbate, seated on wicker stool facing l. holding a lotus with a long stalk with leaves and buds in the r. hand, l. hand empty resting on waist. No symbol. Legend on r. *Ajitamahendarḥ.* अजितमहेन्द्रः । Pl. XXXVII, 57.

No.	Wt.	Size	Obverse	Reverse
			the king and the horse, separated from the rest. पृथिवीतलाम्बरशशी कुमारगुप्तो जयत्यजितः । Metre Upagīti.	
1386	127	.75	Hindmost leg of the horse is off the flan. (I) *Pṛithi* (III) *vītalāmbara* Letters *lāmbara* are very distinct; both the *i* and *ṛi mātrās* of *pṛi* are distinct.	Stool has two bands and the cushion upon it is clear. Pearl girdle of the goddess is distinct. Her earring is rather large. R. hand rests on knee. *Ajitamahendraḥ.* **Pl. XXII. 1.**
1387	125.7	.79	(I) *Pṛithi* (III) *vatalāmbara* .. .. (X) *tyajataḥ.* Letters *vitala* are blurred but *mba* is distinct. One crack in the edge at VIII, but not visible in plate.	Cushion on the stool is distinct. Girdle is just visible and earring is large. R. hand not resting on knee. *Ajitamahendra*; last three letters are blurred. **Pl. XXII. 2.**
1388	127.1	.75	(I) *Pṛithi* (III) *vītalāmbara* .. (VI) *Kumāra-.pta jayatyajita. Ku* is under the horse and only traces of *ma* and *ra* are visible. The medial *i mātrā* over *pṛi* is quite distinct.	Hair tied in a knot behind the head; girdle very clear. Leaves of the lotus stalk quite distinct. R. hand not resting on knee. *Ajitamahendra.* **Pl. XXII. 3.**
1389	127.2	.77	*Pṛithavatalāmbara.* .. .. *tyajita.*	R. hand not resting on knee. *Ajitamahendra.*

No.	Wt.	Size	Obverse	Reverse
1390	126.5	.79	(I)*Pṛithi*(III)*vata*...(V) *śaśa Kumāra*.(IX) *pto jayatyajita*. *Ku* is between the feet of the horse and the *i mātrā* over *pṛi* is quite clear.	Hair of the goddess tied in a knot behind the head. The stool has three bands. *Ajitamahendra*. **Pl. XXII. 4.**
1391	127.3	.79	Hindmost leg just visible. (I) *Pṛithi*(III)*vitalāmbaraśa*; traces of *tyajata* at the end.	*Ajitamahendra*. **Pl. XXII. 5.**
1392	126.6	.76	*Pṛitha*...*mbara*.. ..... .*yatyajita*.	*Ajitamahendra*.
1393	126.7	.72	*Pṛithavītalāmbara* .. ..*ta*.	Girdle of the goddess is distinct. *Ajitamahendra*.
1394	127.4	.75	Nose, two lips and chin of the king clearly denoted by thick dots. (I) *Pṛitha* .... (VIII) *jayatyajitaḥ*. Traces of letters in front of the horse.	Stool of the goddess has three bands. Her hair is tied in a knot behind the head and also plaited round the forehead. Lotus in her hand is not denoted by dots, but looks natural. *Ajatamahandra*, rather blurred. **Pl. XXII. 6.**

Variety B : 1 coin

(Legend, *Jayati nṛiporibhirajitaḥ*)

1395	125.6	.79	King riding on horse, probably uncaparisoned, to l. holding bow in the r. hand, whose	Goddess, nimbate, seated l. on wicker stool, holding a noose in the r. hand bent

No.	Wt.	Size	Obverse	Reverse
			top is visible between the head of the horse and that of the king. Dress of the king is indistinct; his hair is falling over his neck on the back. Circular legend, beginning at XI, *Jayata(i) nṛiporibhirajitaḥ.* जयति नृपोरिभिरजितः। Pl. XXXIV. 24. The flan seems to have been deliberately clipped at the top, perhaps to adjust the weight.	upwards and a lotus of long stalk in the l. resting on waist. No symbol. Legend on r. *Ajaitamahendra (ḥ).* अजितमहेन्द्रः। Pl. XXXVII. 57. **Pl. XXII. 7.**

Variety C : 37 coins

(Legend, *Kshitipatirajito vijayī Kumāragupto divaṁ jayati*)

No.	Wt.	Size	Obverse	Reverse
			King riding on a caparisoned horse to r. bare-headed, wearing a coat, trousers and high boots; he carries no weapons. Items in the horse's saddle and embroidery are of a different type than those in var. A; stars are replaced by beaded strings. Circular legend, beginning at I, *Kshitipatirajito vijayī Kumāragupto divaṁ jayati.*	Within dotted border, goddess seated on wicker stool facing l., holding a noose (in rare cases, a flower), in r. hand bent up, and a lotus with long stalk in the l. resting on waist. No symbol. Legend on r., *Ajitamahendraḥ.* अजितमहेन्द्रः। Pl. XXXVII, 57.

No.	Wt.	Size	Obverse	Reverse
			The letter *Kshi* is usually separated widely from the rest and is between the head of the king and that of the horse. क्षितिपतिरजितो विजयी कुमारगुप्तो दिवं जयति। Pl. XXXV. 25.	
1396	127.3	.8	Coat buttons in the centre are prominent and the armlet is distinct. (I) *Kshatapatarjata vija. Kamaragapa dava jayata.* Letters are small, blurred and truncated.	Girdle of the goddess is distinct. *Ajatamahendra.* **Pl. XXII. 8.**
1397	126.6	.8	(I) *Ksha*(IV)*tapatarajata vaja* . . . . . (IX) *pta dava jayata.* Letters are all blurred.	Goddess holds a flower in her r. hand; it is different in nature from the lotus held in var A. L. hand resting on waist holds lotus with a long stalk. No symbol. *Ajatamahendra.* **Pl. XXII. 9.**
1398	126.6	.78	*Kshitapatara*.. ... . *dava jayata.*	Goddess holds a noose in the r. hand. *Ajatamahendra.*
1399	126.8	.79	*Kshitapata*... ... ...*gupta dava jayata.*	*Ajatamahendra.*
1400	127	.75	*Kshitapata* ... ... *gupta dava jayata.*	*Ajatamahendra.*
1401	127.1	.8	(I) *Kshatapatarajata* ... ... (IX) *gapto dava jayata*; rather blurred.	*Ajitamahendra.* **Pl. XXII. 10.**

No.	Wt.	Size	Obverse	Reverse
1402	126.4	.74	*Kshatapata... ...* *...gupta dava*	*Ajatamahandra.*
1403	126.4	.8	*Kshatapata... ...* *...gupta dava jayata.*	*Ajatamahandra.*
1404	125.2	.78	*Kshatipatira.. ...* *.... pta dava jayata.*	*Ajatamahandra.*
1405	128	.78	*Kshatapatarajata* *...... gapta dava ja-yati.*	*Ajatamahandra.*
1406	126.3	.78	*Kshatapatarajata* *... ... gapa dava*	*Ajatamahandra.*
1407	127	.76	*Khatapatara.. ...* *... gapta dava jayata*	*Ajatamahandra.*
1408	126.2	.75	(I) *Kshatipatara.. ...* ..(VIII) *ragupta diva jayata* Letters on the left are fairly clear.	*Ajatamahandra.* **Pl. XXII. 11.**
1409	125.5	.78	King's face is long-ish and chin pointed. (I) *Kshatipatarajata ...* ....(IX) *pta dava jayata.* Letters on the left are all truncated.	Head of the goddess is truncated. *Ajatamahendra.* **Pl. XXII. 12.**
1410	128	.7	*Kshatapata... ...* *..... dava jayata*	*Ajatamahandra*, blurred.
1411	127.8	.75	*Kshitapata... ...* *..... . va jayata.*	Legend blurred and truncated.
1412	127.2	.75	*Kshitapataraja. ...* *..... dava jayata.*	R. hand bent up to the level of the face. *Ajatamaha.*
1413	127.2	.79	*Kshitapatara*; rest blurred.	*Ajatamahandra.*
1414	126.5	.79	(I) *Kshitapatara .. ...* ... (VIII) *gupta dava jayata.*	Wicker stool rather high and the goddess is tall. *Ajatamaha* **Pl. XXII. 13.**

No.	Wt.	Size	Obverse	Reverse
1415	126.7	.75	*Kshiti..... .... dava jayata.*	R. hand bent up to the face. Legend blurred.
1416	126.9	.75	*Kshatapa .... pta dava jayata.*	Legend blurred.
1417	126.8	.75	*Kshitapata... ... . dava jayata.*	Legend blurred.
1418	126.8	.71	*Kshatapata*	*Ajatamahandra.*
1419	126.4	.74	*Kshatapata... ... ...gapta dava jayata.*	R. hand raised up to the face. *Ajatamahandra.*
1420	127.1	.8	*Kshatapata... ... ... gapta dava jayata.*	*Ajatamahandra.*
1421	126.6	.78	*Kshatapata*	*Ajatamaha*
1422	126.6	.7	*Kshatapata... ... ... gupto dava jayata.*	*Ajatamahandra.*
1423	126.2	.77	*Kshatapata·*	*Ajitamaha*
1424	126.3	.77	*Kshitapata*	*Ajatamahandra.*
1425	127.3	.78	Hair of the mane of the horse is peculiarly shown. (I) *Kshatapatara .... gupta dava jayata.* All letters truncated.	*Ajitamahandra.* Pl. XXII. 14.
1426	127.5	.78	*Kshatapata... ... . jayata.*	Legend blurred.
1427	125.7	.78	(I) *Kshatapatara .....* ... (VIII) *gapto dava jayata.*	*Ajatamahandra.* Pl. XXII. 15.
1428	126.6	.76	*Kshatapata*	*Ajata*
1429	126.4	.81	*Kshitipata ... ... dava jayata.*	Legend truncated.
1430	122	.79	*Kshata· .... pta dava jayata.*	*Ajatamahandra.*
1431	126.4	.7	*Kshatapata*	*Ajatamahandra.*
1432	127.9	.75	*Kshatapataraja*	*Ajatamahendra.*

CLASS II : 258 COINS

(Goddess feeding peacock)

Variety A : 97 coins

(Legend, *Guptakulavyomaśaśī jayatyajeyo jitamahendraḥ*)

No.	Wt.	Size	Obverse	Reverse
			King, nimbate, riding caparisoned horse to r., its mane artistically plaited, bare-headed, wearing coat and probably trousers, holding bow in the l. hand, its upper part being visible just above the neck of the horse. Circular legend, beginning at I, *Guptakulavyomaśaśī jayatyajeyo jitamahendraḥ.* गुप्तकुलव्योमशशी जयत्यजेयो जितमहेन्द्रः। Pl. XXXV. 26. Metre, Upagīti. The head of the horse separates usually the first two letters; some letters are below the feet of the horse also; and some are on the left.	Within dotted border goddess, nimbate, seated on wicker stool to l., holding in her r. hand a bunch of grapes before the peacock in her front. The bunch is usually shown as hanging from a long stalk with one twig on either of its side. L. hand of the goddess rests on waist, holding a lotus with long stalk with leaves and buds. No symbol. Legend on r. *Ajitamahendraḥ.* अजितमहेन्द्रः। Pl. XXXVII. 57.
1433	125.8	.78	(I) *Gupta*....(IV) *śaśa* .. (VI) *tyajayo jitamahendra*; *tya* and *ja* are between the feet of the horse.	Hair on the head of the goddess tied in a knot behind. The bangles on the left hand are rather thick. *Ajatamahendra.* **Pl. XXIII. 1.**
1434	126.6	.77	*Gaptak*...*śaśa jaya-* ... *jatamahandra.*	*Ajatamahendra.*

No.	Wt.	Size	Obverse	Reverse
1435	126.6	.8	(I) *Gupta . lavamaśaśa jayatyajeya jatamahandra.* The legend is almost complete, though many letters are blurred and truncated. It is almost continuous after the head of the horse, some letters being separated by the feet.	Hair tied as above. *Ajatamahendra.* **Pl. XXIII. 2.**
1436	127	.8	*Gupta . . . maśaśa . . . . ya jatamahandra.*	*Ajitamahendra.*
1437	127.7	.81	*Guptaka. . . . . ya jatamahendra.*	*Ajitamahendra.*
1438	127	.82	*Guptakala . . . . jatamahendra.*	*Ajitamahendra.*
1439	126.1	.75	. . . . . *maśaśa jaya*	*Ajatamahendra.*
1440	108.5	.76	. . . . *handra.* A well preserved coin but small in size. Weight remarkably low.	*Ajatamahendra.*
1441	126.7	.78	A coin of crude workmanship; the face of the horse looks like that of a donkey. (I) *Gapa*. . . . . (XI) *ndra.*	*Ajatamahandra*, blurred. **Pl. XXIII. 3.**
1442	129.3	.78	King not nimbate. *Guptakula . maśaśa . . . . tamahandra.*	*Ajatama*
1443	126.7	.79	*Gupta*	*Ajitamahendra.*
1444	126.6	.75	. . *kula . maśaśa jaya*	*Ajatamahendra*, truncated.
1445	127.1	.77	King not nimbate. *Gupta . . . . śaśa*	*Ajitamahendra.*
1446	125.7	.8	*Gupta . lavamaśaśa ja*	*Ajitamahendra.*

No.	Wt.	Size	Obverse	Reverse
1447	125.9	.77	*Gupta*...... ..... .*tamahandra*.	*Ajatamahendra*.
1448	125.7	.77	*Gupta*..*vamaśaśa jayatya*.. *jatamahandra*	*Ajitamahendra*.
1449	125.6	.8	*Gupta*...... .... *handra*.	*Ajitamahandra*.
1450	127.1	.8	*Guptakulavyamaśaśa* .... *handra*.	*Ajatamahandra*.
1451	125.5	.77	.... *handra*.	*Ajatamahandra*.
1452	126	.79	(I) *Gupta*.. (III) *vamaśaśa ja*. (XI) *tya*. *ya* (VIII) *jitamahendra*.	*Ajitamahandra*. Pl. XXIII. 4.
1453	126.8	.7	....*tamahandra*.	.*jatamaha*
1454	127.5	.8	*Gupta*...... ..... *jatamahandra*.	*Ajitamahendra*.
1455	126.8	.78	*Gupta* ....*tamahandra*.	*Ajatamahandra*.
1456	126.4	.8	King not nimbate. *Guptakalavyamaśaśa jayatyaja*. *jatamahandra*.	*Ajitamahandra*.
1457	126.2	.81	(I) *Guptakulavyamaśaśa jayatya*.. *jatamahandra*. Some of the letters are blurred, but fairly distinct.	The anklets on the feet of the goddess are rather big. Peacock is graceful.
1458	127	.8	....*tamahandra*. Edges are uneven.	*Ajitamahendra*. Pl. XXIII. 5.
1459	125.3	.72	......*śaśa*	*Ajatamahandra*.
1460	126.9	.77	*Gu*....... ..... . *tamahandra*.	*Ajatamahandra*.
1461	125.5	.79	*Guptakalavyamaśaśa* .... *mahandra*.	*Ajatamahandra*.
1462	127.1	.75	*Guptakalavyamaśaśa* ..... .*tamhandra*.	*Ajatamahendra*.

No.	Wt.	Size	Obverse	Reverse
1463	126.4	.75	....*tamhandra*.	*Ajitamahendra*.
1464	126.1	.75	*Guptakalavyamaśaśa ja*.... . *tamahendra*.	*Ajatamahendra*.
1465	126.3	.72	......*śaśa ja*	*Ajatamahendra*.
1466	125.1	.75	*Gupta*..*vamaśaśa* ..... . *tamahendra*.	*Ajitamahendra*.
1467	125	.73	......*śaśa jaya*	*Ajitamahandra*.
1468	127.8	.78	....*tamahandra*.	*Ajatamahendra*.
1469	125.9	.73	......*śaśa jayatya*	*Ajatamahendra*.
1470	127.0	.75	*Guptakalavyamaśaśa*	*Ajitamahendra*.
1471	127.1	.75	.....*maśaśa jaya* ... *jatamahandra*.	*Ajitamahendra*.
1472	126.7	.73	(I) *Gupta*.*lavamaśaśa jayatya* ....*mahendra*; last three letters truncated; *tya* is separated by hoofs.	*Ajitamahendra*. **Pl. XXIII. 6.**
1473	127	.75	*Gupta* .. *vyomaśaśa*	*Ajitamahendra*.
1474	126.8	.77	....*vyamaśaśa jayatya*	*Ajitamahendra*.
1475	126.5	.78	.*pta*...*maśaśa jayatya*- .. .*tāmahendra*.	*Ajitamahandra*.
1476	126	.8	*Guptaka*..*maśaśa ja* .... *ndra*.	*Ajitamahandra*.
1477	125.6	.78	*Gupta* ....*śaśa* ..... *jatamahendra*.	*Ajitamahendra*.
1478	124.8	.78	King not nimbate. ....*vyamaśaśī jayatyaja*	*Ajitamahendra*.
1479	125.5	.78	*Guptakulavamaśaśa* .... *ndra*.	*Ajatamahendra*.
1480	125.5	.7	*Gupta*... *maśaśa ja* . *tya*	*Ajitamahendra*.
1481	124.5	.79	*Gupta*...*maśaśa* ....*ndra*.	*Ajitamahendra*.
1482	125.8	.79	*Guptakalavamaśaśa* ..... .*tamahandra*	*Ajitavikrama*.

No.	Wt.	Size	Obverse	Reverse
1483	125.2	.8	*Guptakalavamaśaśa .. .... ya jatamandraḥ.*	*Ajitomahendra.*
1484	126.5	.84	*Guptakulavamaśaśa ja .... jatamahendra.*	*Ajitamaha.*
1485	125.8	.8	(I) *Guptakula* (III) *vamaśaśa jayatya* (VII) *jaya jatamahandra.* The legend is almost complete; but only the lower part of *la* is visible, and the conjunct letter *vyo* is partly visible. *Jayatya* is between two front hoofs.	*Ajitamahendra.* **Pl. XXIII. 7.**
1486	126.2	.75	*Gupta .... śaśa ja ...... mahandra.*	*Ajatama.*
1487	124.8	.74	*Guptakalavamaśaśa ja .... jatamahandra.*	*Ajatamahendra.*
1488	128.7	.79	*Guptakalavamaśa. .... handra.*	*Ajatamaha.*
1489	125.3	.75	*ptakalavamaśaśī jaya—*	*Ajatamahendra.*
1490	126.4	.75	*Gupta .. vamaśaśī .. tya .... mahandra.*	*Ajatamahandra.*
1491	125.4	.73	(XII) *Guptaku..* (II) *.maśaśa jayatya.. ...*(X) *handra.*	*Ajatamahendra.* **Pl. XXIII. 8.**
1492	125.9	.8	*Gu ... vama .. ja .... jatamahendra.*	*Ajatamahandra.*
1493	126.7	.75	*Gupta .... maha*	*Ajatamahandra.*
1494	126.3	.74	*Guptaka . vamaśaśa ..... .tamahandra.*	*Ajatamahandra.*
1495	125.5	.75	*...... śaśa jayatya .. jatamahandra.*	*Ajatamahandra.*

No.	Wt.	Size	Obverse	Reverse
1496	126.7	.72	(I) *Guptaka*. . . . . (VIII) *jatamahandra*. The coin has been considerably rubbed; so the horse appears to be uncaparisoned.	Lotus is conventionally shown. *Ajitamahendra*. **Pl. XXIII. 9.**
1497	128.7	.86	*Gupta*. . *vamaśaśa ja*. . . . . *tamahendra*.	*Ajatamahendra*.
1498	126.4	.75	(I) *Gupta* . . (III) *vamaśaśa jaya* (VI) *tya*- . . . *tamahandra*. Last few letters are truncated.	*Ajitamahendra*. **Pl. XXIII. 10.**
1499	125.3	.78	*Guptakalavamaśaśa* . . . . . *jatamahandra*.	*Ajitamahandra*.
1500	126.5	.81	(I) *Gupta*. *lavamaśaśa jaya* (VI) *tya* . . . . . . (XI) *ndra*.	*Ajitamahandra*. **Pl. XXIII. 11.**
1501	125.9	.74	*Gupta*. . . . . *jayo jatamahandra*.	*Ajitamahandra*.
1502	126.3	.75	*Gupta*. . . *maśaśa jayataja*. *jatamahandra*.	Completely blurred.
1503	126.2	.7	King not nimbate. . . . . . (IV) *maśaśa jayatajaya* . . . . *ndra*. The legend is continuous from IV to VIII and is not interrupted by the hoofs of the horse.	*Ajitamahandra*. **Pl. XXIII. 12.**
1504	126.5	.7	*Guptakalavamaśaśa ja*-	*Ajatama*
1505	126.3	.75	. . . . *tya*	Legend truncated.
1506	126.5	.78	*Guptakalavamaśaśa jaya*	*Ajitamahandra*.
1507	127.6	.79	*Gupta*. . . *maśaśa jayatya*. . *jatamahandra*.	*Ajitamahendra*.
1508	126.5	.8	*Guptakalavamaśaśa jayatya*	*Ajitamahandra*.

No.	Wt.	Size	Obverse	Reverse
1509	106.7	.79	*Guptaka.vamaśaśa jayatya ...... dra.* Well preserved coin, but low in weight.	The string of the girdle between the legs. *Ajitamahandra.*
1510	126.3	.78	*Guptakalavamaśaśa ja.... iatamahandra.* One crack in the edge at X.	*Ajatamahandra.*
1511	126.5	.8	*Guptakalavamśaśa ja- .... .tamahandra.*	*Ajatamahendra.*
1512	125.8	.73	*.....maśasa jaya... ...handra.*	*Ajitamahandra.*
1513	126.2	.71	*Guptaka..... ....handra.*	*Ajatamahandra.*
1514	127.3	.78	*Guptakalavamaśaśa jaya... ...handra.*	*Ajitamahandra.*
1515	127.2	.8	*Gupta .... mahandra.*	*Ajata*
1516	126.4	.75	*Guptakala..śaśa jaya*	*Ajatamaha*
1517	126	.75	*Gupta...... .... mahandra.*	*Ajatamahandra.*
1518	127.4	.79	*Gu..lavamaśaśa jayatya ..jatamahendra.*	*Ajatamahandra.*
1519	126.6	.77	*Guptakalavamaśaśa .. tya ..jatamahandra.*	*Ajatamahendra.*
1520	126.1	.78	(I) *.pta* .. (III) *vama-śaśa jayatya..* .... (XI) *ndra.*	*Ajatamahendra.* **Pl. XXIII. 13.**
1521	126.6	.73	*......śaśa .... mahandra.*	*Ajatamahandra.*
1522	125.2	.78	*.... vamaśaśa ..... jatama*	*Ajitamahandra.*
1523	125.8	.75	*Gupta...... ..tya- .. jatamahendra.*	*Ajatamahandra.*
1524	125.7	.8	(XII) *Guptakula* (II) *vyamaśaśa jayatyaja-*	*Ajatamahandra.* **Pl. XXIII. 14.**

No.	Wt.	Size	Obverse	Reverse
			(VIII) *ya jatamahandra*. The legend is almost complete; only *ja* in *tyajeyo* being incomplete and indistinct.	
1525	125.1	.78	*Gupta*...... ....*ndra*.	*Ajatamahandra*.
1526	126.8	.75	Legend off.	*Ajitamahandra*.
1527	118	.75	*Guptakalavamaśaśa ja*...... *mahandra*.	.*jatama* -
1528	127.2	.8	An artistic coin, showing the plaited hair of the horse. (I)*Gupta*.*lavamaśaśa ja*. (VI) *tya*.. . (VIII) *tamahandra*.	*Ajitamahandra* **Pl. XXIII. 15.**
1529	127.4	.79	*Guptaka*.*vamaśaśa*; faint traces of illegible legend between VII and IX.	*Ajatamahandra*, quite blurred. **Pl. XXIV. 1.**

Variety B : 83 coins

(Legend, *Guptakulāmalachandro mahendrakarmājito jayati*)

No.	Wt.	Size	Obverse	Reverse
			King, nimbate, riding on caparisoned horse to l., bare-headed and with curly hair, wearing coat, waist-band and probably trousers, holding bow in the r. hand whose top is visible between the head of the horse and that of the king and sword on the l. kept in a decorated scabbard. Caparison of the horse is simple and its hair	Goddess seated to l. on a wicker stool cushioned and having a very low back, offering to peacock some fruits hanging from a twig in her r. hand bent up, and holding a lotus with long stalk in the l. resting on her waist. The twig in this variety has fewer grapes than in var. A. Symbol on l.

No.	Wt.	Size	Obverse	Reverse
			is plaited ornamentally. Circular legend beginning at I, *Guptakulāmalachandro mahendrakarmājito jayati*. गुप्तकुलामलचन्द्रो महेन्द्रकर्माऽजितो जयति। Pl. XXXV. 28. Metre, Upagīti. The concluding letter of the legend is usually alone, between the head of the king and that of the horse.	Legend on r. *Ajitamahendraḥ*. अजितमहेन्द्रः। Pl. XXXVII. 57.
1530	125	.78	*Guptaku..... mahandrakama jita jayati*.	Symbol *Ajitamahendra*.
1531	125.1	.73	*..kalamalachadra*	Symbol *Ajatamahandra*.
1532	125.9	.8	*Guptakulamala.. mahandra.. jata jayati*.	Symbol *Ajatamahandra*.
1533	125	.8	*Guptakulamalachandra .... jayata*.	Symbol *.jatamahendra*.
1534	125.6	.73	*Guptakulamalachandra*	Symbol *..tamaha*
1535	126.3	.71	Legend blurred.	Symbol Legend blurred.
1536	123.9	.77	*Guptakala.... . handrakamajito jayati*.	Symbol *Ajatamahandra*.
1537	126.7	.79	(I) *Guptakulamala.. mahandrakamajito jayati*. Last letter is in front of the king's face, separated by the head of the horse from the rest; letters below the horse are blurred.	Symbol *Ajitamahendra*. **Pl. XXIV. 2.**

No.	Wt.	Size	Obverse	Reverse
1538	125.6	.85	(I) *Guptakulama.chadra* (VI) *maha. kamajata jaya-* (X) *ti.*	Symbol ⁝ʃ⁝ blurred. *Ajitamahe* **Pl. XXIV. 3.**
1539	126.8	.8	(XII) *Guptakulamala-chandra ma .. kamajito jayati.* *Cha* is under the tail of the horse and *ndra* between its hind legs. Subsequent letters are almost continuous with the exception of *ti.*	In the upper l. quadrant marginal dots appear like traces of letters. Symbol ⁝ʃ⁝, but blurred. *Ajitamahandra.* **Pl. XXIV. 4.**
1540	122.2	.76	.......*ndra mahandra-kama.. jayata.*	Symbol ⁝ʃ⁝ *Ajatamahandra.*
1541	124.4	.85	(I) *Guptakulamalacha-ndra mahandrakarmajito jayati.* Legend is complete and almost continuous; *cha* is under the tail of the horse. Medial vowels in the latter half are clear.	Upper l. quadrant is hazy; so the fruits are indistinct. Symbol blurred. *Ajitamahendra,* in bold characters. **Pl. XXIV. 5.**
1542	125.4	.78	(I) *Guptakalamalacha-ndra mahandrakamajito jayati.* Legend complete and almost continuous.	Symbol ⁝ʃ⁝, blurred. *Ajatamahendra.* **Pl. XXIV. 6.**
1543	125.4	.79	*Guptakala.... ma-handrakamajato jayata.*	Symbol ⁝ʃ⁝ *Ajatamahendra.*
1544	127.2	.8	*Guptakulamalachandra* ..... *jata jayati*	Symbol ⁝ʃ⁝ *Ajatamahandra.*
1545	123.9	.75	*Guptakalamala.. ma-handrakamajata jayati.*	Symbol ⁝ʃ⁝ *Ajatamahendra.*
1546	123.3	.78	*Gupta....cha.* ....*majito jayati.*	Symbol ⁝ʃ⁝ *Ajitamahendra.*

No.	Wt.	Size	Obverse	Reverse
1547	126.2	.78	*Guptakulamala.ndra ... kamajato jayati.*	Symbol *Ajatamahendra.*
1548	124.7	.74	(I) *Guptakulamalachandra* ....(X) *jayati.* Letters on the right are big and on the left are truncated.	Symbol *Ajatamahandra.* **Pl. XXIV. 7.**
1549	124	.75	*Guptakulamala.......* .. *jayati.*	Symbol *Ajitamahandra.*
1550	126.4	.75	*Guptakulamala*	Symbol *Ajatamahendra.*
1551	125.3	.8	*Gupta.lamala..* ....*jata jayati.*	As above.
1552	123	.8	(XII) *Guptakulamala.* (VI) *ndra* .... *ta.* Letters are blurred.	Peacock is bending back its neck to reach the fruits. Symbol *Ajitamahandra.* **Pl. XXIV. 8.**
1553	121.9	.78	.... *ma..karmajata jayata.* Weight is rather low for this series.	As above.
1554	124.1	.78	(XII) *Guptakalamalachandra mahandrakamajata jayata.* Complete legend, but somewhat blurred; it is almost continuous.	Symbol *Ajatamahandra.* **Pl . XXIV. 9.**
1555	125.5	.78	*Guptakalamalachandra mahandra.. jata jayati.*	Symbol *Ajitamahendra.*
1556	127	.75	*Guptakalama...* .. *ndrakamajata jayata.*	Symbol *Ajatamahandra.*
1557	124	.8	*Gupta .. ma* ... ... *kamajata jayati.*	Symbol *Ajatamahendra.*

No.	Wt.	Size	Obverse	Reverse
1558	125.3	.79	(XII) *Guptakulamala-chandra mahandraka. jata jayati.* Some letters on the left are blurred and truncated. Legend almost continuous.	Symbol *Ajatamahendra.* This side is blurred. **Pl. XXIV. 10.**
1559	124	.71	*Guptaka*	Symbol *Ajata*
1560	125.7	.73	Legend off.	Symbol Legend off.
1561	125.5	.72	Legend off, only the last letter *ta* is visible. One crack in the edge.	Symbol *Ajatamaha*
1562	125.7	.8	*. patakulamala. . . . . ta.*	Neck of the peacock is straight and long. Symbol *Ajatamahendra.*
1563	124.8	.78	*. . . . . mahandra-kamajata jayata.*	Symbol *Ajatamahandra.*
1564	126.9	.78	*. . . . . .chandra maha-ndrakamajata jayati.*	Symbol *Ajatamahendra.*
1565	124.7	.72	Legend off.	Symbol *Ajatama*
1566	123	.73	*Guptakalamalachandra mahandrakamajito jayati.* Complete legend.	Symbol *Ajitamahendra.*
1567	124.7	.78	*Guptakala. . . . ma-handrakamajata jayati.*	As above.
1568	124.9	.75	*Guptakulamalachandra*	Symbol *.jatamaha*
1569	124.2	.75	*Guptaka. . . . . .ta*	Symbol *Ajitamaha*
1570	124.9	.78	*Gupta. . . . . . . .ndra*	Symbol *Ajatamahandra.*

No.	Wt.	Size	Obverse	Reverse
1571	125.3	.79	*Guptakalamalachandra*	Symbol *Ajatamahandra.*
1572	123.8	.75	*Guptakulamala.. ..ndrakama.. jayati*	Symbol *Ajatamaha*
1573	125	.79	(XII) *Guptakulamala.* (VI) *ndra ma..kamajito jayati.* Many letters blurred. A crack in the edge at III.	Symbol *Ajitamahendra.* **Pl. XXIV. 11.**
1574	126.9	.72	*Guptaku............ .. ta.*	Symbol *Ajatamaha*
1575	124.4	.73	*Guptakulamala.. .. ndrakamajata jayata.*	Symbol *Ajitamahe*
1576	124.2	.78	*Gupta .... ta.*	Symbol *Ajatamaha*
1577	127	.75	*Guptakula.... .. ndrakamaja .. jayata.*	Symbol *.jatamaha*
1578	124.7	.75	*Guptakulamala.. mahandakarma*	Symbol *Ajatamahandra.*
1579	124.3	.75	Legend off.	Symbol *Ajatamaha*
1580	122	.72	*Guptakula .... ta.*	Reverse blurred.
1581	123.8	.72	*Gupta ....ta*	Symbol *Ajatamaha*
1582	123.8	.75	*Gupta*	Symbol Legend truncated.
1583	125.5	.74	*Guptakulamala*	Symbol *Ajitamahe*
1584	122.5	.75	*Guptakula*	Symbol *Ajitamahandra.*
1585	125.9	.78	*Gupta...... .... ti.*	Symbol *Ajatamahandra.*

No.	Wt.	Size	Obverse	Reverse
			Characters are big in size.	
1586	122.7	.75	*Guptakula*.... ....*ta*.	Symbol Legend truncated.
1587	125.9	.75	*Guptakula*.... ... *karmajata jayata*.	Symbol *Ajatamahendra*.
1588	126.7	.8	*Guptakula*.... .... *jayata*.	Symbol *Ajitamahandra*.
1589	126	.75	*Guptakalama* ... . *jayati*.	Symbol Legend off.
1590	125.6	.75	*Gupta* ....*ta*.	Symbol *Ajatama*
1591	124.5	.8	*Guptakalamalachandra* .... *jayata*.	Symbol *Ajitamahendra*.
1592	123	.75	*Guptakula*.... ....*ta*.	Symbol *Ajatamahandra*.
1593	125.7	.78	*Guptaku*..... ....*ta*.	Symbol *Ajatamaha*
1594	124.5	.75	*Guptaku*	Symbol *Ajatamahandra*.
1595	107.8	.75	*Gupta*...... .... *ta*. The weight of this coin is very low.	Symbol .*jatama*
1596	125	.7	.*ptaka*	Symbol *Ajatamahandra*.
1597	125.2	.78	*Guptaka*..... .... .. *ta*./	Symbol *Ajitamahandra*, blurred.
1598	125.6	.73	.*pataka*..... .... *ta*.	Symbol Legend blurred.
1599	126.3	.7	Legend off.	Symbol *Ajatamaha*

No.	Wt.	Size	Obverse	Reverse
1600	124.5	.72	*Guptakulamala*	Symbol *Ajatamahandra.*
1601	123.3	.78	Only *ta* of the last letter of the legend is visible.	Symbol *Ajitamaha*
1602	126	.79	Legend off.	Symbol *..tamahandra.*
1603	125	.8	*Guptakulama...* *..ndraka*	Symbol *Ajatamahandra.*
1604	125.1	.78	*Guptaka*	Symbol *Ajitamahendra*
1605	124.6	.75	(I) *Guptakalamalacha*. .. (VI) *ndra* .... (XI) *ta.*	Peacock's neck is rather high. Symbol , but blurred and truncated. *.jatamahandra.* **Pl. XXIV. 12.**
1606	126.2	.77	*Guptaka*	Symbol *Ajatamahendra.*
1607	125.2	.78	*Guptakulamala..* .. .. *jayata.*	Symbol *Ajitamahendra.*
1608	124.7	.73	*Guptaka..... .....* .. *jayata.*	Symbol *Ajatamahandra.*
1609	125.1	.75	(I) *Guptakulamala..* .... *jayata.* Several letters before *jayati* are blurred and truncated.	Symbol *Ajatamahandra.* **Pl. XXIV. 13.**
1610	124.6	.74	(I) *Guptakula....* .... (XI) *ta.*	Peacock's neck is tall and straight; a crest upon the head. Symbol *Ajatamahendra,* rather blurred. **Pl. XXIV. 14.**

No.	Wt.	Size	Obverse	Reverse
1611	126.4	·7	*Guptaka*..... .... *jayata.*	Symbol *Ajatamaha*
1612	125.9	·75	(XII) *Guptakulama*... ....(VII) *majata jayati.* A few intermediate letters are blurred.	Peacock is graceful. It is difficult to say whether this coin had a symbol or not. The symbol was probably the usual one, but ill-engraved; and it has subsequently become blurred. *.jatamaha*, blurred. **Pl. XXIV. 15.**

Variety C : 69 coins

(Legend, *Kshitipatirajito vijayī Kumāragupto jayatyajitaḥ*)

No.	Wt.	Size	Obverse	Reverse
			King, nimbate, riding a caparisoned horse to r., bare-headed with curly hair; dress indistinct, but the ends of the waist-band flying behind. The hair of the horse is plaited and a ring under the neck is prominent in its accoutrement. King carries no weapons. Circular legend, beginning at XII or I, *Kshitipatirajito vijayi Kumāragupto jayatyajitaḥ.* क्षितिपतिरजितो विजयी कुमारगुप्तो जयत्यजितः । Pl. XXXV. 28. Metre, Upagīti. The first letter is usually separated from	Within dotted border, goddess, nimbate, seated to l., feeding peacock in her front with fruits, usually attached to a twig, and holding behind her a lotus with long stalk in her l. hand, resting on the waist. The hair of the goddess is usually tied in a big knot behind her head. No symbol. Legend on right, *Ajitamahendraḥ.* अजितमहेन्द्रः । Pl. XXXVII. 57.

No.	Wt.	Size	Obverse	Reverse
			the rest and is engraved between the head of the king and that of the horse.	
1613	127	.8	*Kshitipatirajito vija*	*Ajatamahendra.*
1614	127.6	.83	*Kshitapata* ... ... *gu*	*Ajatamahandra.*
1615	126.9	.81	(I) *Kshitapatirajata*; blurred letters under the feet of the horse.	*Ajatamahendra.* **Pl. XXV. 1.**
1616	125.5	.88	*Ksha . patarajata* ... ... *ga*	*Ajatamahandra.*
1617	126.3	.8	(I) *Kshatapatarajito* (V) *vijaya* ... (IX) *gu* (XI) *ta*	Goddess is apparently holding a single fruit between her thumb and forefinger. **Pl. XXV. 2.**
1618	126.6	.81	*Ksha*	No stalk to the fruit offered to the peacock. *Ajatamahandra.*
1619	126.1	.78	*Kshatapatirajito va*	*Ajatamahandra.*
1620	127.1	.79	*Kshitapatirajito vajaya* K*u*	*Ajatamahandra.*
1621	126.2	.78	*Kshatapatara*.. ... .*pta ja*	*Ajaitamahandra.*
1622	126.3	.81	(XII) *Kshatapatarajata* ... (VIII)...*gupa jayatyaji*[*taḥ*]. Letters *jayatyaji* are quite distinct between IX and XI, showing that the legend ended, not with *divaṁ jayati* or *jayati divaṁ*, but with *jayatyajitaḥ*. Letters on the right are all blurred.	Legend blurred, but *Aja* is clear. **Pl. XXV. 3.**

No.	Wt.	Size	Obverse	Reverse
1623	126.1	.79	*Kshatapataraja*	Legend blurred.
1624	127.3	.75	*Kshatipataraja. ...* *.... pa*	*Ajatamahandra.*
1625	127.2	.8	*Kshitapataraja* More letters are visible but they are blurred.	The end of the twig is almost in the mouth of the peacock. *Ajitamahendra.* *A* and *ji* are joined together and blurred. **Pl. XXV. 4.**
1626	126.2	.83	*Kshitapatara.. ...* *.... pta jaya*	Legend blurred.
1627	126.7	.82	*Kshitipatarajata ...* *.... pta ja*	*Ajitama*
1628	126.9	.75	*Ksha...... ...* *..ragupto ja*	Legend blurred.
1629	127.1	.76	Crest of the horse is clear.	*Ajatamahendra.* **Pl. XXV. 5.**
			(XII) *Kshatapatirajito va*	
1630	127.4	.8	*Kshatapatara.. ...* *... gapta ja*	*Ajatamahendra.*
1631	129	.83	*Kshitipatirajata ...* *.... pta ja*	*Ajatamahendra.*
1632	127.4	.78	*Kshata*	*Ajatama*
1633	126.1	.79	*Kshitapatara.. ...* *... gapta*	Legend blurred.
1634	127	.78	*Kshatapata* Blurred letters on the l. side.	Peacock is large and its neck graceful. *Ajitama* **Pl. XXV. 6.**
1635	126	.77	(XII) *Kshitapatirajito va*	*Ajitamaha* **Pl. XXV. 7.**
1636	126.2	.78	*Kshatapata... ...* *... ragu*	*...mahandra.*
1637	126.7	.8	*Kshitipata... ...* *.... pta ja*	*Ajitamahandra.*

No.	Wt.	Size	Obverse	Reverse
1638	126.1	.79	*Ksha*	.....*ndra.*
1639	126.5	.79	*Kshatapata*	Legend is blurred and looks like a thick convex line.
1640	127.3	.77	*Kshatapatara*	Legend blurred.
1641	127	.78	*Kshatapataraja*	Legend blurred.
1642	126.6	.76	*Kshatapataraja*, truncated.	*Ajatmahandra.*
1643	129.8	.75	*Ksha...... ..ya*	*Ajatamahandra.*
1644	127.4	.78	*Kshata.......... gupta ja*	*Ajitamaha*
1645	126	.8	*Kshatapatarajata vajaya Ku*	*Ajatamahendra.*
1646	127.1	.82	*Kshitipatirajata va*	*Ajatamahandra.*
1647	127.1	.81	*Kshatapa.... ... . jaya*	Peacock is only half on the flan. *Ajatamahendra.*
1648	127.5	.8	*Kshatapatarajata va- .. .. jaya*	*Ajata*, truncated.
1649	126.8	.79	*Kshapata... ... .mara*	*Ajitamahandra.*
1650	126.2	.8	*Ksha...... vaja*	*Ajatamahandra.*
1651	127.9	.79	(XII) *Kshatapatirajito vijaya*	*Ajatamahandraḥ. Visarga* is distinct. **Pl. XXV. 8.**
1652	126.7	.75	*Kshatapatara.. ... .pta*	*Ajatamahendraḥ.*
1653	126.7	.78	*Kshitipatirajato ... . ja*	Object in the r. hand of the goddess is blurred. *Ajatamahandra.*
1654	126.6	.8	*Kshitapatara .. .. ja*	*Ajatamahandra.*
1655	127.5	.75	*Ksha .... pta ja*	*Ajatamahendra.*
1656	127.3	.78	*Kshatapatarajata ... Kuma*	*Ajatumahandra.*

No.	Wt.	Size	Obverse	Reverse
1657	126.9	.75	*Ksha...... ...* *Kumara*	*Ajatamaha*
1658	126.9	.78	*Kshitipatarajata ...* *.mara*	*Ajatamahandra.*
1659	127.1	.85	*Kshatapatirajata vaja.* *.mara*	*Ajatamahendra.*
1660	126.8	.8	*Kshatapatara*	*Ajitamaha*
1661	126.6	.8	*Kshitapatirajito*	*Ajatamahendra.*
1662	107.8	.79	*Kshatapatarajata* Weight is remarkably low.	*Ajata*
1663	128.7	.78	*Kshatapata... ...* *... gupta ja*	*Ajitamaha*
1664	125.3	.79	*Kshitipatara.. ...* *.... pta ja*	*Ajitamahandra.*
1665	127.4	.8	(I) *Kshi...... ...* ..... (IX) *jayatyaja* Letters following *Kshi* are blurred and illegible, but the last four letters are distinct, though truncated.	*Ajitamahandra.* **Pl. XXV. 9.**
1666	128	.78	*Kshatapatarajata ...* *..... ja*	*Ajitamahandra.*
1667	127.6	.78	*Kshitapatarajata*	*Ajatamahandra.*
1668	127.5	.85	*Kshitipatara*	*Ajitamahendra.*
1669	126.3	.8	*Kshata..ra.. ...* *.. gupta ja* *Ksh* and *ta* are both between the head of the king and that of the horse. Letters following are blurred.	*Ajatamahandra.*
1670	125.3	.79	*Kshatapatirajita va..* *. mara*	*Ajatamahandra.*
1671	126.9	.85	*Kshitapatirajito vaja.* ***Ku***	*Ajatamahandra.*

No.	Wt.	Size	Obverse	Reverse
1672	125.7	.8	*Kshatipatarajata*	*Ajatama*
1673	127.2	.75	*Kshatapatara*	*Ajatamahandra.*
1674	125.7	.79	*Kshitapatirajata*	*Ajitamaha*
1675	126	.8	*Kshitapatara.. ... . pta jaya*	*Ajatamahandra.*
1676	127.3	.8	*Kshatapatirajito vaja. .ma*	*..tamahandra.*
1677	126.7	.8	*Kshatapatara.. ... ... gupta ja*	*Ajitamahandra.*
1678	126	.79	*Ksha.patirajito vajaya Kumara*	*Ajatamahandra.*
1679	127.1	.81	*...... ... ... gupta*	*Ajatamahandra.*
1680	126.1	.85	*Kshitipatarajata vaja. Ku.... ..tyajata*	Object offered held between two fingers. *Ajitamahendra.*
1681	127.2	.8	*Kshitapatirajito*	Goddess crudely engraved; object in r. hand not distinct. *Ajatamahendra.*

Variety D : 1 coin

(Legend as in variety c, but ends with *divaṁ jatyati*)

No.	Wt.	Size	Obverse	Reverse
1682	127.2	.81	King, not nimbate, riding on caparisoned horse to r., bare-headed, with curly hair falling on the neck, wearing coat and (probably) trousers, holding no weapons. Circular legend, beginning at I,[1] *Ksha(i)tipat [irajito vijayī*	Goddess, nimbate, seated facing l. on wicker stool, offering an object held between the thumb and fore-finger to peacock whose neck only is just visible, and holding lotus with long stalk in the l. hand resting on waist.

[1] Letters in round brackets represent the emendations of the previous ones; letters in square brackets are conjecturally supplied.

No.	Wt.	Size	Obverse	Reverse
			Kumāragu] *pta*(*o*) *dava jayati* (*divaṁ jayati*). क्षितिपतिरजितो विजयी कुमारगुप्तो दिवं जयति । Pl. XXXV. 25. Metre, Upagīti.	No symbol. *Ajitamahendraḥ*. अजितमहेन्द्र : । Pl. XXXVII. 57. **Pl. XXV. 10.**

Variety E : 8 coins

(Legend, *Pṛithivītaleśvarendraḥ Kumāragupto jayatyajitaḥ*)

No.	Wt.	Size	Obverse	Reverse
			King on caparisoned horse, riding to r., bare-headed with curly hair, wearing buttoned coat and (probably) trousers, holding bow in the l. hand with string inwards and sword in the r. having a handle. Legend beginning on left at VIII, *Pṛithivītaleśvarendraḥ Kumāragupto jayatya* (*jitaḥ*). पृथिवीतलेश्वरेन्द्रः कुमारगुप्तो जयत्यजितः । Pl. XXXV. 29. Metre, Upagīti.	Goddess, nimbate, seated on a wicker stool facing l. feeding peacock in her front with fruits, usually not attached to twig. Symbol generally on the l. and sometimes on the r. also. Legend on the r., *Ajitamahendraḥ*. अजितमहेन्द्रः । Pl. XXXVII. 57.
1683	125.2	.83	*Pṛithivītalaśvarandra Kuma*	Symbol 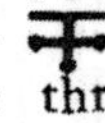, but without the three upper dots. *Ajatamahandra*.
1684	125.7	.79	Sword and bow are both distinct. (VIII) *Pṛithivītalaśvarendra Ku*	Entire peacock is on the flan; its feathers are shown somewhat unnaturally. Symbol 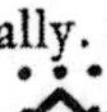, but without the three upper dots.

No.	Wt.	Size	Obverse	Reverse
				Legend blurred and truncated. **Pl. XXV. 11.**
1685	126.6	.8	(VIII) *Prithavatalaśvarendra Ku* .. (III) *gupta* Only faint traces of *gupta* are traceable at III. Letters on the l. are blurred but sufficiently clear.	Feathers of the peacock rather unnatural. Symbol , but without the three upper dots. . . *tamahandra*, blurred. **Pl. XXV. 12.**
1686	123	.84	Legend on the l. is blurred; *maraguptaja* on the r.	Goddess is crudely engraved. Symbol , but without the three upper dots. *Ajatamaha*
1687	125.5	.82	*Prithivītalaśvarendra Ku* Faint traces of letters on the r.	Symbol either hammered out or not engraved; former appears to be the more probable alternative. *Ajatamahendraḥ.* **Pl. XXV. 13.**
1688	125.8	.85	(VIII) *Prithavītalaśvarendra Kuma* (III) *ragapta jaya*	Peacock neat and small. Symbol on the l. 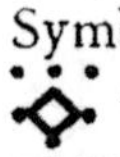 without the three upper dots. Symbol on the r.  *Ajitamahandra*, blurred. **Pl. XXV. 14.**
1689	126.3	.78	(VIII) *Prithavatalaśvarendra Kuma* (III) *ragupta jayatajata.*	Goddess offers a bunch of five fruits. Symbol on l.,

No.	Wt.	Size	Obverse	Reverse
			Traces of the last two letters look more like *ja* and *ta* than *na* and *śa*; hence the legend appears to be ending with *tyajitaḥ* and not with *tyaniśam*.	without the three upper dots. Symbol on r., *Ajitamahandra*. **Pl. XXV. 15.**
1690	127.4	.8	*Prithavatalaśvarendra Kumāragupta jayatya*	Symbol on the l., , but without the three upper dots. Symbol on r., *Ajitamahandra*.

KĀRTIKEYA TYPE : 13 COINS

Variety A : 10 coins

(Kārtikeya three-fourths to left)

No.	Wt.	Size	Obverse	Reverse
			King, nimbate, standing three-fourths to l., bare-headed, and bare-bodied, but with waist-band round the waist, whose ends hang down behind him, wearing short *sakachchha dhoti*, necklace and wristlets, offering by his r. hand a twig of grapes to peacock in his front, l. hand hanging down and resting on hips. Usually king wears a curious conical ornament on the top of his head. Circular legend, not fully read, beginning at I, *Jayati svaguṇirguṇāravindas* (?) *Śrī-Mahendra-Kumāraḥ*. जयति स्वगणैर्गुणारविन्दः (?) श्रीमहेन्द्रकुमारः । Pl. XXXV. 33.	God Kārtikeya, nimbate, three-fourths to l., sitting on peacock perched on a platform, holding a spear in l. hand resting on waist and r. hand bent up, opened out and scattering some round objects, apparently *puroḍāśas*, on an indistinct object before him, probably an altar. The god is bare-headed, has profuse hair and is bare-bodied; he wears ear-rings and necklace. No symbol. Legend on r. *Śrī-Mahendra-Kumāraḥ*. श्रीमहेन्द्रकुमारः । Pl. XXXVII. 60.
1691	126.3	.79	Peacock partly visible. (I) *Jayati svaguṇai* —— (XI) *Kumāra*	Hair of the deity is parted on two sides like those of ladies.

No.	Wt.	Size	Obverse	Reverse
				R. hand open but nothing falling down from it. Altar-like object clear. Legend blurred and truncated. **Pl. XXVI. 1.**
1692	126.7	.79	Entire neck of the peacock is visible and it is actually grasping the fruits in its beak. (I) *Jayata svaguṇaigu*—— (X) *ndraKu*; letters blurred; only traces of the concluding letters are visible.	Peacock's toes are resting on the platform before the altar. R. hand of the deity is apparently holding some objects, which however are not clear. Legend blurred. **Pl. XXVI. 2.**
1693	127.2	.78	Peacock indistinct and incomplete. King's r. hand considerably bent up. (I) ..*ta svaguṇaguṇara*	Altar off the flan. .*Mahendra* **Pl. XXVI. 3.**
1694	127.5	.78	Peacock's outstretched feathers and toes are clear. King is wearing a long *dhoti*. (X) *handrakumara*	Altar (?) is fully visible and the deity is offering something over it. The toes of the peacock are clear, and its plumage can be seen behind Kārtikeya. Legend truncated. **Pl. XXVI. 4.**
1695	124.8	.82	Peacock is almost entire and is catching the twig in its beak. (I) *Jayata svaguṇagu* (X) *ndra*	Altar (?) is off, but round objects like *puroḍāśas* are falling down from king's r. hand. .*Mahandra-Kumara*. **Pl. XXVI. 5.**

No.	Wt.	Size	Obverse	Reverse
1696	126.6	.78	Peacock is only half on the flan. King's *dhoti* is short. (I) *Jayati svaguṇairguṇa-ragra* (?) (IX) *Mahandra-Kumāra.*	Altar (?) is fully visible, as also the peacock's plumage behind Kārtikeya. Legend off the flan. **Pl. XXVI. 6.**
1697	126.5	.79	Peacock is only half on the flan, but its toes are clearly visible on the pedestal. Legend is very much blurred on the right, though several letters after *guṇairguṇa* are visible; but they are indistinct. (XI) *—mara.*	The platform for the peacock is distinct, as also its plumage behind the deity. Neck of the bird is graceful. *.Mahandra-Kumara,* blurred. **Pl. XXVI. 7.**
1698	125.4	.75	Peacock is nearly entire. Legend is blurred; (XI) *—ndraku*	Legend blurred, only *ndraKu* being distinct. **Pl. XXVI. 8.**
1699	126.8	.76	Peacock is nearly entire. (X) *—ndrakumāra.*	*.Mahandra-Kumara,* much blurred. **Pl. XXVI. 9.**
1700	126.2	.79	*Jayata śva—* (IX) *Mahandra-Kumāra.*	Peacock's platform is clear. *....Kumara.* **Pl. XXVI. 10.**

Variety B : 3 coins

(Kārtikeya facing)

			Same as in variety A. But the king stoops forward slightly and wears a coat. He is holding no object in his r. hand; the peacock also is not try-	Same as in variety A. But peacock perched on a platform, facing, with neck slightly turned to l. R. hand of the deity is as in variety A; no

No.	Wt.	Size	Obverse	Reverse
			ing to reach it. Its head is well under the king's elbow. King is perhaps pointing out to some object by the fore-finger of his r. hand drawing peacock's attention to it. Circular legend apparently the same.	objects are however seen falling from it. No symbol Legend the same.
1701	125.9	.73	Fore-finger of the king is pointing out at some object. (I) ... *svaguṇaguṇa*	... *nda-Kumara*. **Pl. XXVI. 11.**
1702	127	.8	Legend is fuller here than on other coins; but not entirely legible. (I) *Jayata svaguṇairguṇa* (*ravindo* ?) (IX) *śrī-Kumāra*.	Peacock and Kārtikeya as above. Legend blurred. **Pl. XXVI. 12.**
1703	126.9	.82	(I) *Jayata svagaṇaguṇa*—(X) *Kumara*	Legend blurred and truncated. **Pl. XXVI 13.**

CHHATRA TYPE : 2 COINS

No.	Wt.	Size	Obverse	Reverse
1704	126.1	.75	King, nimbate, standing to l., wearing *dhoti*, sash, earrings and necklace. Torso and head bare, curly hair hanging down from the latter. R. hand of the king is extended and offering oblations on an altar which is off the flan. Behind the king is a dwarf with	Goddess, nimbate, standing to l., wearing earrings, necklace and bangles, holding a noose in outstretched r. hand and lotus with a long stalk in the l., hanging down by her side. The hair of the goddess is tied in a knot behind her head.

No.	Wt.	Size	Obverse	Reverse
			frizzled hair on the head, standing and holding a *chhatra* by the r. hand, his l. hand resting on the l. leg, bent up. Circular legend, beginning at I, *Jayata mahatala* (*Jayati mahītalaṁ*—) जयति महीतलम्— Pl. XXXVI. 37. Normal condition.	Symbol on the l.  Legend on the r., *Śrī-Mahendrādityaḥ.* श्रीमहेन्द्रादित्यः । Pl. XXVI. 14.
1705	127.2	.72	As above. Altar is off the flan. (I) *Jayata* Normal condition.	As above. Symbol 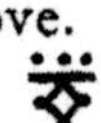 *Śrī-Mahendrāditya.* Pl. XXVI. 15.

TIGER-SLAYER TYPE : 36 COINS

Variety A : 32 coins

(With *Ku* in the field)

No.	Wt.	Size	Obverse	Reverse
			King standing l., wearing a short-sleeved coat, short *dhoti*, turban, earrings, necklace, armlets, wristlets, trampling tiger by r. foot and shooting at it with bow held in r. hand, l. hand drawing the string of the bow; tiger falls backwards with gaping mouth. Crescent-topped banner adorned with fillet to l. *Ku* in field under l. arm with crescent above. Circular legend, usually beginning at X, *Śrīmāṁ vyāghrabalaparākkramaḥ.* श्रीमां व्याघ्रबलपराक्रमः । Pl. XXXV. 35.	Goddess, nimbate, standing l. slightly bent on *makara* (crocodile) holding behind her, lotus with long stalk in l. hand and feeding peacock, usually with fruits, in the r. hand. She wears *sari*, bodice, earrings, necklace, armlets, etc. Symbol on l. Legend on r. *Kumāraguptodhirājā.* कुमारगुप्तोधिराजा । Pl. XXXVII. 67.
1706	126.9	.78	Only fillet of the banner is visible. (X) *śramā* (II) *vyā ghrabalaparākkrama.*	Goddess standing bending forward. Fruit in the hand clear. Symbol  or 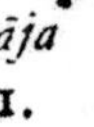 *Kumāraguptodhirāja* **Pl. XXVII. 1.**

No.	Wt.	Size	Obverse	Reverse
1707	127.1	.79	Legs show the *dhoti* sticking to them in an artistic line. Armlets very prominent. Only the fillets of the banner visible. (X) *Śrīmāṁ* (II) *vyaghrabalaparākkrama*; *kra* and *ma* are truncated.	Goddess but slightly bent. Her bangles are rather big. The fruit on the palm is squarish in shape. Symbol , but incomplete. *Kumāraguptodirājā*. **Pl. XXVII. 2.**
1708	125.6	.79	Crescent top of the banner just visible at X. *Dhoti* edge indicated as above. Arrow piercing right into the mouth of the tiger, which is fully visible. (X) *Śrama* (II) *vyaghrabalapara*, truncated.	Hair of the goddess tied in a knot behind the head. Peacock is graceful. The mouth of the *makara* is longish. Symbol,  or  *Kkumāraguptodhirājā*, slightly blurred. *Kku* is a mistake for *Ku*. **Pl. XXVII. 3.**
1709	118.9	.73	Tiger only partly on the flan. King's l. hand almost in the mouth of the tiger. The *dhoti* edge sticks to legs. Faint traces of the crescent of the standard above the tiger's head. (X) *Śrīmāṁ* (II) *vyaghrabalapara* Letters on the r. mostly blurred and truncated.	Goddess standing considerably bent; two fruits (?) in her hand. Lotus denoted by longish dots. Peacock's plumage is attached to its body inartistically. Symbol a variation of , but with a dot in the centre of the parallelogram. *Kumaraguptodharājā*. **Pl. XXVII. 4.**
1710	124.8	.79	Top of the crescent standard distinct at	Peacock fully visible, but object

No.	Wt.	Size	Obverse	Reverse
			IX. King's posture and attitude very energetic. (X) *Śrīmāṁ* (III) .*ghra*	offered to it is not clear. Symbol *Kumāraguptodhirājā*. **Pl. XXVII. 5.**
1711	126.4	.76	Hardly any traces of tiger or standard on the flan. King's figure is blurred. . (XI) *ma* (III) *vyāgh-rabala*	Legs of the goddess too much bent; one anklet is visible. Hair tied in a knot behind the head. Peacock just visible. Symbol *Kamāragaptadharājā*. **Pl. XXVII. 6.**
1712	126.4	.79	Only faint traces of the standard. .. *vyāghrabalaparākra-maḥ*	Symbol off. .*maraguptodirajā*
1713	125.5	.8	.. *vyāghrabalaparākkra*	Legs of the goddess crossing each other. Symbol *Kumāraguptodhirājā*.
1714	126.1	.77	Standard faintly visible between the tiger and the bow-end. *Śrīmāṁ vyāghra*	Symbol *Kamāragaptadha*
1715	127	.78	Crescent top and the fillets of the standard clear. *Dhoti* edges indicated by graceful lines. (X) *Śrīmā* (II) *vyaghra-bala*; letters on the r. truncated.	Goddess, peacock and the plumage all blurred Symbol *Kumāraguptodhiraja*. **Pl. XXVII. 7.**
1716	126.7	.76	Only traces of the standard are visible. *Śrīmāṁ vyāghra*	Symbol ..*raguptadharā*

No.	Wt.	Size	Obverse	Reverse
1717	127.7	.79	Tiger off the flan. .. *vyāghrabalaparākrama*. Two cracks in the edge.	Symbol off. *Kumāraguptadha*
1718	108.2	.78	Only the staff of the standard visible. *Śra. vyāghrabalaparakra* A well preserved coin.	Symbol Legend almost off.
1719	126.5	.78	Crescent standard partly visible. (X) *Śramā* (III) *vyaghrabalaparakkra*	Object offered is clear, but not easy to indentify. Symbol *Kumāraguptodharājā*. **Pl. XXVII. 8.**
1720	127.9	.75	.. *vyāghrabalaparakkra*	Symbol or *Kumāraguptodhirājā*.
1721	127.4	.78	.. *vyāghra*	Symbol or *Kumāraguptodhirājā*.
1722	125.7	.77	Only the staff of the standard visible. *Srīmā vyāghra*	Symbol *Kumāraguptodhirājā*.
1723	126.4	.79	*Śrīmā vyā*	Symbol , but incomplete. *Kumāraguptodhirājā*.
1724	126.7	.77	Only traces of the tiger and no traces of the standard. (X) *Śramāṁ* (III) *vyaghrabalaparāk*; only traces of the last letters are visible.	Peacock is artistic but the legs of the goddess are crude. Object offered is apparently a fruit. Symbol , but incomplete. *Kumāragapta* Die having slightly slipped while striking,

No.	Wt.	Size	Obverse	Reverse
				the legend is blurred and there are two marginal borders. **Pl. XXVII. 9.**
1725	127.6	.78	Crescent standard clear. *Srīma vyāghra.... krama.*	Symbol  *Kumāraguptodhirājā.*
1726	126.6	.75	*Srama vyāghra .... k*	Symbol  *Kumāraguptodhirājā.*
1727	126	.74	Tiger almost off the flan; only traces of the standard visible. *Srīmā vyāghra*	Symbol 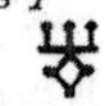 *Kumāraguptodhirājā.*
1728	127.8	.8	Crescent top clear. *Srīmā vyāghrabalaparākrama,* mostly truncated.	Symbol  *Kumāraguptodhirājā.*
1729	124.9	.76	Legend partly blurred but legible. (X) *Sramā* (II) *vyāghrabalaparakra* *Ku* under the arm is only faintly visible.	Hair tied in a knot behind the head. Object offered is not clear. Symbol a variation of , but with four prongs above. *Kumāraguptodhira* **Pl. XXVII. 10.**
1730	125.7	.79	*: vyāghrabalaparākramaḥ.*	Legs of the goddess crossing each other. Symbol 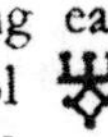 Legend truncated.
1731	126.5	.75	*Srama vyāghra .... ka*	Symbol 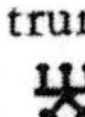 Legend blurred.
1732	126.1	.74	*Srama vya*	Symbol  Legend off.
1733	127.9	.75	No standard is visible. (*I*) *Srama* (*II*) *vya-*	Crocodile only slightly visible. Lotus is denoted by a

No.	Wt.	Size	Obverse	Reverse
			ghrabalaparakrama, partially blurred.	cluster of dots. Symbol *Kumāragupto* **Pl. XXVII. 11.**
1734	126.7	.78	*Srama vyāgrabalaparā-krama*, partly truncated. Crack at IV.	Legs of the goddess crossing each other. Symbol *Kumāraguptodhirājā.*
1735	126.5	.78	*Vyāghra*	Symbol *. . raguptodhirājā.*
1736	126	.79	(X) *Srīmā* (II) *vyā-ghrabalaparākkra*	Goddess is rather tall and not bending. The objects offered to the peacock look like sheafs of corn. The lotus is sufficiently realistic in appearance. Symbol *Kumāraguptodhirājā.* The last three letters are a little above the line of the first five. **Pl. XXVII. 12.**
1737	126.3	.78	*Srama vyāghrabalapa-rākra*	Symbol *Kumāraguptodhirājā.*
1738	127.8	.78	*Sra. vyāghrabalaparā-kramaḥ.*	Symbol *Kumāraguptodhirājā.*

Variety B : 3 coins

(Without *Ku* in the field)

No.	Wt.	Size	Obverse	Reverse
1739	126.1	.75	King and tiger as in variety A; but no *Ku* in the field. Neck of the king is bent down rather characteristically in his effort to stretch	Goddess as in variety A. Mouth of *makara* is wide open. Peacock's neck is artistic. Symbol

No.	Wt.	Size	Obverse	Reverse
			the bow to the maximum. *Srama vyāghrabalaparākra* There is a letter like *ta* or *bha* before *śrī*, but it seems to have been due to a mistake in engraving the top of the crescent standard.	*Kumāraguptodhirā* **Pl. XXVII. 13.**
1740	124.8	.78	Neck of the king bent as on the preceding coin. (X) *Sra*. (II) *vyāghrabalaparākra*, rather blurred.	Peacock stretches up the neck to reach the hand of the goddess. Lotus in the l. hand looks like a cluster of dots. Symbol  *Kumāraguptodhirā*, rather blurred but legible. **Pl. XXVII. 14.**
1741	126.3	.75	Tiger is partially visible; the crescent top of the banner is clear. (XI) *Srīmā* (II) *vyāghra* ..... (X) *ma*. The last letter is enclosed in the crescent at X.	Peacock is completely on the flan. Symbol  *Kamāraguptodhirājā*. **Pl. XXVII. 15.**

LION-SLAYER TYPE : 53 COINS

CLASS I : LION-COMBATANT : 23 COINS

Variety A : 13 coins

(Legend, *Kumāragupto yudhi siṅhavikramaḥ*)

No.	Wt.	Size	Obverse	Reverse
			King standing to r., bare-headed, wearing coat, sash, *janghia*, earrings and necklace and shooting at lion in his front with the bow held in l. hand, r. hand stringing it to the ear. Circular legend, beginning at VIII and ending at IV, *Kumāragupto yudhi siṅhavikramaḥ.* कुमारगुप्तो युधि सिङ्हविक्रमः । Pl. XXXV. 31. Metre, Vamiśasthāvila.	Goddess seated facing on lion couchant to r., l. leg folded and r. one hanging down, dropping down some circular coins, probably of gold, by the r. hand and holding lotus of long stalk in the l. resting on thigh. Symbol on l. Legend on r., *Siṅhamahendraḥ.* सिङ्हमहेन्द्रः । Pl. XXXVII. 59.
1742	126.7	.8	... (VIII) *gupta yudha* (l) *saṅhavakrama*; last letters truncated.	Four circular coins falling down. Symbol  *Saṅhamahandra.* **Pl. XXVIII. 1.**
1743	125.9	.82	... *gupta yadha siṅhavakrama.*	Five coins are falling down. Symbol  *Saṅhamahendra.* **Pl. XXVIII. 2.**

No.	Wt.	Size	Obverse	Reverse
1744	126.2	.82	As above. .... *pta .dha saṁhava-krama.* Last letters very clear.	Symbol *Saṁhamahandra.*
1745	126.5	.8	(VII) .. *yagupta yu-dha.*	Four coins fall down from the r. hand of the goddess. Symbol *Siṁhamahandra.* **Pl. XXVIII. 3.**
1746	126.3	.79	... *gupta yu.* ...*kra-ma.*	Goddess as above. Symbol *Siṁhamahendra.*
1747	126.9	.81	.. *ragupta yadha saṁha*	Goddess as above. Symbol *Saṁhamaha*
1748	124.5	.8	(VIII) ..... *yudha* Traces of letters on r.	Goddess as above, but her palm off the flan. Symbol incomplete, but *Saṁhamahendra.* **Pl. XXVIII. 4.**
1749	125	.81	Lion snatching at the bow. (XII) *yudha saṁhavakra* Only r. side of *yu* has come on the flan at XII.	Goddess as above. Symbol *Saṁhamahandra.* **Pl. XXVIII. 5.**
1750	126.7	.72	(VII) ..*ragupta yudhi* (I) *saṁ*	Four round coins falling from the r. hand of the goddess. Symbol *Saṁhamahandra.* **Pl. XXVIII. 6.**
1751	125	.77	..*ragupta* .. .*ṁha* Poor condition.	Symbol Legend blurred.

No.	Wt.	Size	Obverse	Reverse
1752	126.4	.82	....*pta yudha*	Symbol *Saṁhamahendra.*
1753	123.8	.8	.... *saṁha*	Symbol Legend truncated.
1754	126.8	.75	Lion snatching at the bow. (VII) ...*gupta yudha* (XII) *saṁhavakrama.*	Symbol *Saṁhamahendra.* **Pl. XXVIII. 7.**

Variety B : 6 coins

(Legend beginning with *Kumāra*, but incomplete)

No.	Wt.	Size	Obverse	Reverse
1755	126.9	.77	King's bow touches the lion's mouth; but he is not trampling the lion. He has a diadem on the head. *Kumāra*	R. hand of the goddess open and empty. L. hand bent up and holding lotus with a long stalk. Symbol *.ṁhamahandra,* blurred. **Pl. XXVIII. 11.**
1756	126.1	.78	Diadem on king's head. Arrow piercing the lion's face. *Kumāra*	Hands as above. Symbol *Saṁhamahandra.*
1757	127.4	.76	Diadem on king's head. Lion trying to clasp at the bow. *Kumāra*	Hands as above. Symbol *Saṁhamahandra.*
1758	128	.74	King wears a diadem. Bow touches the lion's gaping jaw and the arrow almost pierces it. *Kumāra*	Goddess as above. Symbol blurred *..mahandra.*
1759	126.4	.75	King wears a diadem. His l. hand is almost in the jaw of the lion. *Kumāra*	Goddess as above. Symbol *Saṁhamahandra.* **Pl. XXVIII. 12.**

No.	Wt.	Size	Obverse	Reverse
1760	128.1	.8	*Kumāra*	Lotus in the l. hand rather blurred. Symbol  or  *Sanhamahandra.*

Variety C : 3 coins

(Legend beginning with *Kshitipati,* but incomplete)

No.	Wt.	Size	Obverse	Reverse
			King, not nimbate, standing r., wearing a diadem, coat, waistband, *janghia*, earrings, wristlets, armlets, and necklace, shooting at lion standing in his front by bow held in l. hand, r. hand drawing the string back to the ear. Arrow visible on the bow. King's posture is rather awkward; he faces to r. but his r. leg is bent behind him. Only the first word of the circular legend, beginning at I, is legible; it is *Kshitipati.* क्षितिपति।	Goddess seated on lion couchant to r., l. leg tucked up, r. one hanging down, reclining on l. arm resting on the waist and holding lotus with leaves with outstretched r. hand. No symbol. Legend on r., *Srīmahendrasinhaḥ.* श्रीमहेन्द्रसिंह:। Pl. XXXVII, 58.
1761	126.1	.73	King has ample hair on the head and the diadem can be seen wound across them. *Kshata*———	Legend blurred, but one can see traces of *Sramahandra.* **Pl. XXVIII. 8.**
1762	126.5	.72	King's l. hand is almost in the jaw of the lion. *Kshatapa*———	*Srīmahendrasinha.* **Pl. XXVIII. 9.**

No.	Wt.	Size	Obverse	Reverse
			Traces of the legend between VII and IX, but illegible.	
1763	124.6	.78	*Kshatapa*	. . *handra*. **Pl. XXVIII. 10.**

Variety D : 1 coin

(King to l. and lion to r.)

No.	Wt.	Size	Obverse	Reverse
1764	126	.85	King standing to l., not nimbate, bare-headed and with frizzled hair, wearing buttoned coat of short sleeves, half-pant, sash and necklace and earrings, shooting at lion in his front with bow held in r. hand, l. hand stringing it behind to the ear. Legend is not sufficiently legible to permit decipherment.	Goddess seated facing on lion couchant to l., r. leg folded up and l. leg hanging down, holding some indistinct object in r. hand bent up and a lotus with long stalk in the l. resting on knee. Symbol on the l. at the centre (and not at the top), *Sra(ī)maha(e)ṅdrasiṅhaḥ*. श्री महेन्द्रसिङ्हः **Pl. XXVIII. 13.**

CLASS II : LION-TRAMPLER : 30 COINS

Variety A : 19 coins

(Legend, *Sākshādiva nārasiṅhaḥ siṅhamahendro jayatyaniśaṁ*)

No.	Wt.	Size	Obverse	Reverse
			King, nimbate, standing r., wearing *pagaḍī* (head dress), *janghia*, ear-rings, necklace and armlets, end of the waist-band floating behind him, and trampling upon and shooting at a	Goddess, facing, seated on lion couchant to r., l. leg tucked up, r. leg hanging down, holding in r. hand, usually bent up slightly, a noose and in the l. hand resting

No.	Wt.	Size	Obverse	Reverse
			lion, which falls back from a leap, with bow in l. hand being strung by the r. stretching it to the ear. Circular legend, beginning at I, *Sākshādiva narasiṁhaḥ siṁhamahendro jayatyaniśam.* साक्षादिव नरसिङ्हः सिङ्महेन्द्रो जयत्यनिशम् । Pl. XXXV. 30. Metre, Upagīti.	akimbo on waist, a lotus treated as a cornucopiae. Goddess wears earrings, necklace, bangles and a circular pearl ornament round the head. Symbol on l. Legend on r., *Srī-Mahendrasiṁhaḥ.* श्रीमहेन्द्रसिङ्हः । Pl. XXXVII. 58.
1765	127	.83	(I) *Sākshādiva narasaṁha* ... (VIII) *handro jaya.naśa.* Letters of the word *narasiṁha*, though truncated, are fairly distinct between IV and V.	Lion's head slightly raised. Symbol *Srī-Mahendrasiṁha.* **Pl. XXVIII. 14.**
1766	126.9	.75	*Sākshādiva nara.* Letters on the l. are blurred.	Lion's head stooping. Symbol *Sra-Mahandrasiṁha.*
1767	127	.83	*Sākshādava* .... .. (VII) *mahandra jayatyansa.* The coin is nearly oval.	Symbol *Sra-Mahendrasasiṁha.* **Pl. XXVIII. 15.**
1768	126.2	.75	Tiger trying to snatch at the bow with paw. *Sākshādiva nara..* ..... *jayatyanaśa.*	Lion's head slightly raised up. Symbol *Sra-Mahandrasaṁha.*
1769	126.8	.78	*Sakshādava* .... *jayatyanaśa.*	Symbol as above. *.Mahandrasiṁha.*

No.	Wt.	Size	Obverse	Reverse
1770	127.5	.76	(XII) *Sākshādiva na-* ... ... (VII) *handra jayatyanaśa.*	Symbol incomplete and blurred. *Śra-Mahendrasaṅha.* **Pl. XXIX. 1.**
1771	126.5	.75	*Sākshādiva na..... ..ndra ..tya*	R. hand of the goddess is stretched out straight. Symbol *Śra-Mahendrasiṅha.*
1772	125.5	.75	*.kshādava na... .... ndra*	Lion is gaping; its head is raised. Symbol, incomplete. *Śra-Mahandrasaṅha.*
1773	126.6	.78	Lion is snatching at the bow by his paw. (I) *Sākshā.. ....* (VI) *saṅhamahandra jayatyanaśa.* Letters on the l. are truncated.	Symbol *Śra-Mahendrasiṅha.* **Pl. XXIX. 2.**
1774	125.8	.75	Muscles of the arm are exaggerated. (I)*Sakshadiva na .... ndra jayatya*; letters on the l. truncated.	Lion's neck is raised and the r. hand of the goddess is stretched out. Symbol *Śra-Mahendrasiṅha.* **Pl. XXIX. 3.**
1775	126.6	.76	Nose point of the king is exaggerated. (XII) *Sākshadava .... .ṅhama* (VII) *handra jayatya.śa.*	Lion's head is drooping down. Symbol *Śra-Mahendrasiṅha.* **Pl. XXIX 4.**
1776	127.4	.79	Wristlet on the r. hand looks like a continuation of the necklace.	R. hand stretched out. Lion's head is drooping.

No.	Wt.	Size	Obverse	Reverse
			(I) *Sākshādava* ..... *ṅhamahandra ja .tya*; legend on l. truncated.	Symbol *Śrī-Mahendrasiṅha*. **Pl. XXIX 5.**
1777	124.8	.78	*Sākshādava na* ... . *ṅha* ..... *tya*	Symbol *Śrī-Mahendrasiṅha*.
1778	125.5	.8	*Sākshādava nara* .... *sa*	Symbol *Śrī-Mahendrasiṅha*.
1779	126.4	.78	*Sākshādava* .... *jayatya*	Symbol *Śra-Mahandrasiṅha*.
1780	127.9	.79	*.kshāda*. ... *ṅha saṅhamahandra* .. *tya*	Symbol *Śrī-Mahandrasiṅha*.
1781	125.8	.79	(I) *Sākshādava* .... .(VII)*ṅhamahandra jayatya* ..*śa*. Letters on the l. are blurred and truncated.	R. hand stretched out. Lion's head drooping. Symbol *Śra-Mahandrasaṅha*. **Pl. XXIX 6.**
1782	126.3	.75	*Sākshādavana* ... . *tya*	Symbol ...*ndrasiṅha*.
1783	127.3	.78	(I) *Sākshā* .... (VII) *ṅhamahandra jayatyanaśa*.	R. hand slightly bent. Lion's neck is raised. Symbol or *Śra-Mahandrasaṅha*. **Pl. XXIX 7.**

Variety B : 11 coins

(Legend beginning with *Kumāra*; goddess holding a garland)

			King standing r. in tense action, bare-headed, wearing waist-band with ends flying behind, *janghia*, earrings, necklace and wristlets, shooting at lion in his front falling back from a leap, with the bow	Goddess, nimbate, seated facing on lion couchant to l., r. leg tucked up, l. hand resting on thigh and holding a lotus with long stalk and r. hand opened out and holding a garland.

No.	Wt.	Size	Obverse	Reverse
			held in l. hand, r. hand stretching it to the ear. King is bare-bodied, but he wears a sash whose ends float behind. Circular legend incomplete, but beginning at I with *Kumāra*, and probably reading as *Kumāragupto yudhi siṅhavikramaḥ*. कुमार [गुप्तो युधि सिङ्हविक्रमः] Pl. XXXV. 31.	Symbol on l. *Siṁha-Mahendraḥ.* सिहमहेन्द्रः । Pl. XXXVII. 59.
1784	131	.79	Arrow is clearly visible. (I) *Kumāra*.. .. ... (IX) *kra*	Posture of the goddess is graceful. Garland is suspended on the fingers of the r. hand. L. hand on thigh. Lion seems to be sleeping. Symbol ⁘, blurred. *Siṁha-Mahendra.* **Pl. XXIX. 8.**
1785	126.7	.78	King's attitude is energetic. Arrow is clearly visible. (XII) *Kumāra*.. .. ...*kra*	Symbol ⁖. Garland held as above. L. hand on thigh. *Siṁhamaha* **Pl. XXIX. 9.**
1786	125.6	.74	Arrow is clearly visible. (XII) *Kumāra*	Garland suspended from fingers of the r. hand. L. hand on thigh. Symbol ⁘, blurred. Legend blurred. **Pl. XXIX. 10.**

No.	Wt.	Size	Obverse	Reverse
1787	127.5	.73	Lion only half on the flan. (XII) *Kumāragu*. .. ...(IX) *krama*.	Garland in r. hand; l. hand on thigh. Symbol ⁂, but incomplete and blurred. *Simhamahe* **Pl. XXIX. 11.**
1788	126.7	.77	King's body is rather bulky. (I) *Kumāra*.. .. ... (IX) *kkra*; *Kumāra* is blurred.	Garland in r. hand. L. hand on thigh. Symbol ⁂ *Simhamaha*, blurred. **Pl. XXIX. 12.**
1789	126.7	.74	(XII) *Kumāragu*	R. and l. hand as above. Symbol ∴ *Simhamahendra*, blurred. **Pl. XXIX. 13.**
1790	127	.79	(I) *Kumāra* Letters are bold and clear.	R. and l. hand as above. Symbol ∴ *Samhamahandra*, very much blurred. **P. XXIX. 14.**
1791	122.3	.75	(XII) *Kumāragu*	R. and l. hand as above. Lion partly off the flan. Symbol ⁂, but blurred. *Samhamahandra*. **P. XXIX. 15.**
1792	126.2	.79	*Kumara* Crack in the edge at IX.	R. and l. hand as above. Lion's mouth is gaping. Symbol ⁂ *Simhamahendra*.

No.	Wt.	Size	Obverse	Reverse
1793	126.8	.77	*Kumāra*	Garland is off the flan. Symbol ⁙ *Simha-Mahendra*
1794	126.6	.75	Legend off.	Garland is visible. Symbol ⁙ *Simha-Mahendra.*

ELEPHANT-RIDER AND LION-SLAYER TYPE : 4 COINS

No.	Wt.	Size	Obverse	Reverse
			King wearing coat and waist-band, bare-headed, riding a caparisoned elephant, furiously advancing to r., raising his r. hand holding a dagger in the posture of attack. Dwarf behind him, holding a parasol over his head: A lion is in front of the elephant, which the latter is trampling with l. fore-foot; the lion tries to bite the r. front leg of the elephant by opening its jaw. Circular legend is uncertain and incomplete; it begins at XII with *Kshata*; very probably it may have been the following :— *KshataripuKumāragupto rājatrātā jayati ripūn.* क्षतरिपुकुमारगुप्तो राजत्राता जयति रिपून् । Pl. XXXVI. 40. Metre, Upagīti.	Goddess, nimbate, wearing earrings, necklace, bangles and armlets, with hair on head tied in a knot, standing three fourths to r. on a lotus, but looking to l., and holding in r. hand some indistinct object, before a peacock looking up towards it; l. hand rests on waist and holds a lotus with long stalk. The goddess is wearing a *sāri*, tied round the waist by a string (*nāḍī*), whose two ends are seen between her legs, and an upper garment, whose ends are hanging on her either side. No symbol. Legend partly on the l. and partly on r. *Siṁhanihantā Mahendragajaḥ.* सिङ्हनिहन्ता महेन्द्रगज :। Pl. XXXVII. 68.

No.	Wt.	Size	Obverse	Reverse
1795	125.8	.79	Top of the umbrella not visible. Elephant is not elegant, but its fury is well depicted. At (XII) *Kshatarapu*, at (II) *trata*. Normal condition.	(IX) *Sanhanaham-* (II) *ta Mahandragaja*. Legend blurred. **Pl. XXX. 1.**
1796	126.8	.82	Elephant is more elegant, but equally furious. The umbrella in the attendant's hand is visible on this specimen. Lion is only half accommodated on the flan. Legend beginning at XII, *Kshata* (*rapa* ?); at (VIII) *yata ra*, at (X) *pun*. Normal condition.	The plumage of the peacock is full and beautiful. (X) *Sinhani* (II) *hamta Mahandragaja*. The first three letters of the legend are very distinct on this coin. **Pl. XXX. 2.**
1797	115.2	.77	Attendant is poorly represented on this specimen and the umbrella in his hand is off the flan. The legend is indistinct and incomplete; it begins at XII with *Kshatara*. One crack in the edge at II. Worn out.	Toes of the peacock are distinctly shown. No symbol. (X) *Sinhani* (II) *hanta Mahendragaja*, rather blurred. **Pl. XXX. 3.**
1798	127	.75	Lion is slightly blurred. At (I) *Kshata*, at (X) *pun*. Good condition.	Peacock is beautiful. No symbol. Legend on the l., (X) *Sinhani* (II) *hanta Mahandragaja*, blurred and truncated **Pl. XXX. 4.**

RHINOCEROS-SLAYER TYPE : 4 COINS

No.	Wt.	Size	Obverse	Reverse
			King bare-headed, with flowing frizzled locks (*alaka*) on head, riding on caparisoned horse to r., wearing buttoned coat, waist-band and trousers, leaning forward and attacking a rhinoceros with the sword in r. hand. Horse raises up its head, slightly frightened. Rhinoceros stands at bay, turning back its head to attack, mouth being open. Rhinoceros is engraved realistically and beautifully, the horn on the head, two ears, l. eye, circular spots on the body, the tail and the four feet being all clear. Circular legend is (XII) (*Bhartā* ?) *khaḍgatrātā Kumāragupto jayatyaniśaṁ*. (भर्ता ?)खड्गत्राता कुमारगुप्तो जयत्यनिशम् । Pl. XXXV. 36. Metre, Upagīti.	Within dotted border goddess Gaṅgā, not nimbate, standing to l. on an elephant-headed crocodile, holding lotus with long stalk in its trunk. R. hand of the goddess is extended, forefinger pointing out at some object, not visible on the coin, l. hand hanging down by the side empty. Hair on the head of the goddess is tied in a knot behind and she wears earrings, necklace and bangles. Behind the goddess a female attendant holding in her r. hand a *chhatra* (umbrella), without fillet, its staff being denoted by a dotted line; her l. hand is on the waist. Symbol to r. Legend on the l., *Śrī-Mahendrakhaḍga(ḥ)* श्रीमहेन्द्रखड्गः । Pl. XXXVII. 63.
1799	127.1	.75	King's head slightly off the flan. Buttons of the coat clear. All four legs of the rhinoceros are visible.	Stalk of the lotus partly visible. Symbol on r., 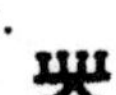 [*Śrī-Mahe*] *ndrakhaḍga* **Pl. XXX. 5.**

No.	Wt.	Size	Obverse	Reverse
			.. ...(l) *ta Kumāra-gupta jayatya* (*tā Kumāragupto jayatya*) Letters in sharp relief. Good condition.	
1800	125.4	.78	The buttons of the coat are very clear. Legs of the rhinoceros are just visible. (X).. *khagatrata Kumāragupta ja*, (..*khaḍgatrātā Kumāragupto ja*), slightly blurred. Normal condition.	As above, but the feet of the goddess are turned, as if she was about to face to r., though actually she is facing l. The pointing forefinger of the r. hand is not clear on this specimen. The elephant-headed crocodile holding the lotus in its snout is fully visible. The lotus can be clearly seen above the r. hand of the goddess. Female attendant is rather tall and blurred, but her breasts are prominently visible. *Śra-Mahandrakhaga*, blurred, but the letters *khaga* are fairly distinct. Symbol on the r.,  **Pl. XXX. 6.**
1801	128.1	.78	Buttons of the king's coat are not clear on this specimen. The feet and part of the lower part of the body of the rhinoceros are	Goddess is turned slightly to r., though she is actually looking to l. Crocodile is fully visible, as also the lotus stalk in its

No.	Wt.	Size	Obverse	Reverse
			truncated. (IX) (*Bha* ?) *tta kha-gatata* (*Bharttā khaḍga-trātā*). The lower loop of the crucial letter *kha* is quite distinct on this coin above the king's r. shoulder. Good condition.	snout, but the lotus is represented merely by four dots. The female attendant is blurred and indistinct. The dotted line of the staff of the umbrella is quite clear. *Śra-Mahandrakhaga*, the last two letters being blurred. Symbol on the right  **Pl. XXX. 7.**
1802	126.1	.78	Buttons of the coat faintly visible. Feet of the rhinoceros off the flan; the fury on its face is remarkable. (IX) (*Bha* ?) *ta kha-gatata* (*Bha* ?) *rtā khaḍgatrātā*). *Kha* above the r. shoulder has a broad triangular base. Good condition.	Crocodile, its tail, and snout holding the lotus stalk, as also the lotus are all very clear. Attendant is dwarfish as usual. Symbol on the r.,  but partly off. *Śra-Mahandakhaga*. **Pl. XXX. 8.**

AŚVAMEDHA TYPE : 4 COINS

Variety A : 2 coins

(Caparisoned horse to right)

No.	Wt.	Size	Obverse	Reverse
			Caparisoned horse with plaited mane standing to right before a *yūpa*, from which a pennon flies above the animal. The *raśanā* (girdle) and *chashāla* of the *yūpa* not shown. There is no string of beads above the horse, nor the letter *si* under it. Circular legend, not completely read, seems to be: *Devo jitaśatruḥ Kumāragupto'dhirāja.* देवो जितशत्रुः कुमारगुप्तो-धिराजा। Pl. XXXVI. 39.	Within dotted border, queen standing to left, wearing *sāri* and upper garment, holding *chouri* in right hand over right shoulder, l. hand hanging down, holding a small towel. In front of the queen is an ornamental *sūchi* with fillet hanging down. No symbol. Legend, *Srī-aśvamedha-Mahendrah.* श्रीअश्वमेधमहेन्द्र :। Pl. XXXVII. 66.
1803	126.7	.82	*Yūpa* and pedestal off the flan. *Deva jataśata* (IX) *Ku* There are three illegible letters before *dava.*	Queen's hair is falling on her back. *Sra-aśvamadha-Mahendra,* blurred. **Pl. XXX. 9.**
1804	127.6	.8	*Yūpa* and a part of its pedestal are partly visible. Pennon flies over the horse. Blurred traces of truncated legend between	Queen's hair is tied in a knot behind the head. No symbol. *Srī-aśvamedhamaha* **Pl. XXX. 10.**

No.	Wt.	Size	Obverse	Reverse
			IX and I, probably reading *Dava jataśata Kuma*. *Ku* is fairly clear at XII.	

Variety B : 2 coins

(Bare horse to left)

No.	Wt.	Size	Obverse	Reverse
1805	126.7	.88	Bare horse, standing to l. in front of a *yūpa* on a pedestal, pennon flying over it. At (XII) jata (?), at (V) *Kumāragupta* Good condition.	Queen as in variety A. No symbol. *Srī-aśvamedhaa-Maha* **Pl. XXX. 11.**
1806	126.5	.83	*Yūpa* and pedestal are more fully visible than on the above. (XII) *Dava jataśatru Ku* (V) *māragupta*. Good condition.	Queen's features indistinct. Towel in the r. hand looks like a rope. No symbol. *Srī-aśvamedha-Ma* **Pl. XXX. 12.**

ELEPHANT-RIDER TYPE : 3 COINS

No.	Wt.	Size	Obverse	Reverse
			King bare-headed, with diadem, coat, waistband, necklace, earrings, armlets and wristlets, riding a caparisoned elephant, furiously marching to l., holding goad in r. hand, l. hand resting on waist. Behind the king, a seated attendant holding an umbrella over him. Circular legend, rather uncertain, but	Within dotted border, Lakshmī, nimbate, standing on a lotus, facing, wearing earrings, necklace, bangles, anklets, a peculiar flat headdress on the head, *sāri* and an upper garment, whose ends fall on her either side. Her r. hand is bent up and holds a lotus creeper with buds

No.	Wt.	Size	Obverse	Reverse
			most probably, *KshataripuKumāragupto rājatrātā jayati ripūn*, *n* being widely separated from *pū*. क्षतरिपुकुमारगुप्तो राजत्राता जयति रिपून्। Pl. XXXVI. 40. Metre, Upagīti.	and flowers; l. hand rests on waist holding a cornucopiae. Conch in lower r. corner. No symbol. Legend on r., *Srī-Mahendragajaḥ*. श्रीमहेन्द्रगजः। Pl. XXXVII. 67.
1807	126	.84	Only the staff of the umbrella is visible on this coin. The legend begins at III; its first four letters are indistinct, but the subscript of *Ksha* is clear. Under the feet of the elephant we have the letters, *(K)umāragupta ra*; *ma* and *ra* are blurred and only the medial *u* of *Ku* is visible. Between the front foot and the trunk, we have *jatrata*, *tra* being quite distinct. Between X and I, there is *jayata rapu*, rather blurred. Normal condition.	Besides the lotus on which Lakshmī is standing there is a half lotus near her r. foot and the plant has two more lotuses, one at X and one near the halo. *Srā-Mahandragaja*; the second and third letters are indistinct and can be determined only with the help of other coins. **Pl. XXXI. 1.**
1808	129.1	.85	The umbrella is fully visible. Legend beginning at II, *n. Kshatara* behind the umbrella bearer; then follow *puKumaragupta*; the letter *Ku* is between the hind legs; the next five	Cornucopiae is indistinct. *Srī-Mahendragaja*. **Pl. XXXI. 2.**

No.	Wt.	Size	Obverse	Reverse
			letters are blurred; above the elephant's head, *yata rapu*. Normal condition.	
1809	125.4	.75	Staff and fillet of parasol visible, but not its top. Legend beginning at III n. *Kshatarapu*, under the elephant's feet, traces of *ragupta*; above the elephant's head, *tarapu*. Good condition.	Legend, *Śra-Mahendragaja*. **Pl. XXXI. 3.**

LYRIST TYPE : 2 COINS

No.	Wt.	Size	Obverse	Reverse
1810	125.3	.75	King, nimbate, wearing earrings, necklace and armlets, sitting on a straight-backed couch (*paryaṅkikā*), whose three sides are clearly visible; r. leg folded on the couch, l. leg over the r. one and hanging below the couch. Fingers of the king's r. hand are playing over a four stringed lute placed in the lap, the l. hand above the lute, its fingers gesticulating appreciation. Legend beginning at I, *Maharajadhirajaśrī-Kumaragupta*. (*Mahārājādhirāja-śrī-Kumāraguptaḥ*.) महाराजाधिराजश्रीकुमारगुप्त : । Pl. XXXVI. 38.	Within dotted border, goddess (or queen ?), with earrings, sitting on a couch with straight back. Two sides of the couch, as also its four legs of the *tāpdār* design are clearly visible. R. leg of the goddess is folded under the couch and the l. leg is hanging down in its front. R. hand of the goddess is bent up and holds a flower of long stalk; the l. hand rests on the couch. No symbol. Legend on the l., *Kumāraguptaḥ*. कुमारगुप्त : । Pl. XXXVII. 61.

No.	Wt.	Size	Obverse	Reverse
			Letters *Kumāra* are under the couch and *gupta* at XI. The beginning letter is just behind the king's head above the back of the couch. Very slightly worn at the edge.	The second letter is doubtful, but it can hardly be any thing other than *mā*. **Pl. XXXI. 4.**
1811	126	.8	As above. Halo visible only on r. Only two legs of the couch are visible. Legend as above, but rather blurred on r. (I) *Maharajadharajaśra-Ku*..(X) *gupta*.	As above. Three legs only of the throne are visible. No symbol. Legend on the l., *Kumāragupta*. **Pl. XXXI. 5.**

APRATIGHA TYPE : 8 COINS

No.	Wt.	Size	Obverse	Reverse
			A male figure standing in the centre, wearing a *dhoti*, with folds hanging between the legs; hands folded at the waist, a protube-rance on the head as on the Buddha images, or hair tied in a knot. To the r., a female figure, standing to l. slightly bent forward, her hair tied in a knot on the head, wearing a *sāri* and tight *kañchukī*; l. hand on the waist, r. hand bent up and raised in the attitude of *vitarka* (argumentation); fingers almost touching	Within dotted border, goddess Lakshmī, nimbate, seated facing on a beautiful, full blown, double petalled lotus, her left hand on waist akimbo; right hand is bent up, holding a lotus with a long stalk. The lotus is conventionally denoted by four thick and elongated dots, looking like the symbol , but as a regular symbol occurs lower below,  is to be taken as a conventional lotus. Crescent in the r.

No.	Wt.	Size	Obverse	Reverse
			the face of the central figure. To the l. of the central figure, another figure a male, standing to r., wearing a close fitting cap, l. hand holding a shield in front of the torso, r. hand bent up and holding *Garuḍadhvaja* just behind the central figure. Legend written horizontally but in lines placed vertically between the central figure and the figures on its either side; on r. side, to be read from top to bottom, *Kumāra*; on left side to be read from bottom to top, *guptaḥ*. None of the figures is nimbate. Circular legend, not yet read.[1]	upper corner in most cases. Symbol on l. in the centre, Legend on the r., *Apratighaḥ*. अप्रतिघ: । Pl. XXXVII. 69.
1812	123	.75	Folded hands fairly clear; no crescent above the king's head. *Kumara* is blurred, but *guptaḥ* is quite distinct. Circular legend, *Papurapaparapa* (?)	Crescent to the r. of the head of the goddess. Symbol *Apratagha*. **Pl. XXXI. 6.**
1813	121.4	.72	No crescent above the king's head. Palms folded at the chest rather	Lower bud on the l. slightly truncated. Crescent on the r. in

[1]For the discussion of the legend, see Introduction pp. cxi-xii.

No.	Wt.	Size	Obverse	Reverse
			indistinct. Staff of the *Garuḍadhvaja* is clear. *Kumāraguptaḥ*, written as above; the *visaraga* at the end being very distinct. Circular legend considerably truncated.	the upper corner. Symbol *Apratigha*. **Pl. XXXI. 7.**
1814	121.5	.72	The bump (*kakud*) or the knot of hair on the head is very prominent. *Garuḍadhvaja* is clear. Crescent above the king's head to right. *Kumāraguptaḥ*. under two arms. Circular legend considerably truncated.	Crescent in the upper r. corner. Left lotus bud only partly visible. Symbol *Apratagha*. **Pl. XXXI. 8.**
1815	120.7	.73	No crescent above the king's head. *Kumāraguptaḥ* under two arms. Circular legend fairly well preserved on the right, but illegible.	No border of dots. Symbol *Apratighaḥ*. Medial vowel of *ti* is quite distinct. **Pl. XXXI. 9.**
1816	121.5	.73	Crescent above the central figure. *Kumāraguptaḥ*, rather blurred. Circular legend not legible.	Crescent in the r. upper corner. Symbol *Apratighaḥ*, quite distinct. **Pl. XXXI. 10.**
1817	121	.71	A crescent between the central figure and the one on the right. *Kumāraguptaḥ*, as usual. Circular legend	No crescent in the r. upper corner. Dotted border on the left. Symbol *Apratighaḥ*,

No.	Wt.	Size	Obverse	Reverse
			fairly well preserved on the l. Good condition.	very distinct. **Pl. XXXI. 11.**
1818	120.5	.78	Garuḍa on the standard quite distinct. *Kumāra* is quite clear, so also *guptaḥ*. Circular legend, indistinct and truncated.	The flan was ill adjusted on the l., and as a result only one of three lotus buds has come out on the l.; the symbol is truncated and only three out of the four dots above it are visible. Symbol  *Aparaṭigha*, very clear. **Pl. XXXI. 12.**
1819	122.3	.75	Crescent above the king's head. Garuḍa standard very distinct. *Kumāragupta* written as usual but *Kumāra* rather blurred. Circular legend indistinct.	Dotted border not on the flan. Crescent in the r. upper corner. Two buds of the lotus stalk are visible. Symbol 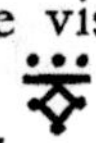 *Apratigha*. **Pl. XXXI. 13.**

KING AND THE QUEEN TYPE : 1 COIN

No.	Wt.	Size	Obverse	Reverse
1820	126.7	.73	King standing to r., bare-headed and with frizzled hair, wearing coat, waist-band, *dhoti*, earrings, necklace, wristlets and armlets. The king's l. hand is on the hilt of the sword at his waist and he is offering by the r. hand, bent up, a bunch of flowers to the queen	Goddess, nimbate, seated facing, on lion couchant to r., holding a lotus in r. hand bent up and leaning on the l. hand resting on the thigh. This posture of the goddess is similar to her posture on the reverse of some of the Archer type coins of

No.	Wt.	Size	Obverse	Reverse
			standing to r. facing him. The queen wears earrings, necklace and bangles; her r. hand is on the waist and the l. one is hanging down. Crescent between the king and the queen. Traces of legend on the r.	this ruler, see Pl. XX. 8. The goddess wears earrings, necklace, bangles, armlets and a girdle. The folds of her *sāri* are clearly visible on the folded feet. Dotted border all round.
			Kamara can be seen truncated from III; *ma* is of eastern variety.	No symbol. Legend on the r., *Śrī-Kumāraguptaḥ*.
			Good condition.	**Pl. XXXI. 14.**

[SKANDAGUPTA] KRAMĀDITYA

CHHATRA TYPE : 1 COIN

No.	Wt.	Size	Obverse	Reverse
1821	130	.8	King with curly hair and bare body standing to l., wearing *dhoti*, waist-band, earrings, necklace and wristlets, offering by outstretched r. hand oblations on altar, (off the flan); l. hand on the hilt of the sword. Behind the king a fat-bellied dwarf with waist-band and curly hair, standing with legs slightly bent, holding a parasol with fillets in the r. hand (invisible on the coin), l. hand hanging down. Only the staff and the fillets of the parasol are visible on the coin. Legend beginning at I, incomplete; *Vijitavana*. Probably its full form was *Vijitāvaniravanipatiḥ Śrī-Skandagupto divaṁ jayati*. विजितावनिरवनिपतिः श्रीस्कन्द-गुप्तो दिवं जयति । [?] Pl. XXXV. 41. Metre, Upagīti. Good condition.	Goddess Lakshmī, nimbate, standing three-fourths to l. holding a noose in the r. hand, slightly bent and extended and a lotus with long stalk in the l. hanging down by the side. The lotus stalk penetrates the nimbus on the l. and the lotus is within it. The goddess wears earrings, a necklace, and bangles. Symbol , incomplete. Legend on the l., *Kk:ramāditya* (*ḥ*). क्क्रमादित्य : । Pl. XXXVII. 70. **Pl. XXXI. 15.**

SUCCESSORS OF KUMĀRAGUPTA I

(Not represented in the Hoard)

Skandagupta

Archer type, small size

No.	Wt.	Size	Obverse	Reverse
1	130.2	.75	King standing left, holding bow in left hand and arrow in right. Garuḍa standard behind his right hand. Under left arm, *Skanda* written perpendicularly. Circular legend, *Jayati mahītalaṁ* ..... *sudhanvī*, only partly visible.	Goddess, nimbate, seated facing on lotus with noose in right hand and lotus in left. Symbol  *Śrī-Skandaguptaḥ*. [*B.M.C.G.D.* XIX. 1] **Pl. XXXII. 1.**

Archer type, large size

No.	Wt.	Size	Obverse	Reverse
2	142.8	.85	King as above. *Skanda* with crescent above under left arm. Legend, not fully read; probably it was *Para-hitakārī rājā jayati divaṁ śrī-Kramādityaḥ*.	Goddess Lakshmī, as above. Symbol incomplete. *Kramādityaḥ*. [*B.M.C.G.D.* XIX. 11] **Plate XXXII. 2.**

King and Lakshmī type[1]

No.	Wt.	Size	Obverse	Reverse
3		.75	Skandagupta standing to right wearing *dhoti* and usual ornaments, torso bare, holding bow by the	Goddess Lakshmī as above. Symbol incomplete. *Śrī-Skandaguptaḥ*. [Bibl. Nat.]

[1] Some scholars regard the lady on the obverse as the queen.

No.	Wt.	Size	Obverse	Reverse
			middle by his left hand near his left knee; right hand, holding arrow, rests on right hip. In his front goddess Lakshmī standing to left, holding some indistinct object in her right hand, to which the king is looking with interest; there is a lotus in her left hand. Garuḍa standard between the king and the goddess.	[*B.M.C.G.D.* XIX. 9] **Plate XXXII. 3.**

Ghaṭotkachgupta

Archer type

No.	Wt.	Size	Obverse	Reverse
4		.8	King, nimbate, standing to left holding bow in left hand and arrow in right. The Garuḍa standard behind right hand. Under left arm, *Ghaṭo*, with crescent above. Circular legend, indistinct.	Lakshmī, nimbate, seated facing on lotus holding fillet in right hand and lotus in left. Symbol  *Kramādityaḥ.* Leningrad Museum. [*B.M.C.G.D.* XXIV. 5] **Pl. XXXII. 4.**

Narasiṁhagupta

Archer type

No.	Wt.	Size	Obverse	Reverse
5	144.5	.9	King, nimbate, standing to left holding bow in left hand and arrow in right. Garuḍa standard behind right hand. Under	Goddess Lakshmī seated as above. Symbol incomplete. *Bālādityaḥ.* [*B.M.C.G.D.*, XXII. 7] **Pl. XXXII. 5.**

No.	Wt.	Size	Obverse	Reverse
			left arm, *Nara*. Between king's feet, *Gō*. Legend, incomplete, ending with *jayati* (?) *Narasiṁhaguptaḥ*.	

Kumāragupta II

Archer type

No.	Wt.	Size	Obverse	Reverse
6	148.7	.8	King standing with bow and arrow as above. Under left arm, *Ku*. Between his feet, *jā*.	Goddess Lakshmī as above. Symbol *Śrī-kkramādityaḥ*. [*B.M.C.G.D.* XXIII. 4] **Pl. XXXII. 6.**

Budhagupta

Archer type

No.	Wt.	Size	Obverse	Reverse
7			King standing to left as above with bow and arrow. Garuḍa standard behind right hand. Under left arm, *Budha*. Circular legend off.	Goddess Lakshmī, seated as above. Symbol Legend off. [Banaras Hindu University.] [*J.N.S.I.* XII p. 112] **Pl. XXXII. 7.**

Vishṇugupta

Archer type

No.	Wt.	Size	Obverse	Reverse
8	149	.8	King standing as above with bow and arrow. Garuḍa standard behind right hand. Under left arm below crescent, *Vishṇu*. Between feet, *ru*. Circular legend off.	Goddess Lakshmī, as above. Symbol off. *Śrī-Chandrādityaḥ*. [*B.M.C.G.D.* XXIII. 9] **Pl. XXXII. 8.**

Vainyagupta

Archer type

No.	Wt.	Size	Obverse	Reverse
9	148	.8	King standing with bow and arrow as above. Garuḍa standard behind right hand. Under left arm *Vainya*. Between feet, *Bha*. Circular legend, not yet completely read; *Para*——— *Dvādaśādityaḥ*.	Goddess Lakshmī as above. Symbol incomplete. *Śrī-Dvādaśādityaḥ*. [*B.M.C.G.D.*, XXIII. 7] **Pl. XXXII. 9.**

Prakāśāditya

Horseman-Lion-slayer type

No.	Wt.	Size	Obverse	Reverse
10	145.8	.8	King on horseback to right, attacking lion in his front leaping at horse, by a sword; bow round his body with string over left shoulder; Garuḍa standard behind right hand. Beneath the horse, *ru* or *u*. Circular legend ending with *Vijitya vasudhāṁ divaṁ jayati*.	Lakshmī, nimbate, seated as above. Symbol  *Śrī-Prakāśādityaḥ*. (Indian Museum) [*B.M.C.G.D.*, XXII. 3] **Pl. XXXII. 10.**

Jayagupta

Archer type

No.	Wt.	Size	Obverse	Reverse
11	131.8	.8	King, nimbate, standing to left; holding bow in left hand and arrow in right.	Goddess Lakshmī seated facing on lotus. On the left, an elephant sprinkl-

No.	Wt.	Size	Obverse	Reverse
			Chakra standard behind right hand, not visible on the present piece. Beneath left arm, *Jaya*. No trace of circular legend.	ing her with water. (Not clear on this specimen). No symbol. *Śrī-Prakāṇḍayaśāḥ*. [*B.M.C.G.D.*, XXIV. 6] **Pl. XXXII. 11.**

Śaśāṅka

Śiva type

No.	Wt.	Size	Obverse	Reverse
12	145.3	.75	Siva, nimbate, reclining on the bull in his front, his left hand uplifted. Moon on the left. On right, written vertically, *Sri-Śa*. Below *Jaya*.	Lakshmī, nimbate, seated facing on lotus with lotus in left hand; right hand empty. Above, on either side of the goddess, elephant sprinkling water over her. No symbol. On right, *Śrī-Śaśāṅkaḥ* [*B.M.C.G.D.*, XXIII. 16.] **Pl. XXXII. 12.**

Samāchāradeva Narendrāditya

No.	Wt.	Size	Obverse	Reverse
13	148.2	.9	King standing to left with bow in left hand and arrow in right. Bull standard behind right hand. Beneath left arm, *Samā*, between feet *chā*. No trace of circular legend.	Goddess Lakshmī, seated facing on lotus, holding fillet in right hand and lotus in left. Symbol on left. *Śrī-Narendrādityaḥ*.[1] (Indian Museum) [*B.M.C.G.D.*, XXIV. 4] **Pl. XXXII. 13.**

[1] This legend has been read as *Śrī-Narendravinīta* by N. K. Bhattasali.

Ancient imitations of Gupta coinage

(Issuers unknown)

No.	Wt.	Size	Obverse	Reverse
14	86.5	.85	King standing to left with bow and arrow. Under his left arm, a horse. Behind right hand, horse-headed (?) standard. *Śrī* in front of king's face.	Within border of thick dots, eight-handed goddess standing. No symbol. On the right, crude imitation of a Gupta legend. [*B.M.C.G.D.*, XXIV.17] **Pl. XXXII. 14.**
15	92.5	.85	As above, but without the horse, on the right and the letter *Śrī* in front of the king's face.	As above. [*B.M.C.G.D.*, XXIV. 18.] **Pl. XXXII. 15.**

DESCRIPTION OF THE FIGURES

On the Bayana Hoard Coins

ILLUSTRATING COSTUMES, FURNITURE AND WEAPONS

(Plates XXXVIII-XLVII)

The reference to the Plate in Clarendon type at the beginning of each entry refers to the Plate where the figure is drawn; the subsequent reference to the plate in the bracket given in the ordinary type refers to the original photograph of the coin in the plates of this work from which the drawing is prepared. This will enable the reader to judge whether the figure drawing is accurate or not.

Male costume

CHANDRAGUPTA I

Standard Type

Pl. XXXVIII, Fig. 1 (Pl. I. 1). Beaded helmet with peaked top; tunic with buttoned or embroidered front and pointed ends; shoes decorated with a vertical series of bosses or buttons.

Pl. XXXVIII, Fig. 2 (Pl. I. 2). Tunic in front has a panel of oblique lines, perhaps indicating embroidered pattern or fasteners; full boots decorated with buttons, reaching little below the knees; the pleated fold of the *dhoti* seen in between the legs.

Pl. XXXVIII, Fig. 3 (Pl. I. 5). Tunic tied securely with *kamarband* in several folds, with one end hanging freely on the right; *dhoti* and shoes.

Pl. XXXVIII, Fig. 4 (Pl. I. 10). Skull-cap decorated with a boss; the tunic decorated on both sides with curved panels of circles, perhaps indicating sequins or embroidered patterns.

SAMUDRAGUPTA

Standard Type

Pl. XXXVIII, Fig. 5 (Pl. 1. 11). Skull-cap with beaded edge; tunic with pointed end, the sleeves folded at the elbows; *kamarband* in several folds; light *chūrīdār* trousers.

Pl. XXXVIII, Fig. 6 (Pl. I. 12). Tunic with pointed ends; sleeves folded; *dupaṭṭā* worn across the chest; buttoned shoes.

Pl. XXXVIII, Fig. 7 (Pl. I. 13). Skull-cap with scalloped edge; tunic with folded sleeves; shoes with buttons.

Pl. XXXVIII, Fig. 8 (Pl. II. 1). Dome-shaped cap with upturned, scalloped edge; tunic with pointed end, its sleeves either folded or pleated; trousers with wrinkles.

Pl. XXXVIII, Fig. 9 (Pl. II. 3). Conical cap decorated with streamers; tunic with pointed ends; *kamarband*; trousers with buttons.

Pl. XXXIX, Fig. 10 (Pl. II. 6). Conical cap; tunic with pointed ends; *dupaṭṭā* wrapped round the right hand; *dhotī* and boots.

Pl. XXXIX, Fig. 11 (Pl. II. 9). Tunic with pointed ends; folded end of *dupaṭṭā* visible on the waist; *dhoti* and boots.

Pl. XXXIX, Fig. 12 (Pl. II. 10). Skull-cap with beaded edge, tunic with pointed ends secured with a belt; *shalwār* decorated with buttons or bosses.

Pl. XXXIX, Fig. 13 (Pl. II. 11). Peaked conical cap; loose pointed tunic; *shalwār* with bosses; shoes.

Pl. XXXIX, Fig. 14 (Pl. V. 6). Skull-cap with streamers; tunic with folded sleeves; *kamarband*; *dhoti*; shoes.

Pl. XXXIX, Fig. 15 (Pl. V. 13). Hemispherical cap; tunic with pointed ends; *dhoti* with pleated end; *kamarband*; buttoned boots.

Lyrist Type

Pl. XXXIX, Fig. 16 (Pl. VI. 3). Skull-cap decorated with pearls running from the forehead to the back of the neck; short *dhoti*.

Archer Type

Pl. XXXIX, Fig. 17 (Pl. VI. 10). Turban with a plaque; tight fitting tunic; *kamarband*; *dhoti* with its pleated end tucked behind.

CHANDRAGUPTA II

Archer Type

Pl. XXXIX, Fig. 18 (Pl. VIII. 10). Skull-cap with streamers, heavily embroidered tunic; *kamarband* tied in a knot on the proper left; *dhoti* with the pleated end tucked behind; shoes.

Pl. XL, Fig. 19 (Pl. VIII. 11). Beaded conical cap with streamers; tunic secured with a *kamarband,* its ends dangling between the legs; *dhoti* reaching upto the knees.

Pl. XL, Fig. 20 (Pl. VIII. 13). Close fitting skull cap; tunic with pointed ends secured by a *kamarband* tied in a knot on the proper left; *dhoti* with pleated end tucked behind; shoes.

Pl. XL, Fig. 21 (Pl. VIII. 15). Tasselled cap; pointed tunic tied with a *kamarband* on the proper left; short *dhoti.*

Pl. XL, Fig. 22 (Pl. IX. 2). Full sleeved tunic; short *dhoti*; shoes decorated with buttons.

Pl. XL, Fig. 23 (Pl. X. 5). Beaded helmet; heavily embroidered tunic; short *dhoti* with its pleated end tucked behind; *dupaṭṭā* on the shoulders; short *dhoti* or shorts; full boots with buttons.

Pl. XL, Fig. 24 (Pl. IX. 14). Tunic; *kamarband*; *shalwār*; shoes.

Pl. XL, Fig. 25 (Pl. X. 5). Tunic embroidered at the middle and the neck; *kamarband*; long pleated *dhoti.*

Pl. XL, Fig. 26 (Pl. X. 13). Tunic; shorts or short *dhoti*; buttoned boots.

Pl. XL, Fig. 27 (Pl. XI. 13). Tunic; *kamarband* tied on the proper left; *dhoti*; shoes.

Pl. XLI, Fig. 28 (Pl. XII. 12). Bare body; shorts; *kamarband* tied on the left.

Pl. XLI, Fig. 29 (Pl. XII. 13). Bare body; shorts (*janghiyā*); *kamarband.*

Horseman Type

Pl. XLI, Fig. 30 (Pl. XIII. 8). Tunic; *kamarband* with its two ends fluttering in the air; shorts.

Pl. XLI, Fig. 31 (Pl. XIII. 12). Shorts; *kamarband.*

Pl. XLI, Fig. 32 (Pl. XIV. 10). Scull cap; tunic; shorts; *kamarband*; shoes.

Pl. XLI, Fig. 33 (Pl. XIV. 12). Skull cap with streamers ; tunic ; *kamarband* ; *dhoti.*

Pl. XLI, Fig. 34 (Pl. XIV. 13). Tunic ; *kamarband* ; trousers ; stirrup.

Chhatra Type

Pl. XLII, Fig. 35 (Pl. XV. 6). Turban with a plaque ; tunic ; shorts secured by a *kamarband* ; shoes.

Pl. XLII, Fig. 36 (Pl. XV. 14). Tunic secured with a *kamarband* ; short *dhoti* or shorts ; *paryastaka.*

Lion-slayer Type

Pl. XLII, Fig. 37 (Pl. XVI. 10). Flowered cap ; half-sleeved tunic without pointed ends secured with a *kamarband* tied on the left ; *dhoti* with its ends hanging freely ; shoes.

Pl. XLII, Fig. 38 (Pl. XVI. 14). Light turban or *tiara* with a plaque ; shorts.

Pl. XLII, Fig. 39 (Pl. XVII. 5). Shorts (*jaṅghiyā*) secured with a *kamarband,* its knotted end fluttering in the air.

Pl. XLII, Fig. 40 (Pl. XVII. 10). *Lañgot* secured with a *kamar-band,* its free ends hanging on the right.

Pl. XLII, Fig. 41 (Pl. XVII. 11). Hair covered with a scarf ; half-sleeved tunic secured by a *kamarband* tied on the proper left ; short *dhoti* with its pleated end tucked behind.

Pl. XLII, Fig. 42 (Pl. XVII. 14). Light turban decorated with a plaque ; half-sleeved tunic secured with a *kamarband* tied on the proper left ; its ends hanging freely ; short *dhoti* with its pleated end tucked behind.

Couch Type

Pl. XLII, Fig. 43 (Pl. XVIII. 13). Beaded hemispherical cap ; *dupaṭṭā* and *dhoti.*

KUMĀRAGUPTA I

Archer Type

Pl. XLIII, Fig. 44 (Pl. XIX. 3). Light tiara ; half-sleeved tunic secured with a *kamarband* tied on the left.

Pl. XLIII, Fig. 45 (Pl. XIX. 12). Tunic beaded at the sleeves, the neck and front ; *dhoti* with its pleated end tucked behind.

Pl. XLIII, Fig. 46 (Pl. XX. 2). Tunic as in Fig. 45; belt; knickers; shoes.

Pl. XLIII, Fig. 47 (Pl. XX. 5). Half-sleeved tunic with pointed ends; *dhoti* reaching the knees with its pleated end tucked behind.

Pl. XLIII, Fig. 48 (Pl. XX. 8). Half-sleeved tunic as in Fig. 45; short heavily pleated *dhoti* with one end tucked behind.

Pl. XLIII, Fig. 49 (Pl. XX. 15). Half-sleeved tunic with beaded sleeves and the front secured with a belt; short *dhoti*.

Swordman Type

Pl. XLIII, Fig. 50 (Pl. XXXI. 8). Half sleeved tunic secured with a belt; short *dhoti* with its pleated end tucked behind.

Chhatra Type

Pl. XLIII, Fig. 51 (Pl. XXVI. 15). Pleated *dhoti* secured with a *kamarband*; its ends hanging freely on either side.

The Costumes of Women

CHANDRAGUPTA I

Pl. XLIV, Fig. 52 (Pl. I. 1). Beaded veil; full sleeved tunic secured with belt; heavily pleated *sārī*; *chādar* or *dupaṭṭā* covering the shoulders.

Pl. XLIV, Fig. 53 (Pl. I. 2). Veil; *dupaṭṭā*; bodice and *sārī* reaching the ankles.

Pl. XLIV, Fig. 54 (Pl. I. 6). Veil decorated with pearls; tunic; *dupaṭṭā* on the shoulders, its free end hanging loose; *sārī*.

Pl. XLIV, Fig. 55 (Pl. I. 6). Full tunic reaching the feet; *dupaṭṭā*.

SAMUDRAGUPTA

Standard Type

Pl. XLIV, Fig. 56 (Pl. I. 11). Bodice, heavily pleated *chādar* and *sārī*.

Pl. XLIV, Fig. 57 (Pl. I. 12). Tunic; *dupaṭṭā* worn transversely on the chest; *sārī*.

Pl. XLIV, Fig. 58 (Pl. II. 3). Beaded veil; heavily pleated *chādar*; bodice; *sārī* reaching the feet.

Pl. XLIV, Fig. 59 (Pl. II. 6). Beaded veil; *chādar*; bodice; *sārī* to which *paryastaka* is attached.

Pl. XLIV, Fig. 60 (Pl. IV. 5). Dattadevī wears a veil; *dupaṭṭā*, *sārī* with its pleated end hanging in front and *kamarband* with its loose end hanging freely on the right.

BATTLE-AXE TYPE

Pl. XLIV, Fig. 61 (Pl. II. 8). *Chādar*, bodice and *sārī*.

LYRIST TYPE

Pl. XLV, Fig. 62 (Pl. VI. 5). *Dupaṭṭā*, long *sārī* and bodice.

KĀCHA

Pl. XLV, Fig. 63 (Pl. VI. 14). Bodice; *dupaṭṭā* on the shoulders with both ends hanging freely; *sārī* reaching down the feet with the pleated end tucked in front.

CHANDRAGUPTA II

ARCHER TYPE

Pl. XLV, Fig. 64 (Pl. XI. 7). Half-sleeved bodice and *sārī*.

Pl. XLV, Fig. 65 (Pl. XI. 11). Half-sleeved bodice; *sārī* with zone.

HORSEMAN TYPE

Pl. XLV, Fig. 66 (Pl. XIII, 12). Bodice; *sārī* with many folds reaching the feet.

CHHATRA TYPE

Pl. XLV, Fig. 67 (Pl. XV, 4). *Sārī*; bodice; *dupaṭṭā* on the shoulders, its ends hanging loosely.

Pl. XLV, Fig. 68 (Pl. XV. 10). Spiralled headdress; the *dupaṭṭā* hanging loose; *kamarband*; shorts underneath.

Pl. XLV, Fig. 69 (Pl. XV. 14). Bodice; *sārī*, broad zone.

LION-SLAYER TYPE

Pl. XLV, Fig. 70 (Pl. XVII. 11). Bodice; *dupaṭṭā*; *kamarband*; *sārī*.

Furniture

CHOWKIS

There are many kinds of stools with machine-turned legs; **Pl. XLVI,** Figs. 71-74 (Pls. I. 12; III. 12, 14; V. 15). Their forms are either rectangular or oblong. Some of the sofas, **Pl. XLVI,** Figs. 75-77 (Pls. VI. 2, 7; II. 14), are provided with high backs and were probably cushioned. The bed resembles its modern prototype ; **Pl. XLVI,** Fig. 78 (Pl. XVII. 12). It was at times provided with a back, **Pl. XLVI,** Fig. 79 (Pl. XVIII. 11).

The *moḍhā* or *āsandī* seems to have been used very extensively. It was hour-glass-shaped, **Pl. XLVI,** Fig. 80 (Pl. VI. 6) or bell-shaped, **Pl. XLVI,** Fig. 81 (Pl. VI. 6). The *moḍhā*, which was apparently made of cane, was decorated with zig-zag and leafy pattern, **Pl. XLVI,** Figs. 82-86. The umbrella was a simple affair without ribs, **Pl. XLVI,** Fig. 87.

The Gupta coins also represent certain interesting types of weapons. The recurved bows are of many kinds, **Pl. XLVI,** Fig. 88, **Pl. XLVII,** Figs. 89-92.

The battle axes, **Pl. XLVII,** Fig. 93, swords and knives **Pl. XLVII,** Figs. 94-100 have also been represented in different forms.

APPENDIX I

BIBLIOGRPHY

General Works

Banerji, R. D., Age of the Imperial Guptas. Banaras, 1933.

Basak, R. G., History of North-Eastern India. Calcutta, 1934.

Dandekar, R. N., History of the Guptas. Poona, 1941.

Fleet, J. F., Corpus Inscriptionum Indicarum, Vol. III. Calcutta, 1888.

Jayaswal, K. P., History of India, 150-350 A.D. Lahore, 1933.

„ Imperial History of India. Lahore, 1934.

Majumdar and Altekar, The Age of the Vākāṭakas and the Guptas, Lahore, 1946.

Ray Choudhari, H. C., Political History of Ancient India, 4th Ed. Calcutta, 1938.

Mookerji, R. K., Gupta Empire.

Saletore, R. N., Life in the Gupta Age. Bombay, 1943.

Upadhyaya, B., Gupta Sāmrājya-ka Itihāsa, in Hindi. Allahabad, 1939.

Books on Coins

Allan, J., Catalogue of the Coins of the Gupta Dynasties and of Śaśāṅka, King of Gauḍa (in the British Museum). London, 1914.

Smith, V. A., Catalogue of the Coins in the Indian Museum. Calcutta, 1906.

Altekar, A. S., Coinage of the Gupta Dynasty. Bombay, 1954.

„ Guptakālīna Mudrāe, (in Hindi). Patna, 1954.

Articles on the Gupta Coinage

Bibliography of Indian Coins, Part I, Bombay, 1950, gives a complete bibliography of the articles on Gupta coinage. Some articles have been published subsequent to 1950 in the *Journal of the Numismatic Society of India.*

Principal articles on Gupta coinage are mentioned here.

Altekar, A. S., Attribution of the Chandragupta-Kumāradevī Type, *N. S.* XLVII, 1937

Bhattasali, N. K., Notes on Gupta and Later Gupta Coinage, *N. S.* XXXVII, 1923.

„ Attribution of the Imitation Gupta Coins, *N. S.* XXXIX, 1925.

Cunningham, A., Silver Coins of the Guptas and their Successors, *C. A. S. R.*, IX. 21.

Diskalkar, D. B., Bamnala Find of 21 Gupta Gold Coins, *J.N.S.I.*, V. 135.

Gupta, P. L., Gold Coins of Kumāragupta II or III, *Ibid.* XII. 31.

„ Attribution of the Coins of Prakāśāditya, *Ibid*, XII. 34.

„ A unique Gold Coin of Chandragupta II, *Ibid*, IX. 147

Mirashi, V. V., A Note on the Khairtal Hoard of Mahendrāditya, *Ibid*, XI. 108.

„ *Apratigha* Type of Kumāragupta I, *Ibid*, XII. 68.

Narain, A. K., Budhagupta and his Gold Coins, *Ibid*, XII. 112.

Saraswati, S. K., A Gold Coin of Budhagupta, *I.C.*, I, 691.

Shastri, H. N., The Aśvamedha Coins of Samudragupta, *N.S.*, XXVI. 152.

Shivaramamurti, C., Chakravikrama Type. *J.N.S.I.*, XIII. 180.

Shitholey, B.S., The Art of Gupta Coins, *Ibid*, X. 119.

Smith, V. A., A classified and detailed Catalogue of the Gold Coins of the Imperial Gupta Dynasty, *J.A.S.B.*, 1884 p. 119.

„ The Coinage of the Early or the Imperial Gupta Dynasty of Northern India, *J.R.A.S.*, 1889, 1.

„ Observations on the Gupta Coinage, *Ibid*, 1893, 77.

Sohoni, S. V., Chandragupta I-Kumāradevī type. *J.N.S.I.*, V. 37.

APPENDIX II

KNOWN DISTRIBUTION OF THE HOARD COINS

In this Appendix, information is given about the distribution of some of the coins in the Bayana Hoard in the different Museums of India. Many of these coins have been identified with those in this printed Catalogue.

Palace Cabinet, Bharatpur

This cabinet possesses 78 coins and includes all the rare and unique types and varieties. The following 68 could be identified.

CHANDRAGUPTA I

King and Queen type, No. 1, Pl. I. 1

SAṂUDRAGUPTA

Standard type, var. A, No. 79, Pl. II. 11
" " var. B, No. 103, Pl. III. 1
" " var. C, No. 110, Pl. III. 3
" " var. D, No. 133, Pl. III. 10
" " var. E, No. 151, Pl. III. 14
Aśvamedha type, No. 159, Pl. IV. 6
" " No. 168, Pl. IV. 15
Battle-axe type, var. A, No. 174, Pl. V. 6
" " var. B, No. 181, Pl. V. 13
Archer type, var. A, No. 184, Pl. VI. 1
Lyrist type, var. A, No. 186, Pl. VI. 3
" " var. B, No. 189, Pl. VI. 6
Tiger-slayer type, var. A, No. 192, Pl. VI. 9

KĀCHA

Chakradhvaja type, No. 207, Pl. VII. 9
Garuḍadhvaja type, No. 209, Pl. VII. 11

CHANDRAGUPTA II

Archer type, class I, var. B, No. 235, Pl. VIII. 13
" " class II, var. D, No. 981, Pl. XII. 8
" " class II, var. E, No. 983, Pl. XII. 9

Archer type, class II, var. F, No. 984, Pl. XII. 10
" " class II, var. G, No. 985, Pl. XII. 11
" " class II, var. H, No. 994, Pl. XIII. 1
" " class II, var. I, No. 1004, Pl. XIII. 3
Horseman type, Class I, var. B, No. 1044, Pl. XIII. 15
" " Class I, var. C, No. 1054, Pl. XIV. 5
" " Class II, No. 1060, Pl. XIV. 8
" " Class II, No. 1061, Pl. XIV. 9
" " Class II, No. 1062, Pl. XIV. 10
" " Class II, No. 1064, Pl. XIV. 12
" " Class II, No. 1068, Pl. XIV. 13
" " Class II, No. 1087, Pl. XV. 2
Chhatra type, Class II, var. A, No. 1099, Pl. XV. 7
" " " " var. A, No. 1100, Pl. XV. 8
" " " " var. A, No. 1105, Pl. XV. 10
" " " " var. B, No. 1111, Pl. XV. 12
" " " " var. C, No. 1114, Pl. XV. 15
" " " " var. D, No. 1130, Pl. XVI. 5
" " " " var. E, No. 1146, Pl. XVI. 7
Lion-slayer type, class I, var. D, No. 1167, Pl. XVII. 10
" " class II, var. D, No. 1173, Pl. XVII. 14
Couch type, var. B, No. 1190, Pl. XVIII. 12
Chakravikrama type, No. 1192, Pl. XVIII. 14

KUMĀRAGUPTA I

Archer type, class I, var. A, No. 1206, Pl. XIX. 5
" " class I, var. B, No. 1236, Pl. XIX. 11
" " class I, var. B, No. 1263, Pl. XX. 1
" " class II, var. B, No. 1312, Pl. XX. 11
" " class III, var. A, No. 1360, Pl. XXI. 1
" " class III, var. B, No. 1376, Pl. XXI. 6
Horseman type, class I, var. B, No. 1395, Pl. XXII. 7
" " class I, var. C, No. 1396, Pl. XXII. 8
" " class II, var. B, No. 1612, Pl. XXIV. 15
Kārtikeya (Peacock) type, var. A, No. 1696, Pl. XXVI. 6
" " var. B, No. 1702, Pl. XXVI. 12
Chhatra type, No. 1705, Pl. XXVI, 15.
Tiger-slayer type, var. A, No. 1706, Pl. XXVII. 1
" " var. A, No. 1740, Pl. XXVII. 14

Lion-slayer type, class I, var. A, No. 1754, Pl. XXVIII. 7
„ „ class I, var. C, No. 1763, Pl. XXVIII. 10
„ „ class I, var. D, No. 1764, Pl. XXVIII. 13
„ „ class II, var. A, No. 1765, Pl. XXVIII. 14
Elephant-rider Lion-slayer type, No. 1795, Pl. XXX. 1
Rhinoceros-slayer type, No. 1799, Pl. XXX. 5
Aśvamedha type, var. B, No. 1806, Pl. XXX. 12
Elephant-rider type, No. 1808, Pl. XXXI. 2
Lyrist type, No. 1810, Pl. XXXI. 4
Apratigha type, No. 1817, Pl. XXXI. 11
King and Queen type, No. 1820, Pl. XXXI. 14

SKANDAGUPTA-KRAMĀDITYA

Chhatra type, No. 1821, Pl. XXXI. 15

Bhārata Kalā Bhavana, Banaras Hindu University

The Kalā-bhavana possesses 78 coins, of which the following 64 could be identified.

CHANDRAGUPTA I

King and Queen type, No. 8, Pl. I. 8.

SAMUDRAGUPTA

Standard type, var. A, No. 24.
„ „ var. B, No. 102, Pl. II. 15
„ „ var. B, No. 91
„ „ var. C, No. 119, Pl. III. 6
„ „ var. D, No. 123, Pl. III. 9
„ „ var. E, No. 149
Aśvamedha type, No. 163, Pl. IV. 10
Archer type, var. B, No. 185, Pl. VI. 2
Battle-axe type, var. A, No. 177, Pl. V. 9
Lyrist type, var. B, No. 189, Pl. VI. 6

KACHA

Chakradhvaja type, No. 208, Pl. VII. 10

CHANDRAGUPTA II

Archer type, class I, var. A, No. 214, Pl. VIII. 2
„ „ class I, var. B, No. 241, Pl. IX. 1

Archer type, class I, var. D, No. 244, Pl. IX. 3
„ „ class II, var. A, No. 823
„ „ class II, var. B, No. 953
„ „ class II, var. C, No. 972
„ „ class II, var. D, No. 981, Pl. XII. 8
„ „ class II, var. H. No. 997, Pl. XIII. 2
„ „ class II, var. I, No. 1007, Pl. XIII. 5
Horseman type, class I, var. A, No. 1008
„ „ „ „ var. A, No. 1018
„ „ „ „ var. B, No. 1036, Pl. XIII. 13
„ „ „ „ var. C, No. 1052
„ „ „ „ var. C, No. 1055
Lion-slayer type, var. A. No. 1149, Pl. XVI. 10
„ „ „ „ var. A, No. 1159, Pl. XVI. 12
„ „ „ „ var. B, No. 1158, Pl. XVII. 2
Lion-slayer type, var. C, No. 1163, Pl. XVII. 6.
Chhatra type, class I, No. 1092, Pl. XV. 5
„ „ „ II, var. A, No. 1110
„ „ „ II, var. B, No. 1112, Pl. XV. 13
„ „ „ II, var. C, No. 1113, Pl. XV. 14
„ „ „ II, var. D, No. 1143
Couch type, var. C, No. 1191, Pl. XVIII. 13

KUMĀRAGUPTA I

Archer type, class I, var. A, No. 1204, Pl. XIX. 3
„ „ „ I, var. B, No. 1259, Pl. XIX. 15
„ „ „ II, var. A, No. 1300, Pl. XX. 7
„ „ „ II, var. B, No. 1308, Pl. XX. 8
„ „ „ III, var. A, No. 1351, Pl. XX. 14
Horseman type, class I, var. A, No. 1394, Pl. XXII. 6
„ „ „ I, var. C, No. 1397, Pl. XXII. 9
„ „ „ I, var. C, No. 1409, Pl. XXII. 12
„ „ „ II, var. A, No. 1436
„ „ „ II, var. B, No. 1538, Pl. XXIV. 3
„ „ „ II, var. C, No. 1665, Pl. XXV. 9
„ „ „ II, var. E, No. 1688, Pl. XXV. 14
Tiger-slayer type, var. A, No. 1710, Pl. XXVII. 5
„ „ var. B, No. 1741, Pl. XXVII. 15
Lion-slayer type, class I, var. A, No. 1745, Pl. XXVIII. 3

Lion-slayer type, class I, var. B, No. 1759, Pl. XXVIII. 12
„ „ class II, var. A, No. 1774, Pl. XXIX. 3
„ „ „ II, var. B, No. 1784, Pl. XXIX. 8
Kārtikeya (Peacock) type, var. A, No. 1695, Pl. XXVI. 5
„ „ var. A, No. 1700, Pl. XXVI. 10
„ „ var. B, No. 1703, Pl. XXVI. 13
Swordsman type, No. 1378, Pl. XXI. 8
„ „ No. 1380, Pl. XXI. 10
Elephant-rider Lion-slayer type, No. 1797, Pl. XXX. 3
Apratigha type, No. 1816, Pl. XXXI. 10
Elephant-rider type, No. 1809, Pl. XXXI. 3
Aśvamedha type, No. 1804, Pl. XXX. 10

The Prince of Wales Museum, Bombay

This Museum possesses twenty coins of this hoard, of which the following 12 could be identified.

SAMUDRAGUPTA

Standard type, var. C, No. 112
Aśvamedha type, No. 167, Pl. IV. 14

CHANDRAGUPTA II

Archer type, class I, var. D, No. 245
„ „ class II, var. C, No. 973, Pl. XII. 5
„ „ class II, var. H, No. 1002.
Chhatra type, class I, No. 1093, Pl. XV. 6
„ „ class II, var. C, No. 1121
„ „ „ II, var. D, No. 1141

KUMĀRAGUPTA I

Swordsman type, No. 1377, Pl. XXI. 7
Horseman type, class II, var. A, No. 1456
„ „ „ II, var. A, No. 1475
„ „ „ II, var. B, No. 1566

In addition to the above 12 coins, the Museum possesses four coins of the Archer type, class II, and one coin of the *Chhatra* type of Chandragupta II and three coins of the Horseman type of Kumāragupta I, which were not possible to identify.

Patna University Coin Cabinet

This coin cabinet possesses the following 18 coins of the hoard.

SAMUDRAGUPTA

Standard type, var. A, No. 55, Pl. II. 3
„ „ var. B, No. 89
„ „ var. D, No. 134

KĀCHA

Chakradhvaja type, No. 107, Pl. VI. 14

CHANDRAGUPTA II.

Archer type, class II, var. A, No. 618
„ „ „ II, var. A, No. 637
„ „ „ II, var. C, No. 978
„ „ „ II, var. H, No. 992
Horseman type, class I, var. B, No. 1041
Chhatra type, class II, var. C, No. 1123

KUMĀRAGUPTA I

Horseman type, class I, var. C, No. 1417
„ „ class II, var. A, No. 1507
„ „ „ II, var. A, No. 1509
„ „ „ II, var. B, No. 1610
„ „ „ II, var. C, No. 1662
Tiger-slayer type, var. A, No. 1718
Lion-slayer type, class I, var. A, No. 1746
„ „ „ II, var. A, No. 1770, Pl. XXIX. 1

The Patna Museum

This Museum has got 59 coins from the Bayana hoard, of which the following 30 were possible to identify.

CHANDRAGUPTA I

King and Queen type, No. 2; Pl. I. 2. Mus. Reg. No. 18575

SAMUDRAGUPTA

Standard type, Var. B, No. 90; Pl. II. 12. Mus. Reg. No. 18577
Aśvamedha type, No. 158; Pl. IV. 5. Mus. Reg. No. 18583
„ „ No. 166; Pl. IV. 13. Mus. Reg. No. 18582
Battle-axe type, var. A, No. 178; Pl. V. 10. Mus. Reg. No. 18584

KĀCHA

Chakradhvaja type, No. 200; Pl. VII. 2. Mus. Reg. No. 18576

CHANDRAGUPTA II

Archer type, class I, var. A, No. 231. Mus. Reg. No. 18599
" " " I, var. B, No. 236. Mus. Reg. No. 18597
" " " I, var. D, No. 246. Mus. Reg. No. 18600
" " " II, var. C, No. 974 Mus. Reg. No. 18588
" " " II, var. H, No. 974, Mus. Reg. No. 18589
Horseman type, class I, var. A, No. 1031. Mus. Reg. No. 18611
" " " I, var. B, No. 1039 Mus. Reg. No. 18609
" " " I, var. C, No. 1055. Mus. Reg. No. 18608
Chhatra type, class II, var. A, No. 1103 Mus. Reg. No. 18603
" " " II, var. C, No. 1121, Mus. Reg. No. 18602

KUMĀRAGUPTA I

Archer type, class I, var. A, No. 1197. Mus. Reg. No. 18632
" " " I, var. A, No. 1198. Mus. Reg. No. 18633.
Swordsman type, No. 1381, Pl. XXI. 11. Mus. Reg. No. 18618
Horseman type, class I, var. A, No. 1392. Mus. Reg. No. 18622
" " " I, var. C, No. 1422. Mus. Reg. No. 18619
" " " II, var. A, No. 1487. Mus. Reg. No. 18629
" " " II, var. A, No. 1510. Mus. Reg. No. 18623
" " " II, var. C, No. 1613. Mus. Reg. No. 18627
" " " II, var. C, No. 1617. Mus. Reg. No. 18625
" " " II, var. D, No. 1683. Mus. Reg. No. 18631
Peacock or Kārtikeya type, No. 1691; Pl. XXVI. 1. Mus. Reg. No. 18621
Lion-slayer type, class I, var. B, No. 1756 Mus. Reg. No. 18607
" " " II, var. A, No. 1775. Mus. Reg. No. 18612
" " " " " No. 1779, Mus. Reg. No. 18615

Among the 29 coins, which could not be identified, are three of the Standard type of Samudragupta, eight of the Archer type of Chandragupta II, two of his Lion-slayer type, three of his *Chhatra* type, two of his Horseman type, two of the Lion-slayer type of Kumāragupta I, one of his Archer type, and four of his Horseman type.

The National Museum of India

The National Museum of India possesses 209 coins of the Bayana hoard; 73 of these, which are among the rare coins of the hoard, were presented by the Maharaja saheb of Bharatpur to the President of India for the Museum, and the rest were acquired by it.

It was possible to identify the following coins.

CHANDRAGUPTA I

King and Queen type, No. 6, Pl. I. 6
,, ,, No. 9, Pl. I. 9

SAMUDRAGUPTA

Aśvamedha type, No. 155, Pl. IV. 2
,, ,, No. 165, Pl. IV. 12
Battle-axe type, var. A, No. 11, Pl. V. 179
,, ,, var. A, No. 175, Pl. V. 7
Archer type, Var. A, No. 183, Pl. V. 15
Tiger-slayer type, var. B, No. 193, Pl. VI. 10

KĀCHA

Chakradhvaja type, var. A, No. 202, Pl. VII. 4
,, ,, ,, ,, ,, 205, Pl. VII. 7
,, ,, ,, ,, ,, 208, Pl. VII. 10

CHANDRAGUPTA II

Lion-slayer type, class I, var. A, No. 1150, Pl. XVI. 11
,, ,, ,, ,, ,, ,, ,, ,, 1152, Pl. XVI. 13
,, ,, ,, ,, ,, ,, C, ,, 1164, Pl. XVII. 7
,, ,, ,, ,, II, ,, A, ,, 1168, Pl. XVII. 11
,, ,, ,, ,, ,, ,, F, ,, 1177, Pl. XVIII. 4
,, ,, ,, ,, ,, ,, G, ,, 1181, Pl. XVIII. 6
,, ,, ,, ,, ,, ,, H, ,, 1185, Pl. XVIII. 7
Couch type, var. A, No. 1189, Pl. XVIII. 11

KUMĀRAGUPTA I

Swordsman type, No. 1379, Pl. XXI. 9
,, ,, ,, 1383, Pl. XXI. 13
Kārtikeya (Peacock) type, var. A, No. 1694, Pl. XXVI. 4
,, ,, ,, ,, ,, 1695, Pl. XXVI. 5
,, ,, ,, ,, ,, 1697, Pl. XXVI. 7
,, ,, ,, ,, ,, 1698, Pl. XXVI. 8
,, ,, ,, var. B, ,, 1701, Pl. XXVI. 11
Chhatra type, No. 1704, Pl. XXVI. 4

Tiger-slayer type, var. A, No. 1715, Pl. XXVII. 7
,, ,, ,, ,, ,, ,, 1719, Pl. XXVII. 8
,, ,, ,, ,, ,, ,, 1733, Pl. XXVII. 11
,, ,, ,, ,, ,, ,, 1736, Pl. XXVII. 12
,, ,, ,, ,, B, ,, 1739, Pl. XXVII. 13
Lion-slayer type, class I, var. A, No. 1742, Pl. XXVIII. 1
,, ,, ,, ,, ,, ,, ,, ,, 1745, Pl. XXVIII. 3
,, ,, ,, ,, ,, ,, ,, ,, 1750, Pl. XXVIII. 6
,, ,, ,, ,, II, ,, ,, ,, 1767, Pl. XXVIII. 15
,, ,, ,, ,, ,, ,, ,, ,, 1781, Pl. XXIX. 6
,, ,, ,, ,, ,, ,, B, ,, 1785, Pl. XXIX. 9
,, ,, ,, ,, ,, ,, ,, ,, 1787, Pl. XXIX. 11
,, ,, ,, ,, ,, ,, ,, ,, 1788, Pl. XXIX. 12
Elephant-rider Lion-slayer type, No. 1796, Pl. XXX. 2
Rhinoceros-slayer type, No. 1800, Pl. XXX. 6
Aśvamedha type, var. B, No. 1806, Pl. XXX. 12
Elephant-rider type, No. 1808, Pl. XXXI. 2
Lyrist type, No. 1811, Pl. XXXI. 5
Apratigha type, No. 1812, Pl. XXXI. 6
,, ,, ,, 1813, Pl. XXXI. 7
,, ,, ,, 1814, Pl. XXXI. 8

It may be added that in addition to the above coins, the National Museum possesses a large number of the ordinary types of the Bayana hoard. There are 9 coins of the Standard type of Samudragupta. The Archer type of Chandragupta II is represented by 34 coins, the Horseman type by 18 coins and the *Chhatra* type by 10 coins. There are 16 coins of the Archer type of Kumāragupta I, 13 of his Lion-slayer type, 6 of his Tiger-slayer type and 63 of his Horseman type.

APPENDIX III

GENEALOGICAL AND CHRONOLOGICAL TABLE OF GUPTA KINGS

N. B.—Dates are given in A. D.

(1) Gupta (C. 270-290)

(2) Ghaṭotkacha (C. 290-305)

(3) Chandragupta I—Kumāradevī (C. 305-325)

Kācha (C. 325-330). (4) Samudragupta (C. 330-370)

(5) Rāmagupta (C. 370-375). (6) Chandragupta II—Dhruvadevī —(C. 375-414)—Kuberanāgā

(7) Kumāragupta I—Anantadevī (C. 414-455) Govindagupta Ghaṭotkacha-gupta

(8) Skandagupta (C. 455-468) (9) Purugupta (C. 468-9)

(10) Narasiṁhagupta (C. 469-72) (12) Budhagupta (C. 475-496)

(11) Kumāragupta II (C. 472-475)

(13) Vishṇugupta (C. 496-505)

(14) Vainyagupta (C. 505-510 ?) Bhānugupta (C. 510-525)

N. B.—Kings are indexed in Appendix VI.

APPENDIX IV

INDEX TO TYPES AND MOTIFS

Kumāragupta I, as above, but holding bow in l. hand and sword in r., xcix-c, 269.
——— riding on caparisoned horse to l. holding bow in r. hand and sword in l., xcix-c, 255-63.
——— as above, but king has no weapons, c, 263-68.
——— to r. and attacking a rhinoceros in his front by a sword, cvii, 296-8.
——— sitting on couch to left, playing on a lute, cx, 302-3
——— standing to l. holding bow at the top in l. hand and arrow in r., *Kumāra* being under l. arm, xcv, 210-13.
——— as above, but holding bow by middle, string outside, Kumāra being outside the bow-string, xcv, 213-224.
——— standing to l., bow being held at the top, and *Ku* being under the l. arm, xcv, 224-33.
——— standing as above, with no letter under l. arm, xcv, 234-37.
——— standing to l. offering oblations on altar by r. hand, left hand resting on sword, xcvi, 237-40.
——— standing to r. and shooting at lion by bow, civ-v, 284-88.
——— standing to l. and the rest as above, civ-v, 288.
——— standing to r. and trampling upon the lion, which he shoots with an arrow, cv, 288-94.
——— standing to l. and shooting at tiger by arrow and trampling upon it by foot, cresent-topped banner being between him and the tiger; ciii, 277-82.
——— standing to l. and feeding a peacock with a bunch of fruits held in wrih hand, l. hand resting behind him, ci, 272-75.
——— standing to l. and offering oblations on altar, dwarf holding an umbrella over his head, cii, 275-6.
——— standing to l. and offering bunch of flowers to the queen standing before him, cxiii, 306-7.
——— standing facing, hands folded waist, in non-royal dress, with a male on his r. holding a

APPENDIX V

INDEX TO SYMBOLS

N.B.—References in Arabic numerals are to the numbers of coins in the Catalogue; references in Roman numbers are to the pages in the Introduction.

 46, 1099

 11, 14, 15, 31, 33, 42, 47, 55, 60, 82, 85, 90, 96, 124, 125, 135, 150, 174, 182-3, 229-30, 242-3, 249, 300, 333, 359, 364, 446-7, 475, 786, 855, 902, 923, 948, 949, 951, 999, 1190, 1191, 1350, 1353, 1358, 1708, 1710, 1718, 1722, 1726, 1732, 1733, 1739-41, 1783, 1799-1802

 34, 44, 54, 60, 65, 80, 128-29, 147-49, 151-2, 176, 308, 1709

 43-4, 58, 217, 337

 102

 2, 3, 212-13, 294, 316, 326, 330, 349, 476, 477, 606, 756, 760, 877, 1150.

 678, 1185, 1188, 1375.

 194-98, 201, 204, 206

 1099

 609, 616, 807, 834

 27, 81, 266, 306, 467, 478, 503, 550, 669, 672, 795, 799, 888, 889, 905, 910, 926.

 321, 332, 467, 1153, 1155

 1716

 1720, 1721

 208

 1188

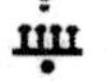 52, 103, 183

 48, 401, 402, 962

 680, 700, 734, 781, 866, 867

 23, 29, 30, 36, 38, 39, 49, 50, 74, 97, 137, 138, 185, 189-191, 211, 221, 231, 240, 250, 253, 310, 340, 524, 578, 642, 691, 729, 774, 1706

 473, 705, 715

 481, 772, 798, 895, 1223.

1025, 1028, 1032-33, 1036, 1039, 1043, 1046, 1050-52, 1058, 1116, 1130, 1134, 1138, 1141-44, 1177, 1178, 1196, 1201, 1204, 1206, 1211, 1213-14, 1224, 1226, 1231, 1760.

 77

 130, 655

 370, 398, 480, 518, 522, 577, 581, 584, 593, 752, 762, 785, 945, 971, 973

 4, 6, 8-10, 64, 104-21, 188, 209, 211, 216, 223, 251-52, 254-58, 259-61, 264-65, 267, 271-74, 277-79, 282-83, 285, 288, 290-91, 293, 295, 299, 302, 305, 312, 318, 320, 322, 323, 325, 331, 334, 336, 338-39, 341-42, 345-48, 357-58, 366, 372-74, 376, 379, 381, 384-87, 392, 394-97, 404-09, 416-18, 420-22, 430-31, 433-34, 436-37, 439, 442, 444-45, 450-52, 455,461-62, 465-66, 474, 479, 482-86, 488, 492, 494-96, 498-99, 501-02, 506, 508, 511, 513-15, 525, 526, 528-30, 531, 533, 535, 537, 538-39, 542, 544, 547-49, 551, 553-55, 558, 560-62, 566, 568, 570, 571, 573, 576, 586, 587, 589, 591, 595-96, 598, 600, 601, 608, 612-13, 615, 618, 619, 622, 624, 625, 627, 631, 634, 636, 637-43, 645-46, 649-50, 653, 656, 657-61, 663-66, 671, 674, 676, 677, 679, 681-83, 688, 697, 698, 701, 704, 706-08, 713-14, 716-17 724-25, 726-27, 730, 733, 737-38, 744, 746, 747, 748, 751, 753, 755, 761, 764, 765-70, 773, 775, 777-78, 783, 784, 787, 788, 792, 796-7, 802, 810, 812, 814-5, 818, 823, 825-6, 831, 833, 835, 837, 840-44, 846-50, 851, 854, 857, 860, 904, 905-09, 912-14, 916-17, 920-22, 924, 930, 941-42, 946, 950, 953, 957-60, 965-66, 968, 972, 979, 980, 981, 985-93, 995, 996-98, 1003, 1005, 1006, 1008, 1013, 1016, 1018, 1023, 1029-31, 1034, 1037, 1038, 1040-42, 1044-45, 1047-49 1074, 1114-15, 1117-22, 1125-26, 1128-29, 1140, 1145, 1151, 1154, 1156-59, 1163-65, 1167, 1174, 1192, 1202, 1208, 1210, 1221, 1234, 1235-49, 1256-57, 1259-74, 1276-85, 1288, 1289, 1291, 1293-95, 1299, 1300, 1302-03, 1362, 1376-80, 1383-85, 1704-05, 1719, 1745-48, 1754-60, 1811-12

 70, 545, 1113, 1197

 794

 1811

 1309, 1311-12, 1331, 1333, 1341, 1345, 1785, 1789-90

 cxxxi

 cxxxi

 Pl. XLVIII

 cxxxii

 cxxxi

 Pl. XLVIII

APPENDIX VI

GENERAL INDEX

APPENDIX VII

CONVERSION OF INCHES AND GRAINS INTO CENTIMETRES AND GRAMMES

A

One centimetre is equal to 0.397 inch

B

TABLE OF THE RELATIVE WEIGHTS OF ENGLISH GRAINS AND METRIC GRAMMES

Grains	Grammes	Grains	Grammes
91	5.896	116	7.516
92	5.961	117	7.581
93	6.026	118	7.646
94	6.091	119	7.711
95	6.156	120	7.776
96	6.220	121	7.840
97	6.285	122	7.905
98	6.350	123	7.970
99	6.415	124	8.035
100	6.480	125	8.100
101	6.544	126	8.164
102	6.609	127	8.229
103	6.674	128	8.294
104	6.739	129	8.359
105	6.804	130	8.424
106	6.868	131	8.488
107	6.933	132	8.553
108	6.998	133	8.618
109	7.063	134	8.682
110	7.128	135	8.747
111	7.192	136	8.812
112	7.257	137	8.877
113	7.322	138	8.942
114	7.387	139	9.007
115	7.452	140	9.072

Grains	Grammes	Grains	Grammes
141	9.136	149	9.655
142	9.200	150	9.720
143	9.265	151	9.784
144	9.330	152	9.848
145	9.395	153	9.914
146	9.460	154	9.978
147	9.525	155	10.044
148	9.590	156	10.108

APPENDIX VIII

ADDENDA

FURTHER HOARDS OF GUPTA COINS.

On p. ix, after 30, add,

BAMNALA HOARD. In 1940, a small hoard of Gupta gold coins was discovered at Bamnala in Nimar district of Madhya-bharat, scattered under the surface of a road, along with a gold bar weighing 11 *tolas* and 10 *māshas*. Out of these coins 8 were of Samudragupta (7 of the Standard type and one of the Lyrist type, var. B), nine were of Chandragupta II, (all of the Archer type, class II), and four of Kumāragupta I (2 of the Archer type, 1 of the Horseman type and one of the Tiger-slayer type). One of the Standard type coins of Samudragupta in this hoard had the *biruda Vikarma* on it; the Horseman type coin had the letter *si* inscribed under the foot-stool of the goddess.[1]

KUSUMBHI HOARD. In 1947 a hoard of Gupta gold coins was discovered at Kusumbhi in the Unnao district of U.P., while digging for the extension of a distributory canal of the Gaṅgā. 29 coins were recovered from this hoard of which 3 were of Samudragupta, all of the Standard type, 19 of Chandragupta II (17 of the Archer type and one each of the Lion-slayer and *Chhatra* type) and 2 of Kumāragupta I, one of the Archer and one of the Horseman type.[2]

KUMARKHAM HOARD. In 1952 a hoard of Gupta gold coins was for the first time discovered in Gujarat at Kumarkham in Viramgaon Taluka of the Ahmadabad district. It consisted of only nine coins, 2 being of Kācha, 1 of Samudragupta, Battle-axe type and six of Chandragupta II, all being of the Archer type.[3]

---

[1] *J.N.S.I.*, V. p. 135 [2] *Ibid*, XV. p. 82 *Ibid*,[3] XV, p. 195

ERRATA

Page	Line	For	Read
iii	33	Kramaditya	Kramāditya
xi	39	;	,
xvi	10	may	might
xviii	34	gupta	gopa
xxvi	26	See.	See
xxxii	19	Pushyamitrās	Pushyamitras
xxxiv	26	more than	nearly
xxxiv	28	Kumāragupta I, (*c.* 454-540 A. D.)	Skandagupta, (*c.* 468-540 A. D.)
xlv	37	*C. G. I.*	*C. G. E.*
xlvi	20	persons	person
xlix	38	pl	pl.
lii	34	Brother	brother
lxvi	36	*C. G. I.*	*C. G. E.*
lxxiii	11	standard	Standard
lxxiii	37	52	lii
lxxiv	36	*B. M. C. G. D.*	*B. M. C. G. D.*, lxxiv
lxxv	6, 11, 19, 20, 25, 27, 32,	Kacha	Kācha
lxxvi	3	off resh	of fresh
lxxx	33	D.,	D.
lxxxii	15	*ri*	*sri*
lxxxvi	15	both	them
lxxxvii	28	*iaya*	*jaya*
lxxxviii	2	'of	of
lxxxviii	5	C, D	C and D
lxxxviii	35	hanging	generally hanging
cxiv	7	coin	coins
cxvi	15	*XXI*	XXI
cxvii	28	The	the
cxxii	12	19 coins	18 coins
cxxiv	26	525	515
cxxv	37	120	121
cxviii	23	*Skandogupta*	*Skandagupta*
cxxx	4	Na is	Na is sometimes
cxxx	7	*Tha* is	*Tha* is sometimes
cxxxv	27	the	these
36	After 3rd line in the last column, add Symbol		

Page	Line	For	Read
41	Folio line	Asvamedha	Aśvamedha
42	24	vatva	.vatva
43	Folio line	Asvamdeha	Aśvamedha
45	Folio line	Asvamdeha	Aśvamedha
47	Folio line	Asvamdeha	Aśvamedha
49	Folio line	Asvamdeha	Aśvamedha
49	29	कृतान्त	कृतान्त
64	Folio line	KACHA	KĀCHA
66	Folio line	KACHA	KĀCHA
66	71	Add at the end, 'but with one horizontal line'.	
74	21	truncated.	truncated
94	14	pearl be-	pearl-be-
164	19	XXIII	XXIV
169	24	....	......
181	Add below folio line		

VARIETY A: 16 COINS.

Lakshmī standing facing, on lotus.

Page	Line	For	Read
222	32	37	42
233	7	श्रीमहेन्द्र : ।	श्रीमहेंन्द्र : । Pl. XXXVI. 56
234	23	श्रीकुमारगुप्तः	श्रीकुमारगुप्तः ।
242	5	जयत्यजितः ।	जयत्यजितः । Pl. XXXV. 23
262	19	seated	seated on a wicker stool.
262	35	28	27
277	2	32	33
277	28	67	62

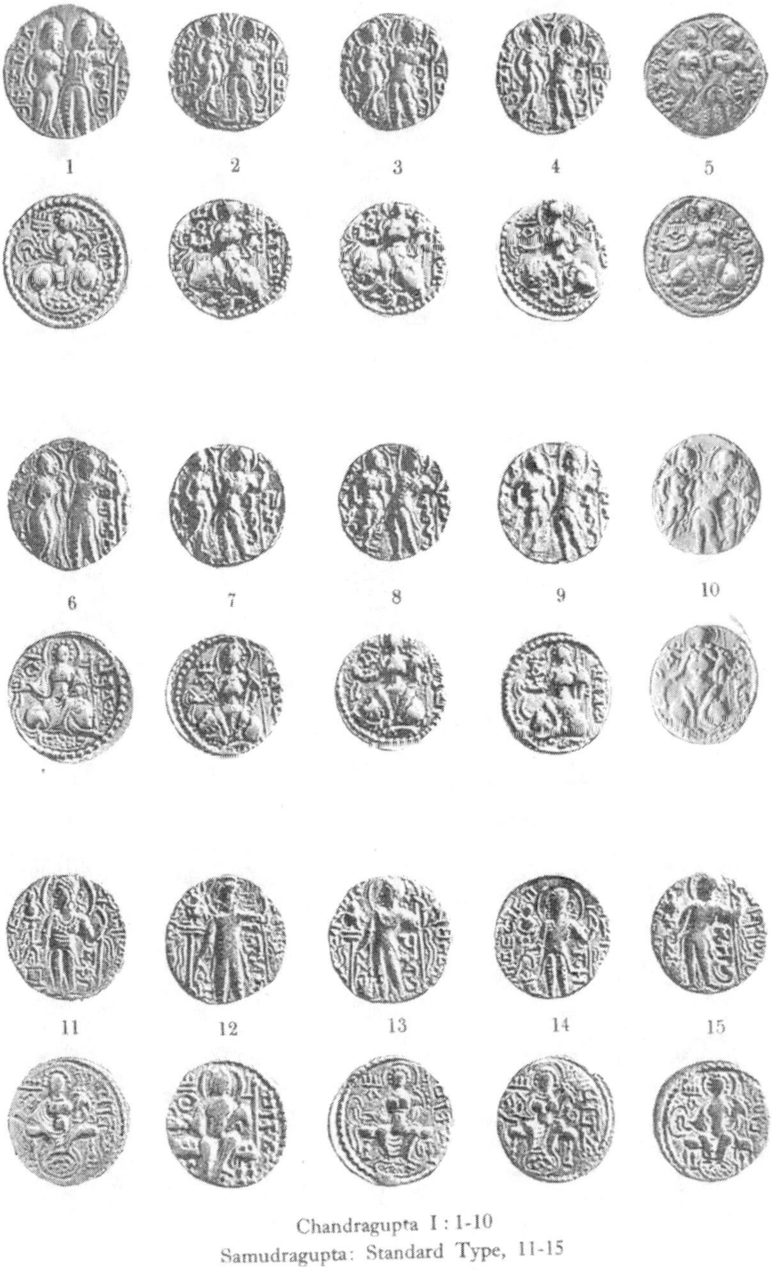

Chandragupta I : 1-10
Samudragupta: Standard Type, 11-15

Samudragupta: Standard Type

Samudragupta: Standard Type

1 2 3 4 5

6 7 8 9 10

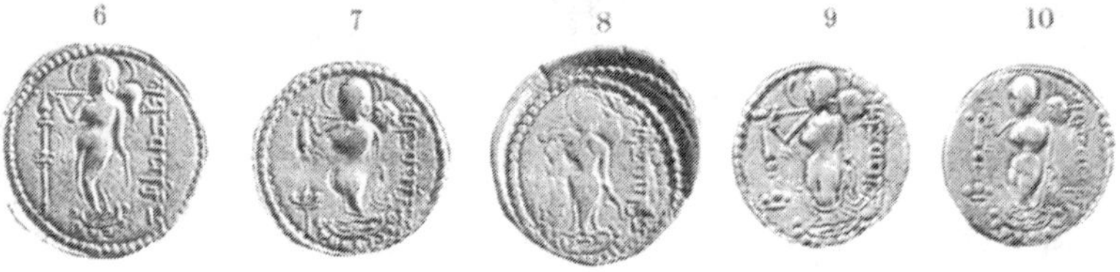

11 12 13 14 15

Samudragupta: Aśvamedha Type

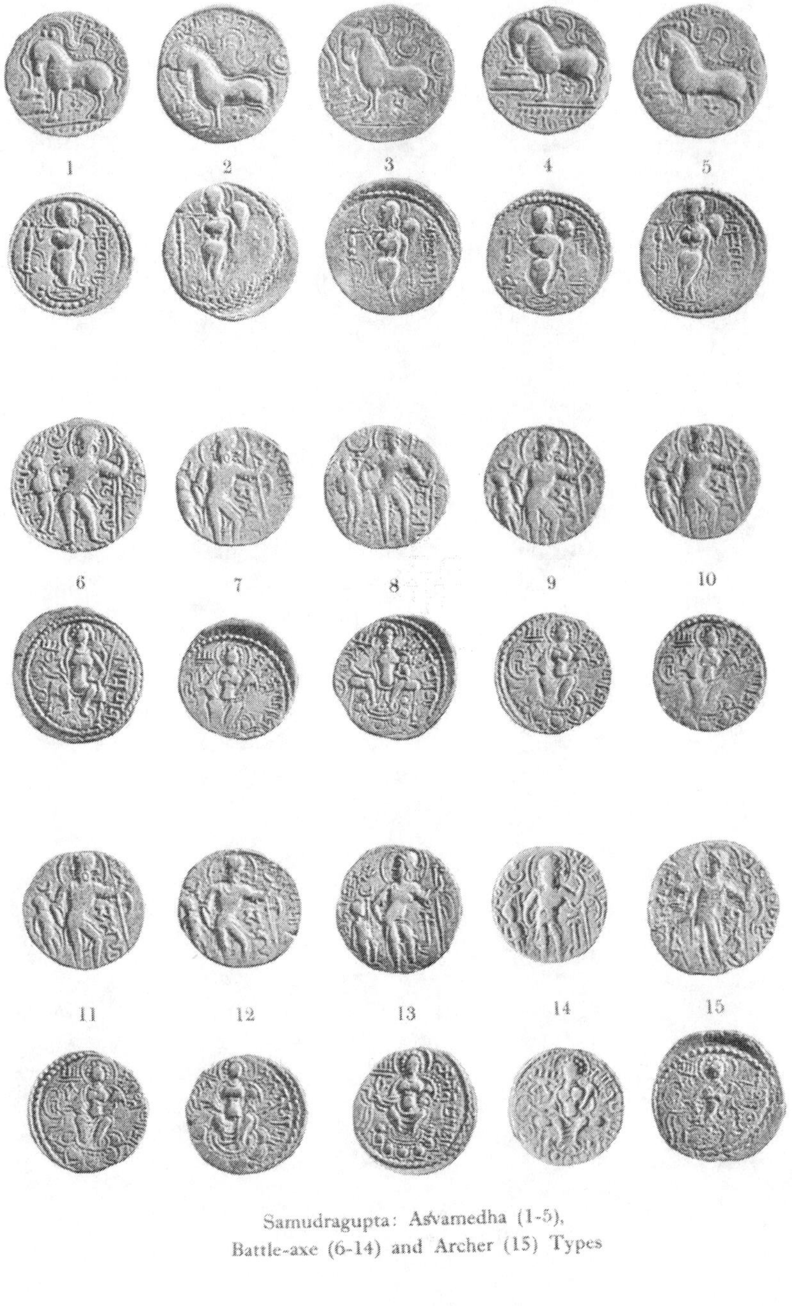

Samudragupta: Aśvamedha (1-5),
Battle-axe (6-14) and Archer (15) Types

1 2 3 4 5

6 7 8 9 10

11 12 13 14 15

Samudragupta: Archer (1-2), Lyrist (3-8) and
Tiger-Slayer (9-10) Types
Kācha: (11-15)

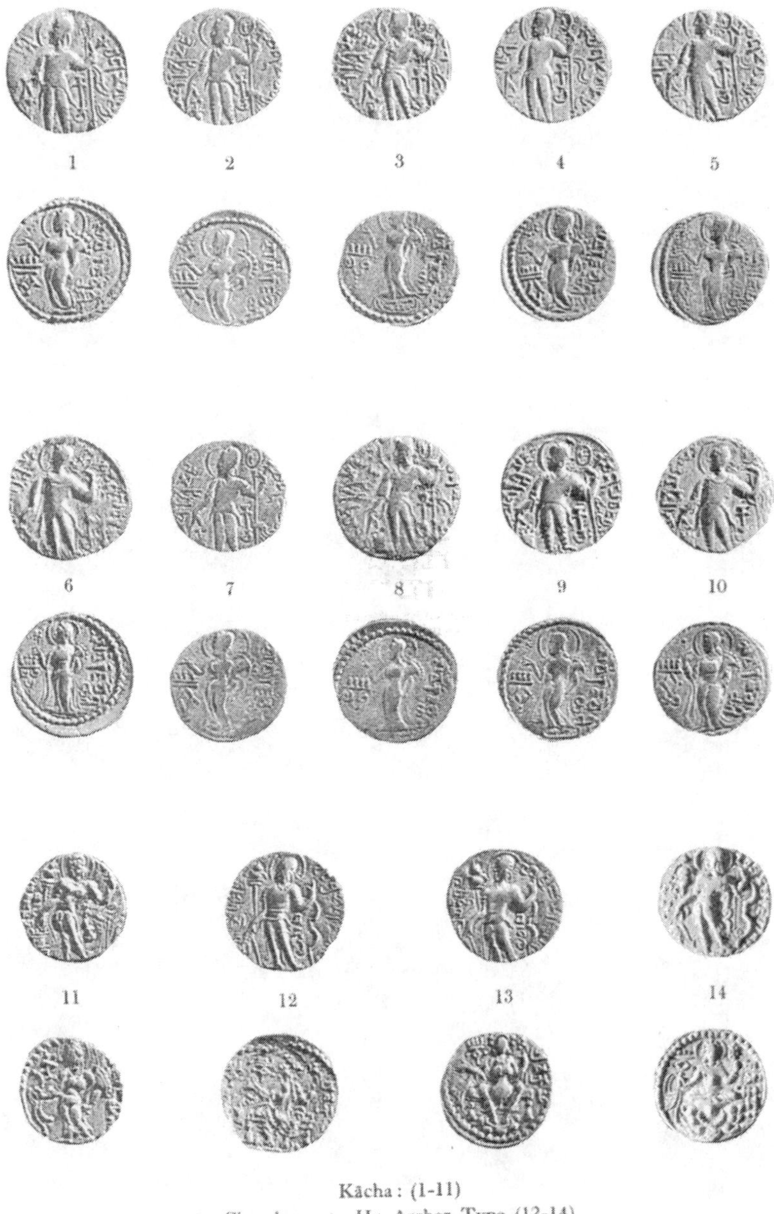

Kācha : (1-11)
Chandragupta II : Archer Type (12-14)

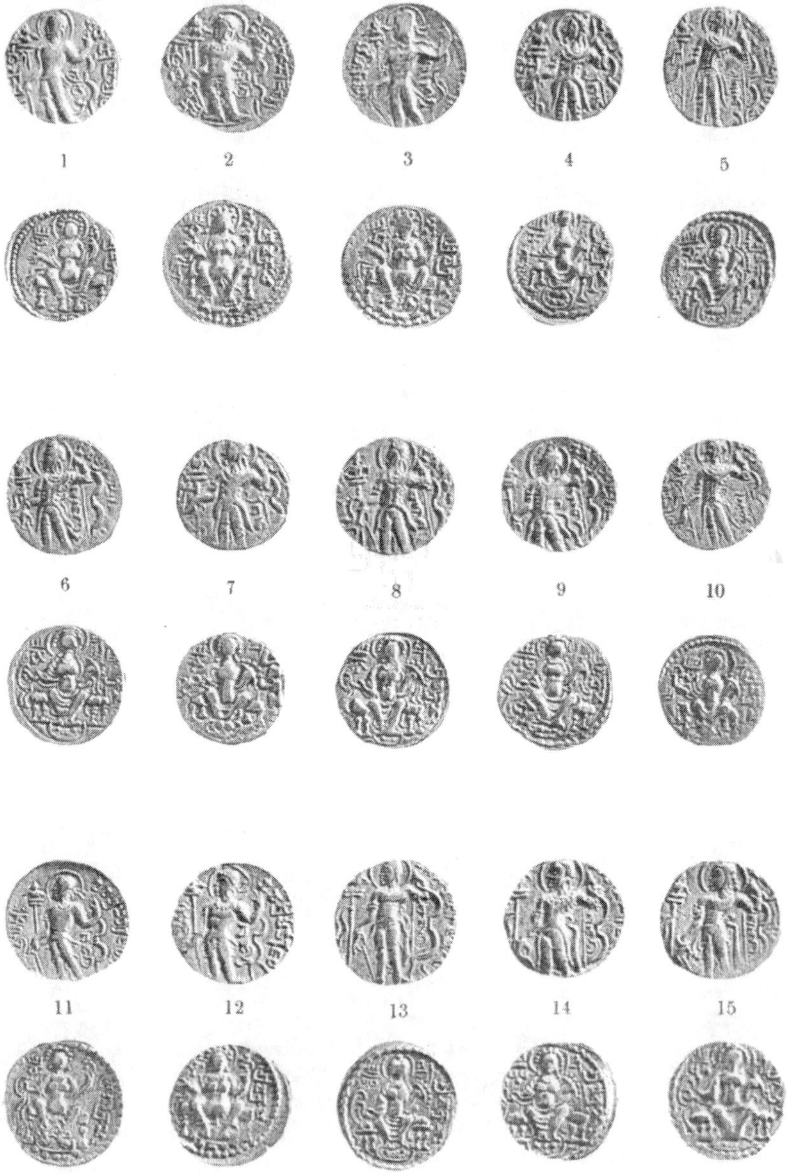

Chandragupta II : Archer Type

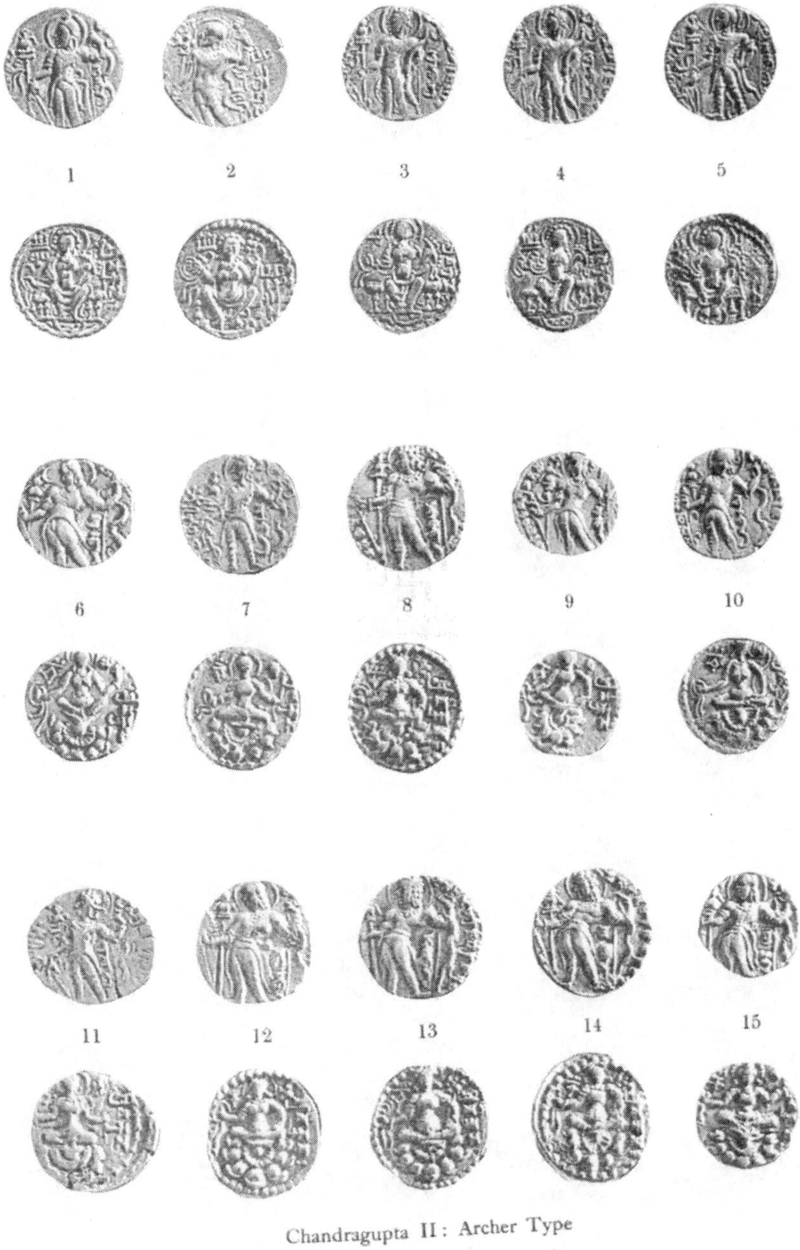

Chandragupta II: Archer Type

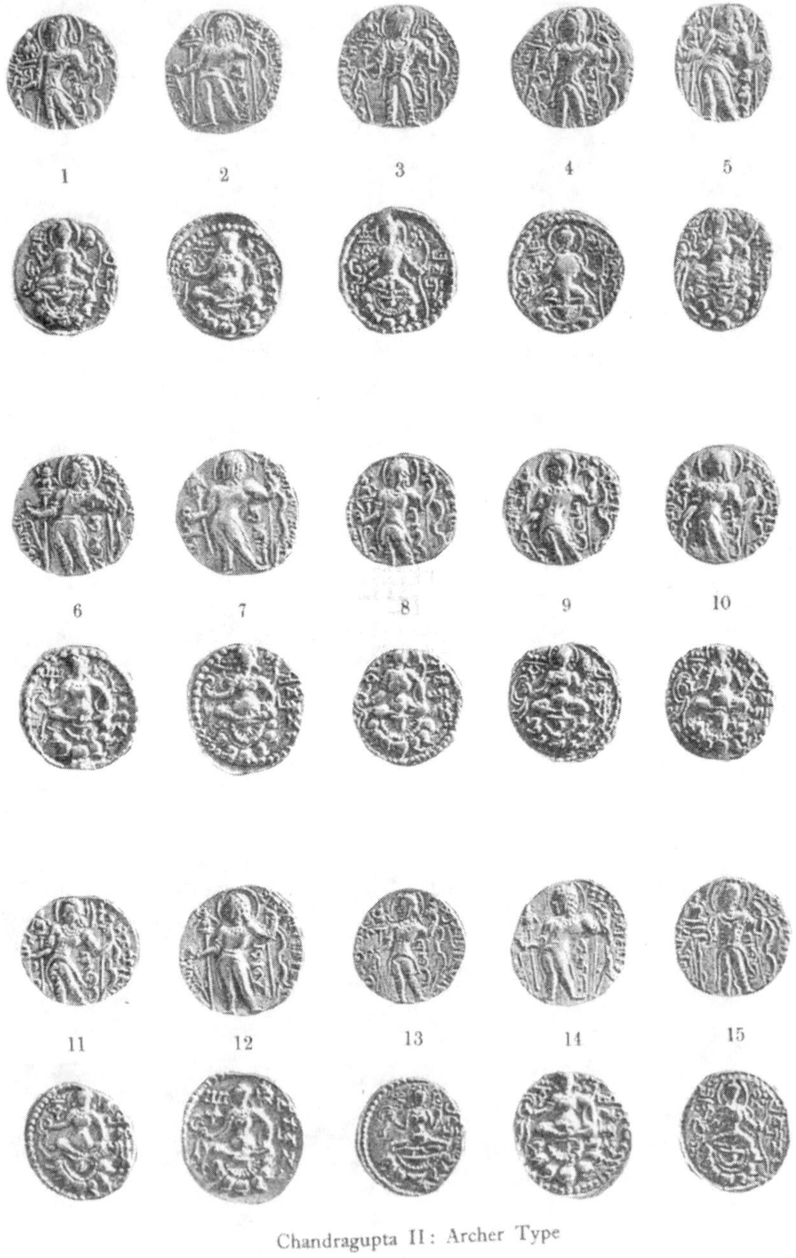

Chandragupta II: Archer Type

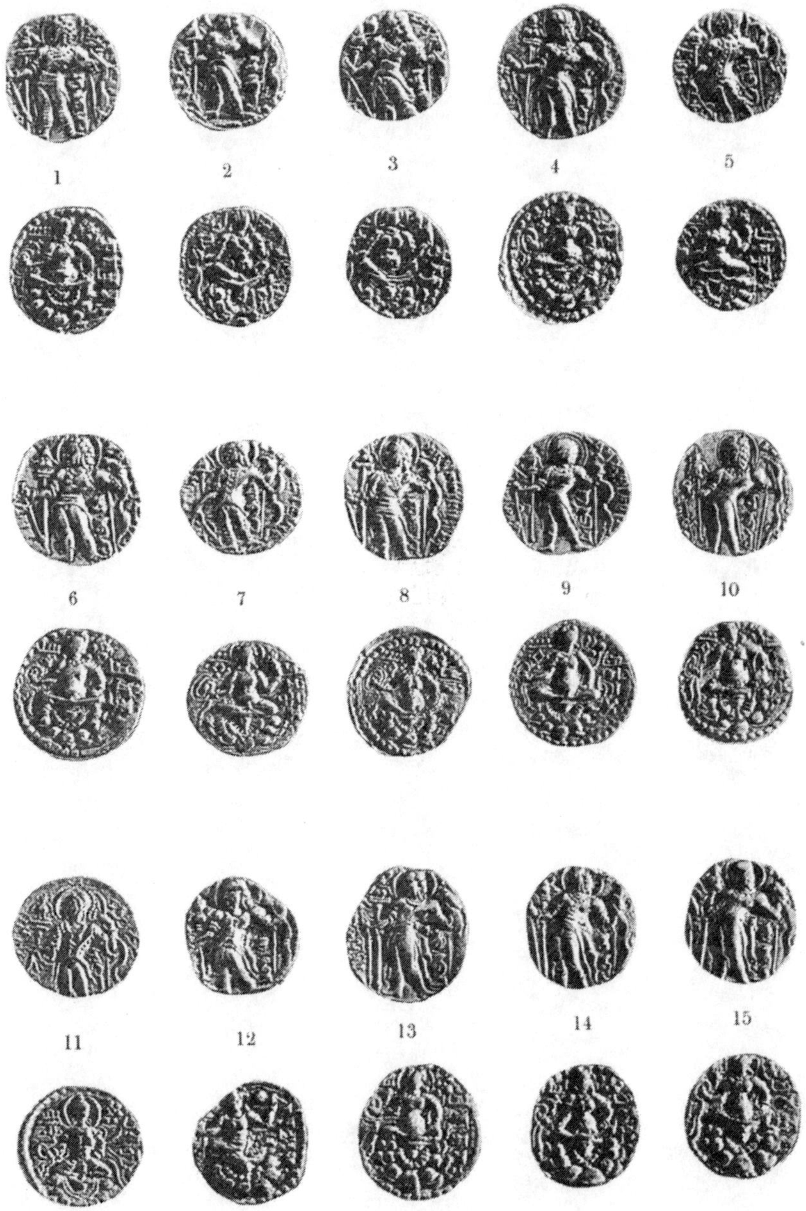

Chandragupta II: Archer Type

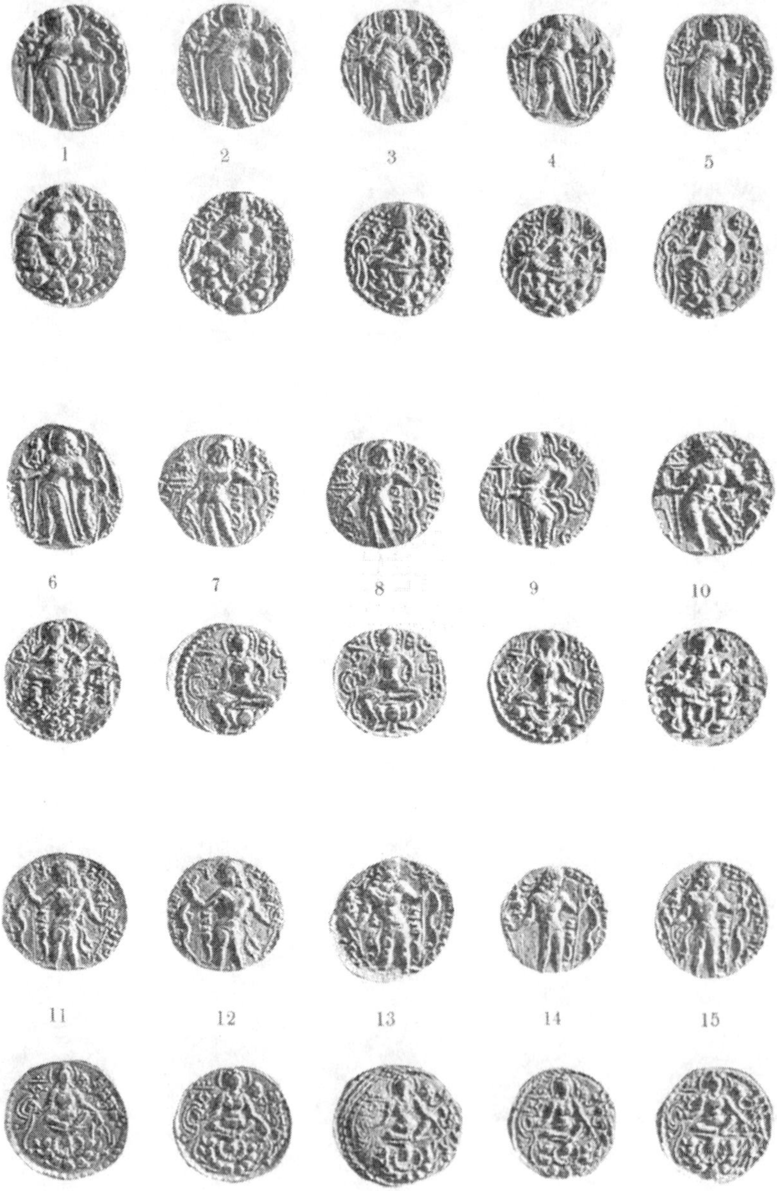

Chandragupta II: Archer Type

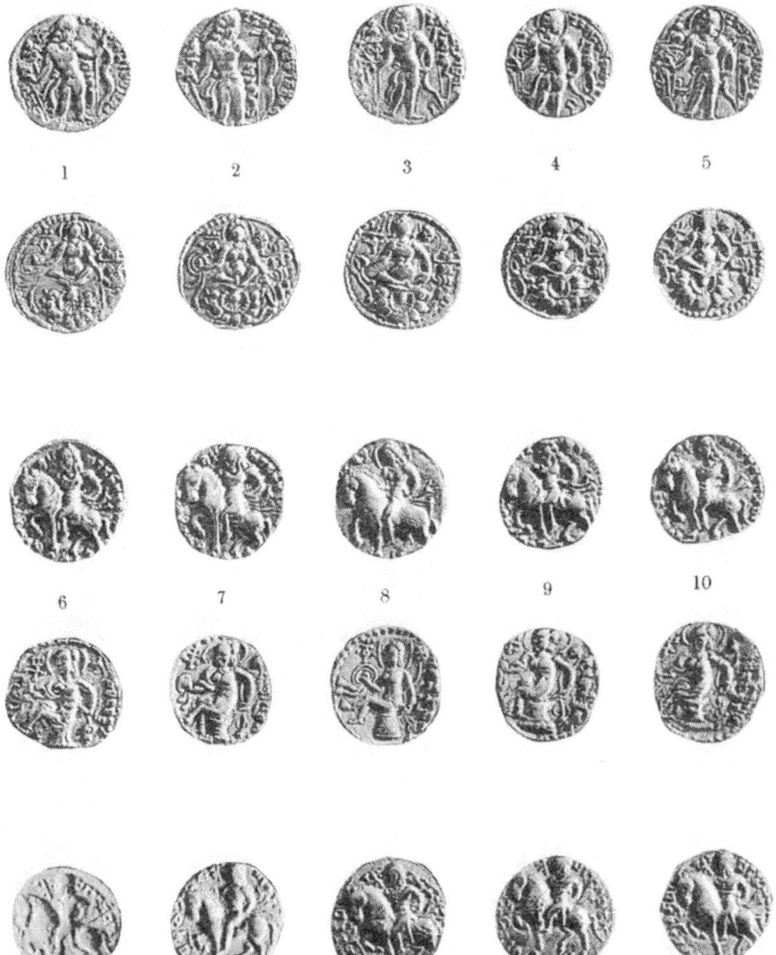

Chandragupta II: Archer (1-5) and
Horseman (6-15) Types

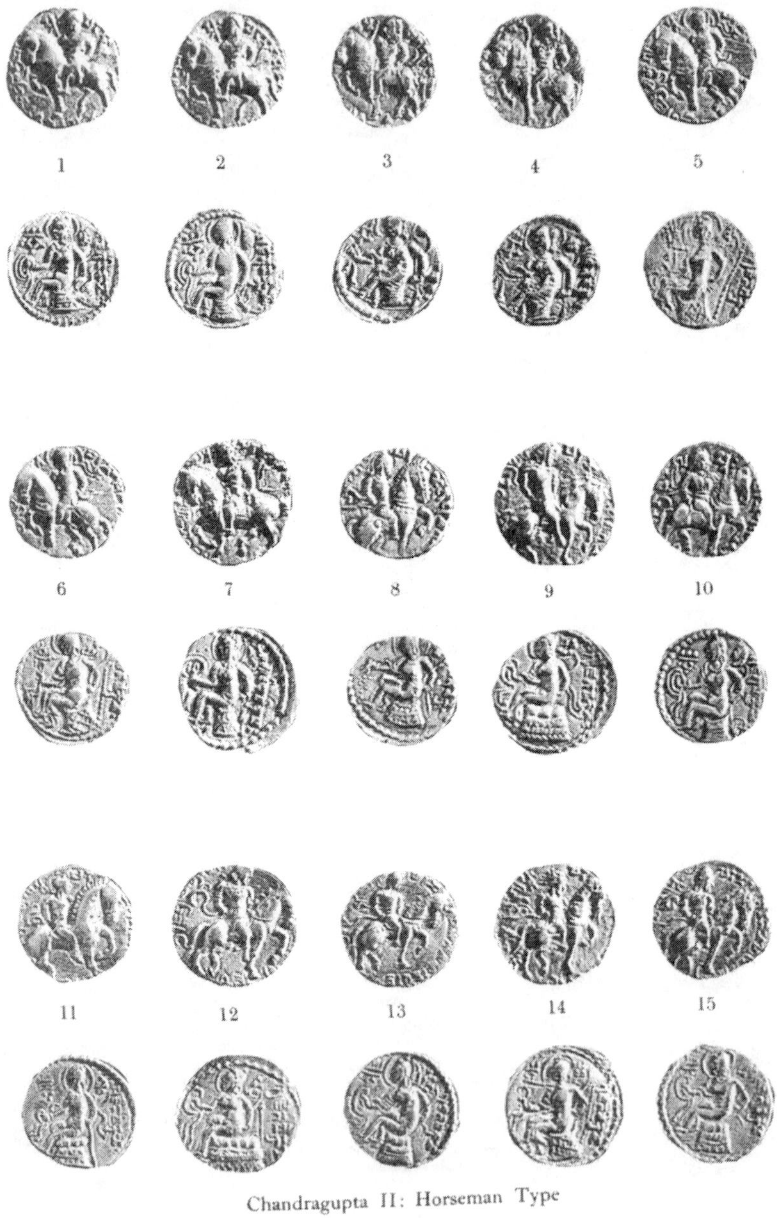

Chandragupta II: Horseman Type

Chandragupta II: Horseman (1-3)
and Chhatra (4-15) Types

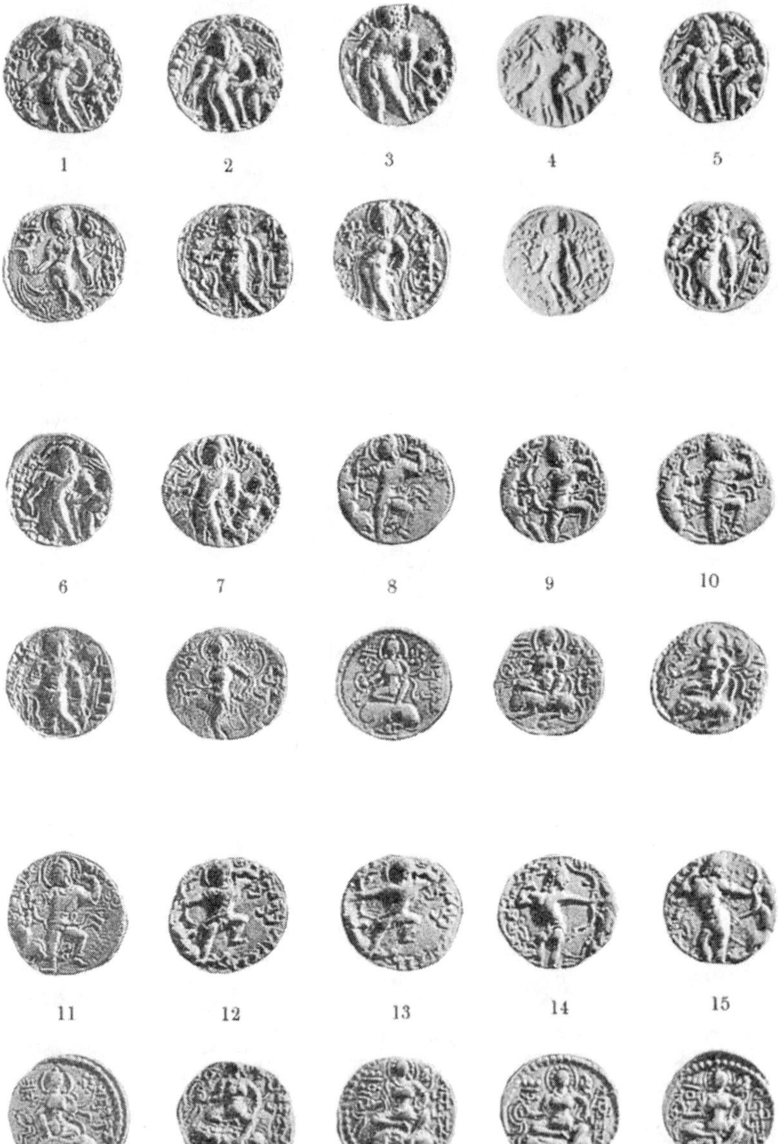

Chandragupta II : Chhatra (1-7) and Lion-Slayer (8-15) Types

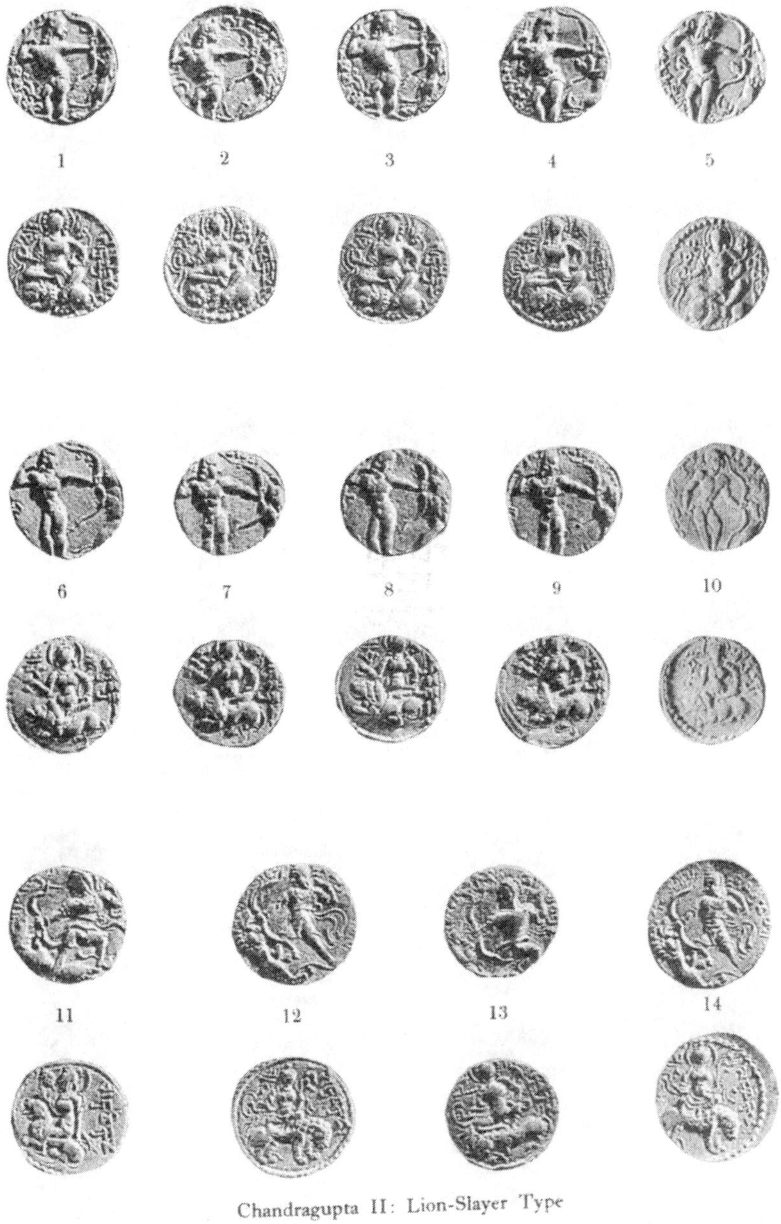

Chandragupta II: Lion-Slayer Type

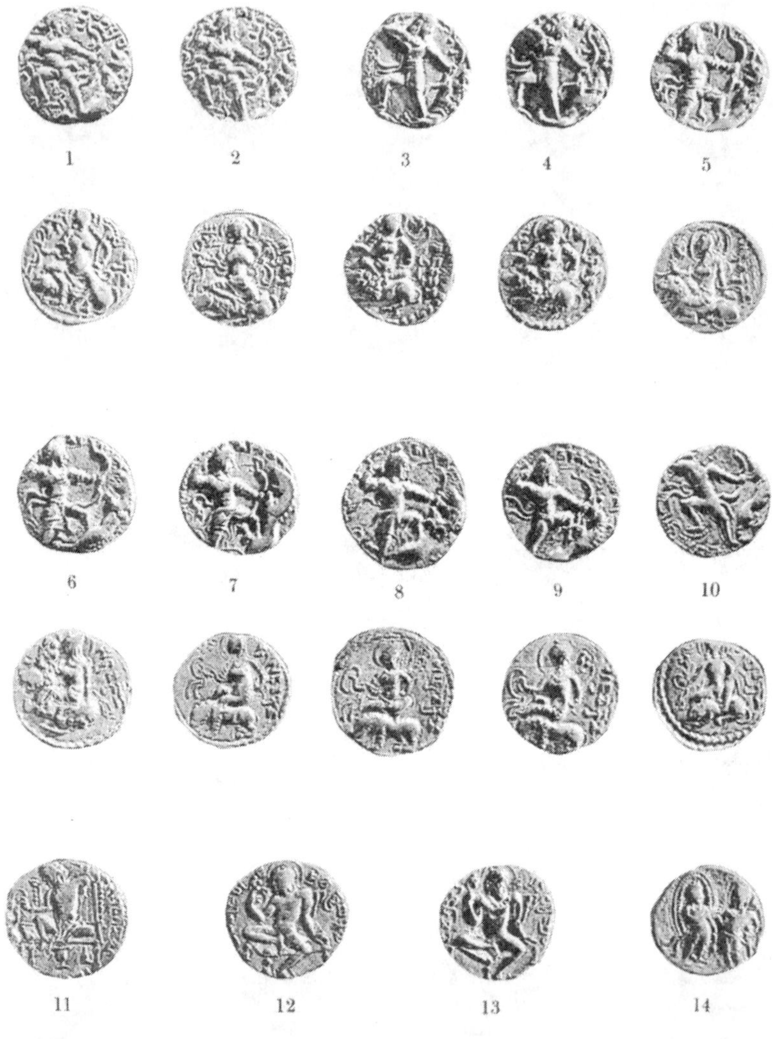

Chandragupta II : Lion-Slayer (1-10),
Couch (11-13) and Chakravikrama (14) Types

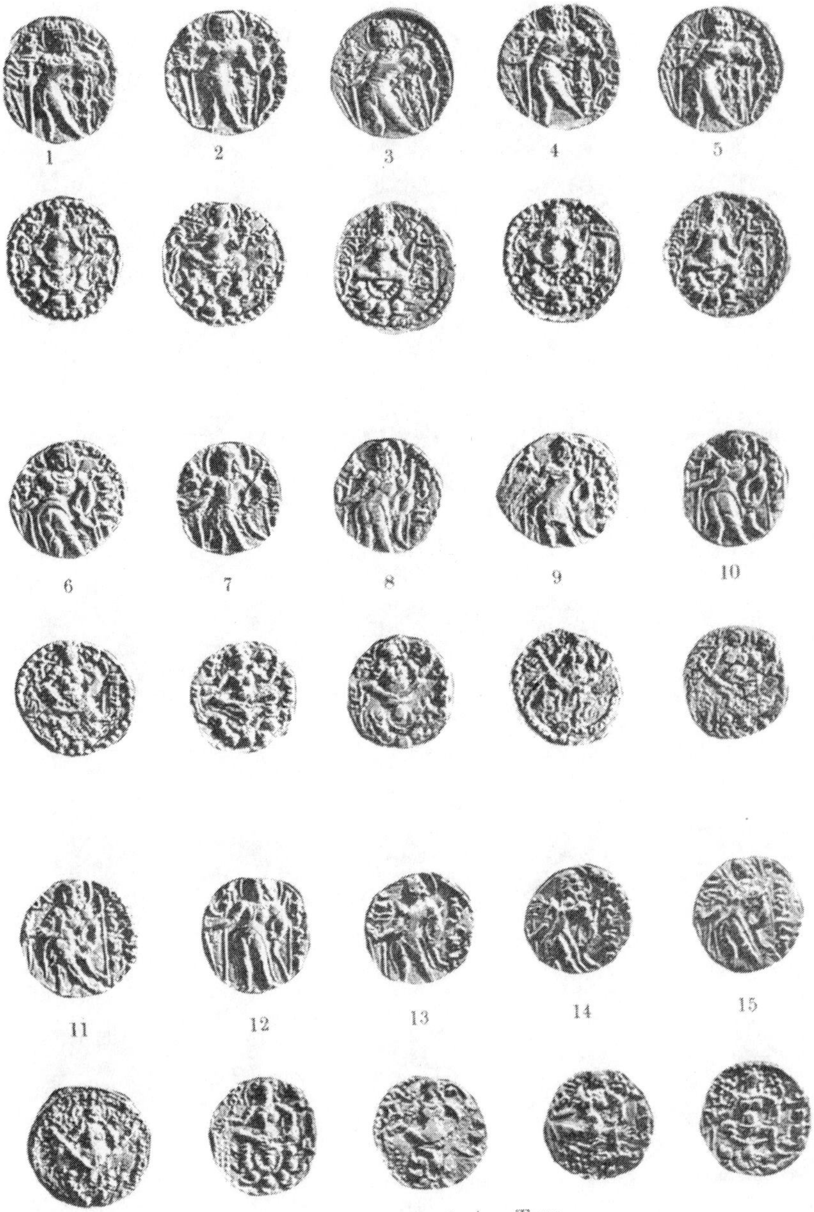

Kumāragupta I: Archer Type

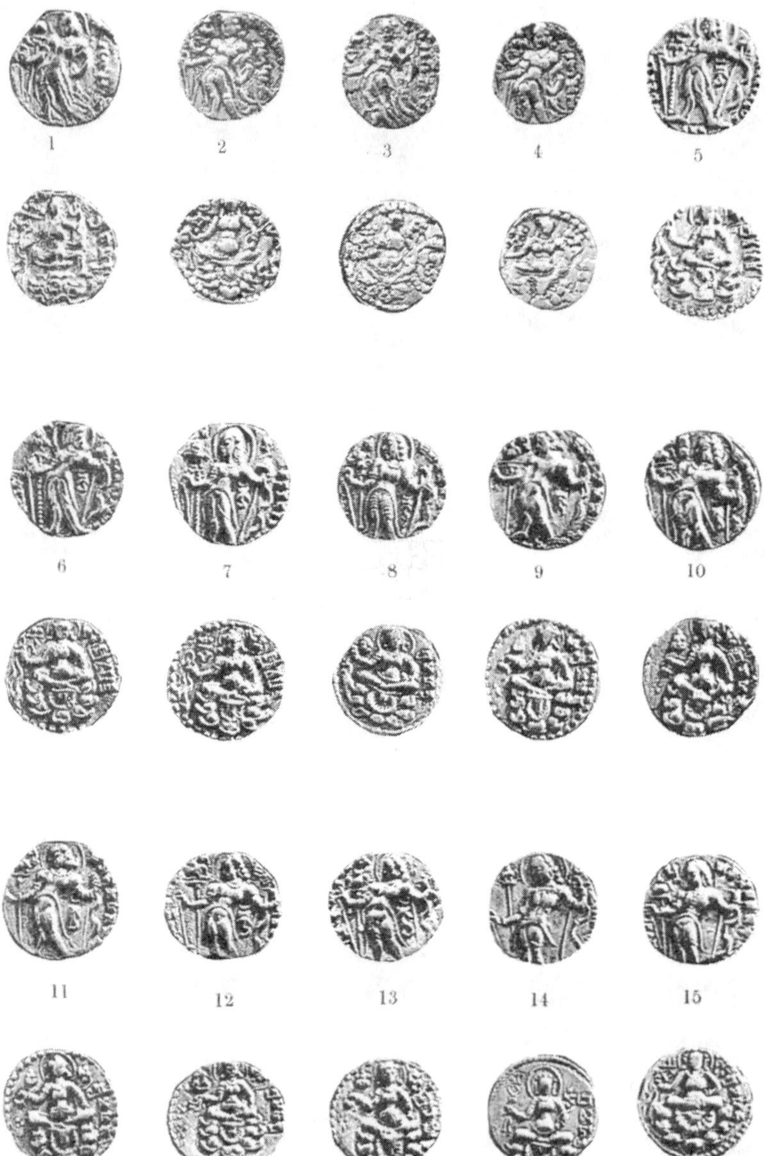

Kumāragupta I: Archer Type

1 2 3 4 5

6 7 8 9 10

11 12 13 14 15

Kumāragupta I: Archer (1-5) and
Swordsman (6-15) Types

Kumāragupta I: Horseman Type

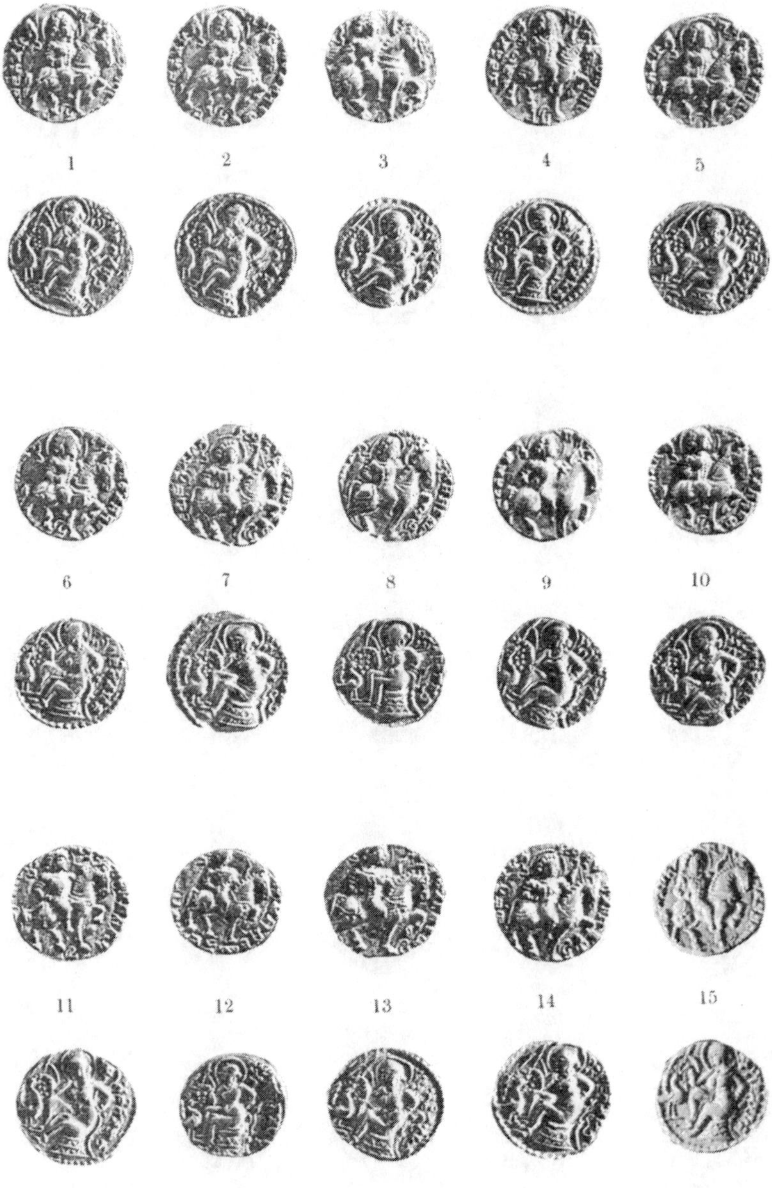

Kumāragupta I : Horseman Type

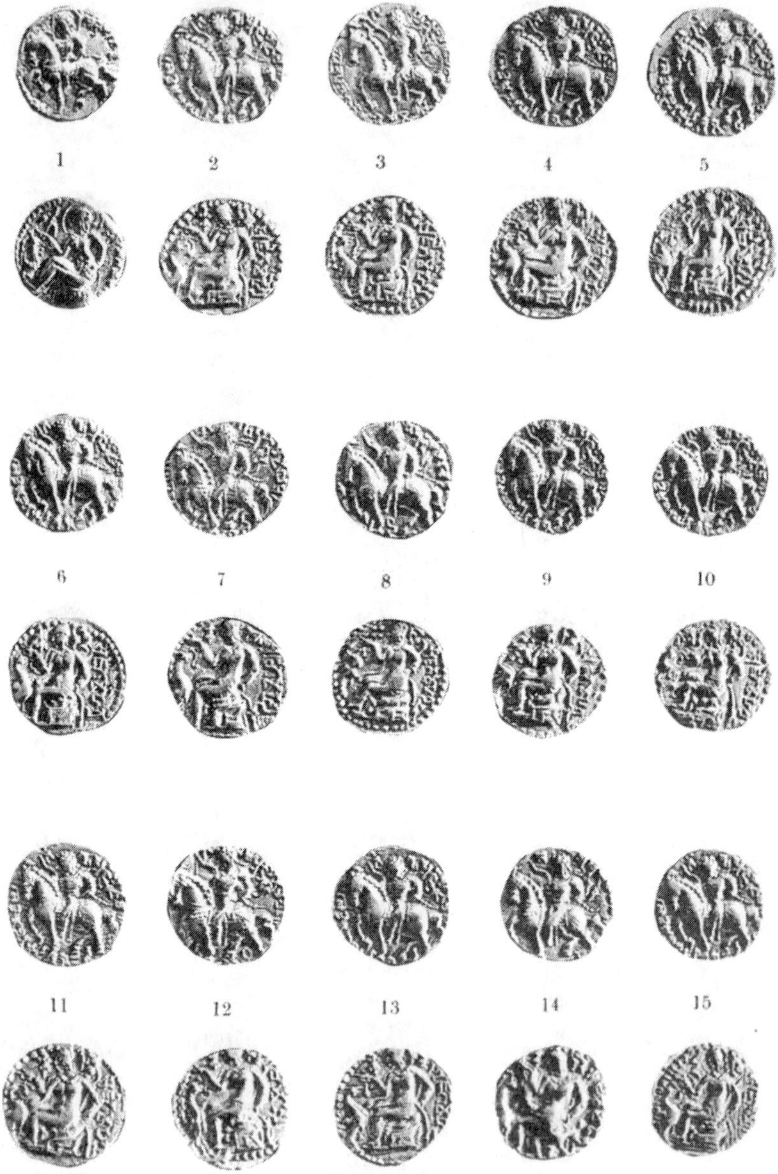

Kumāragupta I : Horseman Type

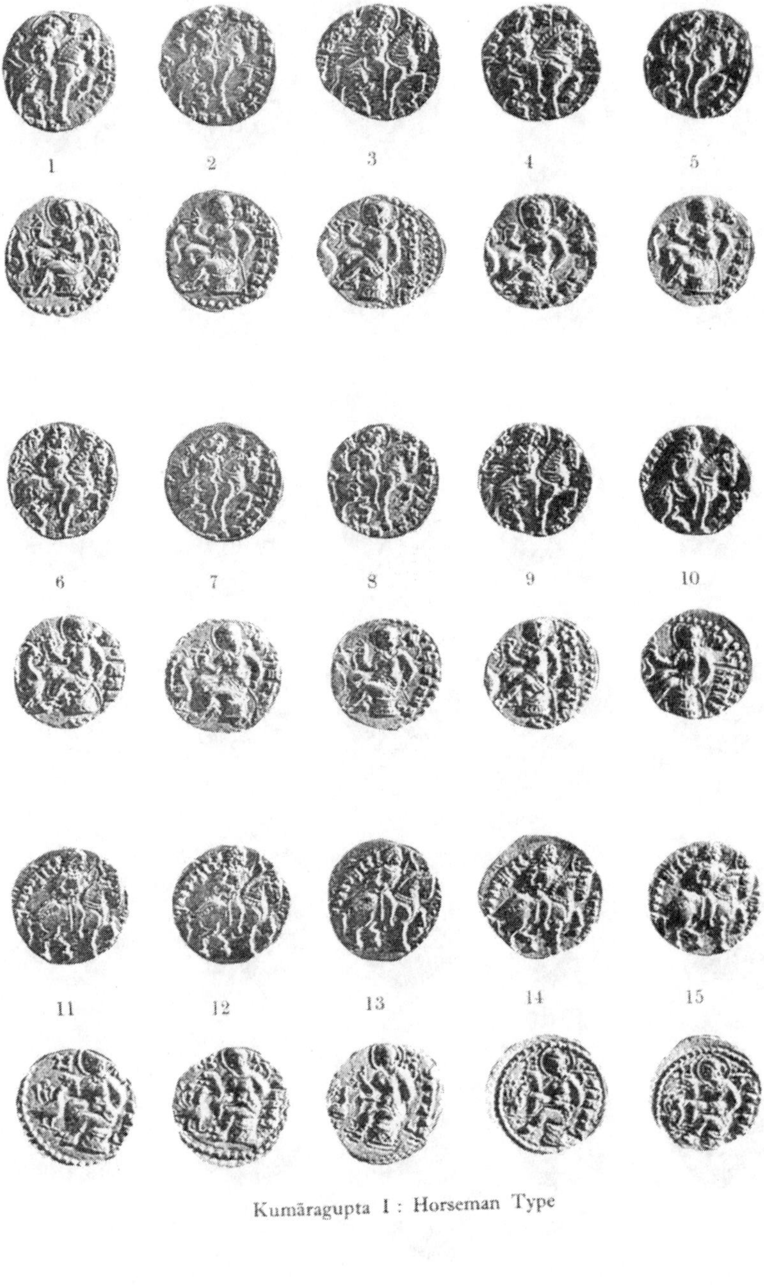

Kumāragupta I : Horseman Type

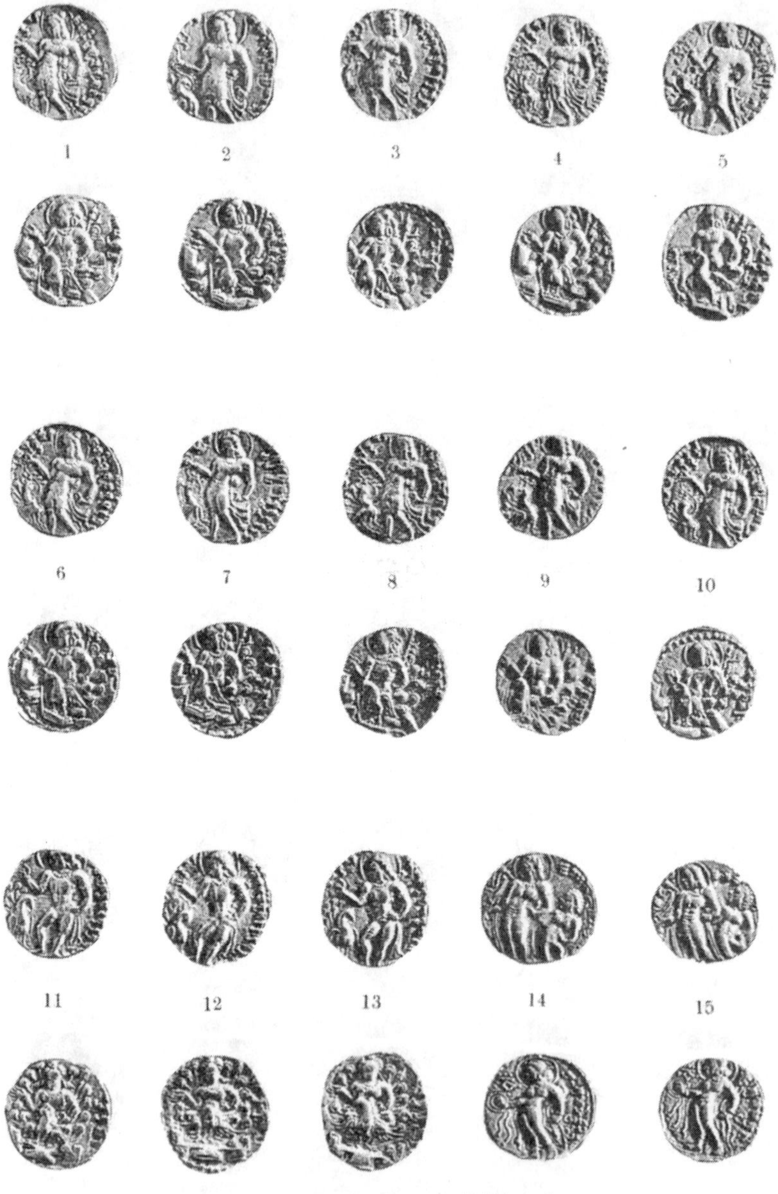

Kumāragupta I : Peacock (1-13) and
Chhatra (14-15) Types

Kumāragupta I: Tiger-Slayer Type

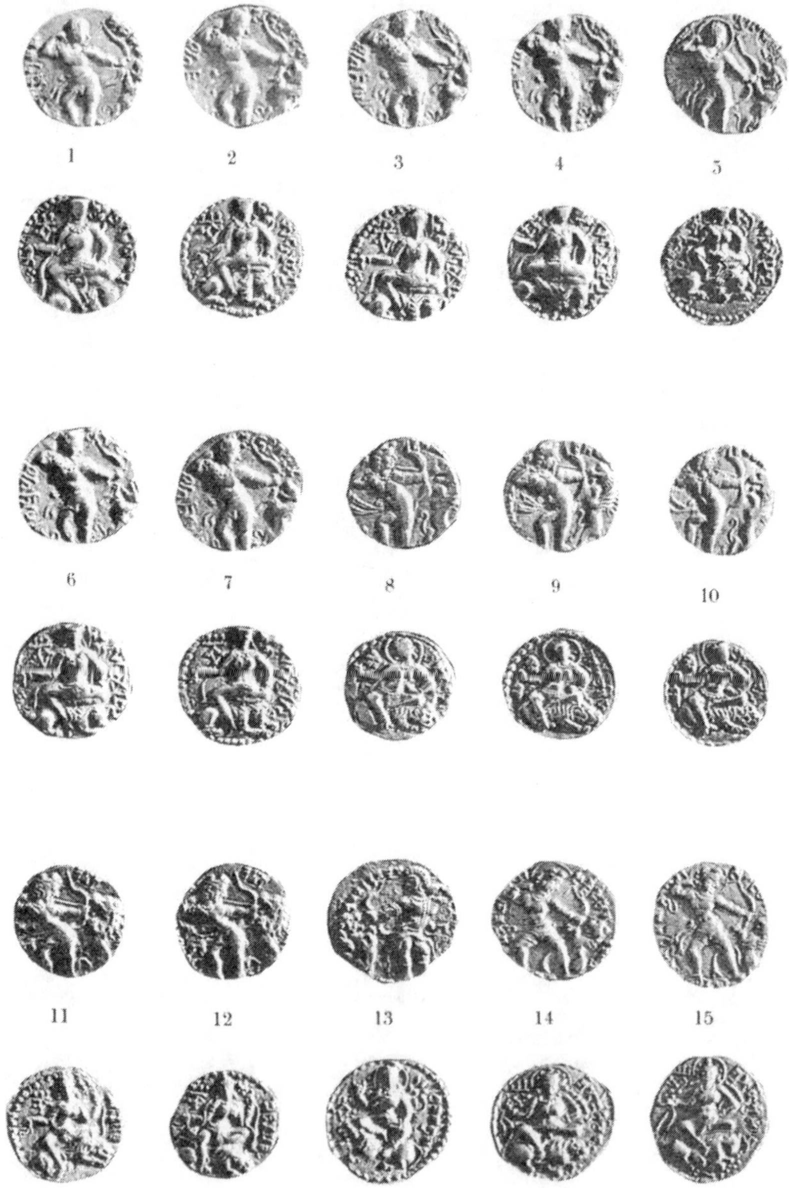

Kumāragupta I: Lion-Slayer Type

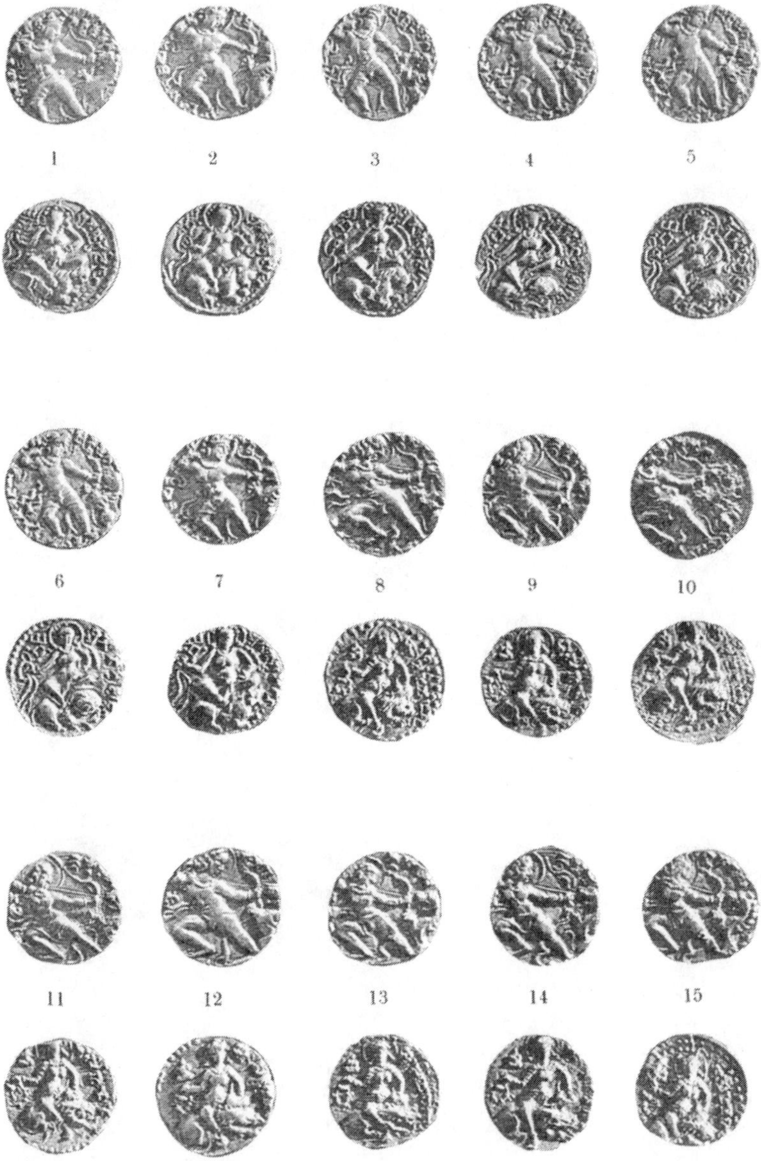

Kumāragupta I : Lion-Slayer Type

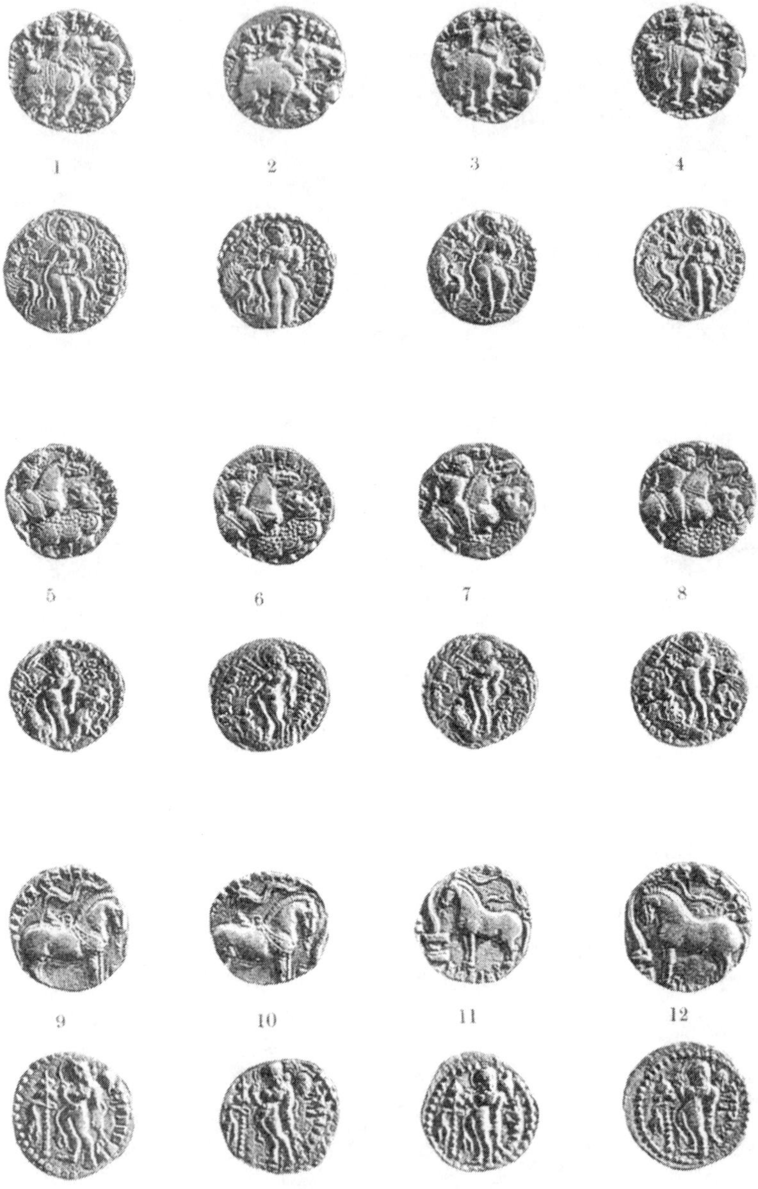

Kumāragupta I: Elephant-Rider—Lion-Slayer (1-4), Rhinoceros-Slayer (5-8) and Aśvamedha (9-12) Types

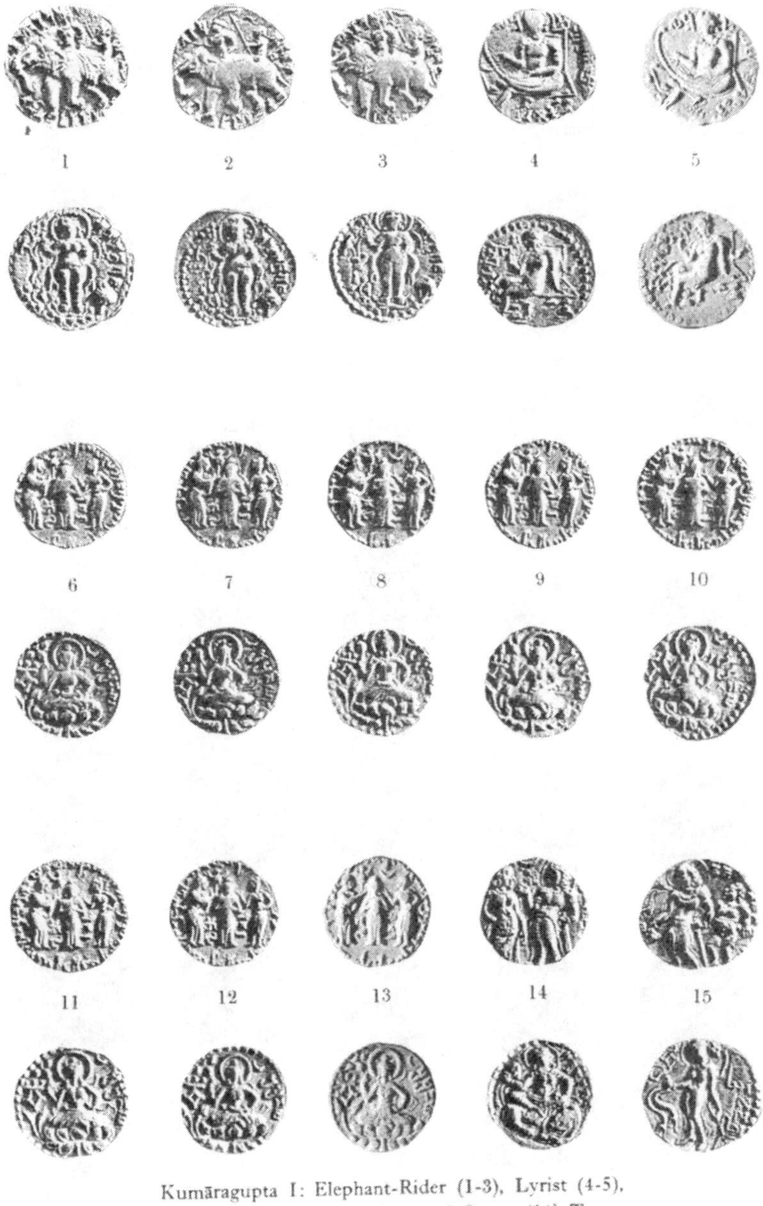

Kumāragupta I: Elephant-Rider (1-3), Lyrist (4-5), Apratigha (6-13) and King-and-Queen (14) Types
Skandagupta: Chhatra Type (15)

Supplementary Gupta Gold Coins PLATE XXXII

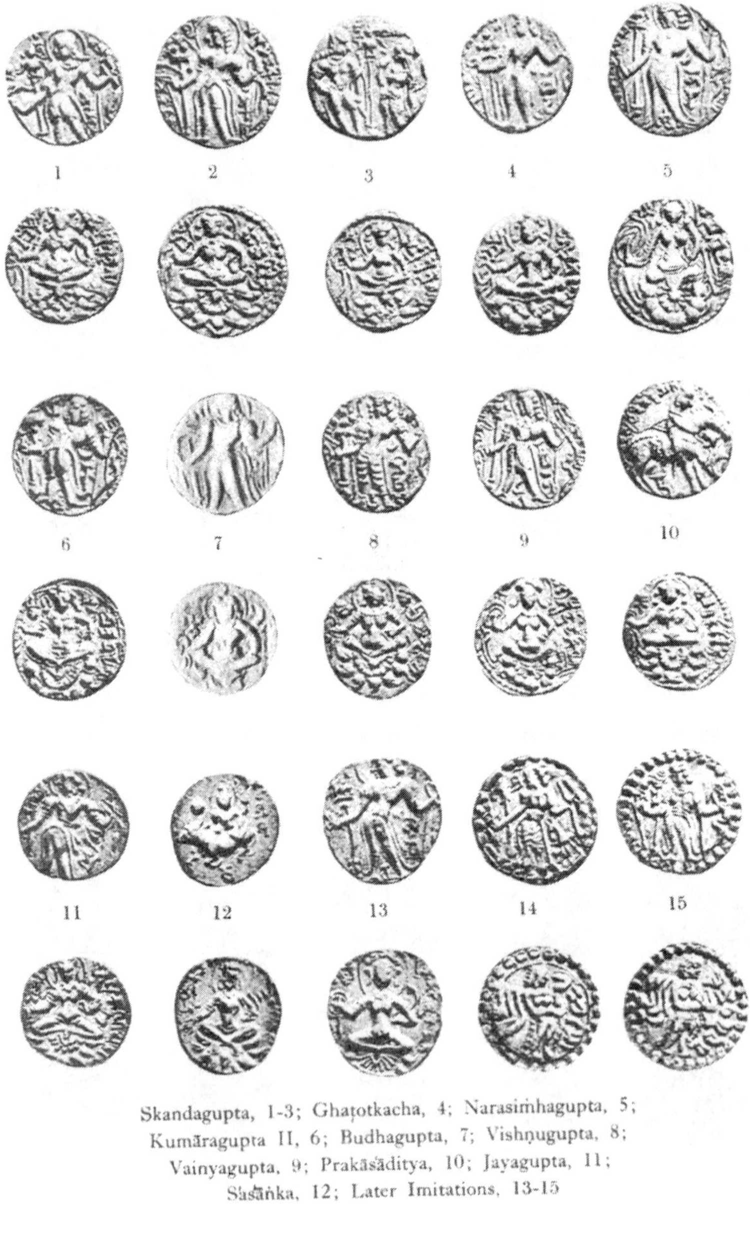

Skandagupta, 1-3; Ghaṭotkacha, 4; Narasiṁhagupta, 5; Kumāragupta II, 6; Budhagupta, 7; Vishṇugupta, 8; Vainyagupta, 9; Prakāśāditya, 10; Jayagupta, 11; Śaśāṅka, 12; Later Imitations, 13-15

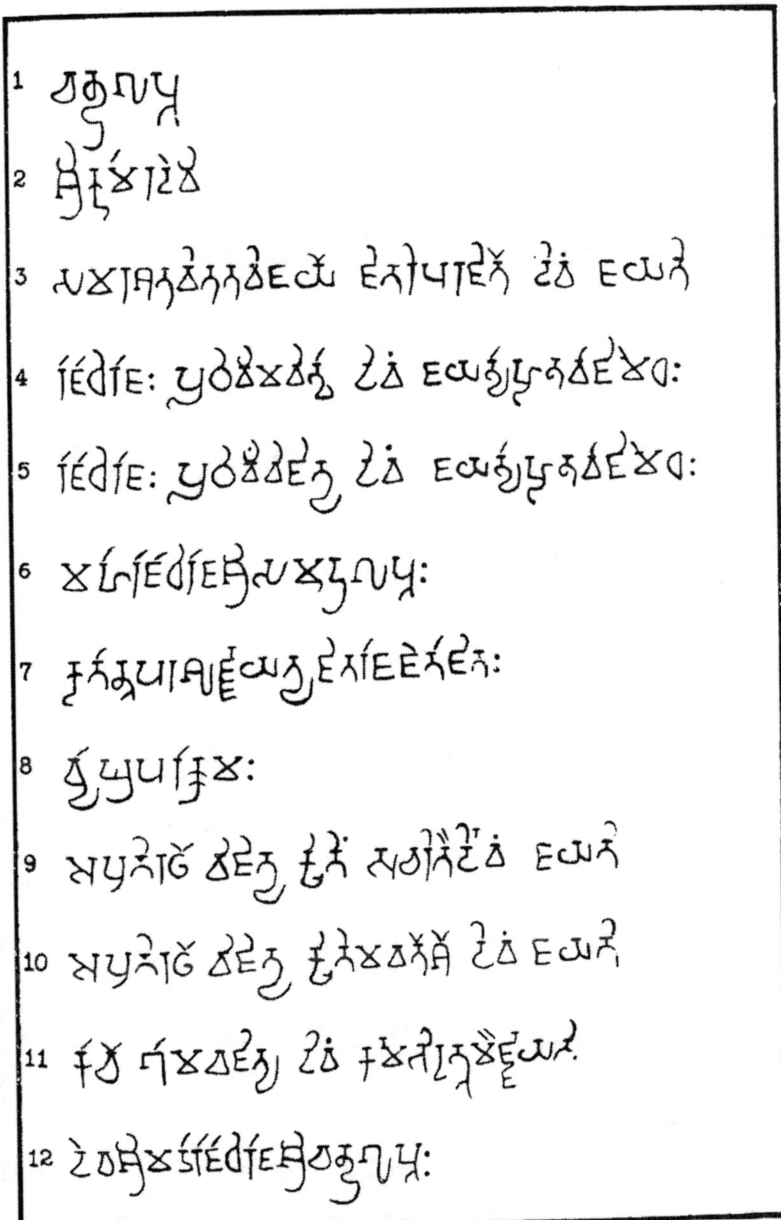

Obverse legends on the coins of Chandragupta I, Samudragupta, Kācha and Chandragupta II

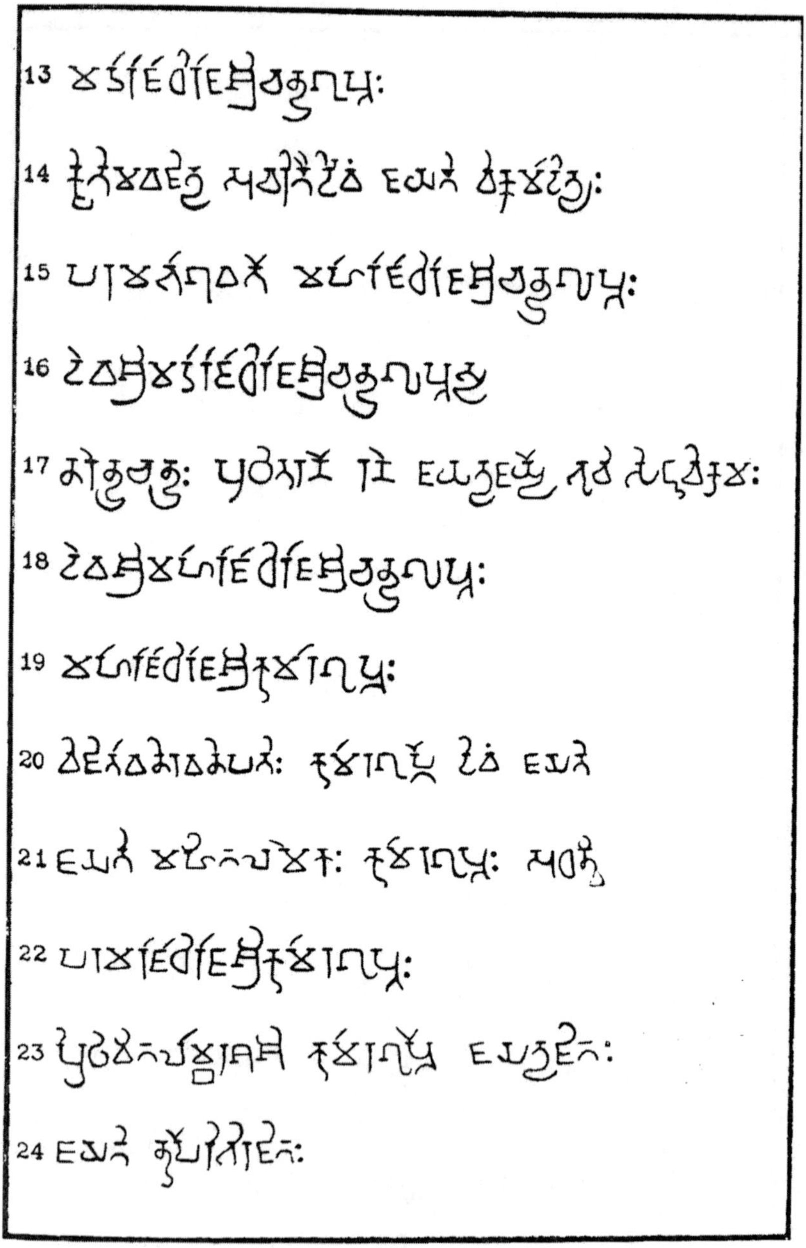

Obverse legends on the coins of Chandragupta II and Kumāragupta I

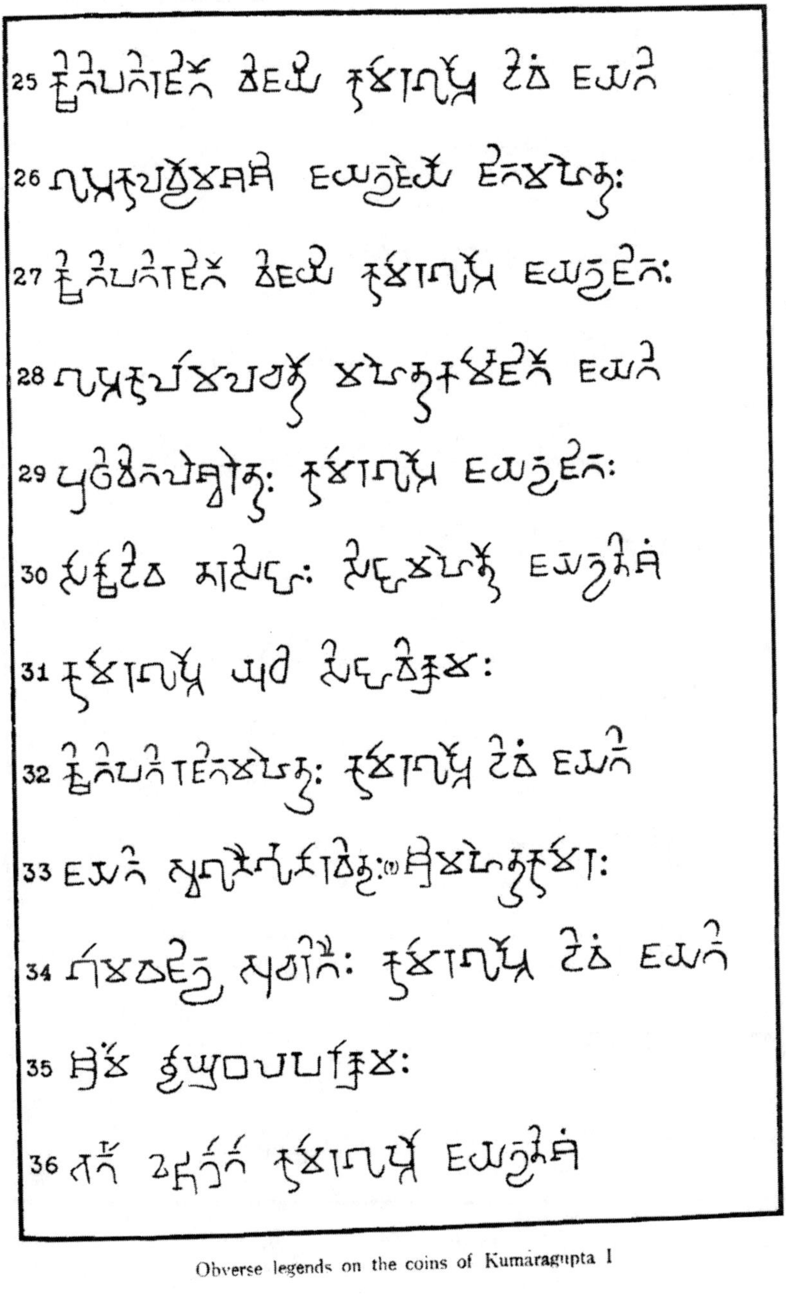

Obverse legends on the coins of Kumāragupta I

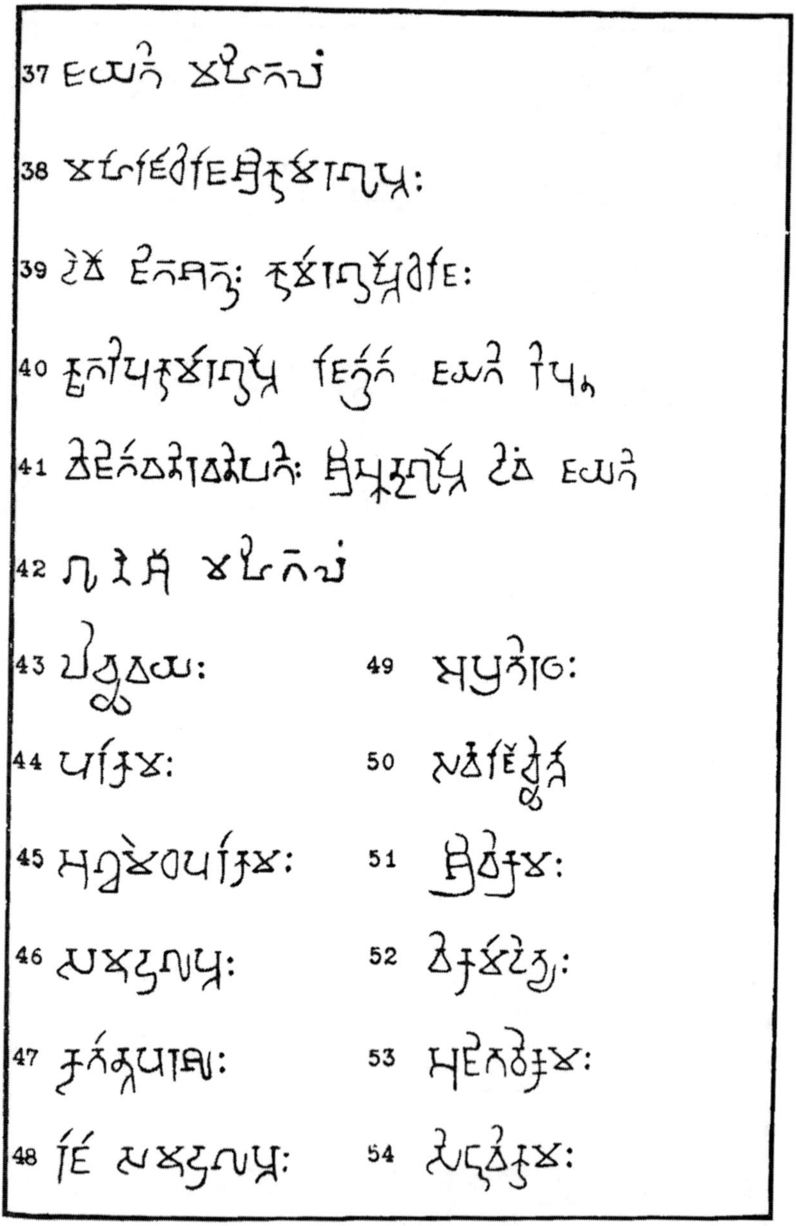

Obverse coin legends of Kumāragupta I and reverse coin legends of Chandragupta I, Samudragupta, Kācha and Chandragupta II

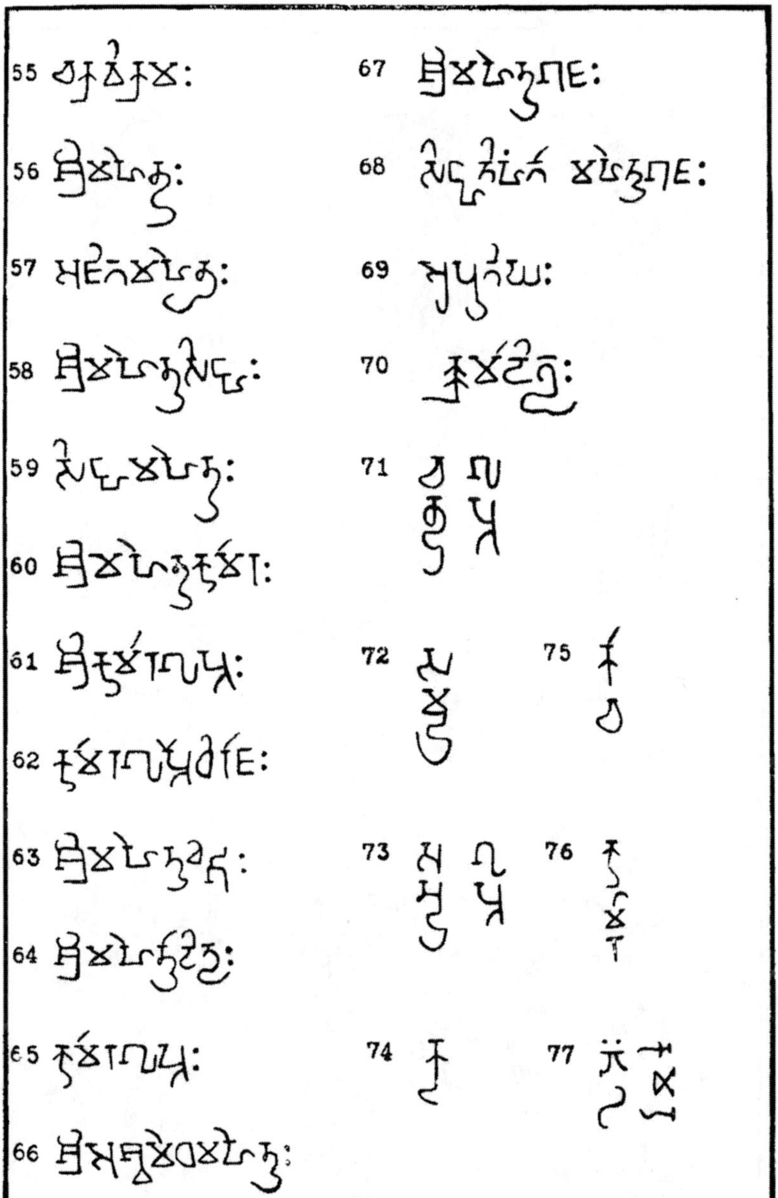

Reverse coin legends of Chandragupta II and Kumāragupta I and legends under the arm.

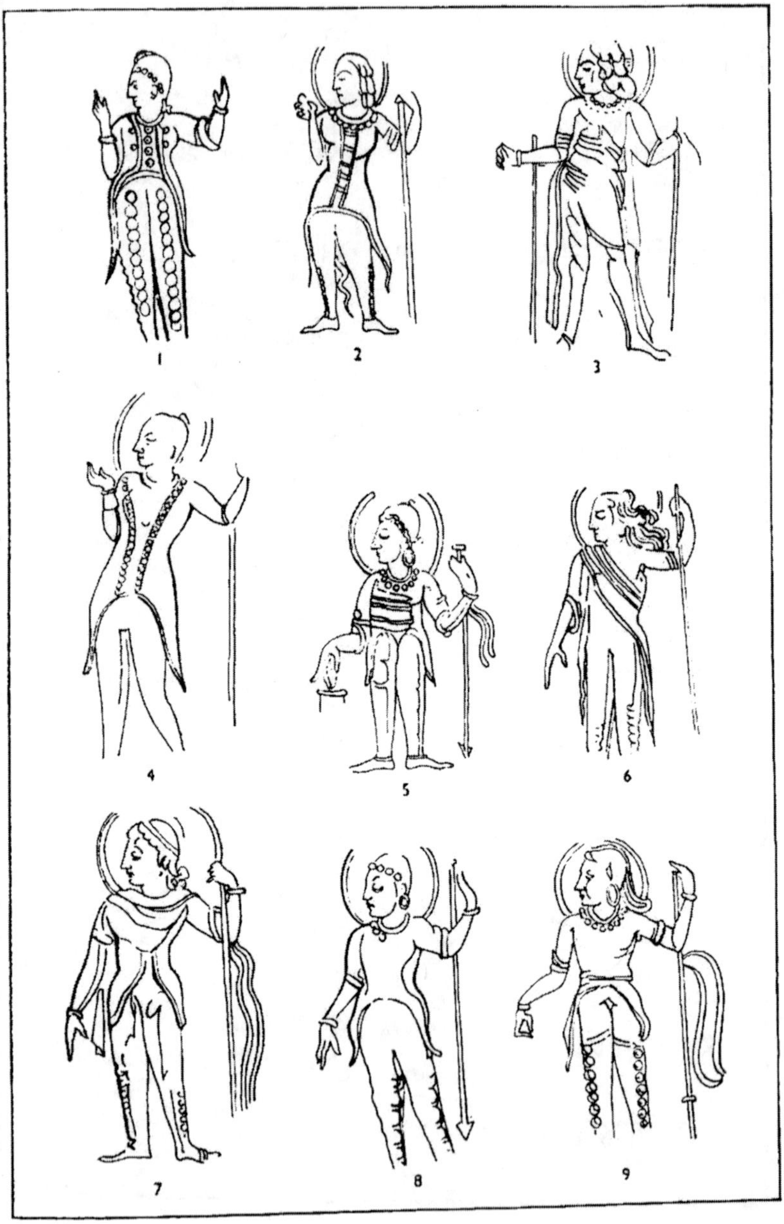

Male Costumes
(From the coins of Chandragupta I and Samudragupta)

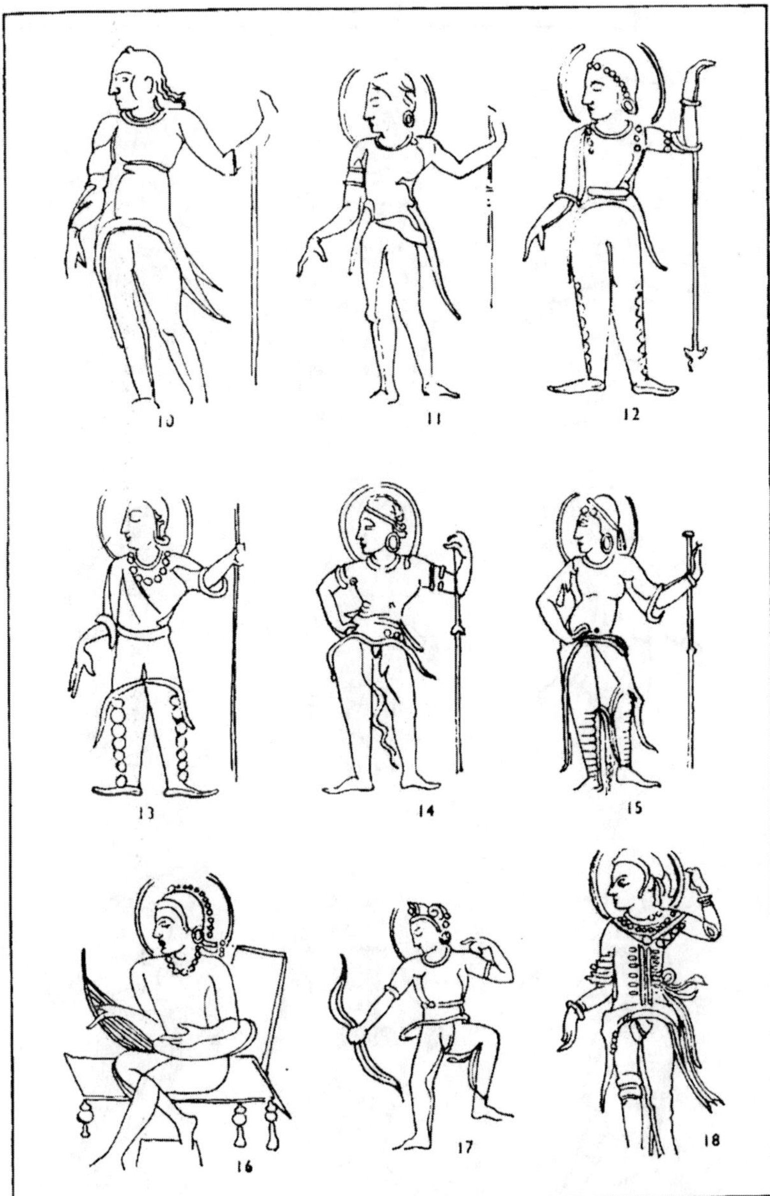

Male Costumes
(From the coins of Samudragupta and Chandragupta II)

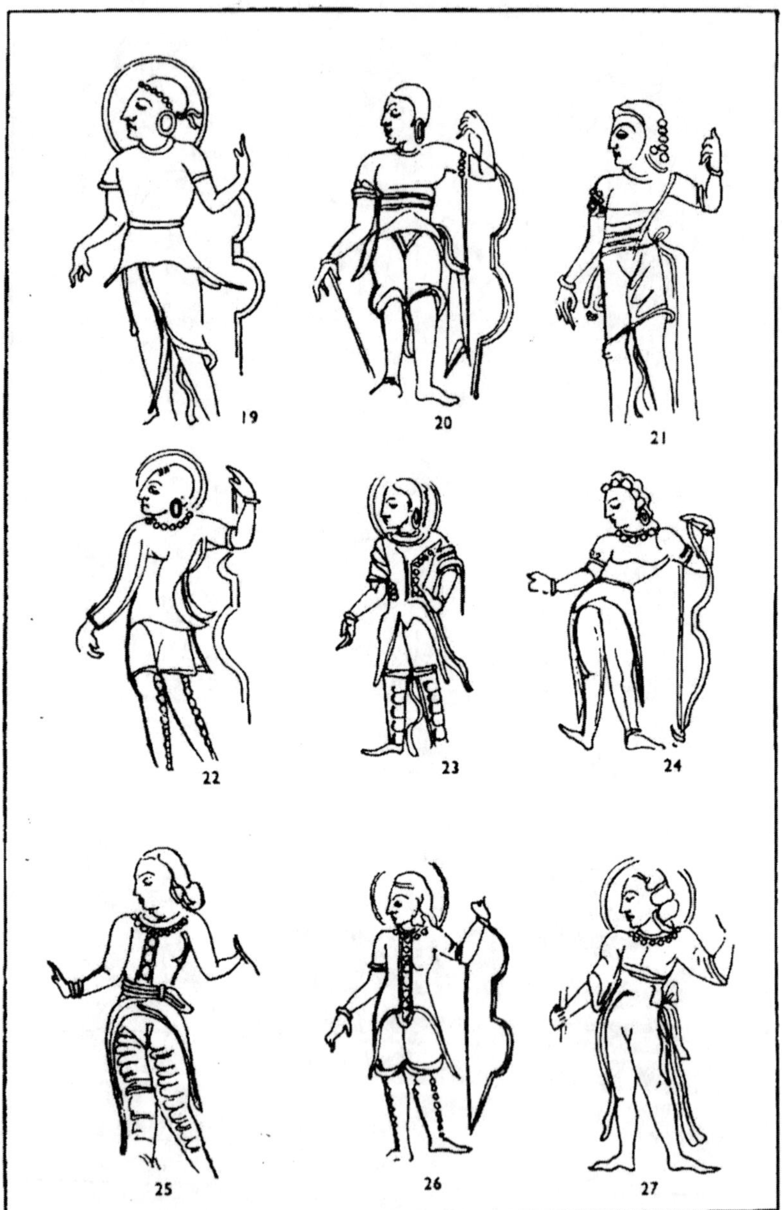

Male Costumes
(From the coins of Chandragupta II)

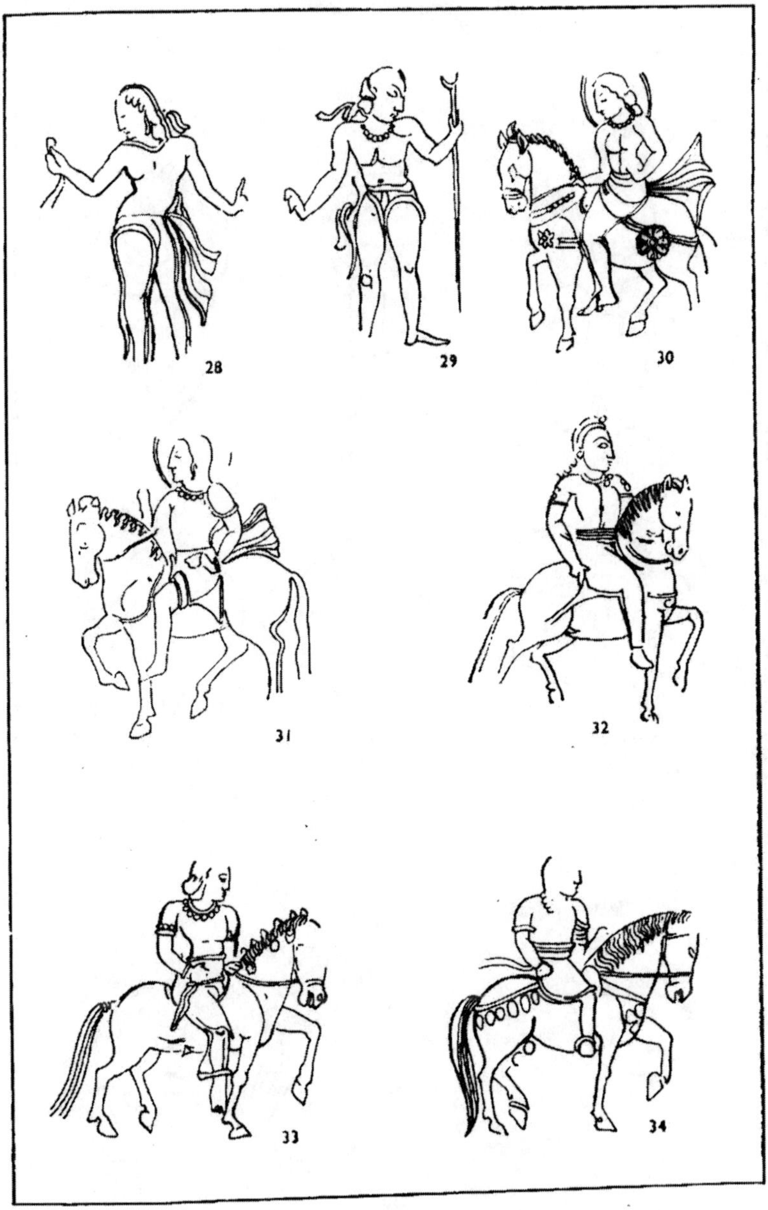

Male Costumes
(From the coins of Chandragupta II)

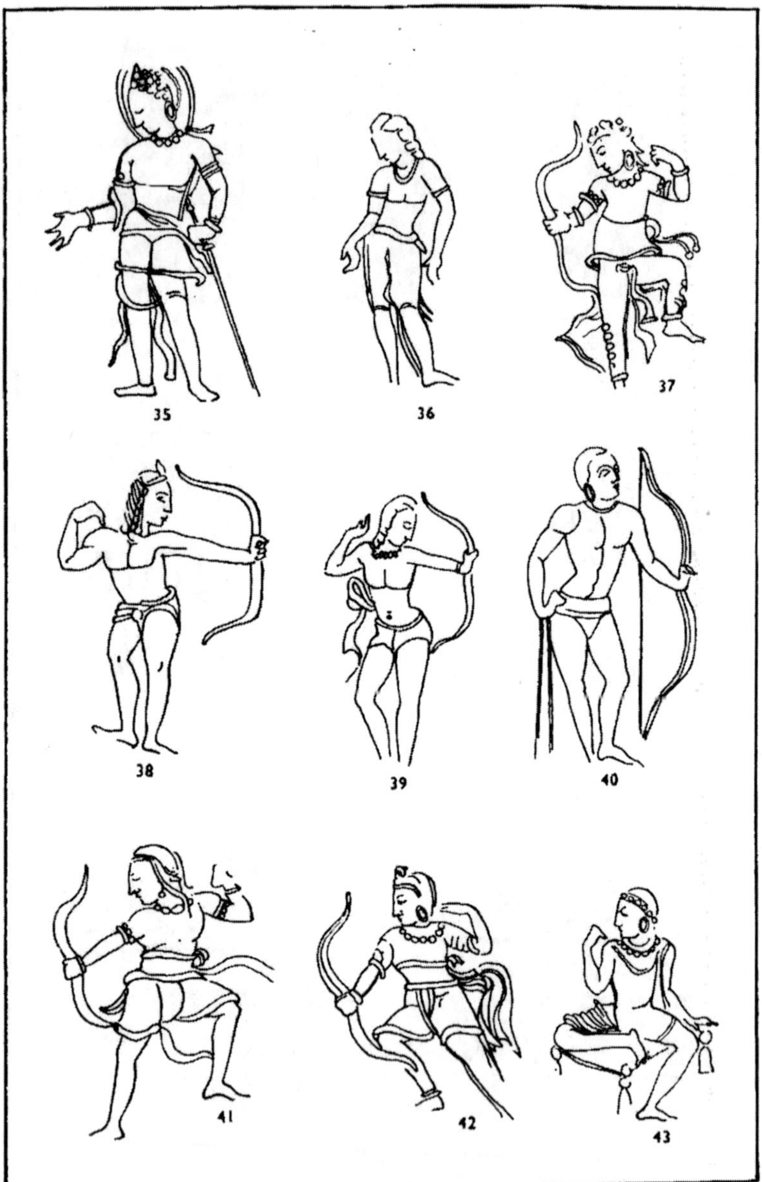

Male Costumes
(From the coins of Chandragupta II)

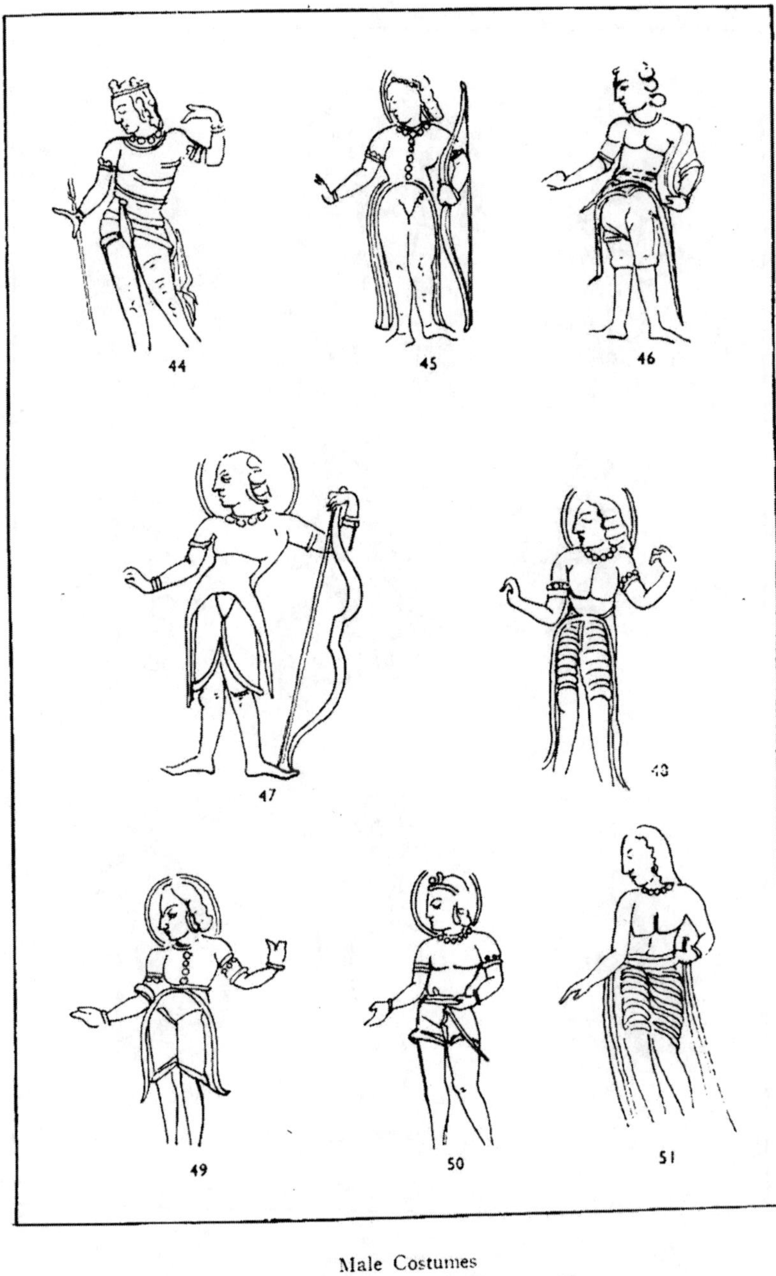

Male Costumes
(From the coins of Kumāragupta I)

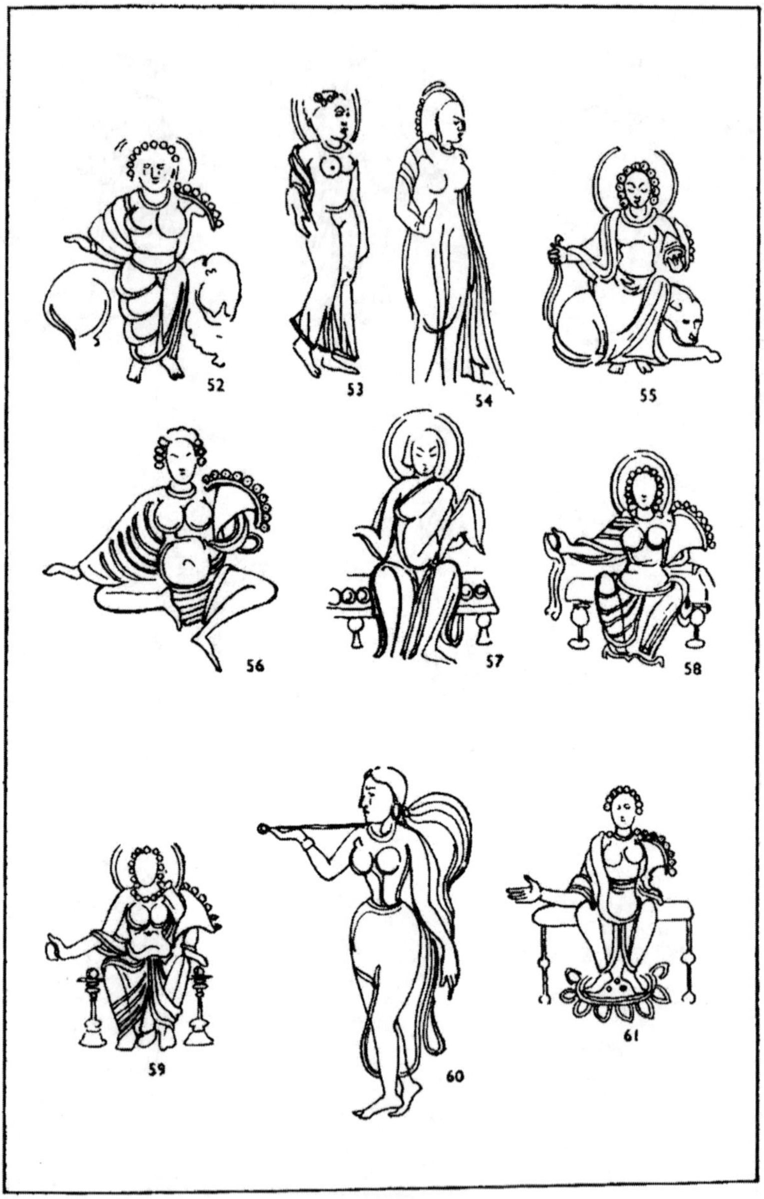

Female Costumes
(From the coins of Chandragupta I and Samudragupta)

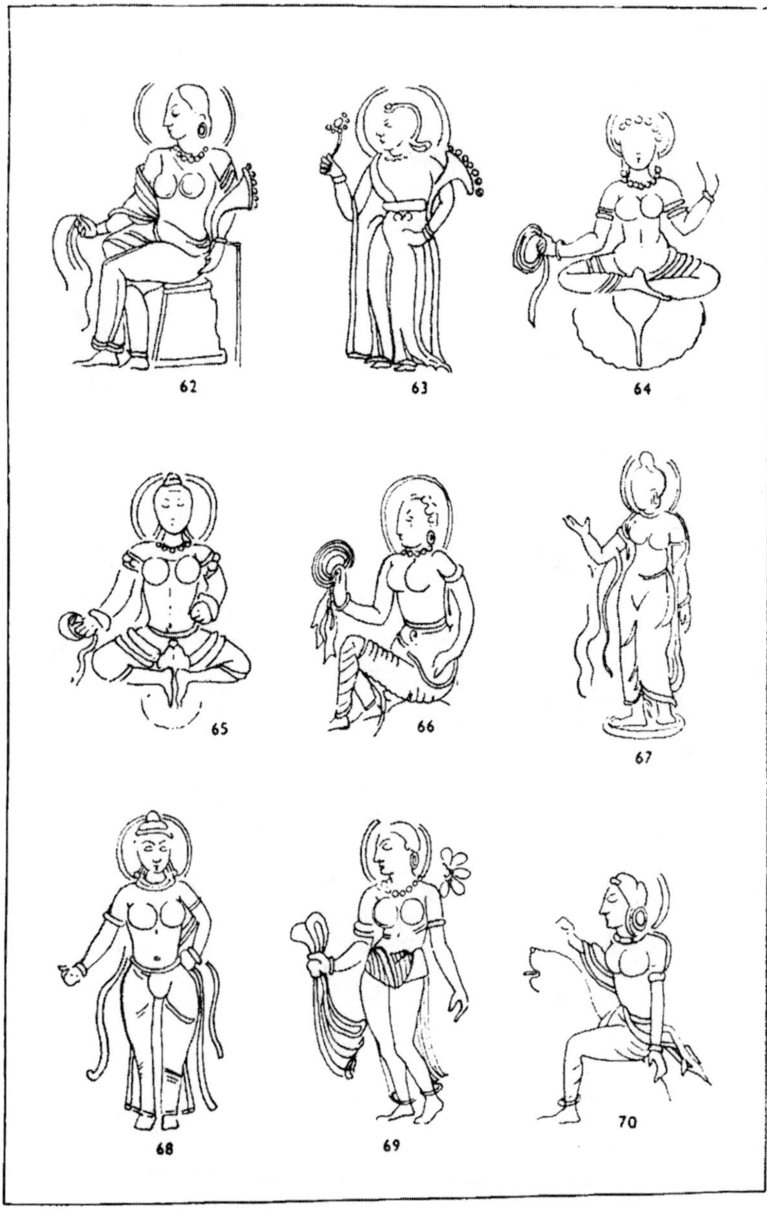

Female Costumes
(From the coins of Samudragupta and his successors)

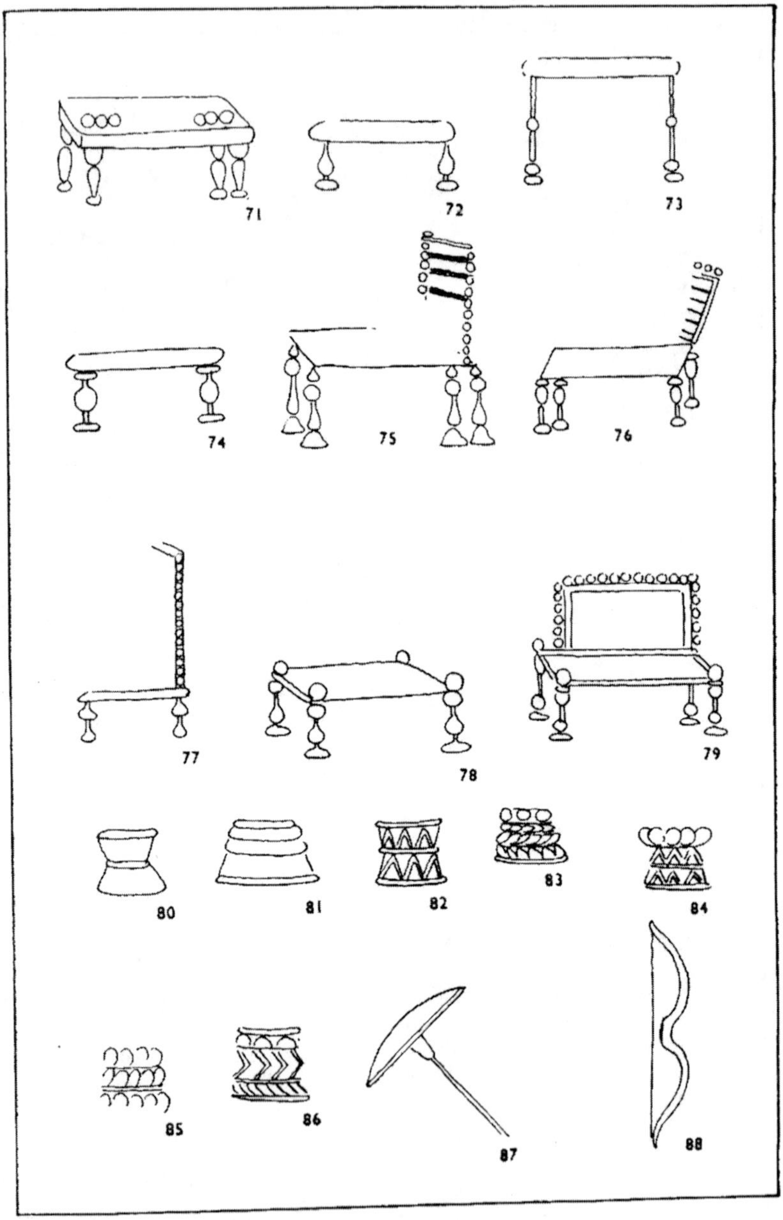

Furniture and Weapons

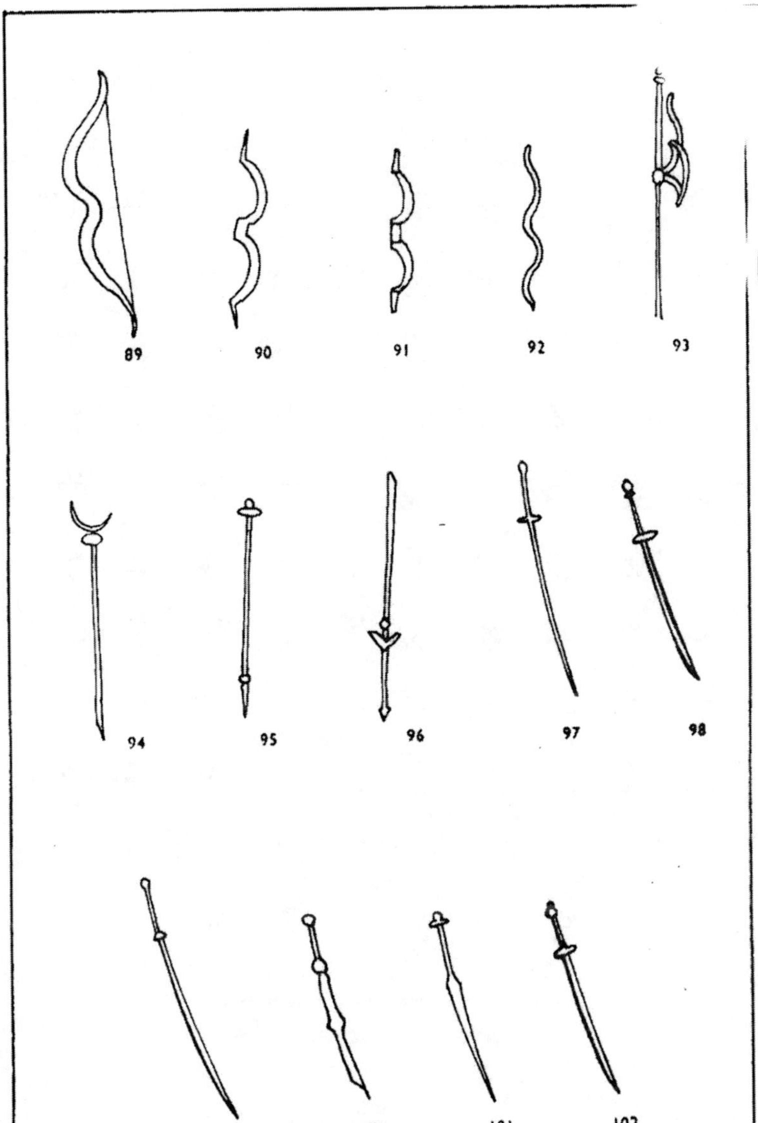

Weapons

PLATE XLVIII

SYMBOLS ON GUPTA COINS

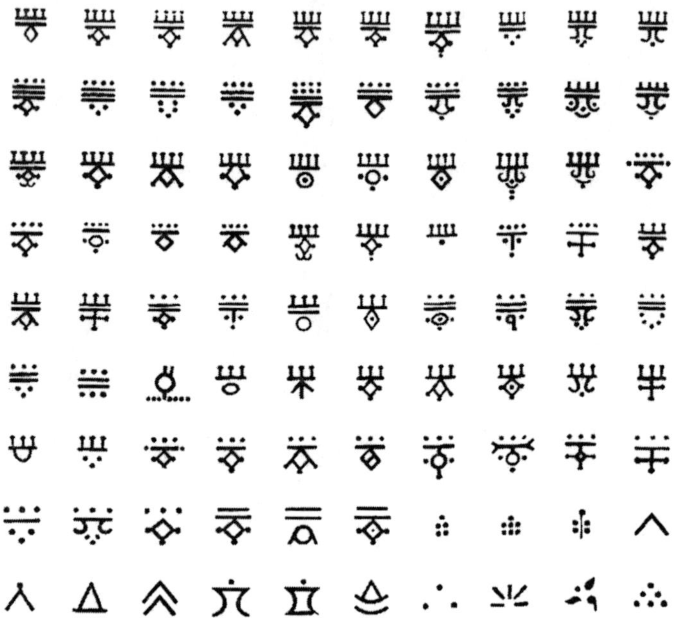

SYMBOLS ON KUSHĀṆA COINS

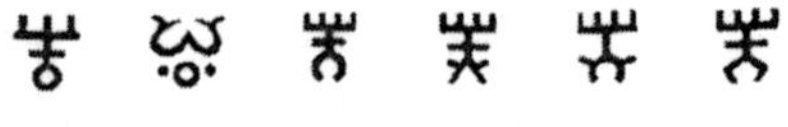

Symbols on Gupta and Kushāṇa Coins